Law and Visual Jurisprudence

Volume 10

Mario Ricca

Intercultural Spaces of Law

Translating Invisibilities

Springer

Mario Ricca
University of Parma
Parma, Italy

ISSN 2662-4532 ISSN 2662-4540 (electronic)
Law and Visual Jurisprudence
ISBN 978-3-031-27435-0 ISBN 978-3-031-27436-7 (eBook)
https://doi.org/10.1007/978-3-031-27436-7

This Springer imprint is published by the registered company Springer Nature Switzerland AG
The registered company address is: Gewerbestrasse 11, 6330 Cham, Switzerland

Contents

Chapter 1
Introduction

The Invisible Pillars of Law, Cultural Mobility and Planetary Socio-Semiosis

1.1 Underneath the Positive Layers of Law: 'One Difference, Manifold Invisibilities'

Law is not a self-generating phenomenon. Its existence germinates from socio-cultural pre-conditions. The positive layer of legal discourse and action is only the visible portion of legal experience as a whole. This visible portion leans on the invisible semiotic landscapes hosting the network of experiential habits and meaning that communities share. The permanence of this implicit dimension is a crucial prerequisite for legal systems to be capable of deploying their effectiveness through time. And yet, no legal system is fully able to maintain stable both the social and semantic ingredients comprising the universe of discourse that, as a communicative and pragmatic ocean, allow it to float on the surface of historical experience.

Far on this side of the is/ought and/or facts/values distinction, the implicit dimension of law equals a submerged semantic continent. The pillars of this kind of Atlantis are made up of the reciprocal and processive relationships between cognitive habits and the constellation of meanings coextensive with each social universe. Despite the claims for its self-referentiality, positive law cannot avoid hetero-integrating itself through the reference to this semiotic ocean, the dynamics of which is beyond its control. The phrastic parts of legal propositions borrow from both common and other specialized languages terms, categories and semantic spectrums that make up their semantic structures. For this reason, the analytical isolation of legal language is to be considered only as a heuristic strategy. It has neither ontological implications, nor premise. On the contrary, it can be treated and considered separately only operationally and as long as the relational semiotic ocean that *keeps it afloat* enters a phase of change. When this occurs, the semantic morphology of positive law is challenged and the basic connections between the legal categorization of facts and the values legitimizing the institutional action morph. The overall process holds a spatial significance insofar as each word, and especially legal words, both epitomize and anticipate the assumption of schemes of

M. Ricca, *Intercultural Spaces of Law*, Law and Visual Jurisprudence 10,
https://doi.org/10.1007/978-3-031-27436-7_1

actions. When the semiotic landscapes underlying legal languages change, the spaces of experience have already undergone a process of transformation. In these situations, the cognitive habits through which people recognize and qualify the 'social facts' as targets of their sensorial empirical attitudes and functions are to be remolded. This is because when the relational backdrop of things and their previous categorizations changes, new semiotic attunements between presuppositions and consequences, human ends and environmental conditions is to be achieved. If this process of re-adjustment and transactions does not take place, the crystallized fixity of previous semantic schemes (or morphologies) will prove to be detached from experiential conditions. Such a functional divorce will therefore make them unable to convey the attainment of results in line with the same values/ends originally driving the shaping of categorical boundaries and, therefore, meaning. From a legal perspective, this diffraction translates into the collapsing of law's language inwards upon itself stemming from the contrast of its semantic and pragmatic implications with the values/ends legitimizing its deontic function.

Western modern legal thought traces the foundation of law's legitimacy, and even existence, in a mythical/rhetorical origin coincident with the 'social contract.' Unfortunately, the political imagination has identified this contract as an agreement focused on axiological and normative aspects. This idea is in line with the 'epistemology of secularization' according to which there is an ontological divide between the external dimension of experience and the internal one, as such paralleled by the mind/world, subjective/objective, values/facts, faiths/reason, politics/law, moral/law and many other distinctions. What such a meta-narration misses, is the indispensable pre-condition of any axiological/political social contract, that is to say the conclusion or the pre-existence of a semantic social contract[1] resulting from the sharing of the cognitive habits that people make use of in construing their universes of co-existence and the related spaces of experience. In the absence of the 'semantic contract' no 'social contract' is conceivable, nor the distinction between normativity and facticity. The construction of a universe of meaning, on the other hand, is a process along which subjective and objective, axiological and factual, teleological and empirical, conflate and reciprocally remold. Only when an interlocutory final step is reached, can each part of this couple of 'dispositions' be distinguished by virtue of the stability of their achieved combinations, which constitute what is usually passed off as 'objectivity.'

The creation of universes of meaning and the related world of experience result from both cultural activity and its dynamic/transformative interactions with the environment: namely Nature. The culturally remolded natural world is the space people live by. And precisely for this reason the encounter and interpenetration between different cultural circuits and spaces of experience stirs up the waters of the semiotic ocean on which every legal system navigates contemporaneity, upsetting the pre-conditions of its effectiveness and (even) validity. Today, human planetary dispersal has intensified the number of threads and relational opportunities so that an

[1] Greimas (1983, pp. 103–113).

intercultural intermingling of 'cultural spaces' concurs to mold the compounds of local ways of life. The 'here' and 'now' is ever more the outcome of the convergence of multiple multi-sited factors that along semiotic/practical corridors engender the emersion of phenomenal effects throughout the planet. Even migration and the cultural mobility inside peoples' heads and bodies is to be understood as semiotic means of the overall process of transformation through which multiple spaces have generated a ubiquitous experiential and semantic *continuum*.

By and large, the whole set of dynamic factors just described alters the cognitive frameworks underlying the positive, explicit surface of law and the related legal systems. The semiotic wave drawing the multidirectional lines of tension animating the spatial simultaneity of intercultural phenomena on a global scale shakes the pillars of the manifold cultural Atlantis underneath the various national legal systems. The consequence is that the intermingling of cultural spaces of experiences, externally perceived as a supervenient multiculturality or superdiversity of local social circuits, is to be thought and managed as a process of inter-environmental 'translation.' This means that new cognitive tools are needed for addressing the result of the phenomenal inter-penetration of multiple cultural universes that can become co-present in each place despite their physical/geographical remoteness. The invisible parts of law and its national/local declinations is to be brought to light. At least interlocutory, the Atlantis underlying and shoring the only apparently stable architectures of positive national legal systems are to be made to surface. Only in this way can the semiotic networks and the resulting habits be rewoven by social subjects cognizant of the semantic warp and weft that give shape to the contemporary tapestry of global and local intercultural dynamics of experience. Law, especially when it is law-in-action, is called to translate in legal/axiological terms the landscapes of factual occurrences fallen under its lens (the construction of the middle term of the so-called judicial syllogism) and cannot work without a renewal in tune with the semantic contract updated anew by the above transformations.[2] The refusal to embody in legal language and categories the results of a semantic renegotiation of the experiential elements of law's validity and efficacy—namely, its function—would run the risk of precipitating the application of legal rules towards an inevitable heterogenesis of ends: that is, putting their practical consequences against their own prerequisites of legitimation. In the medium and long term, the blindness produced by a deceptive self-confidence in the national/local power of institutions, as such fostered by a misleading faith in the iteration of the past, could compromise the responsiveness of legal and institutional action so as to engender a kind of rift between law and the social world (or, at least, large, too large, parts of it).

I think that only an informed and responsible use of values/ends underlain by the cultural gist of local legal systems and experiences, that is to say their treatment as processive means, can avoid the shortsighted clinging to their morphological schematizations and the ossified behavioral patterns (allegedly) derived from them. If

[2]For further investigations about this topic, I refer to Ricca (2022), Ricca (2023a, *forthcoming*) and Ricca (2023b, *forthcoming*).

intended in this way, it might be possible, in my view, to achieve a certain degree of continuity along the line of semiotic and pragmatic interactions that weaves the past and future of the relationships between law and social dynamics that unfold astride our present of deep transformations. And besides, the only way to fruitfully face and control transformations is to undertake an intentional and weighed commitment to an adaptive self-transformation. This is, actually, a strategy—so to speak—to maintain the direction even if through a change of paths, which in legal terms is equivalent to using constitutional ends, as well as the axiological gist of human rights, processively through the new means required by supervenient environmental/contextual/cultural conditions.

The core topic addressed in this book is the possibility to give course to an intercultural use of law together with a *transactional* and *translational* mobilization of the underlying semiotic/spatial connections usually confined to the domain of 'invisibility' or, however, left lying in an overshadowed 'implicitness.' Translating the cultural-semiotic invisibility of morphological appearances, as such shaped and compartmentalized by the grammar of senses, represents the turning point to redefine in a non-ethnocentric way the significance of people's behaviors before the multiplicity of national laws. The relationships between law and senses are considered, at least to date, mainly in terms of the law's propensity to influence and imperatively pigeonhole the socio-cognitive uses of people's sensory activity. Hence legal agencies are criticized for their silent, but not less pervasive, proclivity to bias people to construe outwardly hetero-directed geographies of their sensorial geographies so as to ultimately mold their cognitive imageries about what is and what is not. Nonetheless, the other side of the intermingling between law and sense hinges upon the inner normativity of cultural grammars of the senses and their influence on law and the interpretation of legal statements. Actually, culture-laden sensory patterns imbue the descriptive, or phrastic, components of legal rules if only because they cognitively contribute to shape the morphological features of things, behaviors, phenomena, etc. The activity of senses and its enfolding constitutes the experiential plot that concludes with the fixation of the properties, qualities, denotative and connotative features, etc., of the phenomenal entities of the world. Such constitutive influence of the cultural scanning of the perceived 'reality' often goes completely unnoticed, or alternatively, is drastically glossed over. The consequence is its utter invisibility and the legal agencies' false belief that their assessments and activities include nothing more than neutral categorizations of the world: in short, that they see and categorize things and facts *as they are*. In this way, however, the culturally different grammars of sense are completely silenced, while their consequences on categorizations end up being condemned to be marginalized or, more often, eclipsed to invisibility. The cultural obscuring of the perceptual Otherness leads, inevitably, to the blinding of law to individuals' cognitive differences (even before axiological ones), thus making it impossible to even consider their legal relevance. In order to face this huge problem, my proposal is to dismantle such a regime of sensorial invisibility by means of a specific commitment to the intercultural translation of the different grammars of senses and their 'regimes of invisibility' nestled in the multiplicity of cultural domains. This is, in my view, a necessary step so that equality in law is not indifferent to the multiplicity of sensory grammars and their consequences on the different worlds people 'make present' through their perceptual activities and the related synesthetic connections. In the same vein, the cognitively normative influence of cultural sensory grammars on categorizations, and thereby the legal qualification of the 'things of the world, can be considered as the invisible pillar of a submerged and implicit part of legal experience: precisely the cultural Atlantis which is to be brought to the surface so as to face contemporary difference/equality dynamics before the law. Translating cultural invisibilities results in a renewed and more equitable grammar of visibility and therefore in a trans-cultural objectivity to be taken as the factual ground to be included in the interpretation and application of legal rules. The dis-composition of the semiotic network underlying differing 'cultural visibility/invisibility' can re-determine what is relevant for law, and in this way critically close the loop of the bottom-up and top-down mutual influence between the 'legal' and the 'sensory' or, more specifically, the 'ruled' and the 'seen.' From this perspective, the interplay between the semiotic analysis of the different sensory patterns underlying the cultural worldviews and an intercultural approach to the use of law are two wings of any commitment to legal equality. For this purpose, in the book the intercultural use of law and its methodology are developed through an interdisciplinary approach. Anthropology, semiotics, geography and legal theory are combined to address the inclusion of cultural/religious differences into national and supra/international legal systems. In the same vein, the book draws an argumentative path involving a renewed consideration of human rights and their function in the legal recognition and translation of cultural/legal differences.

1.2 Intercultural Interdisciplinary Approach: Presuppositions and Implications

When cultural diversity is focused on from a legal perspective, the overall matter is usually boiled down to an issue regarding the potential conflicts between norms or, even worse, exclusively legal rules. Nonetheless, despite their axiological and normative significance, cultures cannot be equated with the apparatuses of legal rules and, in any case, their significance does not show the same relevance/pertinence constraints that characterize the language of laws' normative apparatuses. And yet, this is precisely the approach that legal pluralists are prone to assume and advocate, especially when they move from a multicultural perspective. Their point of view coincides, more or less, with the idea that only the maintenance of the original cultural patterns of behavior—taken in their morphological structure—and the related normative apparatuses can keep minority cultures safe from assimilation and, in the end, annihilation. Despite their iteratively bandied about appeal to intercultural dialogue, their overriding concern and target seems to be equivalent to a 'non-contamination strategy.'[3] Of course, both colonial and post-colonial experience exerts a strong influence on the assumption of such a perspective and, in a sense, makes it justifiable and even plausible. Nonetheless, I think that assuming the rigidity of cultural normative apparatuses could turn out to be a hindrance rather than a real advantage point to assure minorities a genuine exercise of cultural autonomy.

Social life is made of relationships and networks of relationships. If these are to be fruitful, developmental, and generative of a shared experiential landscape, then mutual understanding is to be considered as a prerequisite of their unfolding and structuring. Normative and/or legal rigidity is only an apparent medium of such reciprocal understanding and recognition. This is because respecting others' norms or rules and giving them the possibility to follow the related behavioral schemes in leading their lives, does not at all imply that there is any understanding of the meaning of those norms or behaviors, and even less the previous assumption of a translational/transactional disposition. In other words, normative pluralism, if assumed as a corollary of a multiculturalist political recipe, could prove to be a 'poisoned apple.' In the end, it could result in a paradoxical inter-cultural othering stemming from an apparent recognition of Otherness blended with a cognitive distancing from it. As if to say in rough terms: *I allow you to assume the behaviors you prefer and follow your culture-based rules, but I want to maintain myself free to not understand or translate anything of the meaning underlying your patterns of conduct*. The result of this way to manage intercultural encounters is that the majority groups will raise axiological and legal barriers gauged on the morphological features of Others' behaviors and projected onto them from an unilateral and thereby ethnocentric perspective. The identitarian conflicts 'flourishing' beside and around such ultimately *indifferent* treatment of *differences* are nothing but the other side of an organized and institutionally legitimized ignorance of Otherness. Along this path claims for cultural identity, in turn and almost unavoidably, end up amounting, by and by, to nothing more than moves in a social chess game pointing at a defective goal of self-distancing. Inside this play of polarizations each act of recognition of Otherness camouflages the fetishization of 'alienness' coincident with the exteriorizing morphologization of what are, instead, the semiotic networks underlying words, gestures, material symbols, etc. adopted by people.

To put it more simply, we can make this discourse explicit with reference to an 'icon' in cultural 'othering': the veil. When the Western political and legal gaze interprets the wearing of the veil by Muslim women' as 'a religious conduct required by the Qu'ran,' but does not fathom the semiotic webs underneath the assumption of the related conduct, no formal recognition of the freedom to wear the veil in public spaces can be considered per se a measure excluding the 'indifference' for Otherness. In other words, the 'veil' will remain bereft of its meaningful and contextual

[3]Even if such a strategy could appear justified when one considers some kinds of analytical and essentializing approaches to cultural differences, especially with regard to legal experiences: see, as a paradigmatic example, Hannikainen et al. (2021).

implications, its affective, psychological, bodily and aesthetic projections, its being only a means, for example, for Muslim women to live their womanhood. What is worse, the formalistic recognition rooted in a normative pluralism might well hide a discriminatory or dismissive attitude ready to yield its socially toxic fruits by and large throughout the intercultural relationships surrounding the veil and ensuing the formal recognition of the 'wearing of the veil'.

In this book, with the precise intent of avoiding the above pitfalls, I propose to also consider cultural habits besides legal rules. This multifaceted approach is to be deemed preferable for it allows to pursue a polyphonic and multilateral inclusion of differences in the so-called multicultural societies. I understand that such a proposal could be strongly criticized by 'legal pluralists' because of its implicit asymmetry. They could contend that foreigners or people from non-majority cultures should leave behind the normative apparatuses of their countries of origin or cultural circuits. On the other hand, instead, natives or people belonging to the majority could maintain their legal apparatuses even if adjusting them to allow for the intercultural inclusion of Otherness. Legal pluralists, in a characteristic anti-statist fashion, could object that in this way my view implicitly confirms the primacy of the state legal system. Conversely, they could provocatively ask why we should not consider the possibility that natives could abandon their legal rules and try to inscribe their cultural habits within the legal framework of foreigners.

My idea is that no legal system is to be considered as preferable or bestowed with an aprioristic condition of supremacy over others when people from different cultural contexts encounter each other and have to manage their relationships. Actually, legal rules originating in countries or legal circuits different from the 'space' where the intersubjective relationships take shape or have their practical fulcrum can be involved in the legal qualification and regulation of each particular case. The question I raise has to do with the scope of this inclusion and the reasons for which it is, and should be, carried out. The same applies to the application of the hosting countries legal systems when legally relevant relationships involving people belonging to cultural, religious or ethnic minorities are at stake. In this regard, I argue that what is to be primarily translated are the semiotic webs underlying people's behaviors and—if existing—the related normative apparatuses. Only after having undertaken and accomplished this translational and cross-contextual work will it be possible to ascertain what rules and of what legal system/apparatus are applicable to the case in order to arrange a semantic and deontic combination as much as possible in tune with an intercultural declination of human and/or fundamental rights. The whole process is to be intended as a translational and therefore axiologically self-reflexive path. It is to be considered, therefore, as the opposite pole of a hermeneutical attempt[4] to reduce the (cultural) Other to the Self. It can be so, of

[4]See, in this regard, the criticism raised by Ellis, and based on Jarava La Mehta's post-colonial thought (2009, p. 105 ff.; 2013, p. 39 ff.), on Gadamer's (2013) notion of dialogue and 'fusion of horizon' as a strategy still inclined towards the self's edification and enrichment, and thereby imbued with lingering colonial interests. An alternative approach to Gadamer's hermeneutical

course, with the proviso that the epistemological and cognitive/political starting point is the (self-awareness of the) reciprocal incompleteness of each cultural worldview at stake in order to encompass the 'environmental situation.' An environmental situation that is tantamount to the intercultural fabric phenomenally engendered, time and again, by the experiential and semio-spatial interplay between differences. That situation, on the contrary, can be grasped only by means of a bi- or multi-directional involvement of the creative agency of the cultural actors involved in it. Something that can be reached only through a transactional withdrawal designed to make room for Others' contribution to a cognitively cooperative production of a re-semanticized experiential and communicative landscape (or semioscape). This means that no pre-postulated conceptual grid for understanding Otherness can be implicitly and unilaterally assumed as the ground for comparison—and thereby, in such a way, surreptitiously produce the colonial (and, sadly, also post-colonial) asymmetrical gaze and its susceptibility to knowing the Others through the semantic annihilation of their own Otherness.[5] In this sense, the intercultural use of law can be considered genuine and effective only if no ontological presupposition is laid down as a prerequisite for the recognition and the translation/comparison of the Other. This is because 'implicit interculturality' has already taken place in the planetary dynamic and changed the 'composition' of the experiential space surrounding, and interpenetrating with, any local culture, self or identity. In literary/metaphorical terms, it could be said that the apocalypses (if any) of identity and of the myth of self-bounded cultures have already betided our multi-locally interplaying world. Therefore, there is no plausible perspective for a subject-object hermeneutics of Otherness—so strongly echoing an Orientalist psycho-cognitive asymmetry—but only for a *realistic* subject-subject relationship, as such necessarily co-re-originating each of the involved subjectivities.

Understanding Otherness arriving among 'each ubiquitous us' is equivalent to becoming aware of the Otherness that has already penetrated us, remolding our own substance and its space—an ideal and hermeneutical pattern that should be intended in a rigorously symmetrical way and outside any self-centered cognitive paternalism or apriorism and even—as far as possible—beyond colonial and post-colonial events and narratives. In other words, any effort of recognition is to be gauged on the Other that each actor has become, for either *good or evil, to* themselves through the 'Other *than* themselves' and their pro-active semanticization of global spaces of experience. Along the unfurling of the self-reflexive and remolding process coextensive with the intercultural use of law, the values and ends encapsulated in human and/or fundamental rights should be utilized as interfaces of intercultural metaphorization/translation rather than formal patterns of legitimacy overarching in a hierarchical and pyramidal way the qualification of the subjective (and cultural) claims at stake. Applying the rule of one rather than another legal system or circuit, therefore, is not

approach to Otherness can also be found in Glissant (1969, 1990, 1997), on which see also Britton (1999) and De Schutter's (2004) interesting essay.

[5] Mandair (2009).

the crucial point—at least, according to this perspective. This is because the habits formalized in the legal proposition of the involved legal systems are the primary target of intercultural translation, which subsequently is to be used as a foil against which to assess the compatibility of the formal legal rules of both systems with human/fundamental rights. In this sense, the starting point could be the legal rule of one or, alternatively, another legal system, but the norm resulting from the overall process of intercultural translation and attunement with human and/or fundamental rights will be in any case still another one. It could result from both a human rights constitutionally oriented interpretation of the regulatory propositions included in the legal systems involved in this dynamic comparison and interplay, as well as from the remolding of the semantic structure of sentences arising from the judicial review of legislation (and, for example, a partial annulment of a pre-existent statutory rule). What is important, as an outcome of the overall translational/transactional intercultural adjustment succinctly described above, is that the final 'norm' constitutes a balanced and symmetrical interpenetration between the cultural universes of discourse involved in the intersubjective relationships under examination. All this provided that the 'final norm' is to be intended as the result of the interpretation of legal texts in light of the translation of the habits and the semiotic networks underlying them. As such, it should be applied to all the subjects taking part in both the situation and the translational/transactional process not because it is an accommodation between pre-existent cultural repertories but rather as a product of the pro-active exercise of cultural competence by the agents partaking in the relationship fallen under the lens of law.

The transformative 'protension' of the above intercultural use of law is not to be considered as a betrayal of the (quasi-mythical) will of the legislator or the original meaning of legal texts. On the contrary, it is only an alignment with the teleological structuring undergirding the morphological features of both legal categories and propositions when the interpreter is called to cope with the transformation of the cultural/environmental pre-conditions embodied by the semantic social contract that positive law and its validity presuppose. Such a 'culturally engaged' hermeneutic attitude does not imply an abandonment of legal certainty and a departure from a positivistic approach to legal experience but instead an attempt to build logical bridges between past and present through a processive understanding of law's function. In this sense, it is a genuinely 'modern strategy' insofar as it applies a kind of experimental logic to the implementation of the axiological and teleological categories legitimizing the organization of society by means of law. Rather than ossifying the meaning of those categories through the fetishization of behavioral patterns assumed as exclusive and prototypical extensional projections of their meaning, the hermeneutical approach adopted here focuses on the semiotic relations underlying such projections and the *axiotelic* compasses used in weaving their threads. In this way, it is possible to assess how much the environmental changes that have occurred alter the relational landscape and demand a reweaving of the semiotic connections necessary for legal positive categories and rules to maintain their functional efficacy with regard to the values/ends of legal experience. I would like to observe, in this regard, that there is nothing post-modern in this way of proceeding. Conversely, I think that it merely embodies a sort of enfranchisement from a non-modern way of interpreting values, ends and categorization. It is the same which, behind an analytical and positive reading of language and legal propositions, hides the tendency to assume in a dogmatic and aprioristic fashion elements (values, ends, deontic propositions) that cannot be divorced from the experiential situation taken as a relational whole. This is precisely what I intend when I refer to a processive use of legal values/ends as transformative means to be involved in the construction of renewed relational frameworks or situations within which their meaning and systemic function would refresh as part and parcel of an integrated whole. Legal certainty and axiological stability, in this perspective, are granted by, and coincide with, the continuity of the semantic self-transformation of linguistic and legal categories. On the other hand, this way of conceiving legal certainty is the only one which makes sure that categories (both axiological and factual) can adhere to their original function—that is, the attempt to grasp the future and contribute to its construction through and despite inevitable contextual change. In this sense, the maintenance of, and the fidelity to, any original (envisaged) meaning necessarily include a weighed rate of semantic entropy. This is an inescapable and inherent element in the relationship between meaning and time, and therefore in meaning itself insofar as it is an emergence from the combination between past and future semiotic projections/implications. The indeterminacy of future contextual conditions requires that semantic entropy and self-transformative attitudes of values/ends and categorizations are treated as two sides of the same coin. The same indeterminacy that marks, as an inherent feature, the contemporary changes in global environmental relationships and their interpenetration with the local socio-legal circuits. For this very reason, the refusal to make room in legal interpretation and experience for the binomial entropy/self-transformation would trigger the bursting of an unavoidable heterogenesis of ends that would annihilate any semantic stability despite the apparent permanence of the morphological linguistic as well as behavioral structures. Cultural authenticity cannot be considered without the boundary environmental conditions surrounding the concrete and topical use of the cultural means, that is, the set of 'knowing how to do things and achieve ends' of which each culture consists. Translation/transaction with Otherness and its semio-spatial projections is therefore an adaptive pre-requisite if meanings and categorizations idiomatic to each cultural network are to remain consistent with themselves within a changing environment. When this adaptive protension fails to unfold, then cultural habits become divorced from people's 'cultural proactive competence' and their misoneistic iteration ends up disjoining from people's needs and gives course to phenomena of self-alienation.

The above remarks apply to both the cultural and normative frameworks involved in intercultural encounters. This is because Otherness is in itself an environmental condition. When it intervenes as a supervenience, it inevitably intercedes between people's cultural axiological expectations and their achievements. This occurs because the co-presence of Others in experiential landscapes remolds the relational background on which the semantic relevance/pertinence constraints are gauged and the categorical boundaries that have been previously laid down. When the environment changes, the consequences/implications of past habits and their symbolic figurations can lose their attitude to correspond with the teleological patterns so that the extensional or implementational projections of values/ends needs to be reconfigured. This, in turn, will also inevitably import a redrawing of the categorical borders of values/ends insofar as each value/end is a processive epitome of the means leading to their achievement. Such circularity, however, is not a tautological circle, as each end qualifies its own means and in turn is signified by their relational, cumulative, and transformative interpenetration. Outside this dialectic co-adaptation and mutual relationship of 'signification,' values/ends would consist only of dogmatic and ossified patterns fatally destined to sever the human agents, and thereby law, from their own lives and any chance of a truly responsible and responsive relationship with experience.

On the other hand, an openness toward universalization—which is something different from a substantive, essentialized and reified universality mistaken with its historically contingent and local tokens—is ideally and genetically intrinsic to values/ends enshrined in human and/or fundamental rights. This implies, consequentially, that legal systems including such rights as both their foundational pillars and, simultaneously, their pole star are constitutionally extended towards an incremental updating of their meanings in tune with the relational framework that from time to time hosts the implementation of those rights and the related values/ends. Were such relational responsivity absent, no path to universalization would be possible. Such an argument, however, applies to all cultural/axiological patterns connoted by a certain degree of generality. The mutating of surrounding conditions does not at all mean that their generative values/ends must also collapse. This way of thinking hides a misleading and rather naïf conflation between values/ends, as well as principles, and the related patterns of implementation that have already taken shape. Conversely, the general, proactive and projective meaning of values/ends makes sense just by virtue of their self-transformative attitude to cruise through and help manage change, unveiling in this way all their semiotic and meaningful potentialities.

What is to be emphasized as regards the theoretical and methodological proposal I proffer in this book is that the main locus of translational activity is pivoted on habits rather than legal texts. The latter, in my view, can be appropriately taken in account only once the cross-contextual translational/transactional combination of the 'cultural implicits' at stake has been carried out. Moreover, the choice of what legal rules can be applied to the case and therefore the construction of the medium term of the judicial and/or interpretive syllogism can be appropriately made exclusively after the values/ends enshrined in human and/or constitutional rights have been situated within the intercultural translational process as interfaces for translation/metaphorization.[6] Without the previous surfacing of the semiotic landscapes underlying people's conducts and expressions and the checking of their axiological/teleological crossed relevance it is simply impossible—or, even worse, exclusively

[6] See below Chaps. 3, 5.

ideological—to determine the meaning of the so-called *factual side* of the legal syllogism and thereby the legal rule (or better, the norm—to be intended as the result of the interpretation of legal texts) to be applied in the individual case. This is also the reason I think that the pluralist and multiculturalist legal approach to the problem of coexistence between different cultures is not viable.

Assuming that the field of the comparison/confrontation between cultural attitudes boils down to a conflict between legal rules fails to grasp the genuine 'matter' of the intercultural situation. People are not rules or norms. Even if the legal positive schemes play an unquestionable role in the assessment and the solution of the intercultural encounters, what must primarily be considered is the modification of the semiotic relationships with which the cognitive and behavioral habits of each cultural actor must be in tune. If the identification and the interpretation of the legal rules relevant to the case are detached from the analysis of that renewed semiotic terrain, legal rules will be used as merely symbolic fetishes divorced from their semantic context and will be vulnerable, therefore, to any kind of instrumentalization and ethnocentric identitarian misinterpretation. When this occurs, the translational intercultural process is compromised at its very beginning. To be certain: it is not as if no intercultural transformation took place. Interculturality always *happens*. When people realize that cultural difference is among them, interculturality has already taken place. And yet, it is a kind of unintentional, implicit interculturality, very similar to the 'third space/Thirdspace' both Bhabha and Soja,[7] though from different perspectives, discuss in their work. I would prefer to dub the semiotic dimension to which implicit interculturality processes gives birth as an 'indistinct and protean thirdness.' Its hybridity—both semantic and pragmatic-spatial—is mostly out of control and is prone to germinate in the interstices (echoing Certeau's theory of everyday life[8]). For this very reason, it is semi-glorified by the post-modern thought because of its characteristic and sometimes even idolizing being heedful of the spots that creativity and immunity from the mainstream or dominant powers are rhapsodically and indeterminately able to embody. Nevertheless, the ephemeral contingency of this Thirdness has no appeal for me. I find in it a source of both thrilling life moments and burning disappointments, which in many cases in people's minds take the shape of lost illusions and a skepticism dramatically leaning toward an identitarian enfolding. On the other hand, I think that the strict connection that post-modern thought establishes between complexities and the emergence of the above Thirdness is—at least, in my view—only a consequence of a distorted interpretation of modernity. Things could be different, however, if we interpreted categories not as a-priori and semi-dogmatic schemes but rather as proactive operational and procedural guidelines stemming from experience and oriented to unremittingly carry on and renew it through the relationship with the environment and its semiotic texture. Should all that be the case, then we would become immediately aware of how human life is in constant dialogue with a Third dimension. For

[7] See Soja (1996) and Bhabha (1998).

[8] De Certeau (1990).

Thirdness is nothing but the exceedance of meaning gushing out beyond the envisaged horizon of human action and sprouting from its continuous relational interplay with the world.

Categorization is never a mimetic symbolization of the world's structure but rather an enactive disposition and a pro-active response finalized to allow us to fruitfully carry on our further activities in and through the environment. In the same vein, meaning and the symbolic dimension of human subjective attitudes toward the world are semiotically intermingled and interpenetrated with the so-called outer conditions of experience. By resorting to a metaphor, they are only one side of the bilingual, inherently incomplete, and ever-unfinished vocabulary by virtue of which human beings translate/transact the world *into* themselves and vice-versa. What should be caught—following the above metaphor—is that Thirdness is the generative relationship between the two parts of that vocabulary. Something which in turn makes *retrospectively different* the *differences* between the two languages as previously perceived; simultaneously, it produces at its front and beyond itself a spacc of un-contained, indetermined *ulteriority* still in need of being fathomed and grasped. In this sense, the Thirdspace or Thirdness is not at all an idiomatic element of post-modern times as such marked by a sort of super-complexity, but rather an inherent feature of cognition insofar as it is intended as an instrument of life. This orientation toward experience and the revisability of categories and the underlying relational/semiotic habits is a genuine trait of modernity and, at the same time, the most basic improvement assured by the (dream of) secularization—at least, in terms of potentiality.[9] Unlike post-modern thinkers, I consider Thirdness not so much as a kind of epiphenomenon of experience but rather as an emergent implication that should be continually and endlessly pursued with modesty and open-mindedness. Its semiotic exceedance, in turn, should be assumed not so much as a limit to the predictive and dominating power of reason but rather as a self-renewing experiential reserve for the production of the world. Indeterminacy, in other words, precisely because it is a source of both existential and cognitive precariousness is to be taken in its positive sense insofar as it is the doorway to a never-ending and ever-refreshing discovery of meaning—including that related to past categorizations subsequently enlightened by their further consequences. In this sense, Thirdness is not to be understood as a substance or even a substantive framework but rather as a reticular, a-centered and inherently mobile arras of semiotic relationships the semantic/symbolic figurations of which are to be taken as the interlocutory fringe of a perpetually unfinished experiential and cognitive venture.

[9] On this topic and, specifically, the incompleteness of Western secularization and its epistemological missteps, see below, Chap. 2.

1.3 A List of Reasons to Reject as Not Viable the Inter-legal Solutions Proposed by the (Legal) Pluralist-Multicultural Approach

All the above being said, I believe the multicultural proposal and especially its legal projections—in their being oriented towards the establishment of a pragmatic/institutional recipe well summed up by the formula 'one culture, one law', or 'to each culture its own law'—are actually not viable even if they seem to coincide with an abstract logic of cultural equivalence/equity. In support of this position there is a long array of arguments, specifically gauged on social contexts where multiculturality and migration phenomena overlap, which could be synthetized as follows:

1. When people move across national spaces, there is no certainty that they want to bring their legal apparatuses with them; nor that they want to maintain a rigid orthodox conformity to the cultural mainstream of their countries or circuits of origin.
2. Nothing assures that the legal systems of the countries from which people emigrate include a pluralist view of legal and cultural subjectivity. Hence, these legal apparatuses could aprioristically refuse any possibility of intercultural translation/transaction and inclusion of the Others' (in this case the natives of 'arrival countries') cultural habits. And yet, the legitimation of those legal apparatuses to be recognized and/or included by the hosting legal systems, rather inconsistently, cannot avoid hinging on the claim for cultural and legal pluralism. Against this backdrop, what kind of solution could a multiculturalist approach proffer with respect to the relationships between individuals from different cultures? Which legal rules should be applied to a case involving subjects culturally and legally tied, for one reason or another, to different contexts or legal systems? Multiculturalism and its legal versions seem to have no answers for these questions. Indeed, even a bird's eye view of the case law inspired by the multiculturalist approach will show how the areas ruled in tune with the 'multiculturalist tenets' almost exclusively concern infra-communitarian and cultural intersubjective issues and relationships; or, alternatively, matters relating to individual or group claims raised against public institutions and their activity.
3. However much amenable to ethnocentric readings, human rights, as well as their vernacular versions understood as constitutional fundamental rights, express a potential attitude to function as a semantic platform for an inclusive process of universalization. Their contested (exclusively) Western origin does not entirely impede an inner dialectics between their semantic potentials, which could be open to intercultural interpretation. Moreover, the universalizing inspiration of human rights' discourse constitutes the source of legitimacy for constitutional/democratic state legal systems and could be used as leverage to make the same state law provisions collapse in on themselves whenever they prove to be not interculturally inclusive.

4. The legal provisions that people on the move could be interested in bringing with them are part and parcel of a whole, more specifically, part of legal systems taken in their wholeness. What allows their social and pragmatic accomplishment to take place is precisely their belonging to and partaking in an institutional and cultural system liable to assure their effectiveness. Unfortunately, that system cannot be transplanted everywhere in its entirety, and people from different cultures must unavoidably rely upon the host state's institutional apparatuses—or at least on them as well—to enjoy any legal protection of their prerogatives.
5. Consider, now, a reverse solution. Legal norms belonging to the original social circuits of migrants and/or minorities could be assumed as axes for the adaptation and inclusion of the cultural habits underlying them. For this solution to be productive, those norms should be self-sufficient in their effects—provided that, furthermore, all the obstacles mentioned above were previously overcome. Unfortunately, again, this is on average not the case, apart from legal provisions belonging to foreign states or supranational institutions. There are, actually, a few cultural normative systems that besides rules on marriage or inheritance (in many cases however only partially) also include provisions about property, other rights in rem, obligations, contracts law, corporate law, etc. Religious normative apparatuses constitute a paradigmatic case. They, however, seem to be insufficiently complete and too out of date to assure an exhaustive discipline of these areas in contemporary social environments.[10] And yet, even the legal regime of family is strictly linked to the regulation of property, rights in rem, contracts law, obligations, and so on. The same thing could be said about inheritance and other provisions regarding personal rights and duties. It seems therefore rather unlikely that those clusters of rules on marriage or inheritance can be used as normative platforms for the elaboration of intercultural legal regimes applicable to all subjects of the host country (including natives, individuals belonging to majoritarian groups and all those from other cultures or of different faiths). But what is the solution to be adopted for all the rules needed to support and supplement the efficacy of the regulatory clusters and the related areas that seem to be outside the horizon of multiculturalists' concern?
6. Further problems arise from the need to choose a specific cultural legal apparatus for the development of an inclusive intercultural system—provided that, at least for the sake of discussion, we exclude, at this point, the state legal system of the hosting state. Why should the democratic institutions of this hyper-pluralistic and 'allophile-oriented' indigenous community choose one rather than another cultural group's original law to construe an all-comprehensive intercultural legal lexicon?

[10]Even Canon Law, despite the positivistically structured codification of its rules, includes an exhaustive discipline of the major areas in which contemporary legal experience unfolds. In many cases, it avails of state legal apparatuses by means a mechanism of *renvoi*.

7. Moreover, many cultural or religious ethical provisions conflate with state legal systems which migrants or people from other cultures come from. In many cases, at home, they experience these provisions as resulting from such a conflation rather than as ethical imperatives perceived in their own cultural or religious *purity* and considered as such. This is the case, for example, of the rules applied by the religious courts of migrants' countries of origin but, in many cases, not recognized and not even enforced by the respective state judges. The same rules that, in the name of the multiculturalist approach to pluralism, are often invoked as personal laws to be recognized by the host countries and applied by the minority communities' courts: for example, Muslim Arbitration Tribunals, the Sharia Courts, or the Rabbinical Courts. But apart from this trans-local dissymmetry, even the transplants of the state legal system rules enshrining cultural/religious habits should at least include, when the case involves intercultural relationships, also the substitution of the hosting state's legal rules and judges with those deriving from only one foreign/external state legal system. Subsequently, these imported rules should be used as a platform for the elaboration of intercultural hermeneutical solutions gauged on the factual situations including relationships between subjects belonging to the same legal systems of those rules, on one hand, and citizens of the hosting country or subjects from other different cultures and/or religions. Which would simply constitute the suicide, or a masochistic version, of the constitutional pluralism of any state legal system.
8. The last remark, besides being pragmatically unsurmountable, furthermore overlaps with the political unlikelihood that citizens of the host country, the members of majority groups as well as those of other minorities, can agree to use normative patterns from only one non-native or minority culture as the main platform for elaborating intercultural common legal rules.
9. The institutional and thematic incompleteness of cultural or religious normative systems make so that people subject to them cannot avoid resorting to the use the hosting state's legal system as for the regulation of many situations of their life as well as the development of a normative platform for their intercultural inclusion. But at this point, the anti-statist approach advocated especially by the proponents of post-modern legal pluralism would seem to be doomed to collapse in on itself, if only because of its cultural and pragmatic defectiveness.
10. The above collapse could be averted only if the intercultural legal implications faded into the background in deference to a radical and all-pervading multiculturalist policy. This means that migrants or even people belonging to minority cultures could be, alternatively, entitled or obliged to follow exclusively their cultural/religious rules. But the question is, again: do such cultural/religious apparatuses of rules suitable to exhaustively regulate all aspects of life exist? Or is this true only of others' state legal systems? In the latter case, however, the application to migrants of rules pertaining to their state legal system of origin would again raise the issue of the reification of their national/cultural belonging and the rigid identification of people with the legal schemes related to their home country. Let alone the matter of fact that such a solution could not meet the

non-migrant minorities' quest for cultural differentiation, there would be still the problem of how to choose the rule applicable to the inter-subjective relationships involving both a native and an individual from another culture. On the other hand, the insulating and socially polarizing effects of personal law regimes are well-known (but see, on this aspect, the next point). However, as I will show at length below, this outcome would constitute an element of inner inconsistency of constitutional pluralism. This is because it would allow the settlement within a pluralist legal and social 'habitat' of monist legal systems oriented by an exclusivist and rigid regime of belonging based on ethnicity, religious orthodoxy, and the corresponding normative apparatuses.

11. The application of personal cultural or religious laws would take place through the introduction inside the state legal systems of formal legal provisions—and more often than not merely bits and of them—from other normative circuits. However, the need to supplement the efficacy of these rules with (other) state legal provisions would generate, sooner or later, the perception of them as alien bodies or particles, for the absence of previous and full-scale efforts of intercultural translation/transaction would make the application of the foreign rules the source of social and systemic inconsistencies and struggles. In short, the 'foreign *legal* bodies' could stimulate the activation of 'national antibodies,' both political and legal, the action of which usually tends to turn into the neutralization, if not even the annihilation, of those who bear the *alien nomopathogens* (in this case, the Others) rather than the intercultural and dialogic transactions of their reasons and requests.
12. Moroever, it is to be considered that even in the case of personal laws and cultural/religious courts (for example, Sharia Courts) there is nothing that formally urges or obligates the communities' judges to know the national law and have a sophisticated skillfulness in managing it. On the other hand, to be included, or at least adapted, in national legal systems, their decisions should be tested for compatibility with it. And yet, according to this policy of inclusion, what would be integrated into the national legal system would be formal legal statements rather than behavioral habits. This means that engaging in any real intercultural negotiations and translations/transactions—for the same reasons put forward above—would be of the utmost difficulty.
13. Some might argue that taking the national state legal rules as a translational-intercultural counterpart would entail an aprioristic asymmetry in favor of natives' culture. For the reasons already mentioned, however, I believe that even if cultural/religious courts show in many cases a propensity to adapt their community norms to migratory contexts, such flexibility cannot be fully and effectively achieved without the ability and competence to shape and vary the responses of the national legal system to demands for recognition of cultural/religious difference. In any case, the religious/cultural courts would have no competence to rule on the relationships among citizens and immigrant community members; and the same is to be said for the relationships between the citizens belonging to a specific minority group and all the other ones (including those belonging to other minorities and/or immigrant communities). This

implies that the institutionalization of their activity would not be the best way to elaborate an inclusive and culturally non-asymmetric legal language capable of making so that anyone, from any culture or religion, can perceive their social position as equidistant from both the state law and other individuals or social groups.

14. It is important to emphasize that assuming the legal national systems as a counterpoint in order to interculturally include Others' cultural/religious habits rather than exclusively receiving the rules/norms from their contexts of origin does not necessarily imply the assumption of an aprioristic ethnocentric asymmetry. That is, that only Others' cultural or religious dimensions would (be compelled to) undergo a process of adaptative remolding or self-transformation. For interculturality to genuinely take place, the transformational translation/transaction must be bi- or multi-lateral. But that is not all. Actually, the adaptation of others' habits can involve and/or pass through a reaction that take place inside the normative religious and/or cultural systems. Nonetheless, the Others' behavioral habits could self-transform by virtue of a dialectical movement pivoting on the same apical principles of cultural apparatuses or religious norms. As I will try to show below, this collapsing in on themselves of normative cultural/religious apparatuses could pave the way to a co-pollination between their semantic and axiological potentialities, on one side, and those of national legal systems, on the other. Likewise—it must be strongly emphasized—the process of collapse/self-transformation mediated by the axiological cornerstones of cultural and normative systems could and should also involve state law precisely through a convergent path of translation/transaction between it and the cultures and/or religions of Others. Making use of the multi-layered structure of state legal system as a normative/semantic platform for intercultural translation/transaction does not at all preclude the production of a third space, a Thirdness, which can function as a symmetrical and equidistant 'adjustment terrain' among the cultural differences at play. On the contrary, it is exactly such multi-layered normative framework that conveys and, in some sense, prompts the activation of intercultural/transactional practices.
15. I deem that any aprioristic assumption against the use the normative contents of a national legal system as a counterpoint to translate/transact the Others' cultural and/or religious patterns would be a mistake. Being 'state law' is insufficient, per se, to make national legal rules unfit to open the way to multilateral processes of self-transformation—both semantic, normative and anthropological—capable of legitimating the inclusion of foreign habits and/or legal provisions within the semantic spectrum of an intercultural use of law. Conversely, were the parties to the multicultural relationship open to carrying out processes of mutual self-transformation, an intercultural inclusion could genuinely take shape as a result of a previous activity of translation/transaction involving (also) the cultural-semiotic landscapes and encyclopedias underlying formal legal provisions. Only in this way would it be possible to overcome the semantic rigidity inherent in legal provisions and avoid formalistic conflicts doomed to foster the reciprocal identitarian, if not even fetishistic,

interpretations of cultural habits and the related claims to recognition. In this regard, however, it is to be emphasized again and again that the intercultural translational/transactional process should operate, in any case, at the level of habits. Only if cross-cultural transactions are properly carried out at this level can they induce, and in a sense compel, national legal systems to self-transform for reasons of consistency with their own axiological and cognitive prerequisites. Such reflexive variations can be triggered precisely by the profiles of legal semantic relevance stemming from the cross-contextual semiotic landscape engendered by the translation/transaction between the different cultural habits. In the same vein, the national legal rules can become amenable to a process of intercultural self-transformation because of the projections that the above cross-contextual semiotic landscape could cast onto the semantic potentialities of human and/or fundamental rights: which, in this case, should be intended as a horizon of universalization rather than a reified collection of ethnocentric essences surreptitiously passing off a specific, *vernacular* identity as universality. Such a hermeneutical path and its result could avoid the chronic flaws of the legal reading of Otherness, namely the assumption of national legal rules and their cultural (axiological and cognitive) implicit patterns as paradigms to measure, signify, and ethnocentrically annihilate the Others by reducing them to the (Western) self—as is typical in the colonial and post-colonial approaches and their endemic Procrustean inclination. By contrast, the Other would be involved in the translational/transactional process as an agent called upon to participate in the production of intercultural solutions: which, therefore, could embody the 'substance of Thirdness' stemming out from the understanding of the ubiquitous semio-spatial requisites of an equitable, equidistant and inclusive paradigm of socio-legal subjectivity. In this regard, it is crucial to underscore that the main part of any implicit or invisible/mute cultural knowledge, which as such is encapsulated in the form of assumed habits in legal provisions and experience, pertains and is relevant with respect to how meaning *transforms* rather than *what it is*. To be more explicit, it could be said that the implicitness in legal translation has to do not as much with tacit rules and semantic (para-normative/linguistic) structures but rather with the qualitative and dynamic components (values, ends, emotions, habits including their plasticity) that give rhythm to the self-transformation of the linguistic semantic apparatuses in accordance with environmental changes and challenges.

16. Intercultural Law, or better the Intercultural Use of Law, does not coincide either with multiculturalism, or interculturalism,[11] at least according to their socio-political manifestations and the way they are usually intended.[12] Its radical

[11] Nor is it equivalent to other kinds of theoretical and practical approaches suggested in the last decades mainly by sociologists and anthropologists: for example, trans-culturalism and cosmopolitanism—the last one considered in all its various versions and declinations as a bottom-up cosmopolitanism—Mignolo (2000)—or a humanitarian one—Zapata-Barrero (2019).

[12] See, in a huge literature, the comparison/confrontation traceable in Meer et al. (2016), and there for further bibliographical references on this topic.

> difference from these approaches is due to its methodological and interdisciplinary treatment of cultural difference and cognitive-axiological plurality. Correspondingly, the Intercultural Use of Law is distant from the legal practices currently inspired by both multiculturalism and interculturalism.[13]

Meer, Modood and Zapata-Barrero, for example, interpret interculturalism as a methodology mainly designed to support inter-subjective and local social conflicts in which cultural difference is at stake; meanwhile multiculturalism—especially in Meer and Modood's words—would be gauged on and operate at a general societal level, where group belonging is discussed (inevitably, it seems to be assumed) in identitarian terms.

Nonetheless, neither Meer and Modood nor Zapata-Barrero seem to be particularly familiar with legal experience, lawyering, or legal logic. They—but especially Modood—seem not to realize that each legal rule always applies to the individual cases *sub specie generali*. This means, borrowing Aarnio's words, that

> In the legal investigation, the prediction that is formulated is always general as far as its nature is concerned and, consequently, says nothing about the individual attitude of the judge regarding an individual matter. As we have indicated above, a prediction states only that if the state of things belonging to the class is given
>
> H
>
> the court (presumably) will confirm the legal consequence pertaining to the class
>
> G.[14]

The intercultural use of law I propose is oriented to face each individual case as an opportunity to engender a (cultural/legal) third semio-space sprouting from an activity of translation/transaction of cultural habits. This activity is to be carried out by exploiting the axiological contents of human and/or fundamental rights taken as qualitative interfaces in the reciprocal, symmetrical and horizontal metaphorization of cultural patterns involved and situated in each situation in which the relational space of each social actor is already imbued with Otherness. And this despite the individuals' erroneous and illusionary conviction that an identitarian, oppositive and conservative reading of their existential environment isomorphically represents and embodies the actual meaning of their experience and subjectivity: namely the connection between what is 'before' and 'afterwards' the adoption of a specific conduct. Consequentially, any solution that is given to the individual case by resorting to the intercultural use of law methodology—as it is outlined in this book—is to embody a reciprocal translation/transaction and, correspondingly, a re-drawing of the semantic relations between different cultural

---

[13] 'Interculturalism', even when understood in legal terms, coincides, in many cases, with a kind of disguised assimilationism. In my view, this is precisely the case of Québec. Something different could be said with regard to the intercultural approach promoted by some Latin America countries in their most recent constitutional charter. But on these different policies of interculturality I will proffer more detailed considerations in the next chapters.

[14] Aarnio (1987).

universes of discourse. Symmetrically, any treatment of individual cases *orchestrated* without making use of the general cognitive and axiological patterns/categories of each culture as translational means, but rather as absolute and ethnocentric schemes of signification, would give rise to a mere contingent and opportunistic accommodation. The results of such an accommodating attitude, however, would be devoid of infra-cultural relational relevance as well as a genuine intercultural import. As I will try to show later, this is also because in the field of interculturality there can be no room for ontological or operational distinctions between goals and values as well as for formalistic functional equivalences that are 'calculated' regardless of a previous broad fathoming of the semio-relational implications underlying the morphological features of cultural behaviors and the situations in which their translation/transaction must take place.[15]

Against the backdrop of the above considerations, I shall now proceed to briefly illustrate the contents of the book chapter to chapter.

1.4 The Structure of the Book

Following this chapter (Introduction), in Chap. 2, I will address the relationships among secularization, democracy and multiculturality. More specifically, I will try to emphasize the deep and too often ignored connection between Christian moral theology and the conceptual grammar of legal language in the Western legal tradition. As is well-known, Carl Schmitt strongly and icastically underscored the resilience of certain theological schemes in the architecture of modern secularized politics. However, far beyond so-called political theology, there is an ocean of cultural and semantic continuities between the conceptual lexicon of Western legal systems and the principle of Christian moral theology nestled in Medieval Western law as remolded by Second Scholasticism and its rationalist transfiguration carried out by Grotius and other modern legal thinkers. Enveloped in the casing of a secular/rationalist rhetoric, the moral/theological categories can be still traced within the legal apparatuses of contemporary legal systems. What is even worse, they lie in the objectifying shadow of the epistemology of secularization that bestows on them the mark of 'axiological neutrality' and 'universal significance' as expressions of reason. Moreover, this is the same epistemology that underlies the modern distinctions between 'internal' and 'external,' 'objective' and 'subjective,' values and facts, primary properties and secondary (or merely qualitative) ones, 'is' and 'ought,' the public sphere vs. individual freedom, and so on. I will try to trace the cultural and religious origins of the legal language, which still invisibly gives rhythm to daily life in Western legal contexts, to show how it tacitly defeats any possibility of keeping the liberal-constitutional promise of 'neutrality.' In this regard, I will

[15] Against functionalist intercultural translations and (attemps ati) accomodation, see Keane (2007, p. 223 ff.).

emphasize the cultural and institutional incompleteness of 'secularization' and the asymmetrical treatment of cultural/religious minorities and their differences that result from the attempt to pass off Western secularization as complete and all-encompassing. Subsequently, I will explain why a complete secularization is a culturally unviable task, and further clarify the need to veer towards a mature interpretation of the 'secular' in view of the anthropological significance of the religious dimension and its distinction from the denominational one. 'Intercultural secularization' is the label I will propose to suggest a way out from the asymmetrical and conflictive architecture inherent in the anthropological and legal subjectivity engendered by the partisan interpretations and implementations of both the democratic/constitutional ideals of Enlightenment and the efforts to rationalize legal language as they have been carried out in Europe from the seventeenth century onward. In developing this proposal, I will try to show why current problems arising from the lack of inclusion of people on the move are the other side of a colonial and post-colonial blindness to the anthropological significance of religion and the related attempt to superimpose on colonized countries the faith/reason, politics/religion, law/freedom, objective/subjective and external/internal divides incompletely applied in European and other colonizing countries. I will conclude the chapter focusing on translational/transactional processes to be managed by means of a semiotically informed methodology as the crucial ingredient in order to combine the exigencies historically underpinning the secularization project, cultural symmetry and pluralist claims.

In Chap. 3, I propose a methodological approach for what I term 'intercultural use of law.' More specifically, I will illustrate here my approach to intercultural translation/transaction based on the anti-reifying and anti-essentializing argument that *people are not norms or legal rules*. Simultaneously, this view is coupled with an understanding of 'cultures' as dynamic and pro-active competencies rather than repertoires of acquired cognitive and behavioral patterns. Consequentially, I will propose a way to conceive of intercultural translation as a semiotic activity able to parallel the transformative process entailed by people in trans-*lation*, to be etymologically intended as the movement through semantic and experiential spaces that people traverse when they leave their context of origin. Prior to symbolized structures, culture is made of habits: enactive and proactive scripts epitomizing the organisms' relational adaptive schemes that, in turn, are plastically employed in facing environmental challenges. Habits operate tacitly and invisibly, underneath the threshold of consciousness; and even if they present a certain degree of rigidity and resistance to change, they are however denoted by a plasticity far more pronounced when compared to symbolized categories or normative standards. This means that they are capable of maintaining their relational significance even when the contextual conditions vary or fluctuate. A habit, therefore, might go through a metaphorical displacement—which is, actually, a spatial-semiotic transferal from one semantic domain to another—and largely retain its adaptive significance as well as its inner and constitutive teleological hub. Focusing on cultural habits rather than their symbolized and often fetishistically essentialized projections, and bringing to the surface their underlying semiotic relationality, would be a momentous cognitive and axiological achievement. In this regard I focus on the 'invisible and mute' parts of human communicative action and legal experience so as to develop a specific approach to excavate them beyond the morphological features/properties of phenomena and behaviors and, simultaneously, bring to the surface the corresponding underlying semiotic landscapes to be used in order to carry out intercultural translations. Respect for cultures would hinge, in this case, upon the possibility for people to exert their agency in managing a controlled transformation of habits and their relational significance rather than in the formal and symbolized preservation of behavioral schemes metonymically taken for their morphological exterior features. If the recognition of Others' normative apparatuses were gauged on the assessment and adaptive adjustment of the habits underlying individual or collective conduct rather than the formal or morphological iteration of their symbolic and behavioral exterior features, then the translational task inherent in the intercultural use of law could be carried out as a metaphorical and creative interpenetration between different spaces of experience and signification. In short, the respect for culture would no longer be distinguishable from the production of culture, that is, a thirdspace isomorphic to the transformative dynamics ineluctably involved in any intercultural contact. In this pursuit, I have built a methodology for the intercultural use of law articulated in three steps: respectively, cross-cultural narratives, cross-cultural contextualization, and translation/transaction. I will illustrate by means of practical cases the potentialities of this methodology and, specifically, its relevance for what I call a timely intercultural law, which is intended to proffer a recipe for the re-thinking of the overall function of law as a means to the planning of social facts.[16]

In Chap. 4, I will address the dynamic relationship between space and categorization. In this regard I will try to unearth the semiotic *continuum* extant between legal meanings and the scope of people's actions. This continuity depends on the spatial projections implicitly entailed in each categorical frame and, symmetrically, the semantic texture of space's experiential framework. This implies that categories and spaces are semiotic dimensions the form of which is the result of their mutual interplay. The transformation in symbolic schemes of what results from the *semiosical* interpenetration between words and spaces is, therefore, to be continually maintained open to the dynamics of the above interplay in order not to betray the signification inherent in each category, or better in the activities of categorization and spatialization that each epitomizes. This means that any change in spatial experience and, thereby, in the texture of its relational fabric brings a mutual translation of different spaces; but, at the same time, that the interactional spatial dynamics go hand in hand with an unavoidable self-remolding of the categorical borders. Insofar as each categorical frame contains elements that can be also traced among the checklist of other categories, their respective spatial projections are continually exposed to intermingling. In the same vein, any spatial circuit comprises elements that are relationally interrelated with other spaces of experience. This semiotic ubiquity or multi-situatedness of the denotative and connotative components of

[16] See, in this regard, Ricca (2020).

both spaces and categories has a specific import: that spatial and semantic dimensions vary concomitantly and their being in tune is the other side of the process of universalization, namely the ongoing production of signification. The dynamics of spatial experience bring, therefore, a generative logic of Otherness, which is nothing but the unremitting and unrestrainable self-producing phenomenon of translational interplay (to be intended in both categorical and spatial terms) generating an interspatial/intercultural experiential context. With respect to the sprouting of this interspatial/intercultural framework human rights function as interfaces of metaphorical transposition (to be intended, again, in both spatial and semantic terms) rather than as standards of evaluation hinged upon a hierarchical-pyramidal logic of comparison among cultural differences and conflicting claims. The above continuity between meaning and space allows me to propose a move from the fruitful critical approach labeled 'legal geography' to what I term 'legal chorology,' which includes a dynamic and transformative way to conceive of the relationships among meaning, space, human rights and the *transpatiality* of cultural experience.

In Chap. 5, I will address the problem of the ethnocentrism of human rights discourse through an epistemological analysis of the cognitive means proffered by modern art to adopt a dis-compositional approach to categorization. More specifically I will try to show how an understanding of cultural differences based on the translational activity can be carried out by exploiting in a cross-cultural and metaphorical way the semiotic textures underlying the alleged morphological features of Others' behaviors and communicative acts. I propose this hermeneutical and operational dispositive with the aim of supporting a symmetrical and thereby genuinely 'contrapuntal' expression of cultural competences and agencies. Beginning with Gauguin's juxtaposition of categorical/images belonging to different discursive and cultural universes, I then focus on Klee's approach to the function of *figuration* and his dynamic, interactive and transformative theory of categorization. The import of this excursus across the semiotic territories of visibility/invisibility for the intercultural use of law will find its theoretical and pragmatic hub in the translating function that can be bestowed to human rights as *transducers* among different universes of meaning. The *palpable* signification of this methodological outlook will be shown by putting together the spatial implications of intercultural coexistence and the role of human and/or fundamental rights in remolding the cognitive maps of daily experience. For this purpose, I will analyze and try to devise a solution for the issues related to the so-called nuisance law, arising within the multicultural micro-spaces of cohabitation.

In Chap. 6, I will develop the chorological view proposed in the previous chapter with specific regard to the legal profiles of intercultural and interspatial relationships. In this direction, I will come back to the intertwining between cultural categories and spatial categories in order to *make visible* the interspatial and semiosical blurring produced by the individuals' trans-posing/trans-lating through manifold and culturally plural circuits of state/territorial sovereignty.

Subsequently I will focus on intercultural translation intended as a place of convergence for the condensation of categorical properties and connotations used by different cultures for marking space. I will try to show how translating cultures, each into another, by means of law's spectrum could be equivalent to and coextensive with translating different 'spatialities' and vice versa.[17] Reaching this interlocutory target allows for the configuration of inter-spaces capable of working as a platform to assure the legal relevance of different culturally oriented subjective agencies. The theoretical toolkit to investigate these topics will be precisely legal chorology, in this case illustrated through the following argumentative steps: (1) Legal chorology and a timely intercultural translation; (2) Inter-spatial dynamics and cognitive deficiencies of legal qualifications across cultures. To conclude the Chapter, I will apply these methodological tools to envisage a pluralistic legal approach conceived to explore the potentialities of intercultural interplay beyond the exclusive use of inter-normative devices and inter-legality.

In the following two chapters, I will apply the theoretical and methodological approach developed above to two thorny issues of contemporary debate on cultures, rights and space.

In Chap. 7, I will combine the chorological approach developed in previous chapters and the topic of indigeneity. My starting point here will be the epistemological and semiotic relationship extant between the production of culture and spatialization. From this perspective, I will try to turn upside down the widespread post-colonial approach to indigeneity, as such pivoted on a normative and historically contingent conception of the relationship between indigenous people and their territories. My proposal is oriented, instead, to emphasize the anthropological/cognitive co-implication between space and culture, its universal relevance and, therefore, the consequent characterization as 'indigenous of the Earth' of all populations and cultures dwelling, in the past as well as in the present, in planetary spaces. This approach cognitively puts on an equal footing all the cultures dwelling on the planet and their semanticizations of space to confute the idea that indigeneity is only the subjective interpretation of an objective space existing 'out there.' Quite the opposite, I will propose a radical conception of the plurality of spaces, as such isomorphic to the cognitive plurality of cultures. In contrast to the current ontological turn in the interpretation of cultural and indigenous issues, I will emphasize the semiosical transformative relationality and interdependence of all the possible recipes concerning the constitutive inter-penetration between space and cognition. From this assumption stems the necessity to conceive of intercultural relationships as phenomena of transposition/translation intervening among different ways of spatializing human experience. Therefore, ignoring or blindly overwhelming each of these recipes of spatialization is tantamount to a loss in understanding space itself, insofar as it is nothing but an emergence from its semanticizations. From this perspective, the intercultural and chorological use of human rights as interfaces for a metaphorical translation among different 'spatialities' will represent an ingredient

[17] A mesmerizing reading of Lefebvre's (1974) critical work on space, everyday life and the commitment to re-categorization inherent in intercultural approach to both cognition and socio-political issues can be found in Irwin (2004).

for the production of a planetary thirdspace of coexistence that comes as a pro-active synthesis between 'is' and 'ought' along the path leading humanity towards the future.

In Chap. 8, I will bring under the lens of the legal intercultural and chorological approach the much-debated issue regarding the international protection of sacred places. Once again, I will base my analysis on the demonstration that religion and its anthropological/spatial implications are two sides of the same coin and that the logic of secularization—that is, the alleged ontological divide between faith and reason, belief and facts, subjective and objective—is a serious hindrance to any possible solution to the problems related to the international protection of sacred places. I will underline, therefore, the necessity to apply the intercultural/chorological methodology to carry out a translation among the spatializations that religious discourse embodied in sacred places. More specifically, a translation among the projections in the life experience unfolding through the semio-spatial surroundings of sacred places and the trans-local cultural scope of their meaning (consider in this sense, the trans-spatial significations and ways of experiencing attached to sacred places as Mecca, St. Peter Church in Rome, Jerusalem, etc.).

To conclude I would like to proffer a kind of disclaimer to the reader. The intercultural methodology presented in this book is quite different from the commonly applied concepts of multiculturalism and interculturalism. The crucial difference lies in its interdisciplinary prospection, straddling law, anthropology, and semiotics. For this reason, I have intentionally made room for some reiteration of the theoretical and methodological schemes throughout the different chapters. The aim is twofold: improving the acquisition of familiarity with the use of an intercultural legal approach, and facilitating the independent reading of each chapter.

Let me close this introduction with a kind of catchphrase that can serve—this is my hope—as a compass in navigating the text: when multiculturality takes shape in the eyes of any local observer, interculturality has already taken place in their daily life environment and has silently built its headquarters inside their mind.

References

Aarnio A (1987) The rational as reasonable: a treatise on legal justification. Reidel, Dordrecht

Bhabha HK (1998) The third space. In: Rutheford J (ed) Identity, community, culture, difference. Lawrence and Wishart, London

Britton CM (1999) Édouard Glissant and postcolonial theory: strategies of language and resistance. New world studies. University Press of Virginia, Charlottesville

de Certeau M (1990) L'invention du quotidien, vol. I, Arts de faire. Gallimard, Paris

De Schutter H (2004) Gadamer and interculturalism: ethnocentrism or authenticity. In: Powell D, Sze F (eds) Interculturalism: exploring critical issues. Inter-Disciplinary Press, Oxford, pp 51–57

Ellis TB (2009) On the death of the pilgrim: the postcolonial hermeneutics of Jarava Lal Mehta. In: Bilimoria P, Irwine AB (eds) Postcolonial philosophy of religion. Springer Science+Business Media, Dordrecht, pp 105–120

Ellis TB (2013) On the death of the pilgrim: the postcolonial hermeneutics of Jarava Lal Mehta. Springer Science+Business Media, Dordrecht

Gadamer H-G (2013) Truth and method. Bloomsbury, London

Glissant É (1969) L'intention poétique. Poétique II. Gallimard, Paris

Glissant É (1990) Poétique de la relation. Poétique III. Gallimard, Paris

Glissant É (1997) Traité du Tout-Monde. Poétique IV. Gallimard, Paris

Greimas AJ (1983) Du Sens II. Seuil, Paris

Hannikainen IR et al (2021) Are there cross-cultural legal principles? Modal reasoning uncovers procedural constraints on law. Cogn Sci Multidiscip J 45(8):1–13. https://doi.org/10.1111/cogs.13024

Irwin J (2004) Intercultural everyday life via Lefebvre. In: Powell D, Sze F (eds) Interculturalism: exploring critical issues. Inter-Disciplinary Press, Oxford, pp 91–96

Keane W (2007) Christian moderns: freedom and fetish in the mission encounter. The University of California Press, Berkeley

Lefebvre H (1974) La production de l'espace. Anthropos, Paris

Mandair A (2009) Autoimmunity in the study of religion(s): ontotheology, historicism and the theorization of Indic phenomena. In: Bilimoria P, Irwine AB (eds) Postcolonial philosophy of religion. Springer Science+Business Media, Dordrecht, pp 171–191

Meer N, Modood T, Zapata-Barrero R (eds) (2016) Multiculturalism and interculturalism: debating the dividing lines. Edinburgh University Press, Edinburgh

Mignolo WD (2000) The many faces of cosmo-polis: border thinking and critical cosmopolitanism. Publ Cult 12:721–748. https://people.duke.edu/~wmignolo/Interactivecv/Publications/ManyFacesCosmo.pdf

Ricca M (2020) Planning facts through law: legal reasonableness as creative indexicality and trans-categorical re-configuration. Int J Semiot Law 33:1089–1123. https://doi.org/10.1007/s11196-020-09702-z

Ricca M (2022) The 'spaghettification' of performativity across cultural boundaries: the trans-culturality/trans-spatiality of digital communication as an event horizon for speech acts. Int J Semiot Law 35:2435–2479. https://doi.org/10.1007/s11196-021-09880-4

Ricca M (2023a) Cultural constraints of legal interpretation and legal translation (forthcoming)

Ricca M (2023b) The semiotics and the space-time ingredients of legal experience (forthcoming)

Soja E (1996) Thirdspace: journeys to Los Angeles and other real-and-imagined places. Blackwell, Malden

Zapata-Barrero R (2019) Methodological interculturalism: breaking down epistemological barriers around diversity management. Ethn Racial Stud 42(3):346–356. https://doi.org/10.1080/01419870.2019.1538527

Chapter 2
Impossible Neutrality: Cultural Differences and the Anthropological Incompleteness of Western Secularization

2.1 Impossible Neutrality: How Religious Anthropologies Invisibly Make the World Visible

Who can define themselves a secularized (or *laïque*) individual? And what does 'secularization' mean? At first, it could even seem elementary to answer such a question. 'Secular'—one could say—is everything that does not have to do with religion. And in saying that, one would strictly abide by common sense. Nevertheless, in the above answer there is nothing as obvious, clear, or self-evident as one might initially think.

The idea of secularization is quite different from that of '*laïcité*,' the expression used in languages of Latin origin (e.g., French, Italian, or Spanish). Anglophone idioms have no strictly equivalent word. The parallel term is, precisely, secularization, and yet the semantic spectrum does not coincide. Furthermore, the word '*laicus*' can also be traced to the ecclesiastical Catholic domain. Its meaning has more than just a political pertinence, as might be assumed by common sense definitions. In the Catholic church, for example, *laicus* is the 'simple believer', namely he/she who is entitled to the so called 'common priesthood' by virtue of baptism.[1] And besides, in socio-political jargon, *laïque* can be intended as the profiling features of the layman, that is to say s/he who is just a citizen, as such partaking in public life as a human being and not necessarily seeking ideological or communitarian belonging. *Laïque*, in this sense, refers to everything that can be ascribed to the paradigm of socio-political, if not even anthropological, 'normality,' and conjures up the idea of 'equality.' Semantically expanded, 'laïque' transmigrates in the English language as laic and thence lay (or layman), which can be compared to the broadest meaning of 'secular,' insofar as it is intended as equivalent to 'common sense' or 'commonplace.'

[1] Corecco (1999). For a recent comparative analysis with the common priesthood in Protestant tradition see Pouw (2021).

M. Ricca, *Intercultural Spaces of Law*, Law and Visual Jurisprudence 10,
https://doi.org/10.1007/978-3-031-27436-7_2

The semantic expansion of both the words secular and *laïque* unveils, especially with regard to the last articulations, a close connection with 'culture.' This begs the question: what can be labeled as 'normal' outside a cultural frame of reference? Or irrespective of schemes of judgment forged within a social and communicative circuit? Even assuming, according to the natural law tradition, that 'normal' is to be equated to 'natural,' there is no empirical nature, at least conceivable by human beings, other than the one corresponding to the natural world seen through the cultural lens.[2] On the other hand, what other cognitive agency could establish what nature or culture is if not the same cultural understanding conceived as a continuous process through which the human mind and nature reciprocally transform and reproduce? Nonetheless, 'secular' and '*laïque*,' in both Latin and Anglophone languages, find their molar significance in 'not having to do with religion': even if 'secularization' has gained over time a broader significance involving all cultural aspects of life; meanwhile *laïcité*, especially in French experience, assumed a political import, mostly concerned with the relationship between state e denominations considered as institutional circuits and communities of belonging. In any case, a question arises. How is it possible to neatly and ultimately split apart culture and religion? Even if one decided to take the idea of 'secular' as slightly more than a political commonplace or slogan, things would not become any clearer. Deepening the focus of the analysis, one would end up realizing that burning bridges with religion requires a previous definition of what is on the other side.

Where, therefore, does religion dwell? In sacred buildings? In the minds of the religious leaders of all the different faiths? In people's conscience or imagination? In some specific kind of mental disposition? Or rather in people's behaviors, gestures? Or, still, in the intentions underlying their uses of the world? And thereby also in places, garments, food, journeys, words, actions: in short, in any item which can be converted into a symbol or a sign of faith? And, consequently, are there specific spaces religion inhabits, so one could—if so desired—keep a distance? Or, on the contrary, is religion endemic to the world, nestling even where it is invisible and, above all, when and where people suppose its absence?[3] If this were the case, that is, if religion were omnipresent by means of its evident or silent connotative joining to common (abstractly secular) objects, words and behaviors, how might one obtain a 'safe' distance from it? And furthermore, if religion is grafted onto what appears 'normal', 'laic', how can one discern what is religious and what is secular, and vice versa? Or, instead, should one conclude that 'religious' and 'secular' have specular, reciprocally referential meanings, and thereby are devoid of any autonomous significance? All in all, is there a better definition for 'secular' than 'all that is not religious;' and, reciprocally for 'religious' than 'all that is not secular'? All of which is to say that—at the end of this (double) recursive game—the end result is nonsense.

I understand that at this point the reader could suspect a verbal trap. They might rebut that in every life context people can recognize religion, as even children

---

[2]Ingold (2000) and Descola and Pálsson (1996).

[3]Norris and Inglehart (2011).

do. The problem is, however, that all social and communicative frameworks are forged by culture, of which religion is, at least historically, part and parcel. This means that 'the religious' is inescapably destined to be differentiated inside each cultural universe according to criteria that already include religion among their sources of meaning.[4] In the same vein, even what is labeled as secular, normal, common, obvious, self-evident, is the (however interlocutory) outcome of a process of differentiation molded by the picks and axes of culture including its religious imageries.[5]

The interpenetration between culture and religion is nothing but a consequence of history. This is because everywhere in the world, in all the social imaginaries, religions have unfolded over time as an anthropological source and an agency for the production of social meanings. The worldviews coextensive with the present cultural frames have also been developed and carved out through the activity of religious imagination. The world faiths and their categorizations of the experiential universe have run as powerful undercurrents in the making of the cultural habits of the different populations, to the point of blending with them and becoming *invisible*. It is precisely for this reason that, for example, a French person and an Indian person might—nonsensically—represent themselves as rigorously secularized even as atheists, exhibiting through this attitude how they keep what they deem to be religious at a distance. And yet—and this is the point—even when they define something as religious and something else as secular or *normal*, neither of them can avert using categories that are culturally rooted in Christianity and Hinduism, despite—but perhaps, precisely because—these conflate and are diluted in their respective commonsense.

The ambiguities, however, do not end here. This is because not only individuals, but also public institutions or states can declare themselves to be secular and/or *laïque*. Actually, the institutional lexicon designates the word 'secular' as a peculiar feature of public politics. But if it so, what precisely do we mean by a 'secular state?' Does it entail that the public institutions must have nothing to do with religion? That they are to maintain a clean line of separation from it? But how is this possible, beyond and outside the historical and theoretical schemes used to define the dialectics between state and religion, if religion dwells in people's habits and is interspersed even in the minutest folds of their daily life? Which is, *inter alia*, the main reason it is so hard to sharply distinguish what is secular or 'normal' from what is

[4]From this point of view, it makes little sense to consider secularism as marked by a kind of 'correlative secondariness' to religion (Modood 2019a, pp. 196 f.) because without religion per se there would be no 'secularism' or 'secular dimension.' The 'secular' and the 'religious', inasmuch as they are considered the wings of an oppositional couple, are relationally co-defined; neither of them is prior to the other. In turn, secularism is dialectically twinned with denominationalism.

[5]This circularity is the main factor weakening the explanatory model based on a distinction/differentiation process, drawn from Spencer-Brown's (1979) seminal text that undergirds Luhmann's approach to religion: see Luhmann (1977, 1990, 2000). For some interesting considerations about the development of Luhmann's theorization on religion see Laermans and Verschraegen (2001).

religious? What makes things even more complicated, then, is the circumstance that if the (alleged) secular state is to avert any connection with religion, it is consequentially not even adequately equipped to prosecute or forbid it. In this regard, we should consider that the secular state is not an atheist state, and a secularized society is not necessarily an atheist one. A rigorous *laïcité* is an anthropologically almost unviable recipe—as Jacobinism or the most radical Marxist socio-political experiments have shown. Any attempt to stamp out the worldviews ingrained in religious beliefs and in the ensuing orthopraxis—as an intransigent atheism would require—is tantamount to imposing one or more worldviews completely devoid of any religious connotation/contamination. This is the ultimate goal, but also the main dilemma, of all the plans envisioning a completely atheist society and state. But the past experience in this direction raises a crucial question. Beyond abstract claims, what are the real chances at the present stage of human history and culture that a planned construction of individual and collective know-how could succeed in erasing any resilient religious *relics* from its semantic apparatuses?

A complete and radical decontamination of both public life and private imagination from any component directly, or indirectly, related to religion would assume as feasible the *invention* of a psychosocial world that is bereft of its own past and, inevitably, its cultural heritage.[6] Nevertheless the building blocks of cultural innovations as well as revolutions, and therefore of any change in cognitive paradigms, are however themselves 'culture.' Novelty in all knowledge systems is, and can always be, only partial, and more often than not peripheral.[7] In any case, a wholesale annihilation of the past cultural vessels or their radical unmooring from their 'semantic forbearers' is simply impossible to do if only because the tools to complete such a cyclopean enterprise cannot avoid including those past 'cultural items'. The life of culture cannot reproduce, or even survive its self-deconstruction without making use of the means previously embedded in its own previous unfolding. This is the developmental course of both societal and individual life. Precisely for this reason, a serious integralist atheism is not a viable option. Any attempt to implement such a plan would bring with and in itself the semantic resilience of knowledge and practices cognitively embroiled in religious experience and imageries. Conversely, should such a semantic and anthropological legacy be denied or disclaimed (something the historical self-mythicization of secularism in many cases actually tried to do), things could become even worse, if only because it would made occult and ungraspable what would however remain deeply nestled inside the psycho-social grammar and lexicon of the same atheism. The ineluctability of such a historical-cultural paradox makes it so that, in the end, the same atheism misses its declared neutral rationality and transforms itself into an irrational faith, nothing other than fuel for senseless fights against other faiths.

However, if the path of secularism cannot run aboard of the atheism ship, namely under the aegis of an absolute absence of religion, what then are its proper (if any)

[6] Glenn (2014).

[7] van Quine (1980, pp. 20–46).

meanings and its horizon of feasibility? The almost unanimous answer of contemporary political thought seems to coagulate around one word: *neutrality*. The secular state is (and ought to be) *neutral*. This means that it does not fight against faiths. Conversely, it constitutively recognizes people's freedom to profess and practice their own belief. And yet, on the other hand, the state should in any case keep itself at a proper (and wise) distance from all faiths: a distance that is drawn and somehow self-produced by the public/private divide. This means that religious belief inhabits the people's private and intimate sphere, but from there it can freely project its implications into the public domain, at least as long as it does not collide with other public values/ends that the secular socio-legal system qualifies as fundamental and indefectible. To put it more simply, this means that the secular and (allegedly) neutral state should relate to and interact with religions as an uninvolved agent, a kind of metaphysical traffic light.

Although the metaphors 'state/uninvolved agent' or 'state/traffic light' might appear to be somehow evocative, they are however tremendously incomplete. The traffic light does not determine its own colors, nor regulate the timing of red, green and yellow. There is always someone who programs its functions and decides where it is to be placed. By contrast, in secular public life no one could nor should replace the state when what is to be established is *whether*, *how* and *where* religious faith and its expressions are to be interfered with. Only the state itself can accomplish such a task. But to do so, the same state is requested once again to distinguish what is secular and/or *normal* from what is specifically religious. The problem, however, is that it is simply impossible to determine rules about something without simultaneously defining and qualifying it.[8] Moreover, it is impossible to define and qualify something if not by means of criteria and patterns that are culturally determined. This conclusion, however, would take both the state and the people back to the point of departure in so far as culture, in turn, is not free of religious respects and roots; the same culture that, on the other hand, should provide the semantic and axiological standards functional towards the self-reflexive recognition and distinction of what is secular or, *instead*, religious.

The secular state's neutrality postulates that its institutions can cast a gaze on social experience from nowhere, somehow an aseptic one, as such projected by a virtual 'nadir of culture.' If conceived in these terms, however, it seems to be a blindness rather than a neutral gaze. It does not take much to realize that a culturally aseptic neutrality is impossible to achieve. The dream, or better, the miracle of a secular point of view, intended as absolutely neutral and a-cultural, is only an *ignis*

[8]This is also the main problem with so-called 'negative freedom,' as well as the proto-liberal conception of 'property'. However much these prerogatives were meant to be protected in negative terms (allegedly), through a mere withdrawal (or refraining) by the state from its activity, at the same time, state legal rule cannot avoid determining the scope of the limitations of its own activity. But precisely this determination amounts to, or in any case implicitly entails, tacit definitions and/or conceptualizations of the content of negative freedoms (as well as property). In short, it is impossible to legally protect something without semantically, and thereby also pragmatically, forging the 'subject' of protection.

fatuus—at least according to what the state and democratic experience has shown to date. Conversely, its 'persuasive' appearance hinges entirely upon the mimetic semantics of religion and its resilient stratifications inside the secular habits and lexicon. It further depends on each individual, as they make sense of their own experience, sincerely believing themselves to express ideas and adopt behaviors *coded* as 'neutral' and 'purely rational,' while remaining—through this rhetorical artifice (or discursive *code*)—completely unaware of the religious legacy nestled in what they are doing.[9]

A possible objection to the above arguments could be sustained by relying upon a kind of *representationalism*. What matters—it could be contested—is not so much the origin of ideas or behaviors as rather the actual way they are represented. To put it in more topic-related terms, we could say: if Western civilization assumes its own legal categories to be secular, then they must be deemed authentically secular; and this even if they encapsulate a matrix or a nub imbued with religious culture and/or moral theology. I think, however, that such an argument is utterly devoid of plausibility, at least from a psychosocial point of view. It postulates a kind of cognitive self-evidence that is doomed to crumble as soon as the encounter with cultural difference comes upon the scene. The above representationalism is affected by a radical limitation coextensive with its inherent, even if perhaps historically and locally fruitful, cultural relativity. It tacitly states that there is no cognition without representation, and therefore that representation and cognition are indistinguishable. We have, in other words, a kind of absolute and omnipotent semantic performativity.[10] Nevertheless, even if I do not agree with the epistemological premises of such a point of view,[11] I can recognize its rhetorical efficaciousness with regard to the specific topic of secularization. It seems to assert that, inside an assumedly abstract self-bounded and self-reflexive social context, cultural entities are what people believe they are. While conceding that the performativity of representations is somewhat endowed with such an ontogenetic power, nonetheless I think that this should not amount to legitimizing its absolutization. Representations are tools, surely endowed with operational and thereby pragmatic implications, but they are not magically equivalent to some divine 'fiat.' Unfortunately, this is exactly

[9]The idea that *codes* can be used to self-differentiate the sub-systems of the social cosmos belongs to Luhmann's theory of social systems applied to religion: Luhmann (1997, 2000).

[10]Sometimes this performativity is dissimulated in the phrase 'conditions of intelligibility:' De Roover et al. (2011). Nonetheless, the conditions of intelligibility presuppose and encapsulate other cognitive/cultural boundary conditions that have previously plowed the semiotic field hosting the conscious understanding of symbolic categories. It would be enough to consider, in this regard, the metaphysical/meta-epistemological speculations raised by the contemporary development of sub-atomic physics—e.g., the various formulations of string theory. Of course, everything depends on what we assume the semiotic scope of 'conditions of intelligibility' is. See, in this regard, for example, Calinger (1999), Shapin (1994), and Graham and Kantor (2009). Further on I will show how the cognition/translation of 'invisibility/implicitness' underlain by morphological features is the main problem with legal intercultural relationships.

[11]I proposed a criticism of 'performatives' in Ricca (2022b): see there for an exposition of my viewpoints and for bibliographical references on this topic.

what the above psycho-representational objection seems to assume in defense of 'secularization as neutrality.' Moreover, merely expressing different representative modalities would suffice to reveal the pragmatic implications of an exclusively self-centered representation of secularity/neutrality, betraying how beset it is with thorny difficulties. Indeed, this is precisely the situation that contemporary multicultural/multireligious societies are called to cope with throughout both the global North and South—even if along different paths.

What appears secular, rational, self-evident, natural, normal, etc., in the eyes of people who observe themselves or their institutions from inside their own culture can, by contrast, divulge its religious roots before the eyes of Others: namely, those who cast their gaze from a cultural outside or elsewhere. Secularization, or better, the perception (even when genuine) of local secularization processes is culturally relative (or culture-driven). What is important about such a conclusion, however, concerns the possibilities for the coexistence of cultural and religious differences within social contexts that are not homogeneous. This issue—to put it more directly—boils down to the following question: what does the cultural relativity of secularization imply for the alleged religious neutrality of the democratic state and its ability to function as the political hub of equality among cultural and religious subjectivities?

My answer—quite bluntly—is that in any multicultural/multireligious social universe the cultural relativity of secularization makes the neutrality of the state impossible. And, even worse, the practical impossibility of neutrality ineluctably ends up producing social and legal asymmetries for citizens from different faiths and cultures, thereby contributing to the spread of a creeping sense of pervasive injustice. This basically depends upon the naïve (but by no means less recurrent) attempts to impose what is neutral for one person upon Others, as if it should necessarily be neutral for them; the same Others who from the height (or the base) of their difference perceive that alleged neutrality to be culturally and religiously connoted, intrinsically relative, and sometimes even partisan. Once again, any culture, on average, is neutral by default for those who observe it from within and independently from Otherness. Such 'self-centered neutrality', moreover, fatally leans toward an anything-but-politically-innocuous transmutation into 'naturalness,' thence self-evidence and, in the end, universality. The immediate and dramatic consequence of such a conversion is that whoever does not share and transform into practice the behavioral patterns that are coextensive with the 'cultural substance' of that neutrality, puts themselves outside 'nature', beyond the *legitimate* boundaries of the 'human.'

At this point, a rather unequivocal argument could be posited: If the implementation of secularization is charged with so many problems and difficulties, how could it have become an axis of modern and contemporary constitutionalism? Or even a steadfast label to which everyone can ascribe their claims—including the various denominational representatives—by giving their own interpretation and trying to pass it off as the authentic cornerstone of liberal democratic experience?

I think the answer to the above questions can be found in history. Secularization, as a political frame, is an offspring of Enlightenment. The possibility to turn its ideal scheme into an institutional and practical option, however, does not automatically imply Jacobinism or some sort of militant atheism, that is to say an aprioristic hostile attitude to religion. Rather, the very source of secularization is to be found in an alternative faith: trust in the self-evidence of reason and the possibility to grasp truth through rational thought.

The Enlightenment and its secularizing momentum were the political 'incarnation' of modern rationalism that had already arisen in Europe during the seventeenth century. The contemporary struggle against ecclesiastical powers and their cultural bulwarks should be understood as a consequence rather than as a premise to the spread of faith in reason. From the scientific truths related to Galileo's and Newton's discoveries to the alleged self-evidence of the rational-natural law and its universal ethical assumptions, the axioms of Enlightenment secularism orbit a peculiar anthropological prerequisite: the (presumed) ability of all human beings to use their reason to grasp the order of nature, both physical and anthropic.

From a chronological perspective, what triggered the modern polarization between faith and reason was first and foremost the natural theology advocated by the Catholic church and its opposition to the new scientific discoveries.[12] The new interpretations of the universe and its order were considered to be an attack on the centrality of humankind and, consequently, on any theology based on human beings created in the image and likeness of the Creator himself—according to the doctrine of '*Imago Dei.*' The relativization of the human position in the universe was seen as a direct detraction of legitimation to a divine natural-social order of which religion had been assumed to be—up until that time—the ultimate guardian. The new role of the natural sciences undermined the centrality of *temporal* ecclesiastical institutions and posed a threat to their power. Similar dynamics unfolded in the political field. It was not religion in and of itself that was the source of the dualistic antagonism between modern political thought and the universes of faith but rather the ecclesiastical institutions' self-representation in the public arena and the legitimation they assured to the *Ancien Régime* power structures. The socio-political dialectics between reason and faith was fueled by strategic reasons that can only indirectly be traced back to a genuinely cognitive or anthropological source.[13] The fear and suspicion of religious institutions transformed the dispute between science and natural theology into a struggle for power, which had only indirectly to do with knowledge in and of itself. This is why political secularization (and even *laïcité*) and modern rationalism cannot be understood as synonymous.[14]

---

[12] Funkenstein (2018).

[13] In this regard, however, it must be noted that a non-secondary role had been previously played by the 'problem of universals,' and specifically Ockham's individualistic nominalism. Nominalism (since Roscellino), through its debunking of the 'ontological reality of categories,' had threatened to deal a crushing blow to the legitimation of the Church and its intermediary function between the divine order and the worldly one from both axiological and cognitive perspectives.

[14] In this regard, see, in an immense literature, Blumenberg (1985) and Taylor (2007) and, more specifically, Taylor (2011). But see McLeod (2003) for some observations in tune with the distinction between the political and cultural respects of secularization. A different view, at least

Despite appearances, the last assertion should not be considered heretical or eccentric; the same lexicon of secularization substantiates it. On one hand, there is no doubt that modern scientific rationalism produced a radical revolution concerning the image of nature and, especially, the methodologies to investigate its (alleged) inherent order. The same, conversely, cannot be said as for the commitment of Enlightenment and then Liberalism to renew the anthropological grammar of people's patterns of daily life. Of course, the declarations of rights and the defense of 'natural' freedom found in both these ideological and political movements offered tremendous support, if not even their own sources, which propagated their influence to pave a path toward constitutionalism and modern democracy. Nonetheless, the idea of 'natural rights' had deeply ingrained roots in the Western cultural tradition,[15] the same underlying the apparatuses of legal categories later encapsulated in the post-revolutionary nineteenth century legislations—first and foremost, the Napoleonic Code.[16]

Laïcité and secularization are often interpreted according to two semantic spectrums that do not coincide. The *laïque* political orders are connoted, at least historically, for their idiomatic anti-clericalism and the related attitude to emancipate and distance themselves from any religious legitimation.[17] The path of secularization shares this political differentiation from religion only partially because it is more broadly understood as a cultural enterprise. Secularization is interpreted as Western thought's ideal trajectory of enfranchisement from the philosophical-theological categories of Christianity.[18] Nonetheless, within quotidian life, such bifurcation is much less far-reaching than public opinion—due to cultural tradition and political positioning—is generally inclined to believe. This also explains why (as I will emphasize in more detail below) technological progress and secularization are not at odds, and why the resilience of religious or ancestral superstitious beliefs or habits

---

partially, seems to emerge from the very interesting, even if cognitively hybrid, observations proffered by Calhoun (2010), about the ways in which 'secularism' (and its relationship with religion) is both concretely and theoretically 'experienced.'

[15] Tierney (2001).

[16] Todescan (1983).

[17] This is the approach that Asad (2003) seems to propose through his Foucault-inspired interpretation of the anthropological background of the modern state and the ambition of its institutions to be all-comprehensive. I do not share, however, Asad's (2003) emphasis on institutional power and the law-centric reading of modern society. For analogous reasons, even if differently modulated, I am not of the same 'mind' with Taylor (2007) regarding his stance in which the 'religious domain', to be interpreted in both its denominational and anthropological scope is, in contemporary times, a matter of choice. Conversely, I think that even within the most (allegedly) secularized societies, the more people are convinced of the absoluteness regarding the binomial 'faith/free choice,' the more they are *not immune* from the cultural/anthropological influence of religion and its historical cognitive/axiological categories. However, for an acute distinction among different kinds of 'secularism' (political, ideological, institutional) see Casanova (2009).

[18] Blumenberg (1985), Lübbe (1975), and Böckenförde (2020, pp. 152 ff. and 220 ff.).

cannot be taken as a sign of a lack of secularization, or alternatively, de-secularization[19]

Both secularization and laicization were partial (and/or incomplete) cultural and political processes, respectively. Each of them brought out some unprecedented innovations but also slightly remodeled much of the 'know how' already anchored in the cognitive seabed of Western societies. In this regard, however, it is to be recognized that in its unfolding, even the flourishing of the seventeenth century scientific revolution involved notions and schemes already forged by previous cultural circuits (Christian, Hebrew, Islamic, Indian, etc.), as such deeply imbued with religious beliefs.[20] And this despite its explicit refusal to pursue the ancient objective of both of nature's 'first and ultimate causes.' This is particularly true for the political and legal fields. Doubtless, while the general paradigms changed, their building blocks did not. Modern imageries allowed for the socio-political peripheralization of religion, and yet they had no trouble using conceptual apparatuses that had been formerly molded by medieval moral theology.[21] The work of philosophers, lawyers, and theologians of the long European Middle-Ages (Patristic, Nominalism, Scholasticism, Glossators, Commentators, Second Scholasticism, etc.) was not put on the back burner at all. Rather, it was re-purposed under rationalistic pretenses, its theological guises craftily edited out; thus was Grotius' recipe to inaugurate modern legal rationalism brought to bear.[22] The change concerned, once again, much more the dosages of ingredients and the shape of the final product, while the 'raw cultural material' in many cases lay unaltered. The anthropological stuff of the different faiths (mainly, diverse *declensions* of Christianity) remained resilient within the cultural scaffoldings of Western knowledge. But it is hardly surprising. Faith and culture overlap, their pragmatic projections show coextensiveness, especially if observed over long timeframes. In turn, there is no possibility to construe a 'faith in reason' that is not culture laden. Cognitive evidence and 'transparencies' are necessarily connoted by culture, marked and coded by its communicative circuits. Outside the cultural dimension there is neither experiential evidence, nor semantic clarity. The factory of Cartesian 'clear and distinct ideas,' as well as analytical judgments, is nothing other than culture. The same can be assumed

[19] A sharp contrast between technological development and religion is configured by Bubandt and van Beek (2012) in their assessment of secularization in South Asia. But this contrast is not an idiomatic characteristic of non-Western societies. If one were to board an Alitalia plane, one would discover that aisle 17 is absent. This absence is due to the superstitious belief that the number 17 is bad luck. I think that the overlap between technologically marked experiences and behaviors dubbed as 'superstitious' is interpreted as a lack of secularization in popular imagery only if, as observers, we sustain the following two assumptions: (1) Secularization is coextensive with everything that coincides with progress and scientific rationality; (2) Religion is indistinguishable from outward manifestations of the sacred, the spiritual, and the magical. However, both these evaluative standards should be judged as '*modernist* prejudices' radically inappropriate to ethnographically fathom worldwide experiences of secularization.

[20] Grant (1997).

[21] Berman (1985), Prodi (2000), and Schmitt (1985).

[22] See Grotius' *De jure belli ac pacis*.

as regards the image of nature engendered and taken for granted in all the various ages and contexts of human history. In the end, the nature of a human being is—*inter alia*—that of a 'cultural being.'

In contemporary common language, 'secularization' is used as synonym for an imaginary boundary line between reason and religion, almost an emergence of an ontological divide. Nevertheless, this is a false depiction. It relies upon a misleading metonymy, in which a part is taken as the whole. From a political point of view, the secular state develops and is structured as dialectically opposed to all religious institutions (denominations, churches, etc.), at least if they are considered according to their institutional dimension.[23] But denomination and religion cannot be equated. Any identification of one with the other stems from an inappropriate conflation of two different social circuits. Religions are the anthropological source of the denominational groups and institutions, as such more or less circumscribed or circumscribable for their subjective and objective elements. And yet, their cultural effects and projections prove, instead, to be wide-ranging phenomena throughout the cultural map of society. This is because religion, if understood in its anthropological significance, is a much broader phenomenon than denomination. In European history, for example, the same 'wars of religion' retrospectively look like struggles for 'political investiture' and the legitimation of public power rather than being genuinely fomented by basic cultural divergence or incommensurability. They failed to erode the ethical heritage of Christianity accumulated through centuries of quotidian practices. On the contrary, precisely this cultural/ethical platform served as a basis for the idea of a natural-rational law even despite the Catholicism/Protestantism divide.

However, it would be a mistake to assume that the anthropological overlapping between culture and religion is an idiomatic feature of Western societies and their modern development. In a variety of ways, the interweaving of culture and religion, reason and faith, applies to all traditions and social universes, from Islamic to Confucian, Hindu to Buddhist, and so on.[24] In Western history, the path of political secularization, as well as *laïcité*, released political authority from religious influence and ecclesiastical *supervision*. However, the enfranchisement from the cognitive and ethical categories of Christian faith, as such layered in the 'know how' of quotidian life, was far less weighty and wide. This is especially true for both private and criminal law, about which—against Schmitt's term *political theology*, as such focusing particularly on constitutional and public features of the modern state—

[23] And yet, as both Stolleis (1990) and Calhoun (2010), among others, underscore, modernity passed through a process of nationalization that found in the principle 'cuius regio, eius religio' a means for the enfranchisement of territorial political institutions (not only states) from the Catholic Church's legitimation and, simultaneously, a cultural glue useful to ethnicize denominational belonging and transform it in a kind of 'marker' of genuine/authentic citizenship.

[24] In this sense, see the various contributions included in the collection edited by Dean and Van der Veer (2019).

scholars should speak of a 'legal theology.' [25] In any case, it is impossible to start history again from the scratch. Any attempt to understand or represent Enlightenment in this way, as well as any other ideal revolution, can function, perhaps, as a rhetorical strategy but is destined to result in a mere misrepresentation and, in the end, even a mystification.[26] Secularization had to bear some anthropological constraints to be viable as a pragmatic option at a socio-political level. The resilience of the past and its cultural/religious connotation is particularly evident in the legal 'culturescapes' that give rhythm to the concrete and quotidian actions of people as well as their intersubjective relationships. In my view, the anthropological mark left by religion on the grammar of daily life and its legal patterns is far more relevant, pervasive, and invisible than the conceptual transduction of the ecclesiastical schemes of power and government in the modern political apparatuses and public law—namely, what is labeled 'political theology.' As I will try to illustrate, legal theology is anthropologically much more relevant than the 'political one' and, in all likelihood, the primary source of the problems that multicultural democracies have to face today and in the future.

2.2 Secularization with 'Self-reflexive' Modesty and Cultural Equidistance

As observed above, the attempt to assert (and even believe) that the political and/or axiological categories of the modern secularized states are religiously aseptic and purely rational can be efficacious in communicative terms—and it has been so. The effects of such a representative strategy are doomed, however, to fade over time.[27] In

[25] As articulated by, among others, Fitzpatrick (2008), who in this text, at least, does not widen his gaze beyond the institutional structures so as to find the semantic and axiological footprint of religion also in legal schemes and practices that marks the rhythm of people's daily life.

[26] Ricca (2008a, b).

[27] The fading effects of this strategy are also the source of the success met by Asad's (2003) re-interpretation of secularization as well as the post-colonial critical approaches. With regard to Asad's point according to which we cannot take 'religion,' 'politics,' and 'the secular' as neutral or analytical terms, I would propose some remarks if only because the above assertion is, in some sense, a kind of truism. To take those terms as 'aseptic' items would be suspiciously ingenuous. The claims against secularism in the name of a non-Western conceptualization of any religion different from Christianity are propelled by more than an ethnocentric idea of religion hidden within the overarching secular interpretation of the social world to be intended as a power dispositive. This Foucaultian deconstructive approach is to be matched by the cultural incompleteness of Western secularization. The 'true religion' that post-colonial subjects ascribe to themselves seems to be too deeply engaged in a struggle to assert its own abstract or speculative divine uniqueness. The bone of contention is to be traced in the circumstance that post-colonial subjects are aware that inside secularism and secularization are nestled the anthropological remnants of another religion, which under the guise of secular reason aims to occupy their public space. The anthropology of secularization is not only a remapping of a social field stirred by the lust for power or domination. It also involves a cultural nub that the same Western world has not yet reckoned with. The conflict, in other

social contexts, the anthropological aspects of religion are diluted in common culture as a consequence of the mimicking effect induced precisely by communicative habits. From this perspective, religion and practical reason can become so reciprocally enmeshed that they appear indistinct. Such tacit assimilation can certainly be useful for public consent and social control, but eventually there will be a price to pay for it. The showdown comes every time the fabric of social certainties and the communicative/experiential background are deeply disturbed, and the related cognitive cartographies need to be redrawn. When, for example, scientific innovation impinges on the basic patterns of people's quotidian life, cultural conflicts suddenly erupt and, in most cases, they prove to be almost ineluctably prone to assuming religious connotations. But this is nothing more than contemporary history. In such situations, the life of democracies will always inspire many calls for the secularity of state and public discourse as well as symmetric contestations arising from the political socio-political interests of religious/denominational representatives.

I think the point is not whether denominations or religious actors are entitled to publicly express their opinions about abortion, divorce, euthanasia, genetic engineering, public healthcare, and so on. The question is, rather, why even inside secularized societies—Western or otherwise—people are still interested in and concerned with the approach of denominational subjects to certain moral issues. In this regard, several scholars have recently proposed the term 'de-secularization'[28] to describe a resurgence of the 'religious' in public life. I wonder, however, if the notion of de-secularization is not anything more than a specular clone of secularization, as such emphatic and allegedly absolute as its opposite.[29] What is labeled as (a sign of) 'de-secularization,' by contrast, seems to me a repository for all that historically remained outside of Western secularization and subsequently preserved its invisibility under the shadow of secular rhetoric. But precisely this never-secularized portion of cultural experience is today put in motion and buoyed up from the ocean-bed of implicitness because of the subverting impact of both

words, flares up and springs from the vast and dynamic area hosting the cultural projections of religions and their pragmatic/relational collision course. It would be very misreading to assume that the dispute orbiting secularization stems from its pure performativity as a dispositive of power, as such able to forge a new anthropological map of daily social life. Many controversies, by contrast, have their source in the anthropological features that religious axiological and cognitive patterns have maintained within Western secular discourses, first of all the legal lexicon.

[28] See the collection of essays edited, already in 1999, by Berger Peter (1999), Norris and Inglehart (2011); most recently the collection edited by Beaumont (2019) and moreover, Habermas (2006). With specific regard to Casanova's (1994) idea of the 'de-privatization of religion' and the subsequent self-criticism that the same author raised against his previous approach (2008), I have to observe that from a legal perspective and, especially, what I call 'legal theology,' the 'privatization' of religion has never taken place. On the contrary, the public/private divide, officially drawn under the aegis of religious freedom, has appeared viable as a constitutional recipe only by virtue of the cultural resilience of Christian moral theology inside the legal grammar of modernity with specific regard to the legal categories giving rhythm to daily life.

[29] Rosati (2010).

technological innovation and the cultural hybridization (especially) of democratic societies.

In the light of the last remarks, it could be argued that what makes people interested in the public involvement of religious denominational authorities is the deep and never severed ties between religion and culture. This could also be the reason the use of secularization as a red-light against the presumed intrusion in public sphere of religious agencies—according to the old medieval adage '*silete clerici in munere alieno*'—ends up, in many cases, merely fomenting an increase of conflicts. In my view, this occurs precisely because denying 'civil citizenship' to denominational voices equates with silencing the presence within the secular praxis of categories rooted in religious tradition. Following this explicative path, however, a paradox could take shape—even if, I think, it is only apparently so. What is too often underestimated is that the more cultural roots and their interdependence with religion are overshadowed or dissimulated, the more the secular discourse will be vulnerable, if not even plagued, by conflicts. In the same way, the polarizations ensuing all the metamorphoses of social habits tend to commute, very frequently, in religious struggles triggered by the lack of awareness of how much religion is nestled in secular cultural schemes. In this regard, I think that only after a serious demystification of the 'absolute secularization' myth and the exclusive rationality of modern public discourse would it be possible to undertake a real critical assessment of religion's social influence and its tacit presence in the common mindset. In other words, the religion hidden among the folds of social 'know how' should be mined and brought into the light. And besides, it is impossible to wriggle free from something that remains unknown. The 'arcane,' namely what is not intellectually grasped and symbolized, is destined to overdetermine people's minds, at least insofar as it remains silenced and enshrined in the domain of implicitness.

The recent exorbitant attention given by media to issues such as the exposure of religious symbols in classrooms, the teaching of religion in public schools, the statements proffered by clergy of all faiths on bio-medical issues, and so on, result from the deep historical intertwining between religion and culture, rather than being a symptom of their resurgent conflation. The real issue is that topics such as the relationships between life and death, body and person, public ethics and instruction, etc., are inherently imbued in each culture with meanings or entailments related to traditional religious semantics. When the (apparent) self-evidence of some archetypical commonplaces and the corresponding habits is questioned, almost inevitably the underlying religious linkages come to the fore. In each socio-political context, and especially in Western liberal-democracies, the 'secular' unexpectedly realizes its own religiosity and thereby its 'closeness' to one or the other religious-denominational dimension and its cultural influence.[30] Nevertheless this is only a

[30] As I argue below, things are rather different in non-Western societies even because of the mixture of many their institutional structures and languages with the cultural patterns inherited from colonization and post-colonial imageries. For an analysis of this precise phenomenon at work comparing modern secular states with Protestant and Catholic roots (respectively), see Vazquez (2019).

belated discovery. In such circumstances, people become aware of what has always been inside them. On the other hand, it is very hard to know that one knows. Although the rhetoric of a complete and cognitively self-referential secularization has veiled this 'knowing,' it has been lying in the background throughout Western modernity.

The path that could lead Western culture, before any other, to an authentic secularization is to be drawn from the preliminary acquisition of awareness about the resilience of religion within. This tacit presence is sometimes brought to the surface by the analysts of multicultural and multireligious societies that criticize the dogma of neutral secularism. They contest its hidden ethnocentrism and identify a possible remedy to the culturally unbalanced politics arising from it in a secularization to be practiced with moderation.[31] This attitude to moderation is gauged on the exigencies of all the non-Christian minorities and the respect that is due to their cultural differences, in turn rooted in their own religious traditions. I think that the call for 'moderation' is politically very insightful. Nonetheless, in my view, Western secularization needs first of all to be *modest* with regard to the presumed absence of religion from its own categories of thought, and especially the legal schemes that mark common life.[32] I fear that as long as Western secular societies imagine themselves and their institutions to be semantically immunized from religious categories, the invocation of a moderate attitude towards Others' religiosity is not likely to produce significant results. In the same way, on the other hand, some non-Western societies, as for example India, seem to be increasingly and dramatically tempted to mimic the dissimulating ignorance/blindness that Western secularized societies demonstrate with reference to their being religiously aseptic.[33] The strategy is implemented through a double movement: (a) labeling Western institutions, especially the liberal order, as Christian-derived and colonizing systems of thought;[34] and (b) de-religiosizing their own cultural features and qualifying them as apparatuses of non-Western rationalities, in turn assimilated and dissimulated under the guises of national identities.[35] The final result is very close to a legitimation of uneven relationships with other cultural and religious minorities, including Christian

[31] See Modood (2019a).

[32] In this sense I partially agree with Bhargava (2014) and his idea that Western secularization has been 'modest,' even if I reverse the implications of this qualification. Bhargava casts it from without, as reflecting an objective feature of Western secularization and, therefore, as a kind of flaw corresponding to a low degree of achievement. Conversely, I think that the West should hold a *modest* attitude about its alleged 'secularization' and exploit this self-reflexive and critical starting point to relationally and horizontally re-calculate its position towards the projections of Others' religions in the public sphere and within the legal discourse/lexicon.

[33] Losonczi and Van Herck (2015); but, also, Balagangadhara (1994).

[34] See, for example, De Roover et al. (2011). But, more in general, with regard to the 'colonial bent' of the Western philosophy of history and philosophy of religion see Mandair (2009), King (1999), Dressler and Mandair (2011), and Halbfass (1988).

[35] See, Jurgensmeyer (2006) and Van der Veer (2013), with specific regard to the Indian Supreme Court's interpretive guideline, Sen (2007). More in general and for a comparative analysis of the relationship between religions and nationalism in Asian regions see Shani and Kibe (2020).

ones. All this, undoubtedly, is a reaction to colonial domination and the cultural imbalance that the West tried to perpetrate in the post-colonial era.

In many cases, the defense of ethnocentric articulations of secularization by non-Western societies is grounded upon the alleged incommensurability between the Semitic religions and, for example, the Asian or the so-called chthonic beliefs: up to the point of denying the same applicability of the category of religion to the non-Abrahamic faith.[36] Beyond the indisputable differences among the world religions, however, to consider the comparative study of religion and comparative theology as nothing more than imperialistic projections of Western/Christian thought seems, in turn, the expression of an overflowing Occidentalism. This is also because the final result of this rhetorical and ethnocentric para-secularizing strategy is prospectively the specular reiteration of the same mistakes and flaws affecting Western secularization and its mythologization. On the other hand, defining 'religion' as a Western category exclusively gauged on 'Christianity' would presuppose the availability of a wider semantic frame to grasp both Christianity and other psycho-social experiences so far classified as 'religious.' The manifold attempts committed to demonstrating the 'Occidentality/Christianity' of the term 'religion' instead appear, in their unfolding, terminologically clumsy or, even worse, inconsistent, if only because the same term 'religion' ends up reappearing when the related discursive fabric refers to the non-Christian '*non-religions*.' The choice to substitute the 'term' religion with different lexemes, for example 'spirituality'[37] is, however, equally defective, even because the semantic spectrum of 'other terms', at least in many cases, amounts to a selective restriction of the semiotic network subsumed under the word 'religion.' These linguistic transmutations seem to be prompted by the intent to distinguish 'religious phenomena' from the process of domineering processes of inculturation coupled to colonialism and post-colonialism. Behind this approach, there is also the exigency—in many cases more grounded in political ideology than stemming from scientific analysis—to enfranchise the relationship between non-Christian religions and their social contexts from the shadows projected on them by Western secularization/secularism. A secularization/secularism which, in turn, is considered as the specular image of 'Christian religion.' In the end, the stigmatization of the term 'religion' and its analytical/explicative potentiality seems to equal a kind of epiphenomenon of cultural/political dialectics between the West and the Rest. But if this is the case, then the overall 'linguistic' operation runs the risk of making very little sense or being reduced to a vicious cycle, and this if only because 'culture' and 'religion' are not two ontological or anthropological reciprocally secluded domains. The danger of carrying on a merely verbal dispute is increased by the tendency to identify secularism with nationalism—or nationalism as the historical reification of secularism—and through this move to give shape to a sort of implicit argumentative chain unwinding from Christianity to secularism and, in

[36] See Fitzgerald (2000, p. 4), Asad (2003, p. 29), Van der Veer (2014), and Smith (1998).

[37] In this sense, see the interesting discursive proposal elaborated by Van der Veer (2014), who suggests a substitution of 'religious' with 'spiritual.'

sequence, nationalism, colonialism, post-colonialism. And yet, at the *terminus* of this movement scholars cannot avoid observing the phenomenal joining of nationalism and 'non-Christian religions' also in non-Western (e.g., Asian) contexts.[38] The same areas where the 'non-religions' often play the role of cultural hallmarks in the attempt by the non-Westerners (whatever this might still mean) to wriggle free from the long wave of historical colonialism as well as the more recent Western dominance embodying, in turn, national geopolitical antagonistic attitudes.

In my view, 'religion' is, like other terms such as 'world,' 'freedom,' and 'humanity,' an absolute metaphor,[39] whose source is undetermined and shifts continually according to situations, contexts, time, and relationships of signification. Precisely in this vagueness, I think, lies the explicative capacity of these metaphors. The attitude to faith shares with 'sign' the time-space duplication of the signification level. Beyond the divide 'transcendence/immanence,'[40] which is tied to the Abrahamic religions, the duplication/multiplication of the level/stages of signification and its inherent dialectics connotes both religions as well as their axiological/teleological attitude and cognitive import. The projection toward another level of signification, even if merged with immanence and not necessarily dialectically dislocated in some kind of 'elsewhere,' produces an effect of categorical recalculation of the 'existent' together with a relativization of the related schemes of categorization. From this perspective the relationship between culture and religion, knowledge and faith, ideality/spirituality and empirical experience is dynamic, interpenetrating and interchanging.[41] Religions tend to institutionalize, and some aspects of the cultural dimension can transmute in axiological/teleological horizons capable of 'putting within brackets' even the most common categories (perhaps already well-established and embodied in dominant social or institutional structures, and thence corresponding to a common gaze on the world). In this sense, despite the colonial period's 'covering' of religion with semantic features specifically aligned with Christianity—up to the point of transforming it in a kind of anthropological and ontological yardstick to measure the non-Western 'religious' experiences—'religion' is nevertheless not utterly deprived of its explicative potentiality. Rather, it is to be used as an open metaphor, that is to say that the process of metaphorization/signification coextensive to its being an 'absolute metaphor' should be critically engaged. This could help explain why 'religion' remains enmeshed, so frequently, in contemporary confrontations between different secular/national circuits and, at the same time, sometimes it seems to disentangle from secular conflicts—perhaps carried out by the political authorities in the name of religion—to find at a different

[38] See Herzfeld (2012).

[39] Blumenberg (2007).

[40] See Smith (1978).

[41] In this direction as well as with respect to the idea of anthropologically based intercultural secularism—which I label also as a 'mature' and 'intentionally polyphonically *contaminated* secularization—that I will propose below, the writings by Abeysekara, among which see (2006, 2010, 2011) are very inspiring.

level channels of inter-faith translations and ethical allegiances. It could be enough, in this vein, to recall the recent dialogue between the Catholic Pope and the Imam of Al-Azhar; or the interreligious appeals for fasting and prayers for peace, during the war in Syria or in Ukraine; and even, symmetrically, the failed meeting between the Dalai Lama and Pope Francis in 2014 caused by the pressures that China put on the Vatican; and this despite the fact that Pope John Paul II had met with the Dalai Lama eight times previously and had spoken with him about inter-religious dialogue and peace. Similar remarks, for example, could be proposed regarding the ecological commitments of religions, including Catholicism and Protestantism, which is a point of convergence for Christian and East Asian faiths, as such endowed with a global significance that, in a sense, outshines the national/secular embodiment of religion as a dispositive to enhance intercultural and political conflicts. My view on this matter is that the problem concerns less the nomenclature than the semantic openness and the translational/transactional attitude to interculturally and critically renew the signification of the term 'religion.' Even if each word is doubtless marked by its own historical and experiential 'wrinkles,' nevertheless its semantic scope can always be updated to be responsive to the relational and environmental conditions of its signification. Terms, then, as well as categorical frames are to be intended as tools rather than as vitrified portraits of an immutable 'reality' placed out there.

I would here like to iterate my conviction: 'religion' should be treated as the target of an absolute metaphor (and, precisely by virtue of its absoluteness, partially also the source of the 'metaphorization' through which understanding and research proceed). This entails, *inter alia*, that such metaphor should be divested from its tacit psycho-semantic connection to secularization and, more specifically, the public/private, objective/subjective divides that populate and forge the modern social imagery. A self-reflexive gaze, in tune with a cognitive modesty in the understanding of Western secularization, would show that religion is not coextensive with denomination and that religion and culture are placed along a psycho-social *continuum*. On the other hand, even Augustine's *De Civitate Dei*, perhaps the most dated treatise of Christian-centered comparative theology, as such pivoted on the 'spiritual order/temporal order' divide, assumes that the criticized and even stigmatized *pagan* and *polytheist* cults can be named *religion*s (although not *true religions*). And this just to emphasize that the Christian divide between 'spiritual' and 'temporal' does not overlap either anthropologically or historically with the public/private modern distinction. For the correspondence between religion and the private sphere constitutes only a specific fold connoting the endless process of the metaphorization of 'religion' throughout modernity.

Still, the path of emancipation from the self-deceptive and dissimulating representations of secularization and/or rationalization of politics and the public sphere should nevertheless be primarily undertaken by the West. And this if only because Western culture must bear the burden of all the deficiencies inherent in a 'term' (secularity/ism, as such to be distinguished from 'modernity') and the related practices that the West originated and tried to diffuse and impose all over the world. The first step in this direction, I think, consists in the recognition of the inner incompleteness of any attempt to secularize society. Such incompleteness is due to the anthropological significance of religion, and is therefore both unavoidable and indelible, no matter how relativized, in its resilience in cultural schemes. This means that secular societies should represent their relationships with their religious pasts by assuming a disposition of *self-reflexive modesty* towards the possibility of eradicating religion from social knowledge and, in this way, embodying a worldview enlightened by a universal rationality. This does not imply a sort of subjection to the religious traditions but rather their critical assessment to be carried out by assuming an open-minded attitude and avoiding aprioristic prejudices on both cognitive and political grounds.

This *self-reflexive modesty* is of the utmost importance even because the religious 'remnants' nestled in (allegedly only) cultural categories do not pull up anchor from their cultural seabed only because scientific-technological developments occur or because of the influence of factors endogenous to each cultural context. Whatever number of cultures and religions meet, just as many '*rationalities*,' repertories of self-evidence, and '*normalities*' will be under challenge. When different universes of self-evidence and/or normality come into contact, by settling on people's shoulders and in their minds, the related schemes of judgments and categorizations ineluctably undergo processes of re-semanticization, relativization, contamination and critical assessment.[42] Even if unconsciously, the coexistence of people with different cultural backgrounds and mindsets induces in any case a noetic and behavioral decentralization from one's own repertories of self-evidence and their (until then) unquestioned normativity. This is an effect to be assumed as an epiphenomenon of the same realization that Otherness is co-present in any situation a subject can experience—regardless of the positive or negative attitude they assume toward Others. And besides, even racializing hatred is a transformation if it takes shape as a consequence of contact with Otherness. The impact between different galaxies of sense can therefore be traumatic, an event that clouds the future and the consequences of individual actions, at least insofar as crossing another's 'galaxy' cannot be avoided.

Religion has made its contribution to all traditions or civilizations by creating corresponding worldviews, horizons of values, and frameworks for individual and collective behavioral patterns.[43] The vestiges of religious agency may even have been lost sight of or concealed, falling below the threshold of cultural awareness.[44] What remains, however, are the conceptual tracks of the intense activity of religious thought and its pistic (from the ancient Greek: *pístis*) categories.[45] When different worldviews and behavioral habits enter each other's orbit, the stratifications of the past come to light, assuming unprecedented semantic potentialities. But the necessity to face what is 'new' urges people to engage in processes of self-reflection and a

[42] Dewey (2012, pos. 563).

[43] Glenn (2014).

[44] This phenomenon, however, has nothing to do with the 'subtraction stories' against which Taylor (2007, p. 143) launches his darts.

[45] Ricca (2002, pp. 153 ff.).

quest for new identity recipes that are not utterly disengaged from the past—be it real, only imaginary, or even oneiric. In any case, the findings that emerge from this gaze at the past also end up wrapped in the semantic patina and obscure any cultural evidence, and this precisely because its 'efficient cause' is the existential anxiety elicited by the encounter with Otherness. At that point, what begins is a search for the sources of legitimation and 'objects' to believe in, as such needed to give shape to a renewed grammar of cultural and personal knowledge. Realizing that one's own certainties are becoming precarious and feeling the need, primarily for practical purposes, to construe new ones—maybe even invoking the everlasting value of those that have already vanished—materialize as two wings of the same phenomenon. In any case, the objectification of the Self, its linkages to a re-invented tradition, even if just to face the present and the 'unknown' that is cloaked in the Other/Future, are creative cognitive processes. They entail ongoing and iterative endeavors to revise and re-semanticize one's own past knowledge. In this predicament religions are taken as reliable guides along the path towards the rediscovery of the Self. Nonetheless, this folding back on oneself in search of the religious roots of cultural identity is not carried out as a solipsistic act. In that direction, just following the trajectories of faith, the index finger pointing to where to look—paradoxically as it may appear—is mainly that of the Other than Self, the alien, the migrant. It is because from outside the cultural circuits of other people—in this case the 'natives'—show their idiomatic specificity most evidently (which is due to specific and semantically situated reasons strictly tied to the contrastive dynamic of perception). In the same vein, history is perceived—at least potentially—as a semiotic component of the present contextual framework. Hence, before the Other's eyes, the semantic legacies of religions often look like authentic and structural components of a local culture, despite their being perceived from inside as secularized or purely rational elements. On the other hand, it is exactly for a kind of specular dialectical reason that the same secularized West, under the pressure of Otherness, unexpectedly winds up reflexively seeing itself as culturally ingrained in Christian roots.[46] In a symmetric way, however, when facing the long destructive wave of Western modernity, the Rest of the World unearths its own cultural and religious roots as if they were the proof of its non-Westernity and—if nothing else—a 'different' modernity. Orientalism and Occidentalism[47] become, in this way, semantic machines churning out reciprocally specular stereotypes to be used as strategic weapons to face Otherness. We can see that at work as the communicative vectors of the antagonisms among Islam, Hinduism, Christianity, Judaism, Buddhism, and so on.

The strange result of the above processes is that secularization, exactly because of its entanglement in cultural conflicts, fades away. So, it can happen that almost

[46] See, for example, what is reported by Modood (2019a, pp. 199 ff.), with regard to the UK. But the same could be said of many secular states and even of Europe. Consider, in this regard, the long dispute about the 'Christian roots of Europe,' on which see Joppke (2014).

[47] Said (1991), Carrier (1995), Nandy (1983), Venn (2001), and Buruma and Margalit 2004.

offhandedly even Western secularized societies appear prone to declare the religious 'embeddedness' of their public culture and, vice versa, the cultural significance of their religious traditions. Along this path, one more paradox, therefore, takes shape, though it can be defined as such only in analytical terms, rather than from a historical and anthropological perspective: secularized societies and states can more and more often be caught showing off their religious traditions under the guise of cultural features. Through these paradoxical actions, however, they are simply making visible the incomplete substance of the secularization processes they allegedly underwent in the past. Of course, the above incompleteness is not universal but rather culturally relative, as if to say: different religions, different (incomplete) secularizations.[48] On the other hand, that there is a Christian secularization, a Hindu, a Confucian, a (possible) Islamic (for example Ataturk's Turkey) is to be taken as an anthropological-political truism—even because it could not be otherwise. The very issue concerns, rather, the ways that each society or state adopts the re-assertion of their own cultural/religious roots: that is, the discursive artillery that each selects to shore up its own apparatus of self-evidence against the estranging occurrence (sometimes perceived as irruption) of Otherness in its experiential and daily life spaces; even when such Otherness takes the shape of 'Progress' and/or 'Revolution.' When cultural/religious conflicts arise, what is threatened, at least in people's perceptions, is the kernel of silent and implicit certainties, just as happens when facing scientific-technological innovations and their ensuing effects on common life patterns. And yet, the interplay between the core ganglia of cultures and the impact of diversity, on average, is not noticed at the initial close encounters.[49] The inner turmoil produced by the encounter with Otherness up to one point is inclined to maintain a sort of invisibility. The main and decisively negative result of this is in the public eye. Although the true exigency is to preserve the kernel of the different cultural circuits at stake, the struggles are often orchestrated in connection with fetishes or symbols, which are not infrequently merely peripheral with regard to the respective cultural landscapes. With respect to the intercultural comparison they are however striking, endowed with a morphological and immediate recognizability and, precisely for this reason, easily eligible as identity symbols and landmarks of its protection. Veils, turbans, religious buildings, the material paraphernalia of rites, bodies, sexual codices and so on are wielded as ideal sabers to safe identity and eliminate contamination but, at the same time, to dissimulate the real object of concern and preservation: the overall, invisible semiotic network underlying any cultural encyclopedia of 'know how.'

The problem with identitarian fetishization is that it gives utterance and preeminence to prejudicial fears and instinctive reactions to difference—something that is

[48] On the other hand, it has reached the status of a commonplace. See, among a myriad of texts: Calhoun et al. (2011), Rectenwald and Almeida (2015), Berg-Sørensen (2016), Medovoi and Bentley (2021), Mapril et al. (2018), Losonczi and Van Herck (2015), Al-Azmeh (2020), and Verma (2019).

[49] A closeness—to be clear—that is to be considered in both semiotic and geographical terms. But, on the semio-spatial *continuum*, see below, Chaps. 4 and 5.

in and of itself, after all, utterly psychologically explainable. If not channeled in intelligent intercultural interactions, however, these attitudes and their reifying outcomes end up hampering and ossifying the processes of self-objectification: namely, the acquisition of an actual and broad awareness of ones' own cultural traditions, the related know how and underlying semiotic networks, but also the threads along which religious categories are anthropologically intertwined with people's cognitive and behavioral patterns. These identitarian scripts can be traced in both Western and non-Western socio-cultural societies and communities, especially in the post-colonial ones. And yet, if, on one side, the Western socio-cultural circuits seem to be committed to a dissimulating preservation of their alleged secularized apparatuses of self-evidence and commonplaces—in many cases implicitly enmeshed in the ethical legacy of Christian moral theologies—post-colonial circuits must deal with a symmetrically opposed problem. Not infrequently, they must manage institutional and legal apparatuses inherited from the colonial experience and inextricably embedded in the democratic imageries and governance that have fostered, over time, the anti-colonial emancipatory enterprise. What unfolds, in these contexts, is a process of cultural re-appropriation of the conceptual cartography of the public sphere and an attempt to re-codify its language (India, from this perspective, can be considered a paradigmatic case).[50] Such attempts are often undermined by the impending action of capitalist globalization and the pervasive dissemination of information flows and commodities spread by Western culture across the planet. Against the towering of colonial legacies and post-colonial global canvasses, traditional religious symbols and fetishes are frequently used as cultural-political battering-rams because of their morphological distance from the behavioral, institutional, and legal framework imported in those countries from outside. In many cases, however, the result is nothing other than a strategic invention.

A complete eradication of all the 'West-related' features from the quotidian circuits of 'non-Western' people is almost impossible and, ultimately not even really useful to those same people. The rejection of the so called liberal-constitutional model, which includes the public/private divide applied to the relationship between state and religion, is often argued on the basis of its cultural discriminatory effects and its braiding with colonial pseudo-universal ideologies and post-colonial interests. The main argument pivots on the political marginalization of local traditional religions, as such (allegedly) ensuing the adoption of liberal political framework and its use as a means to surreptitiously discriminate against native cultures on behalf of institutional and legal schemes that are semantically rooted in the Western and Christian culture. In this critical view there is, actually, far more *substance* than a few crumbs of truth. The problem—at least, in my view—lies instead in the implications inferred from its assumption. Those who support such a reading of the uneven consequences of secularized liberalism tend to veer their critical premises towards the nationalization of local traditional religions through the following twofold argumentative move: (a) local religions and culture are indistinguishable,

[50] Madan (2005), Menski (2001, 2004), and Sen (2007).

at least against the foil of the co-implication between Western culture and Christianity; (b) the category of secularization is inapplicable to non-Christian (or, at least, non-Abrahamic) religions because of their inner differences, up to the point to assert the *impossibility* of defining (in Western-scientific terms) Hinduism, Buddhism, the various form of polytheism, chthonic beliefs, etc., as religions. Consequentially, the legitimation of a conflation between faith and politics at a national level is presented as a 'done deal.' The idea that in this cultural-institutional scenario a slot for religious freedom or non-discrimination in the dynamics of the public sphere could somehow be preserved seems to be not much more than a vague hope. What is certain, however, is that such a defense of the interlacing between local cultures and religions in some non-Western contexts inevitably brings about some symmetric flaws and incompleteness affecting Western secularization. This can easily be seen simply by surveying ex-colonial institutional experiences of religious nationalization and observing the effective degree of Westernization they have eradicated from the common life of people. The enormous migration fluxes from those areas towards Western countries shows by itself that the above eradication is, at least anthropologically, anything but successful. By contrast, it reveals the huge pervasiveness and emulative draw of Western lifestyles and models with respect to the imageries of people living in those countries; and this, in many cases, even despite the anti-West political rhetoric promoted by local authorities. From a distance, the dialectics between the self-proclaimed secular West and these anti-Western experiments of 'cultural religionization' of state exhibit a kind of entrapment in an ironic two-faceted discursive spell. On one side, the secularized West is unable—also because of its lack of religious self-awareness—to erase the anthropological projections of Christianity from its cognitive and behavioral habits; on the other, many non-Western societies and political apparatuses fail in their intent to 'convert' their public imagery and discourse from the 'Western secularized (but still Christian-stigmatized)' patterns towards: (a) local political cultures immunized from the colonial contagion; or, alternatively, (b) a pluralistic public sphere capable of avoiding the culturally unbalanced neutrality affecting Western secularization.

Beyond absolute political declarations, however, non-Western countries often take the middle path, attempting to 'domesticate' Western influences by identifying a selected few categories and re-editing their meaning according to their compatibility with the autochthonous culture and/or religion. In these cases, religion is used as a device to configure public life in political-anthropological terms. Though this endeavor is designed to unfold broadly, it tends instead to reify its semantic scope by focusing on certain iconic items: namely, symbolic elements raised to the status of 'markers' on the path towards the local vernacularization of so-called Western modernity. Interestingly, these attempts at domestication take place in socio-institutional contexts that are officially theologized, such as the Islamic ones, as well as in those that are formally secularized, such as the Indian one (but this also applies in the absence of pervasive colonial histories, such as Japan, China, etc., according to the local cultural variables).

In some respects, the almost paradoxical and unexpected convergence in and among the different parts of the world between the language of secularization and the discursive strategies designed to vernacularize the icons of Western modernity could be of concern.[51] I think, however, that it is a consequence of the cultural situatedness of any process of secularization alongside its legal categories. Symmetrically, it is to be emphasized that all the attempts to vernacularize cultural Otherness can be only partial and often merely a façade. Any initiative in this direction will produce its effects through its inevitable interplaying with the communicative path drawn by transnational information flows. Precisely for this reason, in its unfolding (if any), it cannot avoid engendering upgraded semantic stages within global contemporary experience. Nonetheless, the endeavor to situate within the local dimensions the 'implications of modernity', for example through the vernacularization of human rights' semantics, should not be considered as a drifting away from their universality but, quite the opposite, the lifeblood of their ongoing universalization.[52] On the other hand, no universality could be taken seriously as such if it were unable to situate, take shape and dwell in different places in tune with people's changing experiences. Precisely these experiences can offer feedback to the semantic and communicative frames that make and keep alive any universalization by inherently and 'processively' remolding its contents. This is the global semiotics (or better, semiosis) of life that the world has always experienced ecologically, and the effects of which we are only now becoming socially aware.[53] What happens in a possible 'elsewhere' can interplay with the same paradigms of meaning inherent in what happens in a possible 'here.' In the same way, if human rights are understood and practiced in a local way in China or in India, this circumstance will affect their semantic status and its practical consequences also at a global level, eventually projecting its effects on the way those rights will be interpreted and applied in Europe or in South America. What conveys the fluxes of semantic contaminations are the relationships among the Chinese, Indian, European and South American people on the stage of the *worldominium* traversed by the vectors of migratory routes and the economic-political interdependence.[54]

The process of self-transformation analyzed above suggests that the reciprocal implications among religion, culture and law are not only 'a thing of the past.' It is, conversely, a past that renews itself and is ceaselessly involved in the definition of the present and its horizons. But this also implies that, at the present time, the notion of secularization can no longer rely on the ontological divide between politics and law, on one side, and religion, on the other. The neutrality paradigm proceeding from this axiomatic assumption, as such required by the 'vulgate' of secularization and/or

---

[51] And this, as just observed, both as a result of and/or simultaneously despite any post-colonial conditions. Provided that—as already noted—secularization and modernity cannot be taken as coextensive phenomena and/or categories. In this regard, see Eisenstadt (2000, 2002), Casanova (2008), Bhambra (2007) and many others; but see also Stoeckl and Rosati (2016).

[52] Clarke and Goodale (2010a, b) and Goodale (2007) and Engle Merry (2006b, 2010).

[53] Covid-19 could be considered plain evidence of the cultural and political relevance of the biological global semiotics that connects the individual bodies comprising humankind: see Ricca (2020c).

[54] On this and its chorological significance see below Chap. 5.

laïcité (despite their different declinations), is unviable simply because religions' anthropological projections are embedded within culture, and vice versa. This means that if local as well as international institutions are to be neutral with regard to religions, then they have to be neutral also with respect to cultures. Consequently, only states, legal systems, and societies that formally respect and responsively include cultural differences in their institutional lexicon can be genuinely deemed to *be neutral.* The further implication of these arguments is that if secularization as well as *laïcité* are to be considered synonyms for the democratic principle of 'responsiveness to differences', then their combination embodies a metaphor of equality. To wit: an equality not only 'before the law'—echoing Kafka's famous tale[55]—but also 'inside law.' Therefore, such equality cannot be only formal but must also be substantive in radical semantic terms. It cannot be limited to laying down clear and equal rules for everybody, while remaining *indifferent* to the universes of meaning and actual conditions people live in. At the same time, it is not enough to design those rules with the intention of overcoming the hindrances and vulnerabilities that hamper efficacious legal protection for all if this is pursued through an abstract and ethnically/ethically aprioristically predetermined template of social and legal subjectivity. A genuine *secular equality* should be inspired to a kind of semantics that is *equi-representative* and *equi-responsive.* Which entails, in turn, that legal rules should embody a weighted and thoughtful synthesis among the manifold cultural semantics corresponding to the different subjectivities extant in the social landscape. In short, the features of the legal subject should be the result of such a synthesis. And only when the legal framework is created as a *condensation* of differences and their universe of meaning, rather than as an uneven accommodating (and often merely commodifying) juxtaposition, could it deserve to be defined as inclusive.[56]

To reach the threshold of a genuinely secularized language—to be intended in the above inclusive and responsive terms—legal rules should result from a previous commitment to the translation and transaction of cultural and religious differences, the related imageries and semantic landscapes.[57] The final outcome of this cyclopean effort, should it actually be successful, can only be a product of creativity and reasonableness rather than the ineludible result of a 'logical' process married to an aseptic and objective rationality. Therefore, legal secularization is not to be intended as a synonym for or coextensive with rationality, or the compartmentalization of the political field by means of the dictates of an absolute reason, as such completely free of cultural inclinations and twists. Secularization cannot hover above differences but must instead stand horizontally in the midst of them, as a (possible) emergence from the flux of their intersections and reciprocal translations. It is thus not neutral, in the sense of 'culturally aseptic,' but rather reticularly in-between, creatively

[55] Kafka's famous tale is titled 'Before the Law' (or. *Aus dem Gesetz*).

[56] Ricca (2013, 2020a). About accommodations see below.

[57] As I hope may emerge below, my idea of 'translation' between the religious and the secular domains, respectively, is quite different from that of Habermas (2006, pp. 10 ff.).

transactional and therapeutic. The prerequisite for the achievement of such an inclusive and self-transforming cultural and political *disposition* is the abandonment of any idea that secular/rational discourse can be imagined as a linguistic/semantic platform that is pre-existing to any translational activity.[58] If the 'secular' is to be functional to equality, then it is to be imagined as a thirdness—and, in any case, not an all-comprehensive one—sprouting simultaneously from the flowing of translational/transactional activity. This means that the 'secular' cannot be understood as a self-reflexive dimension that can learn something from the dialogue with the 'religious' without constitutively renewing itself. In other words, the self-reflexivity allegedly coextensive with the reciprocal learning between the 'secular' and the 'religious' is to be intended as a re-invention of the yardstick to interpret both the sides of the dialogical interplay: at least, as regards the relational areas in which they cannot avoid interpenetrating spatially and semantically. In this vein, it is makes little sense to continue to assert that religions have to translate their conceptions and categories in rational/secular terms, or at least, in a commonly understandable language. This is because 'secular factual/empirical terms' inside the religious dimension, if intended as a universe of discourse, can also assume different anthropological significations that are not automatically or readily interpretable and in tune with the secular language and the related circuits of experience. In any case, such anthropological difference can only be translated by means of an inter-spatial, and therefore also metaphorical, transaction/transposition which can also deeply remold the previous 'semantic state of the art' of the secular universe of discourse.[59] And this precisely because of the danger that labeling as 'religious' a behavioral or discursive set of attitudes is the same as casting a prejudicially differentiating—and therefore *secularistic—veil of ignorance* about the experiential breadth of religious dispositions towards the world and its inherent cognitive import. Without a serious commitment to undertaking a 'probing journey' inside the religious universe of discourse, the appraisal of its own *alternative rationality* and the ensuing anthropological/experiential projections will remain out of reach for any translational action. But in the absence of a symmetrical assumption of the 'different rationalities' involved in the process of translation, any attempt to include

[58] Ultimately, this is the moot point in both the theorizations about the relationship between religion and the public sphere respectively proposed by Rawls (1996) and Habermas (2006). And this even if in the stance expressed by Habermas there is a relevant evolution, especially regarding the self-reflexive and genealogical approach that secular thought should assume in relation to its origins and the anthropological/cognitive role played by religion in molding some categories still nestled in its lexicon. This development in Habermas' approach to secular politics and its interplay with the religious sphere is as interesting as it is inconsistent with the idea that the religious dimension is called to 'render' in rational/secular terms its own 'categories' and 'axiological tenets'. About this profile, see the following arguments proffered below.

[59] About this I refer, here, to Ricca (2020c), where I try to elucidate the reasons why the 'hijab' is not in fact a piece of cloth to be put on face but, rather, something to be 'materially' translated in Western secular language as 'underclothing' with regard to its signification involving personal and sexual modesty, women's self-perception of their corporeality and its inner relationality with the life-environment, their sense of self-esteem and individual distinctiveness, etc.

Otherness—be it religious and/or cultural—will remain undermined by an inner unbalancing from the start. When this is the case—as it sadly is in most situations—even with the best of intentions and the most politically open attitude translation will be marked by the 'ontological supremacy' of an ethnocentric gaze. But this would be—nothing new under the sun—the umpteenth reappearance of the hermeneutical bug already affecting the colonial and post-colonial othering categorization of non-Western cultures and religions. A categorization indissolubly *coupled* with the assumption of Western categories and experience as the tacit but universal yardstick against which any kind of 'knowledge' must measure the world.[60]

The opposite view implies that reason (whatever that is) is, in and of itself, a neutral agency capable of producing meaning and political-normative patterns. Beyond the abstractness and vagueness of such assumptions about the rational attitude, I suspect that they can only increase the cultural and thereby even religious bent of institutional action. Anyone invoking or seeking to invoke the analyticity and semantic transparency of their *reasonable judgments*, is only attempting to pass off their own cultural and religious convictions and habits as universal. Consequently, the more their alleged secularity promises to be unyieldingly a-religious and neutral, the more it will accentuate in the eyes of Others, namely minorities and culturally different people, the cultural relativity of its contents. The outside view, in other words, cannot avoid recognizing in (secular) politics and law of such kind of aprioristic and self-asserting secularity a despotic coextensiveness with the historical-theological legacy of its 'champions.'

2.3 Rules vs. Recognition

The dawn of multiculturality has brought about, in many national contexts and especially all those receiving migratory fluxes, claims for social security and respect for state legal rules. Who is different, culturally Other, seems to generate, as a result of their mere presence, clouds of psychosocial chaos. All this as if the allegedly homogeneous local communities—assuming they exist at all—were not compelled to come to terms with one another within an already diminished planetary space, the distances of which have collapsed in a quotidian dimension affected by creolized and ubiquitously interlaced determinants. The reality is quite the opposite; faith in local homogeneities, in a dreamed social security resulting in clear, general and 'good for all' rules, engenders only a plurality of places perpetually in conflict with one another and inside themselves.

How often today do we hear—from populist politicians and media—the claim for the binomial 'rules and security?' It becomes almost a hendiadys-catchphrase addressed primarily to foreigners and those who are perceived as culturally different

[60] ...which remains, in my view, the flaw affecting also Rawls' and even the most open-to-otherness version of Habermas' approach to the relationship between religion and the secular public sphere.

(from the assumed majority). Its rhetorical message goes more or less like this: who comes here, among us, must respect our rules. And besides, 'everyone must abide by legal rules' is bandied about and coupled with another apparently more moderate adage—in many cases surreptitiously circulated—which calls for the need to join all differences in tune with the ideal of 'unity in diversity.' A slogan also adopted as a kind of 'identity icon' by the European Union, namely the same transnational institution that preaches about 'intercultural dialogue' inside and outside Europe, but only to break into itself and seal its borders against immigrants.[61] That said, the question that arises is: can all these appeals for the respect for formal legal rules legitimately and coherently be assumed as social and political expressions of secularization?

To be secular, the legal and political nomogenetic lexicon should result from—as observed above—a creative and transactional synthesis among the different cultural semantics people live by. Under what conditions, then, can the request to the Other to respect the national legal rules, to partake in a presumed 'unity'—in turn identified as an indispensable axis for peaceful coexistence—be deemed consistent? This question raises the issue of the universality of rules. But for universality to be authentic, it must be coextensive with an ongoing and open-ended process of universalization. To this end it is not enough to elaborate legal statements in general and abstract terms, or according to a rational systemic approach. It is not sufficient to state that 'all are obliged to', 'everyone has the right to', or other equivalent enunciations, in order to wash away any danger of a discriminatory use of law and its practical implementations. Legal rules, even the most general ones, can legitimately aspire to universality only if their contents are responsive and inclusive with regard to the equitably weighed interests of all the individuals and groups partaking in social life. But for this to take shape, multicultural societies must promote the creation of a public lexicon, a semantic social contract,[62] stemming from iterative processes of reciprocal translation and recognition among the social components and their imageries. This task should be progressively promoted and carried out, however, on both national and global levels. This exigency has to do with power and economic unbalances, which make it so that the decisions adopted inside the more powerful national circuits, even if democratically assumed, affect the quotidian life of individuals residing in another corner of the world. In any case, without the development of an intercultural language that can enable translation between differences, it will be impossible to establish legal rules that do not run the risk of being used as means to exclude, make unfair decisions, and give course to a partisan rationality, that is, the 'monster' of a biased universality. Without translational intercultural efforts and a genuine propensity for reciprocal recognition and equality, the universality of legal rules and principles can be only inflicted, with the complicity of institutions ironically presumed as secularized, upon all the Others: namely all

[61] For some semio-spatial remarks about the translational/transactional and intercultural hollowness of both such wording and its implementation in the legal experience of EU, I refer to Ricca (2015).

[62] Greimas (1983, pp. 103–113) and Ricca (2018b, 2022a).

those who are not able to see themselves in the semantic mirror of legal enunciations. Unfortunately, this condition is far from what is generally signified with the constellation of meaning orbiting the terms secularization, secularism and *laïcité*.

As already pointed out, the semantic space of 'secularization' includes (and in a sense '*is floating on*') a kind of self-evidence, something very near to commonsense. But 'common' sense—at least, according to its baseline interpretation—implies a referral to a rough precipitate of the convictions, views, mindsets and habits extant within a social circuit. When the demographic and cultural ingredients of this communicative and existential context change, or their (however precarious) stability goes through deep ferment or turmoil, what was common before becomes 'difference,' albeit still ascribable to the dominant parts of society. This does not in any way mean that the idea of 'commonsense' should be set aside, forsaken as a relic secluded in a past that has ineluctably crumbled: something obsolete and unsuited—to use the post-modern iconology—to a nomadic world, substantiated by a relentless transfiguration, endemically hybrid and protean. These kinds of abstract rejections end up emphasizing the loss of something, eventually becoming more conservative than the same post-modern/avant-garde would like to appear. Conversely, I think that the *warp* of what is 'common' cannot be assumed as something taken for granted in deference to a misoneistic reading of culture. Grasping its *existence* requires continually weaving its *weft* by putting this relational activity under an intercultural open-minded lens and thoughtfully re-sewing the resulting socio-communicative fabric by translating and transacting old and new differences/semiotic threads. According to the way I interpret the interculturalization of social relationships, only after having begun this redesigning of the 'semantics' and pouring it into law, will it be possible to ask for legal rules to be respected. Only when law is the result of a process of polyphonic and symmetric paving of responsive universalization[63] can compliance with formal legal prescriptions be deemed to be a social practice that is inherently responsive to the manifold 'culturalities' and 'subjectivites' extant in the social scenario. Passing off the universalistic linguistic form of the legal rules as the premise and the shell of an indisputably genuine universal content is not only mystifying and unfair but even self-deceptive, if only because, by reneging on the promises of equality, it does nothing but foment social insecurity.

On the other hand, whoever does not see themselves mirrored in the semantic and axiological spectrum of legal rules and feels culturally inhibited will inevitably develop a feeling of seclusion, as if they were kicked out from the range of the benefits allegedly ensuing from the law's application. These individuals (or groups) will be held to the law without any possibility to partake in its meaning. Once again, they will be *before* the law, but not 'semantically' inside it, unlike all the others,

[63] For the notion of 'democratic responsiveness', which in my view is something quite different from 'deliberative democracy', I refer to Dewey (1916); on which see the recent analysis carried out by Räber (2020).

namely those belonging to the majority.[64] This is the contradictory condition that foreigners and minorities must face in many formally democratic and secularized social contexts. But this is also a condition of social amputation, which will compel the 'different' people living before/outside the law to evade as far as possible the public sphere, in search of more hospitable social and communicative circuits. But the mimetic withdrawal (or rather seclusion) of cultural/religious differences in the folds of the private sphere, the same that modernity would protectively surround as an untouchable oasis of freedom, is the outcome of an exodus from the public sphere (which is the province of official appearances) and thence a potential retreat from any social control. Subaltern and hidden circuits and deviance, unfortunately, are quick to redouble, transmuting into a worm in the apple of public life and threatening social safety. Any emphasis on the obedience of 'rules for the sake of rules' should be moderated by a self-aware disposition to cultural modesty:[65] which is, on the other side, a necessary ingredient of any genuine recipe of institutional secularization.[66]

Anyone who is disregarded by the public discourse because of their idiomatic cultural features and differences, despite any aspirations, will be not able to inscribe themselves in the semantic spectrum of law. That feeling, however, will spur their *e*-migration (which is nothing but a forced escape) from both institutional and common spaces. With specific regard to migrants from different cultures, this phenomenon can eventually take the form of a psychological (and therefore not necessarily physical) counter-migration away from the hosting country, carried out in silence, almost with resignation amidst general indifference, but precisely for this reason all the more 'alarming.' To be clear: I use the word 'alarming' not to conjure up the danger of a 'foreign branded' deviance, exactly as the nationalist xenophobic propaganda of many countries hosting immigrants indulges in doing. On the

---

[64] For an analysis of this Kafkian divide—that is, 'before/inside' the law—I refer to Ricca (2020a), and therein for further bibliography on this topic.

[65] Sajò (2004). Of course, any detour from the respect for rules in themselves, regardless of the reasons for abiding by them, is an implicit confutation of legal formalism (Kelsen) or the analytical view of law (Hart). According to both these approaches the play for the 'meaning' and the axiological legitimation of a rule is to be considered as aprioristically over at the moment when the institutional dimension of law takes shape and the framework of the sources of law is fixed through the *Grundnorm* or the *rule of recognition*. But a legal experience based on the idea that all its legitimacy relies on the past, on the *meanings already meant* is inevitably tainted with a surplus of both axiological and cognitive *immodesty*. And besides, logical and chronological apriorisms cannot be other than immodest towards what is *present* or partakes in the supervening future. An immodesty that ineluctably ends up leaning toward a blindness to everything that is Other than the 'already known.' Until the 'direction of correspondence' in legal experience is thought of as something proceeding from past to the present, I fear that the possibility of any intercultural use of law will remain *arrested*. The basic question is: what is law for? Are its categories devices intended to meet and *manage* the future and its charge of unforeseeable novelty or, rather, to neutralize change at any cost?

[66] A self-critical modesty that is, perhaps, the unique, genuine, legitimacy of modernity and a *mature* secularization. That is to say a secularization germinating from a deep awareness of its cultural constraints and the unavoidable 'being enmeshed' in a space-time framework surrounding its processive unfolding.

contrary, I refer to the perception of legal rules as non-responsive, semantically alien, and deceptively universal, something that winds up estranging and de-centering especially the weakest subjects from the institutional dome. People in migrant communities and the circuits connoted by cultural and religious difference, vulnerable to oppression by the most overpowering among both natives and their countrymen and coreligionists are, in this way, ultimately displaced. This a consequence of any 'partisan general rule'—that is, the law of the strongest inflicting on others its irresponsive and thereby mystifying universality—which engenders subalternity and mistrust, ghettoization and disaffection. What is worse, these kinds of rules cast an umbra that prevents the institutional gaze from piercing the cloud of invisibility that covers cultural discrimination, prevarication and exploitation.

The fieldwork I have carried out in foreign communities has made me aware that their claims for justice, especially when infra-communitarian conflicts are at stake, is almost doomed at the start, even before a glimmer of possibility can be seen. In all of my conversations with immigrants about the opportunities for judicial protection when conflicts arise within their communities, as well as between migrants and natives, the reaction has been always the same: 'No, that is pointless! The (national) judges do not understand us!'[67] On the other hand, those who think they can be never 'inside the law' but only before it, namely that equality can be only *inflicted* on them, not surprisingly shun the (national) judges belonging to the majority culture. These individuals and groups already know that they will be misunderstood; or at least, they preventively hold a solid conviction that it will be impossible to find responsive attitudes in the legal circuit. In other words, migrants form other cultures, on average, perceive themselves as overwhelmed by the blind force of legal rules, which demand obedience but are indifferent to Others' *semantic spaces*.

2.4 Diversity, Democracy and Intercultural Sovereignty

I would like to propose, at this point, some questions that could be properly raised by a Devil's advocate.

'Why should foreign people, or even minorities, have the right to receive full recognition also inside the state law, and not only before it? Why should their cultural exigencies curtail the space of the autochthonous people or majorities? Is it not enough that they are hosted and tolerated? That we allow them to break into the sacred space of our territorial sovereignty and even express their cultural dissidence in the private sphere? After all, nobody forced them to come to us or remain here. As for the autochthonous minorities, moreover, it should make at least a little sense to have some respect for the will of the majority! Is freedom—as already stated by Constitutions—not enough in and of itself as a safeguard device? Why should the

[67] In this sense, see Foblets (2005).

public sphere not be the space of common sense—precisely, that steered, in its content and direction, by the majority?'

The above series of questions and somehow snooty assertions, quite widespread today in the national public opinion of many (officially) constitutional democracies, bumps, however, against two axiological and political standards: democratic reflexivity and institutional responsiveness. Democracy implies that the legitimation of the state and its laws is rooted in the reflexivity of the norms enacted by institutions: that is to say, at a basic level, that legal provisions benefit and bind all social actors, including their authors.[68] Nobody should be 'immune' to the law. But this is possible only if laws embody the interests of all people, regardless of whether they are part of the dominant group or a minority group. In turn, this means, however, that institutions must be responsive with respect to the needs, convictions, and cultural exigencies of all people. Conversely, when reflexivity and responsiveness are lacking, democracy is on the verge of transmuting into a dictatorship of the majority or a dominant minority, as such very far from any idea of sovereignty of the people. Of course, this does not mean that the majority cannot make political and normative choices that do not comply with the minorities' expectations. Nonetheless, the thresholds for the legitimacy of the majority's preferences do not allow them to radically compromise the possibility of individuals to recognize themselves and inscribe their own existential horizons within the contents of laws: at least, insofar as the impairment impinges on the fundamental features of individual subjectivity. Despite diverging or contrasting views, a common cultural plafond must be created, construed, and then, respected and assured.

For such a democratic landscape—as just elementarily sketched out—within a multicultural society the common cultural biosphere can only be intercultural. If it were not the case, and thereby the legal rules were determined exclusively by the (autochthonous) majority's culture and interests, how could institutions assert that their laws are in tune with the democratic ideal of the (tendential) coincidence of rulers and the ruled? How could it be said that a legal system arises from the voice of the people and their sovereignty if its rules include only the cultural, ethical, and religious schemes of some individuals but deny representativeness to others?

The lexicon of sovereignty (and therefore the legal system) can be qualified as democratic only if it is capable of proving itself equidistant and inclusive; otherwise, it would be the expression of an ethical/ethnic state rather than a democratic one. Of course, a thousand objections could be raised to the last assertion. They could be utilitarian, communitarian, traditionalist, and ethnic-territorial. Beyond a certain threshold, however, they end up becoming a denial of democratic/constitutional ideals. Even if somewhat provocatively, I would say that there is nothing absurd (at least in absolute terms) about this option. What is at stake, here, is not a fideistic

---

[68] This basic description of the principle of reflexivity can be considered, however, the seminal gist of the subsequent theories of reflexivity—tied to the development of the welfare state and the pluralistic dynamics of equality—developed with regard to democracy and law by Habermas (1995), Teubner (1983), Honneth (1998), and Forst (2011).

defense of the sacredness of democracy. It is, doubtless, a political system full of strengths, but also of as many flaws. Some might even prefer a theocratic system. There is no demonstration that democracy is inherently good or better than other systems of governance. *Inter alia*, the same could be said for human rights. And, certainly, that they have established themselves and (contemporary) history has 'decreed' their legitimation on an almost planetary scale cannot be taken as self-evidence of their high axiological status. History is steeped in sacralized and legitimate injustices.[69] That something exists and is widespread does not constitute undisputable proof of its value. Although philosophical speculation has dwelled for quite some time on the distinction between facts and values, I think (as I will further emphasize below) that they are not neatly separable. This does not imply, however, that facts, in their mere occurrence, can be taken as values: namely that the existing, as such, should be idolized or held valuable.

What I am trying to underscore is only the impossibility of defining a state as democratic and effectively based on popular sovereignty if its laws do not result from a weighed balancing of the cultural voices and differences living in its social landscape. The democratic/constitutional order requires that sovereignty must be intercultural precisely because it is to be popular, that is, an expression of all the people. Every time democracy is institutionally constructed in compliance with a specific ethno/cultural and ethical code, its foundational premise will be purely and simply denied: that is, the principle 'one person, one vote,' which is the main axis of the autonomy of both individuals and groups.[70]

The final outcome of the 'one person, one vote' principle should be that all those who are subjected to laws should be able, at least potentially, to be co-authors of these laws. This can be defined as the ideal democratic 'optimum', or better, the static and radical version of democracy. The implementation of the coincidence of the rulers and the ruled must undergo, however, some adjustments and mitigations in order to avert the risk that it turns into a dictatorship of minority. Indeed, were unanimity assumed as the only criterion to produce legal provisions, it would wind up giving each individual a kind of absolute power over all the others. The disagreement of just one individual would be enough to undermine the approval of political choices and legal rules, despite the consent of all others entitled to vote. Politics and law must unfold through history and their substance should 'engage' with change. This means that the 'unanimity ideal' is to be applied (and understood) in diachronic terms and must be balanced with majority decision-making. Further, though it might seem paradoxical, the adoption of the majority criterion is unavoidable for the principle of equality to be safe. The oscillation from majority to minority and back again, today and tomorrow, is the idiomatic way through which the equality principle can be implemented over time. On the other hand, the effectiveness of that alternation requires that all the social actors, namely both the dominant and

---

[69] With specific regard do human rights see, for example, from an anthropological/legal perspective, Dembour (2006); but, also, Goodale (2022).

[70] Tully (1995).

minorities groups, are culturally equidistant from the semantic and axiological nub of the legal system, so that their relationships with law are not asymmetrical. For this reason, the contents of legal rules are to be informed with anthropological inclusiveness and should encapsulate the semantic features of a public subjectivity that affords everyone the ability to move effectively through the folds of everyday life, giving rise to different future majorities. In other words, no majority—even when its components self-proclaim their status as guarantors of the national tradition and living symbols of an ethnic unity—can claim for the right to cement their condition of supremacy and prevent future change in the political leadership of the state. If this were the case, it would no longer be a democratic majority, and the overall institutional system would have already left democracy behind on its long descent to a condition of cultural despotism.

Unfortunately, the means available to dominant groups to impose their ethical, economic and cultural supremacy are many and extraordinarily effective, also because they are often hidden and masked by the shadow of the rhetoric of power. In some respects, the same idea of a people's legal culture, of its unity and homogeneity, is a striking example of just such an occurrence. For example, in many countries hosting immigrants the distinction between 'who has always been here' and 'who has just arrived' is one of the favorite topics of those who intend to preserve the *status quo* to their own advantage.[71] Its psychological strength rests, all in all, on the subliminal power of the adage 'last one in is a rotten egg.'[72] Nevertheless, this idea, although anthropologically anything but banal, is incompatible with democratic logic. Democracy is a form of *normalization* (although not a 'normativization' or compartmentalization) of social, political and cultural change. The axis of its legitimation and reproduction lies in consensus dynamics and the process of its ongoing self-renewal. Hence, the normative outcomes of a democratic state are and must always be exposed to change and re-evaluation, that is, a continually self-reflexive examination of past social achievements from the height of the present by those who inhabit it now. Any substantive and procedurally frozen relationship of primacy between subjects of democratic states and/or their normative-cultural paradigms would undermine, therefore, the whole democratic order irremediably.

---

[71] It is very interesting, and only apparently paradoxical, that the argument 'we were here before you' is also used by the minorities of natives who support a multiculturalist approach to politics. The relationship of exclusiveness between 'people' and 'space' seems to cut across the rhetorical representations of reasoning for both the ethnic majorities and minorities. I think that such ideas of exclusiveness float on a more general anthropological tendency to categorize/semanticize experiential space by means of its centripetal embodiment and the self-centered worldling of the human body. I developed some observations about the intercultural universalization of human rights, the above tendency towards a semanticizing territorialization, and the possibility to wriggle free from its unconscious influence through an analysis of the experience of astronauts in outer space: see Ricca (2018a).

[72] ...or, to put it in a more elegant and refined way '*prior in tempore, potius in iure*'.

Emphasizing the close connection between democracy and contingency does not at all mean that decision-making power should and could be gauged on ephemeral situations. Policy options are candidates for transformation into norms and norms are designed to grasp the future. They distribute duties and benefits by weighing up previous and future situations. Advantages and costs must therefore be borne by everyone, and their occurrence, namely the moment when they are respectively entitled to knock on the door, is not always synchronic, nor amenable to immediate fulfillment. This means that today's laws can confer advantages that will still have to be balanced by sacrifices tomorrow. The entitlement to participate in the processes of democratic political integration must be calibrated, at least in part, also on this time factor, that is, on the (relative) permanence in a specific territory and a coefficient of demographic stability.[73] Otherwise, those who are here today, because they have just arrived and are already about to leave, will have every interest in maximizing the immediate benefits and, simultaneously, discharging the costs of legislative choices on others, namely those who will remain. But this would precipitate patent inequality in decision-making processes. Foreigners or people of different/minoritarian cultures should be full-fledged active participants in the democratic system and entitled to claim for an inclusive and intercultural reconfiguration of the cultural axes of legal and social subjectivity: but this only on condition that they propose themselves as somehow durable members of a sovereign community. To meet such a prerequisite—though there is nothing in a human beings' life that can be said to be 'everlasting'—the presence of foreigners should in any case be coupled to some probabilistic evidence of stability.

As for foreigners, once again, time, in this case past time, could provide some insightful clues. Participation in democratic processes and full entitlement to political citizenship might legitimately impose a prerequisite that newcomers demonstrate their interest in staying in the host country. Of course, this does not mean that residing in a country for at least 5 or 10 years (as is currently required by many European regulations) can prevent people from subsequently migrating. And besides, the same consideration also applies to those who were born in one country and remained there. In this regard, I think it should be reiterated that there is nothing ethnocentric or nationalist in placing a temporal/demographic threshold as a requisite for participation in the processes of political and cultural integration and the democratic renewal of the social context. Vice versa, at least in my view, such a request satisfies an egalitarian exigency: the same that, *inter alia*, leads to assert the coextensiveness between equality and secular democracy. A democracy that, as such, is to be equidistant from the socio-cultural diversities extant in the social landscape and an expression of a polyphonically weighed intercultural sovereignty.[74]

[73] And this despite all my sincere alignment with the inspirational sources of the criticism raised by Shachar (2009) against the compartmentalizing idea of national citizenship.

[74] Intercultural sovereignty—as will be better illustrated below—is something completely different and radically distant from the 'multicultural nationalism' that has been recently proposed, for

2.5 Traditions, Religions and Everyday Life: The 'Immodesty' of Western Secularization

If cultural equidistance from law is to be considered coextensive to democratic order, why then call for secularism and/or secularization? Would not the grammar of socio-political and constitutional pluralism be sufficient to give foundation to the exigency of symmetrical relationships, mutual recognition and equitable institutions? Why blur, or worse conflate, the plane of politics with that of religion? Why does the first necessarily call into play the second? In one way or another, the terms secularism/ secularization have a very specific historical connotation, which anchors them, *inter alia*, to religious freedom, the fight against theocracy, and the release of modern thought from the chains of theological influence. Although inspired by pacifying intents, secular thought flows from the cultural fault ruptured concomitantly by the eruption of fierce conflicts and unresolved dialectics placed under control but never completely neutralized by Western modernity.

These plausible objections could be replied by arguing that even when not addressing it, pluralism should still deal with the religious factor and its presence in any socio-cultural context. Silencing and hiding, or even expunging it from institutional language would certainly not make religion vanish from the anthropological dimension, from the sphere of experience lived by individuals. To be concerned with religion is a sure source of problems, especially for modern political discourse, but this does not provide institutions with an alibi for ignoring it and avoiding the consequences of this intentional aloofness. In the field of politics and law the maxim of the 'first Wittgenstein' according to which 'what can be said at all can be said clearly, and what we cannot talk about we must pass over in silence' cannot be applied. No one, not even a despot, can fully and efficaciously decide what to keep silent about. Lordship over language is an ephemeral exercise, a façade. The *silences* it can impose would be loaded with much more meaning than the words that are forbidden. This constraint is due to the concreteness of politics and law: they are not exercises in fantasy. Power—as it were—cannot draw freehand, however absolute it is. It, too, must accept limitations to the possibility of its exercise, which operates first on the semiotic and communicative level, and thereby on the pragmatic terrain. If not respected, those limits turn into flaws of institutional effectiveness and the imperatives authorities produce. Pretending that there is no religion, not talking

example, by Modood (2019b). This is because the same word 'nationalism', however much adjusted with multiculturality, can be the harbinger of uncontrollable othering consequences, if anything, for the threatening wrinkles etched into its semantic spectrum by historical events. I agree with Modood's observation that the state recognition of a majority religion, and even its establishment, can be more functional than a 'radical secularization of public sphere' in the recognition of religious difference. An entirely separate issue is that related to the intermingling between nationalism and religion, even because the 'secular nationalism'—to follow Gellner—has proven to be, in turn, an appalling crucible of religious intolerance. I would prefer not to accept the challenge to experience how *staggering* a 'religiously marked nationalism' could prove to be in '*abetting*' the social flourishing of cultural and religious minorities. See also Mandeville (2021).

about it, strengthens its social weight rather than overshadowing it. This is a lesson that secularized modernity has had—or maybe has yet—to learn, almost everywhere in the West and especially in more recent times. But if this is the case, it depends on a paradoxical circumstance, already mentioned in part. Even when democratic institutions intend to keep a strict silence about religion, their existing law still speaks of it.

Public language is drenched with past and tradition. There is no communicative habit that does not sink its roots in thought and behavior patterns unreflectively embodied in people's conduct, inherited from their communities' past. But in the folds of collective memory, tradition and religion are inextricably interpenetrated. Many do not know what they know about religion, and yet they know a great deal; in the same vein, many are not aware of reiterating the meanings of a specific religious tradition through their everyday gestures. Therefore, when the law marks people's public and private life, its qualifications rely on common sense networks steeped in this unreflective knowledge and shaped by it. However, there is not only an extrinsic relationship between legal/deontic language and common language. In regulating life, the rules and the ends respectively enacted and pursued by law intertwine and contaminate with the networks of meaning and the categories of common life.[75] Moreover, the same authors of laws (lawmakers) are part and parcel of the social world they are committed to regulate. From a cultural point of view, therefore, even the secular legal discourse still chooses sides, and these choices follow paths of meaning also shaped by religious knowledge.

The above intersections can be positive, cooperative, but also conflicting or hegemonic. Speaking one or the other cultural dialect, laws end up engendering reactions and echoes of meaning that make the voice of religion ring out from the traditions and the implicit knowledge of the groups living in multicultural societies. In such situations, the mixture of anthropological lexicons and codes of faith can liquidize into political fuel. Under the umbrella of religious freedom and secular fashion of the state, the actors of cultural diversity build the trenches of their resistance to the homologating force of an allegedly *neutral* state law, especially when this is perceived—because it actually is—as an expression of the dominant culture.[76] Religious belonging and interests are thereupon transmogrified into a sort of passe-partout for the political/normative discourse since it can function as a legitimate device for claims and open the doors of the institutional home for cultural difference. On the other hand, religion has always asserted for itself—relying on the 'political code' of Western modernity—a sort of alternativity and competition with respect to the state. This circumstance gives it a kind of a priori and legally/constitutional apical authority, as such inscribed within specific institutional

[75] In this sense I refer to Ricca (2022a).

[76] A more sophisticated discourse is to be developed with regard to many post-colonial contexts. For within their socio-political circuits the legal and institutional lexicon is culturally tied to the cultural imageries and categories of the historical colonizers. About this already mentioned feature of post-colonial political and legal experience, see also below.

pigeonholes (e.g., religious freedom) already existing in constitutional language and capable of triggering effective protection instruments: like, for example, the judicial review of legislation. The advantage ensured by the possibility of giving cultural claims a religious *vestment*—which brings with it an intrinsic intertwining of traditions, personal memories, and faiths—provides the rest. The final result is reflected throughout the current tendency of cultural dialogues and conflicts to commute into religious-based dialogues and conflicts. In this way, cultural claims are somehow enabled to find in religion a sort of argumentative ground and public/institutional legitimacy.

It is the combination of these factors that makes the bulk of problems arising from contemporary multicultural societies unclassifiable, by taking an alleged neutral 'secular perspective' as their observation axis. By contrast, these are the same factors that compel the management of cultural pluralism to reckon with the religious promiscuity inherent in any political choice concerning the issues stemming from multiculturality. As a consequence, law, which is the agency that most punctuates everyday life even in its minutest folds, cannot avoid coming to terms with the hidden, silent cultural import of religion: the same which camouflages its presence in anthropological habits, unreflective gestures, and the unaware knowledge of legal subjects. All this suggests that only through a recalculation of both the spheres of meaning and the semiotic boundaries extant between common life and cultural/religious differences can a lexicon of constitutional pluralism be arranged in order to pacify intercultural conflicts and act as a platform for coexistence between differences. This requires, in other words, a specific commitment to cross the narrative landscapes traced by cultural traditions, religions and the related stores of meaning to achieve three crucial political goals: (a) the creation of a commonly 'viable cartography' of social and legal subjectivity; (b) the elaboration of an inclusive and impartial lexicon of 'daily active citizenship'; and (c) the implementation of institutional and regulatory coordinates to make the previous points effective.

2.6 Institutional Lexicon and Cultural History

The answers proffered so far, however, might raise further questions for someone belonging to a national state. For example: Why is an extra effort needed today to achieve a common institutional lexicon? Did the history of modernity, and secular modernity, not produce normative standards that correspond to universal reason? A reason which is epitomized by rational legal principles, as such ascribable to human nature? Are freedom, equality, solidarity, self-determination—if taken as axes of the democratic-constitutional legal language—not neutral principles/values which, as such, could be traced in all cultures, or adapted to each of them? And when this is not the case, should those principles not be considered, at least against the refractory cultures, an ethically legitimate instrument for the emancipation and the development of the individuals belonging to them? Furthermore, is the assumption of those standards as sources of individual rights not a real support to an authentically secularized legal experience? I am aware that the way the above questions are expressed could appear overly naïve or superficial. Nonetheless, the 'common life rhetoric'—often quite distant from the sophisticated discursive texture of academics and intellectuals—is far from being immune to such political phrasing.

Twentieth century historical criticism and anthropological research have strongly and widely contested the universality of human rights and the rule of law.[77] Both have disputed the alleged universality of human rights, denouncing their Western origin, their acceptance of colonialism in their developmental path, and their being limited to only one small part of humanity's cultural history and geography. In short, critical voices have emphasized their relativity because human rights constitute the expression—historically, at least—of a cultural-political experience that is specifically situated in time and space. The same voices have instead argued for the equal dignity of all cultures and their ethical-deontic apparatuses. The main tenet wielded by such criticisms is that all cultures are endowed with horizons of meaning, as such not always commensurable, but not for this reason to be considered less valuable.[78]

In some cases, anthropological research has been the driving force and sometimes the spokesperson for political struggle. As is well known, these critical voices contend that modernity has used the achievements of the Enlightenment just as if they were ships and cannons. Together with the devices of technological progress, cultural/political achievements have also been surreptitiously exported to strategically curve the discourse of rights for hegemonic purposes. Propagandized as the highest anthropological frontier of human emancipation from ignorance, they have been rhetorically established as an architrave for the legitimization of colonial enterprise. The arrival of Westerners has been portrayed as the historic chance for the other populations on the planet to shed their minority status, and develop beyond their cultural childhood. [79] Under the guise of anthropological aid—the West's self-assigned mission—the domination, exploitation, divestment of entire populations from their lands, the usurpation of their wealth, and sometimes even ethnic extermination, have all been legitimized. All this is true. Modernity has darkened progress with the shadows of death and strewn it with the leavings of merciless plunder. Like it or not, the rhetoric of colonialism is thoroughly modern. Nonetheless the story does not end here.

What has been done, the rhetorical and mystifying use of modernity and its political and ideological arsenal, does not reflect its semantic potential, and even less its overall authentic sources of inspiration. To use a metaphor, that fire may be used to burn does not intrinsically deprive it of its potential to heat or cook, that is, to be employed for beneficial purposes. Post-modern and anti-Western criticism has developed a current of thought animated by the intention to enhance the alternative character of values forged by non-Western Others. Among the multiple variations

[77] For a recent overview see Goodale (2008, 2009); but see also Goodale (2022).

[78] Clarke and Goodale (2010a, b); Goodale (2007); but see also Engle Merry (2016) and, most recently, Goodale (2023).

[79] Among others, this was the famous stance taken by Locke, ch. V, II *Treatise on Government*.

taken on by this critical stance, the movement of so-called Asian Values can be included. But, to date, its diffusion seems to have been as rapid as it has been ephemeral. Compared to the battles waged by indigenous peoples[80]—another relevant label of political criticism—Asian Values were characterized by the alleged cultural homogeneity and geographic-cultural amplitude of their references. The defense of Asian values is not free from a sort of reverse stereotyping, as such an offspring of Orientalism born from the colonial era and converted into a specular Occidentalism.[81] It has orbited the centrality of the community dimension, to be opposed to the individualistic one, as a particular and differentiating characteristic of Asian cultures. The criticism of the ethically catalyzing, epicentral features of the category of the individual has led this current of thought to a radical contestation of human rights and their logic.[82] They take on—it is argued—an individualistic anthropological connotation and pass it off as a universal human condition. Eastern thought rests instead on a completely different version of subjectivity, according to which the defining features of the individual are the consequence and not the source of community order, the bonds of solidarity, and the ethical order, in many cases considered as analogous to an overall cosmic order. These are relevant objections, which force the Western version of human rights and modernity itself to undertake a serious self-reflexive analysis. And it is precisely for this reason that the case of Asian Values is to be taken in account here despite the fading of their critical relevance. When mirrored into Otherness and even if stiffened in schemes that are too sharp and forced within an oppositional and antagonistic logic, modern thought is driven to develop a salutary retrospective and self-critical analysis, which functions as a kind of stress test for the alleged universality of its categories. The dialectic with the West opened by Asian Values, however, shows some genetic flaws due, in my view, to a rough essentialization of the cultural features of the 'civilization fronts' put into conflict.[83] Despite this, however, I would stress again that it produced some relevant beneficial effects.

The progressive fading of the strength and, thereby, the political success of Asian Values coincided with revisionist critiques of human rights and constitutional-democratic lexicons. The semantic structure of human rights was transfigured by this comparison/confrontation—at least, among some critical circuits. It had to abandon its rationalizing apriorism, opening up to the empirical evaluation of the discursive uses of the declarations of rights urged and claimed by non-Westerners. When facing the above reflexive stress test, as evidenced by the changed contemporary attitudes of the anthropologists themselves, human rights discourse had to *take note* of its potentially multicultural significance, its possible role as a platform

[80] A semiotic-intercultural analysis of indigenous people's claims can be found below, Chap. 7.

[81] Buruma and Margalit (2004).

[82] Bauer and Bell (1999) and Bell et al. (2001).

[83] Niezen (2004, 2009).

for the articulation of different subjectivities, its inherent openness to contamination and cultural translation/transduction.[84]

What seems to have removed the *claws*—as it were—from the antagonism preached by Asian Values was an occurrence sprouting from experience: non-Western people have shown that they have no ultimate intention of giving up on human rights. Regardless of whether they are universal in themselves or not, whether they are inherently fair or instead the product of a history marked by hegemonic inclination, omnilateral focus on the 'category' can neither be avoided nor considered worthless.[85] Conversely, the reinterpretation of the enunciative and semantic patterns imbuing the discourse on human rights can improve their universalizing scope, to be intended as an ongoing process, a horizon and therefore a means to set in motion the creation from below of an intercultural and cosmopolitan legal language. On the other hand, the fact that the clash with Asian Values and with the troops of human rights relativists forced an attunement to the voices of Others, of those who talk about them—even if from their own point of view—represents an important beginning for a new way of understanding their ethical and regulatory value.

If they are to renew their legitimacy in the contemporary world to match its plurality, human rights must abandon their self-description as the arrival point of history and icon of an eternal reason. Openness to experience, to the assessment of their possible alternative cultural uses, has highlighted their instrumental potential, that is, their attitude to serve as a means to approach an ever-proceeding horizon of universalization. As I will try to make more explicit further on, it can be said that human rights are starting to be understood as no longer the essence of universality, but rather as the semantic motor of a universalization process open to the inclusion of cultural differences.

Today, it is asserted that human rights and their national twins—i.e., the fundamental rights listed by the constitutions of many national countries—should be interpreted with modesty, namely avoiding apriorism or essentialization.[86] This means that they should *undergo* an inclusive reading, as such receptive of multicultural reinterpretations.

There is, however, another side of the perspectival multiplication of the meanings traceable to human rights. I refer to the circumstance that their universality, in order to provide evidence of its authenticity, should demonstrate that they are able to situate their contents: namely, their ability to adapt to manifold social contexts. Nonetheless, this test of authenticity, including the proof of a kind of *vernacularization* of human rights,[87] reveals a double-edged significance. It is right here that the tendency to a tight interpenetration between the institutional

---

[84] See below Chaps. 3 and 6.

[85] Cowan et al. (2001) and Twining (2009).

[86] See, for example, Sajò (2004).

[87] On the wording 'vernacularization of human rights' see Engle Merry (2006a, b, 2010) and Goodale (2022, 2023).

lexicon and the national history of a given local context deploys both its distinctiveness and problematic connotation. This is because situatedness shows the awkward implications ensuing from its dialectic relationship with a globalized, de-territorialized world, marked by interdependencies capable of contaminating and affecting any circuit of sense and experience articulated at the local level. On one hand, in order to accomplish its necessary conjugation with the various political-institutional circuits, the discourse on human rights cannot avoid measuring itself against the legal lexicons elaborated by each national tradition. But this implies, symmetrically, a reshaping of the previous traditional interpretations of local legal languages, especially in countries that have experienced a recent conversion of previous regimes into political-institutional orders inspired by democratic constitutionalism. Unavoidably, along the ridge of these multi-directional adaptations and re-semanticizations, the determination of what is to be the 'form of the human' on which 'universality' is to be gauged becomes a colossal intercultural challenge.[88]

In the West, however, things go differently, also because they have already gone differently—even if this does not mean they are easier to handle. Many Western democracies are coeval, if not co-extensive, with the invention of the discourse on rights and their implementation at the constitutional level. This chronological and cultural coincidence has meant that the interpretation of human rights has merged and co-developed together with the evolution and the re-interpretation of legislative texts and the categories of national law. Those categories, however, were and are still charged with history and culture, and therefore also with religion—even though this is a disguised presence, hidden by the rhetoric of modern secularization. As already observed, the situatedness of human rights, as such, is certainly the evidence rather than an implicit refutation of the possibility of their assumption as a processive and discursive horizon of universalization. However, in articulating and recomposing their meanings within the semantic landscape of national laws, human rights have inevitably ended up taking on culturally oriented signification. There is nothing wrong in this—I want to iterate—under the proviso, however, that these interpretations are not assumed as prototypical icons. This means that the *vernacularized* understanding and implementation of human rights cannot be passed off as their univocal and essentialized semantic scope. And besides, emphasizing this danger is not just an abstract hypothesis, a mere remote eventuality. This is, rather, a serious peril, which has already produced harmful results on both national and transnational dimensions.

Many Western peoples have historically experienced the implications of human rights discourse at home, and this has often led them to export a provincial version of their universalization potential.[89] They have mistaken—not altogether inadvertently—the particular modalities of implementation carried out in their

[88]Roniger (2016).

[89]This bent in human rights discourse and both its colonial and post-colonial implications is inversely symmetrical to the cultural/political project of 'provincializing Europe' ideally abetted by Chakrabarty (2009).

countries with human rights' absolute meaning, so exchanging universality with the 'identity to themselves' and transforming a product of their history into a sort of aprioristic cosmopolitan (if not also ontological) template. All this has caused political-anthropological disasters, generating a profound disaffection and mistrust in non-Western populations with respect to human rights discourse. If such disaffection is combined with the exploitation perpetrated by Western modernity for hegemonic purposes, then the matrix of hostility shown in other cultures with respect to the banner of rights becomes easily understandable. This is also because the banner of rights has been bandied about by the West as a symbol of its salvific-planetary action and a cornerstone for the legitimation of supranational institutions that are both politically and culturally firmly under its control.

Nevertheless, problems and reasons for controversy do not end there. Contemporary migrations pour the intercultural dialectic of human rights into the national states' social circuits, generating a return effect on the overall structure of the relationship between authority and freedom designed by international declarations and liberal-democratic constitutions. The presence of migrants and, more in general, of people from different cultures within Western national contexts generates an internal crisis delivering a nationalistic reading of human rights. The binomial 'state/culture,' however artificial and discriminatory it may be with respect to the autochthonous minorities themselves, tends to lose plausibility today. The result is that the forms of situated universalization, localizations of rights logic, are now undergoing intense criticism. The conflation between local legal traditions and human and/or fundamental rights is contested from within by the same subjects who coexist with the natives within the national territory embodying different cultures and traditions, in many cases coming from afar. In this situation, passing off the historically located universalizations and the related national implementations of human and constitutional rights as the prototype of human rights themselves, namely for the reified essence of their potential meanings, risks opening up unsolvable fronts of conflict and above all compromises any possible confidence in the universalizing potential of rights discourse.

The inability to face the confrontations between cultures within multicultural democratic contexts is fraught with past and present missteps, including the attempts to forcefully export not only the logic of rights, but also the entire Western legal lexicon, its categories, and its anthropological-religious substratum, artfully camouflaged and vaunted as rational, neutral, and *a-cultural*. The burden of these mistakes finds a rebounding echo in the resulting ethnic-national stiffening as well as in the ensuing refusal of any serious commitment to elaborate a symmetrical and equidistant intercultural legal lexicon within multicultural democracies, with the consequence of throwing these conflicts back towards the migrants' countries of origin and thereby at a transnational level.

In any case, the task of an intercultural conversion of national legal lexicons is arduous and requires the self-distancing of the dominant and/or national groups from their own culture. Equally fundamental is the achievement of an in-depth awareness of the cultural inclination of national legal agencies to imbue their interpretations of human rights with the basic categories of local quotidian legal experience. Needless to say, it is a tough challenge, one that should be underpinned by a widespread sense of responsibility and a skilled ability to make those categories available to translation and intercultural transactional practices. These are propaedeutic and as such indefectible steps in view of the reformulation in an intercultural and therefore authentically universalizing interpretation of human rights and constitutional rights, which is in harmony with the needs of equanimity, institutional equidistance and the alleged neutrality of multicultural secularized societies.

On the whole, what has just been outlined is a tremendously complicated enterprise, also from a psycho-cognitive point of view. And in fact, it is difficult to make people who have grown up in the myth of their own secularization understand that their legal lexicons and the jargon of everyday life are both invisibly full of 'tradition and religion.' Even today, it would leave many somehow puzzled to hear that *(a)* without the basic knowledge rooted in Christian culture, many Western civil and criminal legal categories would be incomprehensible; or *(b)* that, otherwise, they would be subject to interpretative approaches providing results that were extraordinarily distant from national 'law in action.' And this despite the fact that the last statements are immediately verifiable only if one had some interaction with the communities of foreigners present on the national territory and tried to explain to them the implicit meanings, the unspoken, the invisible and silent parts of the host (Western) countries' law. In this regard, the legal system of Italy, one of the countries most exposed to migratory flows and with a strong religious tradition underlying the secular structure of the state, could be taken as a paradigmatic example. From the definition of marriage to the civil concept of good faith or contractual equity, from the idea of legal liability related to criminal offense to the relationship between the individual, personality and corporeity epitomized in the formal figurations of legal capacity and subjectivity, all these categories are deeply imbued with the cultural imaginary of Christianity. The same conclusion would be reached even when analyzing the changes that have taken place in some institutes, such as marriage, which have been heavily affected by secularization processes. Evidence of this is the inability of divorce, which has been legal in Italy for almost 50 years, to overthrow the paradigmatic role of the ethical model of coexistence between men and women encapsulated in the normative fabric of legal marriage. And this although in many respects social practice tends to move away from that paradigm, even if through very contradictory paths. Actually, though more and more people prefer to live together rather than get married, the claims of cohabiting partners to obtain legal guarantees similar to those provided for legal spouses, especially in cases of separation, cannot be ignored; as well as the claim of homosexual couples to have official access to legal marriage and the related opposition of Catholic political representatives.[90] The intercultural interpretation of human rights, as a prospective outcome of contemporary multicultural dialectics,[91] goes hand in hand with the need to rethink national

[90] I analyzed these socio-legal dynamics more in detail and from a theoretical point of view in Ricca (2022b): see there for further references.

[91] Connolly (2009).

legal cultures by giving them a similar dialogical and transactional approach. This task calls secularism into play at a level of anthropological depth never before experienced. It urges social and institutional agencies to delve into the cultural territories of invisible religion to identify the thought schemes historically forged by faith and now cloaked with the common secular language and its legal lexicon. After all, it is the universalizing inspiration of human rights discourse (rather than their aprioristic and essentialized universality) that requires this retrospective and self-reflexive investigation. The openness of daily life dynamics to the planetary dimension is carried, today, on the shoulders and inside the minds of migrants. The same migrants who claim, on the basis of those rights and democratic logic, to be allowed to enter 'into the law'—quoting Kafka once more—by means of a remolding of the legal lexicon, historically produced by the national experience of the hosting countries, in a new legal vocabulary that allows for coexistence among differences inside social and institutional circuits in tune with an intercultural sovereignty.

2.7 Invisible Inequalities and Asymmetrical Secularization

Every legal system has its own lexicon. The language of law epitomizes the history, the tradition of a people. Thus, the regulatory dimension merges and often conflates with social experience. 'How the world should be' and 'how it is' share at least some aspects. But this semantic and cognitive blurring is nothing but the consequence of the above convergence, that is, the slow sliding of values towards effectiveness and the relationship between the state of things with the meaning of values and their reciprocal dynamics.[92] In this respect, it is no coincidence that the legislative texts are mostly conjugated in the present tense. The categories of law are configured in the same normative statements as if they were empirical objects or phenomena. Especially in the civil law tradition, legal statements such as 'the contract is . . .,' 'the sale is . . .,' are only paradigmatic examples of a common linguistic use. Of course, in these enunciations the 'is' means 'must be.' At the same time, however, the conflation between 'is' and 'ought' serves as an indicating clue of a latent and widespread cognitive phenomenon. In many cases, the binding force of the most dated norms in a sense has already worn out, settled and fixed in social habits, which work as cognitive/anthropological proactive schemes. However, this is only one of the many sides of the close interplay between social life and regulatory layers, daily communication and institutional discourse.[93]

Law is a social fact not only by virtue of the implementation of its binding force, and therefore of its propensity to produce and convey behavioral habits. In large part, the opposite is also true. That is to say that law is an expression of social processes, a

[92] On the relationship between facts and values I refer to Ricca (2018b, 2020a, b, 2022a, b, 2023).

[93] With regard to the performativity of denotation and its spatial import see Ricca (2022b).

projection of values/ends that constitute the 'being itself' of society, even prior to being framed as a formalized 'ought to be.'

Law heavily relies on these factual dimensions, which are but the historical-concrete expression of the culture of each community. Without such a pragmatic and cognitive prerequisite, the legal regulation of social life would be doomed to be a construction with a low coefficient of effectiveness. But there is something more. What takes place spontaneously at a social and inter-subjective level, something that law presupposes for both its legitimacy and effectiveness, does not only coincide with what is explicitly stated by legal rules. In its discursive unfolding, each legal system, and any normative act, presumes a semantic background—a kind of semantic social contract—underlying the injunctive force of its provisions: which is also the stoking factor coextensive with the values/ends playing the role of presupposition of both institutional action and the obligations arising from it. If detached from the semantic landscapes comprising cultural knowledge, orders and values/ends would remain incomprehensible, like fragments disjoined from their context of meaning. Their pragmatic implications would become indecipherable, drowned in a marsh of semantic ambiguity and polyvalence. The prescriptiveness of law, conversely, presumes a world, a world of facts, which is however the result of cultural options, cognitive categories, as such shared by a community of individuals and groups living together by virtue of, and *immersed in*, communication. But it is precisely amidst this ocean of communicative continuities that in many cases cultural diversity *befalls*, breaking into it as an unexpected event. Especially foreigners from different cultures, therefore, when they come into contact with national law, end up getting lost in semantic labyrinths that lead them along paths that in their eyes appear haunted by unforeseeable hindrances and hidden inequalities. This is because laws presume knowledge that is not held by those who come from different socio-cultural backgrounds. Nonetheless, these presumptions are assumed as if their object, namely the knowledge tacitly attributed to the Other, were nothing more than a self-evident datum, a sort of universal anthropological coefficient, instead of the product of specific cultural experiences. Those who were not in possession of that implicit knowledge would therefore demonstrate that they are somehow almost *non compos mentis* because of their inability to see things as they are.[94] However regrettable it may be, the autochthonous national institutions seem, in many cases, to assume this conviction as a sextant of their own actions towards foreigners from other cultures. And yet, they rely upon an unfounded demand which turns into a source of injustice. But, once again, that is not all.

Giving implicit self-evidence to one's own cultural categories produces a sort of naturalization and, in this vein, also an ontologization of the cultural options and the judgment schemes underlying them. As if to say, in more direct terms, that one's way of seeing is mistaken for the natural one and, insofar as it is assumed to be natural, as something intrinsically good. This cognitive and axiological attitude is strictly linked to the divide assumed by modern thought between objectivity and

[94] Jackson (1996).

subjectivity, external and internal, public and private, the legally institutionalized sphere and the domain of freedom: a sequence of divides that can be terminologically condensed in the formula 'the epistemology of secularization.'[95] The above way of reasoning about the cognitive resources of foreigners or minorities, evidencing the difficulty of grasping one's own attitudes reflexively, transforms into a wall against cultural Otherness, against the reasons of those who are different from us and, ultimately, in a de-qualification of their differing cognitive and axiological patterns. The power of autochthonous groups, their condition of dominance, provides for all the rest, confusing what stems from mere cultural options with absolute truths. The intertwining of law and cognitive schemes, between 'ought' and social facts, thus generates inequalities destined to remain invisible, not perceived by natives and sometimes not even by foreigners, but nevertheless not infrequently neutralized or worse legitimized, and eventually *normalized*, by the rhetoric of national sovereignty. This situation becomes particularly symptomatic and, in many ways, paradigmatic of a real paradox widespread in many contemporary democracies when cultural diversity is placed under the heading 'freedom' and therefore the domain of 'subjectivity.' Despite the acknowledgment of the so-called rights of cultures,[96] it is still difficult to bring a fruitful contestation against the prevailing forms of legal subjectivity by leveraging one's own simple cultural options. The exception to this silently cognitive discrimination is when Others' behaviors are taken as clearly exotic manifestations, the recognition and apparent legal protection of which—as will be analyzed more extensively—ends up being revealed as a remedy worse than evil because of its inherent othering and alienating effect. All this is to be coupled to the related circumstance that a faster and more effective way, at least in Western liberal countries, to achieve some kind of recognition is to give people the possibility to claim for their cultural prerogatives under the aegis of religious freedom. In this regard, however, it is interesting to observe that this 'religiosization' of cultural difference takes on, instead, different shape in many non-Western countries. This is because there it is more functional to the legitimization of state action than the direct claim for individual prerogatives: which in many cases implies also a critical re-reading, if not even an explicit rejection, of secularism.[97] But let us return, at least for the moment, to the Western countries.

With regard to individual claims, state secularization can be considered as the other side of religious freedom. This means that the need for an equidistance of cultural options from the legal system and its cultural language risks merging and conflating with the claims for religious freedom for reasons that are anything but ephemeral or merely instrumental. In order to grasp the deep reasons for this

[95] For more detailed elements on the epistemology of secularization see Ricca (2020a).

[96] Traces of this recognition at a political-institutional level can be found in both the Convention on the Protection and Promotion of the Diversity of Cultural Expressions (2005) and the United Nations Declaration on the Rights of Indigenous Peoples (2007): see below Chap. 7.

[97] In this regard see above in this chapter.

conflation, however, we must unavoidably start from a rather 'uncomfortable' observation, namely that in many democratic states both socio-political secularization and secularism are asymmetrically conceived and implemented simply because the protection of religious freedom is already asymmetrical.

But what does the above asymmetry consist of and what does it depend on? Its origins are intertwined with the partiality and constitutive incompleteness of the legal secularization processes that have accompanied the emergence of Western modernity.[98] The legal lexicon of the democracies of the West presents itself as rational, theologically neutral, and detached from religious nuances. Nevertheless, the semantics and the anthropological imaginary underlying its categories are imbued with references to Christian tradition and moral theology. In other words, religion, when intended also in its anthropological scope, keeps itself invisible within the cultural lexicon that is pulled into the orbit of legal discourse. This datum, however, should come as no surprise. As has already been observed, the neutrality of secular discourse is a myth because it presupposes a zero degree of knowledge, a gaze cast from nowhere. And yet it is an impossible condition to achieve, at least in absolute terms. On the other hand, religious knowledge inevitably conflates with cultural rationality, so that its anthropological implications end up appearing to members of individual communities as an integral part of their rationality and the facts placed under its lens *and pro-actively projected* on the environment through them. From inside, legal discourse can even appear completely devoid of religious connotations, since its categories coincide with the territories of self-evidence, or better the culturally shared, where the religious imagination is intermingled with the world of common life. It is only when religious or cultural diversity becomes part of existential circuits, when it crosses the boundaries drawn by the territorial sovereignty of nation states, that the obvious makes visible its historical origins, its cultural and inevitably also religious pedigree. Precisely for this reason, the eyes of foreigners, insofar as they are subject to the law of the host state, are the most reliable lenses to bring such ideal genealogies into focus. But this is not because those who arrive from without hold mysterious or more refined cognitive attitudes; rather it depends only on the circumstance that the native box of cultural self-evidence does not match that of Others. And besides, it is precisely when the pragmatic implications of 'cultural obviousness' enter a collision course with experience that it becomes as indispensable as automatic to resort to personal memory, to one's own history, in search of axes of legitimacy and identitarian footholds. Only when the world tells us 'no' do we ask ourselves: "Who am I?" "Where do I come from?" "What is my (legitimate) place in the daily landscape?" namely, "...in my current living environment?" When focusing on the social refusal of their habits, individuals *discover* their difference and try to trace the label, the identikit, or in any case a group of features that make their self-representation recognizable and axiologically valuable (at the very least in their own eyes). Religions, in these cases, are generous with support. They act as imaginary

---

[98] Taylor (2007, 2011).

receptacles, proffering entire stockpiles of certainties, almost endless reserves of meaning and noble genealogies to anyone in search of psychological security. By tracing their self-image in religion, anyone can regain, as militants or members, the ascriptive dignity[99] somehow denied, downgraded by the discourse articulated by the dominant groups or by the laws of the host countries. Conversely, when the religious matrix of one's own cultural self-evidence surfaces, the Other's immediately emerges from its cultural umbra. So it happens that the secular, neutral and rational discourse allegedly structuring Western democracies' legal systems suddenly betrays, in the eyes of those who come from other cultures, a 'crucifix' lying in the background. At this point the thrill of demystification provides for the rest, stoking the tendency to represent cultural differences in a confessional/fideistic way, that is to say, under the guise of behavioral dispositions to be protected by resorting to religious freedom.

However, the asymmetry of secularism practiced in Western democracies is not only a representation that arises from psycho-intercultural dynamics. The semantic continuity extant between the national legal lexicons and the ethical-cultural categories traceable to the Christian moral tradition already strongly relativizes, in itself, the 'alienness' of the religious influence with respect to the public sphere.[100] Modern Western institutions have been built and self-legitimated by relying upon state/church polarity and, in parallel, the dualism between reason and religion. At the dawn of European modernity, these divisions were a projection of socio-political conflicts between religious apparatuses and secular institutions, both struggling against each other for the legitimacy of their respective power. The clash was tackled and partially tamed by delimiting different areas of competence. The public sphere was distinguished from the private one, and the idea of individual freedom was placed as a kind of *customs agent* between the two domains. In this scenario, the state ingrained its legitimacy in the original consent of the people, the mythical social contract. Nonetheless, citizens retained the right to freely interpret behaviors within the private sphere. The framework of religious freedom, together with property, constituted the first runway for this new scheme of anthropological-political organization. Even assuming that history errs,[101] in this case it seems to have been right. Law and religion, public and private, the domain of state institutions and the kingdom of faith, have divided the field and, with ups and downs, from then on have managed to somehow find a recipe for a relatively peaceful coexistence. Nevertheless, it would be naïve to think that the public/private divide and the parallel law/religion divide had as their architrave a real anthropological break, an epochal fracture separating the source of common sense, communitarian culture and

[99] On the distinction between 'ascriptive' and 'agentive' dignity I refer to a forthcoming monograph of mine, which is titled 'Indifferent Freedom and Dignity Excesses.'

[100] Habermas (2006), Waldron (2004, pp. 203 ff.), Wolterstorff (2008), and Hunter-Henin (2020, p. 175).

[101] . . . and I cannot avoid believing that it is so, although it is impossible to prove it since—as the saying goes—the roads not traveled, even if just for this reason, can all appear paved with gold.

individual basic beliefs. On the contrary, deep continuities between legal and religious lexicons were retained, even if concealed by the rationalistic reinterpretation of the principles transferred through the work of the Second Scholasticism and Natural Law doctrine from Christian moral theology to modern legal frameworks. Christians could thus obey the rules of social coexistence ingrained in reason, but which were in many respects completely continuous and commensurable with the imperatives dictated to them by Christian morals. Along and despite the horizon dividing public and private, reason and religion, heaven and earth were still being mingled. In this sense, legal secularization was an extraordinary rhetorical device. It was extremely effective at preserving the anthropological-legal inheritance generated by Christian culture, even if it remained in the shadow of the epochal divorce between religion and politics; it became, for its part, an essential communicative strategy for social pacification.

Each individual was free to believe in his own private god (Lutheran, Calvinist, Anglican, Catholic, etc.) but while obeying in the public sphere the principles of conduct required by a common god, the god of all Christians, disguised as state or natural/rational law. And besides, Catholics, Anglicans, Lutherans, Calvinists, and even European Jews, had commonalities in their understanding of the ethical grammar of contract, marriage, inheritance law, and the various kinds of criminal protection and crimes. It was enough to change *brand* of these ethical and legal standards, replacing God with Reason, and the desire to claim theological origin and legitimation for these categories was minimized. But it was the same belonging that had been very recently contested, battled over in an outbreak of confessional struggles.[102]

The result of these processes aiming at the discursive reconfiguration of old truths proved to be extraordinarily efficacious. It allowed for the articulation of the rhetoric of political-social progress—and not only—without severing ties with the past at the level of daily life, that is, retaining the behavioral habits actually held by people and their common, implicit knowledge. By contrast, a radical reshaping of the deep ganglia of practical mindsets would have been a cyclopean work, as culturally utopian as historically impossible. If read in retrospect, the clean contours of modernity therefore fade—as it were—into semi-darkness. And yet, precisely this cultural low-definition or incompleteness turns out to be a problem today. From being a strategic advantage inside the modern watershed of Western history, it has turned into a serious pitfall for coexistence with other cultures.

The cultural continuity between the current law of Western countries and Christian moral anthropology makes the freedom of Others, and religious freedom in particular, less than equal in Western national contexts. While Christians find minimal hindrances in translating most of their religious language into the legal lexicon of the state, at least as concerns practical behaviors, the foreigners or the autochthonous from different cultures have instead great difficulties in transducing the semantics of their freedom and universes of belief in the discursive circuits of the

[102]Prodi (2000).

allegedly secularized public sphere. The private sphere of the Others, the non-Christians, does not have the same opportunity to project and proceed along paths of commensurability and continuity of meaning within the public sphere molded by the democratic institutions of the state. Unlike the Christians, those individuals will not find their own cultural, ethical and religious codes woven in the weft of legal language, in the institutional lexicon and in the grammar of public life. In this sense, history is not on their side. Consequently, the cultural encyclopedia underlying their subjectivity will be forced to compress its practical implications within a private sphere that will be inevitably perceived as too small; and this because it is gauged on the lesser needs encountered by the Christians in giving voice to their difference with the secular cultural and institutional domain. Hence, all the 'nos' that the allegedly secularized cultural code of the public legal discourse directs against the Others' cultural/religious patterns are destined to be converted into fruitless attempts to express them in the private sphere. Inside this frame, 'aliens' and 'minorities' must compress the imperatives, semantic implications and practical projections that culture and religion wedge, over a wide expanse, within their daily life and in their public relations. In the end, the non-Christian belonging to a different culture will only be able to exercise an amputated, defective freedom, at least if it is considered in comparison with the correspondent freedom of a native Christian. What is of the utmost importance to emphasize, however, is that such asymmetry is not the consequence of an explicit discrimination (even if, in many cases, it is not absent). What makes the difference is the anthropological/cultural *indifference* of the state's legal language with respect to its *incomplete* non-Christianity; such indifference invokes the fictitious religious neutrality of modern legal reason as both its smokescreen and alibi.

Finding a remedy for this 'state of secular affairs' entails a reinterpretation of Western history to be carried out through different cultural lenses. First, it would require that Western Christians commit themselves to taking an appropriate critical distance from themselves. The challenge, which includes also a powerful epochal paradigm shift, amounts to a renewal of the lexicon of equality in the contemporary globalized world. This lexicon is essential for the articulation of a symmetrical secularism. But, for such a formidable task to be accomplished, it should be coupled with an effort of intercultural translation/transaction among the semantics of the manifold subjectivities populating the multicultural and multireligious social contexts. Such tremendous cultural effort should be conducted first and foremost on a political anthropological level. To ensure that it is articulated on a background of consensus, we should consider the phase of nation states—intended not so much as units of territorial power as rather the institutional projection of homogeneous and exclusive ethnic-cultural circuits—to be exhausted. To paraphrase the title of a well-known book of the last century, communities should be *re-imagined*.[103]

[103]The referral is, obviously, to Anderson (1983/2006); see, also, Calhoun (2016) and Taylor (2004).

2.8 Cultural Orthopraxis and the Grammar of Rights

Cultures comprise encyclopedias of know-how (or, knowing how to do), instructions for *the use of life* in its relations with the human and natural environment. Each of them puts together and transmits different cognitive and behavioral recipes. Each recipe proactively draws imaginary features and borders of a world. And yet culture is not about closed, mutually non-communicating worlds. Planet Earth is home to many cultures, therefore many cultural universes. Its physical space functions as a ground, or source material, for interaction and translation among those universes. No cultural universe is pure, totally original, or self-produced because it is *genetically* relational. Nonetheless, despite the communication flows, differentiating circuits of meanings take shape with a relative degree of idiomaticity and closure. What comes from outside is absorbed and vernacularized, that is, interpreted and adapted to the internal dimension. In a sense, it could be said that it is *naturalized.* Even globalization, a common condition of contemporary human experience, is subject to *naturalization* processes—which, in my view, are something different from what is usually called 'glocalization.'[104] In many cases, the global, after and beyond its reception, is reinterpreted, 'reworked' and then returned to the planetary arena. The process works as an alternation between diastole and systole along an uninterrupted flow of communication between local and global. During its emergence, new boundaries and cultural circuits arise and others vanish. Within them, new encyclopedias of know-how are defined, and others are refurbished.[105]

However, in the space/time (or, in some sense, the chronotope) of every culture, 'knowing how to do' is also an 'ought.' The language of culture as well as any kind of 'categorization/denotation' has its own normativity,[106] which is an indispensable tool for optimizing communication processes. Having a shared conceptual dialect makes it easier to carry on with life efficiently. Living as a member of a culture requires knowing how to speak the language, how to recognize its landscapes of sense, and how to use its categories to interact effectively with the surrounding environment. The set of such communicational and behavioral schemes consists of thought processes and practical dispositions, definable as cultural scripts or orthopraxis. Cultural orthopraxes organize daily experience and set their rhythms so as to give it regularity. All of us, whichever culture we belong to, are attuned to similar rhythms, that is, to the *bars* inscribed in the scores of cultural orthopraxes. They permeate the most intimate folds of personal and daily existence. They create time and space and forge the ways through which time and space are experienced and perceived. Human subjectivity is the result of the intersection of the different

[104] In this regard, I refer to Ricca (2010, 2021).

[105] Ricca (2008b).

[106] On the 'performativity' inherent in any denotation, and therefore the relativization of the distinction between performatives and constatives see Ricca (2022b), but also Austin (1962, pp. 52, 137–138, 147–148).

orthopraxes that map individual and collective living. Moving, eating, trading, dying, speaking, even being silent, are the targets of this implicit cartography of life.

In any society, the legal level, endowed with an additional degree of semantic and deontic stiffness, is superimposed over this layer of tacit scripts, as such implicit but no less powerful; or rather, so powerful that the expressed law (be it symbolized in communicative customary patterns or institutionalized formal sources) is entirely imbued with it. After all, it is an inescapable constraint, a kind of all-embracing atmosphere.[107] No legal system could function and develop plausible prognoses of effectiveness if its normative acts were utterly alien to the cultural orthopraxis extant at a social level. The grammar of rights, although expressed in formal, general and abstract terms—as happens in the systems of civil laws—is imbued with custom, with mental and behavioral patterns that are traceable, like a kind of watermark, in the so-called common sense. These weave the semiotic framework, the context of meaning and experience—in a sense, the indexical cloud—surrounding and underpinning the words of the law. Disconnecting normative words from the corresponding orthopraxes would be equivalent to engendering far-fetched social worlds. Precisely for this reason, law and the universe of experience should be considered as an inseparable binomial, however dynamic the mutual relations between its components may be.

It is no surprise that the asymmetric interplay of multiple cultural scripts actively embodied by individuals simultaneously present in the same spatial frames inevitably produces a gap between the grammar of rights and experience. Just to use a visual metaphor, it is as if an image were extrapolated from one background and placed in another. The spatial-semantic transposition will produce distortions of meaning, inconsistencies, metamorphosis of sense and above all—metaphors aside—a sharp discontinuity between normative means and ends, between legal words and perspectives for the concrete fulfilment of the values embedded in the law's statements. Such discrepancies between the regulatory level and cultural orthopraxes can result in a sort of legal de-subjectification of those who do not belong to the dominant groups. The semantic indexes mapping their lives, the sources of meaning of their subjectivity, will find entrenched batteries of denials and obstructions in the legal system. And since culture and religion are closely interconnected, the ability of cultural minorities to give space to the pragmatic projections of their own culture and faith will inevitably be affected and made defective. To be clear: it can result in a relative discrimination rather than an absolute one. In other words, the sense of 'alienness' does not depend on a general and a priori interdiction of cultural and religious orthopraxes of *non-dominant* groups. Rather, discrimination can be experienced in terms of daily micro-practices in view of the different conditions offered to both the individual and groups belonging to minorities when compared to those that are instead assured to people classified within the cultural or religious majority. For dominant groups and their members,

---

[107] See, for the metaphorical application of the word 'atmosphere' to legal experience, Philippopoulos-Mihalopoulos (2015).

law speaks their language, allowing them to carry on their daily existence by conciliating freedom of conscience and obedience to the laws without resorting to laborious translational exercise, wearying accommodations, and tiresome compromises. Semantic syncopes—as it were—and the consequential tacit discriminations will however worm their way into a general situation inevitably marked by a latent tension, if not even incipient clashes.

In the name of the autonomy of cultural groups, religious freedom, and pluralism, a sort of separate, special citizenship will probably be claimed on behalf of orthopraxes that cannot be inscribed in the grammar of rights as it is articulated by majority groups and national legal lexicons. This is the way—as already seen—of multiculturalist pluralism. A way that is as much open to dialogue,[108] at least in terms of sociological theorizations, as it seems to be destined to boil down, at least on a legal level, to an inauspicious project of coexistence among compartmentalized legal circuits, which are in turn regulated by heterochronous legal-cultural blocks.[109] The subjectification or personalization of law is the result of a similar approach, seen by many as a viable solution. According to some recipes in vogue, it would lead to the proliferation of 'personal laws,' as for example ecclesiastical courts, Shari'a councils and Courts of Arbitration: namely judicial or para-judicial structures settled within the communities and delegated to apply the legal rules of the different cultural and religious traditions, but only in 'some areas.'[110] In my view, however, the crucial problem lurks precisely in the expression 'some areas.' Although courts of arbitration have a competence that can also extend to contract relationships, these communitarian decision-making structures mainly deal with issues related to marriage, family life and (less often) inheritance. In any case, their activities cover only the relationships between members of the same community and inevitably bump against serious limits when the same relationships involve third parties not belonging to the same cultural or religious community. In other words, the multiculturalist approach is inevitably unable to envisage the construction of a shared and equidistant grammar of subjectivity, which remains structurally beyond its reach. Its unique horizon coincides with the identitarian underlining of differences against the background, paradoxically, of the dominant group's cultural discourse, to which is left the articulation of the general and comprehensive semantic fiber of social

[108] See in this sense, Modood and his long-term debating with Zapata-Barrero—see Meer et al. (2016)—on the dialectical relationship between each of them label as 'multiculturalism' and 'interculturalism'—adding the needful *caveat* that my approach to the intercultural use of law has very little to do with both these theoretical frameworks.

[109] As regard the dramatic distance between the sociological theorizations of multiculturalism and the alleged openness to dialogue and intercultural interaction, on one side, and its stiffening implications as soon as legal and/or normative patterns are concerned, see above what I observed in the introduction. With regard to the most recent attempts to decline the multiculturalist approach according to a dynamic fashion allegedly relying upon the intercultural dialogue see Modood (2019b).

[110] On religious courts see, at least, Schachar (2001), Bano (2012), Griffith-Jones (2013), Bowen (2016), and Zee (2016). For a critical review of the experience of religious courts and arbitrations, especially in UK, see Walker (2017) and Parolari (2020).

relationships. A task that constitutes, by contrast, the source of the Others' (or minorities) mistrust towards the cognitive and axiological predisposition, if not even the aptitude, of national secular judges to have insightful discernment of their personal issues and the related cultural determinants.

The prompting factors spurring cultural or religious Others to organize infra-communitarian courts or arbitration structures can be epitomized in some of my fieldwork results. As already mentioned, whenever I asked people of minority groups if they would refer to a national court a question involving individuals belonging to their community, the answer has been ineluctably the same. It sounds more or less as follows: 'No, because the national judge does not understand anything about our way of life, our culture, our religion.' The question is: can we consider the national secular judges' 'non-understanding' decried by those who belong to cultural and religious minorities to be a subjective condition depending on psycho-cultural factors? Or is it, instead, coextensive with a kind of 'institutional deaf ear' imposed by the epistemology of secularization and, more specifically, the ensuing public/private, public sphere/religious sphere divides? In this sense, how important is the absence—or the peripherality—of university courses on religious laws and their anthropological background in law curriculums? What about the lack of courses teaching inter-legal and intercultural translation skills? From this perspective, no matter how much religious courts show an open and genuine attitude towards the possible path of harmonization between religious laws and secular legal systems, they will be not able, in the end, to defuse the identitarian reaction triggered by the intentional ignorance of national and, in many cases, transnational courts.[111]

It is no coincidence that legal multiculturalists do not focus their gaze on many aspects of everyday life conduct. More precisely, the conduct without identitarian labels and, instead, ascribable to existential ordinariness, which despite this is not immune to huge communicative difficulties and conflict due precisely to cultural difference. On average, multiculturalists concentrate their attention on the most exotic(ized) practices: in short, all those making differences immediately apparent, sometimes even striking, at least in the eyes of the members belonging to dominant groups. In doing so, differences are perceived and conceptualized according to the external morphological features of objects, gestures, expressions, and behaviors. By and large, Otherness is configured as a collection of empirically self-evident data. It is conceived, therefore, as the furthest 'thing' from what results from the patterns of judgment and the semiotic landscapes that individuals have inherited from their own culture to categorize the world. Nevertheless, if difference is relegated to the narrow limits of exoticism and condemned to a sort of folklorization, it will produce a silent but never previously conceived effect endowed with huge political-social significance. Difference will be evicted from everything that is given as 'normal,' everyday, even trivially ordinary experience. This cognitive disposition, often articulated

[111] Sahyouni v Mamisch: Case C-372/16: Court of Justice of the European Union could be considered paradigmatic (https://eur-lex.europa.eu/legal-content/IT/ALL/?uri=CELEX%3A62016CJ0372).

in an unreflective way, can however have deeply discriminatory implications, all the more powerful and pervasive the more they are perpetrated unawares. Paradoxically, the same claims for difference end up, in this way, falling prey to the trap of the specious and ethnocentric gaze cast on Others by the majority culture. And this happens because, if the 'ordinary,' the 'daily,' are subjected to a sort of immunization from cultural difference and its perception, the distinctive features of those dimensions of experience will inevitably become a sort of implicit, but ever more indisputable, mirror of universality. It is not difficult to see, however, how such a ready universality, tacitly taken for granted in its constituent elements, will necessarily bear the Gorgon face of ethnocentrism. It will tend to silence the voice of whoever is Other, petrifying it in its opposition to the universal one, taken as the ontological yardstick of the human itself. But this assumption will be nothing but an aprioristic essentialization, forged as a mere projection of a personal identity passed off as universality.

What has just been observed makes understandable, moreover, why the legal projections of multiculturalism mainly focus on certain figures of cultural difference and read them through the lens of the systems of rules that regulate the corresponding juridical institutes. Unfortunately, if culture is taken as something equivalent to a system of legal and/or normative rules, it can be recognized and legitimized in its 'differential' significance only when internal relationships within individual cultural communities are taken into consideration. Consider the examples of marriage or the overall experience of family life and the corresponding claims for the possibility of applying parallel regulatory apparatuses: respectively, those of the state and those related to the culture/religion of belonging. Such requests make sense and appear based on the principle of individual freedom and the right to self-determination of social groups only on the proviso that the marriage or family life adjudicated concern people belonging to the same culture. When the cases to be ruled instead involve people belonging to different ethnicities, cultures, or religions, obviously the request for an exclusive and concurrent application of, alternatively, the state or non-state regulations would come into collision with the principles of both sociological and legal pluralism. And this because that claim would favor only one of the parties of the (subjectively) intercultural or interreligious marriage. Under these conditions, and even if the supporters of multiculturalism invoke the intimate openness to dialogue of their approach, multicultural and/or multi-religious pluralism would prove to be alien to any hope of intercultural inclusion. Instead of promoting the coexistence and the creation of a horizon of meaning, also conveyed by law, for the elaboration of an inclusive public subjectivity, legal/cultural pluralism would end up increasing mutual segregation and a partisan compartmentalization of the relationships between people of different cultures.[112] Some sociologists

[112]...which is exactly the 'descent' that, despite and perhaps also because of the invocation of a 'progressive multiculturalism'—see Malik (2009)—is fueling the dispute on Shari'a Councils and Courts of Arbitration in UK. On the argument that the formula '*progressive* multiculturalism' gives just a little too much room to the idea that accommodation within Western models and imaginaries

and anthropologists support socio-institutional strategies inspired to multicultural legal pluralism and still widely consider it the preferred way to manage cultural and religious plurality. Unfortunately, they seem to be rather unfamiliar with legal experience, its technicalities and the dynamics of its socio-institutional unfolding.

Nevertheless, considerable problems also arise in the case of exclusively infra-communitarian implementations of multiculturalist legal pluralism, that is, regarding the relationships between individuals belonging to the same cultural community. I suppose it is not difficult to imagine the lack of operational self-sufficiency of the different disciplines of marriage regulations when applied outside their context of origin. Those disciplines have been designed and foreordained to produce their effects, in their multiple legal-cultural projections, within semantic and regulatory contexts that tend to be internally consistent. Therefore, the semantic and axiological scope of those legal institutes can only be grasped and preserved by adopting a holistic perspective. This means, to put it more simply, that if the discipline, for example, of Islamic marriage works well in countries of (mainly) Muslim culture, this is also due to the fact that that this discipline is part of a whole, which pre-supposes the complementary provision of consistent rules on contracts, inheritance, legal capacity, education of offspring, obligations, categories of crimes, etc. The proposal to apply within a socio-regulatory context, and thereby in a given legal system, bundles of legal rules generated elsewhere, guaranteeing their integrity in the name of the protection of cultural and/or religious identity, does not seem to take in account the dysfunctions they will inevitably run into. By contrast, it takes little—especially for those who are familiar with law in action—to understand that the effectiveness of the matrimonial discipline must be read in coordination with the rules on ownership, contracts, inheritance, etc. Unlike and beyond the initial recognition and preliminary controls regarding formal compatibility or incompatibility of the regulations to be transposed, as well as the more or less aware losing sight of the consequent conflicts, the marriage discipline from a different culture can face inescapable inconsistencies: for example, a lack of coordination with the other activities carried out by each of the individual spouses within the host country, as such subject to the state legal system. How, furthermore, should such conflicts be adjudicated when they involve autochthonous people who, because of their apparently absent 'culturality', seem to remain outside the circle of practices endowed with identitarian signification? Presumably, but it is easily realizable, the imported rules will end up being perceived by the autochthonous and/or majoritarian members of society as a sort of 'foreign matter,' and this more in view of the implications than the matter in and of itself, that is, in light of the normative contents considered abstractly. Similar discourses, in a specular way, could also take shape within the minority cultural communities. Unfortunately, however, such kinds of reactions to *Others' bodies* and their active projections are nothing more than the mobilization of

is a 'signal' of progress with respect to the 'irrationality' of religious universes of discourse see the interesting considerations proposed by Sahar and Yefet (2022).

symbolic anti-bodies (and often not only those), the spreading of which will result in a distancing of Otherness rather than a transaction of reciprocal differences.

Talking about intercultural dialogue within a framework orchestrated in legal-multicultural terms would reveal itself, in short, as yet another fiction. That is to say, yet another pseudo-solution as such fit only to increase conflicts and to cultivate the illusion of being able to make individual cultures and their representatives live as harmonically organized hermits, placed in a fictitious relationship of mutual respect but actually merely enduring the precariousness of their reciprocal indifference, the wave of their resistance reduced to a useless puddle. Meanwhile, the syntax of legal and social equality, which is an inevitable axis—if not of the same origin—of any form of genuine pluralism and inclusive support for differences, would be dramatically eroded. The ultimate consequence could be a pluralism bereft of the rule of equality, doomed to transmute into legal particularism, drifting inevitably towards social and inter-subjective misrecognition.

A possible turn of phrase to be used against the danger of the above negative drift (including its underlying, albeit not entirely intentional, theoretical assumptions) might therefore be: 'not just exoticism.' In the same vein, pragmatic analysis and theoretical speculation should be based on interculturally oriented interpretations of the law of the different traditions and the respective institutions that act as organizational hubs in the management of social relations. All this is to ensure that the determination of the rule to be applied to the individual case is preceded by a commitment to understanding the cultural habits and the related semiotic landscapes underlying the different legal traditions and their categories. In this sense, the main objective should be not so much to prefer one rule over another, one system over another, but rather to identify a semantic-normative platform that can be subjected to a process of self-transformation—as such stemming from the translation of the cultural differences potentially invested by its application—to make possible its intercultural use. But this result can be achieved only if the cultural/normative contents so reviewed can simultaneously maintain consistency with the original cultural universes *and* acquire equidistance from the differences reshaped by the process of mutual translation/transaction preliminary to an intercultural use of law.

Is it possible, therefore, to define an alternative project to legal multiculturalism that does not betray the real and doubtless deserving needs that originally triggered its ideation? More explicitly, is it possible to go beyond the interculturalism practiced in some countries such as Québec,[113] where it seems to equate to nothing but a camouflaged form of assimilationism? Or, still, can theoretical platforms be elaborated that can provide pragmatic recommendations that are less vague than those proposed by post-majority sociological interculturalism? That is to say, guidelines that explain for the benefit of the individual social actors of a multicultural environment how and what to do in concrete cases beyond the generic invocations to dialogue and the need to comply with universal standards such as the principles of constitutional liberalism? In other words, is it possible to wriggle free from all such

[113] See Bouchard and Taylor (2008), Bouchard (2015, 2016), and most recently Wences (2016).

'–isms' by using intercultural translation and its semiotic potential as an aspect that characterizes the various areas of social practice and, above all, the function of law in the construction of everyday life?[114] Is it also possible to use positive law and technical-legal skills to include a symmetrical and anthropologically informed reading of the cultural knowledge of both the Other and, reflexively, the Other than Others? That is to say the collections of 'know-how' underlying the behaviors adopted in the conclusion of contracts, the drafting of wills, the management of family life, entrepreneurial activities and, conversely, in the adoption of behaviors amenable to criminal qualification? And what is the role that religion plays or should play in the articulation of these 'corpora'? What relationships are there between religion, its different and multiple anthropological-pragmatic projections, and the semiotic landscapes that permeate individual or collective action and are epitomized by it? Is it plausible to imagine leaving aside the orthopraxes of religious origin that mark not only the rites but also the common actions of people, and despite this being able to engage an intercultural approach conducive to a daily life that is carried out within a symmetric coexistence among differences?[115] And besides, should not the latter figuration of differences be the first goal to pursue in the attempt to elaborate forms of equitably shared 'bottom-up' citizenship?

The creation of an intercultural legal lexicon appears to be the only way to bring together a grammar of rights, equality and cultural orthopraxes. I think it is so because only through a previous effort of mutual and thoughtful translation among the differing cultural knowledge extant in the social landscape will it be possible to define an inclusive lexicon of legal subjectivity, as such capable of making the law socially and impartially responsive to the multiple manifestations of subjectivity. A secular cultural orthopraxis, which is the indispensable precondition for an effectively secular grammar of rights, could therefore only emerge from a synthesis relying upon a transactional interplay among the different cultural and/or religious subjectivities dwelling in the public sphere. Needless to say, this is not an easy achievement, nor a goal that can be reached at a desk. It requires a continuous commitment to cultural and pragmatic repositioning carried out by the various social partners. Moreover, the achievement of this objective—even in theoretical or ideal terms—does not necessarily imply the need for a radical repeal of the legal systems currently in force in the individual states. The normative methods of modernity, in particular those focused on the generality and abstractness of the legislative statements as in civil law systems, make legal orders prospectively open to an intercultural use of principles and rules. As will be specified in more detail below,[116] this is the other side of generality, often accused of being responsible for the tendency of the 'modern' to create serializations, false universalisms, and

[114] A need not far from that expressed here can be found in Abdallah-Pretceille (2006) and in the proposal to replace the term 'culture' with the word 'culturality' or 'cultural.'

[115] In order to answer to this question I elaborated a proposal in Ricca (2016).

[116] See below Chaps. 3 and 6.

improper homologations disqualifying, in this way, the value of differences.[117] Of course, the generality of laws can be used as a hegemonic device. It can be placed at the service of the attempt to stifle the voice of difference in the name of (a false) unity. It is also true, however, that generalizations are inherently ambiguous, so that their semantic spectrum is, in a sense, amenable to the inclusive claims arising from the territories of cultural difference.

By exploiting the *good side*, so to speak, of generality—too often underestimated by post-modern criticism[118]—foreign orthopraxes could thus be able to draw communicative corridors leading to their emergence and pro-active inclusion in the public sphere. Such a hermeneutic channel—it should be underlined—has a normative value, also capable of binding the Others, the Others of the Others, that is, the autochthonous or those who belong to the majority culture. Ineluctably, however, in this case the legal language functions as a reflecting mirror which, at the same time, deforms. Cultural codes cannot avoid undergoing a process of self-transformation and intercultural transaction. But here, those of foreigners or minorities will not be unique; the cultural orthopraxes of both Others and natives will be involved. The translation and transaction sequences, mirrored in the semantic spectrum of the legal lexicon and its categories, will be reciprocal, even if nothing assures that those sequences will automatically be symmetrical and impartial in their unfolding. If excessive asymmetry is avoided, the grammar of rights can acquire an intercultural curvature, since the existing legal languages themselves are then subject to an intercultural use. The outline of an effective secular and pluralist dynamics, rearticulated from below and in a fair, co-participatory way, could therefore be inscribed within the way of thinking about and doing law. Legal semantics could start, under these conditions, to match the multicultural and multi-religious composition of contemporary societies in such a manner that it could ensure an effectively democratic responsiveness and the molding of an authentically plural and inclusive subjectivity. In the next chapters I will provide practical examples and concrete cases combined to illustrate the ways of rewriting and leveraging the existing legal categories through their *intercultural use*. The analysis of such cases will demonstrate how the process of adapting the current law to cultural Otherness, to the orthopraxes of (reciprocal) Others, presents elements of relevant continuity with the daily activity carried out by lawyers within the single national areas in addressing the protean aspects of social experience and its dynamics. All things considered—and despite the fact that bridging cultural distances represents a huge supplementary problem—the intercultural use of law nevertheless already corresponds to the skill set legal practitioners have always cultivated in their professional experience (especially, lawyers, notaries, and judges).[119]

---

[117] Chatterjee (2004) and Peerenboom (2004).

[118] See, for example, Bauman (1991) and Chatterjee (2004).

[119] An example of the intercultural approach within the legal experience, as such gushing out from fieldwork with legal professionals, can be found in Ricca and Sbriccoli (2015).

2.9 Multiculturality, Universalism and Identity Excesses

If taken as institutional aims, giving an intercultural bent to the current law, or renewing the legal lexicon through culturally polyphonic law-making require the overcoming of an identitarian understanding of the multicultural condition. The perception of a stable, fixed cultural border between the Self and the Other, as well as the corresponding ideological or normative disposition, should both be put aside. The need to go beyond what could be called 'cultural identitarianism' is supported by a plurality of reasons. The perception of the social world as a multicultural space presupposes the identification of cultural difference, that is, of 'the Other' as different from 'the Self.' However, this operation is not neutral, it does not occur within a relationship between the subject and his environment independent from any reflective and self-transformative effects. More explicitly, the subject who recognizes the presence of Other-than-Self in their living space is an agent who has already changed from their original condition. Recognizing the Other as someone different simultaneously implies a renewed perception of the Self. Identity is reflected in the 'different' and is redefined as a consequence of this reciprocal mirroring.[120] This is why multiculturality, even if considered as an abstract mental representation, is always the consequence of an implicit interculturality, that is, a silent transformation that has already occurred inside the Self by virtue of the Other's presence in the scene of daily life. Irreflexive interculturality, unconsciously generated as an undercurrent phenomenon, arises, however, from a condition of psychological crisis: a latent *dumbfounding* elicited by the hunch, often vague but still incisive, of the possible supervening ineffectiveness and unreliability of one's own life habits. When facing the Other, the cultural alien, the mind warns that something of its 'know how' will not work and will be destined to get jammed somewhere along the path towards the accomplishment of its vital ends.

Cultural orthopraxes are integrated in the encyclopedia of know-how that is routinely enacted without self-reflection. Their activation is an automatic behavior, usually triggered and carried out subconsciously. This gives them great efficiency. The price of the above efficiency, however, is paid by the people who experience conspicuous difficulties when called upon to objectify their enactment, focus on their meaningful implications, transform their implicitness in symbolic terms and, in this way, make them available to conscious reflection. Without reflection, however, there can be no intentional modulation or modification, that is, responsive and conscious adaptation. The inability to escape such cognitive defectiveness triggers a condition of pragmatic crisis, and the crisis elicits a propensity to conflict. Crisis and conflict, however, already constitute a change, even if only a defective one. Through and because of it, cognitive and behavioral habits become prone to radicalize, stiffen, and sometimes ossify. In conditions of conflict, cultural orthopraxes almost ineluctably

---

[120] The dynamic of this constitutive relationality is efficaciously outlined, according to an enatic approach, by Di Paolo et al. (2018).

petrify their morphological features, self-transforming into fetishized banners doomed to nourish and legitimize polarizations of identity.

As paradoxical as it may seem, in the above situations the identitarian gaze lands on the most striking and idiomatic aspects of the Others' orthopraxes, and most frequently and ironically on those least open to translation and transaction. In so doing, however, the potential significance of cultural habits is maimed, sometimes to the point of being completely emptied. Their contents end up migrating towards the dreamlike landscapes of ethnic, national, and religious memory. Precisely along this defective and self-protecting path, they loosen their grip on experience, their ability to stir the course of individual and social action. Locked in a game of intercultural confrontation, each subject, both individual and collective, strives to remain itself, unaltered, but precisely by aiming at this result they are destined to change, transforming their 'know how' into weapons of opposition, rather than using them as adaptive instruments to dialectically engage with the world. Sadly, caught in an omnilateral loss of meaning, the struggle for identity turns into a formal clash (precisely) between 'identicals,' that is, between subjects driven exclusively by a petition for power aimed at prevaricating or eliminating *their* Other. Though believing they fight for themselves, for their own identity, each pole of conflict, each contender, fights, instead, against something identical to themselves, that is, simply against their formal opposite. Each part becomes purely and simply a counterpart, condemning themselves to a sort of hetero-determination caused by antagonism. But in that case, when the battle is successful for one of the two or more factions, the winners paradoxically stop being what they believed they were when eliminating their Other. Their culture, reduced to a mere strategic toolkit, a rhetorical device emptied of insightful correspondence and interpenetration with the world, must then be reconstructed, revitalized, should this still be in any way useful.

If what I have just outlined is a potential parabola of implicit interculturality, not far behind there is multiculturalism. I refer to the idea that cultures are circuits of meaning cemented by identity bonds and destined to remain so; as such, paradoxically, they seek self-distancing and non-contaminating dialogue, at most open to tolerating limited relationships with Others. Obsessively averting any danger of assimilation is however the primary concern. The multiculturalist approach, despite possible appearances, is however an ideal offspring of implicit interculturality. All in all, the actors populating the multiculturalist scenario, that is, specified cultural identities, are the product of an underlying implicit intercultural opposition and the ghostly essentialized entities that it gives birth to. The version of the normative pluralism consequent to the adoption of the multicultural recipe, precisely the idea of a coexistence inspired by the identity preservation of cultural groups within the same social sphere, is however also defective. Beyond the feasibility limits already analyzed, this kind of pluralism appears to be both relativistic and universalistic. It proclaims the incommensurability of each culture with respect to the others,[121] but

---

[121] For some interesting considerations on the idea of incommensurability between cultures when based on quantitative 'measurement,' but tempered by a qualitative openness to a translational/

simultaneously asserts the right of each of them to place itself on a level of 'mutual equality' with others. Moreover, the perspective of multiculturalism almost inadvertently passes from incommensurability among cultures to the universality of the common denominator 'Culture.' But this implies that any culture would be entitled to read itself as unique, unrepeatable, idiomatic, and therefore as a species of a 'concrete universal,' a kind of category/genre per se. In this way, however, the alleged incommensurability of each culture to the others, at least from the internal (emic) point of view, would end up running the risk of engendering in the cultural actors a dangerous tendency to perceive themselves as the prototypical interpreters of what 'Culture' is. The next step would of course be the 'naturalization' of one's own culture.

Beyond all the proclamations on openness to dialogue as an inherent aspect of multiculturalism, at that point the seeds for the maturation of suffused even if pervasive blindness towards the Other would have already been sown. Each culture can read itself as the type, rather than only a token, of (the authentic) axiological universality: the incarnation of the 'genuine' equality, freedom, autonomy, solidarity, etc. The Others, precisely because they are *aprioristically* considered incommensurable, can be seen at best as formal projections of that prototype, even if inevitably in a 'less than perfect' way; nothing more than additional units to be parameterized to the original, to its contents, to its meanings. In the end, the true difference of the Other, their know-how and cultural encyclopedias, will simply vanish, at least for the outside observer, that is, the individual of another culture who observes Otherness.

What will take place, in the relational context just outlined, will be an implied effect of homologation, or the serialization of the possible iterations of humanity. In a rigidly and consistently multicultural social world, beyond the borders of their community nobody seeks universality, but only 'alterity.' This is the psycho-relational paradox of relativism that makes it unexpectedly essentializing in its outcomes. This occurs because in a universe dominated by relativist representations, everyone is equal in their radical difference. Everyone will be the same in their form, incommensurable in their content. But, in the no man's land situated at the center of this diffraction, inevitably all of 'us,' all groups, will tend to see themselves as prototypical 'incarnations' of the universal, once again, in terms of content. Such content will end up being dialectically—and in an unbalanced way—attracted to its opposite, that is, it will migrate in form, overlapping and merging with it. After all, to

transactional intercultural resonance, see Goodale (2023). For an example of 'analytical cross-cultural quantification' of legal experience and even people's *perceptions* about law, which goes far beyond the quantitative approach applied to assess the fulfillment of human rights, see Hannikainen et al. (2021). I must confess that when considering this kind of treatment of cultural differences, especially regarding legal experience, I cannot avoid sympathizing with multiculturalism and the antagonist/self-defensive conception of cultures' incommensurability. Despite my criticism, I would like to iterate here that the multiculturalist approach had, at least in its origin, more than valid reasons to put forward a countermeasure against the political and cognitive assimilationism lurking in aprioristical and pseudo-universalist approaches to ethics and human rights.

be more explicit, this is exactly what Westerners have done and (at least, try to) continue to do with the rest of the world. First, they proclaim universal values, such as equality, freedom, etc., and then replace them with their own ways of implementing them. The attempt to impose their cultural values and legal categories on others, in the wake of the dissemination of human rights, was the immediate and most ominous consequence of this way of thinking and acting. The dramatic outcome was that the Others, especially if weaker or subdued, were unintentionally induced to identify—in reverse—those cultural and legal categories with human rights themselves, distorting the potential scope of their attitude to function as semantic platforms of universalization. An epiphenomenon of this distortion is that of the inevitable and already realized claim for alternative codes of universality, namely other regional declarations of human rights.[122] The oxymoron, the contradiction in terms, of the existence of as many human rights standards as there are cultures constitutes the terminus, in a sense, of the multiculturalist vogue—even if it is also a more than justified reaction to Western imperialism and assimilationism. But this final step is an integral part of history, already visible. How is it possible, one only apparently naively could wonder, that things have gone this far? Some explanation can perhaps be attempted.

Despite what is being propagated by its supporters, from a multiculturalist perspective, the possibility of translating Otherness, of finding bridges of communication and common meaning, resides at the beginning. It is so precisely because the inevitable intersection of cultural differences and their pragmatic projections in the common arena of social life, as in the international political arena, will be interpreted and lived in an identitarian and thereby antagonistic way. In the common village of cultural relativism, each faction will try to inscribe its requests within a standard of universality and equality invoked as a unit of measure of mutual tolerance. Once situated within the sphere of practical life, however, the haunting play of contrasts will end up making each party perceive the difference of the Other as incompatible with an equitable division of common spaces and social existence. In this regard, examples can be multiplied. More or less surreptitiously, each party will try to fill the grammar of universality with their own cultural contents, that is, the alleged rule of coexistence among the incommensurables: now disguising its own contents under the lexicon of common subjectivity, now trying to prevent others from doing so. A wonderful world of mutual tolerance and dialogue between cultures, cultivated in the shadow of the recognition of the universal (identitarian) difference of all from all, is the myth passed off by multiculturalism and its attempts at implementation in the national socio-political field. Vice versa, a frontline of permanent conflicts, even if often latent and silent, is its concrete reification: a social world animated by indefatigable tensions between cultural self-representations driven towards radicalization and identity excesses. After all, where the yardstick of public subjectivity becomes the universal of mutual difference articulated in terms

[122] For example, the Arab Charter on Human Rights, the African Charter of Human and People's Rights, and the Asian Human Rights Charter.

of identitarian belonging, it would be almost absurd if this were not the result. The most serious problem, however, lies in the tendency—the legal frameworks of which I will begin to describe in the following chapters—to use the law and the lexicon of rights for strategic purposes.

The very tragic result is the transformation of multicultural coexistence into an obstinate contrast with every division of resources: the same ones needed to cultivate the illusion of maintaining 'uncontaminated' circuits of communitarian belonging. As can be easily imagined, the remaining intercultural translator will therefore prove to be money, the only interface able to translate everything. Unfortunately, however, it does not translate anything but rather limits itself to creating quantitative and financial equivalences between goods, the 'substantial' meaning of which has already been determined.[123] And yet, in the multicultural social field, it is qualitative and anthropological differences that will surface and create conflict. The switching of qualitative differences into quantitative equivalences always takes place through a process of amputation because the choice of what is quantifiable is made according to the standards dictated by markets and prices but leaves aside the 'rest.' And besides, this is exactly what the well-known practice of multicultural *accommodations* does with its intrinsic, even if dissimulated, propensity for the *commoditization* of substantially untranslated behaviors, things, and symbols, taken in their mere morphological appearances.[124] Such a practice does not strive to make these indexes of difference interculturally understandable, justifiable and semiotically re-combinable in relation to the exigencies of multicultural coexistence. Quite the opposite, those who carry on (multi-)cultural accommodations attempt to balance 'entities' that are often the result of antagonistic representations, inevitably crammed with implicit self-evidence or ethnocentric biases depending on whether they are proposed by those who are inside or outside a specific culture. But, unfortunately, the above 'rest' represents a genuine cultural difference: precisely that which multiculturalism would like cultural groups to articulate independently. Moreover, what is worse is that if that 'rest' is not translated, there will be a risk of not grasping its interdependence with respect to the general social context. But not grasping its interdependence will mean, in turn, not grasping what the real chances for its practical implementation there may be, as well as the existing obstacles and the concrete chances of adaptation. Because of this ignorance or lack of awareness, the alternative—in both cases defective—between conflict and surreptitious contingent pacification will be inexorably consumed. At that point, the expressed cultural

---

[123] In short, what could be labeled a kind of Hayek's paradise. See von Hayek (1980, pp. 33 ff and 77 ff.).

[124] On the so-called 'reasonable accommodations' see, in an immense literature, Young (1999) and Foblets (2016). For a criticism and the epistemological causes producing the creeping equivalence between *accommodations* and *commoditization* of cultural/religious diversities, see below in the next chapters. A fruitful source of criticism based on the commoditization of culture and its possible projections in the logic of 'reasonable accommodation' can be found in Appadurai (1986) but also in Dewey (1916, specifically ch. IV). See also, Ricca (2018b, 2020a, b, c) and there for further bibliographical references.

difference will be ready to generate a spiral of identity excesses and cultural radicalizations, anomalous and unintended descendants of the formal relativistic universalism outlined in and underlain by the multicultural approach. Moreover, the transmuting of the so-called accommodations camouflaged as commoditization, as such reifying cultural differences, shows well what kind of dialogue identity claims inspire. It will only be a superficial dialogue, inclined to portray differences as 'they are': meaning refusing any attempt to elaborate a 'cross-contextualizing narration' of them that can bring to the surface the semiotic indexical landscape underlying their 'taking place' on the multicultural social stage. A dialogue, still, which will be epistemologically empty, if only because it will take cultural features as data, appearances considered and claimed in their mere exterior morphology. But on all this, and specifically on how to pragmatically implement the semiotic dis-compositions and re-compositions of cultural habits in an intercultural way, I will return below.

2.10 Routes and (Potential) Outcomes of Intercultural Secularization

'Multiculturalist Universalism', precisely because it is anchored to a relativistic interpretation of cultures, is envisaged to be synonymous with 'neutrality.' Its transformation into a conflict originating from the divorce between the universality of the category 'culture' and the relativity of cultural contents, is the same as what occurs when secularism is understood as radical rational neutrality. Should the law and its grammar of subjectivity assume, in the name of secularism, that they could articulate a neutral, relativistic discourse, devoid of any translation between cultural contents, they would only feed the polarization of identities. But with an aggravating circumstance, which has already been established: namely, that in the shadow of the proclaimed neutrality of the legal lexicon, the prevalence of dominant cultural codes, perceived and imposed by the strongest groups as a mirror of a universal subjectivity, would still remain hidden, invisible. In the case of newly formed multicultural societies, this would give rise—as is the case—to the well-known phenomenon of applying the 'cultural qualification' only onto Others, newcomers, and their habits. That is to say that only foreigners or minorities would be *bearers of cultural or religious differences*, while majorities or the natives would already speak the *idiom of reality* by virtue of their rational, neutral, and natural language. A formula summarized, in the legal field, with the falsely pluralistic formulation: 'our law and Others' cultures.'

The first step in the opposite direction, precisely that of an intercultural and---in my view—*mature* secularization, consists instead in adopting a vision I call a 'planetarian cultural system.' Rather than assuming the dominant culture as the hub of the social cosmos and, at the same time, dissimulating its pervasive presence inside a self-declared neutral national state law, it would probably be necessary (and more consistent) to move forward in a different direction. In order to make law equidistant and responsive to everybody, cultures should all be considered eccentric and—to persist with the metaphor—as if they were all planets placed on one orbit equidistant from the center of the system, the *sun-law*, even if spaced apart from each other, in order to avoid collisions. The gravitational center, in turn, should be assumed to be not an alien body, completely different from the other planets, but instead the weighted synthesis of their masses and their differing chemical composition. This means—to follow through on the metaphor—that the orbital distance of each planet from the *sun-law* should be the same. An allegedly neutral *state law-planetary* system insisting upon a multicultural and multireligious social context would make different cultures or religions respectively correspond to Mars or to Saturn, to Mercury or to Uranus, according to their different cultural distance from *sun-law*: in that system there can be no symmetric secularization.

Metaphors aside, the (state) law should be the synthesis of the different cultural languages, in turn resulting from processes of translation and intercultural transaction. In my opinion, if a constitutional order genuinely aspired to produce a viable model of secularization for a multicultural society, it would have to move towards this point of arrival. The path to be followed to reach the destination, i.e., intercultural secularism, passes through the *invention* of an intercultural lexicon to be poured into the legal language so as to stimulate and make possible, in turn, an intercultural use of law.

The first intermediate step, along the navigation route just outlined, consists in understanding that the experienced reality, the *facts* to be qualified through the tools of the law, are not independent from the culture of who acts or speaks. In other words, being from another culture or another religion does not only mean evaluating the same world, the same empirical reality differently, but also seeing and experiencing a different one and *making different facts*. Understanding that cultural differences can produce cognitive variations about the *world of facts* is the first step along the path toward an intercultural secularization. Deciding which norm to apply when judging the acts of foreigners or minorities requires the interpreter to process in intercultural terms the meaning of their gestures. Decoding the narratives and life situations described by the lawyer's foreign client or by the party in court proceedings, can induce legal practitioners and officials to call into play different rules and transpose inside the semantic spectrum of legal propositions the result of interculturally assessed translations and transactions. As already observed, it does not matter which legal rule is used, be it that of the state legal system or another one. As a result of intercultural translation/transaction between the different habits and the underlying semiotic landscapes, the semantic content of the rule applied will consist, in any case, in a 'third' normative 'substance.'[125] Understanding the possibility (and also the need) to reach this prospective thirdness—through this narrative decoding within judicial proceedings—can induce lawyers and judges to collect and

[125] As for the semiotic translational methodology to be applied in order to achieve such transfigurative 'thirdness' see below Chaps. 3 and 5.

question different rules and transpose within their semantic spectrum the weighted result of the intercultural translations and transactions they will bring about.[126] All this will lead to the progressive bottom-up construction of an intercultural lexicon, as such stemming from translations, metaphorizations and semantic transactions. More in general, this activity could allow a widespread intercultural use of law, becoming a vector of a legislative production modeled on the use of an intercultural legal lexicon. The adoption of an approach to law inspired by interculturality would open up the possibility of using legal platforms as a cultural interface. Disseminating among foreigners or people from different cultures the confidence to inscribe their own cultural codes of subjectivity within an intercultural legal lexicon could elicit a sense of co-belonging to the public sphere. Furthermore, this perspective and the possibility of imagining a legal language that gives utterance to differences could trigger on a social level the willingness to engage in the production of cross-cultural contextualizations. On the contrary, an imperialist, unequal and unfair as well as culturally inadequate use of legal provisions is provoked or at least encouraged by the absence of intercultural translations and transactions. As I have described, this approach to law inevitably enforces the predominance of the strongest social groups and cements the subordination of and discrimination against the members of the weaker groups, migrants first of all. But the inequality of law that results from its non-responsiveness with respect to the different cultural subjectivities extant on the social stage, is the other side of the coin of a deficit of symmetric and equidistant secularization of the legal system. Only the creation of an intercultural lexicon can obviate the lack of social and legal patterns of subjectivity that is equanimous and inclusive of cultural and religious differences. In this sense, it can be said that intercultural legal subjectivity and intercultural secularization are coextensive profiles or, in any case, factors to be considered strictly interconnected in constitutional democratic structures. Their coexistence is essential to guaranteeing adequate standards of pluralism, which are an indispensable prerequisite for any real equality before the law.

The parallel connection between culture and religion, on one side, and secularization and legal equality, on the other, makes so that the *secular path* can no longer be imagined as a rhetorical divide between religion and law, and thereby the public sphere. The anthropological 'stuff' of religious experience and its cognitive projections requires that the secular dimension and religious circuits are imagined outside any hierarchical or polarizing relationship. On the contrary, the interpenetration between the lexicon of legal equality and the anthropological projections of religious experience is not negligible. This should induce a consideration of the 'secular' and the 'religious' as placed on a common horizontal level open to transactional, translational and relational connections. In other words, the 'ideal' of law's neutrality—which so often turns into a mere rhetorical device—should be conceived of as a necessarily anthropologically and polyphonically *contaminated* standard. This means that it should be re-configured as a political formula not

[126] See below, Chap. 3.

designed against religions but rather ordered to the development of discursive instruments to manage the mutual and equitable exchange between cultural and religious imageries. Needless to say, among the processive and implicit aims of such a figuration of 'neutrality,' the exclusion of any form of ideological predominance and/or theological/alethic unilateral radicalization in the construction of legal language also plays an important role.

2.11 Intercultural Legal Lexicon, Equi-coexistence and Modernity

The foregoing arguments, in my view, allow the development of an intercultural lexicon to be framed as a direct implication of the political project of modernity. The attempt to mold a grammar of secular subjectivity has accompanied the emergence of modern thought since its beginnings. It was carved out by stripping the theological vestiges of many of the moral categories generated by the Christian tradition and intertwined over the centuries with the grammar of everyday life and thereby the anthropological vocabulary of European culture. As has already been observed, although modern political rationalism had been attuned to the regulative ideal of universality, its historical achievement was culturally situated. 'Natural Law' was its cultural expression, subsequently transfused into the 'Codification experience' of continental Europe. Nevertheless, the cultural continuities between Christian ethics and moral theology, on one side, and civil and penal institutions of modern legal experience, on the other, remained profound. By dissimulating the presence of religion's imprints with a sophisticated rhetorical strategy, legal modernity could display its discontinuity from the past; a discontinuity that, at least apparently, reverberated with secularity. Colonialism then disseminated this fiction all over the world. It imposed on non-Western peoples a (presumptive) rationalist universalism comprising conceptual schemes, habits and practices of Christian origin, even if they were passed off as icons of an anthropologically neutral reason, as such transparent to itself. And yet, the language of colonial cosmopolitanism corresponded, in its semantic 'substance,' to a cultural dialect: the Western one.

The end of the colonial era and the collapse of its post-colonial political resilience have shown, however, that modernity—for better or for worse—in all its polycentric expressions, has propagated itself all over the planet. Nowadays, the so-called Rest of the world—or at least a significant part of it—has managed to grasp modernity by the handle. Thus, it has started to use some of the strengths in the modern paraphernalia to its own advantage, in some cases undertaking a (finally) equitable competition with the West—as can be seen in BRICS (Brazil, Russia, India, China, and South Africa) with the partial exception, or anomaly, of Russia. This movement, running along the channels of economics, politics and anthropological criticism, has produced a re-interpretation of the legal-institutional implementations of modern thought and in many cases triggered a process of their appropriation and vernacularization. Spanning the so-called Asian Values, African Peoples Movements, the claims of Indigenous Rights, fundamentalist critiques and more, human rights and liberal-democratic institutions—after having been introjected by the political language of non-Western peoples and cultures—have progressively undergone a process of transforming interpretation. Their original universalizing inspiration has been, in a sense, retrieved and used as a device to provide cultural differences with a discursive and normative platform connoted by an immediate international and cosmopolitan resonance. From this perspective, the universality of modern legal categories has been illuminated from a multi-sited 'below' and pushed forward towards a broader and more distant, but at the same time more inclusive, horizon. Doubtless, this phenomenon has not unfolded without stumbling into mystification and exploitative uses. In many ways, however, it has been the harbinger of genuinely emancipatory potentialities. And this not only for those who read human rights or democracy from the perspective of the Rest of the world, but also for the West itself. After all, the a priori as well as surreptitious coincidence between (Western) identity and universality have finally begun to fade, breaking the stifling constraints that the ruthless interests of the colonial and post-colonial power had historically tightened around one-sided processes of universalization. Modernity thus breaks free of its more-dogmatic-than-effective provincialism, from that limiting mark imprinted on it by the (not entirely correct) assumption that it has been in any case an exclusively European invention.[127] A mark that was by no means casual or unintentionally imprinted, and which compromised the authentic realization of the universalizing potentialities of modern thought and specifically the Enlightenment—despite its historical dialectics.[128] Caught between rhetorical dissimulations and exigencies of historical continuity imposed by governance practices, the modern project renounced the dispassionate pursuit of the ideal of a socially responsive and bottom-up cosmopolitanism. Taking place within national and regional contexts—also for organizational reasons—political and legal modernity had substantially abdicated the ideal of universal emancipation of differences together with its aspiration to an inductive and inclusive cultural ecumenism. Quite the opposite, it has become a strategic and deceptive narrative at the service of the expansionist aims of the European national states.

Contemporary religious-fundamentalist recapitulations are also the inevitable counterpart of a mono-cultural and surreptitiously universalizing secularization exported to the four corners of the earth and imposed as a (false) ideal of political and legal neutrality. The populations that have had to endure, in its name, the overtaking of their daily life habits and their submission to the cultural categories conveyed by the superimposition of European legal patterns, have seen in modern secularization only a deception, a factor of estrangement and a caesura between their colonial present and their own cultural past. 'Modern,' in their eyes, has become

[127] Chakrabarty (2009), Bhambra (2007), Eisenstadt (2000) and, for a multi-perspectival assessment of the idea of 'multiple modernities', Preyer and Sussmann (2016).

[128] The referral is, of course, to Horkheimer and Adorno (2002).

synonymous with nationalist statism and expansionism. Criticism against modernity, human rights and even democracy was and still is in fact a critique of their caricature and their aberrant practice, often in stark contrast to their ideal model and inspiration. This is why it is, in many ways, a healthy criticism. It serves to save modernity first of all from itself, from the perverse historical embodiments—and in a sense also the betrayal—of its original vision.

The struggle against all that can be considered 'modernity' is the crucial feature of many theoretical approaches to the inclusion of cultural differences in legal discourse. Yet, at least in my view, eschewing modernity's implications and fully discarding its cognitive achievements would be at least disproportionate and, in the end, even paradoxical. If it is impossible to hide the dark side of generalizations and the domineering use of categories as hallmarks of modernity,[129] it would be equally unthinkable to take seriously the implicit, albeit meandering, post-modern proposal to live without categorizing the world.

In my view, the cultural *guilt* of modernity lies not so much in its commitment to generalizations or general categories as tools for knowing and predicting events, but rather in its tendency to treat categorical patterns as a normative portraits of reality, and hence as cages to be imposed over the world.[130] Particularly in the human sciences, more than in other fields of knowledge, the process of modern universalization has incorrectly, but not innocently, assumed categories as definitively forged concepts rather than as hypotheses that are permanently open to revision and verification. This misconception, in many respects overcome in the analysis of the natural world, has proved instead historically fatal for political inclusion and, ultimately, for the respect of cultural differences in the mirror of legal experience around the world. Nonetheless, the so-called 'Enlightenment Dialectic'—I would like to iterate—should not be considered as the inconsistent consequence of the cosmopolitan ideals of modern political thought taken in and of themselves but instead as their betrayal or, at least, their oblique (mis)interpretation. The paradoxical subversion of the aspiration to universalism inherent in the Enlightenment into an instrument of cultural and social exclusion is not an idiomatic feature of the theoretical assumptions of the modern mind. It is only the inevitable implication of an erroneous and badly rhetorical use of 'the category of universal categories.' The very idea that universality lies beneath the surface of historical events and does not dwell over the horizon of cognitive and intercultural transactions carried out as stages of an open-minded and endless research, is the main cause of the problems and failings occurring along the planetary unfolding of the socio-political modern experience.

---

[129] Bauman (1991) and Chatterjee (2004).

[130] I think the distinction between modernity in its ideal state and the uses of the modernity project would be a good lens for a renewed reading of the *Dialectic of Enlightenment* (Horkheimer and Adorno 2002) and its post-modernist textual epigones. In this sense, it is very interesting what is observed, even if from different epistemological perspective, on concepts and categories by Blumenberg (2007), on one side, and both Dewey (2012) and Bentley (1941) on the other.

In the modern age, the pervading essentialist susceptibility to a conceptual setting of categories has led to the replacement of universality with cultural identity in social and political thought. The subsequent almost ironic effect has been that the potential of inclusiveness—surely intrinsic in generalizations and their semantic abstractness—has been turned upside down and, ultimately, dismantled. The explosion of political and social pluralism in the early twentieth century and the progressive emancipation from colonial powers paved the way for contemporary discourse and claims for difference. In a sense, these phenomena are the deformed progeny of modernity, namely faith in the rational and predictive power of *a priori* categorizations and/or generalizations adopted in ethical fields. The increasing rise of the politics of difference seems to have proven that the project to accommodate the world's anthropological multiplicity within taxonomic orders underpinned by aprioristic categorical schemes is simply unfeasible. Another critical stance has emerged from this theoretical foundation: the incommensurability of different cultural perspectives and thereby, in political terms, their irreducibility under the umbrella of speculatively drawn universal models of subjectivity. In the end, almost inevitably, even human rights, natural rights, constitutional rights and so on have ended up under the broadsides of anti-universalist armies, led by the vociferous critics of modern thinking,

It appears upon closer inspection, however, that achievements marked by pluralist discourse and struggles fought in the name of difference (of culture, religion, gender, etc.) have not been implemented apart from an implicit, even if countercurrent, use of moral or legal universals. On the contrary, historical successes attained by subaltern people have often been reached by using the same moral and legal patterns as devices to make discriminatory schemes of institutional action collapse in on themselves. Actually, bringing out into the open the inconsistency of surreptitious choices taken selfishly by political powers in the name of abstract and universal values or rights successfully discredited these schemes of justification for public action. Such confutation was achieved by comparing public actions to the same universal values invoked to claim the moral and legal legitimacy of the subsequent and inevitably unequal political statements. It has been nevertheless a critical strategy common to the challenges issued and won in the past by the lower classes in Western capitalist societies, as well as for the struggles leading up to decolonization.

Pointing out these historical elements, of course, does not neutralize the possibilities, or better, the danger and the actual occurrence of a treacherous, instrumental, serializing and, ultimately, oppressive use of legal generalization and human rights.[131] The topics related to 'human nature' might impose stifling straitjackets on individuals, and sometimes entire peoples, as has been too often demonstrated by recent history. Nonetheless, if unaided by the power of words, the general statements and utterances supporting normative ideals such as equality or liberty, the voice of

[131] Sajò (2004).

difference and the claims by the weakest, would be hopelessly doomed to a fatal silence.

However, after many years of strict anti-modernism and harsh contempt for the category of human rights, anthropological thought is becoming less negative towards a re-evaluation of the possible emancipatory and inclusive uses of their enunciations.[132] The source of this change, in all likelihood but also paradoxically, was the same fieldwork research, the concerted efforts to listen to the opinions of people, even those most subaltern and apparently distant from Western culture, who were not at all persuaded to discard the support obtainable through the invocation of human rights—the most 'disastrous' generalization to have issued forth from the Enlightenment. Despite the ideological or academic tenets and the claims of political or social movements, the common people of any culture or belonging perceive distinctly enough that the assertion of their autonomy or difference would be helpless against state power without the possibility of appealing to principles like freedom, equality or autonomy.[133] Antagonistic criticism is gradually giving way to a constructive, creative and pragmatic re-reading, designed to make use of the positive and beneficial elements that can come from the inclusive and bottom-up universalizing potential of human rights. All this impels, in a certain sense, the modern project to be coherent with itself, to recover its original and less ethnocentric aspirations. Its universalism is subjected to a process of updating, which identifies universality with a periphrastic universalization, a horizon constantly on the move, rather than an underlying collection of essences, as such reified and substantivized in an aprioristic and therefore unavoidably self-centered way.

The contemporary inclination to transform the discourse of rights into a catalyst for cultural diversity should be greeted positively. However, it needs to be constantly accompanied by a complementary intercultural translation activity. Otherwise, the generality of human rights declarations and their universalizing propensity could turn into a simple support for fueling and conveying antagonistic oppositions. To put it more explicitly, the language of rights, precisely because of its vagueness, could become, as often already happens, a foil, enabling the articulation of differences and claims that are already postulated at the outset as *refractory* to any semantic transaction. In that case, human rights would only be an empty shell; they could be exploited to legitimize any even inarticulate petition aimed at subscribing to their semantic content, but for the sole purpose of allowing cultural identities to compete for an 'other-excluding' space in the political arena. Under these conditions, human rights enunciations would mean everything and nothing, resulting in a mere instrument to underpin an ossifying and antagonistic absolutization of differences rather than a means to promote their inclusive and transactional synthesis. Only a constant

---

[132] Engle Merry (2006a, b, 2010), Clarke and Goodale (2010a, b), and Goodale (2022).

[133] A path towards the ambiguity/ambivalence of categories (one I share) could be traced through the following texts: Bruner et al. (1956), Johnson (1987, 2007), Lakoff (1987), Langacker (1987, 2000, 2002), Bauman (1991), Gibbs Jr (1994, 2005), Talmy (2003), Violi (1997), Andreas (2006), Blumenberg (2007), and prior, the writings and philosophical assumptions taken from Peirce, James and Dewey. About the *exotopicity* of signs see further, Bakhtin (1981, 1986).

commitment to intercultural translation—as has already been observed—can avert such a nefarious drift.

The first step in this direction is, as already observed, to put aside the exoticizing reifications of Otherness unfortunately in vogue today, which reduce the focus on cultures mainly to veils, turbans, infibulations, polygamy, sexual mores, religious symbols and other fetishized items. The above intercultural translational task is, conversely, to start from the patterns of everyday life and the habits deeply imbued with anthropological-cultural signification: the same patterns and habits which are implicitly in tune with the religion-based orthopraxes and their ethical-legal projections, as such sedimented in the mnestic basins of all cultural groups as well as individual subjects. Throughout the translation process, human rights could usefully function as a translation interface, opening up to multi-perspective and multivocal readings. In this case—as I will try to demonstrate in the following chapters—the danger of their self-centered and uncontrolled exploitation can be excluded. This opportunity is strictly linked to the embedding of their argumentative use within a situated framework, that is, a semantic cross-cultural context pre-established by the translation activity carried out among people's daily practices and their different underlying semiotic landscapes. Their being called into play, in other words, would be made coextensive with threads of semiotic continuity surfacing through the translational/transactional activity designed to prompt a proactive and transformative interpenetration between cultural differences. In this way, human rights and the law, taken as a whole, could help carve semantic and axiological channels made to convey a cooperative co-construction of differences, rather than iconizing their morphological features as buttresses for an exaggerated stiffening of cultural belonging and its invocation for antagonistic purposes.

The international and macro-political dynamics that move around intercultural readings of human rights find a sort of projection, a mirroring, in the migratory contexts and in the ensuing multicultural societies. Today, within the heart of these national contexts, the dilemma of having to being consistent with the universalizing cipher of modernity takes place again and again. The same universal cipher that democratic nation states find carved in their axes of legitimacy, that is, in the constitutional lexicon. Here, in the dense core of the national reifications of the 'Modern,' universalization is put in front of itself and its original emancipatory and inclusive import. This self-reflexive process takes place when the Others coming from outside 'propose' their own differences in the public sphere and try to inscribe them in the semantic spectrum of rights and duties as they are delineated by the constitutions and other legal sources. The provincialist reading of constitutional language, allowed by the localism of the previous reifications of political modernity, thus undergoes a sort of stress test. An exam which contemporary national democracies, haunted by xenophobic, traditionalist and pseudo-religious resurgences, appear unprepared to pass. And yet, were the outcome of this historical moment unsuccessful, should the development of an intercultural lexicon not materialize, the prospect of an equanimous coexistence of cultural differences would likely vaporize. This would be tantamount, however, to the collapse of modern ideals and thereby the opposite of a victory for the West, and rather—in spite of nationalist and ethnocentric proclamations and tenets—its definitive decline. In that case, universalistic, democratic ideals and even liberal constitutionalism would demonstrate that they are unable and even unfit to face the (domestic) impact of cultural difference. In the end, they would show themselves to be nothing more than an ethnocentric meta-narration, one of the many founding mythologies created by the most diverse civilizations throughout human history; and still, nothing more than a local recipe exploited for particularistic and hegemonic purposes. But if things were not otherwise... then be it so.

A crucial question, however, remains: what would there be after human rights? Is a critique of human rights possible without human rights?[134] Although they have been used as icons to legitimize global capital and the marketization of quotidian life in all its iterations, how could the injustice resulting from these phenomena be criticized once the language of human rights has been *dismissed*? Once the political and juridical discourse has been orphaned from the inspiring sources that historically united human rights and civil (fundamental) rights, making them semantically intertwined and today, beyond any theoretical sophistication and polarization, unthinkable without one another?

What is more serious, lies in the fact that the above defeat would mature precisely on the ground of daily coexistence. Closer scrutiny would reveal its inability to shape an inclusive social and legal subjectivity, renegotiated through interpenetrative and transactional process of mutual understanding among cultural differences and the cross-contextualization of the anthropological indexes nestled within them. In my view, such inability has recently been further fueled by multiculturalist recipes and their legal projections, often engaged in a form of subjectivization of legal protection, specifically in criminal matters. [135] Precisely in the name of multiculturalism, *exceptional* forms of recognition of cultural diversity are often provided, sometimes aimed at giving exemptive protection to behaviors that are morphologically irreconcilable with the dominant culture and with the axiological code of the Western legal systems. Beyond their apparent pluralistic and relativistic openness, however, these measures hide a bitter essence, which is also its inner price. By giving space to differences without attempting to translate or to negotiate them, they end up reinforcing stereotypes and the mutual cultural estrangement among the various groups. But there is something more. Actually, legal devices inspired by legal multiculturalism such as, for example, the so-called cultural defenses and related evidence tests are often a mirror for a kind of sleight of hand. The strategy underlying the treatment of cultural offences and defenses seems to concede space

[134] See Rosenberg (2016).

[135] I addressed the logic of criminal offense and defenses against the backdrop of modern penal law and the underlying epistemology of secularization in Ricca (2020a). See there for the bibliographical references regarding this topic. In any case, a general examination of the theoretical and pragmatic issues concerning the so-called cultural crimes can be found in Van Broeck (2001), Renteln (2004, 2010), and Renteln and Foblets (2009). For an analysis of the brutal effects of the exceptionalizing logic used in legal assessments of intent and motive when in collision with culture, see Vazquez (2022).

and recognition to cultural difference on one front only to prevent the wide-ranging renegotiation of the basic categories of legal and social subjectivity on the other. Contracts, obligations, trade law, urban law, typology of crimes, etc. remain instead firmly shaped in the image of socially dominant groups and their cultural and historical patterns. On average, instead of being genuine openings, those 'exemptions' indirectly function as *disguised tricks*. Though they are pursued by cultural minorities in exchange for the recognition of behaviors that are often placed at the periphery of the overall social system or symbolically connoted as identitarian fetishes, they are almost never considered for their comprehensive authentic psychosocial signification and their relevance in the way of life of 'those' minorities. Not infrequently, these are 'exempting recognitions' made by the majority culture and its institutions just to contingently obtain instrumental political consensus or, in any case, a partial neutralization of any criticism or contestation raised against the pervading social grammar serving the interests and world views of the dominant groups and the powers that be.

The search for an intercultural social and legal lexicon in support of intercultural secularism, moves in quite the opposite direction. Its goal is the elaboration of a semantic platform inclusive of differences that involves both the core circuits of social coexistence and the related legal categories. The development of such a lexicon within national contexts would be a decisive step towards an authentic and effective implementation of the original modern ideals, including the emancipatory ends inherent in the project of cultural and socio-political secularization. Such an invention/construction undoubtedly implies a herculean effort, especially if considered with regard to the transnational relations and the intercultural confrontations encircling the dynamics it needs to manage. In this respect, migratory social environments are real miniatures of the contemporary planetary experience and its anthropological-cultural variety. Nevertheless, and despite the inherent difficulties, the intercultural legal challenge to be carried out is nothing other than a training/laboratory for the 'future present.'

To focus on the thematic core of this chapter, I would like to underscore that the transformation in an intercultural sense of national legal experience would allow for the overcoming of *visions* of secularization exclusively centered on the West and, therefore, implicitly connoted by orientalist inclinations.[136] The creation and implementation of an intercultural legal lexicon would go well beyond the proposals for the deconstruction of secularization also proposed by post-colonial critics with regard to its taking place outside the West. As I have already tried to emphasize, the project and the very need for intercultural secularization starts from the awareness that all the divides that are idiomatic to modernity—religion and politics, public and private spheres, etc.—are consequences of the need for institutional recipes that could help manage the fight for social space that arose at the dawn of modern era. The resilience of religion, taken in its anthropological meaning and projections, within the secular legal language has become an issue to be faced, in parallel, in

[136] Asad (2003); see also Bubandt and van Beek (2012, esp. p. 8).

multicultural Western countries as well as the post-colonial ones (and not only) outside the West. The impossible absolute neutrality inherent in the constitutive cultural incompleteness of Western secularization is a direct result of the resilience of the Christian religion and its theological-moral schemes within the Western legal language: the same language that colonialism has distributed throughout the world, passing it off as rational and universal, and which remains in force, in its basic categories, in many non-European countries. Until this mixture of legal grammar and religion, which I proposed to term 'legal theology,' is called into question and revised by an intercultural approach, words such as 'rights,' 'freedom,' 'religion,' 'equality,' 'democracy,' etc., will be condemned to operate on the basis of a meta-cultural (provided this adjective has any meaning) misunderstanding: and this both in the West and elsewhere.

The same discourse could be developed, moreover, if we view the situation from the perspective of non-Western countries. Regarding these social contexts, many scholars have deconstructed the idea of secularization and the attempts to export it as a strategy to compartmentalize social spaces for political purposes.[137] Such attempts at deconstruction capture, however, only a portion of the overall phenomenon since they do not consider the aspects concerning legal language and the incompleteness of its secularization. If it were realized to what extent the acquisition of awareness about this incompleteness is also a problem for Westerners themselves, perhaps everything could be seen from a different and more holistic perspective. As long as the mixture of legal categories originating in European tradition and Christian religion is not a target of intercultural assessment, religious fundamentalisms—already in place outside the West but ready to reawaken within it as part of a de-secularization wave—will continue to multiply, paradoxically compromising the achievement of the original emancipatory and inclusive purposes of the same modern secularization. Moreover, it would be a serious mistake to qualify conflicts triggered by fundamentalism as only a question of 'power' (a word that after Foucault has become a sort of universal explanatory device in post-modern discourse). Fundamentalist claims regarding the 'true' religion arise, especially in post-colonial contexts, from the comparison with dated models of secularism due to their cultural incompleteness and their projections through legal forms in the almost planetary daily life. What is often claimed as 'true' religion does not actually fight for the uniqueness of its speculative or abstract truth, but rather against the realization, more or less vague, that there is another religion in contention, precisely a Christian moral theology hidden behind the rhetoric of secularism, which continues to run around the public space of non-Western nations unhindered. It is the plan of cultural projections of religions and the routes of their pragmatic collisions that generate these struggles.

[137] See Casanova (2006), Asad (2003), Warner et al. (2010), Cady and Hurd (2010), and many others.

On the other hand, the claim that the calls for tolerance, freedom and equality within secularized and liberal rhetoric are instruments of power[138] aimed at perpetuating asymmetries of colonial origin does not adequately grasp the cultural connection between the language of secularization and the resilience of religion in modern Western legal culture, subsequently exported globally. What should instead be highlighted is how any secularization process cannot erase the cultural matrices of the societies in which it is ingrained: especially with reference to the categories of quotidian life, the same on which both law and moral theology primarily focus.[139] The same warning could be effectively expressed by the consideration that a secularized (or even atheist) Arab person will always be, in the eyes of Westerners, an Islamic person; just as a secularized (or even atheist) Western person remains, in the eyes of Arabs, a Christian. Many scholars also warn, quite rightly, that one cannot speak of 'secularization' in the singular, taking the Western version as a prototype, but that the word should be re-articulated and conceived of in the 'plural.'[140] As if to say: as many cultures and religions as there are, as many secularizations will there be. In this regard, however, they underline the risk that any comparative analysis of secularization will end up being mirrored in Euro-Christian secularization. When taking this consideration too seriously, however, there is the danger of having to conclude that it is better not to talk about secularization at all, since the term is excessively steeped with Euro-Christian references.[141] On the other hand, its use in a local but not comparative sense too often could wind up—as noted above—making it synonymous with 'a substitution of religious-superstitious knowledge with scientific knowledge.' This assimilation encapsulates a naïve identification of religion with a form of enchantment echoing Gauchet's interpretation of secularization as a process of disenchantment[142] (even if I consider the assimilation of religion and enchantment to be a manifestation of 'modernism'). In my view, however, each culture is a source of enchantment, and certainly this is also the case for the cultural areas of Protestant inspiration to which many ascribe the entry into modernity.[143] Conversely, I contend that the alleged secularizing implications of Protestantism gave rise to dramatic and pervasive forms of counter-enchantment resulting in a tendential ossification of cognitive and axiological schemes assumed as rational, but instead deeply rooted in medieval moral theology. Conversely, the proclaimed detachment of those schemes from any transcendent sources ended up generating the self-illusion of their purely mundane content. An illusion from which germinated a subsequent inability to translate in symbolic terms

[138] See Karpov (2010), Karpov and Svensson (2020), and Smith (2020).

[139] See Abeysekara (2006, 2010, 2011).

[140] See Warner et al. (2010) and Jakobsen and Pellegrini (2008).

[141] Jakobsen and Pellegrini (2008).

[142] Gauchet (1999).

[143] See Taylor (2007).

the religious roots of those cultural patterns.[144] Such a translational task would have been carried out only by drawing from the theological imageries, which were instead largely relegated to a whitewashed past.

The spread of science and technology, on the one hand, and the resilience of various kinds of enchantment/superstition, on the other, do not have much to do with religions and with the ethical/anthropological patterns they have left behind in the grammar of everyday life and its legal forms. Many Western and non-Western scientists, doctors, engineers, etc., engage in their occupation using categories of knowledge that have developed in the context of modern secularized culture and yet retain religious icons at home and sometimes even in the workplace; above all, they obey—albeit in many cases unconsciously—laws loaded with Christian moral theology. Moreover, if it is true that people once used categories of religious origin or supernatural events to make sense of their illnesses, it is false that this was the case for all diagnoses. It is also only a myth that scientific thinking did not proceed through the re-articulation of individuals' beliefs and their pragmatic implications. Often, with the hindsight of the present, we perceive past clashes, dialectical movements and polarizations, whereas historical processes certainly underwent transformative sequences. But this is simply because everyday life is not a theory that requires—or can be managed only after having reached—absolute consistency.[145] Making calculations according to the most advanced engineering knowledge of how best to build a skyscraper does not exclude that some engineer is not praying to a god so that bad luck does not affect the project, their own possibility of making mistakes, etc. Unpredictability wraps around human life and pervades it. Everyone is aware that the 'known' represents only the surface or at least a meager portion of what we consider as nature, the world of phenomena, etc. But all this has little to do with the presence of religion in the ethical-legal schemes of Western secular law and in its relationships with non-Western cultures or legal systems. On the other hand, if secularism means 'moving away from religion,' it is also to be made clear how, in each cultural context, this departure must be measured. If seen from outside, that is, with the eyes of foreigners and through an intercultural approach, the Euro-Christian experience would seem to be able to teach us something in this regard. In obeying state law, for example, French or German citizens can be culturally/anthropologically ultra-Christian, even if unconsciously, precisely because they claim to speak in the name of absolute rationalism. This just to say that the failure to attend church or the disaffection towards priests is not always a symptom of a fading attachment to the cultural substance of the religious tradition that anthropologically imbues the social context in which one has been raised. Moving away from churches or clergy, in any socio-cultural context, can

[144] One give away is the vehemence that can be seen as a response to some behavioral patterns that would seem to betray a worldview with religiously rooted value positions, even within social contexts where secularity is considered a fundamental value. For an in-depth analysis of this pattern from a comparative perspective in the domain of bioethics see Vazquez (2019).

[145] Rescher (1985, pp. 45 ff.).

have a very different meaning from what can be observed 'empirically' (even if is to be emphasized, once again, that there is no 'empirical datum' without the cognitive and thereby cultural schemes required to categorize it). On the contrary, the statements concerning the religious origin and/or meaning of people's actions cannot always be considered a sure indication of the lack of secularization or, vice versa, the secularization of their habits. The exploitation of religion for social, political and economic purposes is as old as the hills. For this reason, at least, the assumption that religion is only a means of political control would amount to making its meaning even more difficult to perceive.

By and large, the approach of those who study secularization outside the West shows, in my view, two convergent problems. (1) Secularization seems to be reduced, on average, to everything coinciding with scientific progress and rationality; (2) Religion seems indistinguishable from the external manifestations of the sacred, the spiritual, the magical.

Secularization is often identified as a project, with a sort of social construction strategy that is differently articulated—in *vernacular*, perhaps—in each socio-political context.[146] In daily practice, however, there is no trace of this project and perhaps it never existed, or in any case it has never been understood as an end intentionally pursued at an individual level—if not in the unrealistic intentions of some militant atheists. There is no project that involves people's daily attitudes in all their manifestations and that can be identified with 'secularization.' Rather, one could speak of political projects—for example, Jacobinism, Marxism, India secularism of the 1950s, etc.—in which the exclusion of religious faiths from the ranks of (psycho-)social agencies represented an implication of something wider and, above all, different. No planning disposition has ever existed that in itself, that is, regardless of an original and alternative 'vision' of society and its possible future order, aimed at the de-religionization of all the elements populating social life and individual or collective imagination—not even nineteenth-century Positivism.[147] After all, everywhere in the world people continue to say that the sun will rise at this or that hour despite having long since abandoned the belief in geo-centrism and its religious offshoots. Rather, the secular subject speaks of the plan to eliminate the Church from politics, from the government of the state. This is certainly—and has been—an explicit and sometimes rhetorically diffuse project. However, traces of it can be also found in the medieval European world[148] despite its domination by theocratic worldviews. On the other hand, confusing 'religion' with 'denomination' or 'ecclesiastical institution' could prove to be an ingenuity as widespread and unforgivable as it is likely to commute into a totally misleading approach. And this, at least, if one wants to treat secularization as a total phenomenon, that is, as a change in cultural

---

[146] See Bubandt and van Beek (2012, pp. 12–13).

[147] On the other hand, Comte's positivist religion, with its positivist catechism, while proposing de-religionization on one side, was construing an alternative theologization of the 'immanent', on the other.

[148] For example, Marsilio da Padova.

paradigms of such magnitude as to cut across both the private and public spheres, blurring their axis of distinction.

Furthermore, the complexification of the analysis framework, where local specificities are also put side by side with the effects of macro-cultural dynamics on a global scale, is undoubtedly a recognizable feature of contemporary experience. And besides, this is also, in many respects, an idiomatic way of presenting issues to the contemporary social sciences; a way that, in many cases, allows scholars to generate a bit of cognitive fog, so that they can keep the legitimacy of their specific approaches intact or, to a certain degree, immunize them from any consistency-based analytical criticism. When everything is mixed and indistinguishable, everyone can defend their micro-truth and/or their own methodological autonomy/exclusivity. Global and local implications, actually, should be not only proclaimed, in order to create smoke screens or perimeter islands of competence immunized by criticism, but assumed as an epistemological ground. The ascertainment of the co-implication between these two dimensions would require the awareness that every observed phenomenon needs a reconceptualization of the spaces of experience. A reconceptualization that scholars operate only in some cases by making use of an adequate theoretical apparatus: first and foremost, a semiotic view applied to the spatialization of the production of meaning. As will be seen, I call this reconceptualization a 'chorological approach,'[149] as it is consubstantial with the postulation of the existence of a semantic-spatial *continuum* coinciding with the semiotic coordinates of the observed phenomena. Secularization cannot be distinguished, if analyzed on a planetary scale, from the processes of multi-sited self-mirroring it generates and in which it is involved. Being and feeling secularized cannot disregard how the Other understands the actions and discursive dispositions of each subject. Nonetheless, this relational dimension does not depend only on conflicts, power relations and strategic choices. My stance in this regard, is that in today's world, the relationship with the Other affects secularization and its political effects mainly on a cognitive level.

Secularization and cultural unfolding are two closely related aspects. However, no one can become aware of their own cultural habits if these habits are not seen through the relationship to the Other. Only along the relational path can individual minds see the implicit, the invisible with which cultural action is imbued. The link between secularization and culture means that nobody can understand if and how much they are secularized without mirroring themselves in other subjects with different cultural and religious backgrounds. That is why I think that the complexification of relations between global and local, contingency and long-term, topography and geography, vernacular and universal, as concerns 'secularization' processes, is the natural and constitutive condition of this path towards cultural self-awareness. Symmetrically, I am led to surmise that it was precisely the lack of understanding of the intrinsic relationality of secularization and its cognitive import

[149] See below Chaps. 4–6.

that made it a source of harassing discriminations, exploitations, imperialist perversions, and injustices.

Moreover, the term 'secularization,' if taken as a sign related to a cultural process, represents an invention that is posthumous to the political and psychosocial phenomena that took place in European history. Flows of fading in religious feeling and disaffection in relationships with sacred authorities have always and everywhere occurred, in all civilizations, without the need to be defined as 'secularizations' or, more broadly, 'de-religionizations.' Even some spectacular historical conversions or inventions of new divinities were preceded, throughout history, by periods of 'disenchantment,' of insurgent skepticism for the religious significance of the practices in use in the various cultural contexts. These ebbs and flows could be spontaneous or, in any case, not be made the object of a reflective and symbolizing consciousness of an ongoing melting away of religion and its cultural significance.

Theoretical consistency, therefore, does not belong to, and would be searched for in vain along the development paths of the secularization process. People often move in multiple universes, or multiverses, and do not always seek coherence, either speculative or praxeological, between their multiple selves. Social life is crammed with contradictions, and the world of facts, in a sense, forgives pragmatic inconsistencies until they turn into unavertable obstacles on the way towards impelling individual or collective needs or aims. The world is broader and, in many ways, previous to the actors who populate it. That is why it can allow them—at least, up to a certain point—to float among logical contradictions.

In spite of any empirical faith in the exteriority of reality, we enactively co-generate,[150] through our dynamic and self-reflective relationships with the environment, the worlds in which (we believe) we live. These worlds, however, hover over many dimensions of experience of which we are not simultaneously aware, exactly as occurs for consciousness and its relations with both the body and thereby the environment. For this reason, acquiring the disposition to see what culture makes 'invisible' is the first step towards emancipation from ignorance deriving from all that is self-evident because dazzlingly visible, making us fatally shortsighted about ourselves and prejudicially blind to who is Other than us. From this perspective, understanding the relationship between culture and secularization implies the previous recognition of the close links extant between secularization and cultural versions of 'objectivity', namely of how 'things are' apart from human subjects.

[150] See Di Paolo et al. (2018). For other and more detailed referrals to enactivism, see Ricca (2018a, 2020a, 2022a, b, 2023).

2.12 Secularization and the Senses: The Invisibility of Otherness as a Consequence of Modern Law's 'Exteriority'

In concluding this chapter on the relationships between secularization and intercultural legal experience I would like to address a topic not frequently focused on by analysts of secularization. More precisely, I refer to the interplay between the cultural consequences of secularization and the cognitive activity inherent in the human senses. The binomial secularization/modernity prompted a great transformation in the interplay between reason and religion. This divide multiplied its effects, giving rise to a kind of replication in manifold areas of social experience. From a political and legal point of view, the separation between internal forum and external forum can be considered a pillar of the modern mindset. The myth of the social contract is a consequence of this new epistemological and political paradigm. It implies that citizens are to abide by political and legal authority not because of God's will but rather as a consequence of their primeval obligation arising from their subscription to that original social contract. People's legal liability is no longer driven by their inner convictions. The constitutional consequences of modernity will bring about, in the end, the ability for individuals to believe in their own God or have no religious faith. Human being's conduct, from a legal point of view, can be judged only with regard to its exterior morphological appearances and evidenced insofar as it can bring prejudice or harm to private or public interests and claims protected by law.

The classic liberal lesson gushing out from the above ideal approach finds its idiomatic expression in von Liszt's theory of criminal liability (but something similar can predicated, in the universe of common law, with regard to Bentham's thought).[151] According to von Liszt, the focus of any legal consideration of people's action from a criminal point of view should be limited to the so-called 'typical conduct:' that is to say, the behavioral scheme described by the legal templates and or in precedent case law. The subjective elements of the criminal conducts, namely intentional fault (*dolus*) and/or misconduct (*culpa*), are to be gauged only on the people's objective and exterior behaviors that are to be categorized and legally qualified by virtue of their *factual* evidence.

This kind of exterior approach to law seems to be inspired by the respect for individual freedom of citizens and, accordingly, the principle of lawmakers' and institutional agencies' neutrality in determining what is lawful and what is unlawful. Both such goals have been considered as exclusively political standards constitutively denoting modern state and legal experience. The possibility to achieve them, however, relies upon a silent cultural assumption involving both the axiological domain and the cognitive one. As for the axiological dimension, the state's legal

[151] See von Liszt (2002); for further bibliography on this topic, also with respect to common law experience, I refer to Ricca (2020a).

qualifications can be considered neutral—for example, with regard to the determination of criminal conduct—only if it is possible to deem some values/goods as endowed with an objective, universal significance. Nonetheless, this kind of objectivity presupposes, in turn, some degree of cultural homogeneity even despite the ideological tenets of the multiple components of society. On the other hand, from a liberal perspective, as such taking the individuals' freedom to be fundamental, it would be impossible to justify any deprivation or limitation of these fundamental rights beyond the cases in which a subject has jeopardized or overridden objective values.

On average, the encounter with different cultures and the problems it entails are considered from the perspective of axiological discrepancies. What is completely disregarded is the close connection between the values domain and the cognitive one. The dominant modern empiricist approach is ingrained in the implicit conviction that the universe of values and the universe of facts are sharply distinct and are to be logically assumed—and *maintained*—as such. The worldview resulting from this divide is that the objective world is somehow placed out there, and it is, at least as in its cognitive features, the same for everyone. What varies are the different axiological and teleological perspectives that individuals or communities project upon that unique world of factual elements.

The objectivity of the world is based on a sort of hypostatic understanding of the senses. Although they can sometime be deceiving, what results from the human sensorial attitudes is taken as the main source of knowledge of the objective, exterior world insofar as the affections of senses are amenable to be revised by means of the logic of scientific research and judgment. Facts and sensory perceptions are assumed as phenomenal dimensions endowed with a kind of 'epistemic/existential' correspondence. Sensory perceptions, in turn, are considered as the rough material further elaborated through symbolic representations. The binomial 'senses and representations' is consequently intended as a sort of camera by means of which human minds are capable of viewing nature, namely things out there, more or less as they are.

The above commonsense approach is actually rather naïve. Nonetheless, the criticism against this ingenuous realism in many cases fails to go far enough. Senses do not give only a partial, imperfect or 'too anthropic' reading of the world out there. They are also non-natural, that is, not pre-cultural. Though senses hinge upon biological and genetic predispositions, their development presupposes, in turn, relationships between the organism and its environment. What senses are, how they function, the perceptions they produce, is not entirely predetermined by the biological and genetic structure the individual holds at birth. What people are able to see, hear, smell, touch and taste, is a consequence of the dance, as it were, between nature and culture, education and biology. In other words, what individuals have learned from their birth, and know at present, is part and parcel of what they perceive through their senses: what the world is (for them). The immediacy of perceptions is only an illusion. The chain of semiotic inferences underlying the dazzling taking shape of a perception in an individual's mind is ordinarily doomed to be silent and unknown. Nonetheless, those semiotic interactive landscapes underlying each perception determine what and how it is. The objectivity of the factual world (or the world of *factish*—as Latour would term it)[152] is anchored in, and sprouts from, these invisible semiotic/inferential connections, which are utterly entangled in each individual's developmental story and memory.[153] The 'perceptual', in other words, is in large part the other side of the 'non-perceived': namely, what individuals do not know about themselves (as organisms) and their cultural determinants. In short: what we perceive is the result of the interplay between our biological attitudes and previous experiential as well as representational activities. The perceived sensory reaction to an environmental stimulus is already a mixture of sensorial and representational/symbolic predispositions and patterns. Moreover, as sensorial activity processively and interactively unfolds through time, it is also, at any given moment, the cumulative outcome of the ongoing adjustment between the mind/body unit and the environment. This means that our biological reactions are also stirred and conditioned by what our brain/mind have previously and pro-actively elaborated. But insofar as the specific interplay between culture and nature influences what people assume the world *is* from a sensorial point of view, for the same reason it affects the making of law and, even more subtly, its application to people's social conduct.

The main implication of the above considerations in its simplest terms is that judges and other legal agencies will only be able to perceive and recognize in the world comprising natural facts and others' conduct according to what they already know. Otherness and Others' worlds, therefore, are always at risk of being obscured by one's own sensorial/cultural apparatuses and categories. The inability to become aware of the semiotic clouds—so to speak—underlying perception blinds people, in one fell swoop, to themselves and Others. What is worse, however, is that such blindness ends up extending even to Others' worlds of facts, objects, phenomena and conduct. Consequently, to the extent that law and legal judgments are to be gauged exclusively on the 'exteriority', namely the objective universe of people's factual conduct, they are dramatically prone to overshadow cultural difference, to be intended as both the cognitive semiotic network and the material components making up Others' worlds.

What seems paradoxical is that the above othering blindness is somehow an indirect—and likely unintended—implication of modern secularism/secularization and its commitment to protecting religious and conscience freedom by means of the political/moral divide and the 'exteriority' of law. Assuming such 'exteriority' as a cognitive frontier presupposes, however, the objectivity of the factual world and its immediate and undisputed sensorial evidence/obviousness. Since a culture-free obviousness of the empirical world cannot be taken for granted (because it has proven to be merely a false implicit assumption), the principle of 'exteriority' could allow discrimination to lurk within it. The secularization of legal qualifications could

---

[152] See Latour (2010).

[153] A synthetic but very efficacious rendition of the relationship between habits and symbolic thought can be found in Dewey (1931); but see also, for the Peircean sources of Dewey's approach, Moorjani (2000).

wind up transmuting freedom into power, more precisely the power to deny the Others' worlds of significations by projecting onto them the umbra of a partisan and ethnocentric objectivity. In other words, the claim for the 'exteriority' of law could authorize judges and all the members of the dominant groups to see in Others only a mirror of their own Selves and the related worldly categorizations.

In a sense, the combining of the presumed objectivity of the exterior world and the 'cultural nature' of sensory perceptions constitutes a prophecy of the discriminative effects inherent in law's secularization. Morphological appearances of the world and Others' conduct are always a semiotic construction. Their assumed self-evidence and clarity stem from the unaware processing of experience by means of pre-shaped schemes of categorization applied, case by case, onto the phenomenal stream. But understanding what Others are making cannot be separated from the unraveling of the semiotic landscapes underlying their actions, their use of words, etc. As I will show below, any intercultural translation of the conduct and habits of Others must include a journey through those semiotic landscapes, as well as through those of the translators. Only in this way is it possible to avoid the transformation of the necessary commitment to translation in the creation of imperfect and domesticating metaphors, which are only more othering and discriminating, the more they are unknowingly produced. The imperativeness of law, then, does the rest by implicitly legitimizing and authoritatively sealing its compulsory power with blindness to Otherness.

In intercultural translation, probing what there is beyond the empirical morphological appearances of Others' conduct, and thereby what are the properties and connotations to be taken as axes of salience in categorizing their actions as well as the values/ends determining their ways of categorizing experience is simply crucial. Without diving into the invisible semiotic background of what is visible and more broadly immediately perceptible, that is to say the implicit indexical context of Others' actions, any genuine understanding of what they are doing will remain wildly out of reach. But if the application of law is gauged on this not-understanding and a complete failure of commitment to the translation of facts inherent in the structure of the so-called judiciary syllogism, then discrimination and the alleged legality will become, inevitably, two sides of the same coin. Under these conditions, secularization and the exteriority of law can even appeal to freedom as their own cornerstone, but only to stress that their combined action annihilates, through the facts, the 'cognitive stuff' of that same freedom. Conversely, the consequences of an allegedly neutral and exterior legal secularism would show that the presumptive objective 'facts' are to be intended as something that 'is made.' And besides, this would be (more than) completely in tune with Latin etymological origin of the word 'fact': which comes, more precisely, from the verb 'făcĕre', namely 'to make.' This linguistic origin somehow provides an interesting clue about the hybrid status of what we call 'facts.' I refer to their being not only *per se*, that is, in and of themselves, but always and however 'for us and from us.' The meaning of facts and their categorization involve, in any case, human action: whether it is only speculative and representational, or also practical, enactive and pro-active. Even the mere observation of a phenomenon contributes to the specific categorization that follows the observational attitude. The empirical objectivity of facts is therefore cognitively unbalanced insofar as their categorization does not result from a commitment to inter-subjective and—when needed—intercultural translation. Translational commitment is required just because 'facts for humans are always made by humans,' pragmatically or, in any case, cognitively.

Someone could contend that such cognitive issues have little to do with religion. But this remark makes sense only if one assumes that religion consists only of the denominational aspects of faith. Conversely, were religion taken in all its anthropological significance, the close connection between the lexicon of secularization, religion and cognitive issues would become apparent. Throughout history, world religions deeply influenced the cognitive dispositions of peoples, their horizons of meaning and perception, hence also the way in which they mold the everyday worlds each of them lives in and by. This influence is nestled in the silent and/or invisible semiotic networks underlying categorization and symbolic representations people use to handle their material environment and give it significance. As for law, therefore, the anthropological scope of religions dwells inside the basic instruments that individuals and groups use to organize their activities, from business to family. Moreover, it has to do not only with the 'legal categories', such as contracts, wills, responsibility, corporations, and so on, but also—and, in an anthropological sense, especially—with the descriptive/phrastic portion of the legal previsions, namely with all the terms concerning the world of extra-legal facts and their perception/representation/categorization.[154]

The cultural unbalance in the interpretation of 'facts' is due to the inclination to perceive and categorize them according to the semiotic network that people pro-actively, but silently or implicitly, activate in their minds and behavior. The modern 'ban' against probing individuals' internal forum can consequently transmute in an excluding overestimation of the semiotic networks underlying one's own perceptual and semantic patterns and, conversely, the complete (and sometimes even callous) disregard for the those of Others. Once again, this almost irresistible propensity to elaborate self-centered cognitive approaches to the world ends up, once again, passing off the identity with oneself as universality and the individual or cultural world views as the world in and of itself. From this point of view, however, it is to be considered that the possibility to plumb the Others' semiotic depths is not only a way to condemn people, but—in some cases—a means to discharge them from responsibilities based on their own worldviews and categorizations.

I well understand that emphasizing this side-effect of the law's exteriority could imply the need for an upheaval of all the modern political and legal projects as well as a number of the doctrinal architraves. Nonetheless, this danger cannot be a justification for concealing the internal collapse that intercultural relationships—if considered in all their implications—can and should trigger, above all from a cognitive point of view. Insofar as people belonging to minorities will be judged according to Others' ways of objectifying their actions and defining 'facts,' this

[154] See Ricca (2022a) for further and more detailed analysis of this point.

objectivity can entail a silent, but for this reason all the more overwhelming, crush of their freedom and cognitive pluralism. This is because the limits to freedom will be gauged on the morphological empirical appearances of Others' behavior but according to the dominant groups cognitive and cultural patterns. The result is that the judgment about the compatibility of Others' conduct and the legal system will be carried out by assuming 'facts' that do not correspond to 'what Others actually meant to do.' Conversely, an emic interpretation and categorization of Others' behaviors (namely, taking in account their *internal* cultural perspective) could show completely different conditions of compatibility, or alternatively incompatibility. All this shows that, in any case, the superimposition of the cognitive/cultural schemes of dominant groups on the Others' action could end up impinging on their freedom by implicit, but no less trampling, constraints. In this way, however paradoxical it may appear, the exteriority of law entailed by secularization could result in a limitation of freedom—including religious freedom—rather than a political-legal device aimed at its protection and improvement. The cognitive flaws caused by the cultural blindness to Others might condemn to invisibility the good reasons encapsulated in Others' actions and make it eventually impossible to grasp the semiotic networks underlying the morphological appearances of what they do.

If the modern world really wants to protect religious freedom, rightly intended in its anthropological projections and full cultural significance, it must assume that religious freedom includes also the freedom to imagine and make (again: in Latin, 'făcĕre') ones' own meaningful world. The imperative commitment to translate Others' ways of categorizing appears, therefore, utterly coextensive with secularization and democratic ideals. But it, in turn, requires a kind of epistemological obligation to understand before judging or condemning according to the 'exterior' morphological appearances of behaviors, things, or words.

From another point of view, it is pivotal to emphasize the spatial metaphor encapsulated in the external/internal divide and its further spatial/political consequences. What is internal and what is external can be compared to the divide between what is completely, and in a sense definitively, individual and what is general, or at least open and amenable to Others' perception. Internal and external reproduce the distinction inside/outside. But such a distinction, in turn, can be considered the source of the separation between the public and the private (spaces of experience and action). Were we to superimpose the conceptual schemes of each of the above oppositional couples—just as a police officer might overlay different translucent sheets upon one another to create a sketch of a suspect—we would obtain the map of religious freedom's topography within the social environment. But just merely seeing this image, we would recognize the asymmetries/discriminations inherent in the current condition of the 'planetary cultural/legal system' analyzed above.

In conclusion, secularization should be read, given the intercultural challenges, as a cognitive enterprise and commitment rather than as an exclusively ethical, political, and legal construction. In some ways, even in these domains a critical approach to the 'empirical world' should be developed, one that is ultimately very similar—as paradoxical and somehow inverted as it may appear—to the revision that took place in the dawn of modernity between natural theology and the emerging logic of scientific research.

References

Abdallah-Pretceille M (2006) Interculturalism as a paradigm for thinking about diversity. Intercult Educ 17(5):475–483. https://doi.org/10.1080/14675980601065764
Abeysekara A (2006) Desecularizing secularism. Cult Relig Interdiscip J 7(3):205–243. https://doi.org/10.1080/14755610601056892
Abeysekara A (2010) The im-possibility of secular critique: the future of religion's memory. Cult Relig Interdiscip J 11(3):213–246. https://doi.org/10.1080/14755610.2010.505432
Abeysekara A (2011) The un-translatability of life: thinking Talal Asad's thought unthought in the study of religion. Method Theory Stud Relig 23:257–282
Al-Azmeh A (2020) Secularism in the Arab world: contexts, ideas and consequences. Edinburgh University Press, Edinburgh
Anderson B (1983/2006) Imagined communities, 2nd edn. Verso, London
Andreas S (2006) Six blind elephants. Real People Press, Lafayette
Appadurai A (1986) The social life of things: commodities in cultural perspective. CUP, Cambridge
Asad T (2003) Formations of the secular: Christianity, Islam, modernity. Stanford University Press, Stanford
Austin JL (1962) How to make things with words. OUP, Oxford
Bakhtin MM (1981) The dialogical imagination. University of Texas Press, Austin
Bakhtin MM (1986) Speech genres and other late essays. University of Texas Press, Austin
Balagangadhara SN (1994) 'The Heathen in His Blindness. . .' Asia, the west and the dynamic of religion. Brill, Leiden
Bano S (2012) Muslim women and Shariah councils – transcending the boundaries of community and law. Palgrave Macmillan, Basingstoke
Bauer JR, Bell DA (eds) (1999) The East Asian challenge for human rights. CUP, Cambridge
Bauman Z (1991) Modernity and ambivalence. Polity Press/Blackwell, Cambridge
Beaumont J (ed) (2019) The Routledge handbook of post-secularity. Routledge, London
Bell LS, Nathan AJ, Peleg I (eds) (2001) Negotiating culture and human rights. Columbia University Press, New York
Bentley AF (1941) The human skin: philosophy's last line of defense. Philos Sci 8(1):1–19
Berger Peter L (ed) (1999) The desecularization of the world: resurgent religion and world politics. Eerdmans, Washington D.C.
Berg-Sørensen A (ed) (2016) Contesting secularism: comparative perspectives. Routledge, London
Berman HJ (1985) Law and revolution: the formation of the Western legal tradition. Cambridge University Press, Cambridge
Bhambra GK (2007) Rethinking modernity: postcolonialism and the sociological imagination. Palgrave Macmillan, New York
Bhargava R (2014) How secular is European secularism? Eur Soc 16(3):329–336
Blumenberg H (1985) The legitimacy of modern age. The MIT Press, Cambridge
Blumenberg H (2007) Theorie der Unbegrifflichkeit. Suhrkamp, Frankfurt a. M
Böckenförde E-W (2020) Religion, law, and democracy: selected writings. OUP, Oxford
Bouchard G (2015) Interculturalism: a view from Québec. Toronto University Press, Toronto
Bouchard G (2016) Quebec interculturalism and Canadian multiculturalism. In: Meer N, Modood T, Zapata-Barrero R (eds) Multiculturalism and interculturalism: debating the dividing lines. Edinburgh University Press, Edinburgh, pp 77–103
Bouchard G, Taylor C (2008) Building the future: a time for reconciliation. https://numerique.banq.qc.ca/patrimoine/details/52327/1565995

Bowen JR (2016) On British Islam: religion, law and everyday practice in Shari'a councils. Princeton University Press, Princeton
Bruner JS, Goodnow JJ, Austin GA, Brown RW (1956) A study of thinking. Wiley, New York
Bubandt N, van Beek M (2012) Varieties of secularism in Asia: anthropological explorations of religion, politics and the spiritual. Routledge, London
Buruma I, Margalit A (2004) Occidentalism: the West in the eyes of its enemies. Penguin Books, New York
Cady LE, Hurd ES (2010) Comparative secularism and the politics of modernity: an introduction. In: Cady LE, Hurd ES (eds) Comparative secularism in a global age. Palgrave Macmillan, New York
Calhoun C (2010) Rethinking secularism. Hedgehog Rev 12(3):35–48
Calhoun C (2016) The importance of *imagined communities* – and Benedict Anderson. Debats 1: 11–16
Calhoun C, Juergensmeyer M, Van Antwerpen J (eds) (2011) Rethinking secularism. OUP, Oxford
Calinger R (1999) A contextual history of mathematics. Prentice Hall, Upper Saddle River
Carrier G (1995) Occidentalism: images of the West. Clarendon Press, Oxford
Casanova J (1994) Public religion in the public world. Chicago University Press, Chicago
Casanova J (2006) Secularization revisited: a reply to Talal Asad in powers of the secular modern. In: Scott D, Hirschkind C (eds) Talal Asad and his interlocutors. Stanford University Press, Stanford, pp 12–30
Casanova J (2008) Public religions revisited. In: de Vries H (ed) Religion: beyond the concept. New York University Press, Fordham, pp 101–119
Casanova J (2009) The secular and the secularism. Soc Res 76(4):1049–1066
Chakrabarty D (2009) Provincializing Europe: post-colonial thought and historical difference. Princeton University Press, Princeton
Chatterjee P (2004) The politics of the governed: reflections on popular politics in most of the world. Columbia University Press, New York
Clarke KM, Goodale M (eds) (2010a) Mirrors of justice: law and power in a post-cold war era. Cambridge University Press, New York
Clarke KM, Goodale M (2010b) Introduction: understanding the multiplicity of justice. In: Clarke KM, Goodale M (eds) Mirrors of justice: law and power in a post-cold war era. Cambridge University Press, New York, pp 1–27
Connolly AJ (2009) Cultural difference on trial: the nature and limits of judicial understanding. Routledge, London
Corecco E (1999) A juridical-institutional reflection on the common priesthood and the ministerial priesthood. In: Corecco E, Borgonovo G, Cattaneo A (eds) Canon law and communio: writings on the constitutional law of the Church. Libreria Editrice Vaticana, Città del Vaticano, pp 124–165
Cowan JK, Dembour M-B, Wilson RA (2001) Introduction. In: Cowan JK, Dembour M-B, Wilson RA (eds) Culture and rights: anthropological perspectives. Cambridge University Press, Cambridge
De Roover J, Claerhout S, Balagangadhara SN (2011) Liberal political theory and the cultural migration of ideas: the case of secularism in India. Polit Theory 39(5):571–599
Dean K, Van der Veer P (2019) The secular in South, East, and Southeast Asia. Palgrave Macmillan, Cham
Dembour M-B (2006) Who believes in Human Rights? In: Reflections on the European Convention. CUP, Cambridge
Descola P, Pálsson G (eds) (1996) Nature and society: anthropological perspectives. Routledge, London
Dewey J (1916) Democracy and education. The Macmillan Company, New York
Dewey J (1931) Qualitative thought. In: Dewey J (ed) Philosophy and civilization. Minton, Balch & Company, New York, pp 93–116

Dewey J (2012) Unmodern philosophy and modern philosophy Southern Illinois. University Press, Carbondale. Kindle edition
Di Paolo E, Cuffaro EC, De Jaegher A (2018) Linguistic bodies: the continuity between life and language. The MIT Press, Cambridge
Dressler M, Mandair A (eds) (2011) Secularism and religion-making. OUP, Oxford
Eisenstadt SN (2000) Multiple modernities. Daedalus 129(1):1–29
Eisenstadt SN (2002) (ed) Multiple modernities. London
Engle Merry S (2006a) Human rights and gender violence: translating international law into local justice. Chicago University Press, Chicago
Engle Merry S (2006b) Transnational human rights and local activism: mapping the middle. Am Anthropol CVIII(1):38–51
Engle Merry S (2010) Beyond compliance: toward an anthropological understanding of international justice. In: Clarke KM, Goodale M (eds) Mirrors of justice: law and power in a post-cold war era. Cambridge University Press, New York, pp 28–43
Fitzgerald T (2000) The ideology of religious studies. OUP, Oxford
Fitzpatrick P (2008) Law as resistance: modernism, imperialism, legalism. Aschgate, Burlington
Foblets M-C (2005) Mobility versus law, mobility in the law? Judges in Europe are confronted with the thorny question "Which Law Applies to Litigants of Migrant Origin"? In: von Benda-Beckman F, von Benda-Beckmann K, Griffiths A (eds) Mobile people, mobile law: expanding legal relations in a contracting world. Routledge, London, pp 297–315
Foblets M-C et al (eds) (2016) Belief, law, and politics: what future for a secular Europe? Ashgate, Farnham
Forst R (2011) The right to justification: elements of a constructivist theory of justice. Columbia University Press, New York
Funkenstein A (2018) Theology and *scientific imagination from* the Middle Ages to the seventeenth century, 2nd edn. Princeton University Press, Princeton
Gauchet M (1999) The disenchantment of the world: a political history of religion. Princeton University Press, Princeton
Gibbs RW Jr (1994) Poetics of mind: figurative thought, language, and understanding. Cambridge University Press, Cambridge
Gibbs RW Jr (2005) Embodiment and cognitive science. Cambridge University Press, Cambridge
Glenn PH (2014) Legal traditions of the world: sustainable diversity in law. OUP, Oxford
Goodale M (2007) Introduction: locating rights, envisioning law between the global and the local. In: Goodale M, Merry SE (eds) The practice of human rights: tracking law between the global and the local. CUP, Cambridge, pp 1–38
Goodale M (ed) (2008) Human rights: an anthropological reader. Wiley-Blackwell, Malden
Goodale M (2009) Surrendering to Utopia: an anthropology of human rights. Stanford University Press, Stanford
Goodale M (2022) Reinventing human rights. Stanford University Press, Stanford
Goodale M (2023) Justice in the Vernacular: an anthropological critique of commensuration. https://www.researchgate.net/publication/358803212_Justice_in_the_Vernacular_An_Anthropological_Critique_of_Commensuration [Forthcoming in Law & Social Inquiry (2023) special issue entitled "Measures of Justice: A Symposium in Honor of Sally Engle Merry," edited by Dixon P, Firchow P, and Vera-Adrianzen F]
Graham L, Kantor J-M (2009) Naming infinity: a true story of religious mysticism and mathematical creativity. Belknap Press, Cambridge
Grant E (1997) The foundations of modern science in the Middle Ages: their religious, anstitutional and intellectual contexts. CUP, Cambrdige
Greimas AJ (1983) Du Sens II. Seuil, Paris
Griffith-Jones R (ed) (2013) Islam and English law. CUP, Cambridge
Habermas J (1995) Paradigms of law. Cardozo Law Rev 17(4-5):771–784
Habermas J (2006) Religion in the public sphere. Eur J Philos 14(1):1–25. https://doi.org/10.1111/j.1468-0378.2006.00241.x

Halbfass W (1988) India and Europe: an essay in philosophical understanding. Motilal Banarsidas, New Delhi

Hannikainen IR et al (2021) Are there cross-cultural legal principles? Modal reasoning uncovers procedural constraints on law. Cogn Sci Multidiscip J 45(8):1–13. https://doi.org/10.1111/cogs.13024

Herzfeld M (2012) Secularity and religiosity: holy spaces and the battle for administrative control over land in Bangkok. In: Bubandt N, van Beek M (eds) Varieties of secularism in Asia: anthropological explorations of religion, politics and the spiritual. Routledge, London, pp 231–249

Honneth A (1998) Democracy as reflexive cooperation: John Dewey and the theory of democracy today. Polit Theory 26(6):763–783

Horkheimer M, Adorno TW (2002) Dialectic of enlightenment: philosophical fragments. Stanford University Press, Stanford

Hunter-Henin M (2020) Why religious freedom matters for democracy: comparative reflections from Britain and France for a democratic '*vivre ensemble.*'. Hart, Oxford

Ingold T (2000) Three in one: on dissolving the distinction between body, mind and culture, published with the title 'Evolving Skills.'. In: Rose H, Rose S (eds) Alas, poor Darwin: arguments against evolutionary psychology. Jonathan Cape, London

Jackson M (1996) Introduction: phenomenology, radical empiricism, and anthropological critique. In: Jackson M (ed) Things as they are: new directions in phenomenological anthropology. Indiana University Press, Bloomington

Jakobsen JR, Pellegrini A (eds) (2008) Secularisms. Duke University Press, Durham

Johnson M (1987) The body and the mind: the bodily basis of meaning, imagination and reason. University of Chicago Press, Chicago

Johnson M (2007) The meaning of the body: aesthetics of human understanding. University of Chicago Press, Chicago

Joppke C (2014) The strange but necessary suppression of Europe's Christian roots. The Hedgehog Review. https://hedgehogreview.com/issues/europe-in-search-of-europeans/articles/the-strange-but-necessary-suppression-of-europes-christian-roots

Jurgensmeyer M (2006) Nationalism and religion. In: Delanty G, Kumar K (eds) The Sage handbook of nation and nationalism. Sage, London, pp 182–191

Karpov V (2010) Desecularization: a conceptual framework. J Church State 52(2):232–270. https://doi.org/10.1093/jcs/csq058

Karpov V, Svensson M (2020) Secularization, desecularization, and toleration: toward an agency-focused reassessment. In: Karpov V, Svensson M (eds) Secularization, desecularization, and toleration: cross-disciplinary challenges to a modern myth. Palgrave Macmillan, Cham, pp 1–39

King R (1999) Orientalism and religion: post-colonial theory, India and "the Mystic East.". Routledge, London

Laermans R, Verschraegen G (2001) "The late Niklas Luhmann" on religion: an overview. Soc Compass 48:7–20. https://doi.org/10.1177/003776801048001002

Lakoff G (1987) Women, fire and dangerous things: what categories reveal about the mind. University of Chicago Press, Chicago

Langacker RW (1987) Foundations of cognitive grammar: theoretical prerequisites. Stanford University Press, Stanford

Langacker RW (2000) Grammar and conceptualizations. Mouton de Gruyter, Berlin

Langacker RW (2002) Concept, image, and symbol: the cognitive basis of grammar. Mouton de Gruyter, Berlin

Latour B (2010) The modern cult of the factish gods. Duke University Press, Durham

Losonczi P, Van Herck W (eds) (2015) Secularism, religion, and politics: India and Europe. Routledge, London

Lübbe H (1975) Säkularisierung. Geschichte eines ideenpolitischen Begriffs. Karl Alber, Munich

Luhmann N (1977) Funktion der Religion. Suhrkamp, Frankfurt am Main

Luhmann N (1990) Society, meaning, and religion—based on self-reference. In: Luhmann N (ed) Essays on self-reference. Columbia University Press, New York, pp 144–164
Luhmann N (1997) Die Gesellschaft der Gesellschaft, two vols. Suhrkamp, Frankfurt am Main
Luhmann N (2000) Die Religion der Gesellschaft. Suhrkamp, Frankfurt am Main
Madan TN (2005) Modern myths, locked minds: secularism and fundamentalism in India. OUP, New Delhi
Malik M, Muslim Legal Norms and the Integration of European Muslims. In EUI RSCAS, 2009/29, MUSMINE - https://hdl.handle.net/1814/11653
Mandair A (2009) Autoimmunity in the study of religion(s): ontotheology, historicism and the theorization of Indic phenomena. In: Bilimoria P, Irwine AB (eds) Postcolonial philosophy of religion. Springer Science+Business Media, Dordrecht, pp 171–191
Mandeville P (2021) Multicultural nationalism? Reflections on the contributions of Tariq Modood. ReOrient 6(2):214–218
Mapril J, Blanes R, Giumbelli E, Wilson EK (2018) Introduction: secularities, religiosities and subjectivities. In: Mapril J, Blanes R, Giumbelli E, Wilson EK (eds) Secularisms in a postsecular age? Religiosities and subjectivities in comparative perspective. Palgrave Macmillan, Cham
McLeod H (2003) Introduction. In: McLeod H, Ustorf W (eds) The decline of Christendom in Western Europe, 1750-2000. Cambridge University Press, Cambridge, pp 1–26
Medovoi L, Bentley E (eds) (2021) Religion, secularism & political belonging. Duke University Press, Durham
Meer N, Modood T, Zapata-Barrero R (eds) (2016) Multiculturalism and interculturalism: debating the dividing lines. Edinburgh University Press, Edinburgh
Menski W (2001) Postmodern Hindu law. Heidelberg University Library. https://core.ac.uk/display/33413473?utm_source=pdf&utm_medium=banner&utm_campaign=pdf-decoration-v1. Last accessed 28 Feb 2022
Menski W (2004) From Dharma to law and back? Postmodern Hindu law in a global world. Heidelberg University Library. https://archiv.ub.uni-heidelberg.de/volltextserver/4410/. Last accessed 28 Feb 2022
Merry SE (2016) The seductions of quantification: measuring human rights, gender violence, and sex trafficking. University of Chicago Press, Chicago
Modood T (2019a) Essays on secularism and multiculturalism. Rowman & Littlefield, London
Modood T (2019b) A multicultural nationalism? Brown J World Aff 25(2):233–246
Moorjani A (2000) Peirce and psychopragmatics: semiosis and performativity. In: Muller J, Brent J (eds) Peirce, semiotics, and psychoanalysis. John Hopkins University, Baltimore, pp 102–121
Nandy A (1983) The intimate enemy: loss and recovery of self under colonialism. Oxford University Press, New Delhi
Niezen R (2004) A world beyond difference: cultural identity in the age of globalization. Blackwell, Malden
Niezen R (2009) The rediscovered self: indigenous identity and cultural justice. McGill-Queen's University Press, Montreal & Kingston
Norris P, Inglehart R (2011) Sacred and secular: religion and politics worldwide, 2nd edn. Cambridge University Press, Cambridge
Parolari P (2020) Diritto policentrico e interlegalità nei paesi europei di immigrazione. Il caso degli shari'ah councils in Inghilterra. Giappichelli, Torino
Peerenboom R (ed) (2004) Asian discourses of rule of law: theories and implementation of rule of law in twelve Asian countries, France and the U.S. Routledge, London
Philippopoulos-Mihalopoulos A (2015) Spatial justice: body, lawscape, atmosphere. Routledge, London
Pouw M (2021) Greatness & limits of common priesthood in 16th century reformation theology. A realist phenomenological priesthood in Luther and Calvin from a roman catholic perspective. Summum Academic Publications, Kampen

Preyer G, Sussmann M (eds) (2016) Varieties of multiple modernities: new research design. Brill, Leiden

Prodi P (2000) Una storia della giustizia. Dal pluralismo dei fori al moderno dualismo tra coscienza e diritto. Il Mulino, Bologna

Räber MI (2020) Knowing democracy – a pragmatist account of the epistemic dimension in democratic politics. Springer, Cham

Rawls J (1996) Political liberalism. Columbia University Press, New York

Rectenwald M, Almeida GL (eds) (2015) Global secularisms in a post-secular age. De Gruyter, Berlin

Renteln AD (2004) The cultural defense. OUP, Oxford

Renteln AD (2010) Making room for culture in the court. Judges J 49(2):7–15

Renteln AD, Foblets M-C (eds) (2009) Multicultural jurisprudence: comparative perspectives on the cultural defense. Bloomsbury, Oxford

Rescher N (1985) The strife of systems: an essay on the grounds and implications of philosophical diversity. OUP, Oxford

Ricca M (2002) Diritto e religione. Per una pistemica giuridica. CEDAM, Padova

Ricca M (2008a) Dike meticcia. Rotte di diritto interculturale. Rubbettino, Soveria Mannelli

Ricca M (2008b) Oltre Babele. Codici per una democrazia interculturale. Dedalo, Bari

Ricca M (2010) Riace, il futuro è presente. Naturalizzare il 'globale' tra immigrazione e sviluppo interculturale. Dedalo, Bari

Ricca M (2013) Culture interdette. Modernità, migrazioni, diritto interculturale. Bollati Boringhieri, Torino

Ricca M (2015) United Europe and the Euclidean pluralism: the anthropological paradox of contemporary UE legal experience. UNIO - EU Law J 1(1):3–26

Ricca M (2016) A modest proposal: an overgrown constitutional path to cultural/religious pluralism in Italy. CALUMET - Intercult Law Humanit Rev 3:1–46. https://calumet-review.com/index.php/2016/09/10/a-modest-proposal-an-overgrown-constitutional-path-to-cultural-religious-pluralism-in-italy/

Ricca M (2018a) Cultures in orbit, or justi-fying differences in cosmic space: on the significance of human rights under conditions of absolute a-territoriality. Int J Semiot Law 31:829–875. https://doi.org/10.1007/s11196-018-9578-5

Ricca M (2018b) *Ignorantia facti excusat*: legal liability and the intercultural significance of Greimas' "contrat de véridition". Int J Semiot Law 31:101–126. https://doi.org/10.1007/s11196-017-9529-6

Ricca M (2020a) Otherness, elsewhere, and the 'ecology' of law's implications: the semiotic oceans surrounding legal signification and its discriminatory exteriority/objectivity. Int J Leg Discourse 5(2):185–237

Ricca M (2020b) Planning facts through law: legal reasonableness as creative indexicality and trans-categorical re-configuration. Int J Semiot Law 33:1089–1123. https://doi.org/10.1007/s11196-020-09702-z

Ricca M (2020c) Don't uncover that face! Covid-19 masks and the niqab: ironic transfigurations of the ECtHR's intercultural blindness. Int J Semiot Law 19:1119–1143. https://doi.org/10.1007/s11196-020-09703-y

Ricca M (2021) The multi-sited/synesthetic taste of the Italian 'Tricolore': time-space transmutations of the Italian flag's colors through the ingredients of Pizza Margherita. In: Wagner A, Marusek S (eds) Flags, color, and legal narrative: public memory, identity, and critique. Springer, Cham, pp 531–552

Ricca M (2022a) Perpetually astride Eden's boundaries: the limits to the 'limits of law' and the semiotic inconsistency of 'legal enclosures'. Int J Semiot Law 35:179–229. https://doi.org/10.1007/s11196-020-09771-0

Ricca M (2022b) The 'spaghettification' of performativity across cultural boundaries: the trans-culturality/trans-spatiality of digital communication as an event horizon for speech acts. Int J Semiot Law 35:2435–2479. https://doi.org/10.1007/s11196-021-09880-4

Ricca M (2023) How to undo (and redo) words with facts: a semio-enactivist approach to law, space and experience. Int J Semiot Law 36:313–367. https://doi.org/10.1007/s11196-022-09912-7

Ricca M, Sbriccoli T (2015) Notariato e diritto interculturale. Un viaggio giuridico-antropologico tra i notai d'Italia. CALUMET - Intercult Law Humanit Rev 1:1–49. https://calumet-review.com/index.php/2015/05/06/notariato-e-diritto-interculturale-un-viaggio-giuridico-antropologico-tra-i-notai-ditalia/

Roniger L (2016) Multiple modernities 'East' and 'West' and the quest for universal human rights. In: Preyer G, Sussmann M (eds) Varieties of multiple modernities: new research design. Brill, Leiden, pp 122–148

Rosati M (2010) Post-secular society, transnational religious civilizations and legal pluralism. Philos Soc Crit 36(3–4):413–423

Rosenberg FJ (2016) After human rights: literature, visual arts, and film in Latin America, 1990–2010. University of Pittsburgh Press, Pittsburgh

Sahar I, Yefet KC (2022) Kadijustiz in the ecclesiastical courts: naming, blaming, reclaiming. Law Soc Rev 56(1):53–77

Said E (1991) Orientalism. Penguin Books, London

Sajò A (ed) (2004) Human rights with modesty: the problem of universalism. Martinus Nijhoff, Leiden

Schachar A (2001) Multicultural jurisdictions: cultural differences and women's rights. CUP, Cambridge

Schmitt K (1985) Political theology: four chapters on the concept of sovereignty. Chicago University Press, Chicago

Sen R (2007) Legalizing religion: the Indian Supreme Court and secularism, with a comment by U. Baxi. East-West Center Washington, Washington

Shachar A (2009) The birthright lottery: citizenship and global inequality. Harvard University Press, Cambridge

Shani G, Kibe T (2020) Introduction: legacies and possibilities. In: Shani G, Kibe T (eds) Religion and nationalism in Asia (Political theories and East Asia contexts). Routledge, Abingdon

Shapin S (1994) A social history of truth: civility and science in seventeenth-century England. University of Chicago Press, Chicago

Smith JZ (1978) Map is not territory. Brill, Leiden

Smith JZ (1998) Religion, religions, religious. In: Taylor MC (ed) Critical terms for religious studies. University of Chicago Press, Chicago, pp 269–284

Smith SD (2020) The resurgence of (immanent) religion and the disintegration of the secularization hypothesis. In: Karpov V, Svensson M (eds) Secularization, desecularization and toleration: cross-disciplinary challenges to a modern myth. Palgrave Macmillan, Cham, pp 135–152

Spencer-Brown L (1979) Laws of form. Dutton, New York

Stoeckl K, Rosati M (eds) (2016) Multiple modernities and postsecular societies. Routledge, London

Stolleis M (1990) Staat und Staatsraison in der frühen Neuzeit: Studien zur Geschichte des öffentlichen Rechts. Suhrkamp, Frankfurt am Main

Talmy L (2003) Toward a cognitive semantics. I. Concept structuring systems. MIT Press, Cambridge

Taylor C (2004) Modern social imaginaries. Duke University Press, Durham

Taylor C (2007) A secular age. Harvard University Press, Cambridge

Taylor C (2011) Why we need a radical redefinition of secularism. In: Mendieta E, Antwerpen J (eds) The power of religion in the public sphere. Columbia University Press, New York, pp 34–59

Teubner G (1983) Substantive and reflexive elements in modern. Law Soc Rev 17(2):239–286

Tierney B (2001) The idea of natural rights: studies of natural rights, natural law and church law 1150–1625. Eerdmans, Grand Rapids, Michigan

Todescan F (1983) Le radici teologiche del giusnaturalismo laico. I. Il problema della secolarizzazione nel pensiero di Ugo Grozio. Giuffrè, Milano

Tully J (1995) Strange multiplicity: constitutionalism in an age of diversity. CUP, Cambridge
Twining W (ed) (2009) Human rights, southern voices: Francis Deng, Abdullahu An-Na'im, Yash Ghai and Upendra Baxi. CUP, Cambridge
Van Broeck J (2001) Cultural defence and culturally motivated crimes (cultural offences). Eur J Crime Crim Law Crim Justice 9(1):1–32
Van der Veer P (2013) Nationalism and religion. In: Breuilly J (ed) The Oxford handbook of the history of nationalism. OUP, Oxford, pp 655–671
Van der Veer P (2014) The modern spirit of Asia: the spiritual and the secular in Asia and India. Princeton University Press, Princeton
van Quine WO (1980) From a logical point of view: nine logico-philosophical essays. Harvard University Press, Boston
Vazquez ML (2019) Secularism, religions, and law: a legal-cultural inquiry. Torri del Vento, Palermo
Vazquez ML (2022) Futile otherness: religion and culture vs. futile motives in criminal law. CALUMET - Intercult Law Humanit Rev 14:35–65. https://calumet-review.com/wp-content/uploads/2022/05/Vazquez-M-Futile-Otherness-1.pdf
Venn C (2001) Occidentalism: modernity and subjectivity. Sage, London
Verma V (ed) (2019) Secularism, religion, and democracy in Southeast Asia. OUP, New Delhi
Violi P (1997) Significato ed esperienza. Bompiani, Milano
von Hayek FA (1980) Individualism and economic order. University Chicago Press, Chicago
von Liszt F (2002) Der Zweckgedanke im Strafrecht (1882/83). Nomos, Baden-Baden
Waldron J (2004) Tribalism and the myth of the framework: some Popperian thoughts on the politics of recognition. In: Catton P, Macdonald G (eds) Karl Popper: critical appraisals. Routledge, New York, pp 203–230
Walker T (2017) Sharia Councils and Muslim women in Britain: rethinking the role of power and authority. Brill, Leiden
Warner M, Vanantwerpen J, Calhoun C (eds) (2010) Varieties of secularism in a secular age. Harvard University Press, Cambridge
Wences I (2016) Quebec interculturalism: a version of Canadian multiculturalism or a model with an institutional structure? Convergencia 23(72). http://www.scielo.org.mx/scielo.php?pid=S1405-14352016000300115&script=sci_arttext&tlng=en
Wolterstorff N (2008) Justice: rights and wrongs. Princeton University Press, Princeton
Young C (1999) The accommodation of cultural diversity: case-studies. Palgrave Macmillan, Basingstoke
Zee M (2016) Choosing Sharia? Multiculturalism, Islamic fundamentalism and Sharia Councils. Eleven International Publishing, The Hague

Chapter 3
Translating Cultural Invisibilities and Legal Experience: A Timely Intercultural Law

3.1 Introduction

'Culture' is ordinarily and almost instinctively grasped as something people belong to. Paradoxically, this is the self-alienating other side of the very idea that individuals and groups have 'a culture.' The general psycho-cognitive implications of this possessive understanding of 'culture' converge at its identitarian declination. 'Cultural heritage,' 'cultural identity', 'cultural tradition,' 'cultural habits,' 'cultural practices' are but a few examples of the overall tendency to objectify and/or commodify what culture means. People show the inclination to reify their cultural attitudes as something that is different from the agent even if, at the same time, these same attitudes concur to define who or what they are. This concoction of reification and distancing results in a dialectical relationship between the agent and the environment, both natural and social, with which individuals and groups have to deal with. The byproduct of such dialectical tension between subject and environment, knowing and known, is a misoneist reading of what culture is: as it were akin to a repertoire the classificatory order of which could be considered as a copyright of the past. Such approach is cause of the unintended, even though not for this very reason less nefarious, idolatry for the so called 'cultural evidence' and the related practice of 'cultural tests' that infect the otherwise precious use of cultural expertise in multicultural legal contexts. The 'authentic culturality' of behaviors, expressions, objects, lands and so on is reduced, in this way, to the evidence of their conformity to prefixed schemes, rules, social imperatives, normative templates, customary linguistic/pragmatic patterns the 'author of which' is the past. The ultimate upshot is that as 'genuinely cultural,' or recognizable as such at least before law, is to be considered only what is equivalent to the morphologically well-defined products of the prescriptive apparatus which culture is considered coincident with. Needless to say, along this hermeneutical ridge the drift towards the exocitization and foklorization becomes a self-realized prophecy. But this is implicitly to mean that the idea of culture is divested of its cognitive nub and ossified in a repertoire with a

M. Ricca, *Intercultural Spaces of Law*, Law and Visual Jurisprudence 10,
https://doi.org/10.1007/978-3-031-27436-7_3

museum-like morphology. The signical 'stuff' of cultural production ends up being annihilated together with its inherent self-transformative potential. The periphrastic, ongoing dimension of cultural experience is fictitiously silenced, denied, with the net effect that people (allegedly) belong to cultures rather than being cultures that come from people.

My approach to culture is at the antipodes of the above anthropological and political conception. The rhetoric of cultural identity inclines, despite its fair anti-imperialistic afflatus, to overshadow the dynamic and self-renewing source of cultural patterns, namely 'experience.' In my view, culture is a collection, or better a semiotic network, of noetic/pragmatic recipes to manage the multifaceted environment that, in different times and places, hosts human life. Even if those recipes are transmitted from one generation to another, they should be intended as a sort of renewable energy source. Their genuine content has to do with the 'know how' they encapsulate, that is to say their noetic/pragmatic semiotic ciphers rather than the morphological features resulting from their historical and/or contingent implementation. Cultural know-how*s* are means that continually reshape their corresponding ends by virtue of their adjustment with the boundary conditions provided by the ongoing experience. In this sense, it could be said that ends qualify the means, and the adaptive self-transformation of means endlessly reveals and reshapes the genuine 'meaning' of ends. Such a protean circularity coincides with the life of culture. From this perspective, insofar as cultures are acted by people, they are inherently and genetically designed to be unremittingly re-signified through the dynamic and inexhaustibly creative cultural competence of human beings.

In this chapter, 'culture' is understood as 'cultural competence,' synonymous to 'human talent' for endlessly modelling the spaces in which we, precisely the humans, construct our lives. Thus, the legal relevance of cultural differences will be taken as an issue of semiotic distance between the realities of how people live in a cultural pluriverse, and the ways in which institutions and legal structures react. In this vein, I propose an intercultural legal approach that aims to bridge two dimensions of experience and thought. It intends to interrelate the theoretical analysis of cross-cultural communication between different legal/cultural universes of discourse and the daily interactions of people and practitioners of law. Focusing on the daily problems faced by individuals with differing cultural competences, the legal intercultural approach proffered here is designed to assess how to better integrate different ways of life with laws, rules and practical schemes of behavior. In this field of inquiry, the anthropology of law and the intercultural approach to law clearly overlap.

Anthropological legal research focuses on the analysis of diverse legal systems and the modalities, more or less jarring, of their interactions. Anthropological legal pluralism is the disciplinary area that addresses these conflicts. It operates both by evaluating events (specific conflict situations) as well as by elaborating more speculatively the research data in an attempt to ascertain and define what is 'law.' In both cases, the lens of observation, although socially participated, focus on 'normative stuff,' namely rules. Precisely for this reason, the collisions among normative and/or legal systems at issue are handled as issues of translation and accommodation within a universe, or better a pluriverse, of normative statements or standards. However much this activity may result endowed with theoretical and cultural cues, this working ground is but an abstraction or the outcome of abstract processes. As such, it seems to assume that the normative encyclopedias and apparatuses might collide and eventually conflate by themselves, namely as if they were intersecting universes of pure norms/rules put in motion by magical forces.

In the cosmos of social events, however, the contacts between universes of rules are triggered by people, their displacements and interactions unfolding through the spaces that host the enaction of their schemes of action, plans and ends. These people are legal *subjects*, but not only in a passive sense. On the contrary, while depending from time to time on the laws that govern them, this does not prevent them from having some room to actively manage their encounter and interaction with others. And besides, the entire practice of law is designed, in all latitudes and in all forms, to make possible at least an average and as peaceful as possible achievement of this comprehensive end. The behavioral constraints placed on individuals by rules are legitimized, and thus spontaneously obeyed, only when they are committed to that outcome. At this general level, the effectiveness of law and the very possibility of its existence as a social phenomenon are matters relying on culture and the efficiency of culturally communicative tools.

When individuals move through space and act, they use normative standards to make their relations with the others possible. However, the action plans of each person are never totally preconfigured by normative statements, since they may have different legal, religious, or more generally, cultural origins. The same normative utterance and statement might be included within very innovative and socially unusual teleological horizons. In such cases, the 'semantic substance' of rules is curved to fit inside new spaces of action that have to be trans-acted within the pragmatic schedules of other people. Toward such a direction, the progressive layering of trans-action activities makes new sense of normative statements, renewing their semantic spectrums. This has the effect of redrawing previous action maps and, in this way, organizing new ones. In a sense, these interactions give rise to trans-actions, which require, in turn, the trans-*lation*—or trans-*duction*—between different interpretations and proposals raised by legal actors and oriented to influence the use of rules. Here, it should be underscored, the word 'trans-*duction*' is to intended in is etymological sense corresponding to 'translation', that is corresponding to both *trans-fero* and *trans-ducere*, 'carrying through space.' Within each legal system, persons or subjects of law, are actors too, and using the rules for their own purposes they continually engender new meanings, new schemes of behavior as well as new spaces of both action and interaction. Along these hermeneutical and transformative paths, people show their ability to make use of legal systems in new ways, engendering new starting points for the whole process of defining social relationships and their spatial implications.

Something similar occurs in each legal system (if any secluded singularity of them, holistically considered, can still be found) where the use of norms is shaped by persons who find themselves in difficult situations caused by encounters between different actors belonging to different cultures and normative orders. The agents of these intercultural encounters, in any case, are people in flesh and blood. They epitomize, through the choices and plans of action they adopt, the causative factor underlain by both the match and interpenetration between the meanings and the related pragmatic projections envisaged by the normative systems to which each of social actor partakes. And yet, it must be repeated once again: people are not norms. They rather *use* the norms. And when they move their minds and bodies to and fro, traversing different systems of meaning, rules and practices, such use can become extraordinarily elastic.

As observed above, inside each socio-cultural normative universe—assuming that it is relatively homogeneous and self-contained regarding its codes—the rules of daily life are over time unawares transformed by the citizens' behavior, carried out through a series of reciprocal interactions, transactions and translations. In a sense, legal rules over-code the actions of individuals because their normative content is imbued with categories and patterns of behavior already spontaneously and even unconsciously adopted by the majority of people. Nonetheless, this overcoding effect is bidirectional, in that it proceeds not only from the top down but also from the bottom up. To put it another way, legal norms are over-coded, in turn, by social action and its self-transformation along a bottom-up process.

In tune what has just been observed, legal rules—insofar as they are intended as the result of the interpretation of legal statements—do change. More precisely, this occurs because their cultural and practical embedding enables the change to take place without breaking the legal system, and this applies to any normative apparatus. Particularly, in the case of law, both legislative production and interpretive judicial activities are fueled by communicative shifts that take place first and foremost within the social practices and living uses of legal instruments and resources. As a matter of fact, this process of change, more often than not, occurs tacitly and seamlessly, at least from an institutional perspective. It is hidden inside the folds of the same galaxy that hosts and fosters inter-subjective interactions. And yet it happens and, bit by bit, it surfaces in public circuits, compelling them to change. Conversely, although amazingly in some respects, this over-coding and transforming process proves itself a failure when the use of norms crosses the boundaries of the semantic-spatial dimensions of each system. This occurs when people *migrate* or displace into new normative contexts. In this situation, the multiple affiliations of individuals can raise conflicts of loyalty or faithfulness. When individuals find themselves required to comply with multiple rules that impose contradictory behaviors, they typically opt out of all of the alternatives. Unfortunately, having arrived at this point, people seem to lose their ability to discursively tailor the normative obligations in a teleological fashion. This takes place, in my view, because individuals perceive themselves to be suddenly lacking any sphere of significance that might allow them to understand the norms coded in legal (as well as ethical, religious, etc.) statements as means to ends. But, as I will try to show, what is missing is nothing more than an overall semantic horizon informed by an intercultural perspective.

3.2 Subjects and Norms Bereft of Context

The discrepancy factor underlying the need for a cross-cultural approach to legal interactions between different legal systems is the sudden disappearance of the cultural context associated with the production of normative effects that result, on average, from the legal norms that people are accustomed to abiding by in their countries of origin. This statement, of course, requires a necessary and further attempt at explanation.

When people move across diverse normative circuits, they may bring with them binding rules and the consequent required behaviors, but as such inevitably uprooted from the original contexts of signification. In the new social environments, those contexts slide down like the fall of a theatrical backdrop. Thus, to reconstitute the meaning of specific life situations, at least from the normative point of view, only the legal statements or the behavior they provide remain (and this, *inter alia*, according to the meaning it produced within the original system). What is worse, such signification is gauged on their alleged morphological evidence and structure. Of course, the normative results of any rule can be re-contextualized so as to make sense during the transplant process. And yet, despite any effort towards inter-contextualization,[1] legal rules tend to maintain a high degree of semantic stiffness; something also applying to the behaviors originally signified by them. As shown below, this occurs insofar as the analysis and the efforts of translation/transactions between diverse cultural and legal systems are carried out only at an inter-legal level: namely, focusing solely on the formal words of the law rather than taking into consideration the meanings and values embodied by people in their conduct.

The interactions between different normative systems, if processed only through regulatory texts or behaviors taken in their morphological objectivity, are fated to bog down in the marshes of conflict situations most oftentimes unsolvable. This is because the normative standards and the related orthopraxes become fetishes, badges for the construction of clashing identities. Inevitably, rather than adjust to the new legal and socio-cultural contexts, they stiffen even further. Furthermore, these instrumental and strategic transformations trigger a circular process of identity radicalization, within which both norms and required behaviors function as the building blocks of opposite subjectivities increasingly frozen in their semantic features. Along this path, the possibilities of both inter-systemic translation and accommodation will be compromised, or at least severely limited, from the outset.

From this starting point onwards, the clash of identities will gradually, but also unavoidably, affect the self-understanding of the subjectivities involved in any intercultural encounter. The result of increasing identitarian and law-based polarizations will be the over-codification of the systems to which individuals belong. In this situation, norms, rules, and behavioral patterns become formal tools (when not actual weapons) for the fueling of cultural contrasts, all the more powerful and dangerous the more disconnected they are from the mobile and creative relations of

[1] See, Cover (1983, 1986) and Melissaris (2009).

meaning in which they are involved in their contexts of origin. From a semiotic point of view, they will cease to function as signs endowed with a dynamic and flexible aptitude for producing semantic connections to be reduced to mere tools exploited to rhetorically support the reproduction of conflicts. As a result, these conflicts end up consisting not so much of an opposition between the multiple meanings of the subjectivities at stake, but rather of a pure struggle for power over social space, which, in turn, is grasped in its mere material consistency and exterior coordinates.

When cultural bonds and constraints (whether legal, religious or otherwise) cross the boundaries between mutually different universes of signification, they lose their connections to the indexical background and relative status as means to socially shared ends. Thus, the plasticity and the flexibility that, at least potentially, connote both norms and legal rules in their original social contexts, making them available to people to cope adaptively with their experiential contingencies, are radically reduced. From another perspective, it could be said that previous connections between means and ends collapse along transplants. Diversities and changes in the target context annihilate opportunities to adapt and redefine the semantic and pragmatic scope of norms and rules, as well as innovative interpretations and manners of applying them. Normative statements and behavioral bonds then appear as if they were indexically unrelated. What is lost is the possibility, traceable in any sufficiently complex system of normative patterns, of reshaping their semantic projections to adapt spaces, times and modes of application.

When the situations of normative and personal dislocation just described occur, the original conditions supporting the signification of rules and their cultural coherence vanish. Consequently, the social actors who cross the borders find themselves surrounded by a confused and hazy landscape inhabited by wretched means of broken ends, contradictory rules and conflicting bonds. Their present becomes a world of displaced and wandering scraps of meaning. Paradoxically, absorbed into the conflict dynamics, the subject vanishes with his own agency, both blurred inside the shadows of opposing normative imperatives. Such war of rules, unfortunately, winds up transmuting human individual (as well as groups) in hard-wired automatons, blindly overwhelmed by normative patterns that remold their different, unique subjectivities. In the dazzling crossfire of the semantic and pragmatic projections of different normative systems what vanishes is the opportunity for each individual to be an agent endowed with creativity, embedded in a network of mobile social relations and, as such, capable of reshaping cultural encyclopedias of meaning and value.[2] The effort to remain loyal to, and abide by, both their moral and legal systems of origin end up being deceptively and instrumentally portrayed as their main reason for living, their anthropological quintessence.

Why does this occur? And, even before that, where does it occur? Is it possible to overcome this impasse by enabling people to turn encounters with Otherness into an

[2] It is interesting to note how something resembling this assertion, at least in style, can be found in Muthu (2003) about how the modes of 'noble savage literature', from the discovery of the Americas up until the Enlightenment, were used to configure the natural life of New World peoples.

opportunity to empower their agency as cultural and legal actors? To answer these questions, I would like to take a step back to examine how individuals manage to use and adapt rules within their own systems. Before continuing, in fact, it is useful to consider the analysis of these activities provided by network legal theory combined with the multiculturalist theoretical approach.

3.3 The Interplay Between Multiculturality and Differences as a Legal Inter-systemic Process

Multiculturalism is a political/theoretical approach to the multicultural composition of most contemporary societies. It is pivoted on the supposed value of each culture in and of itself. It draws upon the legitimacy of the quest for a reciprocal recognition between the different cultures and for the relative independence of respective circuits of existence. These claims are then poured into an idiomatic political formula, which in the name of (the doctrine of) legal pluralism, impels states and constitutional systems to allow cultural communities to organize themselves on the basis of their own values and rules.

From a legal perspective, the manifold cultural differences are held as icons and pillars of so many systems of rules. Commitment to individual and community cultural integrity is limited only by respect for human rights, although this constraint manifests itself differently depending on the more or less radical version of the multiculturalist approach. In any case, the consequent implication of this view is that every relationship between individuals acting according to different cultural codes corresponds to a parallel relationship between normative systems. The intertwining of systemic apparatuses makes the subject a kind of bridge, engaged in combining the efficacy pathways and pragmatic projections drawn by the norms/rules of each system through their interplay. The individual is considered, in this representation, as a knot in a tangle of threads or a clot in a cluster of veins. Hence, their subjectivity is seen as a kind of obstacle to the ordinary flow of normative effects, a snag that nevertheless imparts new directions to them. But this is precisely the result of adopting a postmodern approach in reading the multiple and multi-situated belonging of each individual—which is, on the other hand, an idiomatic characteristic of the contemporary era. In this scenario, the subject seems to resemble an osmotic membrane capable of triggering the circuits and rhythms of interpenetration between different regulatory systems, each of which limits but at the same time flows into the others. The outcome of such processes is not a situation of predictable stability, but rather a state of permanent transformation constantly evolving toward new thresholds of intersystem equilibrium. 'Inter-normative hybridization' is the label devised to describe the resulting metamorphosis of the overall regulatory network, sometimes juxtaposed with the more specific formula 'inter-legality,'[3] coined specifically to refer to the relationships between legal systems.

Intercultural law, in this framework, could not be understood otherwise than as a process of semantic regeneration of the normative content and/or interpretation provided by the norms of different legal systems in their mutual interactions, which in turn would be conveyed by the actions of individuals or groups. Nowadays—this is the basic assumption—the increase in border-crossing activities (migration, international trade, etc.) fosters the displacement and thereby the overlapping of different regulatory 'environments.'[4] In a sense, it is as if the relative weakness 'contracted' by normative systems in adjusting to each other would assure individuals a strategic opportunity for emancipating themselves from regulatory schemes perceived as too rigid and coercive. In this way, crossing the boundaries of normative systems would create a network of binding but mutually limiting rules that would allow individuals to take advantage of the legal provisions applicable outside each system and, consequently, to resort to them as a means to claim and realize their pluralistic aspirations. On the other hand, however, it should be noted that subjective creativity is not conceived as an agency capable of giving precise direction to the continuous flow that should shape the inter-normative adjustments just outlined. As already pointed out, the individual is assumed as a bridge, a mere 'pipeline' of communication between semantic and deontic contents considered as 'actual and real actors' of systemic interpenetrations, as if they were to be assumed as organic entities.[5] The hybrid creature that would seem to emerge from systemic interplay is intended as a post-human entity, almost an epiphenomenon of the unpredictability and chaotic dynamics of adaptation triggered by the indirect interaction between the homeostatic standards of self-preservation inherent in each different system.

In the network approach, there is no space or time for the planning consciousness of individual subjects, which is a crucial and denotative feature of modern ways of thinking. Categories, universals, generalizations and so on, seem to be banned from this theoretical landscape. They are declared definitively failed as a means of forecasting and constructing the future, and thus stigmatized by their 'very nature' as mere instruments of oppression and limitation of the demands for renewal and critique toward the institutional status quo. In place of categorical generalizations, from time to time invoked and exalted, sometimes almost revered, there is room for the hypostatization of the nomadism of individuals or of ideas and the regenerative power of contingency. The main enemies of the perspective outlined above regarding the realization of cross-cultural normative experience are to be identified, according to this theoretical approach, with the modern State (if not the entire project

[3] de Sousa (2020). But, more generally, regarding legal networks Teubner (2004); Joerges et al. (2004); Ost and van de Kerckhove (2002); Riles (2000); from the perspective of private international law, see Wai (2008); and more Schepel (2013).

[4] Eberhard (2001, 2009).

[5] Philippopoulos-Mihalopoulos (2010, 2012).

of Western modernity) and the single-track logic of its hierarchically ordered legal production. A disseminated and multidirectional pluralism of norms and orders, like a loose network, is the underwood above which the effective course of the global social events is imagined. In such a framework, the disentangled fragments of diverse systems are continually subsumed at an all-encompassing level of normativity pervasively wafting through the middle, or the in-between, of the inter-subjective relationships. In such a so-shaped middle, however, the emergence of cross-cultural and pluralistically forged normative meanings is delivered as a hovering conceptual fog so thick that it phagocytizes the multifaceted belonging of the subject in an indistinguishable *continuum*. In this way, the flow of super-individual and post-human hybridizations is fulfilled and, through an almost inexorable process, the planning attitude and the figure of the subject itself finally disappear from the scene.

Taking a closer look at the theoretical proposal just illustrated, the price of individual emancipation from monistic systems of rules seems to be, necessarily, the disappearance of both subjectivity, the schemes for its conceptualization and, consequently, any possibility for individual agency to employ such categories to face the power of intertwined normative orders. Within this overall framework, however, the intercultural normative dynamics bring out an abstraction, and substantially a reification, of alleged processes of transculturation. Through such processes, individuals and their cultural creativity are regarded only as cogs in a holistic entity that overcodes any subjectively elaborated and categorization-based choices as well as the related attempts to manage the future. In the end, the power of subjective agency appears at once as unleashed from single-system constraints and bounds but also overwhelmed by a pervasive meta-systemic dimension by now global in scope, and therefore almost by definition cross-cultural. In other words, cultural differences and habits are assumed to be the very factors that produce social experience and normative interactions, automatically fostering and drawing the paths of their rearrangements, as if they simply travel on the backs of individuals in action. The other side of this coin is that human subjects seem to be represented as mere stepping stones for normative and behavioral patterns that navigate the current of global flows. Ultimately, subjects are reduced to mere supports for intersystemic cultural-normative mixing and adaptation.

3.4 A Step Forward in the Mirror of the Past: The Possibility of a Creative Intercultural Use of Law

The struggle against all that can be considered 'modernity' is the key feature of the network approach to the possibility of an intercultural legal experience. Yet, eschewing modernity and fully discarding its cognitive achievements sounds at least disproportionate and, upon further consideration, even paradoxical. If it is impossible to hide the dark side of generalizations and the domineering use of categories as hallmarks of modernity,[6] it would be equally unthinkable to take seriously the implicit, albeit meandering, proposal to live without categorizing the world.

In my view, the culpability of modernity lies not in its commitment to generalizations or general categories as tools for knowing and predicting events, but rather in its recruitment of categorical patterns as a normative portrait of reality, and hence as cages to be superimposed upon the world.[7] Particularly in human sciences, more so than in other fields of knowledge, the process of modern universalization has incorrectly but not innocently assumed categories as definitively forged concepts rather than guesses permanently open to revision and verification. This error, largely overcome in the analysis of the natural world, has proved instead historically fatal for political inclusion and, ultimately, for the respect of cultural differences in the mirror of law around the world.

Nonetheless, the so-called 'Enlightenment Dialectic' must not be considered as the contradictory consequence of the cosmopolitan ideals of modern political thought but rather as their betrayal or, at least, their misinterpretation. The paradoxical subversion of the universalism of the Enlightenment into an instrument of cultural and social exclusion is not an inherent feature of the theoretical assumptions of the modern mind, but only the inevitable implication of an erroneous and badly rhetorical use of the 'category of universal categories.' The very idea that universality lies beneath the surface of historical events, and does not dwell over the horizon of intercultural transactions carried out as open-minded research, is the main cause of the problems and failings occurring along the unfolding of the socio-political modern experience.

In the modern age, the widespread essentialist attitude regarding the conceptual setting of categories has tended to replace universality with cultural identity in social and political thought. As a result, the potential of inclusiveness surely intrinsic to generalizations and idiomatic of their semantic abstractness has emerged dismantled. Conversely, the universal statements—such as, for example, those regarding natural rights—have been filled with the contents of cultural traditions of colonizing nations or the world visions and values corresponding to the interests of dominant groups. It was, as it were, a political coup de main, but one with huge implications.

From a historical point of view, in the direction just indicated, the decisive factor was that the democratic ideas professed by the Enlightenment and Liberalism primarily found their implementation within state boundaries and national languages. Compelled by these circumstance, universal categories such as freedom, equality, individual autonomy, and so on, were interpreted in the light of local forms, habits of behavior and thought. In each country, universality was thus mingled with national ways of thinking, as well as with the corresponding ethical values and

[6] Bauman (1991) and Chatterjee (2004).

[7] I think the distinction between modernity in its ideal state and the uses of the modernity project would be a good lens for a renewed reading of the *Dialectic of Enlightenment* (Horkheimer and Adorno 2002) and its post-modernist textual epigones.

cognitive patterns. The result was that every national declination of universal principles was taken as the prototype of their realization. The door for the inclusion of cultural differences, in a cosmopolitan fashion, was therefore inevitably obstructed, contriving to cage the plurality of social worlds within the semantic grids imposed by the power of the state.

The respect for liberal principles was thus blurred, not infrequently, with what was essentially a guarantee for the ruling class to freely realize their own interests. Similarly, the dissemination across the globe of values produced by Western civilization was transformed both in the unleashed exploitation and the cultural annihilation of the peoples subdued by colonial powers. It comes as no surprise, therefore, that in contemporary critical generalizations, universal categories, especially if declined by legal standards, epitomize all the evils of modernity. In the end, the dream of discovering the laws of nature and history, so distinctive of the modern faith in Reason, turned out to be nothing more than deceitful normativism—cognitive and axiological—the backwash of both a domineering attitude and an unlimited greed.

The explosion of political and social pluralism in the early twentieth century and the progressive emancipation from colonial powers paved the way to the contemporary discourse and to claims of difference. In a sense, they have mutilated the deformed progeny of modernity, namely faith in categorization and/or generalization itself. The increasing rise of the reasons and rights of difference on the political scene seems to have proved the impracticability of the project to accommodate the world's multiplicity all within taxonomic orders underpinned by categorical schemes. The demonstrated unpredictability of future events, natural and socio-cultural as well, combined with the impossibility of aprioristically knowing Otherness, have provided the ideal and theoretical basis for the emergence of the incommensurability between different cultural perspectives, hence, in political terms, their irreducibility under the umbrella of universal models of subjectivity speculatively drawn. Thus, under the broadsides of the anti-universalism troops, headed by the vociferous critics of the modern way of thinking, human rights, natural rights, constitutional rights, and so on, were inevitably brought along as well. It appears upon closer inspection, however, that the achievements marked by pluralist discourse and the struggles fought in the name of difference (of culture, religion, gender, etc.) have not been implemented apart from the use of moral or legal universals. On the contrary, the historical successes attained by 'subaltern' people on diverse occasions have been won by turning these universal moral and legal patterns into devices to collapse upon themselves the current discriminatory schemes of institutional action. Demonstrating the inconsistency of planning choices taken by political powers discredited these schemes for public action. This was achieved by comparing them to the same universal values invoked to claim the moral and legal legitimacy of the subsequent and inevitably unequal political statements. It was the same for the challenges issued and won by the lower classes, as well as for the fights leading up to decolonization. To point out these historical elements, of course, does not neutralize the possibilities, the risks, and the actual occurrence of a treacherous, instrumental, serializing and, ultimately, oppressive use of human rights.[8] The topics related to 'human nature' might impute to persons, and sometimes to entire peoples, stifling straitjackets, as has been largely demonstrated by recent history. Nonetheless, if unaided by the power of words, of the general statements and utterances supporting normative ideals such as equality or liberty, to be sure, the voice of difference, the claims of the weakest are hopelessly doomed to a fatal silence.

However, after many years of bitter contempt for the category of human rights, decried in the name of the strictest anti-modernism—especially by anthropologists of law—anthropological thought is becoming open towards a re-evaluation of the possible emancipatory uses of these rights.[9] The source of this change, in all likelihood and paradoxically, was the same field research, the listening to the opinions of people, even those most subaltern and apparently distant from Western culture, who were not at all persuaded to discard the support obtainable through the invocation of human rights—the most 'disastrous' generalization sprung up from the Enlightenment. It seems that despite the ideological or academic tenets and claims of political or social movements (such as Asian Values, Subaltern Studies etc.), the common people of any culture or belonging perceive distinctly enough that the assertion of their autonomy or difference would be helpless before state power without the possibility of appealing to principles like freedom, equality or subjective autonomy.

Human and constitutional rights remain of course the icons of Western political culture. Nonetheless, that they could be elaborated in individualistic or communitarian, solipsist or relational keys, is another matter not to be dismissed, nor is it necessarily fated to resolve with the use of human rights as a vehicle for the imposition of Western cultural models. However slowly, the global experience has indeed been showing just the opposite. Increasingly, statements involving human rights discourse undergo culturally alternative readings, namely interpretations suitable to serve as a platform underpinning cultural patterns and needs different from those arising from Western traditions. This is the case because the universal propositions encapsulated within the declarations of human rights have not been shown to be semantically inapproachable by the instances and causes championed by cultural difference. On the contrary, when (and only if) difference can find a suitable platform to make its voice heard,[10] linguistic generalizations, and therefore also those expressed in normative form, appear exposed and even vulnerable to the requests for re-categorization or categorical reshaping. This occurs because all generalizations and categories are inherently ambiguous and consequently have

[8] Sajò (2004).

[9] Engle Merry (2006a, b, 2010), Clarke and Goodall (2010a, b) and Goodale (2022, 2023).

[10] Regarding the conditions for assuring semantic relevance to the voice of difference within general utterances and statements of law, see below.

flexible boundaries with regard to what they include and exclude.[11] This semiotic issue is addressed further below.

At this point, however, it is important to note that in order to reshape legal categories in an intercultural fashion, shrewd legal skills combined with a flexible anthropological awareness are required. This means that the respective competencies of the jurist and anthropologist are not enough, if taken alone, to address the problems that arise when the law is struggling with cultural differences, and vice versa. Devising intercultural solutions fitting for such struggles necessitates a kind of craftsmanship that combines and recombines the meanings conveyable by normative categories and words. And this certainly is (or at least should be) the specific capability of lawyers.

To further underline what has just been said, to maneuver normative meanings it is further necessary to know the facts to which legal rules should be applied. For this purpose, one might think, simply observing the facts might suffice. And it could be, except that facts do not speak for themselves. On the contrary, they are given voice by human beings, who observe, read, and set them through their ability to categorize. But, again, categories are cultural products. It is therefore impossible to understand what the facts in question are without knowing the cultural coordinates that the people involved used in qualifying them, or, even more so, in the way they were performed.

Within situations marked by cultural difference, the lawyers should have a minimal understanding of their client's culture, if they are to successfully carry out their usual work of dynamically adapting the meanings of rules to facts. But this is exactly not the case when cultural difference is at stake, or the client is foreign. It is to be noted that even though only lawyers have been considered thus far, similar questions arise for judges as well. In any event, to solve the inter-subjective problem of cultural discrepancy and to avoid dramatic misunderstandings, the lawyer and their client, or the judge, should seek the help of an anthropologist or, at least, an expert in intercultural communication. In many cases, however, anthropological expertise may not prove decisive, and indeed may even complicate matters. This is because cultural differences, and cultures themselves, are the result of continuous and cumulative transformations, nowadays dramatically increased by the mobility of people and by the facile transmission of information on a global scale. Hence, it is extremely difficult for the anthropologist to explain the culture of the foreigner or the categorical scheme adopted by the latter in reading or acting in the world to a jurist. Last but not least, anthropologists often have no knowledge or skill with regard to the legal system of the country where they themselves live or where they are called for their expertise. Yet, without being able to read the thoughts and behaviors held by a client of a different culture through the lens of the law, it may be extremely

[11] A path (also mine) towards the ambiguity/ambivalence of categories could be traced through the following texts: Bruner et al. (1956); Johnson (1987, 2007); Lakoff (1987); Langacker (1987, 2000, 2002); Bauman (1991); Gibbs (1994, 2005); Talmy (2003); Violi (1997); Andreas (2006); Blumenberg (2007), and prior, the writings and philosophical assumptions taken from Peirce, James and Dewey. About the *exotopicity* of signs see further, Bakhtin (1981, 1986).

challenging to choose which aspects of their mind to consider and which to leave out in order to best confront their life problems, which are often or quickly become legal matters. In order to work effectively, the anthropologist should have in mind the life context in which the client is presently situated, its implications and its meanings, in its full intricacies. Yet, such a context is nothing but the resulting situation of the simultaneous and reciprocal interactions between the client's cultural competence, their expectations about the future application of law, and the cultural categories used by people living in the same country that enacted the legal rules to be applied to the case. In other words, the anthropologist should be able to predict, at least in principle, how the legal system would react towards the meanings and behaviors articulated by the client who acts according to their own culture.

But how can we expect all this from a cultural anthropologist who is neither a lawyer nor a judge, and certainly does not have practical skills as a jurist? Likewise and symmetrically, how can we be confident that lawyers are able to understand the meaning schemes used by a person of another culture without the specific commitment of the anthropologist to distance themselves from their own culture? To unravel such a dilemma, the anthropologist would have to become a lawyer and the jurist an anthropologist. But doing such a crossing metamorphosis takes effort and requires, moreover, a willingness to overcome disciplinary boundaries—in a sense, another kind of intercultural enterprise.

As a rule, anthropologists of law are equipped with theoretical knowledge of legal systems and, indeed, of legal phenomenon as a whole. And yet, it is quite uncommon for an anthropologist of law to know how to cope well with the technicalities of legal practice. When dealing with intercultural legal situations, only consummate skill in using these techniques can help resolve the issues involved. This is because, despite the critical views of many anthropologists, law is not a monolithic system of rigid, predetermined rules that, like a mold, is forged once and for all and imprinted on peoples' daily lives. Instead, the application of legal norms to facts is the result of a work of translation and adaptation.[12] In the relationships between rules and facts, it is not only the social aspect that is bound to be changed.[13] Of course, to modulate the meaning of the law, to shape and steer the reactions of legal systems, specific training is necessary.

To put it straightforwardly, every jurist must be able to touch the appropriate points on the palette of meanings made available by the legal texts, courts decisions and all the other elements of each legal order. This is exactly what any good lawyer does and is able to do for clients of their own culture. On average, they listen to some stories, confused narratives of events, fancy portrayals of facts, all merged with some elements of folk legal knowledge and, naturally, urgent practical expectations. From this tangle of various elements, they have to come up with legally relevant and useful

---

[12] White (1990).

[13] In this regard, I refer to Ricca (2022a, b) for a criticism of the distinction within the so-called *direction of fit* proposed by Searle (2001, p. 37 ff.). Very insightful observations in this regard can be traced in Dewey (1924).

semantic indexes, and at the same time, combine the normative effects to satisfy the client's goals and interests. From this point forward, the lawyers begin their challenging play within the semantic potentialities of the legal system in search of possibilities of meaning-modelling more appropriate to their client's interests. In so doing, they work ceaselessly with legal categories, exploiting all their semantic ambiguity and trying to recombine, in the mirror of the facts, the related boundaries. The very challenge often lies in the possibility of subsuming the behaviors and words of the client under one rather than another category, in one rather than another combination of regulatory schemes. Thus, by and by, the polyphonic actions of legal operators constantly shape and mold the categorical landscape of law, matching rules with facts and vice versa. The product of this unending activity, resembling an immense network of bustling ants, is the so-called 'living law' or law in action.

As difficult as this work may seem, only the lawyers' cultural and legal competence enables them to reach some kind of result in most cases. Even in ordinary circumstances, only the cultural competence shared by lawyer and client makes it possible to find appropriate solutions. Conversely, the lack of this inter-subjective cultural continuity would make the work of translation from the common language of the client's narrative to legal language, as well as the related challenging re-molding of categories, a terribly daunting task. Nonetheless, the translating ability on the part of lawyers is a hidden, silent skill, subconsciously carried on by practitioners of every country. It is only in addressing cultural differences that its indispensability becomes readily apparent. In such situations, the lawyer's skill for translating common language into legal language suddenly jams. Something does not go.

Even so, precisely because the work of translation is usually ignored, almost as if it were out of sight, it remains equally unknown that preventing failure depends on it. Simply speaking, the lawyer is not able to read the cultural backdrop presupposed by their clients for packaging their narratives allegedly based on 'facts'. As a result, mis-translations become a defect, almost an unavoidable pathology, in average situations. Unfortunately, semantic discrepancies often remain virtually invisible. This discriminating effect stems from a kind of 'cognitive law' according to which what is unknown, in most cases, escapes perception. Perhaps only an anthropologist, accustomed to dealing with people's diverse cultural competence, could contrast the translation skills and shortcomings of lawyers by relating them to cultural difference. In handling the necessary dialogue with jurists, the first step anthropologists should take in order to renew the relationship between translation and legal application is to call the attention of lawyers and judges to the importance of not judging individuals and groups from different cultures by their own cognitive schemes and moral norms. Every lawyer should learn to consider the possibility that during the assessment and legal qualification of the Other's actions there may be something that has gone misconstrued; that beyond the morphological and apparently clear features of the Other's action and expressions, something could remain yet to be understood; and that precisely such a 'something' conflates with a semiotic landscape, which is the background underlying each action and word of cultural agents.

This background is the silent side of language and conduct, more technically, the indexical context of signification.[14] Its action is pervasive, even if tacit. That mute portion of communicative activities includes all contextual relationships supporting the emergence of the outer side of meanings. Without the ability to wander within the territories engendered by the intertwining of these relationships, it is literally impossible to mine from them the sense of actions and words as it is intended by human actors. And besides, cultural competence is precisely the magic key that allows people to understand each other through reciprocal journeys in the mute portion of subjective agency.[15] Nonetheless, it would be much too narrow, and fundamentally incorrect, to think of that competence as a tool to display only the mental theatre of human experience. The silent background of conscious meanings is relational in itself because it is the synthesis of pragmatic and semiotic relations with the environment in which the subjects live. This synthesis overcomes, hence, the mental boundaries of individuals because it is the progressive outcome of an unending process of embodiment of their relations with the world. From this perspective, what is inner and what is outer to the subject are components of a single circuit of reality that goes beyond the 'theater of consciousness' and the same individual. This is because the body behaves as a relational membrane between inner and outer dimensions of individuals' life, so that the meaning and the substance of any internal sign depend on its connections with the external ones. These connections also include past and future relationships, to indicate that the process of signification is always open. This means that a single subject, at the end, does not possess by themselves their cultural knowledge. The semiotic components of this knowledge are only hypothetical, inherently incomplete, since the meaning of every sign lies in the future, and within the links constantly renewed between the future and the past. As a result, individuals are never fully aware of their culture in a twofold sense. In one sense, this is because, for the most part, the semiotic elements that constitute cultural competence function tacitly. As a result, individuals are never fully aware of their culture, in a twofold sense. In another sense, this is because, for the most part, the semiotic elements that constitute cultural competence function tacitly. From a different angle, moreover, because the meaning of personal knowledge, both conscious and unconscious, which are pragmatically managed by the individual in the course of their experience, will be the consequence of future relationships with the environment and the signs that populate it.

[14] Bakhtin (1981, 1986); Merleau-Ponty (1964); Gadamer (2013). See, for an anthropological perspective, Denzin (1997, 2008).

[15] On 'mute parts of law', see Ricca (2013c) and specifically chapter 3 (*L'ombra del diritto. Le «parti mute» dell'agire sociale e la traduzione interculturale* [*The shadow of law. The "mute parts" of social action and the intercultural translation*]).

3.5 Time and the Invisible/Mute Parts of Intercultural Legal Experience

The short semiotic digression proposed so far, perhaps apparently distant from legal matters, can nevertheless help to clarify the reasons why: (a) lawyers need to know the invisible/mute portion of the cultural know how of their foreign clients; and (b) (symmetrically) anthropologists must understand the legal implications proceeding from the social implementation of cultural difference and the potentialities of an interpretive intercultural recombination of legal rules and their meaning. In both cases a matter of consequences and dynamic entailments is at stake. And this, in turn, semiotically feeds back on the substance and signification of the cultural competence[16] and legal rules that both the anthropologist and the lawyer are respectively called up to assess and use in their own work.

Any intercultural life situation, when understood in all its potential projections of meaning, stimulates in social actors unexpected efforts to bring out the invisible/mute cultural parts from the darkening shadow cast on them by the morphological features of behaviors and their ethnocentric interpretations. Catching a glimpse of those potentialities allows, on the other hand, the social actors to mine the practical implications of the acted cultural difference from the depths of their possible future implications: the intercultural relationship is intrinsically transformative. Throughout its unfolding, the main actors—foreign clients, lawyers and anthropologists—are stressed to unearth their cognitive tools from their implicit cultural knowledge and to strip away, as far as possible, the hazy veils of the future from the consequences ensuing a 'worldled' implementation of the corresponding cultural difference. Overall, this process or work could bestow tremendous empowerment of personal agency, giving those involved an extraordinary chance to emancipate themselves from the cognitive constraints and psychological overcoding of their own culture. From this perspective, the law transforms into a mirror from which the wide bundle of often less visible elements of the multicultural experience may be reflected, come to light, and display the semantic/axiological signification of its dynamic interlacing with the societal universe. For this very reason, when considering legal consequences, a cross-cultural anthropological expertise should include a cultural report elaborated from a teleological or predictive perspective. In so doing, however, the anthropologist does not in any way betray their professional rule of engagement—so to speak. He would not behave, to be sure, as a prophet out of place. This is because any consideration of the intercultural 'state of affairs' gauged on the specific condition of the client cannot be carried out independently of an analysis of the possible consequences of their conduct. More generally, it is to be said that the present state of a culture, so to speak, if caught in its subjective folds, is not independent or isolated from its future implications. The link between present and future is a constitutive factor of cultural knowledge, which is not an absolute

[16] I have dealt with 'culture' as partly opposed to 'cultural creativity' in intercultural legal experience in Ricca (2013c).

psychological capital that is always true, something even truer in a multicultural social setting. As I will try to clarify below, the representation of possible consequences must necessarily be combined with the anthropologist's participatory observation of the self-transformative and reflexive processes in which the client's intercultural experience is involved. After all, self-objectification constitutes a crucial step for those who are called to talk about their culture and question it. Moreover, in the spectrum of legal experience, the pragmatic coherence of what is to be taken as a cultural fact is vested with even greater importance than in other areas. And besides, all cultural data are essentially and must always be treated as premises and (semiotic) means of possible future outcomes. In the province of legal facts, this is even more true and palpable.

Categorizing an act of speech or behavior in one way rather than another is evoking and triggering one rather than another chain reaction of normative and material effects. One thing should never be overlooked: each solution makes a difference, sometimes dramatic, for people caught in the web of legal constraints. Determining the meaning of a cultural feature should therefore be an open question above the whole horizon of legal and practical paths that each subject should be allowed to follow. If properly informed about the available alternatives, each person might decide to choose one rather than another cognitive or behavioral resource from their cultural background in order to trigger one rather than another reaction from the legal systems. Similarly, the same feature or connotation of an individual's (cultural) conduct could be interpreted differently, both by the client and the anthropologist, as a result of the interplay of personal intentions and pragmatic perspectives afforded to the (cultural) agent by the specific situation they experience.

In addition to the arguments proffered thus far, and to further complicate matters, we must consider the renewing effect inherent to any multicultural social context. Immersed within such environmental conditions, any cultural competence individually considered has to manage not only the difference expressed by itself, but also those deployed by all the cultural actors involved in each situation. This polyphonic *socioscape* can be a source of many problems for a social actor, but it also comes as a perfect occasion for the opening up of new opportunities. Nevertheless, the chance of intertwining cultural devices of various origins also necessarily involves an effort of translation, a course of reciprocal transactions and, in the end, a process of crossed metamorphosis. Therefore, authentically identifying a single cultural feature requires the ability to figure out how it has been transforming and is being transformed through intercultural relationships. But in accomplishing this task, the investigator must move from a conjectural origin, at first to be taken in an exclusively hypothetical way, to reach an only presumable and ever interlocutory end. The likelihood of the anthropologist being able to make fruitful contact with a client who finds himself drawn into the flow of these transfigurations is probably quite low. In most cases, daunted by the difficulties inherent in taking into account the protean mass of probable and cumulative contaminations, the anthropologist might opt for more distanced and objectifying descriptions of cultural features. Alternatively, if epistemologically unfulfilled by this approach, in a typical post-modern pose they could assume that culture, in and of itself, is the same transformation, a continuous hybridizing of knowledge and skill, the restless germinations of differences, in other words, what the client occasionally might say about themselves.[17]

Although both styles of anthropological analysis can deploy in their support arrays of opposing arguments, neither of them would have much to offer to foreigners entangled in the following triple predicament: *a)* facing the multifaceted difficulty of understanding themselves; *b)* making themselves understood by their lawyer; and *c)* getting the legal, but also practical, meaning of what they are doing or have done. Even if merely hypothetical, a possible (however much multi-layered) origin should be postulated by the anthropologists in order for them to communicate and make themselves understood by the client. The very idea of transformation, after all, implies an origin, a departure platform. For the anthropologist, the caveat to keep in mind is, rather, to assume that origin only in a processive way, as a means of knowledge, and not as an underlying reality, an essentialized and unchangeable cultural coinage.[18] Cultural origins cannot be considered as a repertoire of knowledge and practices established once and for all, as a filing cabinet ready to open the correspondence of a world forged symmetrically within its boxes. The seabed where cultural knowledge originates cannot be discovered in its thinghood like mineral sediment, but only questioned by the anthropologist as much as by the client. In this case, looking back to a heuristically assumed source is just a way to dive deeper to gain a useful boost to project the consequences of a culturally oriented action within a new environment. The only way to draw on that source, however, is to talk about it and talk about it with the client, namely the personified mind that supposedly originates from there. Despite all the limits and risks of overcoding interpretations, this is the only way the anthropologist can induce the emergence of a collaborative, interparticipated dialogue with the client about the directions of their *intercultural becoming*—provided that, of course this communicative task is carried out with prudence through an iterative open play of mutual suggestions and responses.

Tracing the backward paths of cultural metamorphosis in search of its hallmarks can, on the other hand, enable both the anthropologist and the lawyer to better assess its legal implications and, more generally, to calibrate their interpretations and support in light of the cross-cultural understanding of the (future) consequences of the client's action within the social environment of the host society. This advantage point is achievable, however, only as long as the lawyer partakes in the overall activity. This is because the traces of the client's self-transforming cultural memory ought to be stretched between past and future, swinging back and forth from past knowledge to possible future practical and thereby also legal consequences. However, the overall activity connecting both the lawyer, the anthropologist, and the client will unremittingly change along a process of mutual adaptation among the channels of this communicative shuttle. Furthermore, as will be seen below, the poles of oscillation between the prospective and respective targets are not merely

---

[17] Appadurai (1996), Hannerz (1996) and Bhabha (1994, 1998). For an analysis of the reifying trend set by the Courts on anthropological expertise, see Holden (2011a, b), and below.

[18] Yelvington (2006), Singleton (2006) and Mintz and Price (1992).

two but at least three. In the triadic relationship between client, lawyer and anthropologist somewhat echoes the parallel relationship between the client's culture, law and the culture/cultures of the host society.

The previous arguments are oriented to support three complementary assumptions, respectively that: (1) the anthropologist is required not so much to look at law from afar, from the skies of theoretical or philosophical jurisprudence, but rather in order to acquire the ability to work within law using the idiomatic and transformative tools through which legal experience unfolds; (2) without a correct and relatively faithful interpretation of clients' words, behaviors, and intentions, no legal skill can guarantee genuine success; (3) both legal and anthropological professional expertise, in the absence of a client who is also an aware, co-designing participant and thus a creative socio-cultural agent, might wander blindly through a fictitious maze of interpretive pathways. So that the inevitable result of this occurrence would be the overwhelming of the client's intercultural agency by the eclipsing shadow of the anthropologist's and lawyer's respective cultural incompetence.

Needless to say, the examination of cross-cultural transformations raises the question of authenticity regarding the cultural options developed by the client. In this case, the right to self-representation of one's own cultural identity[19] and the strategic or deceptive use of arguments related to cultural difference simultaneously face each other on opposite sides. Unfortunately, in daily practice the boundary between the two wings of this oppositional pair is often quite vague. Doubtless, autonomy in defining what one's culture is and what its meanings are must be allowed and guaranteed to each subject. Without this prerequisite, the entire discourse on cultural difference would remain baseless. Conversely, cultural belonging would prove to be a terribly mystifying means of caging people within abstract stereotypes useful only to the social control plans of the most powerful and dominant groups. On the other hand, the possibility that the foreign client provides totally inauthentic representations of their cultural assumptions is anything but remote or uncommon. By virtue of their acquired understanding of the legal and practical consequences produced by their self-representations, foreigners can often be induced to claim for completely invented, or at least reshaped, cultural habits for the sole purpose of gaining undue specific advantages. Failure to recognize these dangers would only indicate an ideologically motivated willingness to blindfold oneself and avoid seeing the dark downsides of intercultural dynamics. But taking risks into account does not authorize ignoring the processual significance of cultural competence. Adopting such an attitude would be like "cutting off our feet when we want shoes"—to use Swift's famous words.

An answer to this riddle has not yet been found, if not to dive into the ocean of social reality, dealing with the density of its relationship web and all its troubling uncertainties. Maybe, a good way to encourage sincerity, thus leaving the client's right to identity self-representation undamaged, is to make clear how misrepresenting truth could foster public ignorance about their cultural mindset. In

[19] Chryssochoou (2004).

any case, if the anthropologist or the lawyer misunderstands their culture, the same client/misleading-teller could find themselves ensnared in the dangerous position of being unable to receive any actionable help to solve their intercultural legal conundrums or dilemmas. Furthermore, gaining undue advantages via the false self-representation of one's own culture will only produce short-lived victories. Once implemented, these falsehoods can unleash semantic chain reactions within the normative system and in the semantic context of host cultures. Consequently, their further implications could run over and overturn the client's (and even their community's) fate in ways they could never imagine.

However cunning, no foreign common person,[20] unless they have consummate legal skill in the public affairs of the host country, masters the knowledge required to predict and control all the legal intercultural consequences. With respect to the law, moreover, it is to be observed how this ability is out of reach even for native citizens. The reasons for this incompetence appear quite plain as soon as one considers the way the common people know and obey the law.[21] What they hold is only a folk legal education merged with ethical norms, ethnic habits or standards of decency. The technicalities of legal rules and courts are beyond their knowledge. What allows people not to breach the legal bindings is exactly the same folk education that unfortunately will turn out to be totally inadequate when the shadow of formal law settles over the events of their lives. When the figure of legal rules looms, then the citizens need lawyers too. A collaborative attitude by the client could promote a fruitful effort of coordination among the three actors involved in the scene assumed here. With the support of the appropriate skills, mutual implications and interactions between cultural differences and the law could be dynamically managed and planned. The client could handle their cultural habits with greater creativity by selecting the targets of self-knowledge in the mirror the legal system and its semantic/systemic reactions. All this would enable them to dynamically adapt such a cultural competence relying on a conscious reading of the social environment, thereby using cultural knowledge to produce culture. Of course, by relating one another, all the actors of the intercultural legal relationship would remain reciprocally influenced. The *cultural toolkit* of the Other as well that of the lawyer, and even the legal templates that might be initially assumed to apply to the case, would no longer be the same at the end of the overall process of translation and transaction.[22] In a sense, any actor involved in intercultural encounters could contribute to transforming the changing identity of all the others. What is peculiar to legal experience, is that such a transformation would enjoy immediate social effectiveness. Having a method to inscribe one's own cultural difference into the fabric of legal meanings offers a not insignificant advantage. I refer to the opportunity of making the results of the so-called psycho-social integration processes matched to the legal effects and, therefore, binding on all the people. For the client from a

[20] Unless, perhaps, s/he is an intercultural anthropologist/lawyer.

[21] Tyler (2006).

[22] Ricca (2008, 2013c).

different culture it means that the collaboration with the anthropologist can produce practical effects allowing them to come to terms with the culture and law of the host society.

In spite of possible nationalist objections, practicing an intercultural use of law does not make it bend down to cultural difference. Conversely, it means that national law performs its function in accordance with its prerequisites of legitimacy. I think that by proceeding in the way just outlined, both law and culture would no longer be seen as objects to know from without, by a theoretical or academic gaze, but as means to engender a social space open to an improving and creative coexistence of people's differences. I am aware of the huge epistemological implications and difficulties that such an approach can have for both anthropological and legal research. For the first, because at stake would be the neutrality of the anthropological gaze, which is a real obsession of the discipline, most recently sought through sophisticated discursive and participatory strategies, supposedly suitable for relativizing as far possible the transformative presence/action of the researcher with respect to the situations analyzed in the field and inside the ethnographic report.[23] However, if compared with the exigencies of the people within the intercultural experience lived in multicultural contemporary societies, these refined epistemic strategies truly appear and may prove to be at least unfruitful with respect to the questions raised by the clients of anthropologists. For the second, the risk is to the certainty of legal knowledge itself, which could collapse as a result of the semantic turmoil emerging from an unavoidable but silent interpenetration between the implementation of rule systems and an unknown landscape of self-transforming cultural differences.

In modern societies, the approach to law is quite positivistic (or a 'black letter' one). Despite the animated theoretical debates, legal rule is still closely considered, on average, to be coextensive with the written words of institutional statements or decisions by the courts. Nonetheless, we should be aware that the possibility of such a narrow-sighted approach is, however strikingly, a direct consequence of the close intertwining of law and culture. That a lawyer or a judge can focus their attention on regulatory contents and separate the categorization of facts as an implicit and relatively unproblematic task depends on the communicative and pragmatic efficacy of legal imperatives, which in turn rely heavily on cultural ground. Precisely, the cultural components of the law are treated as 'invisible/mute parts' and are regularly overlooked.[24]

Without the cultural continuity between the invisible/mute parts of the law and the common standards of conduct, perceived and acted as folk moral *dispositives*, the very idea of being in charge of the infringement of a rule unknown to the agent would seem to be, at least, nonsensical. If not so, it only is because the greater part of legal behaviors is learned from early childhood onwards as customs communicated through quotidian relationships—as it were, people breathe, sleep and eat them

[23] See, among others, Crapanzano (2004, 2010), Lassiter (2005), Tedlock (1983, 1995), Denzin (1997), Clifford (1988, 1997) and Dwyer (1987).

[24] In this regard, for further investigations I refer to Ricca (2022b).

along with their daily bread. Thus, the eventuality that intimate interpenetration between law and custom can break or vanish is to be psychologically rejected as a remote occurrence. It would be enough, however, to subtract the demographic conditions that ensure this close co-implication to see mushrooming, as a result, countless inconsistencies and conflicts. Faced with such kind of subverting effects, formalistically considered legal texts would show all their incompleteness and the urgent need to be integrated through the activity of reconstructing their cultural (now intercultural) background. This should induce to recognize how knowing legal rules and culture-laden knowledge/conceptualization of 'facts' are two sides of the same coin, namely legal experience.[25]

In the event of a cultural upheaval, the invisible/mute (which are more than implicit)[26] parts of legal rules show themselves as the semiotic and pragmatic backdrop essential to ensure the communicative and pragmatic effectiveness of law statements. This is exactly the metamorphosis undergone by the law of societies ongoing transformations in a multicultural direction (as an exemplary case, societies grappling with massive immigration flows). When such contingencies occur, the way of looking to the law and using it as a matter of formal standards alone suddenly short circuits. From that point onwards, the object of legal knowledge ought to change and therefore no longer include an implicit assessment but instead the explicit and critical investigation of the plural cultural/cognitive ground of law and rules application. In this task, law and cultural anthropology inevitably find themselves elbow to elbow and compelled to support and conflate each other.[27] The ability of lawyers to continually reshape normative contents, usually downplayed by the formalistic, straightforward approach to law, is then forced to come out. When addressing cultural differences and their claims, this interpretative and even

[25] For an analytical examination of the relationship between the principle '*ignorantia legis non excusat*' and the other on '*ignorantia facti excusat,*' with specific regard to the semantic/cognitive social contract underlying any constitutional order, see Ricca (2018).

[26] It is to be underlined here that these aspects of legal experience are to be considered and labeled as invisible or tacit rather than merely implicit, and this precisely in order to emphasize that they require a specific methodology to be excavated and understood. In this regard see also Ricca (2012).

[27] See Bryant (2001), Ahmad (2007), Blasi (2008), and the issues raised there regarding the relationship between lawyers, clients and anthropologists. As a result of their pioneering and very valuable research, Bryant (2001) and Bryant and Peters (2005 and the related latest updates [2023] at https://fivehabitsandmore.law.yale.edu/jean-and-sues-materials/habits/) propose a kind of toolbox for cross-cultural lawyering. Although such toolbox is extraordinarily useful for an informed and not unconsciously ethnocentric approach with migrant clients and as a psychological guide concerning the communicative attitudes of lawyers, it appears, however, theoretically and anthropologically not thorough enough to convey an in-depth and pragmatically fruitful analysis of the problems nestled in the relationship between cultural difference before the law. See also Piomelli (2006); interesting steps forwards and suggestions, but no attempt to develop a semio-anthropological theory of intercultural-legal translation, can be found in a more recent collection of essays: O'Leary and Martin-Scott (2021). More in tune with my views about the relationship between law and cultural differences, especially from a cognitive and pedagogical perspective, Tully (2020: esp. 237 ff.). With specific regard to the role of religion in cross-cultural lawyering, see Sonne (2018).

cognitive power can no longer dissimulate its potential, its actions and responsibilities, merging with the cultural overtones and hiding in the shadows of common language streaming. It is so partly because, in order to avoid inconsistent results in the application of the rules, lawyers must necessarily highlight the cultural side of the 'legal' and justify the interpretive choices they take on the basis of its assessment. In this case, as noted earlier, what stands to be of the utmost importance is the participatory presence of clients (be they foreigners and/or belonging to a minority culture) within the process of producing legal effects insofar as they are the privileged interpreters of their own cultural features, of which the lawyer belonging to the host country or majority group is in most cases unaware.

On the whole, the above observations entail a specific epistemological orientation precisely because everything (cultures, legal meanings, subjectivities) in the predicament of intercultural relations idiomatically occurs, not as thing, but as a result. The targets of legal and of anthropological research are, respectively, law and culture, which cannot be considered as entities out there and to be put under the lens of objective knowledge cast from without. Instead, both law and culture are to be seen as constitutively inherent to the research findings and the interplay of their emergence with the ongoing production of intercultural experiences. Furthermore, the two-way and multilateral adaptations taking place among the actors of the intercultural legal scene should not be deemed a defective affection of the analytical work. Both the modifying impact of the action by the subject upon the object of analysis and the converse reshaping of the observer's mind by the feedback from the object are not limits for a hypothetical neutral gaze on the world, but rather processive means towards an inevitably creative and dynamic emergence of the real situation to be examined.[28] From this perspective, the problem of epistemic objectivity, proceeding from the subject-object divide, turns out to be a question of responsibility in handling the co-implication flows of relationships between the multiple components involved in the production of (intercultural) experience.[29]

If compared with aspirations for a de-subjectivized knowledge, imagined as the outcome of a cognitive gaze cast from nowhere, the *epistemic fold* just proposed may seem to be a source of a small gains. The return for such epistemological modesty, however, is the ability to use law and culture as means to create a world open to plurality and co-constructive transformation, rather than one existing only in abstract self-bound concepts and their inevitable conflicts.

---

[28] Dewey (1938) and Dewey and Bentley (1949).

[29] More generally, on "truth" as "responsability" see Bakhtin (1993) and Wyshogrod (1998).

3.6 Intercultural Processes and Legal Translation

In order to be fruitfully developed, the intercultural approach requires the ability for intercultural translations to be made on legal grounds. But first, we must proceed in an orderly manner to sort out some intricate semiotic questions regarding categories. The first step, in this direction, is precisely to sort out the ambiguity of linguistic categories. They are general by definition since they are ordinarily figured—at least, in the Aristotelian, western tradition—just as a type gathering many tokens under itself. In this view, each category self-produce boundaries. These, in tun, help determine which tokens are 'in' and 'out' of the type, that is, not inside the category. In short, the boundaries work as rules of semantic relevance/pertinence. From an analytic point of view, the inclusion into a category is determined in accordance with a checklist. This checklist consists of semantic properties/connotations. Each set of properties/connotations defines, then, the requisites of relevance/pertinence. In this way, the circle closes on itself.[30] Up to this point, categorization might appear to be a very simple matter, and above all a rather abstract issue. But closer observation of linguistic and conceptual transformations shows a very different, if not opposite, state of affairs.

Firstly, it is to be underlined that the various properties/connotations are not exclusive of one category. They tend instead to be ubiquitous, that is, simultaneously retraceable in many categorical checklists. This raises some problems for the univocality of categorical membership. One property/connotation may well appear as a feature of several categorical tokens, respectively placed in and out of boundaries shaped for the considered category. This continuity in the definitional/connotative aspects can make the choice to leave out an element or a token from a categorical perimeter or, conversely to put it inside, extremely difficult and precarious. To solve such a dilemma the checklist of properties, connotations and relevance/pertinence rules is substantially of no use. This is because the question is not a formal one, but a matter of preference, ends, and values.[31] Everything depends on the property/connotation on which one decides to put emphasis, among all of those shown by a given element or token. Assume, for this purpose, the task of having to decide whether or not an *item* belongs to a specific category whose elements/tokens share with it a certain feature. The answer will come from how that feature is evaluated. Therefore, if the shared feature is considered central to understanding (the meaning of) the object in question, then it will be placed within the boundaries of that category. Otherwise, the same element will remain outside and its membership, as a token, will be placed within the boundaries of other categories.

The decision whether a feature is central (that is, endowed with denotative value) to an *item* or not is nevertheless a difficult task, moreover characterized, for many

[30] For a more detailed consideration of categorization theory I refer to Ricca (2022a, b), also for bibliographical references to related literature.

[31] Even Jackendoff (1983), a Chomskyan linguist-philosopher, after all, admits this co-implication between categories and values.

reasons, by ever-changing evaluative parameters. Actually, each element consists of a bundle of properties and connotative features. But the number of its constituents is not predetermined once and for all. On the contrary, it is permanently exposed both to an increase or decrease. The cause of these variations stems from the multiple *valency* of properties and connotations. Each of them may actually be attracted or catalyzed by a different category and, as if that were not enough, one feature, as has been said, can simultaneously be a member of multiple categories. The attractive/trans-categorical effect can be triggered by a qualitative or teleological factor corresponding with values (cognitive, aesthetic, ethical and so on), ends or purposes. For example, a flat surface can be taken as a property/connotation of a table (the top), a chair (the seat), a floor, a deck, a tree stump, and so on. Each of the items just mentioned can be ascribed to a category but its 'being flat' could support its subsumption under another one. At the same time, each of those items includes multiple properties/connotations, each of which, in turn, may justify putting the individual item within the perimeter of a different category. Each category, furthermore, can show itself to be an element of another category in an apparently pyramidal but actually radial, although unstable, landscape of memberships.[32] Therefore, under certain conditions, a stump can *become*, and be used as, a table.

As it will perhaps be clear at this point, the capacity to subitize, namely cull an element or a category from the flowing *continuum* of experience, is a process and not a function of a photographic mind of sorts.[33] The categorical ascription of each item, and ultimately its very existence as *that item*, is forged by the choice of which properties/connotations it binds together. This choice depends on the assumptions about the semantic relevance/pertinence criteria to be adopted in determining what those properties/connotations are and, at the same time, on how to forge the differentiations and polarizations between the semiotic circuits (i.e., the perimeter of the contexts of signification/communication) that pivot around and orbit each of these properties/connotations.[34] Thus, if one item emerges, another could disappear. In other words, when we subitize an item, we draw a line to circumscribe a context of relevance. This operation is accomplished in sight of ends and oriented by values. Hence, the individual feature will function as a means to those ends and values. But,

[32]From a historical point of view this radial and trans-categorical belonging of properties and connotations can be found already in Al-Jahiz: see Ricca (2019). On the other hand, trans-categoriality could recall the Deleuzian rizomathic view. Nonetheless, my approach is very distant from Deleuze's post-modern and nomadic approach, also because the semiosis of categorical transformations does not need the Spinozian holistic whole (namely: Deus sive Natura) looming in the speculative pre-assumptions of this author. As for a radial approach to category and categorization see Lakoff (1987) and, of course, Wittgenstein's theory of *family resemblances* and his *theory of colors*.

[33]About the idea of 'subitization' see Lakoff and Núñez (2000).

[34]The referral is to Greimas' idea of 'contrat de véridition' (1983). On the problem of circularity in construing the relationship between intentionality and the target of its unfolding in determining the meaning of that target—otherwise known as Gricean Vicious Cycle—see, among others, Capone (2019, p. 19 ff), Salmani Nodoushan (2022). This topic cannot be addressed here. On this subject I attempted to propose a way out from the vicious circle in Ricca (2023), *forthcoming*.

since all the means with their interactions qualify the ends, in the same vein, the meaning and substance of the ends and values will depend on the context defined by elements/means. So that it could be said that each end, when understood as relational and dynamic functors, also qualifies its own means. This circular co-implication demonstrates that drawing out elements, forms, and categories from the world-continuum is a holistic and partly creative activity akin to sewing, unstitching and darning the fabric of features (properties, connotative qualities, etc.) shaped by the interactions of mind and world through experience.[35]

If we ordinarily live in a world populated by stable categories it is only because of the loops made and tightened by culture, defining the very warp of the fabric that retains and molds the flow of phenomena. Nonetheless, the migratory attitude and the ubiquity of properties/connotations constantly and irresistibly force the categorical fences so as to remold semantic frames of items, categories and the very same properties/connotations. However, all of this occurs along the tension lines engendered inside the mobile weave of meanings. This is because the ubiquitous presence of properties/connotations functions as a metaphorical ground in the process of moving an item from one categorical range to another.[36] The reasons for such a phenomenon will become apparent more specifically below.

Reality and its meanings appear to us like the surface of a tapestry. The shapes of figures correspond to the categories, the threads and their knots to the relationships between the properties/connotations. The weave of threads lies hidden from sight but is the matter and the cause that brings form to the figures. In the same way, the (ever interlocutory) shape of categories and their boundaries are the visible part of the plots interwoven by the relationships among both denotative and connotative features.[37] Continuing this analogy, the sequential tightening of knots that make the weft visible in the tapestry resembles the work of culture. It forges, links up and ties the relationships between denotative and connotative features to pull out categories and ensure an indispensable grip on experience. But the same experience, its novelties and discontinuities, are in turn the cause of the loosening and undoing of the knots tied by cultural action.

When new contexts of effective or potential relationships rip the fabric of categories open, only the loose ends of denotative and connotative features remain. They will then tend to recover other, renewed connections amongst each other, making new links and setting up unprecedented categorical shapes. Once the surface

---

[35] For the metaphor of 'sewing' I have been partly inspired by Ingold 2007, although our respective visions about modernity and the anthropological potentialities of modern categorizing fashion are radically different.

[36] Ricca (2008) and, more generally, Kövecses (2006), Lorusso (2005), Glucksberg (2001), Gibbs (1994) and Ortony (1993).

[37] As regards the dimension of 'intercategoriality', it is more correct to assume 'connotation' as the general definitional condition of all features. For the choice/assessment of what features can assume a 'denotative' role/position within the 'categorical mapping' is only the result of the transactional re-shaping of categorical spectra and their mutual relationships. See, on this crucial topic, Ricca (2022a, p. 187, nt 15).

of experience has been restored, it will still be ready for a forthcoming metamorphosis.

The outbreak of new semantic landscapes and the bursting of cultural difference into the imaginary and material boundaries of a social group have more than a vague semantic proximity. The 'irruption' of cultural difference on the stage of both the present and the future always produces a rent in the lived environment. The whole, namely the apparent void so made in it, will immediately ask to be refilled. The attempt and, at the same time, the temptation to re-pack it with unilateral cultural denotation/connotations will be as extraordinarily strong as the defectiveness and the inadequacy of ethnocentric action ordered to achieve its result. On the contrary, what is needed in these situations is the ability to look across and under the differences, facing each other, to see the loose ends of the connotative fabric. This will only be possible by engaging in the cross-cultural mending of the rips caused by the appearance of the Other on the multicultural scene of everyday life. But drawing new semantic threads and tying new semantic knots under the surface of the 'resulting reality' are activities similar, if not coextensive, to the work of translating. For translation always implies bringing to the surface the contexts of signification underlying utterances or words. This operation is necessary to enable the translator to identify as many features as possible to disambiguate the potential meanings of words against their background in the source language, and then re-create a context of sense suited to convey an equivalent of original meaning in the target language.[38] Since it is impossible to transplant a word from one world of experience to another integrally and without any alteration, the translator must linguistically produce a situation that can be interpreted in such a way as to generate a representation as close or comparable as possible to the that enshrining the original meaning. But the equivalence will never be complete, even in functional terms.[39]

The words of the target language have their specific, culturally situated disposition to meaning. In effect, it would be extremely misleading to think that the words of another language are fungible as simple and neutral means for achieving the same end, in this case the (translated) meaning.[40] Linguistic transposition always implies a transformation. The aims of translation are achievable not only through linguistic equivalence. On the contrary, the skill of the translator constantly works and even bets on the experiential attitude of the receiving subject involved in the translation process, precisely the attitude to re-invent a 'cross-cultural world.' All this, however, raises the following question: "How is it that two diverse language-worlds can conflate in a common one by translation?" The answer—in my view—is that the only possible conflation brings together an invention of a third world beside the original two, though not over, or through a holistic inclusion, of them. In other

[38] Eco (2008, 2003/2010).

[39] See Keane (2007, p. 223 ff.); but also, from a legal point of view, Teubner (1998, p. 11 ff.) with regard to the legal transplants and the related irritants.

[40] For some interesting observations about the inadequacy of the functionalistic approach applied to legal translation and comparative understanding of different legal worlds see Constantini (2012).

words, if translation does not fail, it is because human beings have the ability to create and recreate worlds of experience and meaning from a complex of semantic features narratively deployed even across diverse languages. Of course, this ability never provides perfectly reliable or complete results, but neither does it miss the mark entirely.[41] Despite the omnipresent dangers of misleading or misunderstanding caused by incorrect translations, humans have been shown to prefer the danger of not understanding some things over the certainty of not understanding anything. If it may be put so, the novelty of the third (intercultural) world resulting from translation is the good side of the imperfection and of the limits inherent in translation itself.

Moreover and once again, if from a philosophical or epistemological point of view this modest achievement could be considered to be a poor reward for what might be some quite onerous translation efforts, yet and still it holds significant pragmatic value in the intercultural spaces of experience. This can be appreciated by taking into account the consequences of translation as a communicative act rather than as a form of essential and static semantic correspondence between the source language and the target language. In fact, this second criterion for evaluating translation quality is especially found in literary translation, which is assessed not so much as regards its immediate and remote practical implications as for its inherent fidelity in transposing the original text into a foreign language. Intercultural translation, particularly when related to legal issues, is focused on and aimed at the resolution of social issues. It is, and should be, conceived as a means of controlling and shaping the environmental consequences of one's actions.

As noted above, the meaning intended by social actors (native or immigrant) as pointed to by their behaviors or words, always strives to fit into a new situation, precisely, the multicultural situation, which will in turn inevitably transform that meaning. The authentic significance of those words or behaviors is thus to be read not only by looking back or according to a faithful interpretation of the subject's intention, but also from the imagined future, or in the mirror of the potential subsequent implications of social actors' conduct. And if it is true in general, it is even more so within the intercultural predicament, where the act of meaning has to necessarily go through a process of cultural translation. In other words, in such circumstances, the object of meaning and the semantic transformation induced by subsequent practices show the utmost co-extensiveness. Not being able to transfer the original message as a 'whole' is therefore, in a sense, the other side of the coin of the fruitful transformativeness inherent in intercultural translation oriented to achieve pragmatic goals. Its epistemological modesty embodies its characteristic reality in the very way in which it occurs.

As shall be shown, the creation of a 'third world of meaning' goes through a process of metaphorical transposition between diverse schemes of categorizations. But shaping a metaphor always implies choosing a semantic ground suited to join certain features of categorical spectra at stake. Hence the metaphorical ground is never discovered, but rather devised or re-invented. Therefore, when the translation

---

[41] With reference to intercultural translation in the legal field, see Van Brakel (2006).

has practical, social, and legal consequences, the metaphorical transposition encapsulated within it is politically connoted. The social actors are then called to produce the metaphor collaboratively, because only a good degree of symmetrical participation can provide a reliable process of translation (meaning semantic transformation) for all the subjects involved. By remolding the categorical boundaries through the metaphorical transfers between semantic fields, people shape a world of practical consequences and possible intercultural ways of cohabitation. In so doing, each social actor does not merely represent his own cultural features but, so to speak, oozes culture through their creative living. It is so because culture is not only a repertoire of practices modelled on the past or defined according to pre-acquired knowledge. Producing culture is coextensive to living. The cultural function is a natural attribute of human beings. It is continually in the making and proceeds by feeding on meanings woven and rewoven, straddling past and future, the new and the old, existential horizons and memory. However, engendering intercultural spaces of experience by translating words and behaviors into legal schemes is neither a simple task nor a scene that can be drawn freehand. On the contrary, intercultural legal translations require the setting in motion of specific processive activities without which they could disintegrate. As to what these procedural passages, in my view, could be, I now turn.

3.7 Three Methodological Steps Towards the Intercultural Use of Law

3.7.1 Crossed Narratives and Semiotic Dis-compositions

The multicultural situation requires the production of an intercultural context of signification, namely an inter-contextual ground. But stimulating the unfolding of such a communicative backdrop presupposes initiating an intensive effort of crossed-narrative practices. The aim of this first step, in order to obtain an intercultural legal translation/transaction, is to promote the surfacing of cultural knowledge unreflexively and/or unconsciously acted out by the people. This step is necessary to prevent legal qualification from being limited to a mere accounting of the morphological features of words and behaviors enacted by the people, whether foreigners or belonging to cultures other than that of the dominant groups. The danger lurking in an exclusive consideration of morphological evidence is that of an ethnocentric interpretation of the so-called deep semantic referents of actions conducted by the Other.[42] This is because the processes of categorization, as well as those of legal qualification, are selective and value-oriented. Moreover, the phonetic or material features of the Other's conduct are only the tip of the iceberg kept afloat by a huge submerged plexus of semiotic implications. These implications

[42] On the "deep reference" within translation processes, see Eco (2003/2010).

form the context of signification without which it would be impossible to disambiguate the meaning of what an individual says or does.[43]

In order to assess the context of signification, however, it is completely insufficient to simply observe the material scenario that hosts the situation currently under consideration. The constituent components of the context are also imaginary. They unfurl in the semiotic environment experienced by social actors, unfolding along the traces of meaning and experience etched in the landscapes of memory. Indeed, in every gesture or word enacted by an individual, countless traces (a network of signs) are condensed and managed unconsciously by the brain to give rise to an act of meaning concentrated in an (at least apparently) instantaneous perception of meaning. An example can make this idea more explicit.

Suppose that an individual identifies a deep, broad ditch in the ground by calling it an 'impact crater.' Any individual of average education looking at that ditch could say they are seeing an impact crater, as if its semantic constitutive features were concentrated in that thing dug in the earth. Nevertheless, their eyes see only a ditch, while the categorical features of 'impact crater' require them to make a long journey through time and space, imagining at a minimum a large meteorite that came from remote outer space and struck the Earth millions of years ago. Actually, they see the impact crater with their mind's eye.[44] The context of meaning related to the words "impact crater" is thus to be identified with a 'mentalized environment,' consisting of signs organized to produce meaning.

If previously unknown, understanding the expression 'impact crater' when uttered by someone demands the illumination of all the darkened (and mute) parts of the discourse, the so-called implicit, stored in the speaker's mind and integrated into the context of signification. Consequentially, limiting the inquiry on meaning to the external or material components of a communicative scenario would be utterly narrow-minded. That ditch, however broad and deep, would remain merely a ditch. Of course, to establish that a ditch is an impact crater is not only a 'factual-material' description. It contains instead several normative indications to engage future practices. For example, filling that big hole could be prohibited, since it would constitute the elimination of an important source of data about Earth's history. Something similar occurs to the sentences spoken or the behaviors enacted by people. To correctly (but always approximately) interpret them, we must travel to the memory landscapes as suggested by the vision of a meteorite; as well as project ourselves into future horizons to be painted with the brushes of imagination. If we are to unravel the skein of semiotic connections underlying the words and behaviors of Others, we must construct narratives that can provide contextually appropriate scenarios to support the communication of meaning. Within infra-cultural communications, all actors are potential builders of narrative scenarios. People's main

[43] I further developed this argument in Ricca (2018, 2022b).

[44] Furthermore, only the eyes of the mind are seeing even the simple ditch without and before qualifications. The eyes as sensory organs receive only signs in the form of light stimuli. But it is the brain that infers from those stimuli the vision of a ditch.

purpose, at least on average, is to disambiguate the potential meanings of words or behaviors, since none of them are capable, in absolute terms and by itself, of conveying precise meaning. Of course, elaborating scenarios is a delicate work, and it must, at all costs, avoid the danger of superimposing biases or stereotypes, or simply errors of judgement regarding the intentions of the 'speaker' or 'actor.' For this reason, it is important to listen to and promote the production of explicative narratives from the individuals who are to be interpreted.

In intercultural encounters, it is extremely important to improve the production of narratives. Everyone has a spontaneous tendency to surround the words or the behavior of other individuals, sketching semiotic backgrounds, namely plots, yarns and stories. In general, these assumptions tend to be more or less correct. Nevertheless, misunderstandings are widespread even among people belonging to relatively homogeneous cultural circuits. When dealing with subjects from different cultures, the 'narrative filling' of the Other's semiotic background with one's own cultural knowledge can often be fatal to the understanding of Otherness. On the other hand, good or bad, narrative filling occurs in any case. Therefore, to avoid biased overlapping or ethnocentric readings, it is of utmost importance to urge the Other to become a narrator, that is, an active semiotic agent.

Narratives make so that entire populations of semantic elements come to the fore, so as to give backdrop and experiential surroundings to words or behaviors when previously only morphological appearances and definitions were considered. The abundance of features (properties, qualitative connotations, etc.) thus acquired reveals the invisible/mute contexts of signification, the landscapes of overtones, that would otherwise remain imperceptible, making it impossible to conceive of the indexical background unconsciously employed by Others. In addition, the greater breadth of 'semantic ingredients' allows creative semantic equivalences and analogies to grow and flourish between the cultural and linguistic systems of the individuals involved in the intercultural relationship. The more detailed the contextual background, the more the disambiguation of actions' and words' meanings becomes possible. Only under the condition of a sufficient level of inter-contextualization are social actors likely to achieve an adequate ability to understand the deep references hidden within the actions of Others. Of course, even in this case, there remains the difficulty of culling from the bundle of semantic ingredients those most salient and conducive to intercultural translation/translation. Discovering what is critical or salient and what is not, however, necessarily constitutes an intercultural undertaking. Precisely because of this intercultural aspect, the issue requires a commitment to distance oneself from one's own cultural background. At the same time, it should be underscored that any possibility of interpreting Otherness can only stem from a pre-existing knowledge of the interpreter. This means, in other words, that it is not possible to provide a culturally and cognitively neutral point of observation.

In light of this conclusion, should it be inferred that all efforts to immunize oneself from the tendency toward ethnocentrism are in vain? The answer is far from obvious. To escape such a paradox, it seems that the only way forward is to systematically take into account the possibility of intercultural contamination, which

I nevertheless regard as coextensive with any work of (cultural) translation. I believe that the chance of achieving an intercultural and politically symmetrical outcome is not a matter of all or nothing, but rather of degree and method. To distance ourselves from our cognitive schemes and cultural habits, we should read the narratives of the Other against the many elaborated by us and about us, so as to clarify ourselves why our own cultural schemes are the way they are. This work would generate a critical disposition capable of paving the way for the production of one's own narratives to be addressed, then, to the Other. The goal of this discursive activity should be to explain to people from different cultures what we recognize in ourselves or what we see as similar to them in relation to what they have told us about themselves. This exchange of self-descriptive narratives could trigger a potentially endless ping-pong effect that, nevertheless, could enhance the actors' ability to assess the salience of the connotations (to be selectively taken also as denotations) considered when trying to understand the Other.

Engaging seriously in self-trans*duction* (trans-*lations*) into the semiotic landscapes of the Other, if carried out in a truly bidirectional way, wills likely produce an estrangement effect. Consequently, one could find traces of the Other in oneself. Yet, despite hasty judgments, this would not be the epiphenomenon of discovery activities, but rather an act of creation and/or self-modification. The transplant of some semantic ingredients (properties, connotative qualities, etc.) from the Otherness' universe of discourse would be an effect of the cross-narrative process and its self-transformative proceeding. In any case, reaching this stage-it should be reiterated-is a matter of degree and method, rather than a true/false alternative. For the reality and truthfulness of this interplay of mutual interpretations is the creative result of the same continuous and potentially endless process.

The use of cross-narrative methodology is not new to anthropologists, who have dwelt at length on its distorting effect and, at the same time, its inevitability in the construction of ethnographic reports.[45] Actually, the very presence of the researcher in the field produces a semiotic effect of changing the modes of self-representation and narrative for both her/him and the subjects under investigation. This presence, even when mute, would already constitute by its mere being part of the experience, as an implicit narrative. The reality of ethnographic experience will result as implicitly co-construed regardless. Nor have the post-modern technicalities of editing and drafting the ethnographic texts escaped this co-construction effect and its possible, distortive consequences. This is the case both for (a) minimalist and multivocal narratives, where the corresponding report tends to relate without filters or clarification the original voices of the studied subjects; and (b) for the collaboration of the 'native' in writing the ethnographic account with the researcher (collaborative ethnography).[46] In my opinion, however, these problems will continue to haunt scientific anthropological inquiry and its imagery as long as it is still assumed to be an epistemic strive to reach towards objectivity. More precisely, an objectivity

[45] Clifford and Marcus (1986), Bibeau and Corin (1994) and Zenker and Kumoll (2010).

[46] See above, in note.

intended as a result achieved through a methodology of hermeneutical inquiry of the subject aimed at providing a final cognitive 'product' to be packaged discursively in analytical-descriptive terms.[47] What if, conversely, the transformative subject-object relationship and its dynamics were no longer regarded as a limitation of knowledge, but as a constitutive element of both itself and its object? And again, what if the object of anthropological inquiry itself was understood as an ever-open outcome of that dynamic relation (though not in the sense of a normative and/or ontological phenomenological entity)? Compelling though the question may be, I will not examine this from the general point of view of epistemological foundations of cultural anthropology. It seems to me that this would be, in the end, a pointless exercise, since trying to deny or at least demythologize the problem of the factual description of cultures would be to call into question the very same discipline of cultural anthropology, wrapping the entire discourse in a circular chain of self-contradictions. Rather, I hazard the guess that it is preferable to point out how the inherent self-transformation of the object of anthropological inquiry is perfectly suited to the experiential dynamics of intercultural relationships placed within the legal framework.

The inclusion of cultural differences in the semantic spectrum of legal provisions, achieved by having narratives travel to and through the minds of others, is in itself an inescapable need in any social situation characterized in a multicultural sense. Immersed in this situation, every cultural element, as a sign, is necessarily vulnerable or open to inherent transformation. Multicultural society is itself a new context of signification, at least when viewed from an inner cultural perspective. In a sense, 'multicultural' is necessarily already 'intercultural,' if only because interculturality itself is an effect of the inevitable multicultural relationships that occur within social space. Actually, when the 'multicultural' or 'cultural Otherness' appears in the horizon of individuals' quotidian life, 'interculturality' is already happened. In this scenario, bringing to the surface one's cultural background to intercept legal effects and, before that, legal qualifications, becomes a means to realize environmental and reflexive changes. The authenticity and the truthfulness of cultural accounts should be evaluated not on the grounds of their conformity to essences forged in a hypothetical ethnic past, but rather according to the degree of self-recognition allowed to the social actors by the legal and practical effects taking shape within their intercultural relationship. This is because the real significance of cultural characteristics placed in a new multicultural context is not given by their rigidity or static nature, but, on the contrary, by the actual possibility they offer people to change in order to (somehow) maintain their 'being themselves:' that is, to adapt.

The task of adaptation, however, is a necessity for everyone, both natives and newcomers, dominant and weaker groups alike. Everyone contains their own culture (viz, is from a culture), but the very pith of 'culture' is the 'production of culture.' In other words, cultural competence is not something possessed, like a collection of instruments, but a creative ability by which people live, reproducing through

[47] Ricca (2022a).

cumulative and renewing modifications none other than themselves. Cultural narratives are thus the consequence and at the same time the ingredients of the intercultural context of life, and thereby of its transactional transformations.

In legal experience, the degree of reflexivity inherent in narratives and processes of synchronic metamorphosis is extraordinarily high. Since law generates normative effects, the redefinition of categorical boundaries, whether related to language tout court or specifically to law, affects all those involved in intercultural relationships. Adjusting the semantic implications of the 'letter of the law' means changing both the signification and the chorology of social world(s).[48] In many cases, cross-cultural translation produces a shift in the determination of which among the features of a legal category should serve as the salient axis of its semantic spectrum. This shift will, from then on, have a general scope. That is, it will impact, at least potentially, all subjects of law, including the lawyer or judge who has been dealing with a foreigner's case. And it is even (almost) superfluous to mention that the same applies to the anthropologist engaged in intercultural legal assistance, since they too are a citizen and subject of law. This polyphonic interweaving of narratives leads, therefore, to direct consideration of the second step in the intercultural use of law, namely cross-contextualizations.

3.7.2 *Crossed Contextualizations*

The iteration of narrative efforts, on both sides of the cross-cultural relationship, allows each involved social actor to proactively interpenetrate with the contexts of signification used by the Other. In each case, ongoing iterations are usually accompanied by narrative shifts as well as extensions or reductions in recounted facts, underlying semiotic circuits, and the related semantic ingredients. These communicative shifts are not only strategic, but often have cognitive value. The retrieval of the individuals' knowledge from the landscapes of their memory, when carried out with the goal of making it understood by the Other, takes shape in the mirror of their narratives. This means that both the Self and the history of the Self are reread in sequence as a response to the symmetrical attempt at self-understanding made by the Other. But the Self also implies the world within which the mind is embodied. What takes place, then, is a latent re-creation of one's own life context oriented to dynamically interplay with that of the Other. This process, however, never comes to a close. While maintaining the self-consciousness of difference in each part of the

[48] Each word encapsulates instructions about the 'use of the world' and draws, in this way, the features of the space we are living in. Every word or utterance, therefore, molds the space and the spatial dimension of experience by projecting its guidelines of action through time, both backwards into the past and forward towards the future. Since culture is a bundle of meanings, then space and culture are therefore coextensive, in the sense that every cultural doing engenders its space. On this topic, however, see below, Chaps. 4, 6. See also Ricca, Semiotics and the space-time ingredients of legal experience cit.

relationship, it fosters the emergence of an inter-subjective context, or rather, a crossed context of meaning and action. This is precisely the arising of a thirdness coextensive with intercultural social and legal space.

As the semiotic contours of a context of cross-cultural experience begin to emerge, the possibility of a potential horizon of universalization simultaneously looms. But universalization profiles can only be the result of creative activity, and not a semantic framework arising from the mechanical overlapping of the respective cultural repertoires at play; or even the discovery of a buried pre-existing essence, as if it were an archaeological find. The possibility of (as well as the propensity for) universalization, if present and implemented cross-culturally, hovers up astride the frontier of social encounters between current social differences, rather than in the sky of abstract comparisons between the social actors' respective past. This is because crossed contextualization is to be regarded as a discursive response to a new, multicultural, situation. Similarly, and also by virtue of legal tools, symbolic circuits can trigger further reactions within social, pragmatic dynamics, along a circular and infinite process that unfolds dialectically between material action and communication. This means that each stage of this transformative game will not achieve a final synthesis of differences. Rather, it will function as a reflective dome suitable for relentlessly promoting socio-cultural differentiation in a multidirectional way. Like a flight of stairs, each step trod will simultaneously be the point of arrival and departure for the next (socio-cultural) step. The skyline of cross-cultural universalization will thus be destined to continually move beyond itself.

Within a circuit of cross-contextualizations developing along the communicative paths described above, no one will be the same as before. In this regard, however, it should be noted that the social actors involved in the relationship could not have remained unchanged, even without the unfolding of a purposefully and symmetrically managed cross-cultural encounter. For the intercultural relationship and the related metamorphosis take place in any case. Even those who become racists or xenophobes, when facing the irruption of Other in their lived space, are however involved in such kind of transformation. 'Racism,' after all, is a verbal icon that summarizes a number of subsequent behaviors arising as reactions from the appearance of Other on social stage. This 'figure' of interculturality can be described as unreflective or unconscious, as it does not rely upon translation and the cognizant understanding of difference, but rather on deliberate ignorance and the discriminatory stereotyping of it. The penchant for static identities, from both sides of the intercultural relationship, is the constant and inevitable landing place for similar chains of uncontrolled psycho-cultural reactions. Often, the identities portrayed throughout these behavioral sequences are presented as ingrained in the authenticity of a cultural past, which is not so much a historical entity, but rather a communicative and strategic dispositive—an invention that has its roots more in the depicted diversity of the Other than in the actual past or memory of either party.[49] The bitter reward of such a unintended interculturality is, however, nothing but conflict.

Cross-contextualizations, when actually coming out from symmetrical discursive exchanges, involve a primary role of the social actors throughout the process of reciprocal submission and negotiation of their cultural features and claims. Using the law's power to claim and implement their respective needs can, however, bump against several hindrances. Within all new contexts or life environments, cultural meanings change as a consequence of adaption. The implications of Chinese culture in Uganda are surely different from those transpiring in Germany. This is almost a truism. In other words, there is no such thing as a description of a culture at play that could be considered as objective and helpful anywhere and at any time. Precisely this circumstance gives a cognitive basis to the right of self-representation of the features inherent in one's own cultural identity.

The recognition of the right to cultural self-representation can seem obvious, for no culture is a monolith; conversely, each holds a pluralistic semiotic kernel. Actually, everyone can live *in* and *through* the same culture in different ways and yet not to cease to belong to it. Culture is a living phenomenon, and self-transformation is integral to its continuity and self-recognition over time and through different spaces. Within multicultural encounters, very significant and substantial alterations can result, however. Above all, it is to be noted that they do not progressively mature within a (relatively) homogenous communicative circuit. On the contrary, these changes are often abrupt, unpredictable, and exposed to the contingency and various opportunities of negotiations that the case casts on individual existences. Although contemporary cultural life as defined by post-modern anthropology is inherently and conceptually diasporic and uprooted from a specific sense of place,[50] I do not think, however, that the transformation, the fact of being embedded in an un-located in-between, can acceptably be considered as an ontological condition. The reification of transformative flows-as the "transcultural" paradigm seems to presuppose-would make them mere frozen tautologies. Hence, their representation could become nothing more than a sequence of apodictic statements, not least because their semantic ground of departure and their condition of arrival would remain indecipherable or by assumption, out of sight. However much creolized, the transformation process etches traces into the memory. Traces that, in turn and if necessary, are mobilized as semiotic tools to deal with the individual's personal present. In other words, the putative *in-between* is not independent of any time and space. Time and space, as semiotic dimensions, are condensed inside the memory process and dynamically presentified/actualized by the subjects to adapt to the challenges of the environment. But in order to be understood, they must be taken

[49] Regarding memory and cultural devices, see Meusburger et al. (2011); Cattel and Climo (2002); Wyshogrod (1998); Boyarin (1994); and, more generally, Schacter (1995).

[50] See Appadurai (1991, 1996) and Gupta and Ferguson (1997a, c). From these texts forward, the multilocal and diasporic fashion of cultural identity is a sort of mantra of cultural anthropology. For a survey of this question and its developments within literature, see Khagram and Levitt (2008).

for their own 'whence and whither,' even though these semiotic space-time reference points may be only hypothetical, both for an outside observer and-as shown above-for the *wayfarer*'s mind.

However, it cannot be ignored that, when confronted with law and its power, individuals claiming for their cultural differences often use the 'diversity argument' strategically. Here, then, an uncritical and superficial recognition of the right of self-representation can give rise to communicative conduct bordering on strategic mystification, aimed at evading legal obligations or gaining undue advantages. Nowadays, cultural self-defense has become not only an argumentative tool for lawyers' reasoning, but also a rhetorical and psychological instrument to position oneself in the public domain. It is well known that its use may yield practical and weighty consequences. Cultural features can modify the legal qualification of a fact, thus also its binding consequences. People know this. And it is precisely because of this know-how that whenever the law has to cope with cultural differences, the collaboration between lawyer and anthropologist cannot be disregarded. Falling prey to the deception of a mystified representation of cultural features or, on the other hand, ignoring the Other's cultural needs, are opposite situations equally fraught with problems. Both could lead to a certain degree of 'heterogenesis of ends' in the application of the rules (indeed, to a change in their original motivational patterns), as they would be used to ground misrepresentations and mis-categorizations of the psychosocial situations at stake and the actual meanings they are made of. In any case, the lawyer, whether multiculturally well intentioned or instead deaf to the Other's cultural difference, can make huge *blunders*. To avoid this, the support of the anthropologist may be very useful insofar as it is oriented not to portray a figure of granitic cultural evidence, but rather to assess the paths of transformation traced by the cultural knowledge of individuals.

The last point is, in my view, of the utmost importance and shows the deep divide between the intercultural legal approach I propose from the multicultural one, the same from which also originates, *inter alia*, the judicial practice of the so-called 'cultural defenses.' The argument undergirding the so called cultural evidence, along with the use of cultural tests, are some of the most typical tools used by courts inclined toward a multicultural approach (e.g., Canada, the United States, the United Kingdom, and others) when addressing the claim of cultural difference.[51] The confirmation of cultural evidence, obtained by specifically arranged screening tests, is directed precisely to verify that the self-representation of one's own culture is not a strategic dissimulation. The danger in this practice is, though, that evidence can be achieved according to normative and frozen patterns of culture, against which any alteration, negotiation or transformation acted by the social actors could be branded as an inconsistent deviation. The question hovers around what is to be considered as 'evidence.'

The tendency to assume an empirical concept of evidence tends inevitably to reduce the 'proof of authenticity' of cultural features to a morphological matter. This

[51] Foblets and Renteln (2009a), Renteln (2004) and Ruggiu (2020).

implies that the cultural claim is taken as authentic and genuine only if a correspondence can be found between the representation given by the individual and the usages certified by the cultural tradition of belonging through rituals, normative or religious texts, codified practices and so on. Following this line of reasoning, the likelihood of going down the path of stereotyping and the reduction of cultural competence to a repertoire of frozen patterns is unfortunately extremely high.[52] Not by chance, this is the very rise and fall shown by the multicultural experience of many courts of law. What is worse, it ends up forcing even professional anthropological expertise onto the tracks of folkloric or exotic accounts about the authenticity of cultural claims and related culture.[53] When anthropologists attempt to provide explanations of cultural behaviors and related material evidence that are not immediately recognizable as signs of diversity traceable to dominant canons in different cultural circuits, they run the risk of being accused by the judge of complicity in the minority's alleged attempts to escape legal consequences. If such problems arise, it is because the logic of the multicultural approach is grounded on an experience and often a tragic past of conflicts, where the clash of cultures is catalyzed by the opposition between identities reified around outward symbols or features of diversity (skin color and embellishments, veils, garments, rituals, sexual behaviors, buildings, and so on). In this way, cultural competence and its dynamics undergo a kind of metonymic treatment, in which culture is reified as a thing and reduced to the subset of its material projections.[54] But this thinghood is only the epitome of the fictive boundaries of identities strategically forged for self-distinction against the enemy and, in most cases, it has nothing to do with the meaning actually expressed, and perceived, by the individuals or groups through their cultural spectrum. When material features are used as contrastive symbols for the purposes of struggle the real reasons behind their cultural significance result semantically transfigured. Often the icons of difference become weapons in the war for power over social space, so much so that they almost completely lose their original anchors to the entire semantic backdrop of the cultural life of those who wield them. The only meaning of these cultural symbols, or at least the predominant one, reflexively becomes that of a tool of self-identification to be used to orchestrate antagonism among social actors from different cultures. Thus, the flaming apparition of the identities and their figures on the proscenium of social conflict causes original cultural background and their meaning to vanish. The substantive reasons for cultural and social polarization, the very ones that could lead to a solution, then become invisible and give way to a purely formal clash between identities deprived of their meaningful roots: a clash fueled only by the desire to superficially assert themselves against each other.

The radicalization of instrumental contrasts between reified identities, however, is to be seen as a pre-existing object and not merely an effect of cultural tests. Nevertheless, in the end, the request of empirical and/or normative evidence only

[52] Foblets and Renteln (2009b).

[53] Holden (2011a, b).

[54] Appadurai (1986).

encourages the emphasizing of morphologically reified and essentialized cultural characteristics, which become dangerously prone to show an irreducible incommensurability of the pre-asserted differences. Suffice it to consider, in this regard, that one of the most decisive criteria for passing evidence tests is the demonstration that the failure to implement the habit claimed for cultural reasons would provoke a sanction for the individuals belonging to a particular minority group. Cultural behavior is thus assumed to be equivalent to normative/legal behavior, and thus in the most rigid and immutable version that it is possible to assume. But this of course triggers, in turn, a circular effect which cements the cultural stiffness. [55] In an attempt to find a space of idiomatic legitimacy within the general public space, cultural communities often engage in hyper-orthodox self-figuration, dressing up and making their own, to some extent, the same stereotypes indirectly imposed by the courts of justice through the search for outwardly recognizable and fixed cultural evidence. But along this path, culture officially considered within legal discourse ends up becoming a caricature of itself, nothing more than a set of folkloric practices and exotic behavioral habits often traced back to religion only to reinforce their legitimacy vis-à-vis secular legal systems and influence related claims of religious freedom. And yet, when the multicultural social landscape has already been transformed into a confusing puzzle of paratactic juxtapositions between incommensurable actions and untranslatable meanings, cross-cultural contextualizations inevitably become pure chimeras. In this context, even the so-called 'cultural accommodation,' so often invoked as a tool for resolving cultural disputes, ends up being nothing more than a kind of machine that churns out compromises based not so much on the transaction of meanings, but rather upon the 'commoditization' and instrumentalization of (almost fictitious) cultural representations.[56] In this political and ideological milieu, so often bandied about as a positive result of multicultural judicial accommodations, the correspondence between the term 'cultural' and the lenses through which people view the world can get lost.

'Culture' is not just this or that behavior, thing or word. Before that, it signifies the aptitude of the semiotic eye itself to adaptively decipher the environment through which the organism carries on its life. Only by virtue of its pervasive action does cultural knowledge function as a mute agency embodied in the relationships between people and the world around them. In short, nothing is found outside of culture, especially those activities that are carried out without awareness because of their being embedded in previously acquired life habits. Ultimately, the crucial issue posed by 'culture' probably lies in the 'non-evidence' quality of its real characteristics, those that are ceaselessly at work in human beings' grappling with the problems of daily life. The main issue to be investigated when 'multiculturality' (to be intended as a state of affairs, as distinct from multicultural*ism*) makes its

[55]The same problem of reification and ossification of cultural traits affect the definition of 'indigeneity' involved, as a premise, in the protection of indigenous peoples' rights. I will address this topic below, Chap. 7.

[56]Ricca (2013a).

appearance on the social scene is the semiotic distance between different modes of representing and making the world. Since the categorical and conceptual schemes that people use are largely invisible/mute, the intersubjective semiotic distance can only be bridged through deliberate commitments and efforts to extract the semantic coordinates of cognitive and behavioral habits from implicit cultural landscapes. Multicultural contingency can only be overcome by giving utterance to the invisible/mutual parts of cultural competence almost unawares put into action by individuals.

However deeply hidden from the agents themselves and managed unconsciously, knowledge of the world is in any case a tool for being in relationship with a world, in this case the multicultural world inhabited by Others. This is tantamount to saying that within the multicultural social and communicative environment, world features are forged, at least partly, by the actions of Other people and, therefore, through their behavioral and conceptual schemes. It is precisely for this reason that any understanding of that lifeworld aspiring to be recognized as authentic can only be intercultural: namely the result of a thoughtful and transactional combination of the ingredients that are indispensable to give rise to processes of cross-contextualization. In the same vein, it should be reiterated, the correspondence of cultural feature to an authentic cultural background is not akin to membership in a morphological catalogue, identifiable and certified by some kind of reliable labeling. On the contrary, the authenticity (and reliability) of self-representations must be assessed by carefully weighing the pragmatic consistency displayed by the involved individuals during the process of transformation of their respective cultural knowledge. Undoubtedly, assessing the plausibility of intercultural transformations is a thorny issue. But it would be at least absurd to make this difficulty a reason, or even an alibi, for limiting cultural competence and reducing it to a folkloric record of stereotyped forms. Culture is an ongoing creation whose continuity is rooted in its change and its change, in turn, in a cumulative experiential (though underground and often tacit) continuity. When viewed from above, the current global cross-cultural process is simply the 'normal' cultural process, and it will probably appear that way from a future historical perspective, when the globalizing effects of contemporary migration flows will already be 'the past.'

Human history has been constantly marked and brought forward by cultural encounters and exchanges. The exceptionalism of multiculturalism today is only a contingent aspect,[57] as its appearance on the theater of public awareness is an

[57] Such contingency, however, does not mean that cultural differences coexisting in social landscapes can be dubbed 'superdiversities.' The linguistic sliding from 'contingent' to 'super' is tantamount to that from 'contingent' to 'exceptional.' But differences are neither 'exceptional' nor 'not-normal'. Contingency is only a step along history and new situations that will represent a future normality. 'Super-' or 'exceptional' evoke, instead, a sort of ontological being-out-of-order. But no cultural difference can be labelled as out of order or abnormal, even because the implicitly supposed 'normality' could prove to be, at a closer historical inspection, only illusory. Differences 'are', and so being, they are also to be understood and translated to allow their coexistence. See Vertovec (2007, 2014). Despite Vertovec's (2014) efforts to give the formula 'super-diversity' a merely methodological and classificatory signification, it remains much less epistemologically and politically innocent than he would like to make it appear. See, in this regard, Spickard (2017).

inherently intercultural phenomenon. Another question, however, is whether implicit interculturality is apt to omnidirectionally mobilize the invisible/mutual parts of cultural knowledge so as to give rise to the emergence of intercultural contextualizations. For all of the reasons outlined above, I am inclined to answer this question negatively. The objectification of invisible/mutual parts of cultural competence, when oriented toward cross-contextualizing interculturality, requires deliberate efforts to translate and transact one's knowledge. Interculture itself should thus constitute a public purpose, symmetrically and polyphonically pursued. Giving voice to the invisible/mute parts of the Other's culture is actually an extremely difficult task. It requires the utmost care to avoid silencing differences in the accidental cacophony of an unconscious overlapping of one's own criteria of judgment and values with Otherness.

Being deaf to the Otherness of the Other is a pervasive danger in intercultural relations because power differences often and inevitably divide the groups and individuals involved in both the social dialectic and the related transcultural process of translation/transaction. All the more so, the looming 'opportunity' of domesticating translations regarding the invisible/muted parts of cultural competence increases significantly within legal discourse. Indeed, the basic legitimacy provided by the use of the authoritative words of law ends up fueling the temptation to ignore or at least 'tame' foreign languages and cognitive categories. However, this last further reference to the invisible/mute parts of cultural competence and their role within legal categorization leads directly to the third stage of the cross-cultural use of law outlined above.

3.7.3 Intercultural Translations/Transactions

At times, and not unreasonably, scholars of literature and semiotics have advanced critical doubts about the political and ethnic neutrality of the translator's work. Some of them have emphasized the partisanship of the translator's gaze and its tendency to 'othering others,' going so far as to call this event a scandal, indeed, the scandal of translation.[58]

Despite the impossibility of absolutely faithful translation, the commitment to respect rather than overshadowing Otherness can cause a kind of cultural alienation in translators.[59] This is because each language is historically intertwined (and, in a

Changes are always contingent but not for this reason can they be labeled as 'super' or extraordinary (taking this last word also in its etymological sense). All in all, I think that the expression 'super-diversity' could be fruitfully allowed to dissolve despite, or instead precisely because of, its worldwide diffusion and success.

[58] Venuti (1995) and Cronin (2006).

[59] Eco (2003).

sense, also embedded) in a world of experience.[60] Therefore, the translocation of one world of meaning into another can be extremely arduous and estranging. In order to avoid these troubling effects, it is not uncommon for estrangement to be placed against the Other, that is, the translated and the meanings lived by them. Needless to say, the misunderstandings or semantic transfigurations are not always innocent, nor can they be said to arise from a naïve cultural self-defense on the part of the translator. In some circumstances, indeed, it would be incorrect to speak of misunderstanding, if only because the alleged 'mistakes' are many times (perhaps, too many times) entirely intentional, or even strategically planned as tools for the exercise of power.[61] The political relevance of translation activities, and their sometimes dominant tendency, is somewhat co-extensive with the ethnocentric gaze that each of us (also) unconsciously activate when looking at the products and expressions of other cultures. To emancipate themselves from the centripetal attraction of their own culture, translators must distance themselves from their cognitive and behavioral habits.[62] But apart from the intrinsic difficulty and the defective nature of such an attempt—no matter how ethically indispensable—the translator often has to face rigid constraints of linguistic relevance/pertinence in order to accomplish his work. With regard to literary translations, these constraints may arise from the different syntactic structures, conceptual patterns, linguistic tropes or stylistic requirements (e.g., constraints to adhere to the rhythm of the poem or the figurative mode of certain expressions or descriptions) that are constitutively inherent in the original work. To the extent that they strive to make the source text comprehensible to the target audience of the translation, the translator engaged in literary translation has, however, the opportunity to create neologisms, metaphors and idiomatic expressions to achieve their communicative goal.

When the target language is technical, however, and therefore full of stipulative meanings and definitions, the task becomes much more challenging. In the various fields of scholarly research, these problems are partly prevented because language clauses are worked out within international circuits of scholars and, more importantly, the relevant definitions refer to abstract concepts and practices. But the issue is already very different in the case of sociology, philosophy, anthropology and so on. In these areas, theoretical knowledge is based on provinces of experience steeped in historical and mnestic imagery that are absolutely idiomatic in their semantic 'substance.' The abstraction that runs through scholarly discourses can thus conceal, or otherwise keep in a cultural shadow, the living worlds that are, precisely, the object of research. The linguistic creativity of translators, as well as that of the recipients of their work, can therefore come up against some barriers. This is particularly notable when source and target language words cover semantic areas that correspond to sets of experiences assumed to be facts: more precisely, as facts that are deemed to have been shaped by the past within spatial boundaries, which in

60 Deutscher (2010), Heeschen (2003) and Silverstein (2003).

61 Ricca (2013b).

62 Budick (1996) and Iser (1996).

turn coincide with the geographic scope of each research program.[63] It is not uncommon, therefore, for translations of this type of text or spoken phrase to make heavy use of parenthetical citation of the original words or phrases. Nevertheless, all the examples given so far do not illustrate the particular problems arising from the translation of texts or speeches with immediate practical consequences. When people speak within pragmatic contexts and for concrete purposes, misunderstandings or mistranslations can produce tragic effects. The iteration of discourses and thus the ability to adjust misinterpretations might be of some help. However, this semantic and communicative plasticity tends to vanish when discourses or texts directed to convey immediate practical effects are characterized by a high amount of relevance/pertinence constraints. This is precisely, and dramatically, the case of law.

The standard situation of a trial before a court can be taken as a paradigmatic example. The judge must first examine the case by assessing the facts/case at issue. To accomplish this task, they have to use the epistemological tools at hand. Although they are already addressing legal patterns, in the first instance, at least, the judges have to recognize the subject matter in and of itself. At this stage of case assessment, they are likely to listen to accounts of the facts and events to reach a decision. The language with which these facts are reported will not be the legal language, but rather the language commonly used by people. Of course, such speeches could be geared in some way toward achieving a legally qualified result, and thus be shaped specifically for that purpose. However, on average, people think and act in a world understood through their common language. Therefore, to ascertain what 'really' happened, the judges must put themselves on the same cultural wavelength as the parties involved, because only then can they understand people's thoughts and actions. But this is only possible if judges are able to manage the cultural patterns used by the parties at trial; otherwise, the whole work of legal categorization might start off on the wrong foot.

What has just been illustrated is not meant to suggest that the law is a superstructure of social life. On the contrary, the overall proposal concerning intercultural law aims to demonstrate and enable exactly the opposite. I do however intend to point out that not everything in legal discourse is the result of technically elaborate stipulations. The words of law and their usages constantly fluctuate in a semantic ocean co-extensive with common culture and language, with which they are continually blending and conflating both symbolically and practically. Common language, as well as the social life thought and acted through it, is shaped by the law, and

[63] See Descola and Pálsson (1996) and Lloyd (2007). However, with specific attention to anthropological research, personal experience is ever more characterized by the global circulation of semantic tools and schemes as well as the linguistic competence travelling above the shoulders of people who live astride many cultural-geographic domains. At least from a semiotic point of view, anthropological research and the related translation activity ought always to be adequately multi-situated if they are meant to grasp the meaning of human experience. Anyway, all this means only that cultural translation is, in most cases, an activity that is floating above an ocean of sense where intercultural transformations are already in place. For a theoretical survey of multi-sited anthropological analysis, see Gupta and Ferguson (1997a, c); Marcus (1995, 2006); and with specific reference to legal anthropology, Goodale (2007), Gingrich and Fox (2002) and Sousa Santos and Rodríguez-Garavito (2005).

changed as a consequence of its ruling action. In turn, however, law adapts in its contents and meanings according to the changes taking place in society and through the symbolic means used to realize them. In any institutional system, however complex and articulated it may be, law relies heavily on common culture and its semantic codes/models. Adapting to this semantic continuity is a communicative imperative even in non-democratic contexts. At stake is the very effectiveness of legal rules. Statements that are not comprehensible to legal subjects or that are deeply at odds with conceptual patterns commonly used by people would inevitably fail to accomplish their task. On the other hand, law covers almost every social moment and includes even the most intimate folds of daily life. Therefore, legal texts must necessarily assume many things implicit, referring to common language dictionaries in order to mold their content and significance. If this were not the case, legal texts, whether civil law or common law, would have to be huge encyclopedias describing and prescribing every aspect of experience and the world.

In a sense, then, every judge cannot avoid being a translator, even within relatively homogeneous cultural contexts, if only because they are called upon to translate the facts told by people into legal patterns and categories. This translating work, however, is not a one-way activity. In fulfilling this translative task, the judge's mind shuttles (or at least it should) between the legal-conceptual perspective and that related to common-sense narratives, in search of new and more specific semantic aspects of the case. Such aspects may emerge either from the ongoing hypothetical reconstruction on the legal side or from the insights that are gradually provided by the in-depth study of the facts relevant to the legal categorization of the situation to be legally qualified. The game of iterative questions and interactions between the two sides of issue (legal and practical) will go on until the judge believes they have reached a bi-directional adjustment between them. It will be, precisely, an adjustment through the translation of factual narratives into legal terms and vice versa. It is very likely, however, that if the parties involved are not familiar with each other's cultural codes, the implementation of this work will be very onerous. On average, a judge lacking transcultural expertise will tend to disregard the cultural and cognitive views of the subject of another culture and surreptitiously substitute for these their own categorical schemes of conceptualizing the world. The most serious problem in these circumstances is that the judge's ignorance of other cultural patterns blinds them in the sense that they are unable to decode their meaning. This occurs because what they do not know about the culture of Others is simply beyond their understanding, and therefore out of the picture. On the contrary, familiarity with their cultural schemes makes people who use them believe that reality is as it appears through those conceptual schemes. These standards of judgement become, therefore, a kind of inner lens or glass, which is essentially impossible to remove without specific intercultural training/skills.

A judge who is able to see of the Other only what their own culture barely allows them to glimpse is likely to discontinue the examination of the case at hand. This happens because they believe, on average, that they have already recognized in the situation examined the morphological features that could be taken as the basis of a plausible factual finding. Unfortunately, such morphological aspects do not reveal the full semantic content of the facts, but only the cultural and cognitive projections that inhabit the judges' minds, who cast them onto the factual ground of the legal issue. In other words, no reality can, by itself, tell the observers anything.[64] It merely answers the questions they are able to ask. It is not possible to understand the idiomatic 'matter' that constitutes human behaviors without first looking into the purposes, cognitive values and practical patterns conceived and practiced by individuals. Modeling morphological appearances according to one's own criteria of judgment (rather than trying to translate others) closes the door in the face of understanding. In the same vein, this attitude induces the judge to fail in their task of elaborating the middle term of the judicial syllogism, caging them (and unfortunately not only them) into a distorted and mystifying knowledge of Others and the situations they experience. The false knowledge stemming from this kind of hermeneutical practices, when considered in and of itself, is undoubtedly liable to produce psychosocial harm. But it has practical consequences as well, which in the case of law can prove to be exceedingly dramatic. Cross-cultural misinterpretation of factual narratives, which arises from the misuse of commonsense concepts belonging to the judge's culture, can generate huge errors in legal categorization.

In the mirror of those improperly assumed facts, the judge singles out which legal statements and normative meanings are to be implemented to rule the case. The combination of the representation of the 'facts' forged by the judge's mind and what will be regarded as the official normative reaction of the legal system will, in turn, have individual and, hereafter, social consequences. In the end, the result of the entire judicial procedure could rest on a paradoxical intercultural misunderstanding. Which would make the exercise of the judicial function, at least in these cases, a complete failure and, in the end, an outright betrayal of even what is called 'positive law.' This is simply because a false understanding of the facts will lead the judge to choose, as the main premise of the judicial syllogism, a legal rule not appropriate for the case. Symmetrically, what of the facts performed by people of another culture will not have been translated, for this very reason will be deprived of the profiles of legal relevance corresponding to the actual semantic/normative potential of the positive legal system. Thus, the judge who acts ethnocentrically and heedless of the task of translating Otherness will prevent positive law from producing its effects because of his own conduct. With a play on words, one could say that in their claim to act as 'positive jurist' or 'black letter jurist,' that judge would prove to be a 'negative jurists.' But the issue is even more intricate than has been shown so far.

Ignorance of Other's cultural universe is also relevant in other respects. When the judge translates facts into norms, that is, factual representations/narratives into legal rulings, they give utterance to the mute parts of law, that is, its cultural/factual implicit meanings. As an example, the legal word 'marriage' assumes, if it is to be effective, that everyone knows the social meanings and practices epitomized by that word and the underlying semiotic indexical spectrum. However, beyond some legal definitions, most of these practices, as well as the meaning of the words and gestures

[64]To quote Abelardo, "*res de re non predicatur*".

through which they are signified, are neither expressed nor specified in legal statutes and related rulings. The landscape of those practices taken as signs and semiotic relationships constitutes a perfect example of what I call 'the mute parts of law.'[65] Almost tautologically, it must be admitted that law does not say what it presumes *should* be known. The tautology, however, is only apparent.[66] The reason is that requiring compliance even with what is not expressly commanded constitutes a legal provision crammed with innumerable pitfalls for ordinary people. But, as will be seen, what is inconveniencing for a native often proves to be a fatal trap for a migrant.

When the judge considers the morphological features of a case, such as those of a 'marriage' or a 'family,' they project onto the situation both the meanings and mute parts encapsulated in the words and statements of the law to be applied to the fact as it has been previously categorized. The problem is that, albeit tacitly, these silent elements cast a shadow over the meaning of the (cultural) conduct enacted by the individuals to be judged, who understand their activity according to cognitive and axiological patterns that are culturally different from those of the judge. Despite these crucial discrepancies, however, the institutional power of the courts in many cases ends up giving their misinterpretations the allure of authority, with the result that the outcomes of intercultural breakdown can become enduring and a source of similar future decisions. Actually, the judge's translational task can be irreparably compromised by their lack of cultural knowledge. Moreover, along the slippery ridges of a misunderstood intercultural relationship, there is little hope that the activity of the courts can emancipate itself from the ethnocentric 'lapses' induced by the inherent rigidity of legal language. Unlike the literary translator, every jurist must work under a lexical constraint, namely the inalterability and immutability of the words that make up judgments and judicial decisions.[67] Even if a judge is able to recognize cultural difference nestled in the behaviors and speeches of the Other, in order for these to acquire legal relevance they must be categorized under the semantic umbrella of terms already used and prescribed by the lawmaker or case law. That judge, as well as any lawyer, cannot invent or choose the linguistic expression they hold preferable or more suitable to an effective translation. The law's words are inalterable and must be kept and employed as they are.

[65] In this regard it is worth noting that the above 'tacit parts of law' are to be understood as semiotic networks, in some senses traceable to cognitive and behavioral habits, but as such quite different from the sets of tacit rules otherwise referred to as 'mute law': see, in this regard, Sacco (1995, 2015). The rules included in 'silent law' sometimes combine with those provided by explicit law, sometimes have autonomous efficacy, and sometimes even operate contrary to explicit rules. However, the overall intertwining of these paths of combination/interplay between explicit/written and tacit/implicit law, at least in the way Sacco sketches it, makes his conception of 'mute law' ultimately turn out epistemologically rather nebulous and ultimately inherently inconsistent.

[66] The same argument developed in the text with regard to marriage applies to innumerous other legal institutes: for example, theft. As for the relevance in multicultural social and legal contexts of the difference between *ignorantia facti* and *ignorantia legis* see Ricca (2018).

[67] See Pommer (2008), Cao (2007), Mattila (2006) and Legrand (2005).

A famous adage speaks of "translator, traitor," underscoring with this expression the impossibility of full transplantation of meaning from one language and its related universe of experience to different ones. It is no accident that the transfer of word meanings from one categorical circuit to another is called, precisely, metaphor, to signify the displacement of a word from its usual (source) semantic domain to another (target) semantic domain usually proper to a different word (according to its molar significance). The benefits of this language transfer include not only rhetorical effects, but also a cognitive increment helpful in decoding new situations that would otherwise be difficult to categorize under already established language patterns. If applied in this cognitive way, and not only rhetorically, metaphor produces a third domain of sense sprouting from the creative (not mechanical) overlapping of the previous two semantic domains.[68] On the other hand, translation itself, as a cultural process, is always, at least in part, a metaphor, if only in the sense that it is ineluctably transformative. The meanings transplanted from one language and its world of experience to another inevitably go through a kind of transmutation, within which something is lost and something is gained.[69]

A serious danger that metaphor shares with translation concerns the power relation between the source and the target domain. Throughout the process of translating, as well as metaphor-making, each of the involved domains could somehow colonize the other, exerting a semantic supremacy. Between the metaphor domains this effect occurs almost as a rule.[70] Metaphors are generally not reversible, so that, for example, the phrase "that man is a fox" cannot be reversed to "that fox is a man" without changing its meaning. On the contrary, a good translation should be reversible. Nevertheless, the semantic transfiguration might sometimes be so severe that it prevents an ordinary reader from intuitively moving backwards from the translated text to the original. This is the case, precisely, with all domesticating translations.

Some scholars, relying on the irreversibility of metaphor, have contested its cognitive nature.[71] If this took place, they argue, then the emergence of a third semantic domain, as a result of the interplay between the previous ones, should allow reversibility in all cases; but this is precisely what does not occur. Against these arguments, however, it should be observed that the metaphor is not always irreversible. 'Childhood is innocence,' for example, is reversible to 'Innocence is childhood.' Or better, 'Life is a flower,' is reversible to 'A flower is life.' The question then is: in what cases are metaphors reversible? I propose that the kernel of the question lies in the cultural centrality and strength related to the literal (molar) meaning of the words. If the target word (in the first example: 'fox') has a literal meaning that is culturally established and resistant to semantic reconfigurations,

[68] Lorusso (2005), Eco (2003), Glucksberg (2001), Gibbs (1994), Ortony (1993) and Lakoff and Johnson (1980).

[69] See, for an almost paradoxical, but intriguing approach to this issue, Apter (2005).

[70] Crapanzano (2010).

[71] See Gibbs (1994).

reversibility tends to fail. On the contrary, if the literal meaning is culturally plastic, vulnerable to the changes and liable to the adaptation, then reversibility can occur.

The alternative between irreversibility and reversibility is played on the ground of experience and its contexts. The possibility to generate reversible metaphors is, at the end, a social issue. Whenever the linguistic use of metaphors is coupled with the possibility of engendering a relatively autonomous circuit or is so powerful as to change the *generalist* context of communication and experience, then metaphorical reversibility can take place. This means that the subject (ground) of the metaphor—that is, the result of the mapping of the connotative correspondence creatively established by the bridge between the domain of the source word and that of the target word—has acquired a central salience within the two semantic spectra of the categories involved in the process.[72] Such a denotative shift, though, is a sign of an ongoing metamorphosis of social behavior related to linguistic use. To put it more simply, the social and pragmatic context of signification has embarked on a process of transformation. It might be useful to give two examples to clarify what has just been asserted.

To make the '*generalist* change' hypothesis explicit, it is possible to draw on the metaphorical phrases, 'globalization is the future,' and its reverse, 'the future is globalization.' As can be seen, here the meaning remains (relatively) constant in spite of the reversal.[73] This is because in the psychosocial imagery of the world population average, 'future' and 'globalization' have progressively and diffusively acquired common semantic aspects, such that their metaphorical blending gives rise to a third category that includes both 'future' and 'globalization.' It is a creative synthesis of the previous ones, but nevertheless distinct in its semantic scope.

To illustrate what I mean by 'autonomous context,' telling a kind of story could be of value. Imagine that a group of young friends become accustomed to meeting near a particular (architectural) column, which over time comes to earn for them the epithet 'our column.' Moreover, suppose that among them there is a very tall, robust

[72]Once again, here it is to be emphasized that within the metaphorical process 'denotative' and 'connotative' elements conflate and the distinction among them 'evaporates'. In this regard, see Ricca (2022a, p. 187, spec. nt 15) and again there for further bibliographical references among which, however, see Ricoeur (1975, 1978).

[73]Some might observe, in this regard, that the coincidence of meaning may not be absolute, depending on the point of view assumed by diverse readers. The argument proves too much, however. Many times, even the literal tautologies can become metaphors just through the variation in the meaning of a same word. Take, for example, a well-known Italian adage: "*Domenica è sempre domenica*." It is the title of a hit song from a few years ago, still very much present in the collective memory. In English—but from a grammatical point of view in Italian, too—it would be, if literally translated, more or less: 'Sunday is always Sunday,' which is nonsense. But that nonsense is full of cultural implications because it conjures up all the traditional rituals of life related to the Sundays spent in almost the same ways by people raised in (predominantly) Christian countries. Perhaps, it is precisely this (culturally) rich play on words, swinging between tautology and metaphor, which has given that song great and long-lasting success. In any case, it demonstrates that interpretative variations can affect even tautologies, transforming them into metaphors. The rationalization that interpretive variations prevent the reversibility of ordinary metaphors is thus shown to be too broad and therefore too weak an argument.

boy, and the friends begin to call him 'our column,' also, perhaps, for his firmness as a leader. The story continues, and the boy, whose name could be James, but is most frequently referred to as 'the column,' eventually lends his given name to the actual column, until one fine day, said column is finally dubbed 'James.'

This little tale sketches a space of experience contextualized by the emergence of a metaphorical blend that progressively gains its reversibility. After a while, the utterances 'James is our column' and 'our column is James' could be clothed with so much reversibility so as to bring on the possibility of misunderstandings. Still, sentences such as 'See you at the Column's house' or, 'We'll meet at six o'clock under James,' albeit inherently metaphorical in themselves, could be understood, in spite of the reversal, without hesitation. Of course, the peculiar ability to understand such utterances would be limited exclusively to that group of friends. The reason is that the real column and James have assumed in the eyes of the friends and their discursive plots a common connotative ground, which has provided an axis of salience for the creation of a new categorical set including both the 'column' and 'James.' If such a communicative phenomenon can occur, it is useful, however, only for the new semantic ground that serves that group of friends and their communication and interaction practices. In other words, in correspondence with a new category resulting from a metaphorical coalescence, a new world will have been shaped within a bi-directionally reflexive semiotic relationship. Such communicative situations are tantamount to those (hopefully) occurring in multicultural societies on their way to intercultural metamorphosis, where communicative transformations are being driven by changes occurring in the experience of inter-subjective relations.

The sequel of such a digression about metaphors and the condition for their reversibility leads directly back to the matter of legal intercultural translation. However, I will momentarily set aside the metaphorical implications of intercultural legal practice and instead return to the activity of the courts. When a judge puts the situations lived and displayed by people of other cultures under the umbrella of the word of the law, they perform, certainly, an act of 'hermeneutic charity.'[74] Recognition of foreign persons' cultural differences, when it occurs, is not sufficient to ensure that their situation is treated as legally relevant. Not infrequently, somewhat out of cross-cultural ignorance, and somewhat intentionally, courts overlook the invisible/mute parts of the Other's cultural mind, but this is for the sole purpose of being able to declare, almost sincerely, that the party's position is worthy of legal protection. There is no doubt that such attitudes can revolve around a core of ethnocentric paternalism, if not even slide toward the most engulfing assimilationism, which, in turn, sometimes even borders on intolerance for cultural difference. Nonetheless, it must be recognized, the judges' position is unquestionably problematic. To resume and paraphrase the adage cited above, it could be said that in the face

[74] As is well known, this principle, defined for the first time by N. L. Wilson, has been the object of multiple philosophical examinations by Quine, Davidson and Dennet (the latter speaks of a 'principle of humanity'). The kernel of that principle consists in the ethical efforts to recognize the conduct or words of others as making some *kind* of sense, rather than none. From an anthropological angle, see Delpla (2002).

of cultural difference, 'the judge translator is and must be a faithful traitor.' In other words, they should be faithful to the cultural meanings intended by the individuals from different cultures despite having to translate/betray them through the mandatory use of the national legal language. At the same time, they must keep their institutional fidelity to the words of the law despite their obligation to translate/betray through them the meanings intended by the parties of the proceedings. In most cases, the result is that the judge, especially if lacking intercultural skills, creates an imperfect or unbalanced metaphor, within which the vehicle domain—in this case embodied by the legal national word—overshadows completely the invisible/mute parts underlying the Other's discourses or behaviors. This is also what occurs when the judge has to assess the compatibility of the laws of the Other's country of origin or cultural/religious/ethnic group with the domestic legal system according to the standards set by private international law.[75] The final outcome of such hermeneutic processes can often boil down to be a bitter defeat for the law because of the inevitability of its false and unjust application.

What it is of utmost importance, is that the detriment is not only for the person of another culture and their rights, but also for the axes of legitimation of national law, its purposes, and the accordance between its application and its foundational values. The irrational misuse of legal statements (as a result of misunderstood facts) produces institutional mistakes and delegitimizes behavioral aspects worthy of protection from a legal-axiological point of view. In countries whose legislation is based on a rigid Constitution, these axiological profiles can legitimate a challenge to the statutory laws' contents because of their relevance in the mirror of constitutional statements. This consideration applies, of course, both to fundamental rights under the national Constitution and to human rights protected by supranational/international charters and declarations.

The high level of generality and the semantic vagueness of statements provided by national Constitutions and human rights provisions should, in theory, allow for great receptivity to features/connotations related to cultural difference. The use of the constitutional level as a semantic map on which to inscribe events stemming from cultural differences could also compel a re-interpretation of statutes and case-law through the lens of the constitutional and human rights, therefore more attuned to the needs of intercultural legal protection and translation. Alas, these same constitutional and human rights may undergo a strongly ethnocentric interpretation forged by elevating the patterns for legal subjectivity provided by primary/statutory national legislation to the rank of prototypical implementations of those rights.[76] The most serious implication of this way of thinking and doing is the fundamentally exclusionary use of human rights. As a consequence of adopting such a hermeneutic approach, from being an instrument of cosmopolitan and pluralistic inclusion, they are transformed into an ideological-discursive mallet used to stigmatize others for

[75] On these aspects, however, see below Chap. 6.

[76] Ricca (2008), Cowan (2006) and Verkuyten (2001).

their alleged inhumanity, insofar as their behaviors do not correspond to the models of legal subjectivity provided by national legislation and the underlying cultural tradition.[77] On the other hand, if an effort is not made to promote an intercultural ability to translate Otherness when using the legal semantic schemes encapsulated in statutory laws and jurisprudential guidelines, human rights declarations could be involved in a high level of conflict and biased exploitation. This is because their enunciative vagueness can support claims triggered only by a polarizing and purely assertive logic, uninterested in implementing intercultural and equitable models of coexistence.[78] Cognitive ethnocentrism combined with a clashing and potentially hegemonic use of either human or constitutional rights could then become the rule.[79]

To avoid such serious consequences, the challenge of engaging lawyers in the effort to put human rights into practice through processes of intercultural translation of common categories of legal experience must be addressed. To be clear, these categories are none other than the same ones that in most countries and traditions of justice are provided by legislation and courts in the areas of civil, criminal, and commercial law, and relating to property, contracts, inheritance, theft, murder, fraud, comparison, and so on. Perhaps it is needless to point out that the word 'translation' is used here not only to mean linguistic translation, but also conceptual. Indeed, it may well be the case that a migrant, even if perfectly able to speak, for example, English or Spanish, uses the vocabulary of these languages to rely upon semantic spectra very different from that typically used by English or Spanish citizens. When this occurs, the difficulties, and the consequent necessity of a widespread commitment to intercultural translation, are then considerably increased. But this only shows how the central issue is not linguistic translation, but rather cultural translation, that is, a translation between semiotic relational circuits and worldviews that can be revealed to be necessary, even when the party belonging to another culture speaks the same language as the judge.

When intercultural translation does not take place, the parties involved (including the judge) often try to categorize the meanings and behaviors at issue by drawing on the rules of legal systems enacted by states, religions, or ethnic groups.[80] Presumably this approach provides the courts with a sense of certainty. But it only fuels an illusion: rubber-stamping statements or formal rules guarantee nothing. It is just a way of packing people's cultural competence into pre-packaged linguistic formulas from a designated and recognizable authority. Afterwards, problems will pop up again. The norms and statements of other systems or traditions also have and rely, in turn, on their invisible/mute parts. And there is nothing to certify that the meanings produced and understood by the parties within the host society are the same as the norms assumed to be implicit in the system of origin. On the other hand, people who

[77] Chryssochoou (2004).

[78] Douzinas (2000).

[79] Ricca (2013c); see, for an interesting analysis of the conflation between market neo-liberal framework and the 'promotion' of a conflictive use of human rights, Whyte (2019).

[80] Foblets (2005).

belong to different cultural or religious systems try to make use of the supposed formal norms of their systems of origin because they seek an axis of legitimacy as a means of coping with the assimilationist and centripetal force exerted on them by the law and culture of the host countries. Actually, the underlying reason for such an appeal to a formalized normative level of cultural patterns often resides in a double-faced insecurity. The judge is uncertain about managing cultural difference in a reliable way, and conversely foreigners and people from different cultures fear they will be unable to make their (culturally oriented) life choices understood through the lens of law. It is probably as a result of this multilateral lack of confidence if cross-cultural law (when misused in a multicultural*ist* way) resembles and, at the end, boils down to a disciplinary mix of comparative law and private international law. But this approach is incorrect and off-axis from the genuine judicial function of fact-finding. It completely neglects to consider that those who cross the physical and political borders of states are human beings with creative cultural competencies, not mere general rules or reified and normatively objectified cultures.

Migration and attempts to claim minority recognition of differences, at least in themselves, are not attempts at normative colonization and cannot be aprioristically addressed as such. From another point of view, then, the translation of rules may suffer the same obscuring effect that often occurs in cross-cultural translation, but with the additional burden that the judge must make the entire translation effort—which is also a cognitive one—only through them. The voices and thoughts of the people involved are thus in danger of being condemned to silence, as passive subjects of a performance with only legal norms as actors. In the end, people are subjected to one of two defective alternatives: (a) submitting themselves to the statements of their system of origin applied to the case according to the connecting factors provided by private international law; or (b), accepting the legal provisions of host countries 'as they are,' with all the semantically distortive shadows silencing their cultural invisible/mute parts. In this purely inter-normative scenario, however, any public relationship with the law of the host state would be ruled according to a formal hierarchical principle, namely the prevalence of national sovereignty and, therefore of the domestic rules. And yet, along this path, the inter-legal approach just outlined would almost inevitably make a somewhat ethnocentric idea of national sovereignty and the exercise of power related to it prevail over everything, even over the pluralistic inspiration of the very constitutional principles that function as its axis of legitimacy—at least, in constitutional democracies.

The intercultural remedy that can foil this normative or legal essentialization of cultures is precisely to give voice to the invisible/mute parts of cultural competence and to listen to them. Adopting it, the semantic features of the self-represented narratives of the parties can be used to generate a metaphorical interplay between the semiotic landscapes underlying the words included in the legal provisions. This activity would give rise to a kind of semantic turbulence, which could, in turn, trigger an inter-contextual resonance phenomenon among the relational semiotic networks extant and 'fluctuating' beneath each word. What might be likely to happen, specifically, is that some metaphorical and cross-cultural shifts may take shape and prove suitable to produce a reshaping effect on the categorization and interpretation of the words used, respectively, by national law itself and, consequently, by legal practitioners. An effect that, as noted above, could be further strengthened through constitutional and human rights provisions. More precisely, when actually pursued, the possibility of determining such semantic rearrangements is achieved by changing not only the categorical topography of individual words, but also the systematic choices about the normative combinations to be used in deciding the case. Things can take this course because legal categorization operates not so much through a strict correspondence between individual words and facts, but rather by extracting new categorical patterns from the overall semantic landscape of legal provisions; in turn, these new patterns are obtained and shaped by interweaving various principles, rules and arguments through a multi-level normative evaluation gauged on the social situations that arise through experience.

Mapping the semiotic landscapes underlying the self-representation of the Other through a transcultural approach inevitably involves excavating, extracting and, thus, rereading in a self-distancing way the invisible/mute parts nestled in national legal text(ure)s. This operation can trigger creative cross-mapping among the cultural landscapes deployed—including those below the discursive surface—by the actors involved in the intercultural relationship. The possible outcome of this activity could be, in turn, the emergence of a metaphorical-translational ground[81] which coincides with a shifting in the axis of salience of previously employed 'factual and legal categories,'[82] or even with the emergence of new ones. Such phenomenon would correspond to the needs arising from the social situation and its multicultural ingredients. In a sense, the results of cross-cultural categorizations would represent the emergence of cognitive metaphors shaped precisely for the purpose of making sense of new social situations. These metaphors, in turn, could produce new social meanings and—it may be assumed—could become, little by little, increasingly reversible. Ultimately, the evoked reversibility would be nothing less than a cosmopolitan bottom-up conversion/transmutation of national law.

Carrying out the general translation task incumbent upon judges in the intercultural manner outlined thus far would, among other things, allow them to foil a polarizing use of constitutional and human rights. A use that too often proved prone to support claims of protection classified under the label of cultural difference but completely out of context with respect to the actual circuit of lived experiences within multicultural societies and migration experiences. Human rights and their invocation would still retain their guiding role but would be simultaneously used within the cross-cultural translation process in such a way as to operate as criteria for reciprocally adjusting common legal categories (e.g., property law, contracts, crimes, etc.) and cultural differences. In that case, they would not be instruments

[81] It could also be expressed as "translationally transactional ground" according to the icastic formula proposed by Bermann (2005, p. 8).

[82] As for the exceedance of natural language with respect to legal language despite the unavoidable involvement of the former in legal enunciations/provisions I refer to Ricca (2022a, b) and there for further considerations about the illusory self-referentiality of law (and its language).

to fuel disputes and ideological clashes, but rather axes to promote the internal critique of national legal-cultural systems, as such aimed at realizing an experience of universality grown organically from everyday life and to be developed cumulatively from bottom-up.

From the perspective of comparative/anthropological analysis, the intertwining of human rights and other general categories of law, realized in the mirror of cross-cultural translations triggered, in turn, by multicultural social contexts, could prove to be loaded with relevant effects on a global scale. The capacity acquired by migrants and people from different cultures to reshape their cultural habits through intercultural legal translation could be re-purposed in their contexts of origin to promote change, empowerment, updating, and dialogues for global dissemination of cultural and legal forms (including not ethnocentric readings and implementations of human rights). The cross-cultural legal skills that people might acquire during their migration experience could function as an antidote to colonial and post-colonial impositions concerning the use of 'heteroctonous' legal schemes that their social and political systems have suffered in the recent past and even today. The laws of many non-Western countries (including a political economic giant like China) have imported Western legal frames, categories and structures. But all these 'materials' still need to be handled, and with great care, if they are to coordinate effectively with local anthropological customs. Often these 'foreign materials' are simply superimposed on the landscapes of cultural signification, in many cases imbued with religious views, and thereby generating political and social discrepancies that ineluctably lead to conflict. The intercultural solutions processed within multicultural and/or migration contexts could therefore echo fruitfully also in countries people have left. Turning transcultural translation into a kind of laboratory for political capacity building could also help tow the global hybridization of cultural habits out of the misty waters of political vagueness in which they currently find themselves. A condition that is even being hyper-celebrated by scholars with buzzwords like 'in-between' or 'nomadic,' which smacks of fashionable postmodernism, while just outside the cloud of their intellectual allure, the populations of emigration countries are left to wander in foggy conceptual deserts, without sophisticated skills or institutional pathways, in search of political and legal solutions to problems caused, at least in part, by the cultural and economic colonization of Western powers. Learning to weave connecting threads between cultural habits and legal statements, even if they are of Western origin such as human rights, could embolden these populations mobilize their cultural resources and generate political-legal lexicons suitable for placing them on the stage of both domestic and global affairs. They could become capable of acting as culturally creative and politically original subjects—partly because they would be trained to use legal communicative tools—and not just as individuals alternately subjugated and at the mercy of their communities or invincible national and international dynamics.

All this considered, how then is it possible to avoid falling into the temptation or psycho-cognitive trap of passing off one's identity as universality when handling the law and, through it, the lives of people from other cultures? For a judge, achieving this goal is a real institutional conundrum. The issue is usually perceived and couched in these terms because the creation of a cross-cultural metaphors against a legal background necessarily involves an activity of reflexive selection among the conceptual domains involved in the translation process. But the burden (which is also a leeway) of acting creatively should not only be on the judge. Unfortunately, the opportunities for parties to participate in the intercultural production of legal patterns and experiences during court proceedings are significantly limited. This depends on the circumstances and facts of the case that the judge is considering. Unfortunately, these facts also include actions the parties already have performed. Simply put, if there is damage, it has already happened. But let me explain right away. When people come to court, the situation has already taken on the feature of a conflict that is already in place and partly consummated. Within this framework, the understanding of the cultural patterns enacted by the Other must compete in the mind of the judge with the legitimate expectations of people who share the cultural standards encapsulated in the invisible/mute parts of the national legal provisions. Even so, however, much can still be done, especially to avoid blatant categorization errors due to ignorance of the Other's cognitive patterns. Nonetheless, by that time, the virtual possibility for the party to choose other means to achieve their ends, adopting different behavior so as to produce different legal consequences, will have unfortunately already vanished. No matter how many intercultural efforts can be made in retrospect, they will be hopelessly ineffective in changing the (acted) past.

Once a process starts, the possibility for anthropological expertise to promote far-reaching intercultural legal transformations will also remain inevitably limited. In my view, however, the very hindrance to a widespread intercultural use of law should probably be sought in the common approach to the legal phenomenon. When legal scholars think about legal issues, they focus their attention alternately on legislation or court decisions. From this perspective, in the elaboration of the issues at stake, the whole subject-matter of law seems to be framed by an oscillating movement between the analysis of textual legal provisions and the pathological moments (the violations of law) that come to the fore when one ends up on trial. The *other lives* of the law, those that inhabit the folds of people's daily existences, seem remote, almost silent, evanescent. But it is precisely in those circuits, in these too often overlooked areas that culture and legal discourses conflate into one another and give rise to new communicative and practical habits. There, if supported by lawyers and anthropologists working together, people from different cultures could participate in a creative and intercultural process with complete cultural competences at their disposal. In this too-often overlooked space, those who belong to other cultures or are part of a minority would not be doomed to be latecomers—as is the case in court proceeding—in their attempts to choose new culturally blended schemes of behavior.

3.8 A Timely Intercultural (Use of) Law and Its Places: Two Open Case Studies

The courts are ordinarily concerned with conflicts already erupted and almost completely defined by their own morphological, exterior terms. Conversely, intercultural law, at least as I mean it, focuses primarily on devising solutions that can prevent potential conflicts from arising. A comparison with some salient features of the legal-multiculturalist approach may help in highlighting the difference.

Multiculturalism is concerned with 'cultures,' while the cross-cultural use of law tasks itself with improving people's opportunities to exercise cultural competence. In my view, each legal subject must be given the right to use its own culture, and even before that, the right to understand, judge and choose what their culture is. This is why intercultural law is meant to elaborate a co-produced lexicon of subjectivity rather than a subjectification of legal protections, as is the case for cultural defenses.

Multiculturalists argue that people turn to things, not to meanings or rather to semiotic pathways oriented to support processes of adaptive reconfiguration of meanings. But people's attitudes focused and emphasized by multiculturalism may be, in part, due to the fact that people believe (and often know from experience) that they do not have the space and time to process cross-cultural arguments with expectations of responsive reactions from public institutions. I believe, however, that this is also a consequence of the already entrenched application of multiculturalist practice in the judging style of courts in countries marked by a colonial past or affected by migration flows dating back to the early twentieth century.[83] What is at stake is a kind of circular effect or, in part, a self-fulfilling social-theoretical prophecy. The tendency to seek cultural evidence, demonstrated over time by these courts through their cumulative activity, has progressively given its features to a jurisprudential tradition—partly by virtue of the logic of leading cases practiced by common-law countries—so much so that it is very difficult to dismantle or criticize it today.[84] In this socio-institutional scenario, since people from different cultures know their cultural claims will only be recognized if they are arranged and proposed as relying on almost folkloric patterns or rules, it looks perfectly understandable that they seem to incline toward the material or normative reification of their cultural claims. Somehow even jurisprudential trends have become culture, or rather, an active factor in the multicultural situation, leaving room for the unfolding of a circular effect induced by the overwhelming communicative power of dominant groups. And yet, the Other, in this way, ends up being caricaturized rather than genuinely understood making room for an authentic understanding of its difference. It almost seems as if cultural belonging and related habits of behavior were a kind of psychosocial pathology, to be considered and managed as an exception to the 'normality' embodied by culturally dominant groups. This being the case, difference

[83] Renteln (2004).

[84] See, about this, Eisenberg (2009).

tends to change over to diversity, and the latter to cultural incommensurability. As with the sick, culturally diverse fellows—sometimes even to exorcise the guilt inherited due to colonial sins—are allowed behaviors normally forbidden to all others.[85] Of course, to access this special treatment, one must pass all the anamnestic and diagnostic checks of symptoms, pathogenesis, protocols to be followed, and so on, designed to ascertain the patient's 'abnormal' status. Otherwise, in the absence of an accurate diagnosis of cultural diversity, an invalid (the Other thus imagined), passing off their fictitious pains (differences) as true, might enjoy undue care (advantages and exceptional treatments).

Regarding legal multiculturalists' concerns about the authenticity of cultural features and the appropriateness of the resulting care, we must observe, however, that understanding the Other's culture and its dynamics of adaptation does not necessarily mean legitimizing all its strands. On the other hand, cultural belonging does not exclude a reasonable negotiation of one's own cultural competence and its constitutive elements. The multiculturalists, too often, fail to see that the multicultural environment is also an opportunity for the cultural life of all individuals, whether they are immigrant or native. Conversely, each person should be entitled to design innovative solutions, which can coalesce past and present, previous meanings and new possibilities of (life) sense. Only in this way can culture be protected and implemented as an existential resource.

From what has just been observed, it would seem legitimate to deduce that multiculturalist claims are usually based, despite their proclaimed openness to dialogue, on polarizing opposition and the rejection—even if often disguised—of the axiological patterns of the majority; in contrast, cross-cultural solutions aim instead to work out solutions to dissolve the potential conflict between cultures and legal norms that arises in connection with inter-individual disputes.[86] Moreover, not everything that is characterized as being culturally different must for this reason be admitted, just as not everything cultural must necessarily be labelled as diverse and therefore inconsistent with the axiological lexicon of the legal system.

In my view, however, the intercultural (use of) law is not meant as a construction of justifications exclusively suited to exempt some individuals from legal common liability, hence relegating the cultural factor in law to merely an exception to general legal rules. Rather, it is addressed to a cross-cultural reconfiguration of categorical boundaries encapsulated within general rules or principles and, at the same time, designed to re-elaborate the semantic ingredients of a legal subjectivity capable of encompassing cultural differences. Legal interculture is thus a political action to be carried on through legal experience. But this is possible and legitimately pursuable only if social actors in multicultural societies are entitled to equal discursive and participatory agency through the implementation of living law or law in action. The focus of an intercultural approach applied to the law is the overcoming of ignorance

[85] Foblets and Renteln (2009a).

[86] As for the terms of this presumed bifurcation, see above Chap. 1 and therein for the related bibliographic references.

on the part of migrants about cultural and legal meanings, as well as from legal practitioners or authorities about the Other's patterns of judgment and behavior. Of course, this overcoming should not be undertaken for its own sake. The ultimate goal, which is also the instrumental thrust of the entire cross-cultural process, is to convert this mutual ignorance into a creative and participatory capacity geared toward devising solutions that prevent conflicts from arising between reified and frozen cultural identities.

As mentioned above, the right stage to initiate a timely intercultural legal practice is not when matters have already reached court. Instead, anthropologists and lawyers should engage in social work within communities of migrants to inform individuals and groups about the opportunities for intercultural and inclusive uses of law. This effort would respond to the silent and widespread demand for legal protection by migrants and cultural minorities, which often arises before they have made legally relevant decisions and sometimes gets entangled in fearful and confused not-knowing, leading in many cases to irretrievable legal mistakes and missteps. The most important loss, in this situation, coincides with the effects of an unaware and aprioristic renounce to the opportunities, for both the individual and society as a whole, at least virtually stemming from an intercultural use of law. These opportunities, however, are not simply present, as things at hand, but must be invented through the interaction of specific knowledge and skills that the migrant cannot grasp if left to their own devices. On the other hand, every migrant knows something indispensable to a genuine cross-cultural use of law that neither anthropologists nor jurists can perceive without an investigation carried out involving their active participation. The active involvement of the migrant and, more generally, of people belonging to other cultures or religions than those of the majority, is not only a requirement for using the law in a democratic and pluralistic way. The participation of the Other is a cognitive matter. This is also because ordinary people, despite media propaganda, are on average rather indifferent to recognizing the formal rules of the legal, religious or community systems to which they are attached. In most cases, they do not even know the corresponding rules. What they know is how to put in practice the behavioral habits and the purposes codified and communicated by those rules. But habits, and their moral precipitates, are much more semantically flexible and pragmatically plastic than formalized norms, when considered with specific regard to the rigidity of their enunciation. In reality, although regulatory provisions convey culture, religion, tradition and their contents, in many cases people merely abide by them through patterns of practical conduct as they have learned it through extra-legal channels of cultural transmission. In the same way and without betraying or exploiting their cultural tenets, people avail themselves of the plasticity intrinsic to their habits in order to deal with the life environment through the most various circumstances, including the case of multicultural co-existence. Nonetheless, the range of plasticity and the corresponding practical projections cannot be assessed in terms of their suitability to an individual's adaptation needs except by that same individual, who is also the only one ultimately entitled to represent them before the law.

A taxonomic and descriptive knowledge of cultural, religious, and traditional rule systems is radically insufficient to steer the intercultural translation/transaction process.[87] While this knowledge is useful, and even necessary, it must nevertheless be supplemented with the concrete use that people are willing to make of it whenever facing the various contingent contexts. And because the law of host countries is integral to their living contexts, knowledge of the cross-cultural legal possibilities conveyed by national statutory laws and court rulings will have a direct impact on their choices in asserting their own cultural claims. As argued above, it is precisely for this reason that the intercultural law process is distinctly different from international private law and comparative law practices and methodological approaches. Through cross-cultural translations/transactions people do not negotiate normative effects, or at least not only these; rather they use much more creative ways to become aware of and interpret their own cultural meanings. Their role of translating key players is a consequence of their irrepressible exposure and openness to the transforming action deriving from their contact with other semiotic and pragmatic landscapes. The anthropologist involved in intercultural translation processes, therefore, should put much more consideration into the way in which people retain the meanings of rules across the metamorphosis engendered by migration paths rather than the normative apparatuses regarded in their historical or textual fabric. In other words, the anthropologist in the lawyer's office should turn his or her gaze to the culture and/or religion of which people are actually bearers. More specifically, anthropologists engaged in supporting individuals in multicultural contexts cannot overlook that those same people are agents reflexively responsive to the possibility of becoming aware of their culture and religion an interculturally creative interpretation. This means that, from a genuinely intercultural perspective, individuals must be afforded the opportunity to provide retrospective yet adaptive readings of their original cultures, as well as to make themselves proponents of the use of host-state legal rules open to the inclusion of Otherness.

Through intercultural encounters, people simultaneously (even if, inevitably, at first relying on their own cultural encyclopedias) learn reciprocally from each another.[88] Semiotic apparatuses transform cross-cultural adaptive actions carried out by people in their relationship with Otherness; in addition, people are capable

[87] And besides, one wonders what the scientific import of merely taxonomic knowledge would be, considering that, in its often asserted descriptive and cataloguing neutrality, the pseudo-scientific inclination inspiring this approach neglects to determine the epistemological assumptions underlying their classifications. On the other hand, how would it be possible to articulate a critical assessment of the epistemological assumptions of a research path if not through a thoughtful and falsifying verification of the relational and pragmatic implications of them? Which then is exactly what remains outside the generally (only) assertively tautological reach of all descriptive and merely classificatory approaches. Regrettably, many comparative analyses, when not entire disciplines, in sociology, anthropology and especially law, fall prey to a kind of classificatory and taxonomic vertigo, so much so that in their mere descriptiveness they seem to lose sight of the meaning of any genuinely scientific enterprise.

[88] The reader is kindly, as well as resolutely, requested to take the word 'learn' strictly in its least functionalist and Luhmanian definition.

of adapting their minds by means of new ways of using cognitive tools drawn from previously acquired cultural and semiotic equipment. This circularity is the living and very substance of semiotic gear that shapes cultural competence and its unwinding. To put it differently, cultures and religions do not change because of deviations imposed by confrontation with Otherness, but rather make themselves by changing. The culture and religion herein accounted for, at least in these situations, are mainly those in action, living through people's gestures and thoughts, not printed in books or previous ethnographic reports related, for example, to investigations carried out in migrant people's areas of origin. As 'matter' made of signs, cultures (as well as religions) are inherently exorbitant to any attempt to cage them within semantic rigidities and ontological essentialisms.

Too often, the obsession with cultural authenticity, which also underlies the multiculturalist approach to the protection of cultural differences, ends up overvaluing 'in-the-books' culture or religion to the expense of those actually experienced.[89] Even worse, the 'culturalist' and 'hyper-orthodox' implication of that obsession boosts inner conflicts within the same cultural or religious circuits, causing outbreaks of polarizations between traditional practices and innovative ones. Paradoxically but not so much, the political willingness to expend energy on recognizing different and opposing versions of cultural or religious knowledge, so much supported and implicitly encouraged by multiculturalist practices, can sometimes become the watershed between different factions within the same culture or religious group. And so, as a reflected effect of the multiplication of differentiation criteria (sometimes fueled by a kind of taxonomic frenzy) used by some Western institutional and cultural agencies to account for and recognize cultural and religious differences, the problem of protecting individual and minority rights ends up taking shape within social minorities themselves.[90] At this stage, however, constitutional

[89] To be honest, scholars do bear some responsibility for the occurrence of this effect. Their research on cultural and religious normative systems seems often focused, if not limited, to historical data, such as studies in the field of Islamic Law or Hindu Law, and only rarely sensitive to the real adjustments by which the people embody these traditions in their everyday contemporary life.

[90] Tavani (2012), Eisenberg (2005), Kymlicka (2003), Tully (2002) and Jones (1999). Sometimes scholars talk about an alleged 'added value' of community rights: see, specifically, Tavani (2012). My position on this issue goes beyond the division between individual rights and group rights. I simply think that culture is a creative medium for life. Although some rights and needs necessarily belong to the groups or cultures that make them their own, interpretations and representations of 'cultural' or community characteristics can only be available to personal creativity, however much respectful and attentive to the sensibilities of others its exercise should be. The conflicts to which scholars so often turn their attention, such as that between individualistic and communitarian conceptions of rights, often find a transfigured echo in the struggles waged by minorities within minorities; antagonisms that often spring from the confrontation, sometimes bitter, regarding the way in which group tradition or culture should be lived and embodied by individuals. In my view, if an intercultural legal perspective is to be taken, the key question becomes, 'How do people want to live and translate/transform their individually and collectively inspired cultural habits?' And this is simply because identity and creativity, both cultural and personal, should never be aprioristically taken for granted. In any case, collective rights cannot be understood and branded as political-ideological weapons at the disposal of a few individuals, who are self-appointed 'authentic'

pluralism is confronted with monist claims advanced by cultural and religious communities. And since these are protected as such by international norms and the constitutions themselves, pluralism based on constitutional rights and recognition of differences ends up appearing divorced within itself.

Undoubtedly, from a public policy perspective, constitutional democracies ensure the articulation of multiple and diverse claims raised by the various social components. At the same time, however, in doing so, they end up paving the way for the eruption of fractures between aspirations for infra-cultural transformation and constraints inspired by attempts to preserve and affirm monistic and often hyper-orthodox versions of each culture and religion. Then, camouflaging itself among these anthropological or theological skirmishes, the claw of power almost inevitably begins to cast its shadow over the life of cultural and religious communities and their relations with law and state policy, thus indirectly generating leaders and underlings, winners and losers, truth-keepers and heretics.[91] Conflicts within communities become the symbolic place where the construction of boundaries between the domain of cultural differences and the domain of the ethos and lifestyle of the majority begins. However, the 'inner' communitarian conflict should be recognized, at least in part, as a symmetrical image of the 'external' one between people belonging to minority cultural and religious communities, on the one hand, and the state, national society and its axiological and legal patterns, on the other. Causes and effects, in a sense, conflate into each other.[92] Multiculturalist political and legal approaches, on the one hand, and infra-cultural or religious conflicts between individuals and communities, on the other, all together co-construct a growing bundle of hindrances for the self-development and the local positioning of cultures and religions. This combination gives rise, paradoxically, to the so-called problem of prevalence to be assured by state institutions to communities rather than individuals, and vice versa: each taken at the time as the sole genuine cultural agents. On this socio-political stage, constitutionalism and its legal dispositive risk becoming absurdly transformed into enforcers of cultural and religious orthodoxies supported by often only self-proclaimed voices of tradition.

The dissemination of sufficient awareness about the possibilities of intercultural use of law (and lawyering) should be a task widely promoted by institutions. Universities, research departments in law and anthropology, as well as public

---

interpreters of a particular culture or community and, solely by virtue of this, feel entitled to crush the choices of others belonging to the same group.

[91] It is no coincidence that interpretations of cultural traditions and religious normative systems appear in many cases much more rigid and intransigent in migratory circuits than in the contexts of origin. The 'folklorisation' and the overemphasizing of the culture's customs and religious beliefs are steps inherent to the logic of differentiation 'switched on' by the difficulties of migrants in their psychosocial re-positioning. The multicultural paradigm, especially its legal version, increases and fosters the politicization of those transformations so that the burden of the resulting conflicts falls upon the shoulders of individuals. Regarding the most distorting consequences of so-called ADRs ("Alternative Dispute Resolutions") see Nader (2010), Shachar (2008) and MacKinnon (1995).

[92] In this sense, see Dick (2011, p. 148 ff.).

institutions in general should develop social survey programs and action plans aimed at surveying legal protection needs related to cultural differences of minorities and migrants. At the same time, they should embark on a parallel project to spread intercultural skills among associations of legal practitioners. Since people's awareness and lawyers' competence regarding the intercultural use of law are two sides of the same coin, the above two courses of action should be pursued simultaneously. This also because, when confidence should spread among people in the possibility of inscribing their cultural differences in the pages and words of legal texts, the best place and time to initiate the cross-cultural use of law would be, in my opinion, the lawyer's office and prior legal advice, respectively. From an educational perspective, academic courses could and should train specific professional skills in the (legal and anthropological) areas of intercultural activities. Currently, anthropologists and lawyers work together, but as separate professionals. However, they already face some documented problems related to clients' lack of trust in the anthropologist's presence and cooperation while the lawyer provides legal assistance.

As noted above, when the native clients enter the lawyer's office to solve their legal problems, they implicitly ask the practitioner an effort to translate from their common language to legal technical language. Something similar occurs if the client is a migrant or a person from a different culture. In both cases, the clients do not ask—*I'd like article x of the civil code applied to my situation or a specific court ruling y for the case in which I'm party*. They spin, conversely, a yarn made of intersubjective struggles, personal grievances, financial claims and so on. Then, the lawyer has to draw from these conversational elements and mine only what will serve them to meet the needs of the client by weaving some plausible texture of legal arguments. But to accomplish this hard task they must first know the world of meanings that inhabit the client's mind. Accomplishing this with a foreigner, even if they speak the same language, is extremely difficult, if not impossible, without the help of someone who knows at least the broad outlines of client's cultural knowhow. Once the lawyer has understood the client's narrative, the intercultural legal translation work can finally begin. It can occur, however, that the lawyer must translate something very unusual and not corresponding to social patterns ordinarily subsumed in normative statements. As stressed above, lawyer has to become, in such cases, a sort of anthropologist of themselves. However, it is not only the foreign client who is called upon to mine their own cultural patterns to self-represent their own needs and instances before the law. During the translation process, the lawyer should undertake a symmetrical retrospective and introspective path. Even so, it is likely that they would not be able to do it without the support of someone endowed with historical and anthropological knowledge about their culture.

It could be argued, at this point, that no black-letter lawyer would be willing to undergo a training course that would enable them to acquire such knowledge. At the same time, however, this is the most interesting aspect of the intercultural use of law. It requires different notions and, with them, also a particular predisposition or know how to handle them all together. Theory and practice, culture and legal skill, should be deeply joined in order to attain the end in view, namely a genuine intercultural legal translation. It is noteworthy, moreover, that this intertwining of such diverse cognitive tools is not equivalent to a mere conflation between the, so called, law-on-books and law-in-action. The issue is far more encompassing. At stake, there is the same possibility of a consistent action of law, and thus the extent and the systemic role of legal practitioners' activity. The concrete problems raised by multicultural coexistence cannot be solved without first gaining appropriate awareness of the cultural implications stemming from the legal categories provided by law texts, and then creatively synthesizing them by means of new intercultural legal solutions. On the other hand, a lawyer so equipped could suggest multiple possibilities to the client, and these could, in turn, trigger in the latter new ways of elaboration and self-representation of their own cultural competence and patterns in order to face the multicultural social environment. This work, if embarked upon, would have to cover huge cultural and social latitudes. It should run through all fields of the legal experience anywhere the intercultural semiotic distance could produce problems of understanding interlaced with the behavioral plans adopted by people. Unlike the multiculturalist legal approach experienced so far, the intercultural legal approach I propose would be not confined to face only ethnical and religious questions such as those implicit in veils, infibulations, *kirpan*, and other cultural uses marked with exotic or folk labels. All issues, the ones just mentioned, that appear inexorably destined to remain peripheral to social life and the places where individual identity is daily challenged and attempts to take shape. Conversely, intercultural law stresses the central topics of legal experience, those which forge everyday life, such as contracts, marriage, inheritance, theft, fraud, corporations, trade, labor, ecology, sustainability, disability, and so on. If it were a widespread practice, well known along the flows and post stations of planetary migrations, it could slowly engender an intercultural legal lexicon able to influence not only interpretative activities but also the conceptual patterns adopted in the production of statutes and court decisions.

Not infrequently, intercultural legal solutions show a genuinely universalistic attitude deriving from the reflexive cultural reading they have been requested to achieve. In practice, what sometimes occurs is that in translation outcomes, devised to face and interplay with the cultural difference, the natives see an interpretation of legal values able, generally, to best meet their own needs. In this way, therefore, the life of law could change just by undertaking the pathway towards a cosmopolitan dimension of legal experience within the boundaries of individual national states. Even before pervasive change, however, the spread of cross-cultural practices within state borders could in itself provide an extraordinary vantage point for avoiding many socio-legal cases that currently end up before the courts because of the reciprocal ignorance, both cultural and legal, on the part of both natives (ordinary people or legal experts) and migrant peoples belonging to other cultures. Last but not least, such practices could encourage many migrants to use available legal tools rather than be wary of them a priori, thus condemning themselves to a sort of legal clandestine condition, lived socially underground and fated to converge in the circuits of segregated ethnic 'justice' and, very often, of deviance.

However, I must admit that the cross-cultural use of law is something new. And like all ideas to which we are not accustomed (including the discourses that present them) it might be rather difficult to understand without the support of practical examples. For this very reason, I will try to illustrate the 'how' of the intercultural cultural use of law by providing two cases I came across during my fieldwork.

3.8.1 Case#1: The Question of Inheritance Rights After Intestate Succession, Astride Ghana and Italy

A girl from Ghana immigrated to Italy, and, perfectly able to speak Italian, came to see me to discuss issues concerning her citizenship. Talking about family relationships, she suddenly said, 'You know, at home my parents always prefer my brother!' 'Why?' I asked. 'Because he is male!' came her angry reply. 'But what is your faith?' I continued. 'Christian', she said, 'who is not Christian is not from Ghana!'. 'But do you know', I asked, 'that there is also an Islamic minority?' 'Yes, of course. But they are so few...'

At that point, I went back to the topic of her brother. 'How are inheritance matters in your family determined? If you are not Islamic, you and your brother have the same inheritance rights, I suppose.' But her answer was surprising. 'I don't know,' she said, 'but I think my brother is entitled to a larger part than mine'. 'How much larger?' I asked. She answered, 'I think approximately double'. 'As in Islam...,' I said, laughing. 'Yes,' the girl answered, 'it is for marriage. Yes, for that, perhaps... I don't know the details very well. I don't know the inheritance laws of my tradition... not even those required by the statutes of Ghana.'

'But what do you think would be a fair amount for both?' I then asked. 'Fifty-fifty', was the immediate and peremptory response. 'Are you sure?' I urged her... 'Your brother and you will already be Italian citizens when your parents die. So, on that day, will you go before an Italian court to claim your share according to Italian inheritance law if your parents leave more to your brother, in this way encroaching the forced heir share provided by Italian statutes?' 'To what extent can your parents provide for you?' I continued. 'I suppose that your traditional inheritance rules are designed to allow the male sons of family to present their wives with a marriage dowry. And if you divide the whole inheritance fifty-fifty, then will your brother no longer have the money for the dowry, and thereby be denied the possibility of marrying?'

As soon as I finished saying these words the girl's face suddenly changed its expression. She went silent. Then, slowly, she said 'No. I can't help thinking of all my relatives. It would be a tragedy if my brother could not get married because of me. I ought to run away. No, no, for Heaven's sake'.

Meanwhile, her eyes betrayed a mind divorced from itself, split off in two parts totally paralyzed. 'Anyway, it is not fair,' she added, strengthening my impression. True, if asked to choose, she would not know what to do. Facing such a situation, an anthropologist could probably understand more than a lawyer, but they would not know how to provide a solution. Inside the girl were two alternative models, both forged by her life relationships with the multicultural environment she lived in and by. In other words, her mind was extended, but interpenetrating between worlds in conflict. And it was within those worlds and their semiotic landscapes that she needed to find an interface to enable them to communicate. The law was part and parcel of the problem, not only a superstructure imposed over the cultural ground. To achieve an intercultural solution for that inner struggle, all the potentialities of legal recombination skills would have to be set in motion.

My proposed solution, addressed to the girl, was processed in a participatory way and step-by-step. First, I told the girl that Italian law provides two kinds of inheritance. One reserved for legal heirs and another at the free disposal of the testator's will. Probably, in the case of only two children of different genders, even if the parents had reserved a double allocation for the male son, the required inheritance for the other child would not have been encroached. 'Anyway, if you desire an equitable distribution between the two children, Italian law can provide a possible solution to your intercultural struggle,' I argued. 'What solution?' she asked with an inquisitive gaze.

Actually, the Italian Civil Code (art. 785) provides the so-called "Donation on behalf of marriage," otherwise defined and translatable as "obnuptial donation." This is perhaps a legacy, with an anthropologically dense taste of ancient customs. In some ways, it resembles the public and communitarian role of family so widespread among cultures such as Islam, Hinduism and some African traditions. Differently from other cases of donation, the obnuptial one is irrevocable, even if the donee proves to be unworthy of the donor. The intrinsic value of family and its social importance appear within this statement more deserving of protection than the individual interests of the donor. The subject, taken as individual, is subject to the group, the family that they themselves contributed economically to create. Modern Western individualism seems, therefore, to take an unexpected step back. It would be very interesting to trace the cultural genealogy of this rule, steering the journey back in the European legal imagination, taking as an intercultural sextant the relationships between individuals and families in other cultures. To stick to the case at hand, one could fathom the traditional memory of Ghanaian ethnic groups which the girl of this story belonged to and try to ascertain if and to what extent the dowry—probably corresponding to the ancestral custom of bride price—on behalf of the wife may be intended as a tool for assuring the formation of new families. In any case, through the obnuptial donation the parents of the girl of this story could reserve a sum for the male son taking it out of the free portion of the whole inheritance. In this way, the destination of that sum would be linked only to the marriage of the male son and would not be a sign of aprioristic discrimination between the children. Furthermore, this solution would not violate the provision of Italian Civil Code regarding the portion to be reserved to the forced heirs.

I explained to the girl the possibility I have just described, but she, after a fleeting smile, looked at me wryly, asking with sly eyes, 'What if, in the end, my brother decides not to marry? What a great solution! He will keep the extra-money, and I will feel passed over.' 'Don't worry', I said, 'the statement about the obnuptial donation provides that it takes effect only if the marriage is celebrated.' At that point, the girl stood for a moment speechless. Then, wincing with surprise, she asked 'Really? Really, the Italian law says that?' 'Yes, certainly,' I assured. 'Well! I like this! Now, I'll go tell my mother! But...,' she added with a veil of worry, 'if my mother makes a will, can I still go before a court in case my family wants me to leave extra money to my brother, even if he remains a bachelor?' 'Yes, certainly,' I said. 'O.K.', replied the girl, 'Thank you very much.'

Our meeting ended shortly afterward. A few days later, the girl returned to see me, telling me she had asked her mother to explain to her the traditional rules of succession. At that point, I mentioned that perhaps she should have already been aware of the rules of succession under the law of Ghana. With her sparkling character, the girl blurted out, a bit annoyed, 'But then we foreign immigrants, what should we do? Study the laws and tradition of our countries in order to solve our problems with Italian law?' 'Maybe not study, but at least inquiring a little could be useful', I responded calmly. 'Inquire, and with whom?', the girl immediately added. 'I know, vaguely, that we have a matrilineal system of succession, but only because my mother told me. I don't know the relatives of my father, for me they are like strangers. My mother told me about matrilineal succession when she divided the rooms of our house between my brother and me for the future.' 'What has your mother divided?' I asked. 'The house for our future inheritance!' said the girl. 'Only by telling you so?' I asked. 'Sure!' the girl added. 'Do you know that those words would not be worth anything in court, in future?' 'I had a hunch...' answered the girl, 'but we have our traditions, and my mother did not explain why the division was made in that way. She just knows all of us must do so. As, for example, we know that when she dies, we cannot change her decision or sell what she leaves to us, because we, the heirs, take her place with and by the things she leaves. But I don't know very well why. I just know and feel that it is so.'

'I suspect,' I answered after listening to this narrative, 'that you will have many difficulties making these words understood by an Italian notary or lawyer in the future. You know, for the Italian mind there is a clear divide between persons and things. If you told a lawyer that you couldn't sell the goods that your mother left you, he would probably not understand. The very issue is that in your culture persons and things are not radically different. Some things are part of a vital relationship of the person and her body, and this relationship will continue even after death. The same person, then, is not only an individual, a body separated from the others, like in the imagination of Western people, but is part and parcel of the whole extended family group, including the things 'belonging to' its members'. 'This is true' continued then the girl, 'because when one becomes the heir of her mother, all the mother's relatives ask continually for help. In the end, indeed, sometimes the heir hands over some portion to the relatives directly, so that they doesn't have to continually receive requests for support or gifts. However, here we aren't in Ghana. So, some people, even if few, indeed, often sell the goods of their deceased mother and don't give anything to the relatives. Generally, though, this is a problem because all the family begins to curse the heir, and many people are superstitious, they believe in malediction...' 'Do you, too?' I teased her. An embarrassed smile was her only reply. 'Anyway, the claims of relatives would be a serious problem in Italian succession law,' I considered. The division of portions resulting from the application of Ghanaian law would have to be carefully assessed (statements or traditional rules) and then, if and insofar as you believe them binding, you would need to combine those stipulations with those indicated by Italian law. But you would have to talk with a lawyer or a notary, about all of this, simultaneously asking for help from an anthropologist or a lawyer from Ghana who knows the traditional rules of your group.'

'But what does it matter...' said the girl suddenly, 'fortunately there is plenty of time.' With these words, this second discussion ended. I was told the girl made further inquiries. What will happen in her future, however, is an open case. Much, I think, will depend on what all of us will do towards the formation of an intercultural law experience and the dissemination of the requisite skills.

If I used storytelling to render my experience with this case, it is because the narrative plot can show the contingency of intercultural traces that may be taken. The logic of intercultural translation-transaction is distinctively different from that of multiculturalist accommodation. The choice of obnuptial donation is not a tool for a strategic adjustment where the migrant exploits the interstices left open by law statements. On the contrary, the idea of digging out such an obsolete and now socially peripheral institution would never have occurred to anyone if it had not been worked out upon a metaphorical carpet (ground) between the sense of the male/female discrimination in the traditional succession pattern of Ghana and the supporting family function also traceable within the historical folds of Italian legal culture, embodied, in this case, exclusively by the nuptial donation. But the recognition of this metaphorical ground is the outcome of a creative, and then political activity, not the discovery of a previous common ontological or universal essence. Moreover, such a ground is a building block for the categorical shaping of a new intercultural subjectivity, not a mere secondary implication of possible accommodation reached in an empirical way between cultural and legal patterns fated to remain semiotically and politically cut off from each other.

The intercultural items produced by similar experiences could, in the future, overcome the boundaries of legal interpretation to reach the domain of legislative enactment. As a logical-temporal interface between these two phases, the creation of an intercultural legal lexicon could generate useful work. But such work calls for another (enormous) prior commitment that should see as its pioneers academic and institutional cadres. Much could and should be done. Very little is being done. Of course, an intercultural legal lexicon should not be intended as a collection of intercultural legal statements. It ought instead to provide only semantic standards elaborated by metaphorical translations at a legal-anthropological level of cross-cultural understanding and doing.[93] The sole function of all these materials is to

[93]More precisely, through an intercultural legal approach the anthropologist-jurist should not so much assess how people from other cultures think about the (their) world, but rather try to understand how they and we could become able to conceive a future world—recursively including the same anthropologist-jurist—which we can live in, all together.

allow for an efficient interfacing between different cultural competences or semiotic universes in order to facilitate the creation of legislative patterns or, more generally, legal interpretations (by judges, lawyers, notaries, public authorities, and so on) which are interculturally substantiated. To be sure, making law intercultural requires a commitment from public authorities and would have to result from the dynamics of political processes, everywhere situated and developed by a logic of consent determined by history and dependent upon the contingent local composition of social forces. The specific content of legal statements must remain a product of historical and geo-political factors. An intercultural legal lexicon could be, however, a tool for guiding this social function onto a pluralistic and democratic path. The world emerging from an intercultural translation of semiotic universes is not virtually the same as something hovering above the pluralistic landscape of differences and overshadowing them by means of a dialectic inclusion. Rather, the intercultural social world is to burgeon and evolve beside the worlds of differences, working as an interface for the dynamic and interpenetrating iteration of them. Fundamental to underscore is that all these worlds are an emergence, not a plannable construction, from experience, therefore unforeseeable in their transformative interactions, features and outcomes. The intercultural approach, and legal-intercultural too, are only pathways for cultural creativity to follow, not recipes to achieve predetermined or pre-packaged results. We can only participate in the changing of worlds, influencing the ways in which they interact. The deliberate construction of the world is only a dramatic self-deception. The fact that there is not only one objective world out there, and that the internal/external divide is just an operational scheme without any ontological purport, does not mean we can build our worlds in all their respects; would they even be cultural or social worlds. The invisible intermingling of our minds and actions, and what lives within them, is too wide to allow us to entirely mold the world(s). Before we move out there, the constraints and resistance to carrying out such endeavors are within the unfolding of experience itself and its dark strands, including the opaque matter of which we are made.

The discursive style I decided to adopt in rendering the above sample case is also part of the methodology intended to construe the intercultural lexicon. The girl from Ghana has a somewhat confused awareness of the patterns that structure her cultural competence. Ghanaian tradition, Christianity, and Islam, local customs, are all woven and wrapped together in an absolutely idiomatic way of thinking, which the girl enacts and tells. But she does not know all that well what she actually knows. The work of lawyers-anthropologists could, and perhaps should stop here, leaving as a second step the task of interpreting, systematizing and even appealing directly to the reader for its completion. After all, such a choice would correspond to an epistemological attitude that is fully justified by the intent to avoid ethnocentric intrusion within the ethnographic report. From an epistemological point of view, the role required to the lawyer-anthropologist in the intercultural legal translation/transaction is, in a sense, deliberately incorrect. To support the migrant or the Other to use legal instruments in an intercultural way, anthropologists must help them to understand themselves, and disentangle the Other's own cultural competences and knowledge. This intervention could be invasive, even conditioning, I must admit, but it is the only way to set in motion the Other's cultural creativity in confronting the law and, through it, the multicultural environment. The intercultural lexicon ought not to be a table of equivalence theoretically decided by scholars comparing legal texts or ethnographic reports. It should rather come out from the culture, nay the interculture emergent in the making of a 'transactional world,' through self-interpretations produced by the actors of the multicultural situation, along the possible and hoped for paths of collaboration between migrants/individual belonging to minorities, native citizens, anthropologists and jurists.

3.8.2 Case #2: Residence Permits and 'Legitimate' Income for Islamic Religious Leaders Residing in Italy

The second case I will illustrate perhaps displays a practical example of the need for the above collaboration between lawyers and anthropologists, even beyond the epistemological tenets of critical anthropology. Everything stems from a research project aimed at promoting integration processes and conducted in an Italian city by the local university, joining the Police Office for Immigration and the local immigrant communities. The matters confronted during the activities were concerning immigration law analyzed from an intercultural point of view. The research team was composed of lawyers (practitioners and scholars committed to study the law of religion), anthropologists and cultural psychologists. The research methodology provided, *inter alia*, the implementation of meetings, including the staff of policemen and members of migrant communities. The meetings were supported by the presence of the research team and its components. During one of these meetings a question arose about a residency permit for one of the imams belonging to the Islamic community who still resides in that city. I say 'one of the imams' and not 'the' imam, because actually the official imam of that community was someone else.

The reason for that strange duplication is as follows and depends on the Italian legislation for a residence permit. The legislation requires that in order to apply for the residence permit, a non-EU citizen must specify the motives for entering indicated on the visa and, if they have no other special motivations, must prove to earn a regular income. The imam of this big community has a lot of work to do, and to make matter worse, he effectively has to work two jobs, since the imam occupation is not considered to be a job by the state thus forcing him to have another occupation as well. The imam of our story, unfortunately, albeit much loved by his brothers, was getting on in years, and therefore lacked the physical strength needed to perform those two jobs. Still, without earning an income, it is impossible to renew the residency permit. So, the old man tried to search for a job in addition to his role as imam. He was not able to find one. Meanwhile, the community hastily appointed another person to perform the duties of the imam.

A Syrian man, a member of the Islamic community, recounted the plight of the old imam to the participants of the meetings, explaining all the difficulties the whole

Islamic community had to endure. The policemen appeared to consider the problem but declared not to know how to devise a possible solution. A lawyer, present at the meeting, listened to all the discussion, then replied to the Syrian 'Are you certain the old imam cannot acquire another source of income? I ask this because Italian migration law states that the income required for a residence permit can also be 'personal income,' if the foreign subject is able to provide evidence.' The Syrian answered that he did not know anything about other possible sources of income for the old imam, but he was sure, in any case, that the community could provide for him. Hearing this, the lawyer pointed out that this support would have to be demonstrated, verifying a secure and certifiable income. The Syrian fell silent, shaking his head slowly.

Next it was the anthropologist's turn. He observed that the presence of an esteemed imam, loved by his community, is a very important element for the successful coexistence between community members and their larger social context. The lack of such guidance could have wide-ranging effects—and as he said this, he turned towards the police officers. Even so, many of them simply shrugged their shoulders, almost as if to exonerate themselves, meanwhile murmuring in low voices, 'The law is the law; there is nothing we can do.' In a sense, the problem was taking on theatrical dimensions, when a scholar of religious law and I intervened with a suggestion. We told the others about the *zakāt*, its significance in Islamic law and customs, and its actual use, for example, in the construction of mosques, even in migration contexts. We explained the charitable character of *zakāt*—resembling a kind of self-assessment—and the binding value it has for all the faithful. Then, we hypothesized whether or not it was possible for members of the community to pay a *zakāt* portion, which the community would then certify as a reserve for sustaining the imam. Of course, we addressed this question to the Syrian. The answer was immediate and clear. 'Certainly, I think it wouldn't be a problem,' he said, following with a personal description of the religious and social meaning of *zakāt* in the context of migration for the benefit of all present. After this positive response, we—the scholar and I—turned to the lawyer to ask if the income from a certified *zakāt* could be considered as 'personal income' according to the Italian law's requirements. The lawyer's answer was also positive. At that point, the most difficult hurdle remained, that is, the consent of police officers. Unexpectedly, all of them showed a sincere interest in the whole discussion and its subject matter, declaring finally that if the Islamic community had officially certified the financial support—through *zakāt*—for the old imam, for their part there would be no hindrance to considering the resulting stipend as 'personal income.'

I don't know how the relations between the Islamic community of that city and the Migration Office progressed. It is another open case. However, the kind of solution devised is interesting not only for the use of the intercultural method, but also because it provides a model for many other cases and similar plights, relevant even for natives and where in the place of *zakāt* there might be, for example, a *trust*. The connection between trusts and migration processes could then give rise to an array of legal devices to support the problems woven into the constraints and requirements concerning the residence of foreigners inside the national borders of the host country. But that is another story.

I could relate many other cases I have faced along the road of my legal-intercultural commitment. Some of these unfold in hospitals, where many problems arise from the discrepancies between the conceptual maps used by foreigners for their own bodies, and those usual among native medical staff. Sometimes the semiotic distance created by both the self-description of a patient's illness and the physician's ignorance of the folk medical language of the former—especially when the latter is confronted with unspecific symptoms or poly-semeiotic diagnostic results—can bring dramatic consequences. In those cases, the absence of anthropological support at the hospitals may encumber not only patient compliance to health care treatment, but also the possibility of making the appropriate diagnosis, and therefore (not) serving the essential purposes of biomedicine. The problem may seem to be only epistemological. However, it is an institutional and legal issue, too, which involves the legal responsibility of medical personnel and, well before, the general provision of anthropological support inside hospitals. The matter extends, moreover, to the timing of health care and the related economic organizational aspects, also reserved to the provisions of law.[94]

Now I turn from the hospital to the workplace. Here, a host of questions are determined by the invisible/mute parts within the grammar and semantics of value and behavior standards, such as good faith, normal due diligence, loyalty between employee and employers, standards and rules for disciplinary actions, and so on. Working with Japanese clients, for example, I discovered that a lot of difficulties in the workplace are caused by the intercultural asymmetric significance of silence. For European employers, it is inconceivable that to make evident his own disagreement a worker would adopt a kind of ambiguous, silent attitude, which an employer must note and properly interpret. In Europe on average, silence, especially in the case of hierarchical relationships, is synonymous with consent. Hence, a Japanese worker, unaware of this cultural and ethical difference regarding silence, could wait forever and in vain for an appropriate response from a European employer. On the other hand, the Japanese mind considers official protests and claims as leading to irreversible damage of harmony within workplace relationships, not to mention, then, recourse to a court for justice. The outcomes of such cultural assumptions about silence and, in a sense, the diverse attitude about disagreement are all ignored at the expense of Japanese workers, who invariably fail to take advantage of the opportunity to present their cases before the law. An intercultural solution for these difficulties could move in several directions. It should involve lawyers, trade unions, employers and employees, in an effort to develop communication standards likely to assure an intercultural synthesis between the invisible/mute parts of cultural competences at stake and their related legal consequences.

[94] I address such issues in Quaranta and Ricca (2012).

3.9 Interlocutory Conclusions

All of the cases illustrated above could benefit from being specifically mapped to the theoretical considerations developed in the initial parts of this chapter. But it is my intention to leave this task to the reader. Rather, I prefer to conclude my exposition by underlining the dynamic features of the intercultural approach, which tend to avoid opposition between state law and cultural or religious normative systems, in the name of a post-modern legal pluralism.

The relationship of law—including state law—with culture and everything that could be considered non-law[95] appears, through the lens of the intercultural legal approach, as an immanent tendency towards self-transformation that may be checked in all of the normative systems. The 'exorbitant' signification of legal texts and decisions, as well as the ties of meaning with the mute parts of their linguistic matter, are only manifestations of the intrinsic exceedance or 'self-beyondness' of signs. As communicative tools, the law has a signical consistency and hence it refers always to the other than itself to produce its meaning. In a sense, the modern legal project, in its bent for generality, enhances this intrinsic ambiguity of language, making its rules, statements and words vulnerable to the molding effect of interpenetration with other signs.[96] Comparative law studies showcase—in its deepest, albeit not frequent instances—the dependence of formal law on its backdrop of social meanings but with theoretical and descriptive aims. Instead, the intercultural legal approach is pivoted on how positive legal statements are irresistibly transformed when they come into contact with new cultural semiotic landscapes. In this way, it is metaphorically astride the making of that transformation.

This same transformation is, however, inherent in the modern project as well as its related generalizations because of the 'good ambiguity' they derive from the intrinsic Otherness of signs. To put it more simply, the issue is not generalization in and of itself, but the use made of it. If generalization, normative as well as descriptive, is intended as a concept, definitively shaped and ended in all its pragmatic and signifying consequences, then it will result as aprioristic, imperialistic, serializing and reifying. Conversely, if generalization is taken as synonymous to 'hypothesis,' open to an unfettered space of pragmatic and semiotic projections, then its outcomes will be the production of new semantic traces and the disclosure of creative forces functional to the inclusion of Otherness in the making of words and their meaning. All this is to be conceived not so much through the lens of an analysis of the dialectic interconnection between the spoken and the unspoken inside legal discourse, but rather by a fair account of the relationality immanent in the signs of which law is made. This will reveal, in turn, the semiotic exposure of law's words to Otherness, which is, at the same time, the very condition for their effective, authentic semantic scope to unfold in and through social experience. An authenticity that lies in the future and can be grasped, today, only as through the retrospective consideration of

---

[95] Goodrich (2012).

[96] de Certeau (1990) and Bauman (1991).

the implications that the linguistic categorizations included in legal predictions produce within the entire landscape of signs and person-signs that populate a global multicultural space. If so understood, modern law, including state law, will not obscure the differences, but rather will be conducive to them and will work as a device and a mirror by which to thematize cultural instantiations and allow them to acquire public recognition. The 'remote humanity' that Western anthropologists often study in their exotic and distant places of fieldwork has shifted and infiltrated their own countries of origin. It is therefore time they turn their gaze. Otherness has been poured into the geographical, political and social landscapes of Western modernity. Other humanities and their cultures thereby call into question and strike 'at heart' the original cosmopolitan kernel of modern thought. Coherence within ideals and praxis is ceaselessly claimed in democratic societies by people belonging to non-Western cultures or other-than-Christian religions. But if this is the case, and with a hint of plausibility or legitimation, it is only because of the consequences of modern thought. Despite all its sins, perhaps modernity alone can save us from itself.

References

Ahmad MI (2007) Interpreting communities: lawyering across languages differences. UCLA Law Rev 54:999

Andreas S (2006) Six blind elephants. Real People Press, Lafayette

Appadurai A (1986) The social life of things: commodities in cultural perspective. CUP, Cambridge

Appadurai A (1991) Global ethnoscapes: notes and queries for a transnational anthropology. In: Fox RG (ed) Recapturing anthropology: working in the present. School of American Research Press, Santa Fe

Appadurai A (1996) Modernity at large: cultural dimension of globalization. University of Minnesota Press, Minneapolis, MN

Apter E (2005) Translation without no original: scandals of textual reproduction. In: Bermann S, Wood M (eds) Nation, language, and the ethics of translation. Princeton University Press, Princeton, pp 159–174

Bakhtin MM (1981) The dialogical imagination. University of Texas Press, Austin

Bakhtin MM (1986) Speech genres and other late essays. University of Texas Press, Austin

Bakhtin MM (1993) Toward a philosophy of the act. University of Texas Press, Austin

Bauman Z (1991) Modernity and ambivalence. Polity Press/Blackwell, Cambridge

Bermann S (2005) Introduction. In: Bermann S, Wood M (eds) Nation, language, and the ethics of translation. Princeton University Press, Princeton, pp 1–10

Bhabha HK (1994) The location of culture. Routledge, London

Bhabha HK (1998) The third space. In: Rutheford J (ed) Identity, community, culture, difference. Lawrence and Wishart, London

Bibeau G, Corin E (eds) (1994) Beyond textuality: asceticism and violence in anthropological interpretation. Mouton de Gruyter, Berlin

Blasi G (2008) Lawyers, clients, and the 'Third Person in the Room.' UCLA Law Rev CVI. https://www.uclalawreview.org/lawyers-clients-and-the-third-person-in-the-room/

Blumenberg H (2007) Theorie der Unbegrifflichkeit. Suhrkamp, Frankfurt a. M

Boyarin J (ed) (1994) Remapping memory: the politics of TimeSpace. University of Minnesota Press, Minneapolis

Bruner JS, Goodnow JJ, Austin GA, Brown RW (1956) A study of thinking. Wiley, New York

Bryant S (2001) The five habits: building cross-cultural competence in lawyers. Clin Law Rev 8: 33–107. https://academicworks.cuny.edu/cl_pubs/258/

Bryant S, Peters JK (2005) Five habits for cross-cultural lawyering. In: Barrett KH, George WH (eds) Race, culture, psychology, and law. Sage, Thousand Oaks

Budick S (1996) Crises of alterity: cultural untranslatability and the experience of secondary otherness. In: Budick S, Iser W (eds) The translatability of cultures: figurations of the space between. Stanford University Press, Stanford, pp 1–22

Cao D (2007) Translating law. Multilingual matters. Cleveland

Capone A (2019) Pragmatics and philosophy: connections and ramifications. Springer, Cham

Cattel MG, Climo JJ (eds) (2002) Social memory and history: anthropological perspectives. Altamira Press, Walnut Creek

Chatterjee P (2004) The politics of the governed: reflections on popular politics in most of the world. Columbia University Press, New York

Chryssochoou X (2004) Cultural diversity: its social psychology. Blackwell, Malden

Clarke KM, Goodale M (eds) (2010a) Mirrors of justice: law and power in a post-cold war era. Cambridge University Press, New York

Clarke KM, Goodale M (2010b) Introduction: understanding the multiplicity of justice. In: Clarke KM, Goodale M (eds) Mirrors of justice: law and power in a post-cold war era. Cambridge University Press, New York, pp 1–27

Clifford J (1988) On ethnographic authority. In: Clifford J (ed) The predicament of culture: twentieth century ethnography, literature, and art. Harvard University Press, Cambridge, pp 21–54

Clifford J (1997) Routes: travel and translation in the late twentieth century. Harvard University Press, Cambridge

Clifford J, Marcus GE (eds) (1986) Writing culture: the poetics and politics of ethnography. University of California Press, Berkeley

Constantini C (2012) The iconicity of space: comparative law and the geopolitics of jurisdiction. In: Monateri P (ed) Methods of comparative law. Edward Elgar, Cheltenham, pp 230–241

Cover RM (1983) The Supreme Court, 1982 Term -- Foreword: Nomos and narrative. Harv Law Rev 97(1):4–68. https://digitalcommons.law.yale.edu/fss_papers/2705

Cover RM (1986) Violence and the word. Yale Law J 95:1601–1629. http://digitalcommons.law.yale.edu/fss_papers/2708

Cowan JK (2006) Culture and rights after "Culture and Rights". Am Anthropol CVIII(I):9–24

Crapanzano V (2004) Imaginative horizons: an essay in literary philosophical anthropology. University of Chicago Press, Chicago

Crapanzano V (2010) Textualization, mystification and power of the frame. In: Zenker O, Kumoll K (eds) Beyond writing culture: current intersections of epistemologies and representational practices. Berghahn Books, New York

Cronin M (2006) Translation and identity. Routledge, London

de Certeau M (1990) L'invention du quotidien, vol. I, Arts de faire. Gallimard, Paris

Delpla I (ed) (2002) L'usage anthropologique du principe de charité. Kimé, Paris

Denzin NK (1997) Interpretive ethnography: ethnographic practices for the 21st century. Sage, Thousand Oaks

Denzin NK (2008) Symbolic interactionism and cultural studies: the politics of interpretation. Blackwell, Oxford

Descola P, Pálsson G (eds) (1996) Nature and society: anthropological perspectives. Routledge, London

de Sousa SB (2020) Toward a new legal common sense: law, globalization, and emancipation. Butterworths, London

Deutscher G (2010) Through the language glass: why the world looks different in other languages. Metropolitan Books, Henry Holt and Company, New York

Dewey J (1924) Logical method and law. Philos Rev 33(6):560–572

Dewey J (1938) Logic, the theory of inquiry. Henry Holt and Co, New York

Dewey J, Bentley A (1949) Knowing and the known. Beacon Press, Boston
Dick P (2011) Perils of identities: group rights and the politics of intragroup difference. UBC Press, Vancouver
Douzinas C (2000) The end of human rights: critical legal thought at the turn of the century. Hart, Oxford
Dwyer K (1987) Moroccan dialogues: anthropology in question. Waveland Press, Prospect Heights
Eberhard C (2001) Towards an intercultural legal theory: the dialogical challenge. Soc Leg Stud 6 (1):171–201
Eberhard C (2009) Law and anthropology in a 'Glocal' world the challenge of dialogue. In: Freeman M, Napier D (eds) Law and anthropology: current legal issues, vol 12, pp 67–88
Eco U (2003) Dire quasi la stessa cosa. Esperienze di traduzione. Bompiani, Milano
Eco U (2008) Experiences in translation. University of Toronto Press Incorporated, Toronto
Eisenberg A (2005) Identity and liberal politics: the problem of minorities within minorities. In: Eisenberg A, Spinner-Halev J (eds) Minorities within minorities: equality, rights and diversity. CUP, Cambridge, pp 249–270
Eisenberg A (2009) Reasons of identity: a normative guide to the political and legal assessment of identity claims. Oxford University Press, Oxford
Engle Merry S (2006a) Human rights and gender violence: translating international law into local justice. Chicago University Press, Chicago
Engle Merry S (2006b) Transnational human rights and local activism: mapping the middle. Am Anthropol CVIII(1):38–51
Engle Merry S (2010) Beyond compliance: toward an anthropological understanding of international justice. In: Clarke KM, Goodale M (eds) Mirrors of justice: law and power in a post-cold war era. Cambridge University Press, New York, pp 28–43
Foblets M-C (2005) Mobility versus law, mobility in the law? Judges in Europe are confronted with the thorny question "Which Law Applies to Litigants of Migrant Origin"? In: von Benda-Beckman F, von Benda-Beckmann K, Griffiths A (eds) Mobile people, mobile law: expanding legal relations in a contracting world. Routledge, London, pp 297–315
Foblets M-C, Renteln AD (eds) (2009a) Multicultural jurisprudence: comparative perspectives of the cultural defences (Onati series in law and society). Hart, Oxford
Foblets M-C, Renteln AD (2009b) Introduction. In: Foblets M-C, Renteln AD (eds) Multicultural jurisprudence: comparative perspectives of the cultural defences (Onati series in law and society). Hart, Oxford, pp 1–6
Gadamer H-G (2013) Truth and method. Bloomsbury, London
Gibbs RW Jr (1994) Poetics of mind: figurative thought, language, and understanding. Cambridge University Press, Cambridge
Gibbs RW Jr (2005) Embodiment and cognitive science. Cambridge University Press, Cambridge
Gingrich A, Fox RG (2002) Introduction. In: Gingrich A, Fox RG (eds) Anthropology by comparison. Routledge, London
Glucksberg S (2001) Understanding figurative language: from metaphors to idioms. Oxford University Press, Oxford
Goodale M (2007) Introduction: locating rights, envisioning law between the global and the local. In: Goodale M, Merry SE (eds) The practice of human rights: tracking law between the global and the local. CUP, Cambridge, pp 1–38
Goodale M (2022) Reinventing human rights. Stanford University Press, Stanford
Goodale M (2023) Justice in the Vernacular: an anthropological critique of commensuration. https://www.researchgate.net/publication/358803212_Justice_in_the_Vernacular_An_Anthropological_Critique_of_Commensuration [Forthcoming in Law & Social Inquiry (2023) special issue entitled "Measures of Justice: A Symposium in Honor of Sally Engle Merry," edited by Dixon P, Firchow P, and Vera-Adrianzen F]
Goodrich P (2012) Interstitium and non-law. In: Monateri P (ed) Methods of comparative law. Edward Elgar, Cheltenham, pp 213–229

Gupta A, Ferguson J (1997a) Culture, power, place: ethnography and the end of an era. In: Gupta A, Ferguson J (eds) Culture, power, place: explorations in critical anthropology. Duke University Press, Durham, pp 1–29

Gupta A, Ferguson J (1997b) Culture, power, place: explorations in critical anthropology. Duke University Press, Durham

Hannerz U (1996) Transnational connections: culture, people, places. Routledge, New York

Heeschen V (2003) Linguist and anthropologist as translators. In: Maranhão T, Streck B (eds) Translation and ethnography: the anthropological challenge of intercultural understanding. University of Arizona Press, Tucson, pp 115–134

Holden L (ed) (2011a) Cultural expertise and litigation: patterns, conflicts, narratives. Routledge, New York

Holden L (2011b) Expert report writing: professional commitments and legal outcomes. In: Holden L (ed) Anthropological expertise and litigation: patterns, conflicts, narratives. Routledge, London

Horkheimer M, Adorno TW (2002) Dialectic of enlightenment: philosophical fragments. Stanford University Press, Stanford

Ingold T (2007) Lines: a brief history. Routledge, Abingdon

Iser W (1996) Coda to discussion. In: Budick S, Iser W (eds) The translatability of cultures: figurations of the space between. Stanford University Press, Stanford, pp 294–302

Jackendoff R (1983) Semantics and cognition. MIT Press, Massachusetts

Joerges C, Sand I-J, Teubner G (eds) (2004) Transnational governance and constitutionalism. Hart, Portland

Johnson M (1987) The body and the mind: the bodily basis of meaning, imagination and reason. University of Chicago Press, Chicago

Johnson M (2007) The meaning of the body: aesthetics of human understanding. University of Chicago Press, Chicago

Jones P (1999) Human rights, group rights, and peoples' rights. Hum Rights Q 21(1):80–107

Keane W (2007) Christian moderns: freedom and fetish in the mission encounter. The University of California Press, Berkeley

Khagram S, Levitt P (eds) (2008) The transnational studies reader: intersections and innovations. Routledge, New York

Kövecses Z (2006) Metaphor in culture: universality and variation. Cambridge University Press, Cambridge

Kymlicka W (2003) Multicultural states and intercultural citizens. Theory Res Educ 1(2):147–169

Lakoff G (1987) Women, fire and dangerous things: what categories reveal about the mind. University of Chicago Press, Chicago

Lakoff G, Johnson M (1980) Metaphors we live by. University of Chicago Press, Chicago

Lakoff G, Núñez RE (2000) Where mathematics come from: how the embodied mind brings mathematics into being. Basic Books, New York

Langacker RW (1987) Foundations of cognitive grammar: theoretical prerequisites. Stanford University Press, Stanford

Langacker RW (2000) Grammar and conceptualizations. Mouton de Gruyter, Berlin

Langacker RW (2002) Concept, image, and symbol: the cognitive basis of grammar. Mouton de Gruyter, Berlin

Lassiter LE (2005) The Chicago guide to collaborative ethnography. Chicago University Press, Chicago

Legrand P (2005) Issues in translatability of law. In: Bermann S, Wood M (eds) Nation, language, and the ethics of translation. Princeton University Press, Princeton, pp 30–50

Lloyd GER (2007) Cognitive variations: reflections on the unity and diversity of human mind. Oxford University Press, Oxford

Lorusso AM (ed) (2005) Metafora e conoscenza. Bompiani, Milano

Mackinnon CA (1995) Reflections on law in the everyday life of women. In: Sarat A, Kearns TR (eds) Law in everyday life. University of Michigan Press, Ann Arbor, pp 109–122

Marcus GE (1995) Ethnography in/of the world system: the emergence of multi-sited ethnography. Annu Rev Anthropol XXIV:95–117
Marcus GE (2006) What is at stake – and is not – in the idea and practice of multi-sited ethnography. In: Moore H, Sanders T (eds) Anthropology in theory: issues in epistemology. Blackwell, Malden, pp 618–621
Mattila HES (2006) Comparative legal linguistics. Ashgate, Aldershot
Melissaris E (2009) Ubiquitous law. Ashgate, Farnham
Merleau-Ponty M (1964) Le visible et l'invisible. Éditions Gallimard, Paris
Meusburger P, Hefferman M, Wunder E (eds) (2011) Cultural memories: the geographical point of view. Springer, Dordrecht
Mintz SW, Price R (1992) The birth of African-American culture: an anthropological perspective. Beacon Press, Boston
Muthu S (2003) Enlightenment against empire. Princeton University Press, Princeton
Nader L (2010) Epilogue: the words we use: justice, human rights, and sense of injustice. In: Clarke KM, Goodale M (eds) Mirrors of justice: law and power in a post-cold war era. Cambridge University Press, New York, pp 316–322
O'Leary KE, Martin-Scott M (eds) (2021) Multicultural lawyering: navigating the culture of the law, the lawyer, and the client. Caroline Academic Press, Durham
Ortony A (ed) (1993) Metaphor and thought. Cambridge University Press, Cambridge
Ost F, van de Kerckhove M (2002) De la pyramide au reséau. Pour une théorie dialectique du droit. Facultés Universitaires St. Louis, Bruxelles
Philippopoulos-Mihalopoulos A (2010) Spatial justice: law and the geography of withdrawal. Int J Law Context 6(3):1–16
Philippopoulos-Mihalopoulos A (2012) Law, spaces, bodies: the emergence of spatial justice. In: de Sutter L, Mcgee K (eds) Deleuze and the law (Deleuze connections). Edinburgh University Press, Edinburgh, pp 90–110
Piomelli A (2006) Cross-cultural lawyering by the book: the latest clinical texts and a sketch of a future agenda. Hastings Race & Poverty Law J 4:131–179. http://repository.uchastings.edu/faculty_scholarship/637
Pommer SE (2008) Translation as intercultural transfer: the case of law. SKASE J Transl Interpretation (on line) 3(1):17–21
Quaranta I, Ricca M (2012) Malati fuori luogo. Medicina interculturale. Raffaello Cortina, Milano
Renteln AD (2004) The cultural defense. OUP, Oxford
Ricca M (2008) Oltre Babele. Codici per una democrazia interculturale. Dedalo, Bari
Ricca M (2012) Natura inventata e natura implicita nel diritto. Incursioni interculturali. In: Marrone G (ed) Semiotica della natura (natura della semiotica). Mimesis, Milano, pp 309–358
Ricca M (2013a) Il tradimento delle immagini tra kirpan e transazioni interculturali. Cultura vs. competenza culturale nel mondo del diritto. E|C Rivista dell'Associazione italiana di Studi semiotici: 1–31. http://www.ec-aiss.it/index_d.php?recordID=678
Ricca M (2013b) La fabrique coupable des malentendus innocente. Étrangers, diffractions culturelles et strategies politiques du non savoir. Revue des Sciences Sociales, Malentendus 50:60–68
Ricca M (2013c) Culture interdette. Modernità, migrazioni, diritto interculturale. Bollati Boringhieri, Torino
Ricca M (2018) *Ignorantia facti excusat*: legal liability and the intercultural significance of Greimas' "contrat de véridition". Int J Semiot Law 31:101–126. https://doi.org/10.1007/s11196-017-9529-6
Ricca M (2019) Signs across races: Al-Jahiz's cosmo-semiosis and his trans-racial mapping of the "human." CALUMET - Intercult Law Humanit Rev 8:21–40. https://calumet-review.com/index.php/2019/06/11/signs-across-races-al-jahizs-cosmo-semiosis-and-his-trans-racial-mapping-of-the-human/

Ricca M (2022a) Perpetually astride Eden's boundaries: the limits to the 'limits of law' and the semiotic inconsistency of 'legal enclosures'. Int J Semiot Law 35:179–229. https://doi.org/10.1007/s11196-020-09771-0
Ricca M (2022b) The 'spaghettification' of performativity across cultural boundaries: the trans-culturality/trans-spatiality of digital communication as an event horizon for speech acts. Int J Semiot Law 35:2435–2479. https://doi.org/10.1007/s11196-021-09880-4
Ricca M (2023) Processive hoping (forthcoming)
Ricoeur P (1975) La metáphore vive. Édition du Seuil, Paris
Ricoeur P (1978) The metaphorical process as cognition, imagination, and feeling. Crit Inq 5(1) Special Issue on Metaphor:143–159
Riles A (2000) The network inside/out. University of Michigan Press, Ann Arbor
Ruggiu I (2020) Culture and the judiciary: the anthropologist judge. Routledge, Abingdon
Sacco R (1995) Mute law. Am J Comp Law 43(3):455–467
Sacco R (2015) Il diritto muto. Neuroscienze, conoscenza tacita, valori condivisi. Il Mulino, Bologna
Sajò A (ed) (2004) Human rights with modesty: the problem of universalism. Martinus Nijhoff, Leiden
Salmani Nodoushan MA (2022) Breaking out of the Gricean vicious cycle: let's divorce semantics and just agree that there is no meaning in language. Int J Lang Stud 16(3):33–60
Santos BS, Rodríguez-Garavito C (2005) Law, politics, and the subaltern in counter-hegemonic globalization. In: Santos BS, Rodríguez-Garavito C (eds) Law and globalization from below: towards a cosmopolitan legality. Cambridge University Press, Cambridge, pp 1–28
Schacter DL (ed) (1995) Memory distortion. How minds, brains, and societies reconstruct the past. Harvard University Press, Cambridge
Schepel H (2013) Rules of recognition: a legal constructivist approach to transnational private regulation. In: Jurčys P, Kjaer PF, Yatsunami R (eds) Regulatory hybridization in the transnational sphere. Martinus Nijhoff – Brill, Leiden, pp 189–202
Searle J (2001) Rationality in action. The MIT Press, Cambridge
Shachar A (2008) Privatizing diversity: a cautionary tale from religious arbitration in family law. Theor Inq Law 9(2):573–607
Silverstein M (2003) Translation, transduction, transformation: skating "glossando" on thin semiotic ice. In: Rubel P, Rosman A (eds) Translating cultures: perspectives on translation and anthropology. Berg, Oxford, pp 75–105
Singleton TA (2006) African diaspora archaeology in dialogue. In: Yelvington KA (ed) Afro-Atlantic dialogues. Anthropology in diaspora. School of American Research Press – James Currey Ltd, Santa Fe, pp 249–288
Sonne JA (2018) Cross-cultural lawyering and religion: a clinical perspective. Clin Law Rev 25: 223–268
Spickard P (2017) Comment: super-diversity? What super-diversity? J Am Ethn Hist 36(4):62–66. https://doi.org/10.5406/jamerethnhist.36.4.0062
Talmy L (2003) Toward a cognitive semantics. I. Concept structuring systems. MIT Press, Cambridge
Tavani C (2012) Collective rights and the cultural identity of Roma: a case study of Italy. Kononklijke Brill NV, Leiden
Tedlock D (1983) The spoken word and the word of interpretation. University of Pennsylvania Press, Philadelphia
Tedlock D (1995) Interpretation, participation, and the role of narrative in dialogical anthropology. In: Tedlock D, Mannheim B (eds) The dialogical emergence of culture. University of Illinois Press, Urbana, pp 253–288
Teubner G (1998) Legal irritants. Good faith in British law or how unifying law ends up in new divergences. Mod Law Rev 61(1):11–32

Teubner G (2004) Societal constitutionalism: alternatives to state-centred constitutional theory? In: Joerges C, Sand I-J, Teubner G (eds) Transnational governance and constitutionalism. Hart, Portland, pp 3–28

Tully J (2002) Reimagining belonging in circumstances of cultural diversity: a citizen approach. In: Hedetoft U, Hijort M (eds) The postnational self: belonging and identity. University of Minnesota Press, Minneapolis, pp 152–177

Tully LD (2020) The cultural (re)turn: the case for teaching culturally responsible lawyering. Stanf J Civil Rights Civil Liberties 16:201–258

Tyler TR (2006) Why people obey the law. Princeton University Press, Princeton

Van Brakel J (2006) De-essentializing across the board: no need to speak the same language. Rechtstheorie & Rechtspractijk 35:263–284

Venuti L (1995) The scandals of translation: towards an ethics of difference. Routledge, London

Verkuyten M (2001) "Abnormalization" of ethnic minorities in conversation. Br J Soc Psychol 40(2):257–278

Vertovec S (2007) Super-diversity and its implications. Ethn Racial Stud 30(6):1024–1054

Vertovec S (2014) Super-diversity. Routledge, London

Violi P (1997) Significato ed esperienza. Bompiani, Milano

Wai R (2008) The interlegality of transnational private law. Law Contemp Probl 71(3):107–128

White JB (1990) Justice as translation: an essay in cultural and legal criticism. University of Chicago Press, Chicago

Whyte J (2019) The morals of the market: human rights and the rise of neoliberalism. Verso, London

Wyshogrod E (1998) An ethics of remembering: history, heterology and the nameless others. University of Chicago Press, Chicago

Yelvington KA (2006) Introduction. In: Yelvington KA (ed) Afro-Atlantic dialogues. Anthropology in diaspora. School of American Research Press – James Currey Ltd, Santa Fe, NM, pp 3–32

Zenker O, Kumoll K (2010) Prologue: opening doors beyond writing cultures. In: Zenker O, Kumoll K (eds) Beyond writing culture: current intersections of epistemologies and representational practices. Bergham Books, New York, pp 1–38

Chapter 4
Rights, Space and Categories: An Introduction to Legal Chorology

4.1 Rights, Space and the Horizontal Relation Between Legal Meanings and People's Spaces of Action

This essay proposes an intertwined reading of social spaces and the inter-subjective/horizontal implementation of human rights, to be addressed from a legal semiotic perspective. Intersubjectivity and horizontality immediately evoke the idea of spatial distinctions and conjunctions. When applied to social and legal experience, a horizontal recognition/apportionment of rights means that one subject is entitled to replace another subject in a specific position. More specifically, a subject horizontally replaces (or supersedes) another whenever the latter is legally required to withdraw, so as to leave room (or better: *space*) for the former. The same result, however, obtains when people question the validity of a legal rule because of its contrast with human and/or fundamental rights and the invalidity is recognized in hierarchical terms through a judicial review of legislation. Actually, the invalidation of statutory law's rule in most cases turns into an inter-subjective replacement. In this sense, human and/or fundamental rights seem to produce their normative effects according to both a *vertical* and a *horizontal* logic. Nonetheless, as I shall show, the horizontal logic ends up absorbing the hierarchical/vertical one. This is because inter-subjective conflicts, if analyzed under the lens of law, tend to commute in inter-normative and thereby semantic ones. The consequence is that solving inter-subjective disputes based on human rights is equivalent to settling normative contradictions or semantic tensions.

The inter-subjective replacement resulting from the vertical and/or horizontal implementation of human rights comprises a shifting of subjects and the spaces of their legitimate conduct. From the legal point of view, the sequence *takes place simultaneously*, therefore, in and across the semantic and pragmatic domains. This occurs because law's words are designed to simultaneously define both subjects and activities. Consequentially, the legal words project their meanings across space—

M. Ricca, *Intercultural Spaces of Law*, Law and Visual Jurisprudence 10,
https://doi.org/10.1007/978-3-031-27436-7_4

even when it is only a perspective space—thus inherently embodying spatiality within their signification.

More generally, it can be observed that all words encapsulate a list of instructions *for using the world*. Therefore, despite their apparent 'thinghood,' the nouns defining objects also include and provide guidelines for managing dynamic relationships within the world. Just to give an example, in its semantic scope the word 'car' epitomizes a whole range of activities connoted by teleological and instrumental characteristics. 'Car' implicitly communicates the means needed to construe and use what it signifies, and this according to what we will assume its meaning to be. Those means, in turn, constitute the elements of its semantic structure, its form or even its semantic checklist. By virtue of this checklist, we can say that something is a car if it implies those elements/features or, at least, a number of them. We can call these elements implications, or even consequences. They can unfold in the symbolic and/or pragmatic domain. But, in either case, they will be signs.

When the words are legal ones, their pragmatic implications do not need to be excavated by means of a dis-compositional anamnesis of the semiotic relationships and experiences epitomized by and implicitly inherent in each term. Law makes use of the words to shape the social environment: it *takes place* not only to qualify facts and behaviors, but also to trigger human reactions and achieve social/empirical results.

Beyond its political-theological origins, the exteriority of modern law—that is, its incompetence in ruling the conscience domain—strongly conditions its attitude toward molding the living space of subjects. Laws rule space, but by doing so, they pragmatically connote and cooperate to shape it. The active role played by the law makes it so that legal meanings and purposes do not produce their consequences within a semantically empty space. For legal meanings to be implemented, they need to be enacted by people embedded in concrete experiential frameworks. This means that the semantic relationships proactively encapsulated in legal words inevitably encounter other semantic circuits and experiential spaces whose agents are, in turn, the same legal subjects. To be lived, these spaces also involve words and signs, which connect with legal ones, so engendering new semantic relationships. As in a circle, therefore, every semantic relationship can engender space by potentially involving and conjoining spaces produced either by law's prescriptions or subjects' existential experiences. Hence, the choice of whether to apply a specific legal rule, when and how to implement and interpret it, if and in what way to coordinate it with other legal statements—implicated by the semantic indexes involved in every situation that must be legally qualified and lived by subjects of the law—all these activities require the drawing of semiotic and, at the same time, spatial lines. The resulting semio-spatial solutions, if they are to be effective, will constitute a synthesis of potentially 'concurring/competing spaces' and, on the other side, a modeling of a semantic scope of words (including legal words) that proactively envisage them.

Legal practitioners (especially lawyers and judges) continually mold semantic-spatial trends. Through their interpretation of laws, they translate and transact ends, means, and spaces, mapped out by common people and/or institutional subjects. Even the well-known paradigm of subsidiarity is involved in such semio-spatial activities and is implemented in accordance with the general features of legal practice. The implementation of the subsidiarity principle constitutes one of the main legal hubs where the plurality of social meanings finds a normative-institutional modality of coordination.[1] It is the outcome of a cartographic activity designed to determine the reciprocal borders between linguistic categories, and the spaces of subjective conduct marked out by those categories. These borders (or con-fines, intended in the etymological sense of the word: from Latin *cum-fines*) will simultaneously function, therefore, as semantic boundaries and pragmatic borders, as such intended to inscribe themselves *within* the space and to write it—namely, to forge spatiality by filling it with human actions and fashioning the spatial articulations to be in tune with the rhythm of social subjects' various behaviors.

It would be sufficient to decline in the plural the normative implications of the trinomial word/action/space to see a sort of syntax of replacement—namely the parameter to set social roles according to their order of meaning and value—immediately take shape. In a sense, we could even forgo the distinctive mention of hierarchy, division of competence and subsidiarity since each of these terms is only a way to epitomize and convey the idea that social roles and their related meanings are legally and axiologically ordered and differentiated. If we assumed this unifying perspective, we could catch with one look all the 'replacing implications' vertically and horizontally ensuing from the application and/or annulment of legal rules.

As I will try to show, if we were to observe the distinction between vertical and horizontal implementation of human and fundamental rights[2] from a semiotic-spatial point of view, it would prove to be a mere rating-descriptive typological divide, devoid of any deep-rooted signification.[3] Ultimately, we could say instead that all declinations of subsidiarity rely upon the horizontal relationship extant between the spaces-meanings acted by the different subjects moving in and across social landscapes. Such a statement, however, needs further examination and demonstration. For now, I foreshadow its contents only to point out how even the private/public divide underlying the liberal view of human and/or fundamental rights and its implicit authority/freedom dialectics becomes relativized when it is understood within the perspective of the horizontality between values and meanings that constitutional and/or supranational legal systems adopt when ordering social relationships.

The distinction between what is public and what is private, what is pertinent to the state and what to individuals or groups, does not only depend on the subjects whose

[1] On the principle of subsidiarity and its multifarious projections, in a vast literature, see, at least, Millon-Delson (1993), and the collection of essays edited by Evans and Zimmermans (2014); with specific regard to EU legal experience and human rights, see Christoffersen (2009, pp. 235 ff.) and van Zeben and Nicolaïdis (2019).

[2] This distinction parallels that between a 'vertical' and a 'horizontal' subsidiarity. On the theoretical presuppositions of this distinction, fruitfully analyzed from a theoretical and sociological perspective, see Donati (2009, spec. pp. 228 ff.).

[3] With specific regard to the relationship between subsidiarity and human and/or fundamental rights protection, see Carozza (2003) and Alleweldt (2019).

conduct we consider. Even private subjects, in pursuing their tasks and goals, can assume behavior with public and constitutional legal signification. Moreover, through their activities, private actors weave social relationships that continually remap the situations within which legal statements and values produce their effects, and dynamically interact with each other. All in all, whoever acts creates new spaces. However, 'new spaces' also means 'new signs,' new semantic relationships, and thereby new legal meanings, and ultimately an unprecedented unfolding of constitutional scenery. Private activities, precisely because of their *spatiographic* significance, hold therefore an inherent public import.

The principle of horizontal subsidiarity, as an example, is commonly intended—perhaps a little too schematically, especially within national legal systems—as a paradigm for distinguishing the respective areas of competence between public and private action. Nonetheless the border separating these two circuits should not be considered to be automatically drawn by means of an aprioristic paradigm that distinguishes one from the other. There are no rigid distinctions that are valid once and for all to accomplish this task. On the contrary, that border is to be considered the result of a continuous commitment to the spatial-semantic re-configuration of relationships engendered by the intermingling of private and public actions. The possibility of drawing clear-cut conceptual borders/confines and precise distinctions between public and private is only a final, even if always interlocutory, result. It can take place only when the semantic-spatial landscape woven by the various subjects' activities reaches a relatively stable settling, so that its cartography—however transient—becomes viable, at least. Such distinctions and differentiations, however, will always and inevitably remain amenable to being re-mapped. This is because however much 'private' and 'public' can be divided and differentiated for practical purposes, namely from a functional perspective, they keep, in any case, an underlying interlacement and co-embeddedness due to their axiological signification and the processes of social implementation of their respective meanings.

The actions of subjects and, by extension, the *life of law* are constantly exposed to the changes and transformations of experiential contexts. The legal system is never utterly self-referential. In other words, there is no single nomosphere that is completely self-sufficient and capable of autopoietic self-sustaining. The attempts to read the legal experience (or the legal dimension of experience) in this key of radical unrelatedness or self-constitutivity lead to a partial view. A view—to wit—that may prove useful and even legitimate for heuristic or practical contingent purposes, but which is unable to explain why legal experience transforms or keeps still, and in what directions or sense it does.

The signs of legal discourse partake in a semiotic universe, indeed a semiotic-spatial pluriverse. They appear, at a first glance, as inherently and constitutively endowed with performative and cogent power. However, legal signs (and thereby law's symbolic enunciations) are not able to self-produce the framework conditions essential to convey and host their signification; ultimately, they are not even able to control the occurrence of all the factual elements needed to assure their unaltered effectiveness. The processes of legitimation underpinning the life of any legal system can never stop the game of signifying that engenders a semantically closed world, immune to the self-transformation of meanings. Put diversely, the performative attitude of law is always and intrinsically incomplete.[4] It is so because of its inevitable vulnerability to the semantic fluctuations fueled by continuous contact with the semiotic landscapes drawn by social experiences, and the unforeseeable directions undertaken by innumerable individual actions (which must be adjudicated).

Semiotic landscapes can be compared to the contexts of application—to use a language more comfortable to lawyers—and the signification of legal rules. If law, by virtue of its deontic charge/power, is undoubtedly ordered to *imprint* a specific pragmatic bent on social contexts, in the making of this achievement it is, in turn, reflexively connoted by the *semiotic matter* these contexts are made of. A constitutive and, at the same time dialectical, condition of law's function is the existence of a social basin populated by subjects, relationships, and situations, that is capable of receiving and implementing legal words/meanings. Legal communicative acts are designed to rule something that is 'other than law,' and eventually, even conflicts with and/or resists its pretensions of conformity. Even if laws could generate their own effectiveness, they would be utterly useless or even inconceivable, because their binding features would make little sense. Just like values, moral and legal imperatives feed on a sort of dialectics of absence. 'Values' are only that which may also *not be*. In the same vein, a legal rule or imperative is only that which may also be infringed or disobeyed, namely what may eventually not occur. Otherwise, facts and values, *facticity* and *deontic factors*, would coincide from the outset, but in this case both the axiological and the legal discourse (or more generally: deontic discourse) would be bereft of their own objects and devoid of any purpose.

This observation does not exclude, however, that a coincidence between 'value' and 'fact' (or, 'ought' and 'is') could pragmatically function as a horizon of possibility, as such placed at the end of a process of coordination and transaction within a legal and social/empirical world. In the midst, in any case, an experience is produced, a pragmatic path, which can take shape through a process of cogeneration and reciprocal transaction between legal enunciations and social contexts, deontic signs and empirical signs. The final synthesis or adjustment between norm and fact will constitute an outcome of the semiotic 'work of integration' that both subjects bound to law's application and other social actors—in their capacity as legal subjects—will have carried out. Facts/cases must be identified with legal categories and interpretations, just as legal statements must be selected in tune with the meanings ascribed to facts/cases. Only in such a processive and transactional sense is it tenable to argue that law contributes to the production of the factual dimension, that is to say that facts assume new features when placed under the (lens of) legal categories. Within legal experience, facts/cases are not 'as they are' regardless of the laws that (will eventually) rule over them. Symmetrically, the law's words are not immune to the *contaminations*, a sort of semantic cross-pollination, emanating from the situations they rule. Outside their application and the related adjustment to

[4] On this incompleteness I refer, for further investigations, to Ricca (2022).

protean and unpredictable features of the world, legal statements and their meanings are not the same as those which will emerge at the end of the process of their interpretation/implementation/application. Along this path, their semantic potential will re-form, as it is tested by events and cases, responding to them through variable and differentiated feedback.

Changes in experiential contexts remold the consequences of legal statements and thereby their meanings. However, both individual conduct and institutional behavior often cross and re-draw previously established spatial borders, including those traditionally defined as 'territorial.' By means of their actions, people trace new semantic frontiers through activities that cut across the pre-existing public/private divides. When this occurs, the relations of interdependence between these two domains are recalculated. The redefinition of the substantial matter of both the public and private spheres will inevitably have axiological-political features (which do not exclude the hermeneutical-cognitive ones). In any case, only at the end of such an effort of re-definition can the distinction between the public and private dimensions be pragmatically re-articulated; only then can that distinction be attuned to the signification of each of these spheres by taking in due account the possibility of implementation of the relevant constitutional principles.

Drawing borders between public and private spaces of competence and power is much more than a mechanical operation or a taxonomic classification performed according to fixed, predetermined patterns. Quite the opposite, it is an extremely discretional task that finds its rhythm through value choices and semantic remolding; these are in turn spurred by experiential contexts engendered in each case by the unfolding social actions and the semantic implications they assume under the lens of law. What is at stake, ultimately, is a continuous re-negotiation of the geography, or better, the chorology of subjectivity.[5]

What occurs within the area of human and/or fundamental rights protection in terms of spaces and meanings constitutes only an expression of a large-scale process, traceable among the modes of legal cognition. It pertains inherently to the connection between space, activity of categorization, and time. A general analysis of the relationships between space and categories could be extremely useful to show the spatial implications of human rights and their *substitutive* implementation. It is precisely to this that I now turn.

[5] As for the term 'chorology' and, more specifically, the expression 'legal chorology,' and the reasons that lead me to this linguistic choice, see below.

4.2 Spaces and Categories

To begin, I would pose a question. When legal categories project themselves through multiple spaces, or better, are analyzed through a chorological (namely spatial-semiotic) lens, they immediately show an increase in their meaning potentialities: why does this occur?

The answer to this question might start with terms used as stepping-stones, placed to create a path towards an explicative framework. These terms are: 'categories,' 'pragmatic projections,' and 'emergence of semiotic contexts.' Legal and linguistic categories are both endowed with semantic borders, or more precisely, they define themselves by means of semantic boundaries. Likewise, in common and legal languages, each category and its use imply some pertinence constraint that is set out according to a topographic logic resulting, ultimately, in an *in/out* device.[6] What is to be included *in* or, instead, excluded *from*, the list of elements defining each categorical set, however, is not to be considered so much a *datum,* as rather an outcome that stems from an activity of interpretation and representation.[7] An activity that, in turn, is carried out in view of specific ends, taking into account the past, present, and potential relationships between each categorical *product* as well as the related context of experience and signification.

In the current language, however, each category tends to show itself as a monolithic entity, a sort of in-one-piece and all-round semantic sculpture, nearly absolute, in such a way as to eclipse either the activities presupposed for the definition of its semantic borders, or the underlying and connected semiotic relationships.[8] Each category, therefore, looks like a form that in turn comprises a checklist, including essential or *molar* elements/features/properties. If compared to the other semantic implications, those elements are placed in a sort of hierarchical or preferential position. This means that those elements are treated as if they could soar above the secondary/accidental semantic implications and the boundary semiotic relationships, even if these must both substantiate the semantic consistency of the category at issue, its gushing out of experience, and its continuous slipping into the stream of experience. The categorical silhouette—as it were—casts a shadow over all the rest, allowing this 'rest' to resurface in the use of language only when the literal meaning

[6] For a systematic analysis of the literature from the cognitive sciences concerning categories, particularly with regard to conceptual creative metaphor and its use, see Gibbs Jr. (1994) and Bauman (1991).

[7] It is possible to find similar ideas even in the work of scholars who belong to the line of analytical thought otherwise known as 'cognitive grammar.' For example, see Jackendoff (1983).

[8] The overall target of undermining the granitic stiffness of categorical abstraction that is already culturally settled and in regular use is the theoretical and programmatic bridge between legal chorology and critical geography. The common challenge issued by both approaches is to go back to the process of production of sense/meaning to restart it, to trigger and legitimate new categorizations and semantic/experiential molding. Among the several voices in geographical theory, see Olsson (2007; 2011, pp. 35 ff.) and Anderson and Harrison (2010). A similar theoretical vein can be traced in Blumenberg (2007).

is accompanied or substituted by the phraseological or metaphorical one. In these cases, the discontinuity between the denotative and connotative elements inside the category and those outside of it relativizes, and the individual element (feature/ property) start to function as bridging transducers. In this way, by exploiting the simultaneous presence of a denotative and connotative elements in more than one exclusively categorical frame, the category and the word used to signify it share a sort of 'semantic promiscuity.' They are employed—in other words—in overcoming their own usual boundaries, as if the verticality of their hierarchical and definitional differentiation gave way to both the horizontality of its constitutive elements, and the semantic relevance of their simultaneous presence in more than one categorical frame. So, the withdrawal of the denotative/connotative hierarchy constitutive of each category allows for the remolding of the categorical silhouette to take shape (a new shape) and, of course, to produce unprecedented meanings. Hence, the grammar of the in/out divide could be deeply changed by such processes, though much the same could be said about the experiential possibilities coextensive to the pragmatic implications of the renewed categorizations. To this, however, I shall return below.

As a matter of course, the constraints of semantic pertinence that follow the culturally settled use of a category are perceived and function as if they were abstract rules, that is, only *linguistic stuff.* Under this assumption, the normative feature inherent in the use of categories finds a sort of iconic expression. In effect, any categorical scheme envisages a world, and implicitly involves action plans, visions of the future, renewed representations of reality—and this occurs even when it is dissimulated or overshadowed by static definitional structures or allegedly complete semantic checklists. If taken together, all these functions are in tune with the consistency constraints inherent in their embodiment within experience, and the symbolic representation of their life environment. The breach of such constraints means, somehow, and to different degrees, opening the way to the collapse of categories and generating the necessity for their redefinition. The psychological and cultural resistance (sometimes 'hostility') to remolding categorical borders is not due, however, merely to a formalistic *devotion* to the imperative to respect the already settled criteria of semantic consistency. Such a consistency is led by values and ends, moreover it is gauged on the possibility (reiterated and re-iterable) of their effective achievement. So, what actually stimulates and fuels the normative use of categories is the fear, often unconscious, of seeing opportunities to achieve the values/ends that underlie (and are promised by) the (already settled) semantic borders of each categorical definition instead, fade. And the more this danger is envisaged, the more it is perceived almost unawares, as if somehow overshadowed by the formalistic and abstract words' power of signification. Another source of this attitude is the idea, so typical of dualistic epistemology, that language and reality constitute two different and separated domains, rather than complementary and interplaying aspects of experience that are dynamically involved in its unfolding. Besides, the tendency towards maintaining and reiterating 'what has already been' feeds on myths and symbols, which often dissimulate the real interests at stake, but precisely for this reason are extremely powerful in rhetorical and psychosocial terms.

Having demonstrated the psychological and teleological reasons for the denotative rigidities of categories, we can now address the second term of the triad outlined above. I refer to pragmatic projections. Any word conveys meaning—potentially, at least. In so doing, it functions—as I pointed out above—as a sort of instruction for the 'use of world.' It anticipates what will happen and what may and ought to happen according to its implications. Words serve to steer human action. So, when—for example—we say 'table,' inside our brain, even if unconsciously, a series of neuronal connections activates, corresponding to the possible scripts related to that thing we have learned to call 'table.' Those scripts are stored in our memory and, at the time of storage, they are forged *by* and *in* experience through a dynamic, transactional and co-generative exchange carried on between our organism and the world. Within the unfolding of such scenarios, a web of relationships between objects and subjects takes *place* and thereby it transforms *in* and *draws* symbolic landscapes. The form of symbolic relationships tends to assume, by and by, a normativity corresponding to the possible reiteration of an experience and its accomplishment through the interactions between our bodies and the environment. Although words seem to be different from things and the events whose meaning they convey, still each of them is loaded with pragmatic implications. At the same time that a word is emitted through the various media that can embody it (voice, writing, etc.), it engenders in our minds a space of existence populated by relationships between signs and objects (in turn, proactively transfigured in other signs), set out according to patterns of categorical relevance/pertinence.

In this regard, it is important to stress that the space as perceived does not preexist its symbolic molding. It is not an empty dimension within which objects, actions and their transformations carried out by means of symbolic representation will take place. The void, intended as an absolute essence, is not 'just there' or, at least, is always 'related to something else,' although it is embedded in our cultural imagery.[9] It should be understood as a horizon of possibilities, but one which includes within itself a series of symbolic and pragmatic relationships (even though presupposed and implicit) that can underpin the achievement of those possibilities. I understand that it could be somewhat difficult to immediately intuit the ramifications of this point. We are so accustomed from childhood to imagine the presence/existence of spaces defined as 'void,' and to the very word 'space' as a synonym of 'emptiness,' that the difficulty of considering this idea critically is understandable. Simply, we take it for granted. The 'emptiness' of space is usually considered an implicit assumption, but which precisely because of its implicitness, is doomed to remain outside our attention and therefore immune to our critical analysis. If we try to imagine something approaching a true 'void,' such as extra-planetary cosmic space (even if it is actually fully imbued with radiations), and try to assess its pragmatic properties/implications, we will immediately realize that for human beings, outer space presents tremendous barriers to action. Its lack of oxygen and heat constitutes an

[9] On 'void,' and for a short overview of the main philosophical and scientific issues, see Close (2009).

overwhelming existential obstacle for us. It has nothing to do, therefore, with the empty spaces of our daily experience, which we can call 'empty' precisely because they are imbued and replete with semiotic elements (both empirical and symbolic) suited to host our action. This observation seems to convey, then, an interlocutory inference. The dialectic 'empty space/replete space' has a pragmatic scope, and stems from the possibility/impossibility to engage in meaningful experiences. This more extensive explanation allows us to return to the starting point and consider it from a more informed perspective.

Any word, as well as any set of signs, engenders a semantic and pragmatic space.[10] So, if we consider the spatial dimension of 'saying' and, more generally, acts of signification, this will be equal to bringing to the fore the context, namely the web of relationships, entities, and signs that host the semiotic implications of language (both symbolic and pragmatic) and the use of each word (or, more comprehensively: the semiotic activity). The *surfacing* of the spatial context of words corresponds precisely to the third term of the original triad.

The context and its relevance suggest that any word and, progressively, any enunciation or semiotic relational web, is mirrored back by the generation of worlds and their (potential or effective) practical projection. The pragmatic transposition of signs and their significations 'disengages' the words from their (apparent) abstractness and self-bounded absoluteness—however pivotal to them their categorical normativity may be—so as to trigger further processes of extensive implication involving other properties, features, denotations, connotations, categories and contexts. Being able to grasp the extent and plurality of spaces implicated by words and their semiotic projections opens the mind's eye to other semiotic elements that populate those spaces. In other words, the contiguity engendered by, and extant between, the spaces traversed by experience results in unprecedented contiguities or continuities between denotative and connotative elements that were previously inside and outside the categories. Conversely, the extensive abstraction—namely the semiotic connection traceable between the properties and connotations simultaneously included in different categorical frames—brings out unknown continuities between multiple, and previously unrelated, spaces of experience. This is the dynamic of reciprocal and bi-directional implication and transformation between signs and spaces.

By taking up this argument, we could say that 'not seeing' the underlying semantic context functions as a psycho-cognitive device that supplies the worlds-drawn-by-words with their (relative) absoluteness. An attribute which is, however, destined to vanish as soon as the contextual backdrops, the plurality of their

[10] In this regard, it must be stressed that this semantic and spatial implication is not necessarily (or, however, not exclusively) tied to pragmatist philosophy or Peircean semiotics. That every sign engenders significant relations, which only by virtue of a retrospective gaze appear as 'condensed' in categories or objects, is quite a general idea. As such, it is configured under the label 'abstractive extensions,' which can be attributed to A. N. Whitehead. For similar remarks, which *inter alia* were argued within a legal essay on the history of the idea of 'corporate legal personality,' see Dewey (1926, pp. 655–673).

constitutive elements, and the cross-cutting ubiquitous occurrence of their properties and connotations come to the surface.[11]

As the contextual components of categories come to light, along with their connotations and semiotic relationships, they open the way to the appearance (in some respects psychologically uncontainable) of other circuits and spaces of sense that are, at least potentially, competitive or subsidiary. Their conjoined flowing into our perception and representation, however, is not to be presumed to depend on the circumstance that pragmatic constraints compel us to turn our imagination (that is, a mental phenomenon) into factual action (therefore, the outside world). This is because such an intuitive view relies upon the underlying idea of an empty space within which different visions of the world, conflicting interests, and so on, can compete to take possession and transform it into a 'place,' namely, their exclusive existential habitat. In this regard, it could be useful to stress again what I pointed out above. The convergence and competition between different 'spaces' gush out from an elusion of strict in/out logic which is performed by the constitutive elements of each categorical scheme as soon as it is re-placed within the overall underlying contextual landscape. This can occur because each property or connotation proves to be equally traceable in more than one category. Such ubiquity or features multi-sited collocation ends up transfiguring each denotative and connotative element into a (potential) inter-categorical and inter-spatial bridge. Along such inter-categorical

[11] By picking up again, but simultaneously capsizing, the Foucaultian idea of 'heterotopy,' we can say that, in a sense, every categorical use of properties/features gives rise to and contours a heterotopy. Foucault defined heterotopies as those sites or spaces "that have the curious property of being in relation with all the other sites, but in such a way as to suspend, neutralize, or alter the set of relations that they happen to designate, mirror, or reflect," (see Foucault 1967/1994). An antonomastic example of heterotopy is the mirror, a *place* where real features appear remolded such as to alter the *normal* state of things and the underlying relationships that produce it. In the same vein, other heterotopies include trains, the cinema, etc. Nevertheless, every category draws and contours a space, by allowing only some relations of sense to dwell within it. This means that the features/elements compounding the categorical set are subjected to relevance/pertinence constraints that *suspend, neutralize* or somehow *alter* the potential connections that they themselves could trace outside and beyond the particular space mapped by each category. It implies that any categorical dimension that constitutes itself according to a relation of semantic and spatial Otherness to everything else is outside its semantic borders. This relational aspect makes the stability of each category and its contours arise from and depend on the context. However, the (*good*) reason underlying this Otherness could, in turn, alter. Semantic distinctions and relevance/pertinence constraints could require, at that point, a sort of *recalculation*, that is, a process of translation and transaction between the same spaces and semantic frames previously made discontinuous, namely heterotopic. This new common, reciprocal, Otherness between the features or elements that are 'in' and those that are 'out' could lead to include within the categorical contours what was outside and exclude what was inside. In other words, where previous semantic discontinuities had been forged, new continuities could come to light, and vice versa. So, in order to be maintained, consistency between meanings and categorical spaces would require a transformation regarding denotations, connotations and their relationships; which, in turn, would be a process of reciprocal translation between different and multiple Otherness. In the end, in a world that is ubiquitously heterotopic, translation proves to be an efficacious motor for the continuous, essential, renewing of life spaces of sense to have at least some possibility to unfold.

lines, the (perception of) a competing plurality of spaces and meanings, their only relative dis-continuity, and the possibility of their intermingling, is taking shape. The existence of a vacuum, an empty space, is a mere retrospective inference engendered and motivated by the oppositions, antagonisms, and fighting, which we should consider as coextensive to the intertwining of the spaces of 'significant experience.'

In the same vein, the inverse phenomenon may also occur, and I will immediately try to explain why and how it happens. Not infrequently, the multi-sited features commute the (potential) function of semiotic bridges into that of iconic fetishes, which are assumed as semantic and political-topographic places that raise conflicts between different ways of spatializing and, therefore, appear as divergent cultural and axiological options (for example, women's bodies, religious buildings, media portrayals, and so on, through a virtually endless and ever updating list). Precisely as icons, those features become the subject of polarized, and polarizing, interpretations and practices that give rhetorical structure to the inter-subjective struggles. The obsessive focusing on such features as sites of contention produces, however, alienating effects because it tends to cast a cognitive umbra[12] over the equally crucial importance of other contextual elements. So, the competition for territory, women's bodies or fetishized economic benefits overshadows the context of signification within which such reified/cosified icons are placed by the different competitors, as well as the different semantic scope that those 'things' assume in each experiential framework.

Conversely, if the reliance on the categorical salience of features within each different context were properly taken into account, then the spatial-semiotic contenders could find, at least in many cases, that they are not fighting for the same things/features and, thus not even for the same space. People run afoul of each other *on* women's bodies rather than *for* them; *on* religious buildings or *on* garments rather than *for* them. All these are only rhetorical supports, and as such they are *reified/cosified,* and made visible to orchestrate a polarization that is rooted, instead, in other aspects of experience that are subsequently obfuscated by the (artificial) dazzling brightness of the material bone of contention. If people were able to tear the veil off such semantic shadows, what would come to the fore would be the overhead ends and values that direct the choice of semantic domains and the related contexts of signification. Then it would become clear that the struggle is not for any particular thing or feature but rather for the achievement of the ends and values that, in turn, have been drawing the choices of contextualization and the construction of webs of semiotic and pragmatic relationships: that is, the same ends and values underlying the categorical generalization and ultimately the meanings of words. Evidence could be acquired, thus, to support the supposition that the antagonistic polarization between different people and their spatial projection stems, basically, from a lack of translation and transaction between the different value options at stake and the

[12] Neutralizing, suspending, subverting... we could (almost) say again with Foucault.

related habits of categorization.[13] Such translational failure has many important facets and implications, also from a dialogical/strategic point of view. The surfacing of underlying values and ends, as well as the denotative and connotative landscapes, enlarges the scope of possible alternatives to the conflict. These alternatives should no longer coincide with a merely instrumental compromise, so often euphemistically called 'accommodation,' and ultimately resulting in an economic quantification of reciprocal renunciations among intransigent competing positions[14]—which could also be defined as absolutely opposite claims for sway over space. A different way out of these conflicts could be paved by the ability to relativize opposing categorical constructions by means of the translational condensation[15] of the underlying contexts of signification and the related value choices. This essentially means exploiting the semantic continuities extant within and between the denotative and connotative frames or checklists of each category. For example, and just to provide an illustration of this kind of translation, people could discover that the primary reason for conflict between Islam and Western secular thought over a woman's body is not so much a claim for sheer male power over it, nor for an absolute non-negotiable conceptualization of its signification, but rather a different way of giving expression to the idea of dignity and, more generally, a moral order capable of ensuring the respect of subjects. The passage from a morphological or iconic polarization to an assessment and evaluation of difference would include, however, an activity of linguistic translation and transduction of gestures and ends across manifold spaces of signification and action. This is because from this angle, the matter would no longer coincide with the fragmented fencing of social spaces, a sort of socio-cultural allotment, designed to ensure an insulated circuit of power to each faction or individual, but would instead consist in the co-construction of a pluralistic space. If carried out in the wake of values and ends capable of inter-categorical relevance, this trans-*lation* among different contexts of experience and signification would bring with it the necessity of a transaction between the different claims and their related categorical schemes. This would occur, at least, for reasons of consistency and inter-contextually crossed axiological 'resonance.' By that I mean that it would be very hard to deny legitimate spatial 'citizenship' to actions and words which, despite all their morphological difference, were oriented toward the achievement of

[13]For more on inter-categorical and intercultural translation see Ricca (2008, 2013, 2014, 2016, 2019).

[14]. . . and, therefore, between irreconcilable or even incommensurable claims to exclusively occupy space.

[15]I am using the term 'condensation' with the same significance it holds in the practice of photographic composition. More specifically, I refer to when two different images which were previously printed on translucent paper are overlapped thereby engendering a third image, resulting from the conflation—involving bidirectional losses and gains—of the original ones. Something similar occurs when we taste different ingredients combined and mixed in a recipe. We are able to recognize the presence of the original ingredients but within a new overall flavor, precisely something third, that is the result of the combination of the original flavors.

ends at least partly shared by all the stakeholders involved in the conflict situation, namely by each spatialized subjectivity.[16]

More broadly, any translation among different spaces of signification and action inevitably implies some form of semantic transaction. This is a direct consequence of the renewing of the relationships among the categorical elements that accompanies each translational effort. But if this is the case, then trans-*lating* will produce the creation of new (potential and/or practical) contexts of experience and, at least to some extent, a re-writing of the semantic spectrum of both values and ends. The final outcome of such processes of semantic-pragmatic remolding will be neither the annihilation of categories, nor an axiological plasticity completely out of any control. They imply only the need to shift and refocus the axis of semantic salience of categorical features. Put more simply, this means that categories, by virtue of the continuity/ubiquity of their constitutive elements could blend and conflate into one another. It is an occurrence we might define as a kind of 'semantic contamination or connotative migration' that goes beyond the pre-existing divides in/out or inside/outside individual categories so as to redefine, consequentially, the inter-categorical borders as well. This overall transformation will be accompanied by the generation of a third space. This will not be, however, an all-encompassing new space that transcends and dialectically engulfs the pre-existing and now remolded one. It will *place*, rather, alongside them. In this sense, its function will be to not over-determinate the relationships with the other spaces, as traditionally is intended in any form of thirdness. It will work, instead, as an interface for coordination and continuous translation among other spaces of significant experience.

The semantic and pragmatic inter-space engendered and endowed with such thirdness should function, in short, as a mirror that can give back to each social party a recognizable (and thereby translatable and transactional) image of Otherness and the related semantic-spatial claims. Of course, the horizontality of the juxtapositions among the different and multiple spaces implies that none could remain immune to the changes caused by the translational stream flowing through all of them. Nonetheless 'change' does not at all mean annihilation, if for no other reason than because, on the contrary, the ability to change and also self-preserve are two sides of the same coins. Besides, all meaning and so all pragmatic-spatial implications rely on the experiential framework and contribute to forge it. Any transformations of semiotic spaces involved in the overall environment will inevitably produce, therefore, a more or less wide and profound metamorphosis of the general context, as well as the individual categories and meanings constitutive of it.

[16] Such a teleological coincidence is not to be assumed absolutely in a functionalist vein. Translation/transaction is a creative activity, as such it moves along a process of adjustment that also involves the meaning of the ends. On processes of intercultural translation, the related methodologies and technicalities, and the processivity of means/ends dialectics see above Chap. 3.

4.3 Human Rights Protection, 'Logics' of Otherness and Legal Chorology

Horizontality, if intended as a constitutive feature of the relationships between *different spaces* and, further, as a direct consequence of the categorical ubiquity of semantic features, is traceable as such, and is surprisingly analogous to the articulations as well as the problematic aspects of the human rights protection and implementation. This is because the individual subject (both public or private) can autonomously draw their own space precisely because the human rights provisions or constitutional statements grant them an independent and somehow original agency.

The reading of their own context of action by each subject must align with human rights and/or constitutional values but, at the same time, it has the power (at least legally) to influence their interpretation. Such axiological standards, however, are the same ones that institutional actors are required to respect and implement. This shows, then, that any changes or differentiations in reading and interpreting those contexts—that is to say, the semantic variations in the use of words and their pragmatic projections—reverberate across the configuration of the multiple regulatory planes as well as the definition of the legitimate spaces of the other subjects involved in the social relationships. The spatial-semantic relationship, consequently, seems to rely less upon on a binary logic concerning the distribution of competencies and/or entitlements between two (public or private) subjects and agents than on a triadic or multilateral pattern: subject/rules-words/subject. According to this different scheme, the change or shifting of a particular subjective position and the related actions by virtue of the human and/or fundamental rights protection can pull the trigger on a sequence of re-assessments regarding all the other positions, actions and, therefore, their semantic-spatial 'placement.' This extreme *motility* is the main factor that underpins the horizontality among the different subjective roles, and correspondingly tends to turn any hierarchical relationship into a circular one, as such involving a reciprocal interdependence and an *open inter-spatiality*.

This kind of 'open inter-spatiality' is an extremely interesting result for Legal Geography. It can help to overcome the dualism still lingering even behind the reading *Legal Geography* proposes and, more generally, in the underlying theoretical framework of *Critical Legal Studies*. *Legal Geography* scholars are commonly committed to unveiling the politically strategic function/aim of any referral to place, territory and space that is traceable within legal discourse.[17] According to such readings, any apparently neutral and thing-like (or cosal) word or statement regarding spatial elements dissimulates an exercise of power. Beyond the veil of empirical discourses, each legal statement including spatial elements or features would serve,

[17] See Blomley (1994, 2003a, b), Blomley et al. (2001), Delaney (2003, 2010, 2014), Philippopoulos-Mihalopoulos (2010, 2012, 2015), Butler (2012), and Braverman et al. (2014). See, also, from an anthropological point of view von Benda-Beckmann et al. (2009) and Bennet and Layard (2015, pp. 405 ff.). For a specific focus on urban planning see Layard (2010).

instead, to corral individual action and pursue institutional aims oriented to further social control in support of dominant groups' interests. So, every time legal acts refer to places or spatial entities (houses, streets, prisons, zoos, bodies, public or private areas), they pack the social dynamics with implicit orders and imperatives by dissimulating them behind the apparent obviousness and neutrality of terms that are commonly used to describe 'what is,' namely, merely empirical situations. To put it diversely, any referral to places or objects embodying spatial dimensions encapsulates an implicit, silent mapping of what people can or cannot do. In this way, prescriptions and social constraints are passed off as mere descriptions that serve to deceptively legitimate apparatuses of social control and spatial allocation.

However, while law instrumentalizes space in order to forge it and maintain its grip over the bodies and actions circulating inside it, on the other hand it cannot avoid remaining affected and re-semanticized by its own spatial implications. Spatial metaphors abound in legal statements and academic discourse on law, if for no other reason than that both are full of 'scansions,' boundaries, areas and limits of all kinds of competence and power, patterns of linguistic pertinence, etc. Such regimentation of space by means of a maze of boundaries is nothing other than the imprint mirroring linguistically engendered maps, which through an apparent process of de-materialization aim, instead, to keep an overarching control of the subjects' actions in the physical space. The overall approach of *Legal Geography* is efficaciously summarized by the assertion that law is a 'thing of this world' . . . *of things*.[18] It is therefore neither something abstract, nor purely linguistic. Its definitions cast practical effects over and across space thereby colonizing it. Thus, rights abstractly recognized or denied to people end up bumping against spatial barriers—silently engendered by the same legal discourse—and, in this way, undergo restrictions, exceptions, and reductions, that serve as forerunners of social exclusion and subalternity.[19] The task that *Legal Geography* seems to have assigned to itself—

[18] See Delaney (2003), who uses this expression in order to stress that *Legal Geography* makes it possible to demystify the quotidian commitment of legal practitioners who seem, instead, to care almost exclusively about their *word games*, which they carry on by playing on the mobile borders of the categorical semantic spectrum: see, *ibidem*, 67. Most recently, Delaney seems to share the view of Braverman (2014, p. 120), who argued that analysis concerning law/space relationships should be carried out by taking law as a process rather than a 'thing.' Such a transition from 'thing' to 'process' would be—at least, as it seems to be intended—better capable of capture the spatial implication of legal words. From a semiotic point of view, however, everything is the result of signical relationships. In the same way, the *condensation* of such relationships in the representations of some *things* is a *not-insignificant* step along the process that leads to the production of *meanings*, and thereby also of the implied relationships between (both those signs that are) word and space. The epistemological transition proposed by Braverman and shared by Delaney implies a dichotomy of *thing/process* that is read only in instrumental or heuristic terms but excludes any ontological signification. 'Thing' and 'process' are, in short, two faces and moments of the same cognitive/experiential phenomenon. So, it would make little sense to take them alternatively and talk about one rather than the other. Such a choice could result, ultimately, in a merely linguistic and unnecessary censure that is, all *things* considered, cognitively defective.

[19] See Delaney (2003), who explains this view by developing a syllogistic argument that deserves to be extensively quoted because it illustrates very well the current approach of *Legal Geography*

based on Foucault's theoretical guidelines—is to lay bare how law carries on the operations of allocating and marking space. The main purpose of such an approach seems to be oriented to making people aware of such legal-spatial devices so as to trigger, at the same time, a process of emancipation from the grip of a wired world authoritatively (and to some extent surreptitiously) reduced to a nomosphere.[20]

The emphasis that *Legal Geography* puts on the space/law relationship is consistent with the theoretical strain of *Critical Legal Studies* and their primary task of unveiling the presence and action of power hidden in law's structure and rules. It should be welcomed as a beneficial and fruitful turning point with respect to the more traditional reading of legal phenomena. Indeed, it could represent a step towards the promotion of people's understanding of the close interconnection between social life and regulatory policies. In this way, it could also spur the dissemination of an attitude toward democratic criticism of legal categories, which are too often considered by common people, instead, as artificial, remote, and somehow alien to the ordinary course of life and education.[21]

In my view, however, this kind of approach to *Legal Geography* still relies too much on a latent 'thinghood' of space in its conception, while underestimating its signical import. It is no coincidence that the subjects and areas of legal experience which legal geographers typically address (at least to date), relate mainly to that which retains immediate spatial empirical features in the categorizations of common language: territory, property, bodies and corporeality, streets, urban areas, peripheries, political and administrative districts, borders and frontiers, buildings, supermarkets and malls, zoos, and so on.[22] In this regard, it may be observed that houses, prisons, and streets, are not only physical places but also words, and this duplicity is embodied by them in a synchronic and horizontal way. This is because properties/features, as well as the perception of spatiality itself, are influenced and co-constituted by the semantic implications of words; in addition, the semantic features are, in turn, co-related with spatial perceptive/experiential implications. The relationship between these two dimensions (namely, space and words) is

(at least, in the US): "...if the legal is constitutive of the social, if the social is irreducibly material—in a *non-reductionist* sense—and if we carry the social in our very bodies, then there is no a priori way of dematerializing 'the legal.' Any effort to effect a dematerialization of law must be regarded with suspicion. It must, that is, be at least examined as a political maneuver. To the extent that the material world is *as* it is as it is constituted by the legal, so the legal is *what* it is as it participates in the process of constituting the material: reorganizing it, transforming it, preserving it. These processes include, but are by no means limited to, those directly operating on the corporeal. Moreover, as Cover suggested, the legal is *as* it is as it participates in projects that reinforce its own rhetorical dematerialization." Cover's essay cited within Delaney's text is *Violence and Word*: Id. (1986, pp. 1601 ff.)

[20] See Delaney (2010).

[21] See Sarat and Kearns (1995a, b).

[22] From a private law perspective, see Jackson and Wightman (2003, pp. 36 ff.). Things do not improve with regard to the recent practical turn' of legal geography: see, in this regard, Martin et al. (2010) and Brickell et al. (2021); for some fruitful critical remarks see, instead, Orzeck and Hae (2020).

co-generative, and stems from experience and its unfolding. It seems, therefore, to make little sense to rigorously reify (or cosify) and *de-symbolize* the house, the prison, the street, only to assert immediately after that law and legal words are ordered to surreptitiously de-materialize spatiality and physical substance of such *things*. All the more so, when we consider that these efforts of reification/materialization are intended to unveil how the legal use of such *thinglike* terms is primarily pre-ordered to dissimulate still further implications behind their descriptive and materialistic features that, in turn, are culturally forged and hegemonically piloted by agencies of power. This seems to me a rather convoluted argumentative spin, in many respects prone to turn into an ideological or, in any case, partisan use of the chorological implications inherent in any sign and thus even in legal words. What is more, this argument fails emphasize and support the potential transformative dynamics that could instead flourish if there were a widespread awareness of the tight conjoining of language, law and (categorization of) space-time.

A Cartesian mind/world dualism and the related referential conception of language functions seem, despite everything, to continue to punctuate the cognitive background of *Legal Geography* and many of its proponents. Even so, in a Cartesian universe, the *fact* that law colonizes space (a full space according to the philosopher) still would not be terribly surprising or scandalous. Even if lacking post-modern and post-structuralist theoretical awareness, it is a more or less latent datum, and after all, widely accepted. It is likely that most people do not have the critical consciousness to protest the shadows of power that lie within legal categorizations and enunciations, which are only apparently descriptive. Nevertheless, it is a *fact*, an anthropological phenomenon knowable by all human beings, that the activity of *saying* or *designating* something transforms the world and, therefore, is co-constitutive of it. The weak spot in the current *Legal Geography* approach lies in the consequences that stem from an empirical emphasizing of the practical effects of the legal word and its alleged metaphysical referentiality towards the social distribution of space: in short, that law is a thing among the other things of this world. If taken as a mere matter of fact, though as part of a broader critical perspective, this view could paradoxically end up increasing the dualism between 'word' and 'spatial dimension.' This is because once space is designated as a colonized dimension, and then hetero-molded by word, the ensuing emancipatory criticism can convey nothing but a triggering and, eventually, legitimizing of competing plans for colonization. The outcome of *Legal Geography*'s project could be in danger of resulting in a blind and bitter antagonism *over* spatiality, however much it thrives on claims raised in the fair name of demystification, equity, freedom, dignity, pluralism, democratic participation, and so on. Notwithstanding all these praiseworthy intentions, what seems to lie beyond the current horizon of *Legal Geography* is an explication of the deep-seated *reasons* for co-extensivity between the use of words and the forging of space (and time),[23]

[23] Perception of time, as well as of space, relies on what happens within each of these dimensions, which simultaneously forge them. Time, just like space, is not 'void,' despite the abstractions of Newtonian physics. It is a function of events and the *modes* implied to categorize them. Perception

and thereby a cognitive genealogy of the relationships of co-determination between law and the spatial dimension. I suppose, instead, that if all of us could shed some light on this relation of reciprocal inherence and co-implication, so as to bring to the surface its causes, then together we might find a smoother path to defuse the dark and surreptitious collusions between the use of legal discourse and the dominance of the most powerful subjects over space.

The aims that *Legal Geography* so commendably pursues could be achieved more effectively, in my view, if we were to subvert the equivalence and the relation of co-extensiveness between law and 'things of this world.' So, rather than claim that law is a thing among the other things of this world, I propose we draw our attention to how space and everything in it are signs within a universe filled with, and ultimately constituted by, signs and semiotic factors. If we could agree that: (a) every *perceived* reality is the result of an elaboration of signs, even in those respects that usually are taken as 'material,' and, (b) the divide between representation and world is operative rather than ontological, (c) then, we could directly grasp the co-implication between saying and doing, words and actions, imagining and perceiving. The same materiality or 'thinghood' of the world outside would reveal itself to be a *mode of signification*, a way to read, interpret and reconstruct what we perceive, through a sensory activity that is then driven, given rhythm, and modulated according to patterns of judgment that are culture-laden and not at all immediate. This means that even what we see—since 'being visible' is the primary mode in which space appears to us, even if mainly in Western culture—epitomizes and synthetizes our reactions to the world, which in turn are oriented by and to both pre-acquired patterns and ends.[24] The matter we perceive is imagined matter,

---

and understanding of change are conditioned by categorization and the discontinuities it engenders, as well as by the continuities it projects by abstraction onto the stream of phenomena. Words, and especially legal ones, punctuate time precisely because they unify and distinguish the stream of events, thus *oozing* meanings. Normative prescriptions and the related charges of prescriptiveness cast a net on the future, attempting to capture it into normalizing regularities. From a certain point of view, however, the word of law—if endowed with effectiveness—aims to give shape to an eternal present, much like the religious word. What is said in the normative language, by definition, and because of its simply being said, is already *being*, and as such it also self-defines by means of a presumptive retrospective gaze. However, what happens, namely events, besides unfolding through time, spread within and through time. Law is, therefore, a dispositive of spatio-temporal modeling. Its generalizations (try to) grip space and time, they seem to describe—by use of the present tense—what will happen, and where and how it will *take place*. They are, however, description in appearance only. The legal present tense is merely an assertion of normality, which instead dissimulates an implicit presumption of reification of legal prescriptions, already taken for granted and endowed with effectiveness. As for the spatialization of time as a constant inner feature of time perception, see Tenbrink (2007) and there for further literature references on this topic. See also Ronsenberg and Grafton (2010).

[24] See Gibson (1986), and *ibidem* on what concerns the elaboration of the concept of 'affordance'; Goodwin (1994, pp. 606 ff.; 1995, pp. 237 ff.; 1996a, pp. 62 ff.; 1996b, pp. 370 ff.; 1997, pp. 111 ff.); Gregory (1997), where the author proposes and develops the idea that through their perceptive results, "The senses do not give us a picture of the world directly; rather they provide evidence for the checking of hypotheses about what lies before us. Indeed, we may say that the

without exception. It is the outcome, the co-generative relationship among signs, words/representations and the perceived/imagined world, which stems from the unfolding of experience and cumulatively takes shape through a stream of dynamic interactions. That matter is not a datum but instead a result, gushing out from the ongoing adaptive interplay between subject and object, both intended as entities consistently in mutual communication and partaking in a world that is simultaneously engendered (also) by both the occurrence and the progression of their relationships.

The relational patterns between organism and the world, which are gradually achieved and culturally communicated, cumulatively accrete to engender pro-active reactions or affordances in response to environmental stimuli.[25] The result is that we see, hear, smell, and touch, through what we know. It is an embodying and embodied knowledge, in the sense that it gives rise to apparently immediate perceptions which are, instead, related to and pre-ordered by, or to, the interactions between organism and world already attempted, or else in the making. In other words, the perception of the material world and, ultimately, the material world itself, result from the synthesis between the schemes to make the body 'worldled' and those to embody the world.[26] When we perceive matter or material spatialities—to use the terms of *Legal Geography*—we perceive a result (although interlocutory, in any case) of adaptive processes. Metaphorically, we can say that our images/representations of the world could be considered—as already pointed out above—like the figures of a tapestry that is woven with threads that interlace past and future, memories and plans, all of which become invisible when we look at the overall drawing and its iconized shapes. This all-encompassing and self-bounded frame is, in turn, brought to the surface of our conscience by the brain as a set of ready-made, pre-defined entities.

If we acknowledged that we see and live the world according to our biological and cultural, as well as cognitive and ethical, values and ends then, perhaps, we could be less *reticent* to realize that each subject moves in their own space and, furthermore, generates it by means of their *signs-oriented* activity. If viewed from this perspective, the issue would no longer be to show how words—and especially legal words—colonize a partisan space, considered in its exterior materiality, even

perception of an object is an hypothesis, suggested and tested by the sensory data." (*ibidem*: 13–14); furthermore "The seeing of objects involves many senses of information beyond those meeting the eye when we look at an object. It generally involves knowledge of the object derived from previous experience, and this experience is not limited to vision but may include the other senses; touch, taste, smell, hearing and perhaps also temperature or pain. Objects are far more than patterns of stimulation; objects have pasts and futures; when we know its past or can guess its future, an object transcends experience and becomes an embodiment of knowledge and expectations without which life beyond the simplest is not possible." (*ibidem*: 10).

[25] On the unconscious pro-active anticipation see Gibson (1986) and Gibbs Jr (2005).

[26] Regarding the relationship among mind, body and cognition, *inter alia* with respect to the 'affordances theory' proposed by Gibson, see, for a wide-ranging discussion, Gibbs Jr (2005). On the relationships among mind, language and embodiment, see the broad overview of the current different theoretical approach to this topic provided by Ziemke et al. (2007) and Franck et al. (2008).

going so far as to pass off imperatives and prescriptions as descriptive terms. Rather, the matter would be making sure that people can perceive how space and word conflate and merge in view of action, and how the whole world comprises—at least, from a human point of view, ultimately the only one available to us—a polyphonic interweaving of relationships between multiple spaces of (effective and/or possible) action.

My proposal, inherent in the chorological approach, is to try to subvert the tapestry of categories by observing its reverse side, where the figures and their spaces appear dis-composed into the webbing/plot of multicolor threads/connotations (caught in a condition in which they cannot yet be defined as denotations) and can finally be offered up to our mental sight in all their connotative plurality and reciprocal interpenetrating continuity.[27] In other words, we should read the weft underlying the figures—namely, categories—to capture the story that each thread draws along its *path* as it interlaces and connects with the others. This work could enable us to discern the possibilities for dis-composing and recomposing by re-drawing the continuities and/or discontinuities through which colors and forms take shape.[28] Words and space—stepping away from metaphorical language for a moment—should be understood as the components of one common experiential ground within which both remain, and reciprocally interplay in a horizontal way rather than according to the traditional top-down/hierarchical relationship coextensive to the abstract/concrete distinction. So, in short, if taken in its effort to signify, word is space; and space, if seen in its relational articulations, is word or, more generally, sign. As a result, the analysis of the relations between the spatial dimensions of experience and law should also focus on the ways in which spaces (as pro-active and embodied affordances of words) reciprocally interweave and co-generate with words, in turn considered as embodied experiences and therefore previously carried out across, and by means of, space. Playing with words—as lawyers (too) often do—is really playing with spaces. And it is precisely by being cognizant of the inherent spatiality of words—rather than merely emphasizing it in a polemical-demystifying vein—that people could adopt practices of categorical remolding to urge a non-hegemonic and instead polyphonic, and transactional, redrawing of social spaces (including their empirical perception.)[29]

[27]On the relativity and reciprocal conflation between denotations and connotations within the metaphorical (and therefore both inter-linguistic and inter-spatial transformative) processes I refer to Ricca (2022) and there for further bibliographical and theoretical references to this topic.

[28]For a legal intercultural use of the metaphor of the subverted tapestry, see above Chap. 3, and Ingold (2007), even if I do not share the overall post-modern approach of this author.

[29]The adoption of this perspective gives weight to a subversion of Delaney's quasi-syllogism: see above, note 18. So, we could, and should, say: "if the legal is constitutive of the social, if the social is irreducibly **signical**—in a non-reductionist sense—and if we carry the social in our very bodies, then there is no a priori way of **materializing** 'the legal.' Any effort to effect a **materialization** of law must be regarded with suspicion. It must, that is, be at least examined as a political maneuver. To the extent that the **signical** world is *as* it is as it is constituted by the legal, so the legal is *what* it is as it participates in the process of constituting the **social signifying**: reorganizing it, transforming it, preserving it. These processes include, but are by no means limited to, those directly operating on

I would like to point out that in titling this chapter, I preferred to avoid the expression 'legal geography' so as to immediately wriggle free from the oppositional dialectics or divides, word/space, abstract/material-concrete. This is because the Greek term *graphìa* (writing) conjures up—although erroneously—the act of inscription on the Earth, namely the superimposition of signifying grids and often real cages on something (taken as) placed outside there, a sort of preexisting support, or some kind of palimpsest.[30] I think, on the contrary, that *-graphìa* embeds the earthly support and, at the same time, forges it, so as to *co-generate* the 'thing' from which the same *-graphèin* (writing) stems, since it is to be understood as a synthesis of a human action responsive to the world, and a world dynamically reacting to the symbolically-driven action of human beings.[31] Nevertheless, I know that the meaning of *-graphèin* I have in mind is far from the most common one,[32] and presumably also does not correspond to the meaning of space intended by *Legal Geography*'s theoretical assumptions, and this also because of their alignment with the stigmatization of the hegemonic features of 'writing' contended by post-modern thought.[33] In view of all this, I focus my argument from the Earth (signified by the prefix *-geo*) to *kóra* (space), as well as from *graphìa* to *lògos*. The result is the borrowing of the term *chorology*,[34] a word deeply engraved by historical lines and used, with respect to geography, for the analysis of places when considered for their dynamic, organic, ethological and cultural semantic projections.[35]

In the geographical disciplines, and essentially for reasons of historiographical accuracy, chorology was distinguished from geography because scholars assumed the former to pertain to the study of specific regions whilst the latter to the analysis of

---

the corporeal. Moreover, as Cover suggested, the legal is *as* it is as it participates in projects that reinforce its own rhetorical **materialization."** [emphasis, mine].

[30] Whereas it is instead the writing in itself, and even before, the *simple* act of signifying, that transforms into a support for the means used for inscription.

[31] See Sini (2003) and Dematteis (1985). On Dematteì's pioneering essay see also Fall and Minca (2013, pp. 542 ff.).

[32] Otherwise, I would define the theoretical approach suggested here as "spatiography," which may be more generic, but is certainly less esoteric than "chorology."

[33] For geographical theory, see Olsson (2007), Farinelli (2003, 2009), and Pickles (2004). See *ibidem* for more bibliographical references.

[34] See Olwig (2011, pp. 44 ff.). For a thoughtful survey on the genealogy of the word 'chora' in Plato's Timaeus, see Sallis (1999); most recently, see Heritier (2023) for a historical reconstruction of the philosophical and theological 'transfiguration' of the idea of 'chora'.

[35] For an examination of the development of both the term and the concept of 'chorology' in geographical theory see Dikshit (2006) and Moreira (2014). More specifically, in these texts the authors analyze the relationships between the chorology of Ritter, von Richtofen and Hettner (*Die Geographie Ihre Geschichte, Ihr Wesen und Ihre Methoden*, 1927), the last of which gave the following definition of chorology: "The goal of the chorological point of view is to know the character of regions and places through comprehension of the existence together and interrelations among different realms of reality and their varied manifestations, and to comprehend the earth surface as a whole in its actual arrangement in continents, larger and smaller regions, and places." For further declinations of the chorological approach see also Hartshorne (1939).

global phenomena. Nevertheless, and for reasons I will explain later, the massive and widespread increase of global processes and 'global thought' significantly relativize the above distinction. This is because the most serious implication from the maze of globalization discourse is precisely a newly acquired—or perhaps newly acknowledged—awareness that any local event is the result, the epitome of relationships that have interwoven and unfolded on a global scale (but, following Mach, I should perhaps say 'universal scale'), and vice versa.

At this point, it could be useful to recapitulate the argument so far, to further illustrate the practical implications of the operative assumptions of a legal-chorological approach. I will try, therefore, to re-start from an interlocutory point. Working *with* and *on* words is, at least potentially, a way to move them, and simultaneously, to mold (new) spaces; carving and chiseling new experiential spaces, symmetrically, is to set words, signs, and categorical borders in motion. This means that space and sign could be defined by two coextensive terms, namely *signi-space* and *space-sign*. To make the spatial distinctions produced by legal discourse collapse in on themselves, we should do more than point our finger at the colonizing and dissimulating power of legal-spatial statements. What we need is the ability to manage law's words and their inter-contextual constraints to promote categorical, and thus also spatial, re-modeling.

From this perspective, legal chorology would no longer be competent only in issues (and legal words) that involve or evoke, explicitly or implicitly, entities or concepts connoted as space-related according to common language—as is the case for *Legal Geography*. If every word is a project, an instruction for use-of-action through the world, and epitomizes, in turn, events and experience that took place along the unfolding of the same world, then any legal statement, since by definition designed to steer human conduct, will be space-relevant or spatially meaningful and can be analyzed from a chorological perspective. Looking at things from this angle, each legal category, as well as any categorical web, could be eviscerated and dis-composed in its components by taking these denotative and connotative elements as pragmatic, and therefore *spatially-spread* implications, so as to simultaneously compare them with those produced by other categories. Continuity and co-extensiveness, as well as previously invisible discontinuities and oppositions, will suddenly come to the fore. Spatial contiguity of phenomenon thus will turn into categorical co-inherence due to the trans-categoriality of their features. At the same time, the ubiquity of elements included in the checklist of each category can make spaces that were previously perceived to be reciprocally remote instead contiguous and experientially continuous, so connecting them in ways that were inconceivable before. The result of such processes could imply both the re-semanticization and re-spatialization of categorical distinctions and borders. Categorical differences, in short, could undergo a real transfiguration. This will occur because of the increase in our perception of the reciprocal relationships and analogical connections between the semiotic and experiential landscapes beneath each category. This will take *place* because the semantic and pragmatic implications (or, per Peirce: effects and bearings), intended as a synthesis of space and word, will be seen to interplay, horizontally, on a common semiotic ground. This common semantic playing field will allow, thus, the many semiotic contexts that underlie all categories to communicate with each other more openly, exploiting their multifaceted meaningfulness. In this way, new potential contiguities, similarities and possibilities of reciprocal pollination/combination among the features of each context could come to the light. The dynamics of the overall spatial-legal framework could be strongly spurred by the emergence of new semantic/spatial contiguities and/or oppositions, leading to categorical remolding and new critical paths—however paradoxical this may seem—in line with both axiological coherence and respect for the law.

By moving in this direction, I believe, the semantic and spatial constraints inherently imposed by the normativity of words (not only legal) on the landscapes of semiotic relationships underlying categories would suddenly trail off. More specifically, the constraints of utterly linguistic pertinence, even more rigid in legal language, would *loosen their grip* over the array of contextual semiotic factors that support, like domesticated servants, the shiny categorical neatness and semantic absoluteness of single words. So, too, the strict *valency* that the sculptural canopy of words imposes on the potential motility of semantic relationships would probably slacken. Social subjectivities could then find new paths to unfold, and this improvement—even more importantly—could be achieved by using, precisely, the legal discourse as a 'launch platform' to engender, as openly and pluralistically as possible, a semiotic space I would like to term, ecologically polyphonic.[36]

The chorological approach assumes that space and time are not independent from the categories used to experientially situate and thereby conceptualize them. Correspondingly, it highlights that the reliability and stability of categorizations are supported by the space-time signical relationships that fuel experience and put it in motion. This means that every subject creates and moves along their own plots of signification, namely their own space-time horizon. Therefore pluralism, and subsidiarity as well, assume cognitive substance. People, in other words, do not cast different visions of the world over a common 'outside there,' which exists for itself and is taken in its material texture in the same way by everyone. It is not the case that different individuals have different perspectives on a single world. Rather, each person and, to differing degrees, each group, and civilization, gives birth to different worlds. Nevertheless, these worlds do not meet or collide within a void space which hosts their competition. On the contrary, they become perceptible because of the features that they have in common, and their reciprocal relationships—or, to return to the metaphor of the subverted tapestry, one could say: because of the threads that connect and span across their semantic frames/checklists of categories.[37]

[36] In this regard, and on the intertwining between critical geography and law, Olsson's reading is very inspiring (2007; 2011, pp. 35 ff.)

[37] The combination of experiential spaces, intended as an activity of translation, does not exclusively concern the various spaces engendered by different subjects; that is, this activity is not only about managing inter-subjective relationships, as if the issue were primarily political. In my view, the activity of translation holds a cognitive significance, although cognition is also to be viewed as a social process. Translation concerns the experiences carried out by an individual subject, as such caught within a sort of *uni-subjective* relationship among the semiotic events that we differentiate respectively as perception, representation, etc. For example, consider the idea/intention of going through a brick wall, and a representation of the material impossibility of carrying out the necessary action. At this point, many will observe that between these two things (precisely, thinking and doing) there is a clear difference. Nonetheless, what matters in both cases is our loyalty to our senses

and the representations related to their functioning (as well as that rather undefined function that we ordinarily identify with each of those senses). In the end, we can give preference to one sense over another. So, we might believe in the physical impenetrability of the wall, which we assess through the resistance encountered by our bodies to amalgamate with its material, rather than privileging our ability to hear what is beyond the wall and the figurations produced by our imagination in seeing ourselves on the other side. In any case, our believing is the result of a choice, the same one that we make when we convince ourselves that the vision of a ghost is necessarily unrealistic *only* because we are unable to touch it. In that case, we have chosen sight over touch. And yet how often do we refuse to believe in touch by privileging sight? And how much more often do we refuse to believe in our senses, instead relying on instruments that record and elaborate data by means of symbolic representations—even if these will also ultimately be accessible through our sensorial perceptions? A wall, after all, could be got through also by opening a door! Or, alternatively, by putting a camera in the next room, or even by listening to what happens in it. Now, someone might argue—this is all well and good, but dematerializing and rematerializing on the other side of the wall is something that we are unable to do; it is *reality* that shouts at us that we are unable to do it–as if *our* reality were not a representation, and each representation—even if deemed incorrect—were not a reality in and of itself, an event that has occurred in the world. The basic question is that we are unable to ultimately determine in absolutely dichotomous terms that *something* is a mere representation, and something *else* is a reality. To do this, we would need a sort of ground zero, a neutral gaze cast from nowhere, which could distinguish between inside and outside in an absolute way, and not through merely operational or heuristic assumptions. Unfortunately, we have no such ground zero of knowledge. Even if we find it useful to differentiate representations from reality, symbols from their references, such distinctions can take shape exclusively among things or events, all of which happen, and are present, before us. In a nutshell, we could conclude that everything *is*. And whatever *is*, if taken in its protean signical being, is translatable. Consequentially, imagining doing something and experiencing the impossibility of doing it, are both semiotic events, as well as representations. One day we will find a way to disentangle them from both the true/false and reality/imagination oppositions. Then, maybe, we will be able to devise a method to pass through walls, and that method will be nothing but a translation between the idea of the wall, and the idea of being beyond it. These possible translations, taken in their diversities, focus on different connotations; and if some of them are inefficient and/or incorrect, it is because they do not *work on* the salient and disambiguating elements of the signifying contexts. In the same vein, thinking that magic can modify the world means not considering the 'right' connotations of it or, at least, overlooking some of the most salient. In this case, there will be an imperfect translation, and thereby a fallacy. Nonetheless, in methodological terms—that is to say, as a form of translation—magic is not wrong in and of itself. What is wrong is the way the activity of translation is carried out. In writing this, I am thinking of the possibility of instantaneously and immaterially travelling by teleportation. Today, one possible form of translation between imagination and reality is for example—Skype. When I talk with my friends on the other side of the world, see their faces, their houses, hear the clatter of pans, the slamming of doors, and glimpse through the remote camera the light of their homes... then Skype functions, precisely, as a possible translation between the actual space (at least until today) and the imaginary one, that is, as 'a metaphor.' And by means of Skype, as occurs in every metaphorical process, I am losing something just as I am gaining something else. The day we invent teleportation, it will be in any case accompanied by a transaction, a balancing between something lost and something gained: and this holds true even if we consider only the use of energy (even exclusively mental) needed to achieve it. I think on that day—but we could do it even today—we will discover that the rigidity of walls is not secondary to the rigidity of our cognitive values. Indeed, it is only by reciprocally molding again and again both physical and cognitive walls that the passing through, the *trans—wall-uating* translation can become possible: a bit as was the case with human flight. Today, we are able to fly, even if we have not yet become birds.

Below, I will try to provide some concrete examples related to the most traditional legal problems to explain step by step how people and lawyers can draw new categorical (and inter-categorical) implications that achieve axiological-legal consistency. Now, instead, I propose just two snapshots, for explanatory purposes, to make the overall exposition more intuitive, and to ease the realization of some possible, concrete implications of a chorological approach.

Let's assume someone is interviewed about what kind of connection they discern between intestate succession (wills), and legislation concerning the demographic distribution of the population within a given city (urban planning). The likely response would be 'no connection.' The individual questioned—even more so if they were a legal professional—would probably answer that intestate succession and planning legislation are two reciprocally distant categories. And yet, if we were to consider, in terms of spatial implications, the consequences of the inter-generational transfer of ownership of real estate by means of intestate succession, most likely we could easily identify a connection between the presence of elites in some areas and its maintenance over time, on one hand, and the regulation of succession, on the other. The 'inheritance' ideology of our past—when wealth was related to real estate—made it so that buildings placed in the 'strategic location' of cities remained the privilege of the most powerful and prominent families and their networks. Their presence in those locations also meant political power, the creation and maintenance of communicative *enclaves*, relationships of proximity, contiguity, socio-economic influence, and so on. In that light, urban policy and 'inheritance regimes' are seen to be closely connected. Or course, it is not only an inter-categorical connection of the teleological kind. What I mean is that the 'inheritance regime' could prove to be more than just an indirect instrument of urban policy and control over territory that runs along an inter-generational axis. The inclusion of such a regime within the semantic frame of the right to territory or housing immediately focuses our gaze on unprecedented, but possible, connections between succession and citizenship. It seems quite straightforward to say that an egalitarian citizenship should include the entitlement to live and enjoy the city equally. The exigencies of an equitable demographic distribution could trigger claims for a reform of both the hereditary features and phenomenology of the urban allocation of people. These brief points are enough to show how by uncovering the semantic co-extensiveness of categories that are only apparently distant, the axiological axes underlying those categories are almost abruptly called into question, with transformative effects of reciprocal compatibility, and ensuing possibilities of their interplaying.

A similar and mirroring back—as it were—observation could be proposed regarding claims for the remolding of space, and the distance between spaces stemming from a responsive gaze to the (at least potentially) ubiquitous presence of some categorical components. And while we are addressing the demographic distribution of space and its contents, I propose to focus on two further areas usually considered to be unrelated: wage levels and the center/periphery dialectical divide between residential property and right to housing.

During medium-long economic downturns, so often characterized by decreased wage levels for both middle and lower class workers, new family units gravitate towards lower cost urban areas. These areas are generally peripheral.[38] This kind of displacement could result in a drop in demand for housing in city centers, followed by an inversion regarding the territorial direction of house hunting. Nonetheless, the necessity of transport, either public or private, constitutes a significant expense in family budgets. As a result, those workers who are not employed in the city center—and this is usually the vast majority—are likely to remain in peripheral residential areas to avoid additional costs. This kind of socio-economic dynamic could, and often does, impinge on the urban anthropology, so much so that it can transform central urban areas into elite reserves, continuously perceived as privileged locations only for wealthy families; a virtually inelastic property prices curve accompanies the transformation. The possibility of these processes occurring shows how it is not spatial contiguity that engenders the contamination between *remote* categories, but rather its opposite, and more specifically semiotic and experiential continuity. The level of wages and the price of houses can strictly connect spaces that are physically and categorically distant, turning them into direct and continuous implications of a single phenomenon/category, which is, precisely, economic citizenship. If public institutions decided to intervene in order to socially enhance equity, it would involve dismantling both the spatial rift and the semantic caesura between center and periphery. These spaces should thus be considered continuous and distributed within a range of differentiations orbiting wage levels. Public measures should, therefore, cover—and simultaneously resonate across—urban demographic distribution, spatial policy planning, citizenship value definition, and so on.

The above implications can be brought to light by different subjects, each of whom will envisage, draw, and categorize individual spaces according to the various situations they live, and in their own ways. Everyone, for their part, is capable of stressing qualifying profiles of their own experience that could upset long-settled categorical frameworks, the very same which, not infrequently, dominant groups have managed to reify in order to immunize them from social criticism. Such processes will undoubtedly become crammed with issues involving equality or economic equalization, as well as competition, and even social envy. However, I am going to avoid the various aspects of distributive justice or quantitative wealth assurance, for the moment. Rather, I prefer to focus on the plurality of the world people live in and across, and this in order to show the cognitive aspects and legal-axiological potentialities of transformation that are often overshadowed, or even neutralized, by current modes of categorization. The assertion that everybody lives *in* and also pro-actively engenders their own space is equivalent to arguing for a radical plurality of experience and hence subjectivity. [39] This point—I think—comes

[38] This hypothesis, of course, is based on a city model that is widespread in contemporary Western urban areas, even if not homogeneously. This means that it cannot be assumed as a trans-epochal or planetary standard.

[39] In this regard I should like to say how, in my view, radical cognitive plurality is not the accessory of an evolutionist functionalism, which can somehow be assimilated to a Luhmanian or autopoietic approach. Any idea of systems or sub-systems that exchange information by means of processes of functional differentiation, namely through a form of interpenetration that is inherently unable to

into play even before any discourse on equality and the equitable distribution of goods. If inter-subjective equality is to be used to establish a legitimate allotment of goods, then the authority would have to work from an average social subject to determine the eventual degree of equality or unevenness for people based on the situations everyone typically faces. The real point is that subjectivity constitutes a sort of *emersion*, that is, it is the result of a weighted synthesis of different life situations and their corresponding semantic features, completely at odds with any kind of psycho-social straitjacket or Procrustean bed, instead designed to apportion the world.

In many cases, the arguments made in favor of cognitive pluralism, and thus the irreducibility of subjective experience to general schemes or patterns, leads to a fierce criticism of modernity. Nor has modern legal discourse avoided the attack of the post-modern troops. Its serializing and generalizing features were stigmatized as tools used by dominant groups to mystify their dominance. This is a far cry from the image of an instrument designed to mirror and extend the equality ontologically engrained in human nature and capable of embodying the choral expression of popular sovereignty. According to this view, the *puppet* of subjectivity carved out by modern legal discourse would be, in other words, a mere cast of Western bourgeois features,[40] subsequently passed off as a universal icon of human nature. General and abstract laws and their sovereign 'speech' would therefore have functioned only as a means of power, meting out a measure of equality *under* which only the most vulnerable and subaltern people would reside. The law and legal statements, in short, would not have been a mirroring dome of social life and people's interests, able to collect and give utterance to individual exigencies, but rather a map,

---

achieve any possibility of cognitive reciprocity, is distant from my reading of social experience. Rather, the relationship of re-cognition is—in my understanding—the outcome of a process of intercultural translation and transaction, and is therefore a result of human beings' practice of producing culture, or better yet, of their "*gnoseogenetic*" competence. This competence is not based on universal essences, categories, forms or meanings. Universality is instead to be considered as a set of cognitive potentialities inherent in humankind and communicatively circulating among human beings. The *emergent expression* of such potentialities can move along different paths, engendering thus a radical plurality of experience and its products. Universality, in and of itself, cannot be assumed as a regulative and/or teleological horizon. Such an assumption, however, is acceptable only if it is conceived as constantly renewable, that is, capable of spurring further iterations of relational and inter-subjective translations and transactions, which are precisely the expressions of universal potentialities. In this way, every human being can try to retrace the experiential paths which others have previously drawn, giving rise to inter-subjective efforts of objectification and crossed contextualization. However, that re-tracing is to be intended, at the same time, as mimesis and metaphor, understanding and creation, interpretation and production of culture. This is because moving along paths that others have already traced is also, and inevitably, a way to re-draw them. What is crucial, in this respect, is that the re-writing activity be carried out through a polyphonic, inter-subjectively symmetrical and cross-contextualizing approach. See Ricca (2013) and *ibidem* for further bibliographical references.

[40] . . . assuming such a figure exists at all, and can be found somewhere, embodied by real subjects—something that is, however, highly questionable.

designed by dominant groups to assure top-down social control, a kind of partisan cartography ordered to immunize their power from political challenge.

In the same vein, contemporary geographic theorists have also unveiled the normative features of the modern idea of 'map,' and the prescriptiveness inherent in this act of *representing* the world. They have argued that such an imperativeness of representation is dissimulated under a smoke screen of alleged scientific accuracy in the symbolic *reproduction* of territory, the empirical neutrality of patterns and criteria used to make geographic projections, and so on. Conversely, maps *translate* the Earth and make visible (only) what each cartographer wants to show. They are almost a distorting lens that remolds reality and presents itself as the true image of it. The result of such surreptitious substation is that he who reads a map, looks at it and thinks it is the real world, in so doing blinds himself to all the features of the world that the map does not include.

The use of simple present in legal statements serves, in many respects, the same purpose of maps. It passes off the '*ought*' as '*is*', obligation as empirical datum, imposing a sort of tyranny of legal discourse because it makes people perceive imperative acts as descriptive ones. What shall occur and be fulfilled appears as something that has *already* happened in a kind of *eternal present*. Post-modern criticism and post-colonial approaches[41] have been vociferous in calling out the dark side of generalizations, which the Frankfurt School had already identified and given the well-known label, the 'Dialectics of Enlightenment.' It is certainly difficult to deny that the totalizing ambitions of modern thought and the related idea of (the possibility of) a cognitive and normative mapping of the world have frequently produced mystifying counter-effects. Nonetheless, we should not conclude that any generalization is, in and of itself, necessarily false or deceptive. On the other hand, the same idea of radical difference among the various inflections and experiences of subjectivity implies some form of generalization, at least because that idea cannot help but involve categories, if only to be formulated. More broadly, without generalization, categorizations, or cognitive and behavioral habits, we humans—but also other organisms—cannot live. If every human experience were a unique self-bounded event, we would be unable to learn anything, and even the personal identity of subjects would become inconceivable through time because of the incommensurability of each lived situation with all the others. Generalizing is as crucial as differentiating; likewise, mapping is as important as being free to always draw new and unprecedented paths. This means nothing more than that the attitude to generalize/categorize must be accompanied by a commitment to cast a gaze on the world that is open to new experiences and ready to be continually renewed by them. There is something else to be said, however. Most likely, a widespread refusal to use generalizations and maps would run the risk of silencing our critical thinking forever. Individual experiences, if not generalized and thereby exposed to a critical-symbolic comparison with other subsequent experiences, would inevitably

[41] In the huge literature on the relationship between modern law and political-social serialization, see Chatterjee (2004).

incline to turn into stiffened rituals, difficult to alter. Those experiences would transform from vital processes into recipes, authoritatively certified by tradition (or, what has already been done) and mechanically reiterated. Those experiences, if bereft of generalizations, could probably elude categorical serialization, but they would also lack the ambiguity inherent in abstractions. In this way, however, they would cease to enjoy the *good effects* of such ambiguity. Actually, it is what allows us to include under the umbrella of each category many different experiences, which may be *made* analogous precisely through connotative continuity[42]—as illustrated above—so as to create the opportunity for the previous categorical borders to be remolded.

I would like to suggest that the real issue here is not about categories and generalizations as such, but has to do, rather, with the ways we use them. If we gave up generalizations and maps, it could become very difficult for us to conceive of paths different from those already drawn in the past. But the same would happen if we took generalizations and maps for reality in itself, because such an attitude would make us blind to the indexes of novelty stemming from experience. If used in such a way, both generalizations and maps would fail in their cognitive function, and transfigure into mere tools for a narrow-minded attempt at dominance. On the contrary, if we opened our minds and practices to a radical plurality and recast it in chorological terms, I think that generalizations could be exploited as discursive interfaces to translate the different spaces lived by subjects.

The assertion that spaces and circuits of meaning engendered by subjective experience draw a plurality of space-time frameworks does not imply that they cannot communicate or have any commonalities or connotative continuities. Categories and semantic features can partake in broader, or simply different, situations as well as categorical sets. The 'tree' constitutes a category, but it is (or better, can be) also and simultaneously a constitutive element of the 'forest.' In many cases, people live situations within which an element, for instance a house, is related to other, previously assumed features (both denotative and connotative) that could transform the significations of the category 'house.' Nevertheless, it is still the word 'house,' by virtue of its generalizing scope, that conveys such semantic contaminations, not infrequently triggered by exigencies of axiological/teleological consistency. It is values that make enlarging or enshrining categorical borders seem reasonable, because they show, by means of their semantic plasticity and trans-categorical relevance/pertinence, new semantic and pragmatic implications. The semantic/axiological common axes can allow, in such cases, acts of translation and transplantation, not infrequently of a metaphorical kind, between circuits of meaning and experiences that are so far unconnected. Of course, in any translational path—even if never repeated—something is gained and something else lost; this is the price of innovation. This condensing form of intermingling between different categorical

[42]It would be useful to underline, once again, that—at least, ideally and according to the Platonic idea of kóra—such 'continuity' is exclusively connotative (or, populated by connotative elements) because it precedes the stage in which it is possible to speak of denotations.

circuits does not at all constitute a holistic or all-encompassing synthesis. This is because it comprises, I argue, the emersion of a horizontal thirdness, as such capable of *placing* itself besides the other pre-existent categorical circuits, maybe modifying but certainly not engulfing them, in any kind of meta-categorical absolute. People's experiences, when they retain their own difference, can be translated, and so enabled to peacefully combine and coexist, but this need not lead to a reduction of their plurality. Instead, the effects of any translation and re-categorization can turn into an opening for new steps along the overall path of the differentiation process.

The presence of generalizing devices within the legal landscape means that interfaces for translation and re-categorization between different situations can be found, and even before, makes it possible to read and recognize them as experiential situations that can be taken as semantically continuous or discontinuous. In this sense, generalization seem to function in the same way as maps. In saying this, I mean that maps, despite their representative rigidity, can serve as a palimpsest on which endless possible paths can be traced, which over time—perhaps—end up impressed on the territory such that deep and salient marks urge legal *mappers* to rethink, recalculate and redraw the initial socio-cartographical representation. From a pragmatic point of view, both legal generalizations and maps could be considered as means to 'write the world.' Both can function as media for the unfolding of experience and, at the same time, as possible subjects of remolding activities, as a consequence of their unprecedented practical implications.[43]

Before proceeding further, I will try to summarize what I have elucidated so far. Any genuine and effective translation between spaces or symbols always gives rise to a third world. It is not, however, a kind of thirdness that includes the original spatial/semantic circuits and their differences by annihilating them. It is instead a horizontal one, in the sense that it makes it possible to identify the signical interfaces that are suitable to support the coexistence and the intermingling condensation of these spaces of meaning by preserving their recognizability. The process through which such thirdness will take shape will inevitably produce some changes, and make itself a hub for further semiotic relationships. This step, however, will fuel, in turn, new differentiations that trigger the request for new translations along a semiotic direction, virtually without end.

The thirdness I outline is certainly not all-comprehensive; nevertheless, it does not share the same features that characterize the models of 'third space' proposed in post-modern criticism.[44] It is not defined by its being lateral, occasional, nomadic, latent, nor other similar features. Quite the opposite, it retains a feature (or aura) of

---

[43] Some seminal suggestions have been provided by the critique of cartography proposed by Olsson (2007) and his analysis of the connections between mythical-religious thought, categorical stability—along with the ensuing mapping of reality—and social power, and/or sovereignty concepts (2011).

[44] See de Certeau (1990); Soja (1996); and, from a different perspective, Lefebvre (1974), who reads 'thirdness' as an inherent connotation of modern space, almost an epiphenomenon of its advent, as such open to processes of political objectification as well as to attempts at intentional programmatic re-reading of public space.

open generality and, therefore, of openness to its own reshaping through ongoing discursive practices. Without such a characterization, to be sure, any third space will assume traits of untranslatability and absolute diversity. Such a condition, however, could only be virtually postulated, since the 'connotative continuity' among the different circuits of experience engender, in the long term, an inevitable overlapping and thereby, at least in the absence of skilled practices of translation, an unavoidable predisposition to conflict. But this is the same kind of conflict that would mark the arrival point of a post-modernist absolutizing of differences, as well as a radical pluralism, if slated towards self-referential relativism. It should come as no surprise, therefore, that the crooked offspring of such epistemological(-ideological) overstatements are deliberately non cognizant of the 'connotative continuities' that ineradicably bring together the relationships among different circuits of both meaning and experience. Indeed, it is nothing but the revenant idea of a void space—as fictitious as the traditional one—where all the disconnected differences seem to be destined to struggle for the occupation of a vacuum, to the detriment of others.

The plastic representation just drawn of the struggle for space ignores, however, another constitutive element of experience and signification. I refer to the inter-categorical relatedness and contextual dependence of meaning. The occupation of space as a consequence of the eviction or neutralization of Otherness does not ensure the assertion of one's own identity. Conversely, the unexpected result of such 'victorious enterprises' is often a sudden realizing that the contended space was not void or amenable to be emptied after all. The eviction of Otherness can engender, instead, an unforeseen change in the environmental conditions that transfigures the coveted victory and, along with it, the overall subjectivity of the winner. There is an unexpected finding: the Other was an integral part of the space for which the struggle was fought. This is precisely the finding, as surprising as it is bitter, that lies beyond the horizon of the aspiration to an exclusive and excluding dominance of space. The evaporation and/or annihilation of Otherness co-generates the transformation of both space and Self, resulting in a heterogenesis of ends. These kinds of occurrences are not unusual, and they show how important it is to know the Other. And this is precisely because 'ignoring' someone or something is equivalent to obscuring, or making them disappear.

The relationship Self/Other interpenetrates the semantic space-time schemes of law, even if it undergoes, through legal patterns, a sort of *domestication*. The authorities' efforts to tame subjectivities and their connections can never succeed in a permanent confinement. Each subject, as Other-than-someone-else, continually produces meanings and experiences, and thereby new spaces. These new meanings, experiences and spaces, bursting with novelty, can inscribe themselves within the semiotic-discursive dome *traced* by legal texts, particularly the apical ones, since these are endowed with a higher degree of generality, and thereby semantic plasticity/ambiguity. Such possibilities of inscribing subjective spaces within legal semantic frames result from action plans, but assume more than a strategic meaning, and this because they also impinge reflexively on the social and legal sense of the behaviors adopted by anyone who is Other *of* Other, namely the same subject of any action. What I mean is that in a socio-institutional context in tune with the principle of constitutionalism, the inter-subjective relationship takes (or should take) shape in a multilateral and polyphonic way. Since the semantic elements of situations lived by Others can inscribe in, and even remold, legal categories, they will fit into the universe of meaning of each subject. When someone makes themselves blind or deaf to such *inter-categorical resonances*, it does nothing but demote the Other's action and related subjectivity to a condition of subalternity. As a consequence, they will become insulated in a different space from the common one, as well as in an a-synchronic time dimension incommensurable with the time lived by the majority, and all this because neither the Other's time nor spaces are aligned with the dominant social subject's *semantic apparatuses*. These kinds of segregating strategies could produce a neutralizing effect on the Other and, at least in the short term, even an immunization of the more powerful subjects, with respect to the Other's reactions. What ultimately cannot be annihilated—even outside the liberal-constitutional framework—is, however, the Other's ability to transform their own signs. In other words, that specifically human ability to strategically re-categorize one's own actions, as well as those of Others, to subvert a disadvantaged situation (as, mythically, Ulysses did to Polyphemus the Cyclops in the Homeric Odyssey, by transforming an olive tree trunk into a sort of blinding harpoon).

In societies organized by means of legal texts, what makes possible the reversal of situations (or, at least, should) are the written legal words and principles, which indeed should function as a trigger. However mystifying, or used with this diverting bent, modern declarations of human rights serve as critical axes to counter dominant powers. From the struggles of the socialist proletariat to the contemporary critical/renewing reading of Human Rights claimed by post-colonial cultural communities, we can trace, always and everywhere, recurrent attempts to redefine spaces of coexistence and their semantic features on the basis of new interpretations of legal standards of universalization.[45] On the other hand, it is individuals and their lived spaces that continually *regenerate* the categorical borders of legal discourse and its specific areas, as well as its words. In this transformation, we can find the hub around which the dynamics of contemporary sovereignty revolves. Semantic and pragmatic coordinates of sovereignty, its space-time, govern the conduct of individuals who move across ever renewed spaces, a phenomenon that takes place either within or beyond the geo-political frontiers of states. This occurrence has made the exercise of a completely vertical control of social actors and actions by means of rules, supposed a priori to be efficacious, instead, impossible. But this is simply because the categorical stability essential to achieve this aim is absent not only for economic-geopolitical reasons, but also for semantic and cognitive ones.

Disregarding the presence of new semantic features within the situations lived by legal subjects and resulting from their extra-national or multi-situated circuits of

[45] As regards such an approach to human rights, even in opposition to majority thinking within anthropological studies, see Bhambra et al. (2009), Sajò (2004), Muthu (2003), Clarke and Goodale (2010), Meckled-Garcìa and Cali (2006), Messer (2002), Goodale and Merry (2007), Engle Merry (2006a, b: p. 10), Cowan et al. (2001), and Riles (2006). For a broader analysis of the topic I deal with in the above text, see Ricca (2008, 2013).

interests, would be equivalent in many cases to misunderstanding the significance of the same institutional decisions enacted precisely to rule their conduct. But misunderstanding the significance of those decisions also means not envisaging their consequences. Unfortunately, however, failing to see these consequences makes it impossible to assess whether they will be consistent with the axiological and constitutional axes of legal institutional action, and thereby with the legitimate exercise of sovereignty.[46] If sovereignty is not absolute (and unrelated), but rather consists of a sequence of political-legal actions aligned with constitutional values and ends, then it must constantly address the spaces engendered by individuals, including them within its teleological commitments. Moreover, if and when such spaces move beyond the national framework, then sovereignty will have no choice but to hetero-integrate itself, to achieve its ends. In other words, sovereignty must include anything from the outside that aids in the accomplishment of constitutional values as embodied by the actions and spaces of sense drawn by its legal subjects.[47]

In a globalized world, where each local (chorological) space has turned into a crossroads, interconnecting webs of relationships ubiquitously spread over the earth's surface, constitutional values—and even more human rights—end up functioning as norms of presupposition (a specific kind *renvoi*) to the frameworks of sense that are molded within different spaces of experience. As a result, legal systems and regulative areas, especially if they include high levels of teleological signification and inter-temporal scope, require hetero-integration precisely to assure the effectiveness of their legal provisions, and to support the essential prognostic consistency between legal statements and their effects. To put it diversely, every legal system that includes pluralism as part of its axes of legitimation, be it local or global, national or supranational, is intrinsically and structurally incomplete, hence necessarily open to trans-late (so, also transport) Others and semiotic-spatial Otherness. Further, including what is outside and elsewhere also serves as a means of interweaving webs of relationships, or enabling active participation in the creation of global chorological coordinates. If what is outside can become something inside, then what is inside can, in turn, become something outside, or migrate toward supranational dimensions. I think that as regards these semiotic and normative fluxes, much depends on the use of inter-faces of translation, and, therefore, the opening up of a third space between the Self and Other, between 'in' and 'out.'

If considered from this perspective, subsidiarity assumes a huge normogenetic and, even more, semiotic-cognitive signification. In effect, it shows itself to be a vehicle of translation between the exigencies and claims of a multiplicity of actors; this applies also to the translation between the spaces engendered by people's

[46] I addressed this topic in Ricca (1999).

[47] See Ricca (1999). My approach to the issues concerning sovereignty moves along an argumentative path that is very different from the geography of sovereign power developed by Brunner, in *Land und Herrschaft Power* or by Schmitt in *Nomos der Erde*; it is even more distant from the logical-legal coordinates of Kelsen's formalism. This warning is offered to emphasize the differences extant between the legal chorological approach I propose here, and the geo-politics of law, or geo-law, put forth by some voices of contemporary thought, be they legal, political or geographical.

conduct, in view of an ever-renewed *de-finition* of inclusive features for a legal subjectivity resulting from ubiquitous processes of production and legitimation of law. At the same time, focusing the analytical gaze on the ubiquitous chorology of contemporary sovereignty urges us to draw our attention simultaneously to both the top and the foundations of each institutional and legal system to address the definition of, and the differences between, 'public activity', 'activities carried out by private subjects,' 'actions that can be entitled to subsidiary subjects,' 'public interest,' and 'individual interest.'

The strict criteria so often employed by courts in interpreting the principle of horizontal subsidiarity are in danger of revealing themselves to be outside out of time and *real* space *in* and *across* which legal experience actually unfolds. On the other side, however, we must consider that the choral and polyphonic convergence of claims involved in—and, in this sense, subsidiary to, and then replacing—state hierarchical-pyramidal interpretations and implementations of legal statements may raise some concerns. In this scenario of horizontal shifting of subjects and *spaces of competence*, the idea of a common good connoted by (an alleged) anthropological homogeneity, taken as the general frame to rule the rhythms of interaction between public and private, seems to have been overthrown by a socio-political integration driven by private actors, often motivated by a scarcely camouflaged self-interest. Hence, recognizing the cognitive import inherent in the plurality of semiotic-spatial experience can be a source of concern precisely because it puts into question the spatio-temporal unity of sense somehow assured by the 'not realized,' even if real, violence of the 'word of modern state's sovereignty.'[48] This is because the Gorgon face of modern sovereignty is captured not so much in what is said, as rather in what is not silenced: the voice of difference. Despite the consistent failure of these attempts to silence, legal rhetorical assertions succeed in reassuring populations by blurring and conflating the features of 'legal ought' with those of 'social being'—even by means of the not surprisingly widespread use of the present tense in legal statements.

Today, however, it becomes increasingly apparent how the political project of a subjectivity tamed in the shadow of an autarchic sovereignty is just an illusion.[49] The price of the (hidden and unmentionable) temptation to keep cultivating it could turn out to be very high, and ultimately far more difficult to tolerate than even extraordinary efforts to find interfaces of translation in a world engendered by the plurality of individual experiences and cultures. As I have been arguing, it is not the *perspectives on* the World, but the worlds themselves that must be *trans-duced* inside each other, a bit like what happens when galaxies collide. It must be a creative effort, which is to be engaged without support from an ethics of reciprocity[50] nor

[48] See Philippopoulos-Mihalopoulos (2011, pp. 187 ff.).

[49] See, within the vast literature on this subject, most recently, Glenn (2013).

[50] This idea is proposed by Donati (2009).

from an ethics of freedom,[51] let alone the pseudo-ethics of the market.[52] This is simply because these paradigms presuppose the existence of an anthropological/cultural ground of sense that has already been shaped, and is ready to mold the physiognomy of legal subjectivity. The semiotic intermingling among experiential spaces urges us to re-imagine and re-draw that ground through essentially 'freehand' creative efforts, with an anthropologically creative attitude and, therefore, an extremely demanding commitment to ethical responsibility and cognitive depth. Besides, adopting a chorological view, and implementing a corresponding path of legal subjectivity, is driven by an understanding that what we do not make happen cannot happen (or, as the saying goes, 'do nothing and nothing happens'): in short, there is no destiny granted by any philosophy of history that can take the place of people's responsible choices and actions. At the same time, however, such awareness makes it clear that any wrong done will produce its own dramatic consequences, and nothing can assure a happy rescue from the disastrous implications of our mistakes.

The dark side of horizontal subsidiarity[53] is a pulverized and individualistic, as well as disordered and self-interested, flowing of social claims within the always protean framework of 'the common good.' It evokes a hazy murkiness of the landscape of the individual, and a common fate that is coextensive with our blindness to our future, and possibly even to our present. Nonetheless, we must avoid at all costs any attempt to cross such an abyss of ignorance by means of false truths or aprioristic top-down generalizations that lead to mechanistic and deceptive implementations of subsidiarity. Our main task should be to fuel our projects by staying aware of the consequences that inevitably result from a lack of creative synthesis between the pluralities of physical and semantic spaces engendered by individual chorological conduct.

References

Alleweldt R (2019) Avoiding another Brexit: the subsidiarity principle, the European Convention on Human Rights and the United Kingdom. Commonw Comp Polit 57(2):223–241. https://doi.org/10.1080/14662043.2019.1574011

Anderson B, Harrison P (2010) The promise of non-representational theories. In: Anderson B, Harrison P (eds) Taking-place: non-representational theories and geography. Ashgate, Farnham, pp 1–36

Bauman Z (1991) Modernity and ambivalence. Polity Press/Blackwell, Cambridge

Bennet L, Layard A (2015) Legal geography: becoming spatial detectives. Geogr Compass 9(7): 406–422

[51] According to a Kantian framework.

[52] I refer to the economic liberal paradigm based on competition and considered in all its historical declinations.

[53] I am echoing here the title of Costa and Pizzolato's book on subsidiarity (2013).

Bhambra G, Shilliam R, Baxi U (eds) (2009) Silencing human rights. Palgrave Macmillan, Basingstoke
Blomley N (1994) Law, space and the geographies of power. The Guilford Press, New York
Blomley N (2003a) From 'What' to 'So What?' Law and geography in retrospect. In: Holder J, Harrison C (eds) Law and geography. OUP, Oxford, pp 17–33
Blomley N (2003b) Unsettling the city: urban land and the politics of property. Routledge, New York
Blomley N, Delaney D, Ford RT (eds) (2001) The legal geographies reader. Blackwell, Oxford
Blumenberg H (2007) Theorie der Unbegrifflichkeit. Suhrkamp, Frankfurt a. M
Braverman I (2014) Who's afraid of methodology? Advocating a methodological turn in legal geography. In: Braverman I, Blomley N, Delaney D, Kedar A (eds) Expanding spaces of law: a timely legal geography. Stanford University Press, Stanford, pp 120–141
Braverman I, Blomley N, Delaney D, Kedar A (eds) (2014) Expanding spaces of law: a timely legal geography. Stanford University Press, Stanford
Brickell K, Jeffrey A, McConnell F (2021) Practising legal geography. Area 53(4):557–561
Butler C (2012) Henri Lefebvre: spatial politics, everyday life, and the right to the city. Routledge, Abingdon
Carozza PG (2003) Subsidiarity as a structural principle of international human rights law. Am J Int Law 97:38–79
Chatterjee P (2004) The politics of the governed: reflections on popular politics in most of the world. Columbia University Press, New York
Christoffersen J (2009) Fair balance: proportionality, subsidiarity and primarity in the European Convention on Human Rights. Martinus Nijhoff, Leiden
Clarke KM, Goodale M (2010) Introduction: understanding the multiplicity of justice. In: Clarke KM, Goodale M (eds) Mirrors of justice: law and power in a post-cold war era. Cambridge University Press, New York, pp 1–27
Close F (2009) Nothing: a very short introduction. Oxford University Press, Oxford
Costa P, Pizzolato F (eds) (2013) Il lato oscuro della sussidiarietà. Giuffrè, Milano
Cover RM (1986) Violence and the word. Yale Law J 95:1601–1629. http://digitalcommons.law.yale.edu/fss_papers/2708
Cowan JK, Dembour M-B, Wilson RA (2001) Introduction. In: Cowan JK, Dembour M-B, Wilson RA (eds) Culture and rights: anthropological perspectives. Cambridge University Press, Cambridge
de Certeau M (1990) L'invention du quotidien, vol. I, Arts de faire. Gallimard, Paris
Delaney D (2003) Beyond the word: law as a thing of this world. In: Holder J, Harrison C (eds) Law and geography. OUP, Oxford, pp 67–83
Delaney D (2010) The spatial, the legal and the pragmatics of world-making: nomospheric investigations. Routledge, Abingdon
Delaney D (2014) Legal geography I. Constitutivities, complexities and contingencies. Progr Hum Geogr 39(1):1–7
Dematteis G (1985) Le metafore della terra. La geografia umana tra mito e scienza. Feltrinelli, Milano
Dewey J (1926) The historical background of corporate legal personality. Yale Law J 35(6): 655–673
Dikshit RD (2006) Geographical thought: a contextual history of ideas. Prentice Hall, New Delhi
Donati P (2009) What does "Subsidiarity" mean? The relational perspective. J Mark Morality 12(2): 211–243
Engle Merry S (2006a) Human rights and gender violence: translating international law into local justice. Chicago University Press, Chicago
Engle Merry S (2006b) Transnational human rights and local activism: mapping the middle. Am Anthropol CVIII(1):38–51
Evans M, Zimmermans A (eds) (2014) Global perspectives on subsidiarity. Springer, Heidelberg

Fall J, Minca C (2013) Not a geography of what doesn't exist, but a counter-geography of what does: rereading Dematteis' Metafore della Terra. Progr Hum Geogr 37(4):542–563
Farinelli F (2003) Geografia. Un'introduzione ai modelli del mondo. Einaudi, Torino
Farinelli F (2009) Crisi della ragione cartografica. Einaudi, Torino
Foucault M (1994 [1967]) Des espaces autres. In: Foucault M Dits et écrits. Éditions Gallimard, Paris
Franck RM, Driven R, Ziemke T, Bernàrdez E (eds) (2008) Body, language, and mind. II. Sociocultural situatedness. Mouton de Gruyter, Berlin
Gibbs RW Jr (1994) Poetics of mind: figurative thought, language, and understanding. Cambridge University Press, Cambridge
Gibbs RW Jr (2005) Embodiment and cognitive science. Cambridge University Press, Cambridge
Gibson JJ (1986) The ecological approach to visual perception. Lawrence Erlbaum Associates, Hillsdale, NJ
Glenn PH (2013) The cosmopolitan state. OUP, Oxford
Goodale M, Merry SE (eds) (2007) The practice of human rights: tracking law between global and local. CUP, Cambridge
Goodwin C (1994) Professional vision. Am Anthropol 96(3):606–633
Goodwin C (1995) Seeing in depth. Soc Stud Sci 25:237–274
Goodwin C (1996a) Transparent vision. In: Ochs E, Schegloff EA, Thompson S (eds) Interaction and grammar. CUP, Cambridge, pp 370–404
Goodwin C (1996b) Practices of color classification. Ninchi Kagaku (Cogn Stud Bull Japanese Cogn Sci Soc) 3(2):62–82
Goodwin C (1997) The blackness of black. In: Resnick LB, Säliö R, Pontecorvo C, Burge B (eds) Discourse, tools and reasoning: essay on situated cognition. Springer, Berlin
Gregory RL (1997) Eye and brain. Oxford University Press/Princeton University Press
Hartshorne R (1939) Nature of geography: a critical survey of current thought in the light of the past. Association of American Geographers, Lancaster
Heritier P (2023) Understanding legal semiotics: chorologies (forthcoming)
Ingold T (2007) Lines: a brief history. Routledge, Abingdon
Jackendoff R (1983) Semantics and cognition. MIT Press, Massachusetts
Jackson N, Wightman J (2003) Spatial dimensions of private law. In: Holder J, Harrison C (eds) Law and geography. Oxford University Press, Oxford, pp 35–64
Layard A (2010) Shopping in the public realm: a law of place. J Law Soc 37(3):412–441
Lefebvre H (1974) La production de l'espace. Anthropos, Paris
Martin DG, Scherr AW, City C (2010) Making law, making place: lawyers and the production of space. Progr Hum Geogr 34(2):175–192
Meckled-Garcìa S, Cali B (eds) (2006) The legalization of human rights. Routledge, Abingdon
Messer E (2002) Anthropologist in a world with and without human rights. In: Macclancy J (ed) Exotic no more. Anthropology for the contemporary world. University of Chicago Press, Chicago, pp 319–337
Millon-Delson C (1993) Le principe de subsidiarité. PUF, Paris
Moreira R (2014) Para onde vai o pensamento geográfico? Para uma epistemologia critica. Contexto, São Paulo
Muthu S (2003) Enlightenment against empire. Princeton University Press, Princeton
Olsson G (2007) Abysmal: a critique of cartographic reason. The University of Chicago Press, Chicago
Olsson G (2011) Mapping the taboo. In: Daniels S, DeLyser D, Entrikin JN, Richardson D (eds) Envisioning landscapes, making worlds: geography and the humanities. Routledge, London, pp 35–43
Olwig KR (2011) Choros, chora and the question of landscape. In: Daniels S, DeLyser D, Entrikin JN, Richardson D (eds) Envisioning landscapes, making worlds: geography and the humanities. Routledge, London, pp 44–54
Orzeck R, Hae L (2020) Restructuring legal geography. Prog Hum Geogr 44(5):832–851

Philippopoulos-Mihalopoulos A (2010) Spatial justice: law and the geography of withdrawal. Int J Law Context 6(3):1–16
Philippopoulos-Mihalopoulos A (2011) Law's spatial turns: geography, justice and a certain fear of spaces. Law Cult Humanit 7(2):187–202
Philippopoulos-Mihalopoulos A (2012) Law, spaces, bodies: the emergence of spatial justice. In: de Sutter L, Mcgee K (eds) Deleuze and the law (Deleuze connections). Edinburgh University Press, Edinburgh, pp 90–110
Philippopoulos-Mihalopoulos A (2015) Spatial justice: body, lawscape, atmosphere. Routledge, London
Pickles J (2004) A history of spaces: cartographic reason, mapping, and the geo-coded world. Routledge, London
Ricca M (1999) Metamorfosi della Sovranità e ordinamenti confessionali. Giappichelli, Torino
Ricca M (2008) Oltre Babele. Codici per una democrazia interculturale. Dedalo, Bari
Ricca M (2013) Culture interdette. Modernità, migrazioni, diritto interculturale. Bollati Boringhieri, Torino
Ricca M (2014) Sapore, sapere del mondo. Tradizioni religiose e traduzioni alimentari. Daimon. Diritto comparato delle religioni 2014:33–66
Ricca M (2016) Klee's cognitive legacy and human rights as intercultural transducers: modern art, legal translation, and micro-spaces of coexistence. CALUMET - Intercult Law Humanit Rev 3: 1–40. https://calumet-review.com/index.php/2016/09/10/klees-cognitive-legacy-and-human-rights-as-intercultural-transducers-modern-art-legal-translation-and-micro-spaces-of-coexistence/
Ricca M (2019) Signs across races: Al-Jahiz's cosmo-semiosis and his trans-racial mapping of the "human." CALUMET - Intercult Law Humanit Rev 8:21–40. https://calumet-review.com/index.php/2019/06/11/signs-across-races-al-jahizs-cosmo-semiosis-and-his-trans-racial-mapping-of-the-human/
Ricca M (2022) Perpetually astride Eden's boundaries: the limits to the 'limits of law' and the semiotic inconsistency of 'legal enclosures'. Int J Semiot Law 35:179–229. https://doi.org/10.1007/s11196-020-09771-0
Riles A (2006) Anthropology, human rights, and legal knowledge: culture in the iron cage. Am Anthropol 108(1):52–65
Ronsenberg D, Grafton A (2010) Cartographies of time: a history of timeline. Princeton Architectural, Princeton
Sajò A (ed) (2004) Human rights with modesty: the problem of universalism. Martinus Nijhoff, Leiden
Sallis J (1999) Chorology: on beginning in Plato's *Timaeus*. Indiana University Press, Bloomington
Sarat A, Kearns TR (1995a) Beyond the great divide: forms of legal scholarship and everyday life. In: Sarat A, Kearns TR (eds) Law in everyday life. University of Michigan Press, Ann Arbor, pp 21–62
Sarat A, Kearns TR (1995b) Editorial. In: Sarat A, Kearns TR (eds) Law in everyday life. University of Michigan Press, Ann Arbor, pp 1–20
Sini C (2003) Teoria e pratica del foglio mondo. La scrittura filosofica. Laterza, Roma
Soja E (1996) Thirdspace: journeys to Los Angeles and other real-and-imagined places. Blackwell, Malden
Tenbrink T (2007) Space, time, and the use of languages. An investigation of relationships. Walter de Gruyter, Berlin
van Zeben J, Nicolaïdis K (2019) Polycentric subsidiarity. In: van Zeben J, Bobić A (eds) Polycentricity in the European Union. CUP, Cambridge, pp 78–107
von Benda-Beckmann F, von Benda-Beckmann K, Griffiths A (2009) Space and legal pluralism: an introduction. In: von Benda-Beckmann F, von Benda-Beckmann K, Griffiths A (eds) Spatializing law. An anthropological geography of law and society. Ashgate, Farnham, pp 1–30
Ziemke T, Zlatev J, Frank RM (eds) (2007) Body, language, and mind. I. Embodiment. Mouton de Gruyter, Berlin

Chapter 5
Human Rights, Legal Chorology and Modern Art: The Dis-Compositional Approach to the 'Visual' and the Worldwide Dynamics of Cultural Spaces

5.1 Human Rights and the Protopypical Assumption of Their Local/Ethnocentric Implementations

The universality of Human Rights is a matter of relentless contention.[1] Among the several critiques, many argue that Human Rights inherently convey an anthropological view of subjectivity that is deep-rooted in Western culture, with an individualist bent. As I suggested above, in many cases, such criticisms arise because the meaning of these rights is understood through the spectrum of historically realized implementations within the West and, subsequently, forcedly transplanted throughout the world. These implementations take shape through the filter and combination with forms and institutes provided by the statutory laws and legal traditions of the West (in the related areas of family law, inheritance law, contracts, ownership, and other real rights, crimes, etc.). Hermeneutical blending[2] with the legal categories of Western tradition makes it such that these are assumed as prototypes of human rights implementation. The consequence of such prototypical assumption/reduction is that claims for cultural recognition raised by non-Western people and individuals are parameterized to human rights in an ethnocentric way.

What are the practical outcomes of the adoption of such a method of parameterization? Unfortunately, they are easily understood, even if obstinately dissimulated. The compatibility of non-Western cultural habits and forms with the discourse on rights is assessed by taking as real parameters the historical implementations of the latter, precisely those accomplished by means of Western state legislations and legal

[1] Sajò (2004).

[2] Such a convergence is increased tremendously by the activity of Constitutional and Supreme Courts. This is because the judicial review of legislation tends to project the contents of human and/or fundamental rights statements over and within the normative fabric of each national circuit, and vice versa, so engendering a sort of welding, if not conflation, between these two levels of legal discourse.

M. Ricca, *Intercultural Spaces of Law*, Law and Visual Jurisprudence 10,
https://doi.org/10.1007/978-3-031-27436-7_5

institutes/categories. In this way, however, the far more inclusive semantic potentialities of human rights statements—be they from international, supranational, or national sources—end up being inevitably overshadowed and, at last, neutralized.

Human rights implementations realized in Western countries are, in any case, only 'one' and not 'the only' way to interpret and put them into effect. Substantially, therefore, the assumption of Western implementations as prototypical 'incarnations' of rights is like taking the part for the whole, that is, a kind of metonymical substitution determining inevitable hermeneutical strabismus and discriminations.[3] Discrimination takes shape because the legal categories of Western legal systems are furrowed with cultural wrinkles, not infrequently rooted in the religious imagery prevalent at an anthropological level, even before a theological-political or denominational one. It is almost fated, therefore, that different historical-cultural experiences and habits bump into obstacles of compatibility and even commensurability when compared with those categories. In this regard, just think of conceptualizations of corporeality, marriage, the dynamics of inter-subjective recognition inherent in bargaining (for example: 'good faith,' equity), and so on. The final outcome is that human rights are utilized as an interface to assert the universality of legal-cultural Western categories. The direct implication of such a *misuse* of statements of rights, their universalistic vocation, and their authority, is an implementation of them that results in an exclusive rather than an inclusive practice. This occurs precisely because the compatibility of legal claims and cultural habits of non-Western people is assessed according to human rights by using—tacitly, covertly and sometimes unawares—the civil and penal institutes from legal Western traditions as a *medium* of their legitimacy. Conversely, the indirect, dramatic implication of this hermeneutical attitude is that what is commensurable and aligned to these institutes is precisely for this reason deemed to be compatible with human rights; what is asymmetrical or incommensurable with them is automatically considered to be not in compliance with human rights and branded, in the worst cases, as a 'sign of inhumanity.'[4]

Such hermeneutical institutional practices inevitably have consequences and cause specular reactions. If 'consistency with human rights' becomes 'conformity to Western culture,' taken as a whole, including its more idiomatic and normative folds, then it is almost predestined that Others' cultures feel spurred—in a bitter, ironic sense—to dismiss any human rights discourse. Human rights will be perceived to be and classified as—as actually occurs—weapons of cultural imperialism.[5] Their universalism will be grasped as a merely rhetorical device, surreptitiously moving towards a homologation of Western culture carried out on a global scale (iterating, in a different way, the 'deeds' of colonialism).[6] Against this 'Universalism Western Style,' a great deal of antagonistic universalism has emerged (Islamic, Asian, Pacific, African, and so on). The proliferation of human rights

[3] See Ricca (2008).

[4] See Chryssochoou (2004).

[5] See Bell et al. (2001); Hastrup (2001).

[6] See Baxi (2002); Bhambra et al. (2009).

regional declarations, although maintaining, somehow, a pathological and inconsistent attitude, betray nevertheless an underlying interest in the topic of universality, even above and beyond the paean to relativism intoned by the champions of postmodern thought. This interest in universality seems to be embodied, especially in recent times, by the voices of cultures qualified as subaltern or, in any case, in antagonistic positions with respect to Western universality: voices that appear to be not in the least captivated by the idea of giving up the possibilities of emancipation or criticism supplied by the *existence* of the human rights discursive platform.[7]

5.2 Intercultural Uses of Human Rights and the Metaphorical Translation of Differences

After noting the multicultural/multilateral revival of interest in human rights, even within anthropology of law—until just recently all fallen in line, contending and stigmatizing the imperialist modernism 'irredeemably' inherent to them—scholars have little by little taken the path of a critical, inclusive re-reading of legal universalism. An anti-essentialist reading within which the semantic spectrum of rights statements is understood as an inclusive means capable of precipitating a generative move towards a grammar of subjectivity of an intercultural kind, making use of multilateral and reciprocally symmetrical translations of difference.[8]

The possibility to inscribe one's own difference within the lexicon of universality, so regenerating it, could actually mean conferring legitimacy and effectiveness to this lexicon. An intercultural use of human rights could supply law and legal discourse with the power and substance of devices of emancipation, and not only, or no longer, those of the means for the rule of the strongest and the exploitation of the weakest. Before outlining the contents and methodology of this 'use', it must be stressed that it constitutes only a possibility. No law of historical necessity assures that this route will be followed, and that the intercultural use of human rights ships will be brought into port. The risk of a homologating or serializing use of rights statements is always lurking. Avoiding it requires the construction of a ground of semantic continuity between behavioral habits that could be legitimate if properly declined according to different cultural perspectives. For this purpose, the activity of translation, and a corresponding commitment to it, is crucial.[9] Inscribing behaviors and related legal institutes carried out by people of Other cultures *within* the semantic spectrum of human rights statements is an indispensable step. The main issue, of course, is what to translate and how to translate it.

The assumption of an intercultural prospective implies adopting, at least as an operational device, the idea of a phenomenon called 'culture.' Whatever approach is

---

[7] See Goodale and Merry (2007), Clarke and Goodale (2010), Engle (2006a, 2006b).

[8] See Cowan et al. (2001).

[9] See Ricca (2013b).

chosen, 'culture' is destined to remain an open concept, with blurry borders, essentially a sort of 'absolute metaphor,'[10] targeted at orienting experiences and their possibilities. This is because whatever idea of 'culture' we adopt, it will be reflexively inscribed, as in a circle, into a world in which the cultural dimension is simultaneously both outcome and motor. An 'objective' definition of culture, shaped by an observing eye that is 'relatively' culture-exempt or assiomatically pre-configured as a homunculus, is substantially unachievable. Hence, it seems to be preferable to rely upon an idea of culture that corresponds to dynamic encyclopedias of 'knowing to do,' oriented to draw routes of mutual relationships between subject and environment.[11]

Such an approach allows us to grasp the cultural dimension in processive and dynamical terms, so as to ensure its symbolic and material components, its consistency as a sign, and thereby its openness to signifying, its readiness to be supplemented through experience and its charge of novelty.[12] This is a non-essentialist and, at the same time, non-functionalist perspective. It is so because the encounter between different signifying dimensions is (assumed as) co-constructive and creative. The potentialities of signification encapsulated in each sign renew through their ongoing relationships with other signs, thus producing a third dimension that is innovative, and also encompasses axiological parameters (intended in both the symbolic and biological-material senses) that can bring the process of intercultural integration to a successful conclusion. In short, we could say that the process of coordination and interpenetration between signs renews, through production, its own development criteria as well.

The creation of new dynamic relationships between cultural encyclopedias can unfold by means of an activity of translation/transaction. A global and all-encompassing understanding of intercultural translations implies that human rights cannot be assumed as an external axiological and legal parameter with a universal and culturally neutral and/or inherently transversal scope. Rather, these kinds of rights should be intended as a *means of universalization*, that is, as a semantic potential capable of promoting and increasing inclusive processes of translation/transaction. For this to be possible, it is necessary to overcome the fact/norm divide. According to this dualist scheme, which is basically the classic pattern of legal qualification, every determined behavior (along with its regulative statement provided by the competent legal system[13]) is assumed in its morphological configuration and, relying on this, is anchored to one or another principle statement nestled within the human rights platform. However common throughout the world, this

[10]This expression has a Kantian 'ancestry'. 'Absolute metaphor', to be intended as an (at least, potentially) all-comprehensive metaphor, is key concept in Blumenberg's 'Theorie der Unbegrifflichkeit' (2007).

[11]See Ricca (2008, 2013b).

[12]See Ricca (2013a).

[13]In this regard, it is important to consider that, from a legal point of view, all laws/rules that do not belong to (or are external to) a specific legal system, are to be assumed to be mere facts.

approach inevitably produces interpretations of rights with an ethnocentric bent. This hermeneutical curving is due to the tendency of each cultural circuit to inscribe within the semantic spectrum of human rights its own behavioral patterns, already morphologically determined, categorized, and essentialized by means of as many normative/legal codes. But in so doing, the translation between different cultural perspectives results—as noted above—in antagonistic confrontations on the 'proper significance' of statements regarding human rights.[14] Such an interpretive polarization will be followed, therefore, by the use of each right as an authoritative source of legitimation to exclude the Other and their conduct from the social scene (the judgment of the Grand Chambre of the ECHR on the wearing of the *niqab* in public spaces is an emblematic case of such a result, as inevitable as it is absurd[15]).

Intercultural translation should start instead from the semiotic dis-composition of categories, usually considered for their morphological and exteriorly more evident features (in their 'presentified' formal appearance), and in all their components (axiological, contextual, teleological, qualitative, emotional, implicational, and so on). How it has been illustrated above, this operation is feasible only by carrying out an intersection of narratives, oriented to bring to the surface the contexts of sense underlying the adoption of determined behaviors and the related normative standards. All of this can have a doubly beneficial effect. From one side, it averts infra-cultural blindness, that is, the attitude to read in one's own way of acting and thinking the hallmark of self-evidence, naturalness, and even (surreptitious) universalism due to the belief that things could not be but as we (believe we) 'see' them. From the other side, intersecting narratives of reciprocal Otherness can inhibit an innate tendency to understand Others' behaviors and symbols—including ethical and legal apparatuses—through one's own cultural and conceptual schemes. Put in icastic terms, cross-contextual narratives can prevent 'our culture' from camouflaging as 'human nature,' while Otherness undergoes a process of translation hampered by imperfect metaphors, in which the equivalence between the two metaphorical terms results in a complete overshadowing superimposition of the denotations/connotations of the word chosen as a source domain over those of the word taken as target domain.[16]

A striking example of this (aberrant) translational approach can be found in the usual legal translation of the Arab word *nikah* into the English word 'marriage.' As a rule, the 'semantic ingredients' of *nikah*, as it is understood in Islamic culture, are entirely overwhelmed, and uncritically obscured, by the superimposition of the

---

[14] See Douzinas (2000).

[15] See ECHR, decision 1st July 2014, S.A.S. *vs.* France (n. 438351/11). On this, I refer to Ricca (2020b) and *ibidem* for further analysis and bibliographical references.

[16] See Chap. 3, Ricca (2008), and *ibidem* for further, wide bibliographical references on metaphor. On the conflation among 'denotations' and 'connotations', see Ricca (2022, p. 187, spec. nt 15) and there the referral to the theoretical debate between Ricouer and Jakobson (1960, p. 350 ff.) with specific regard to the 'dichotomy of signs and objects' (1960, pp. 357, 351): the same dichotomy that Ricoeur contested precisely in connection with the cognitive/creative processes involved in metaphorization.

categorical features of marriage as ruled and intended in Western legal systems and cultures. The creation of this ethnocentric semantic umbra is that the legal recognition conceded to *nikah* is reduced to its transition towards the domain of unlawfulness as soon as a second wife shows up. The expression 'polygamous or polygynous marriage,' precisely because of all the charge of negative value that it has in Western culture, represents a perfect synthesis of the consequences of such imperfect, asymmetrical metaphors and the related attempts of domesticating translation.

Making the emersion of 'contexts of signification' possible through a process of intercultural communication, instead, requires the extraction of all the semiotic (both denotative and connotative) components that are nestled within and manifested by each word or behavior. This effort tends to spur a strong self-distancing and the disposition to produce crossed contextualizations, which are, in turn, generative of a new, third context: that of a coexistence co-construed precisely in its premises. The germination of a process of crossed contextualization triggered by efforts toward the interpretation and mimetic mirroring of narratives from the Other, constitutes the most immediate path to an intercultural inclusive translation.

Intersecting narratives display existential scenarios that are intensely ramified and thereby very complex in their semiotic relations. If they are to be understood, such narratives require the social actors to generate contextual interfaces as incentive for the configuration of sense landscapes accessible to both narrator/narrated. Through such 'stories,' it is highly likely that the communicative exchange that takes place brings to light reciprocal continuities of life experiences that are enshrined within the cultural context of each of the tellers, even if these were previously completely outside the semantic horizon envisaged by each of them. This *bridge of continuities* can be construed, in such situations, by relying upon a metaphorical ground, constituted by a connotation or a connotative set, suited to work as a vehicle of analogy or correspondence across two cultural domains. In this regard, it is important to point out—once again—that such correspondences are not the same as archaeological findings or things uncovered, lying on the seabed of experience, or events endowed with their own previous ontological consistency. On the contrary, they stem from creative and innovative cognitive-conceptualizing activities, which only retrospectively—as is the case in all the metaphorical processes—seem to be endowed with objectivity. In many cases, the metaphorical ground comprises axiological and qualitative connotations that are inclined to produce and legitimate re-categorization processes calling into play both cultural encyclopedias. This is the consequence of the immersion of such encyclopedias within a new context of experience/signification, which is precisely the intercultural one.[17] Intercultural transformations take place, so, along a track of continuity with respect to the cultural past of each actor of the encounter; in other words, they come into being substantiated as self-transformations prompted by the need to adapt the cultural encyclopedias initially at the disposal of individuals.

---

[17] For further comments on this topic, see Ricca (2008, 2013a, d, 2016b).

Of course, not everything can be translated. Along the translation path, something will be gained and something else lost, as occurs, on the other hand, in all metaphors and translations. They will be, however, transformations and transactions that are quite inevitable, which would take place even if the translational/metaphorical commitment were hampered or refused in the name of a radical cultural conservatism or fundamentalism. Actually, the exigencies of translation arise from changes in the stream of experience and the emergence of contexts of coexistence and relationships where mutual Otherness' find themselves nevertheless involved and 'compromised.' The attempt to remain immune from any 'contamination,' untouched (if indeed such a thing were possible) despite dwelling in a new environment, induces a transformation of the meaning of how an individual acts and thinks regardless, along with the practical consequences that this implies. A change will occur in any case, perhaps underground and unawares, and thereby out of any control, possibility of anticipation, or adjustment. The heterogenesis of ends is inherent to the options of cultural integrality indicated above, often entailing self-contradictory and, sometimes, self-defeating effects.

Along intercultural translation paths, passing through the selection of metaphorical grounds, human rights can play a crucial role. Precisely because of the highly axiological charge and the categorical vagueness that characterize their statements, they can work as axes of semantic continuity bridging different domains of sense and behaviors that may appear otherwise distant and morphologically incommensurable with each other—and destined to remain so, at least, as long as they are read from an ethnocentric perspective. The Others' stories, through their unwinding, enriching and adjusting through processes of cross-contextualization, can shed light on indexes of sense and value amenable to be inscribed within the semantic dome of human rights. These semantic ingredients, moreover, can be simultaneously embodied within the Others' cultures by means of *metaphorical* (therefore, *creative*) *equivalences* with morphological behaviors that could be even completely different and seemingly opposite to those assumed by natives. The axiological and semantic features enshrined in rights statements can act, in other words, as metaphorical grounds of intercultural translation.[18]

The advantage provided by this use of human rights consists, mainly, in the possibility of avoiding their essentializing and/or reifying readings. In this way, they are no longer assumed as hierarchical, top-down parameters for assessing the compatibility of behavioral patterns and related normative schemes taken in their morphological shape. Rather, human rights semantics can become a means of *transduction* of the 'signs of Otherness,' in view of the creation of semantic-categorical categories characterized by an attitude of inclusiveness. Their referral to behaviors, words, and legal figures derived from different cultural circuits, in comparison, will no longer have a pyramidal structure: almost as if human rights constituted a sort of

[18] Space constraints do not allow me to explain the use of metaphorical ground in intercultural translation more extensively, nor to supply practical examples. For both these topics I refer to Ricca (2008, 2013a, d, 2016b).

watershed to determine what side of the cultural confrontation would be legitimated to occupy through its claims and categories the space of coexistence. As noted above, actually, such a hermeneutical approach often leads to ethnocentric and exclusionary outcomes. Rather, if rights statements are involved as processive means into the 'plot' of intercultural translation, they can work as interfaces, as axes for semantic mediation, so as to draw new horizons of universality, new inclusive guises of subjectivity, modelled bottom-up through horizontal transactions among the basic categories of everyday life as interpreted and lived by different (members of) cultures.

The use of such an intercultural key to interpret and implement human rights and, more generally, all the legal categories, can transform law into a powerful means of integration among cultures. The delineation of metaphorical grounds, carved out from the relationships between both different behaviors and normative sets, give cultural claims a chance for effectiveness, directly supplied by the legal-institutional dimension; a chance that, otherwise, would remain entrusted exclusively to the rhapsodic and often asymmetrical course of the merely factual processes of crossed acculturation. Somehow, the 'discovery' of the possibility of drawing out metaphorical grounds from the discursive platform of human rights allows for morphological incommensurability to be overcome by engendering effects of *cross-contextual resonance*. Put simply, this means that behaviors, or symbolic expressions that are apparently incompatible and/or incommensurable can actually merge into paths of metaphorical correspondence so as to legitimize the inclusion of Otherness within the normative-semantic meshes of host legal systems.

In this framework, the metaphorical ground works, somehow, as an axiological/teleological category able to support the construction of intercultural bridges. In this way, it opens and legitimizes the chance that the same value or end is realized and implemented by means of behaviors or symbolic devices that are morphologically different. Such a semiotic 'mechanism' is capable of enabling the possibility that assumptions for the legitimacy of different legal systems, and so the very same human rights, collapse in on themselves, and this even when they would appear, at first, incommensurable with Otherness. Couched in terms of plain *discursivity*, this cross-contextual resonance illustrates the inconsistency in which the denial to Others of the possibility of adopting behaviors or symbolic options that are oriented towards the same values/ends that legitimize other actions, even those that are morphologically different or contrary, is assumed within one's own cultural circuit. Of course, the cross-contextual resonance device is to be activated in a bi-directional way, so as to trigger a process of continuous adjustment and therefore periphrastic paths of intercultural translation/transaction bound to remain ever open and wriggle free from any presumptive merely functionalist equivalence between the cultural differences at stake and the pragmatic means to achieve their ends.

In this regard, a few crucial points should be made. The above method of legal-intercultural translation, and thereby the idea of intercultural law, is quite distinct from the forms of translation typically utilized in comparative law and in international private law. These disciplines are focused on inter-normative comparisons, even when the rules considered for the case are made the object of cultural contextualizations. A consideration for cultural surroundings of legal statements and rules does not merely coincide with a systemic analysis of the normative and para-normative relationships but is to fathom the semiotic-cultural landscape on which tacitly formal positive law and its efficacy float. Without such a cognitive effort, which is far beyond the contextualizing survey that comparativists and international-private law scholars flaunt carrying out, they, in the end, will work from normative statements produced by specific legal/territorial circuits and their related semantic rigidity and completeness. Thus, after conducting their predominantly and almost exclusively inter-legal, albeit systematic and undeniably relational, analysis, and acquiring the results inevitably lacking a genuine and broad consideration of the underlying cultural-semiotic landscapes, only then will one proceed to assess the mutual commensurability and/or compatibility between the different legal categories previously considered form the outset.[19] Conversely, the intercultural use of law (at least, in my view) starts from the premise that even under the lens of the 'legal,' people are not norms, and their involvement in integration processes does not necessarily entail legal transplants to be intended in their formalistic-positivistic meanings. People often aim (because of migration or transnational projections of their interests) to inscribe within the semantic platforms of other legal systems their own ethical-cultural ciphers and habits, but this can happen also regardless of the legal formalizations shaped by the countries or legal systems of origin. Now, ethical-cultural ciphers are much more flexible than legal rules and, above all, adapt themselves to new social contexts retrospectively. This means that such adaption is (or, at least, could be) an outcome of self-reflexive and self-transformative processes of cultural awareness attuned with the emergence of that semiotic inter-space drawn by the exorbitance of sense oozing from cultures and people 'on the move' across both geographical and categorical borders.

The creation of a legal-intercultural lexicon on a global scale—in my view—could be based on the intercultural and symmetrical conversion and/or transduction of different legal experiences that are horizontally and metaphorically interfaced through human rights within each territorial-political circuit. As long as this anthropological-cultural conversion is not set in motion, as the other side of intercultural and trans-*local* processes of trans-*lation*, international-private law will inevitably bump into problems of intercultural commensurability and will provide them with asymmetrical solutions. This is because every national or international private legal system will be inclined to make assumptions about the cultural code that is encapsulated in the 'receiving' legal system, which is, however required to incorporate foreign rules as conveyed by people's claims. On the other hand, I do not think that an overcoming, and even less, a moving away completely from the state-based model, often called for within post-modern thought in the name of an anomic

[19] Needless to say, my remarks are gauged on the hermeneutic attitude that both legal comparativists and private international law scholars have on average. In every field of research there are 'bright' exceptions, which are all the more valuable when it is clear that they are only exceptions. It is precisely for this reason and to adhere to politically correct style that I intentionally avoid nominal references here.

or rhizomatic legal plurality, can lead by itself and without the deliberate, skilled work of intercultural/anthropological translation to peaceful coexistence among cultures. The lack of *general and abstract* discursive platforms, notwithstanding the danger of their serializing and imperialistic uses, would not assure any protection for the most weak and subaltern voices of the social ground. On the contrary, such a semantic and normative void would represent a 'customs clearance' on behalf of an uncontrolled overflowing power of the strongest, beyond the limits of any possible criticism. Silence, the discursive void, as well known, is always on the side of the powerful.

5.3 The Experiential Space We Live in: Rights and Intercultural Legal Chorology

An intercultural use of human rights can promote a process of re-categorization of subjectivity powerful enough to rewrite the grammar of sovereignty. Otherness that appears and breaks into the horizons of everyday life is capable, if underpinned by an axiological interfacing supplied by human rights, to redefine the semantics of subjectivity and thereby the coordinates of quotidian conduct within the borders of national states. This means that being remolded, they would be the spaces of coexistence because of an inevitable, even when contrasting, re-semanticization/re-categorization of facts and behaviors. These changes, moreover, look like self-transformations triggered by the projections of the semiotic components constitutive of cultural difference that inscribe themselves within the paradigms of legal/axiological legitimation of each national/territorial context. It is as if the claims that the subjects and social actors raise would draw, through words, new cartographies of existential space; and this by crumbling and urging the reshaping of frameworks of sense and value serving as a kind of sextant of social geographies of sovereignty. Besides, such an implication derives immediately from the observation that each word, in its 'signical complexion,' is a source of pragmatic consequences. It epitomizes and condenses at a semantic level all the sense relationships that synthesize the already traced experiential paths and design all other possible ones. As an example, in the word 'pen' are included, as it were, 'invisible/mute parts' of its signification, the actions required to create it, as well as those that will potentially be involved in its future use and taking place in the world. These experiences—in part effective, in part imaginable—substantiate the space and concur to configure it: by connoting, scanning, and molding it.

The space perceived by each individual is a synthesis of what he has learned to include within it, pro-actively and protensively, in terms of events, facts, objects, actions, etc. The existential space, in short, is 'full' of semantic relationships engendered through semiotic processes, that is, by means of the creations of relations among signs, of maps transmuted in behavioral habits and, subsequently, embodied in the same perceptions of the world. This means that we see a given space, in and across this space, drawing on what we know about it and according to the cartographies that we develop to understand it.[20] For precisely this reason, symbolic implications transmute into perceptions, so as to co-determine the 'things' that occupy, fill, shape and scale the space.

The processes of space embodiment join the corporeal projection of the processes oriented to the production of meaning. On the other hand, the same work of imagination is intrinsically embodied, in the sense that it stages relations of significance and/or virtual situations within which the body is an active and dynamic factor. The corporeal/spatial metaphors that populate language are salient signs of the bodily projection of symbolic functions. Body is a dynamic and inclusive entity/process always immersed in and interplaying with the environment. The self-perception of one's own body, as well as one's proprioception, manifests as a synthesis of its proactive extensions: namely the inter-relationships that an organism weaves with and through the world, mediating them by means of symbolic representations.[21] This implies that the bodily projections of symbolic-imaginative activity are, at the same time, proactive articulations of space and world, contributing to their categorization. The body works, therefore, as a metaphorical map of the world and, in turn, is mapped according to spatial metaphors that are a sort of retroaction of the dynamic inter-relationships between it and the environment.

If on one side world and meanings are embodied, on the other side the body/mind itself is 'worldl-ed' through the spatial projection of its perceptive and categorical articulations. The modalities of processing and contents of such intersecting metaphors between body and space can significantly differ according to the cultures involved and, therefore, require a commitment to intercultural translation/transaction.[22]

To provide examples of the above observations, a sequence of four argumentative steps can be proposed.

(1) Space (its perception and knowledge) is not separate from what happens and what we make within it. The space we experience is not a thing or a meta-thing, but rather the perceptive effect of semiotic relationships.
(2) What occurs within space as well as within the spectrum of knowledge is not separate from the categories we use to give meaning to our spatial experience.

[20] In this regard, see Ricca (2018a), and *ibid.* further bibliographical references. As for the creative and not (only) descriptive connotation of maps and cartographical activity, see at least: Olsson (2007, 2011), Pickles (2004); Farinelli (2003, 2009).

[21] See Anderson and Harrison (2010).

[22] On the embodiment of meanings, see the overview contained in Gibbs (2005). As regards the function played by emotions and qualitative perception within the activity of categorization, owing in part to the embodiment of signification and its processes, see Kövecses (2003). As for the law, the useful connections between intercultural translations based on metaphorical overlapping and the semantic plasticity of emotive and axiological categories, especially for their 'overexposure' within the legal discourse (unlike the factual discourse where the presence of values is overshadowed by the stability of empirical perceptions), see Ricca (2008, 2018b, 2020a).

(3) The boundaries of each category and their denotations/implicative connotations[23] are exposed to a process of intercultural translation and the effects of cross-contextual resonance conveyed by metaphorical grounds of an axiological/qualitative kind—the same ones traceable in human rights statements.
(4) Any process of re-categorization implies and turns into a re-mapping of the space of experience, namely the space that is imbued with perceptions, understanding and actions.

From a chorological perspective, spatial proximity is implied according to a semiotic point of reference. The Other-than-me that is contiguous (or adjacent) to me in the physical and semantic-categorical space-sign constitutes the horizon, the foil against and across which the features (namely, the denotations and connotations) inhabiting *my* space of sense, *my* subjectivity will assume and produce meaning. Hence categorical boundaries will appear much more flexible, relativized and exposed to transduction processes;[24] the same thing, with perfect parallelism, can be said about the rigidity of spatial articulations in spite of the greater intensity in their perception, almost as if this were a reflection of their *thinghood* and their partaking in the empirical/external world.

The outbreak of Otherness within the semantic/territorial warp of sovereignty might be thought of as a rip, or unstitching. Conversely, the processes of intercultural translation/transaction undertaken relying upon human rights used as a metaphorical ground are comparable to the reweaving of the inter-space articulated and embodied by the coexistence of differences, relations of proximity and distancing, contiguity and separation, between both the forms of subjectivity and their respective spatial projections.

Through the prism of an intercultural use of human rights, spatial proximity transmutes into categorical contiguity/co-extensiveness; the categorical contiguity (conveyed by semantic and connotative ambiguity)[25] available in spatial proximity. And this is because each space is the consequence of what we do within it; and, conversely, what we do within it is an effect, a projection of the categories that work as vehicles, mediums of our action. The blurring of categorical borders caused by connotative and spatial contiguity/proximity entails thus the generation of new spaces, or rather inter-spaces, of experience, new implicative maps and webs that eclipse, in many cases, the existential spaces as previously imagined and lived. This phenomenon can go as far as to bring close what is culturally remote and, often, to make something that was only recently considered to be remote spatially near. We can imagine, for example, satellite televisions within the houses of migrants who live next door to us. Their cultural distance, by means of an adequate commitment to

[23]... for example: this is a chair if it has a horizontal plane and some support that distance this plane from the floor, it was constructed, it is made of wood or iron, etc., it is suited to allow human beings to sit upon, and so on.

[24]See Ponzio (2007).

[25]This spatial interpenetration involves the same conflation between 'denotation' and 'connotation' produced by the metaphorical processes. See, again, on this topic (Ricca 2022: 1987, nt 15).

intercultural translation and an aligned use of human rights, can turn into 'proximity'. It will be embodied in migrants' conduct and in the ideal and pragmatic inclinations they can show as a consequence of information drawn upon from the TV stations of their countries of origin. The presence of those who come from far away places, their physical proximity, is actually a sign that something distant is becoming close: an event that occurs beyond bodies intended in their mere materiality and takes shape simultaneously here *and* in countries of origin, in this way drawing and encompassing a multi-sited, trans-territorial context of sense for peoples' actions. The meanings that such people process by means of television communication will contribute to determining their daily conduct, the very same that they will carry out within the field of their spatial proximity to us. So, what is (previously considered) distant can abruptly manifest itself as constitutive to the 'here and now.' Conversely, the physical presence, apparently destined to be consumed in its material proximity, can provide a clue that the 'distant' is becoming close.

On the other hand, it should be pointed out that even physical distance is a product of our particular way of making experience out of space and, therefore, an implication of the cognitive/cultural categories we use in figuring out and living it (just think of the cultural component encapsulated in 'perspective vision' *practiced* by modern Western culture[26]). This is because the space really experienced is not only that which we define as the *physical one,* and that is the result of the cumulative sedimentation of abstraction processes. Rather, the space people live in is that to be found within time ranges—in turn 'subject to' and 'a product of' activities of categorization—which host the web of the semiotic implications woven by their conduct (both actual and planned).

The intercultural use of human rights can thus transform them into *pantographs* for the remapping of planetary space through the spectrum of law: which shows itself, at this point, as a cluster of semiotic devices characterized by a very significant chorological propensity. A 'law' that *even* in its state or national dimension is anyhow involved as both part and agency in the redrawing of spatial and, therefore, sense relationships. But this is nothing but the phenomenon that entails: (*a*) the approaching and integrating of what is politically and culturally remote within the circuits for the production of daily life sense; and, at the same time, (*b*) the projecting of everyday local activities along the semiotic web unwound on a global scale.

The last observation suggests that globalization is, first of all, a semiotic phenomenon. But if this is the case, it is because the implicative contiguity among categorical elements (and thereby frames of experience) engenders new spatial proximities, so relativizing physical distances and even their 'presentiality' or their (previous) remaining temporal *remoteness*.

Against this backdrop, what results as essential to avoiding intercultural conflicts is the translation/transaction between spaces of experience. And this translation can be conveyed, precisely, (also) through an intercultural use of human rights. Such an

[26] See Belting (2008).

alternative introduces new possibilities for the relationships between legal systems and, above all, paths of inter-constitutionality, and this is because the human rights lexicon is part and parcel of any constitutional language and is tied by an inevitable complementarity with fundamental rights.

The polyphonic and simultaneous emergence of an intercultural lexicon of intercultural experience, rising synchronically in different and distant political-territorial circuits as a consequence of claims for the translation of differences, could appear to be the immediate effect of trans-territoriality and globalizations of social experience. Above all, almost as if hovering like an epiphany of the entire chorological process, the physiognomy of a trans-territorial subjectivity seems to be taking shape and constantly transforming before being de-territorialized with respect to the logic of state-nations and then re-spatialized according to chorological dynamics spread on a planetary scale. Whether humankind will be able to venture out on such a route will depend not—as noted above—on the realization of an alleged historical necessity, but rather only on the unstable force of hypothesis, and the brittle caveat of responsibility.

5.4 Modern Visual Art and Its Figurative/Categorical Dis-Compositions

How I tried to illustrate above, the multiplication of anthropological voices on the global arena as well as in multicultural contexts of communication and coexistence implies their reciprocal translation, mirrored in the semantic potentialities of human rights. To achieve such a level of translatability, the interpretants' voices must be *dis-composed* by narratively opening the connotative landscapes that underlie their morphological aspects. This means that culturally-based behaviors, symbolic expressions, and discourses that can be potentially inscribed in human rights and translated by using rights provisions as metaphorical interfaces, should be de-articulated in their semantic elements and then creatively re-composed and interculturally synthetized.[27] This is the only way to attain a periphrastic universality, or an open universalizing process, that is co-construed within a horizon of sense that holds the potential to be used as a renewed ground for a peaceful coexistence among diversities and cultural differences.

A sort of inter-semiotic toolkit for intercultural translation can be found in the cognitive paths traced by avant-garde artists, especially painters, in the late-nineteenth century and early twentieth century. The driving force behind avant-garde painting research can be considered a reaction against Impressionism. The subjectivist anti-realism approach of the Impressionists, in direct opposition to the perspectival-realist school that had developed after the Renaissance, drew a parabola which soon led to the search for objective criteria underlying human perception.

[27] On this methodology see Ricca (2013b, 2018b).

Assuming perception to be a phenomenological event resulting from a dynamic interpenetration between world and mind, the avant-garde movement followed the notion of *genetic determinants* giving rise to 'the perceived.' The result was an idiomatic commitment, an ideal and practical attitude toward dis-composing forms, that is, appearances taken in their *morphological fashion.*

The crumbling of the natural form and its usual meanings is achieved by virtue of representations that dis-compose, dis-aggregate or factorize the semantic elements of images. This outcome is pursued either through figurative simplifications inspired by primitive art or the de-contextualization of images and, as an alternative, a disarticulated/fragmented representation of their semantic components.

To illustrate the *common thinking* underlying intercultural translation and twentieth-century avant-garde artists, I have chosen to select works from four painters: precisely, Gauguin, Gris, Klee, and Savinio.

In Gauguin's paintings we can recognize the categorical crumbling produced by the juxtaposition of figurative elements belonging to different cultural, naturalistic or narrative contexts. As happens in our dreams, Gauguin shows us heteroclite fragments to trigger in the observer's mind a process of de-contextualization of forms and figures. In this way, every portrayed object is engulfed in a sort of metaphorical vertigo.[28] Therefore, everything can, at the same time, signify something else and move across different categorical circuits. What supports such a process is the breaking free of semiotic elements (both denotative and connotative) from predefined contextual frames established by and within specific cultural habits. But as soon as those elements lose the link of semantic implications with a specific category and/or context of signification, they become potentially ubiquitous and omnipresent. As such, they serve as bridging factors, transducers of sense, liable to give rise to a process of categorical re-generation and new semantic synthesis. The paintings of Gauguin spur the observer's mind to operate semantic re-workings by means of markedly intercultural combinations and transpositions. They are static representations only in appearance. On the contrary, they are designed to re-origin, through their dynamic relation with the observer, the creation of new meanings, a new sense of the world.

The pioneering paths of Gauguin inspire, subsequently, Cubism and its different stages.[29] Echoing—as is well-known—the *warnings* of Cézanne, who invited the painters to grasp *the real,* to be represented in their constant and geometrical features, Cubism opens the way to a semantic-perspectival *dis-composition* assumed

---

[28] Consider, for example, the following sequence of Gauguin's famous paintings: *D'ou Venons Nous, Que Sommes Nous, Où Allons Nous (1897), The Brooding Woman (1891), Contes Barbares (1912).* In each of them there is a sort of extra-contextual and/or disturbing presence. It gives to the observer the estranging perception that a dystonic blending of forms and elements has taken place within the pictorial frame. The paintings of the four artists considered here are widely available on the Internet. In any case, the paintings cited in this chapter can be easily found in another work of mine, Ricca (2016b), available at https://calumet-review.com/wp-content/uploads/2021/08/mat_51-1.pdf.

[29] On Gauguin as a precursor of Cubism, see Messina (2006).

as an interpretive criterion to analyze and portray/render the constitutive elements of every perceived form. Juan Gris, even more than Picasso or Braque, makes dis-compositions that unfold to synthetic re-compositions of new forms and meanings.[30] His paintings appear easily intelligible. This immediate but only apparent intelligibility—so much more pronounced than in Picasso's figurative dis-compositions—is, however, a result of the coordination of pure geometrical forms, assumed in a sort of Platonic fashion. Gris used to say that if Cézanne started from reality, with the aim of representing and rendering it to the observer as something reduced and transfigured in geometrical forms, he conversely began with geometrical forms to obtain, by means of their combination, recognizable images resembling the forms of living experience. Gris was somehow trying to have access to a sort of connotative-semantic repository,[31] as if it enshrined the *building material* of the Platonic demiurge, to engender forms, to invite the observer to see the forms while they were still taking shape. Gris' synthetic representations actually remain open.[32] His images and figurations *are and are not* those which one might recognize at first.

This sort of saying but not saying, affirming and simultaneously veiling, are the constitutive canon of Paul Klee's conception of art. He thought that the main purpose of art was to make visible the invisible. But this is possible—he argued—only by putting in motion pictorial figuration through the active participation of the observer's mind. Klee's paintings bring to the surface the polyphony of connotative elements that lay beneath the form and its morphological appearance: which, in turn, is intended as a result, the conclusion of a hermeneutical/constitutive process ordered to produce sense.[33] Klee's influence on phenomenological thought (above all

[30] On Juan Gris, see Ponce de León (2008). But see also Gris (2013).

[31] This repository is populated only by connotative elements insofar as it precedes the semantic dimension of 'categories.' On the 'continuity' between connotations and denotations see, again, Ricca (2022, p. 187, nt 15) and above in nt.

[32] See, for example, the subsequent series of Gris' paintings: Botellas y cuchillo (1912), La mesa de café (1912), El lavabo (1912), El Velador (1918), Casas de Beaulieu (1918), Caveza de Hombre (1916), Naturaleza muerta con placa (1917), El Reloj (1912), Vista sobre la bahia (1921), La Ventana abierta (1921).

[33] In this regard, Schuback (2014, pp. 124–125) makes some very insightful remarks: "Klee is not preoccupied in drawing lines but in *drawing the drawing of lines*. This *drawing of the drawing* shows that for him the question is not about movements but about the moving of movements, about movements in their "being-moving." In its continuous form, in its being-moving, a movement cannot be seized through a linear representation of movements as passage from one point or state to another. Thus while moving, movement comes from nowhere, not having anywhere to come from; it is moving. In this sense, that which from a nonmoving standpoint could be seized as the difference between a before and an after-that is already before, as erstwhile after-while, expressions that Klee uses himself to entitle a series of drawings, as for instance, *Eidola Erstwhile Philosopher* (EIDOLA: *der weiland Philosoph*). Appearing as ends still ending, as endings that have no end, and as beginnings already there but still to begin, the is-moving of a movement appears as "multidimensional simultaneity," as "aphoristic multibranched," to recall Klee's own expressions. Klee's theory of the line is about the "multidimensional simultaneity" of drawing lines that draw the drawing of lines, the appearing of the appearing in everything that appears. It unfolds his principle

Heidegger and Merleau-Ponty) was remarkable.[34] He thought the artist's main commitment was as an educator. When the painting is observed,[35] the figurative transfiguration must be aimed to trigger the process of *Gestaltung*: a sort of writing of the world, a path of *re-origination* capable of showing reality as *forma formans* and not only, *figuratively*, as a *forma formata*. In Klee's poetics, the artist is committed to usher the observer into the forging of the world and its forms, giving him the creative pleasure of conjoining Heaven and Earth through the rite of re-categorization to which he is invited. Also in this case, the dis-composition is

of principles, so to speak, in which "to draw and to paint is to learn to see behind a façade, to grasp something in its roots, to recognize the underlying forces, to learn the pre-history of the visible, to 'unveil, to ground, to analyze'." What matters is the making visible of the *meanwhileness* and *in-betweeness* of the is-moving, is-drawing, is-painting, where the underlying forming forces can appear as such. Klee sees, that is, Klee makes visible, the impossibility of seizing in forms the meanwhileness and in-betweeness of the forming, *Formende*, since human senses, both sensible and sensitive, are usually accustomed to focus solely on formed forms, on *Form-ende*, on finished forms. Human senses are too conditioned to objectifying and reifying the is-being, so that first of all what they sense are beings and not the is-being, appearances and not the appearing as such, figures and not the drawing, the said and not the saying. In order to make visible the appearing as such, "the underlying forces", or "pre-history of the visible," in order to draw the drawing, to make visible the making visible, senses must un-learn habits of sensing, must de-form the formed. Thus it is while de-forming forms that forming forces appear in their "being-forming." This means that while the formed dis-appears the appearing can appear as such, that is, in an "it is appearing." I proposed to define as *sketch* this appearing while dis-appearing, this making visible while detaching from the visualized forms, this becoming while in dissolution. The sketch is neither a preparation for a painting to come nor an unfinished drawing. It is the gesture of drawing the drawing of lines, of making visible the coming to visibility in its own withdrawal. Understood in this manner, the sketch is a hovering in the gerundive in-between and meanwhile. It can be further understood as a nuancing of Heidegger's understanding of truth as *aletheia*, insofar as it puts the accent on the *meanwhile* and *in-between-ness* of the is-happening, or to speak in more Heideggerian terms, of *das Ereignis*, of the event of the making visible. What Heidegger loved in Klee was above all the sense of the event as the is-happening, is-being, and not as a to-come, the way Klee shows the gerundive mode of the event rather than its infinitive tense."

[34] See Cappelletti (2003). As for a philosophical "tour" through the philosophical interpretations of Paul Klee's works, see Watson (2009).

[35] See Boehm (2014, p. 23): "The formations of the distinct configuration take place in a scene whose borders or whose totality respectively displaces the represented into an ambiguous space of the possible, of associations, of a surplus of meaning, and of interferences. It was of great importance to Klee not to restrict the genesis of form to the sphere of artistic activity: namely, not to treat it as a question of the "aesthetics of production." Genesis, after all, addresses at least equally the moving eye of the observer whose activity Klee quite literally characterized as the "pasture of the eyes" (*Augenweide*), comparing it to the cow grazing on the pasture. Yet totalization brings the kinesis and stasis of formation into an interrelationship. Following the self-unfolding form, the observer recognizes a succession, while, in a totalizing turn, he mobilizes *simultaneity*. The two compositions of time (*Zeitgestalten*) never fully overlap. To the contrary: the image always gives the eye sufficient incentive to realize the suspenseful intersection of the two times anew and differently. The standstill that cosmic movement experiences in the image thus proves to be an impetus for an unending play of movement."

not static but rather designated to promote a dynamic movement.[36] Klee's works are as *sheets of notes*, almost recognizable figures barely sketched out, a door ajar towards the staging of semantic genesis, endlessly repeated, the constant re-generation of the world's meaning.

My inter-semiotic overview concludes with Alberto Savinio. Brother of the more famous Giorgio De Chirico, he also inscribed his poetics along the lines of symbolism and the related tendency to juxtapose figures (objects, buildings, landscapes, individuals) apparently unrelated from a semantic point of view. However, the relationship extant between De Chirico and Savinio is somehow equivalent to that

[36] As regards the relationships of Klee with Cubism and his progressive distancing from this style of painting, consider the interesting observations of Baumgartner (2014, p. 72): "The process of artistic abstraction is accompanied by a growing tendency in Klee's theoretical reflections to conceive of his relationships to nature and natural processes in a wider metaphysical and at the same time analytical context. In a diary entry, he thus distanced himself programmatically from the famous definition of Franz Marc's "passionate variety of humanity," by writing "he [Franz Marc] places himself on the same level with plants and stones and animals. In Marc, the bond with the earth takes precedence over the bond with the universe. . . I place myself at a remote starting point of creation, whence I state a priori formulas for men, beasts, plants, stones and the elements, and for all the whirling forces." This "remote starting point of creation" also meant rejecting a directly perceptual relationship with nature. In its place, Klee developed between 1914 and 1918 a growing interest in structural patterns of the characteristics of processes of growth and development, which he saw as analogous to the genesis of a work of art: There is, in the first place, a kind of structural inventory of plant organs, which has to be seen in the context of Klee's examination of Cubism. This new analytical look at the visible world that the Cubists had presented manifested itself in Klee's oeuvre—as in *When God Considered the Creation of the Plants*, 1913, for example, a work whose title equated the idea of a new world created through artistic means with the idea of divine creation. It is clearly visible how Klee finds, by his own means, his (own) kind of synthetic Cubism, after having engaged himself in the previous years in possibilities on how to break down the world of objects into prism-like component parts and then recombine and interweave them in accordance with purely compositional requirements. Klee had seen Pablo Picasso's early Cubist works in Munich as early as 1910 at the exhibition of the *Neue Künstlerverereinigung* (New Artists's Association), and what impressed him about them was the boldness with which painting managed to gorge beyond the mere outward appearance of the visible to an analysis of inner structure.

Although variously inspired by Cubism, Klee's attitude remained ambivalent. He certainly recognized Cubism as a breakthrough in modern pictorial construction; at the same time, however, he lamented the formal destructiveness that occurred when objects were reshaped. In this regard, he was especially critical of Picasso's arbitrariness when reducing the human figure to "primitive forms of projection such as the triangle, rectangle, and circle" that "lose some of their viability with each conversion. Klee's association with Cubism is limited almost exclusively to abstract constructions of space—from which he developed his metaphor of the "crystalline"—and to occasional depictions of nature in which he dared to deconstruct the organic world, as in *When God Considered the Creation of Plants*. However, after having dismantled the objects in the sense of analytical Cubism, it was rather the structural analysis of natural organisms that mattered to him in terms of the depiction of nature. It is what he described as a remote starting point of creation and *a priori* formulas for men, beasts, plants, and stones."

The transformation of Klee's approach to the dis-composition of objects and images, from an analytical cubism-inspired fashion to a processive synthetical one, can be caught, for example, in the following two paintings: *When God Considered the Creation of the Plants* (1913), *Time and Plants* (1927).

which is recognizable between Picasso and Gris. The former two dis-compose the forms (Picasso) or juxtapose them in a dystonic or heteroclite fashion (De Chirico); the latter two re-compose images starting from connotative singularities (Gris) or by means of a combination between real and well-known figures and fantastic elements (Savinio). Specifically, in Savinio the 'fantastic' brings to the surface, as in a Bachelardian *rêverie*, the implicit semantic potentialities encapsulated within each categorical semantic set.[37] His iconic representations open the doors to a virtual maze of interpretations, re-configurations, re-semantizations.[38] In Savinio's paintings, rather than the invisible that becomes visible, it is the unpredictable that opens the observer's mind to the regeneration of sense.

The lesson these great artists give us holds a very insightful cognitive meaning. The spectator of paintings—as well as the cultural agent involved in this intercultural relationship—is the co-construing actor of a dynamic *reality*. The painting functions somehow as a mobile interface, a metaphorical fuel that bridges two reciprocal Others by producing a sort of genetic conjunction, a cooperative re-writing of signification and its paths. In the same way, an intercultural use of human rights could promote the elaboration of new traces, new plots of *experience and reality*. The outcome would be a new scenario, within which both the 'symbolic' and the 'pragmatic' would reciprocally inseminate. What is engendered in this way is a new world obtained by writing, painting and figuring new shapes of experience: namely the *real* that inhabits and makes itself throughout history. All of this would constitute, in other words, an open synthesis between word and object, minds and worlds, 'nature*s*' and culture*s*.[39] But this would be also nothing but a 'becoming,' utterly in tune with the dialectics of sense, of the same human rights (epigones of natural rights), and the relations between the manifold natures generated by culture, indeed by the inner cultural and thus plural nature of human action. The paintings of the four artists cited above are, in a sense, like human rights statements. Both constitute discursive platforms, possible horizons of signification, semantic agendas that serve as means and thereby processive ends to draw polyphonically, through the unfolding of interpretive differences and their reciprocal translations, new inscriptions and declinations of sense, new plots of history written through an intercultural interweaving of quotidian life stories.

[37] On Savinio's poetics see Fabbri (2007); Jewell (2004); Savinio (1992).

[38] Savinio's synthetic and renewing approach to representations is well shown by the following series of paintings: Objects dans la forêt (1927), Abandonné (1929), Marina (1929), Ulisse e Polifemo (1929), Paesaggio Tropicale (1931), La notte della città (1950), Il Fiume (1950).

[39] Some suggestions in this sense can be found in Henare et al. (2007).

5.5 Paul Klee's Cognitive Approach to Painting: His Artistic Workshop Paraphrased from a Legal Point of View

Hereinafter I will continue with some further insights on Klee's philosophy of representation, with particular regard to his methodology of dis-composing the morphological appearance of images to recover—somehow through a cognitive archeology—the constitutive, original ingredients (connotative underlying landscape) of *things* and, more generally, of the world. References to Klee's paintings will be paired with excerpts from his writings and my side-comments about the meaning of these paintings observed from a legal intercultural point of view. I invite the reader to substitute the words 'art, artist, etc.' with 'intercultural lawyers and/or interpreters.' This sort of metaphorical transposition can help better and almost plastically understand the continuities between Klee's cognitive legacy and the work of translation/transaction required by intercultural encounters, above all when these encounters are analyzed and managed through the spectrum of law and its practical use. To further support an understanding of Klee's thought I will make use of some quotes from other authors who focused their work on the philosophical implications of this great painter. In this way, I hope to give jurists and lawyers an immediately available view of the wide theoretical implications of Klee's work across various disciplines and their importance and fruitfulness in facing intercultural legal issues.

5.5.1 Paul Klee, Creative Confession (1920)

> I have mentioned the elements of linear expression which are among the visual components of the picture. This does not mean that a given work must consist of nothing but such elements. Rather, the elements must produce forms, but without being sacrificed in the process. They should be preserved.[40]

[40]To put together movement and representation, becoming and stasis, Klee draws his inspiration from musical thought. In this regard, see Schuback (2014, p. 128): "In Bach's polyphonic chromaticism and his art of the fugue, Klee could recognize the one differentiating itself as "multidimensional simultaneity" and "aphoristic multibranched" movement. His search for a "linear active polyphony" finds in Bach's polyphonic chromaticism a lesson about the one in itself differentiated, the becoming while in dissolution, where simultaneity is not only of presences but also and uppermost of present and absenting voices, appearing to begin, the realm of in-between and meanwhileness of a coming to form and image, of a coming to be. It is indeed as "polyphony" that Klee will describe what could be called his *archaeology of the gerundive structure of becoming visible*. In following Klee's pedagogy of the line in his work, in which he shows how the drawing of lines draws the drawing of lines, the being-drawing as such, it is possible to see how his work makes visible this multidimensional and aporistic-multibranched simultaneity of before and after, of yesterday and tomorrow. This pedagogy of the line, of line's activity or *agens*, is the basis of making visible the invisible coming to visibility, and not of reproducing the visible. The task is

> In most cases, a combination of several elements will be required to produce forms or objects or other compounds—planes related to each other (for instance, the view of a moving stream of water) or spatial structures arising from energy changes involving the three dimensions (fish swimming in all directions). See, for example, Klee's painting *Fish Image* (1925).

I think that (at least) lawyers, anthropologist and philosophers can learn many things about intercultural translation from the Klee's painting titled 'Fish Image.' The representation shows the tension between verticality and horizontality. Using images of fish as animal metaphors of vertical lines and horizontal lines, Klee points out the creative struggle between stasis and movement. In the center of the picture there is a grey dot: in Klee's cosmology, the grey dot is the impossible and inconceivable that becomes possible, the beginning of all beginnings from chaos. Another germinative contrast is that between the deep blue and the luminosity of white. In yellow, we can recognize two sketches of sea birds. The whole picture seems to explain a sort of evolutionary transformation, a history of the living world: from the ocean bed towards the skies, and back again.

The use of lines and the dis-compositions of a life story into representative elements come to make it so that the painting evokes to the observer a sort of Genesis. But this is nothing but a metaphorical transformation and, at the same time, a deep insight, an archeological survey, into the implicit knowledge that people have of the underwater world and its inhabitants. Consider how many translational and trans-categorical continuities such a painting could convey. The starting image, precisely its morphological appearance, is simply that of fishes moving in all directions. However, it reveals itself as a real epitome of a life story and alludes to so many of its connotative, phenomenal, qualitative, etc., ingredients. If we undertook to dis-compose and re-compose the morphological appearance of Other's behaviors in view of their legal qualification, this could pave the way to metaphorical intercultural translations and the recognition of Otherness.

Klee continues by saying:

> Through such enrichment of the formal symphony, the possibilities of variation and, by the same token, the possibilities for expressing ideas, are endlessly multiplied.[41] [...]

---

therefore to make visible the multidimensionality of a line, its non-successive but "polyphonic" nature, and this has to appear in the very line. Several works by Klee show the polyphony of the line, as for example in *Polyphonic-moving* (1930)". See, for example, Klee's painting *Ad Parnassum* (1932).

In her interesting essay, Schuback traces a parallel between Klee's representative theory and the musical work of Webern. However, I do not completely agree with this hermeneutic and reconstructive proposal. We can find some similarity in the dis-compositional approach of both Klee and Webern to morphological forms: respectively, images and sounds. But if Webern's works aim to make perceptible to listeners the composite structure of every (apparently) simple sound, Klee's paintings, conversely, try to use dis-composed connotations to propose new synthesis, new forms open to the co-constructive and creative activity of the observers.

[41] See Boehm (2014, pp. 22–23): "To describe the potential exposed by the animate form, Klee also repeatedly employed the (easily misunderstood) term "function." With it he refers essentially to the *surplus* of expression and meaning that a form exposes beyond its components in the formative process of opening up, in the scene of the image, room for play that the artist freely composes, in

> Movement is the source of all change. In Lessing's Laocoon, on which we squandered study time when we were young, much fuss is made about the difference between temporal and spatial art. Yet looking into the matter more closely, we [artists and intercultural lawyers] find that all this is but a scholastic delusion. For space, too, is a temporal concept.[42]

In this regard, consider the painting 'Main Road and Side Roads' (1929). This work interprets the ongoing and, at the same time, contrastive development of space. The inner temporality of every spatial representation, at least if considered for its significance, is beautifully explained and displayed by this painting. To understand the 'represented,' the eye of the observer must wander/graze (in Klee's words: *einem weidenden Tier abstenden Auge*) cumulatively among the vertical and horizontal lines driven by the different colors. The sense of the main road is a sort of contextual emergence of the dynamic relationship with the context constituted by the lateral, sometimes tiny, colored horizontal frames of space. The space shows its periphrastic consistence, its existence as an epitome of time and the temporal occurrence of distinctions. According to some interpreters, this painting is a dis-composition and subsequent re-composition of the Nile and its meanings. But, mirrored in the dis-composition of the Nile, we can recognize the sense and protean matter of which human life is made. The main road is the synthesis of manifold stories, imperceptible events, even breaths, which occur in the unfolding of existence. But

---

which also the external influences of culture or of history, and not least, of music and of literature can participate. An observer of one of Klee's studies that is dedicated to presenting the logic of form cannot mistake it for one of the works of the artist. An enormous gap separates the two. For example, he who observes *Vast* (*Harbour of roses*) will recognize the elementary repertoire of the self-unfolding line as Klee discusses it in his theory of composition, and at the same time he will discern interferences that relate horizontal lines to the ocean and waves, or musical notation to ships; he will observe the mirroring of top and bottom and simultaneously see a plant develop that directly references morphology. The sum of these interferences opens up a space of possibilities, of possible meaning, and distances the work from rule-governed construction. "The work," says Klee, "stands above the law."

[42] See Boehm (2014, pp. 20–21): "...in order to develop the process of form, Klee measured it up to the infinite *movement of the cosmos*. His own standpoint, however, does not just lie somewhere in the universe but on the "crust of a planet" called earth and under the conditions that reign there. These conditions are of a constraining type; they emerge from the "singular case of our human being," a cosmic "episode," as he occasionally remarked. The stasis under earthly conditions introduces a decisive and new moment in the question of form. It restricts cosmic movement, prescribes it, and endows it in works with a specific *face*—a process, as equally conflict-ridden as productive, which, as Klee says, plays out in the scene of the image. Forces meet counterforces, and they arrive, on the plane, at an equilibrium. *Cosmic becoming*, striving into the infinite, assumes a *gestalt*, organizes itself as a "parable of creation." This, of course, introduces the question as to how it was possible for Klee to reconcile the *priority of becoming*, which he strongly emphasized, with such *standstill*, in which artistic formation inevitably ends. Stasis is not simply a physical, but rather much more an anthropological, measure that bears on the entirety of corporeal existence and its cognitive and sensory economy; and stasis is no less mirrored in the composition of an image. Klee couches this stasis also in an imperative, namely, a maxim for action: Let the plumb line be the law (*Lot sei das Gebot*!). The upright walking human being adapts himself to gravity, insofar as he maintains equilibrium, and gains a perspicuous view. What he always sees "there," refers to a corporeal "here," which he does not have," but "is." In his embodied state, he is a *point*."

such stories, as they are thought of and reflectively considered, are narrative plots, landscapes that host the connotative elements of life, or better the meaning of life. So, by learning from the constructive philosophy of this painting, we can think of the behavioral morphological appearances of Other's conduct, which every intercultural lawyer has to face, as the 'main road'; conversely, the contextual connotative landscape surrounding such conduct and its semantic components become the 'side roads.' Merely by following this cognitive pathway, we could discover that across an intercultural legal translation the peripheral could become 'essential.'

Klee goes further and writes:

> Formerly we [the artists, therefore the lawyers committed to the qualification and translation of Otherness] used to represent things which were visible on earth, things we either liked to look at or would like to see.[43] Today we reveal the reality that is behind visible things, thus expressing the belief that the visible world is merely an isolated case in relation to the universe and that there are many more other, latent realities.[44] Things appear to assume a

---

[43] As regards the relationship between Klee's representational thought and the Western representational tradition, see again Boehm (2014, p. 8): "The temporalization of form also refers, however, to the *history of discourses on form*, which spans from antiquity into the present. At the end of the eighteenth century, a far-reaching transformation of this discourse begins, a transformation in which Paul Klee also intervened with important contributions. His emphatic defense of time and movement becomes comprehensible only if one recalls his *adversaries*: they are, first and foremost, the inheritance from antiquity of *morphé* and *forma*, which combine with the criterion of *duration*. In virtue of this form, the non-sensible *idea* (eidos) enters into a connection with the visible *manifestation*, a *concept of form* that has also been characterized as *eidetic*. Its artistic substantiation consisted in permitting a moment of *timelessness* to emerge from the current of change, a moment to which an experience of the beautiful also becomes tied. In any case, *eidos* generates *stasis*: a concept that has developed and varied through the centuries." [Klee said: Space too is a temporal concept].

[44] The cognitive and philosophical projections of such a vision of 'figuration' are interestingly investigated by John Sallis in a wide argumentative passage that fords the stream of Klee's creative imagination by using some quotes from the painter's essays as stepping-stones. See Sallis (2015, p. 93 ff.). I would like to reproduce, here, the Klee's words (put in Italic) by punctuating them with Sallis' words: 'In his essay "Creative Credo," which is literally framed by references to imagination, Klee writes almost at the outset': *"The essence of graphic art lures us to abstractions readily and rightly. The schematic and fairytale quality that belongs to its imaginary character is given and is expressed with great prevision. Abstract though it may be, the formal figure readily comes to be associated with natural forms."* As Klee says in the Jena lecture: *"For every construction, if its articulation is complex, can with a bit of imagination be brought into comparison with some natural form."* 'The abstract formal figure lets us, through the play of imagination, see the natural form transposed into pictorial space. A line suggests a road taken. [...] It is in Klee's account of this final ascent to the level of artistic expression that he again invokes imagination: *"Born on the wings of instinctual stimuli, imagination conjures up states of being that are somehow more encouraging and more inspiring than those known on or beyond the earth. Symbols console the spirit by letting it see that for it the earthly with its possible intensifications is not the sole possibility."*

In a Bauhaus lecture entitled, *"Things in nature investigated with regard to their inner being: essence and appearance,"* Klee says: *"But life's way is something more. Life engenders and bears [...] the imaginary is indispensable. Art plays unknowingly with ultimate things, and yet it reaches them!"* [...]

For—in Klee's words—*[...]"What impresses him—in place of the finished natural image—is the solely essential image of creation as genesis." Thus, in his work the artist would display the*

> broader and more [see p. 21] diversified meaning, often seemingly contradicting the rational experience of yesterday. There is a striving to emphasize the essential character of the accidental.[45,46]

The best translation/comment to the above words is provided by Klee himself in his painting *Main Road and Side Roads* (1929).

5.5.2 *Paul Klee in Ways of Nature Study (1923)*

> The artist [the intercultural jurist][47] of today is more than an improved camera; he is more complex, richer, and wider. He is a creature on the earth and a creature within the whole, that is to say, a creature on a star among stars. Accordingly, a sense of totality has gradually entered into the artist's [intercultural jurist's] conception of the natural object, whether this object be plant, animal, or man, whether it be situated in the space of the house, the landscape, or the world, and the first consequence is that a more spatial conception of the object as such is born.

The last excerpt could be better interpreted by analyzing, for example, the painting titled 'Kairuan' (1914). The painting gives an 'ecological' representation of Kairuan, the northwestern city of Tunisia, well known as a place of holy

---

formative forces that would have shaped the present natural appearances, in this way "lending genesis duration."

With a penetrating look the artist would probe beneath the present visible form to the underlying process of taking form, of coming forth, of forming. In his Bauhaus lectures Klee returns again and again to this imperative, that vision be shifted from form to forming. He says: *"Forming determines form and therefore is superior to it."* If the very sense of the word is shifted in accord with this imperative, then form will be understood *"as genesis, as becoming, as essence."*

The effect of this shift from surface appearances to their underlying genesis is seen in various guises in Klee's works. Among these is the deformation of natural forms; though Klee often links the effect to the formal character of pictorial art, it also functions in many instances to present visibly the genesis of particular forms. A dismembered animal or human form, which despite its dismemberment, is recognizable as the whole form it could be, appears thereby in its genesis. The picture shows it coming into form as its detached and deformed parts move—or at least suggest movement—toward coherence and formation. By displaying it in the tension of not yet having its form, the artwork presents the form in its forming.

In the essay *"On Modern Art,"* Klee poses for the artist—and this means primarily for himself, as his own aim—the task of probing still farther beneath the visible form. The artist would strive to realize *"some sort of proximity to that secret ground where the primordial law nourishes every development."* The artist would seek to penetrate even beyond these developments, beyond the genesis of visible forms, so as to entice into visibility *"the womb of nature, the primal ground of creation, which holds the secret key to all things."'*

[45] Klee ([or. 1920] 2013).

[46] With regard to the limits of reason in Klee's "figuration theory", see Sallis (2015, p. 42): To put Sallis' remarks in semiotic terms, we can say that in *Limits of Reason* (1927) Klee is telling us how light and formalized objects can conceal the creative process, the web of connotations, the contextual relationships among signs, that is to say, all the generative factors liable to bring forth the visible and morphological appearances of things.

[47] Hereinafter, in this paragraph, the text in Italic within the square brackets is mine.

pilgrimages. The semiotic ecosystem is figured like a space that shows dynamically its meaning and materiality crossing the borders of the city in many directions: horizontally and vertically, towards the desert and towards the heaven. The sky and the earth appear chromatically conjoined. The city and its buildings, in turn, appear as if emerged from life and motion (including moving animals) in the desert crossing the spiritual and dreaming aura of the night skies. Heaven, moreover, tinges and suffuses the desert's surface with its colored reflections, camels and other living presences. Klee seems to tell us that Kairuan can be understood only if we consider it as a semiotic funnel, a place of convergence and re-composition of signical elements distributed in time and space. Will we also be able to see and legally qualify mosques in urban Western intercultural landscapes by casting a similar chorological gaze?

And Klee again:

> The object grows beyond its appearance through our knowledge of its inner being, through the knowledge that the thing is more than its outward aspect suggests. Man dissects the thing and visualizes its inside with the help of plane sections; the character of the object is built up according to the number and kind of sections that are needed. This is visible penetration, to some extent that of a simple knife, to some extent helped by finer instruments which make the material structure or the material function clear to us.[48]

In this regard I refer the reader, once more, Klee's painting Kairuan (1914).

5.5.3 *Paul Klee in On Modern Art (1924 [1945])*

> May I use a simile, the simile of the tree? The artist has studied this world of variety and has, we may suppose, unobtrusively found his way in it. His sense of direction has brought order into the passing stream of image and experience. This sense of direction in nature and life, this branching and spreading array, I shall compare with the root of the tree.
>
> From the root the sap flows to the artist, flows through him, flows to his eye.
>
> Thus he stands as the trunk of the tree.
>
> Battered and stirred by the strength of the flow, he molds his vision into his work.
>
> As, in full view of the world, the crown of the tree unfolds and spreads in time and in space, so with his work.
>
> But it is just the artist who at times is denied those departures from nature which his art demands. He has even been charged with incompetence and deliberate distortion.
>
> And yet, standing at his appointed place, the trunk of the tree, he does nothing other than gather and pass on what comes to him from the depths. He neither serves nor rules—he transmits.
>
> His position is humble. And the beauty at the crown is not his own. He is merely a channel. [...]

[48] Klee ([1923] 2013).

"I have already spoken of the relationship between the root and the crown, between nature and art, and have explained it by a comparison with the difference between the two elements of earth and air, and with the correspondingly differing functions of below and above.

The creation of a work of art—the growth of the crown of the tree—must of necessity, as a result of entering into the specific dimensions of pictorial art, be accompanied by distortion of the natural form. For, therein is nature reborn." [...]

"I would like now to examine the dimensions of the object in a new light and so try to show how it is that the artist [intercultural lawyer] frequently arrives at what appears to be such an arbitrary "deformation" of natural forms.

First, he does not attach such intense importance to natural form as do so many realist critics, because, for him, these final forms are not the real stuff of the process of natural creation. For he places more value on the powers which do the forming than on the final forms themselves.[49]

He (the artist [intercultural lawyer]) is, perhaps unintentionally, a philosopher, and if he does not, with the optimists, hold this world to be the best of all possible worlds, nor to be so bad that it is unfit to serve as a model, yet he says:

"In its present shape it is not the only possible world."

Thus he surveys with penetrating eye the finished forms which nature places before him.[50]

The deeper he looks, the more readily he can extend his view from the present to the past, the more deeply he is impressed by the one essential image of creation itself, as Genesis, rather than by the image of nature, the finished product.

[49] To understand the closeness between the processive analysis of forms carried out by Klee and the dis-composition that intercultural lawyers should bring forth, consider the following remarks by Boehm (2014, p. 13): "Klee's temporalization has, in parts, explicit morphological characteristics, to which several theoretical notebook pages and more than a few images refer. A further important document in this respect is his collection of natural artifacts and his herbarium. A photograph shows that he produced several preparations—such as those of shells, mollusks, corals, and algae—in the form of an image between two glass plates. Only the morphological gaze recognizes more than death and ossification in these graveyards of past life; it recognizes, namely, the stages of genesis. If a compositional form comes to light in this way, then it also relativizes a familiar difference that accompanies the surface: the difference between outside and inside, between skin and skeleton, between body and soul. The prehistory of the visible concerns entirely new patterns of experience. Indeed, many of the artist's images seduce us into a magical "intermediate realm" that angels also inhabit as transitory beings; or we enter spheres within which inside and outside interlock and interact with one another."

[50] See Boehm (2014, p. 11): "Klee's penetrating gaze corresponds to an "opening of the eyes toward the inside". A viewer of his images is familiar with the unobstructed transitions, not just between outer and inner spheres, but also between all possible worlds. After all, this reality that we know is "in this fully formed gestalt... not the only one." The possible strikes him as more real than the real itself and he "wants... to portray man not at all as he is, but only as he could also be." The penetrating gaze thus grasps, in addition to morphology, the traces of memory, sensation, dreams, phantasy, or of an expressive motor activity that reveals itself in smiles, mourning, wit, and irony, and moreover, in music and poetry as well as even in political events, a "range throughout the... field.""'

> Then he permits himself the thought that the process of creation can today hardly be complete and he sees the act of world creation stretching from the past to the future. Genesis eternal!
>
> He goes still further!
>
> He says to himself, thinking of life around him: this world at one time looked different and, in the future, will look different again.
>
> Then, flying off the infinite, he thinks: it is very probable that, on other stars, creation has produced a completely different result.
>
> Such mobility of thought on the process of natural creation is good training for creative work.
>
> It has the power to move the artist fundamentally, and since he is himself mobile, he may be relied upon to maintain freedom of development of his own creative methods.
>
> This being so, the artist must be forgiven if he regards the present state of outward appearances in his own particular world as accidentally fixed in time and space. And as altogether inadequate compared with his penetrating vision and intense depth of feeling."

The last excerpt from Klee's essay 'On Modern Art' could be further illuminated by observing his painting titled 'Cosmic Composition' (1929). This work perfectly represents the (semiotic) relational meaning of every empirical appearance. Trees, flowers, houses, stars, the moon, stairs and manifold multidirectional lines are involved in a polyphonic orchestration. The painting is shaped by an ascensional movement that draws its rhythm, however, from a sort of genetic burst placed perspectively and chronologically before the scene, before the moving. The cosmic features represented in the painting and their recognizability are to be considered only a contingent 'meanwhile' along the continuous process of transformation/generation of Being. Forms are caught along the pathways through which all their possibilities unfold, from a just looming beginning towards an openness with unpredictable outputs. So, the observer can figure out the meaning of any represented form only by a reiterated and cumulative roaming (grazing) in the space of the pictorial frame. This space and its dynamic components will be, therefore, the (ever interlocutory) result of the temporally layered sequence of the observational acts. Understanding cultures and cultural items (behaviors, words, objects, artifacts, etc.) should follow a similar approach. In this way the observer/lawyer could avoid the reifying thinghood of culturalized meanings. Conversely, he could 'read' behaviors and words as semantic convergences of the fluxes of sense and semiotic relationships that simultaneously stem from both the past and the future, the origin and the horizon. In such a way, the understanding and the legal qualification of people's conduct could be performed as a creative act, a renewal and an execution of the genetic momentum that gave rise to it in its original cultural context. Obviously, the overall process is to be multilateral and multi-directional.

But Klee further observes:

> And is it not true that even the small step of a glimpse through the microscope reveals to us images which we should deem fantastic and overimaginative if we were to see them somewhere accidentally, and lacked the sense to understand them?

Your realist, however, coming across such an illustration in a sensational magazine, would exclaim in great indignation: "Is that supposed to be nature? I call it bad drawing."

Does then the artist concern himself with microscopy? History? Paleontology?

Only for the purpose of comparison, only in the exercise of his mobility of mind. And not to provide a scientific check on the truth of nature.

Only in the sense of freedom.

In the sense of a freedom which does not lead to fixed phases of development, representing exactly what nature once was, or will be, or could be on another star (as perhaps may one day be proved).

But in the sense of a freedom which merely demands its rights, the right to develop, as great Nature herself develops.

From type to prototype.[51]

Presumptuous is the artist who does not follow his road through to the end. But chosen are those artists who penetrate to the region of that secret place where primeval power nurtures all evolution.

There, where the powerhouse of all time and space—call it the brain or heart of creation—activated every function; who is the artist who would not dwell there?

In the womb of nature, at the source of creation, where the secret key to all lies guarded.

But not all can enter. Each should follow where the pulse of his own heart leads.

So, in their time, the Impressionists—our opposites of yesterday—had every right to dwell within the matted undergrowth of everyday vision.

But our pounding heart drives us down, deep down to the source of all, the origin.

What springs form this source—whatever it may be called, dream, idea or fantasy—must be taken seriously only if it unites with the proper creative means to form a work art.

Then those curiosities become realities—realities of art which help to lift life out of its mediocrity.

For not only do they, to some extent, add more spirit to the seen, but they also make secret visions visible.

I SAID 'with the proper creative means.' For at this stage it is decided whether pictures or something different will be born. At this stage, also, is decided the kind of the pictures.

With regard to the last considerations proffered by Klee, it could be very instructive to analyze the painting titled 'Arab Song' (1932). It is a simple

[51] Boehm (2014, p. 24): "The artist represents the trunk of the tree, who has plunged his roots into the earth's ground and thereby entered a metabolic exchange. We know that Klee did not make a relation to visual reality the foundation of his work, that it does not take optical paths, that it submerges into the prehistory of the visible. Precisely this rhizomatic communication is intended here, and its "fluids" rise through the trunk and constitute the forking branches of the crown. At the same time, the trunk is the seat of the eye, through which the rising energies flow. The crown, with its height, makes visible the artistic work, which in no regard stands in a mirror relation to the roots. Instead, it is subject to "deformatic necessities," that already emerge through the "arrival of a specific iconic dimension.""

representation and, at the same time, an enigmatic figuration. First of all, most observers of this painting might say that it is a portrait of a woman. However, this is only a possibility, partially induced by the rose nuance of the garment. Nothing within the pictorial frame compels us to exclude the masculinity of the portrayed subject. This openness is an inner feature of Klee's representation. Furthermore, the title is linked to the curvilinear form of the line painted in the middle of the garment's fabric. In Klee's geometrical/cosmological poetics, curved lines are equivalent to free pathways, namely without a precise destination, walked for the sake of moving around, like a game. These kinds of lines convey a laid-back attitude. As Klee explains (*Das bildnerische Denken*, vol. I. Basel 1971: Schwabe), in musical terms a curved line is similar to a melodic, popular song, which requires a harmonic accompaniment. This is the reason for the title 'Arab Song:' it is enshrined in the enigmatic and magnetic tension between the orange figure and the brown one. Their polarized positions draw the dynamic opposition figured on the garment. And then, the eyes: they emerge from the invisible body as dunes in the desert at the sunset. Finally, the black strap over the eyes that evokes the secret darkness of thoughts. In legal contemporary terms, we could title this picture "the resonating world behind and beyond the veil." What would have happened if in 2014 ECtHR (S.A.S. v. France 695) had dis-composed the Islamic world swarming behind the niqab and its intercultural signification in the same way in which Klee let it sing, so as to stimulate, through its semiotic dis-composition, our cultural creativity? Could cultural creativity take the place of reified/cosified culture? Could the connotative landscape extant behind and beyond the veil be transduced by means of an intercultural use of human rights, so leading to different judicial (and political) results?

In my view, the last lesson we can draw from Klee's critical writings, also in the light of 'Arab Song' is wonderfully summed up by his following words:

> The unsettled times have brought chaos and confusion (or so it seems, if we are not too near to judge).
>
> But among artists [intercultural jurists], even among the youngest of them, one urge seems to be gradually gaining ground:
>
> The urge to the culture of these creative means to their pure cultivation, to their pure use.
>
> The legend of the childishness of my drawing must have originated from those linear compositions of mine in which I tried to combine a concrete image, say that of a man, with the pure representation of the linear element.
>
> Had I wished to present the man 'as he is,' then I should have had to use such a bewildering confusion of line that pure elementary representation would have been out of the question. The result would have been vagueness beyond recognition.
>
> And anyway, I do not wish to represent the man as he is, but only as he might be.[52]

[52] See Paul Klee "On Modern Art", in Herbert Robert (2000).

Klee's dis-compositional and, at the same time, re-compositional approach to representation and figuration gives contemporary jurists a powerful cognitive tool to face cultural Otherness. Notwithstanding the sophisticated theoretical arguments of this artist, his way to see the world and things *inside* it is very close to intercultural legal methodology I propose. Klee teases out the narrative/connotative/temporal fabric of things, images, events. In his paintings, everything is dis-composed so as to deploy a story. But it is an open story. Every step of the plot is treated and figured as a connotative item amenable to be projected towards the future so as to acquire new significations. In the same way, jurists and lawyers would have to read Otherness involved in everyday life and in relationships marked by cultural difference among people. Dis-composing the morphological appearances of objects and behaviors/phenomena is an intermediary step to overcome the ethnocentric gaze and creatively project the connotative materials resulting from this operation into the legal semantic landscape. If such a task is accomplished, then the law's prescriptiveness can be used as a chisel to pluralistically carve out the future features of coexistence.

5.6 Practical Implications of the Intercultural Transposition of Human Rights: Coexistence, Legal Chorology, and Nuisance Law

Klee teaches us how it is possible to see beyond morphological appearances, beyond a psychologically and culturally self-bounded 'thinghood.' The pathway he aesthetically undertook could seem complicated, but this is only because he saw and tried to dismantle the granitic and almost impermeable certainties of vision and conceptualization related to the objects and experiences of quotidian life. Actually, the more something is taken as simple and obvious, the more psycho-cognitively difficult it is to gain a critical and renewing view of it. In tune with Klee's focus on the objects of everyday life, I would like to show the continuities between his figurative philosophy and an intercultural methodology applied to the most (apparently) trivial issue imaginable: the challenge to coexistence stemming from the propagation of bad smells, or stinks, in condos. This could appear to be a silly example. But it can reveal, as few other situations can, how the solution to intercultural problems of coexistence calls for an attitude that seeks to look beyond morphological appearances. Besides, narratively dis-composing a stink and interculturally re-composing its meaning and legal relevance could sound, at a minimum, like an impossible task. I submit, however, that it—namely, transmuting 'things' in re-shapeable 'stories'—is nothing but the currently 'possible' challenge of intercultural coexistence.

How can people therefore coexist with differences so as to involve in their conduct an intercultural implementation of human rights? How to manage a geographical and cultural distance that turns into proximity by virtue of the behaviors and gestures of those who live beside us? How can we devise a code of 'normal tolerability' that does not mark difference as unlawfulness? How can individuals and groups prevent the proximity of those-who-are-different from transfiguring into segregation, and thereby into the re-establishment in cultural terms of a distance that migration has already traversed? How to avoid that the 'elsewhere,' which has become 'close,' be *exiled* in another space of experience that is still topographically 'close' but doomed to be culturally distant?[53] How can all of us keep the law from becoming a weapon to be wielded within the struggle for a unilateral conquest of space? How can we prevent the use of legal rules to position the dominance of particular cultural schemes in an ethnocentric fashion? How can we avert the danger that words of the law are complemented by 'invisible/mute parts,' implicit meanings, so as to signify and re-assert only the natives' or dominant groups' habits? How can we make evident, publicly recognizable, the implicit and sometimes surreptitious substitutions of singular cultural patterns with the alleged objectivity and

[53] As regards the semantic co-implication between space and time in the spectrum of the categorization processes, see the remarks proposed some time ago by Fabian (1983). He argued such considerations with respect to the allochrocnic strategies adopted during the colonialist era to cast non-Europeans into another time and, consequentially also into categorical spaces deemed to be different from those allegedly lived by Western people. This author, actually, extended his epistemological criticism also to include the contemporary anthropological gaze—at least, up to the early 1980s—and the writing style of anthropological texts. Following Fabian, allochronism inevitably turned into strategies aimed at justifying Westerners' occupation of space. All these strategies relied upon the de-legitimation and the cultural backwardness (*childhood*) of non-Western peoples' lifestyles and, consequently, their practices toward engendering their existential spaces. In other words, what mattered was not so much the physical space in and of itself, as rather the incompatibility between it and how to produce the experience of it, to live it. The colonial occupation and its strategies of legitimation were triggered precisely by such experiential and existential differences. If the culturally different lived spaces had the same experiential meaning, they could have been coordinated or, at least, colonizers might have devised other 'arguments' to legitimately compete with natives. Doubtless, in some cases huge mystifications were at work. Europeans emphasized the diversities of custom and the Others' ways of living spaces only to justify, or rather create an alibi for, the eviction of natives. In some respects, the cause of conflicts and competition for space would have been equality of spatial connotations and aspirations rather than their discontinuity: space was however a common object of possession and domain. Nevertheless, colonizers focused their rhetorical strategies on differences so as to legitimize encroachment and plunder. But such an emphasis on differences dissimulated a radical refusal to translate Otherness. Once this move was made, the homology in possession of spaces was contextualized in a framework of sense ('barbaric civilization') that delegitimized the natives' entitlement to it and, at the same time, the anthropological, ethical, political and economic uses they made of *their* spaces. As if to say, by presentifying the overall discourse: their (namely, natives') being equal to us (colonizers) as regards the will to occupy and possess '*the* space,' is unlawful precisely because they are different from us. They dwell in *another room of time* and, therefore, in *another space*: both of which, in turn, were interpreted and signified as sources of disvalue. Consequentially, it is right to engulf them *inside* our space and functionalize them to it: all of this without any effort of translating them, but rather by silencing any possible, recognizable equality/homology between them and us.

Plunder and enslavement were, in other words, the direct implications of categorical evictions, the semantic annihilation of Others, and the nullification of their space-time. Similar considerations, even if in geographically reversed terms, can be argued with respect to the space-time of contemporary migrants when they partake in the space-time circuits of natives (like condominiums). See Ricca (2010, 2017, 2016a), and *ibidem* for further bibliography.

universality of law? And furthermore, in light of such a 'public recognition' of the ethnocentric declinations of space and their political influence, how can we foster a constructive criticism that is interculturally oriented? What is, therefore, the pathway for keeping cultural distance from engendering spatial distance within shared material-geographical spaces? And, again, how can we make it so that the distance among the different geographical contexts from which people of different cultures come, does not block our understanding of the semiotic juxtaposition that multicultural coexistence engenders among physically distant places and the related circuits of experience?

The whole set of the above questions uncoils, actually, the skein of problems encapsulated inside the issue and placed at the top of the list: how can people coexist with differences? I do not believe, however, that there are any possible solutions other than translation. A word—'translation'—that is to be intended according to the meaning emerging from its etymological roots, the same that conjures up, precisely, the idea of passage and going through space as well as linguistic and categorical borders. The translation of habits, meanings, and patterns from different cultures comprises the discovery of synthesis among their practical implications: the consequences of the assumptions that acquire materiality in and through existential space. In this sense, an intercultural translation functions as an inter-spatial translation.[54] And since spaces that host the implications of words are often distant from one another, intercultural translation, in turn, has to occur in an inter-space capable of transcending physical distances, so engendering a sort of *trans-spatial* semiotic *continuum.*[55]

All of this will become possible only if spatial proximity is taken as the premise to recognize the configurability of a categorical continuity among differences; and, symmetrically, the categorical proximity or implication is conceived as a semio-spatial continuity. In a practical sense, this means that any possibility to genuinely grasp what my neighbor-from-another-culture is doing requires a translation of their space of existence into mine, so as to forge another semantic and spatial frame to peacefully host our coexistence. When such a translation does not take *place* between the 'meanings acted' by people, it will inevitably precipitate a fight for the exclusive occupation (or 'filling') of space or more precisely, the forced assimilation (and thereby the annihilation) of Otherness within the space of the mightiest (neighbor).

The first step towards intercultural translation coincides with the narrative dis-composition of the Other's appearance, namely the morphological shape of their presence. What does it mean, however, to "narratively dis-compose or factorize a morphological appearance"? An example drawn from quotidian life could make this semantic operation explicit and show how to make it operative in practice. Suppose that in a condo conflict, inter alia connoted by multiculturality, the smells

[54]For more on intercultural translation, see the theoretical approach developed in Ricca (2008, 2013b). See *ibidem* for further bibliographical references on this topic.

[55]See Ricca (2016a, 2017, 2020a).

emanating from the kitchen of a neighbor are perceived and judged by the owner of an adjoining apartment as a disturbing and invasive emission. To assess the validity of the requested claim to prohibit those emissions, authorities will have to ascertain that such smells exceed 'normal tolerability.' The parameter of 'normal tolerability' and its range, however, are deeply influenced by cultural habits. What is considered to be a stench for one person, could be an appetizing odour for someone else, or even a positive sign of recognition, an emblem of the 'normality of their life.' We might imagine some food typical of a particular religious festival. It would be enough for an Italian and an Indian (or a Chinese person, a Pakistani and so on) to live side by side in the same hallway for perceptive effusions to register in people's perception with regard to smells and invasive exhalations from their kitchens.

The immediacy and relevance of perceiving something as a smell and categorizing it as a stench or, alternatively, as a 'good aroma' could appear to be an entirely empirical and indisputable phenomenon. And yet, as is the case for taste, such immediacy is not tied (at least not exclusively) to biological predispositions but rather, or at least primarily, to culturally acquired habits. [56] The perception of flavors or smells is a synthesis, in many respects metaphorical, of previous firsthand or transmitted experiences. Those experiential paths plot life contexts and dynamical spaces molded by individual and/or collective existence so as to host the individuals involved in them in a relationship of reciprocal symbiosis with their (spatial) environment. This is because human beings fit themselves to their environment and (try to) adapt it to their own needs. This process gradually engenders existential spaces, which can otherwise be defined as cultural habitats. Nature and culture, perception and knowledge, are two sides of the same coin, namely a whole process. It unfolds by the production of constants and variables, and then transforms those variables into constants, and vice versa, along the pathways of a dialectic relationship between that which will be assumed, from one time to the next, either as nature or culture, as objectivity or subjectivity.

Narrative dis-compositions of the morphological appearance, of the 'perceptive existence' (*Dasein*) of smells (as well as flavors, noises and other phenomena substantiating possible invasive emissions) can be carried out by means of a discursive effort to draw out what a specific smell represents and synthetizes. In the case of the kitchen, what matters is not just the description of the ingredients used, but also the significance that each holds in the cultural life of individuals or their communities.

Such an unfolding of narratives will show, little by little, experiential contexts crammed with semantic fragments and frames (or better: bubbles) of lived spatiality. So, for instance, this or that food smell could interplay with specific life situations, geographical-environmental coordinates, traditions, anniversaries, social conditions, sanitary and or dietary needs, religious orthopraxis and duties, and so on. Each of these 'ingredients' could have its semantic equivalent within the life contexts of

[56] See Mahalansan IV (2006), Hyde (2006), Jim Drobnick (2006); on the relationship between culture and taste, see Ricca (2014).

those who perceive the smell of a particular food as 'stink' and judge its propagation like an invasive emission and a nuisance. Such equivalences will be, of course, metaphorical rather than analytical. The *ground* of these metaphors—technically the theme that semantically bridges metaphorical source and target—can comprise qualitative or emotional properties or, in any case, flexible or conceptually vague categorical elements. In this way, the difference between the 'smelling perceptions' of people can fade out, thus relativizing its neat evidence, obviousness, its 'thinghood.' In other words, the 'stink' could doff its morphological empirical absoluteness as a consequence of the emergence of continuities and analogies between the meanings of experiential contexts lived by people; what emerges is an inter-contextual landscape of sense. It goes without saying that this process of inter-contextualization will only be as powerful as the narrative dis-composition implemented by both parties of the 'smell conflict,' that is, insofar as the process remains interculturally bi-directional.[57] Specifically, this means that the exoticism

[57] As I said above, something similar to the narrative dis-composition of connotative elements and their metaphorical re-composition through the creation of 'synthetic figures' could be found by means of an analogy, a sort of trans-duction with representational pathways traced by avant-garde painters across the nineteenth and twentieth centuries, and specifically during the first part of the latter. Also in painting, the plots of narrative de-contextualization and representational dis-composition were triggered by encounters with different cultures. The enfranchisement from the representation of morphological features and the consequential opening, under the painters' gaze, of the connotative landscapes lying behind the natural images and appearances found their early expression in Gauguin's works. He achieved this narrative and connotative dis-composition through the juxtaposition of symbolic/figurative elements from both the Western and Polynesian culture in the same painting. This intercultural parataxis could engender in the observer's mind an interpenetration among distant connotative landscapes, which in turn paved the way to new spaces of sense where figures and objects from different cultural traditions came to be attracted, re-contextualized and re-semanticized. Cézanne followed, inviting the viewer to geometrically de-compose natural figures. Thereafter, the process of connotative rooting-out found its expression in Cubism, and especially in Juan Gris's 'synthetic Cubism,' even more than in Picasso and Braque: all of them, however, were deeply influenced by so-called primitive art and the *transfigured naturality* of its forms, images and figures, so different from those produced by the Western iconic traditions. Gris made use of cubist dis-composition not only to simultaneously present the various, possible perspectives on an object, but also to give shape, by means of color, to new metaphorical objects: all still recognizable by the common observer and yet open to and urging her/his creative ability in figurative and semantic re-composition. Something similar can be traced in the works of Paul Klee, who utilized abstract forms and colors to paint equally recognizable figures (unlike his contemporary Kandinskij) which were yet transfigured. All this was done in an attempt to make visible the invisible, that is, the connotative—we could say *chorological*—richness (*Gestaltung*) that teems in the shadows of the apparent morphological obviousness of natural figures (Sallis 2015, p. 77 ff.). Another version of such a dis-compositional and synthetic re-compositive tendency, as such oriented to make understandable the non-visible, the hidden connections that connotatively join culturally distant objects, can be identified in Alberto Savinio's paintings (even more than in the works of his brother, Giorgio De Chirico, who gave prevalence to the *estrangement*, the unveiling of the unknown and the unpredictable relationships that lie beside and below the normality of objects). Actually, Savinio achieved the re-compositive effect by means of weird assemblages of things and images generally considered plausible, rational, *normal* but so as to show the incoherence of the usual combinations and semantic webs in which they were involved. A quick look at these artistic works and individual intellectual enterprises would be sufficient to obtain a plastic

and the morphological 'inappropriateness' of a smell, which just for this reason is perceived as a 'stink,' could be the material implication, the final phenomenal outcome of the implementation of meanings, ends or values recognizable as such also by the claimant of the spatial conflict, even if experienced by her/him them in morphologically different ways, producing other kinds of 'emissions and propagations.' Once the axiological, teleological, or semantic continuity is recognized, even if in metaphorical terms, then the stigma caused by the morphological difference will be difficult to justify. This difficulty stems from a cognitive-linguistic phenomenon that could be defined as *cross-contextual resonance.*[58] Actually, if we assume a symmetrically discursive level as a framework of comparison between the differences at stake, making claims that inhibit the behaviors of Others will become increasingly uncomfortable. This discomfort will occur at least in all the cases in which the Other's different behaviors can be inscribed within the same values, ends or categorical schemes that serve as a (semantic) compass for the claimant's conduct. Of course, anything is possible if we consider this matter from the point of view of pure, absolute power. But it is precisely another matter when power needs to be justified and there are semantic and normative platforms with a general and universalistic scope that are intended specifically to legitimize the use of power.

In the social contexts within states, people's lives flow through, and by virtue of, legal coordinates. Law is not only an instrument used to rule the habitually determined actions of people but also a *medium* to support the configuration of those habits through the planning of individual and collective actions and the definition of a social horizon of ends. Drawing out and narratively unwinding the connotative landscapes that underlie the production of noises, smells, fumes, etc., can unveil

---

representation of connotative dis-composition (mentioned above) and the related ability to go beyond morphological appearances and categorical boundaries. I have to point out that the use of such analogies with pictorial art specifically relates to the process of morphological dis-composition inherent in the practice of intercultural translation. It is something very different from some analogical uses of contemporary art—for instance, Cubism—aimed at showing in post-modern terms the pluralization of legal experience, the decline the inner consistency of national legal systems, the alleged reticular and multi-perspectival character of contemporary legal subjectivity and sources of law. See, for example, Douglas-Scott (2014, pp. 84 ff.; 94 ff., 101 ff.). These theoretical paths simultaneously lead to a legal inter-systemic pluralism and multiculturalism or, by contrast, towards the search for legal-national unity presented as a sort of antidote against chaos and anomy. In both cases, these approaches are very different from intercultural law (as I intend it) and a value-based pluralism as such capable of promoting a *bottom-up* and inclusive interpretation of values through the spectrum of different cultural perspectives. Intercultural law involves a dis-composition practice pursuing a possible re-composition stemming from the actual exercise of cultural and individual creativity rather than a fragmented juxtaposition of differences, which often—too often—results in nothing but compromises and *commoditizing accommodations*. When the space for cultural and individual creativity is denied, what remains are not differences but only *snippets* of them, fetishized and wielded exclusively to pursue material goals and power. On the dark side of these so-called 'accommodations,' see Ricca (2018b, 2020a), but already Dewey (1916, p. 56), who distinguished 'accommodations' from 'active adjustments.'

[58] As regards 'cross-contextual resonance' in legal-intercultural issues, see above, Chap. 3, and also Ricca (2013b).

unsuspected threads of legal relevance concerning such phenomena. The behaviors from which a specific emission and its morphological appearance stem can thereby reveal features viewed positively or negatively depending on the legal apparatuses applied and their semantic potentialities.

In this way, for instance, a particular smell could result from the use of materials prescribed for the fulfillment of a religious practice and/or duty. This is included, however, within the normative legal and axiological category 'religious freedom' and denotes an individual prerogative, that is, a power to act in, and across the space, that is deemed worthy of recognition and protection by democratic-constitutional legal systems as well as international law and human and/or fundamental rights declarations. One neighbor's perception of a 'stench' should be balanced, therefore, with the Other's right to exercise their religious freedom. This comparison/adjustment of the different subjective prerogatives arising from the *fact* of spatial coexistence requires a commitment to undertaking efforts of inter-subjective and intercultural translation/transaction. It inevitably flows into the re-definition not only of the subjects' power in using their space, but also into the semantic re-qualification of the standard of normal tolerability and thereby of the existential features of social space. And since space—in view of the above arguments—consists of what occurs in it, then the coordination among its possible, different subjective uses, and thereby the re-modulation of legal subjectivity, will correspond to, and result from, a re-conceptualization of what the space *is* in itself.

The religiously connoted 'stench'—the 'stink' of which exclusively depends on the perceptive and cultural schemes of one of the struggling parties—will end up impinging on property rights or rights of possession only insofar as it is judged, after an axiological balancing, not to exceed normal tolerability or, instead, is justified by the necessity of allowing the exercise of a human and/or fundamental right. In both cases, what will end up undergoing a re-categorization will be the space itself and, therefore, also the ensuing separations, divides, regimes of exclusion of Otherness related to the exercise of ownership or possession. In other words, the 'stink' to be tolerated will become part and parcel of the common space within which the inter-subjective distinctions and separations take *place*. This means that the stink at issue cannot be excluded by the space that, in turn, is made object of ownership or possession and, as such, is reserved in an exclusive way to each of the subjects concerned. Perhaps we could summarize in this way: if I may use my (possessed) space so as to introduce into your (possessed) space the emission stemming from my action, then your space, only with reference to those actions and their invasive consequences, will have already (partly) become *also* my space. This will occur notwithstanding walls, fences, divisions, and in spite of them. So, these too, in the end of such a process of re-categorization, will have changed their significance because also their object and premise will have transformed, namely which space they can or cannot divide.

The work of re-semanticization achieved through the legal qualification of spatial uses will have forged, therefore, an experiential inter-space. It is, precisely, the outcome of the work of intercultural trans-*lation* (to be intended also in an etymological sense, that is, as a 'shifting,' 'displacement,' or 'migration'). Within the process of translation, words and spaces are not caught in a relationship of dialectical opposition similar to the well-known subject/world or ought/be divides. Conversely, verbal symbols and spaces are unified, or better, are placed along a *continuum*, and they interplay horizontally/mutually by virtue of their common features as signs. Their inter-relationships engender experience, to be intended precisely as the horizon and the arrival point (though always interlocutory) of the process of reciprocal fitting between subjects and their environments: precisely, an environmental dimension of which also the plurality of subjects partake, and, notwithstanding this self-reflexive inclusion, is made an object of representation and, therefore, becomes a means of human action. All of this points out that the *practice of space* or *spatial praxis* is reflected throughout the meanings of words and, symmetrically, that linguistic practice—in this case legally connoted—transforms experience and the signification of space, up to the point of re-forging even our empirical and irreflexive perception of it and of its 'scansions' of sense.

Such changes take *place* because spatial perception is pro-active and pre-dictive: it draws the cultural and experiential *Umwelt* of subjects, the potential *bubble of existence* out of each of them.[59] For the same reason, the occupation of a space to the detriment of someone else does not mean taking over a space that is abstractly void, or which becomes void (therefore at the disposal of those who have the power to occupy it) as soon as Other is evicted from it. In the dimension of inter-subjective relationships and their socially organized spatial projections, space is always dense, filled with the actual or potential projections stemming from subjectivities that contribute to molding and defining its meaning and thereby also the scansions of its empirical/material perception.[60]

Evicting the Other from a space that is taken to be void is therefore and in any case an act of the annihilation of their subjectivity, an attempt to silence and disregard the Other's human demand for space and the possibility of their existential projection in and through it. When human beings struggle for space, they (as well as the living beings of different species) are never contending for a void space but rather for their own individuality or community, against the individual or collective spatial patterns or claims of someone else. The true quandary and the site of the conflict is the connotative and teleological overlap between the symbolic and pragmatic projections of differing subjectivities, that is to say, the perceived space and the matrix of conflict. What remains outside the representational and pragmatic horizons of the subjects involved in every specific spatial relationship—from a semantic and teleological point view—is not even perceived or considered as a space worth struggling for. A lion in the savanna fights for *its* territory (where it hunts, mates, establishes its group-domination, etc.) *first of all against the other lions* by fighting, killing, tearing them to pieces precisely because it shares patterns of action with them. The same lion

[59] See Pallasmaa (2005, p. 40 ff.; 2011).

[60] From a historical point of view, a deeply fascinating lesson comes from Zumthor (1993).

does not *see* within *its* potential space the presence of lizards, birds, ants, hippos, etc.[61] No matter how many of these animals inhabit the same physical space in which the lion acts, they do not impact the lion's activities, the pragmatic *domain* coincident with the dimension in which it lives. Now, the choice to become a lion or rather a human being (although, as for cruelty and ferociousness there is no guarantee that the second alternative might not be even worse) is up to the latter. The option depends on the ability, which is presumed to be idiomatically human and symbolic, to reciprocally translate 'subjective' spaces and the related subjectivities, so as to engender by virtue of fantasy and creativity an inter-space of coexistence: a renewed *natural* space that is so just because it is *cultural*, since 'cultural' *is (or should be)* human *nature*. In other words, it is up to us to choose what kind of animal we want to be: one that invents new spaces for a shared and cooperative coexistence, or rather one that slays others in order to occupy spaces defined by predetermined cognitive and teleological (and at least partly biological) schemes.

Making room for dialogical narrative exercises regarding the semantic landscapes and stories that underlie each invasive emission and its particular 'matter' (smells, noises, gasses, and various fumes), has a twofold signification. On the one hand, it allows us to overcome the 'thinghood' of perception, its morphological appearance, so as to unwind the skein of semantic connotations and experiential relationships which comprise emissions. On the other hand, the openness to listening to and sharing stories, makes it so that the actors in condo conflicts of invasive emissions and the institutional agents committed to their resolution engage in direct 'journeys' through space and time.

Crossing the borders of morphological 'thinghood' that stem from irreflexive perception means unravelling the weft of actions and relationships that lie in the shadow of the behaviors directly responsible for invasive emissions, namely the gestures designed to fill spaces. This is made possible precisely by an unwinding of narratives and an act of listening to them that people accomplish in a critical and self-reflective way. When someone explains why he is performing particular actions, these simultaneously transform and take the shape of epitomes, final summaries and translations of chains of meaning or significant acts. In this way, people—nay, storytellers—discover that 'behind' an invasive emission lie a number of recollections, necessities, obligations, duties, identity features, familiar and communitarian ties, historical and geographical projections: an observation that applies both to those who perceive the emission and those who feel victim to it. The multicultural

[61] I hope it is not scandalous to compare condos/co-owners and lions. Experience shows how many individuals live the condo experience almost as any 'good' dominant lion rages in the savanna. The environment of the 'condominium' is a useful laboratory to ascertain and measure the constant danger of a drift towards the feral aggressiveness that characterizes the spatial projection of 'humanity': from an urban to a planetary scale. (I understand, however, that sometimes lions *notice* the presence of isolated and diseased elephants, and so include them within the set of their possible prey to be attacked rigorously by means of a group strategy: of course, provided that the group is large enough to balance the unbridgeable gap extant between the physical strength of one lion and one elephant).

dimension of coexistence, if considered through the spectrum of disputes for space, unfolds all the weft of the 'human' caught in diverse folds. The making of that which to the eyes (or nose) of neighbors in conflict can be perceived as a stink, might prove to be, in turn, a constitutive feature of gestures, objects and events which, as such, partake of a categorical frame endowed with axiological relevance. This dialogical emergence can trigger, then, a sort of *categorical migration*. A phenomenon that can take shape even under the (cultural) lens of the same subjects that previously responded to the olfactory stimuli of an emission by qualifying it as a bad smell. Let me explain.

By virtue of unfolding narratives and contextualizing interculturally translated actions, the previously alleged 'disturbing emission'—precisely, the stink—can turn into a connotative element of a complex phenomenon that comprises it as only one of the many articulations of a landscape of sense and/or web of semantic connections. If we consider the inter-subjective relationship between neighbors and their spatial claims, it could be the case that the 'stink' is not the salient connotation (and thereby, a central denotative element) to determine the category to be used in order to qualify in both empirical and legal terms the conduct carried out by the 'emitting party' of the conflict.

Realizing that the bad smell is an 'accident' or an 'epiphenomenon' of the necessity to satisfy—for instance—religious exigencies, health care needs, or other high-value and legally protected purposes, might produce a decrease and/or shifting of its salience within the semantic frame initially denounced as an invasive emission. In other words, the purposes of the 'emitting' neighbors, as such a disturbing agent of the peaceful enjoyment of their ownership/possession, might prove to be worthy of protection on the same level as the respect for living standards claimed by the parties that presume themselves to be victims of an invasive emission. All of this will exert some influence on the work of categorization regarding both the situation and the behavior that is producing the alleged 'stink.' In short, this means that the behavior at stake will not be included within the category 'invasive emission of disturbing smells,' namely 'stenches,' but rather in another category, corresponding to 'health care practices,' or 'religious orthopraxis,' etc. Such categories, in turn, are included in the same institutional and legal provisions (constitutional, human and/or fundamental rights, statutory laws) that recognize and rule ownership, possession and the related entitlements to claim the use (exclusive and excluding) of space. The respect for religious habits and freedom is an inherent feature of ownerships—at least in democratic-constitutional states. So, if the emission of smell/stink is re-categorized as an expression of religious freedom, then that specific stink and its toleration will be inherent respects of ownership, a sort of inner and constitutive features of its legal significance. So, religious freedom, precisely because it is merged and involved in the translational intercultural process, can serve as a metaphorical ground and will be used in a 'horizontal and situated' semantic interface rather than in terms of a higher-level principle of legal absolute hierarchy. Consequently, the authorities responsible for deciding the conflict will have to make space for a balancing of claims, both of which are based on legal provisions and their semantic scope. Such a balancing will give nothing but a redefinition of the categorical borders of the respectively claimed rights and the situations these rights rule. This outcome will be reached precisely by enabling some or prohibiting other behaviors, which from that point onward will be considered as semantic features to be lawfully included in or, conversely, excluded from those particular situations and the related legal provisions.

We can imagine a case, for example, in which a judge considers the human right to 'health care' or 'religious freedom' as prevailing over possession. In this case, he triggers a migration in the social language of the 'stink' (and all the related semantic and pragmatic implications underlying its production) into another category, so displacing the denounced 'stink' from the semantic class of 'ownership or possession-related disturbances.' In this way, the judge gives rise to a renewed standard of 'normality' in the use of ownership, thereby also of space and, ultimately, in the conceptualizations of the same space. But such an arrival point will have been precisely the outcome of a process of intercultural translation/transaction. In this regard, it is of the utmost importance to emphasize that categorical migrations do not constitute an epiphany of pre-existing truths. Such migrations, even when institutional rhetoric labels them as the result of 'acts of ascertainment,' are rather the final step of creative processes, that is, the ultimate consequence of axiological choices that mold categories, and ongoing semanticization and re-semanticization activities that, in turn, carve out their borders from the stream of experience. Intercultural translation and the related unveiling of the implicit connotations underlying the conduct adopted by people from different cultures are acts of invention, just as in the generation of metaphors. Because of its inventive feature, intercultural translation is equivalent to a political act. This characteristic cannot be successfully eluded, even though its results cannot be aprioristically predetermined or prearranged.

No single party to such kinds of disputes, nor any apparatuses of categorical schemes—inevitably culturally determined—can possess the objective truth, the 'winning' evidence, so powerful that it can silence and *evict* Others' cognitive schemes and uses of spatial dimension, in turn, mirroring the existential projections of Others' subjectivities. Objectivity, universality and, consequentially, the related thinghood' of space can be—even if only in an interlocutory fashion— nothing but the outcome of a symmetrical comparison, reciprocal listening and translation/ transaction between different connotative landscapes. But these are precisely the constitutive elements of categorization processes carried out along the pathways of an inclusive interculturality, that is, one that is approached in a symmetrical and bottom-up way.

Along the above outlined narrative unfolding of meanings and implicit connotations of people's behaviors—the *invisible/mute parts* of the morphological appearance of cultural habits—human rights can serve as a sort of semantic magnet and, at the same time, an intercultural bridge. By virtue of their outstanding axiological qualities, the inherent plasticity of value categories, and the vagueness/ambiguity of legal statements on human and/or fundamental rights, they can readily serve as interfaces of translation between different cultures and be used as a metaphorical ground to support the *categorical migration* [62] of people's behaviors. If intended in this way, they can serve as factors of inclusive universalization, namely as teleological horizons and, at the same time, as a semantic underpinning liable to trigger creative generalizations. Moreover, if so envisaged, human rights could also escape from their current configuration as hierarchical and aprioristic paradigms of legitimacy, as such too often exposed to ethnocentric declinations.

Some readers could contend, at this point, that a 'stink' always remains a 'stink.' Nonetheless, the topic of categorical migration processes does not refer so much to a seemingly magic modification of people's immediate sensory perceptions—a phenomenon that, however, can occur and actually does take *place*. Rather, by means of such migrations, 'stink' ceases to be *only* a disturbing entity—and thereby amenable to be qualified as an invasive emission—and repositions itself, along with the overall chain of semantic and pragmatic relationships conveying its production, within another categorical frame (for example: health care, religious symbols or rites, cultural-identitarian implications, housing needs, people's freedom, and so on). Of course, this argument can be extended to noise, fumes, etc. In any case, to undertake the categorical migration pathway, all such events—including the sound of bells or the invocations of the praying muezzins spreading throughout space from religious buildings—will have to inscribe themselves within the margins of reasonability and through a balanced negotiation between the exigencies of all of the parties to each particular dispute.

However, reasonability is merely another name used to label a process that continually re-defines categorical borders, spaces of subjectivity and, therefore, spatial categories and scansions: this is ultimately a process of semantic negotiation. Legal leverage enables people to obtain social effectiveness for their claims aimed at the reconfiguration of categorical borders of a specific action, for example encapsulated in a demand for legitimation regarding a particular emission. If used for such purposes, human and/or fundamental rights can really become concrete resources for

---

[62] As regards the intercultural use of human rights, see also Ricca (2008, 2013b) and *ibidem* for further bibliography on this topic. In these texts, I stress the necessity to use and situate human rights within the practices of translation in a horizontal way, precisely as interfaces or metaphorical *grounds* to translate the meanings acted by people, rather than in a vertical/hierarchical way, that is, as axes ordered to the hierarchical assessment and control of individual actions. The danger of an aprioristic, essentializing, and hierarchical-pyramidal use of the discursive fabric of human rights is that each 'cultural faction' apodictically assumes its own behavioral patterns as the prototypical implementation of those rights. An almost unavoidable result is that the claim for human and/or fundamental rights takes place without any process of translation/transaction of meanings and connotative webs underlying the behaviors carried out by the conflicting subjects. Consequently, in these cases, the inclusive potentialities related to the universalizing inclination inherent in the discourse on rights will inevitably transform into both a premise and an alibi for social seclusion and ethnocentrism. So, those who will not adapt or do not coincide with the prototype of 'humanity' carved out by each 'cultural faction' on the basis of the discursive fabric of rights, will be judged precisely for this reason to be *in-human*. This means that such people will be implicitly and radically delegitimized in their claims for renegotiating the patterns of coexistence and the script to use social spaces in an intercultural way. For a case of 'categorical migration' with regard to intercultural controversies, and specifically the 'veil issue,' see Ricca (2013a, pp. 198–202).

allowing and supporting processes of intercultural translation and transaction. Such kinds of categorical transformations can also occur within infra-cultural dynamics. People tend to adapt to new smells, noises, etc. If this takes place, it is because of 'reasonable-ness' and a recognition of the 'worthiness' of behaviors that produce 'new' emissions. Through such processes of adaptation, social actors develop new habits that little by little can transform into new perceptive *habitudes* and *customs*, that is to say, the nub of new cultural standards of *normal tolerability*. On the other hand, social history teaches us that all thresholds of 'normality' in any field of experience undergo processes of re-negotiation.

The spreading of a social awareness that law, if properly called into question and utilized, can serve as a means to convey intercultural translations and the renegotiations of spaces and their meanings would represent a significant improvement in the managing of pluralism and a way to avert the power devices shrouded in the alleged thinghood/empiricism of spatial categories.

In contexts concerned with massive and recent immigration waves, social plurality—as shown above—takes the shape of the multicultural use of spaces in which people coexist. In these spaces of coexistence—just as in a multicultural and multi-religious condominium—the ability to understand the meaning of Others' conduct and, therefore, the web of sense underlying neighbors' emissions implies a re-examination of the spatial and temporal threads that go beyond the 'here' and 'now.' The narrative plots epitomized by each 'emissive action' go far and beyond the walls of condominiums. They call into play, as part of their connotative and legally significant elements, what simultaneously takes *place* in the original countries of each co-owner. Examples include religious festivals, familiar relationships that are multi-situated and thereby carried on astride the arrival and departure places of migration, social practices engendered and framed by the interspaces of experience opened by the use of contemporary technological communicative tools. All of this creates an interspace capable of making semiotically close and synchronous what happens, had happened and will happen in the other hemisphere, and so on.

Moreover, people act within the space-time topicality of condominiums by relying upon cognitive schemes that are enshrined in their memory, which in turn is nothing but a dynamic recollection of cumulative knowledge achieved and transmitted by their community of origin. So, once again, understanding and legally qualifying what individuals are doing in a dimension of spatial and temporal proximity requires a sort of trip towards and through the *territories* of the physical and semantic 'remoteness;' the same remoteness that is presentified, namely made topical, by the actions and *promanations* of human actors. All of this looms as a chorological dimension, in which space and word stay together, are co-extending, along a semiotic *continuum*. The same space and its experience appear, therefore, as a semiotic framework that stems from the pragmatic reciprocal crossing of physically distant circuits within the topicality of the lived present to which the proximity in condos exposes. When and insofar as such a phenomenon is mediated by a skilled use of the law, we could say that condos are living (or might live) within an interspace, the creation of which would be conveyed by law and especially by human and/or fundamental rights if and to the extent that they are used as intercultural translation interfaces and inter-spatial transducers.

The legal chorology of coexistence in condos, if seen through the experiential spectrum of invasive emissions, transforms condominiums, therefore, into (potentially) mobile *places* for the epiphany of a planetary ubiquity of both different subjectivities and manifold existential spaces. Within these contexts of coexistence the 'elsewhere' becomes close, contiguous and even intimate, as if what is *here* and *now* would be abruptly displaced and intermingled with other remote places, so as to acquire new meanings precisely as a result of these new semiotic relationships.

The last sentence could sound counter-intuitive. It is, however, precisely such a semiotic inter-space (in some respects to be considered as *trans-geographical*) that substantiates the real dimension in which experience unfolds, namely the environment that condos/subjects actually live in. In multicultural condominiums, it is almost as if the whole world has found (or, at least, sought to find) a spatial and semiotic synthesis precisely through the law's qualifying function.

Adjusting to the 'worldominium' environment requires, however, an intercultural cognitive commitment. In a sense, the multicultural 'worldominium' is a kind of metaphor and, at the same time, a laboratory to test coexistence among cultural diversities on a planetary scale. A failure in understanding and making the most of the potentialities tied to an intercultural use of human rights and, more generally, the law (even within condominiums) could hover like a dark omen of our human capacity (or incapacity) to avert global conflicts. If it is true that the world is a stairway, it would be wise for us to learn to run peacefully up and down (as in Escher's recursive drawings or Picasso's multi-perspective pictorial representations) the staircases of the condominiums that host our *apartments*. Our hopes for a peaceful coexistence in that particular condominium that the world has become might have already begun on the landings of our *worldominiums*.

Condos and 'worldominium' are, however, chorologically related places. They transmute one into another. In Klee's terms, we can say that every condominium, if multiculturally populated, is an icon and an epitome of many stories previously widespread all over the world. At the same time, those stories can serve as 'weaving threads' for the germinal *figuration* of new worlds of coexistence. To achieve this result, the temporal dis-composition and the intercultural re-composition of things, events and conducts is an unavoidable passage. But it requires, precisely in Klee's terms, the use of our human capacity for creating culture, namely a renewed polyphonic commitment to retread and prolong the Genesis of possible worlds in which humankind can live.

References

Anderson B, Harrison P (2010) The promise of non-representational theories. In: Anderson B, Harrison P (eds) Taking-place: non-representational theories and geography. Ashgate, Farnham, pp 1–36

Baumgartner M (2014) Paul Klee: from structural analysis and morphogenesis to art. In: Sallis J (ed) The philosophical vision of Paul Klee. Brill, Leiden
Baxi U (2002) The future of human rights. OUP, Oxford
Bell LS, Nathan AJ, Peleg I (eds) (2001) Negotiating culture and human rights. Columbia University Press, New York
Belting H (2008) Florenz und Bagdad. Eine westöstliche Geschichte des Blicks. C. H. Beck, München
Bhambra G, Shilliam R, Baxi U (eds) (2009) Silencing human rights. Palgrave Macmillan, Basingstoke
Boehm G (2014) Genesis: Paul Klee's temporalization of form. In: Sallis J (ed) The philosophical vision of Paul Klee. Brill, Leiden, pp 5–24
Cappelletti P (2003) L'inafferrabile visione. Pittura e scrittura in Paul Klee. Jaca Book, Milano
Chryssochoou X (2004) Cultural diversity: its social psychology. Blackwell, Malden
Clarke KM, Goodale M (2010) Introduction: understanding the multiplicity of justice. In: Clarke KM, Goodale M (eds) Mirrors of justice: law and power in a post-cold war era. Cambridge University Press, New York, pp 1–27
Cowan JK, Dembour M-B, Wilson RA (2001) Introduction. In: Cowan JK, Dembour M-B, Wilson RA (eds) Culture and rights: anthropological perspectives. Cambridge University Press, Cambridge
Dewey J (1916) Democracy and education. The Macmillan Company, New York
Douglas-Scott S (2014) Law after modernity. Hart, Oxford
Douzinas C (2000) The end of human rights: critical legal thought at the turn of the century. Hart, Oxford
Drobnik J (2006) Eating nothing: cooking aromas in art and culture. In: Drobnick J (ed) The smell culture reader. Berg, Oxford, pp 342–356
Engle MS (2006a) Human rights and gender violence: translating international law into local justice. Chicago University Press, Chicago
Engle MS (2006b) Transnational human rights and local activism: mapping the middle. Am Anthropol CVIII 1:38–51
Fabbri P (2007) Transcritture in Alberto Savinio: il dicibile e il visibile. il Verri, "lettera/immagine". www.paolofabbri.it/saggi/savinio.html
Fabian J (1983) Time and the other: how anthropology makes its object. Columbia University Press, New York
Farinelli F (2003) Geografia. Un'introduzione ai modelli del mondo. Einaudi, Torino
Farinelli F (2009) Crisi della ragione cartografica. Einaudi, Torino
Gibbs RW Jr (2005) Embodiment and cognitive science. Cambridge University Press, Cambridge
Goodale M, Merry SE (eds) (2007) The practice of human rights: tracking law between global and local. CUP, Cambridge
Gris J (2013) [or Paris 1946] Posibilidades de la pintura. Casimiro, Madrid
Hastrup K (2001) Legal cultures and human diversity: the challenge of diversity. Brill, The Hague
Henare A, Holbraad M, Wastell S (2007) Introduction: thinking through things. In: Henare A, Holbraad M, Wastell S (eds) Thinking through things: theorising artefacts ethnographically. Routledge, London, pp 1–32
Herbert Robert L (2000) Modern artists on art: second. enlarged edition. Dover Publications, Mineola
Hyde A (2006) Offensive bodies. In: Drobnick J (ed) The smell culture reader. Berg, Oxford, pp 53–58
Jakobson R (1960) Closing statements: linguistics and poetics. In: Sebeok TA (ed) Style in language. The MIT Press, Cambridge
Jewell KJ (2004) The Art of enigma: the De Chirico brothers and the politics of modernism. Pennsylvania University Press, University Park
Klee P (2013 [1923]) In: Gale M (ed) Creative confession. Tate Publishing, London

Kövecses Z (2003) Metaphor and emotion: language, culture, and body in human feeling. Maison des Sciences de l'Homme – CUP, Paris – Cambridge
Mahalansan MF IV (2006) Immigrant lives and the politics of olfaction in the global city. In: Drobnick J (ed) The smell culture reader. Berg, Oxford, pp 41–52
Messina M (2006) Paul Gauguin: un esotismo controverso. Firenze University Press, Firenze
Olsson G (2007) Abysmal: a critique of cartographic reason. The University of Chicago Press, Chicago
Olsson G (2011) Mapping the taboo. In: Daniels S, DeLyser D, Entrikin JN, Richardson D (eds) Envisioning landscapes, making worlds: geography and the humanities. Routledge, London, pp 35–43
Pallasmaa J (2005) The eyes of the skin: architecture and senses. Wiley, Chichester
Pallasmaa J (2011) The embodied image: imagination and imagery in architecture. Wiley, Chichester
Pickles J (2004) A history of spaces: cartographic reason, mapping, and the geo-coded world. Routledge, London
Ponce de León PG (2008) Juan Gris: La Pasión por el Cubismo. Libsa, Madrid
Ponzio A (2007) Fuori luogo. L'esorbitante nella riproduzione dell'identico. Meltemi, Roma
Ricca M (2008) Oltre Babele. Codici per una democrazia interculturale. Dedalo, Bari
Ricca M (2010) Riace, il futuro è presente. Naturalizzare il 'globale' tra immigrazione e sviluppo interculturale. Dedalo, Bari
Ricca M (2013a) Pantheon. Agenda della laicità interculturale. Torri del Vento, Palermo
Ricca M (2013b) Culture interdette. Modernità, migrazioni, diritto interculturale. Bollati Boringhieri, Torino
Ricca M (2014) Sapore, sapere del mondo. Tradizioni religiose e traduzioni alimentari. Daimon. Diritto comparato delle religioni 2014:33–66
Ricca M (2016a) Spazi di conversione. Una lettura corologica. Daimon – diritto comparato delle religioni 2016:91–144
Ricca M (2016b) Klee's cognitive legacy and human rights as intercultural transducers: modern art, legal translation, and micro-spaces of coexistence. CALUMET - Intercult Law Humanit Rev 3: 1–40. https://calumet-review.com/index.php/2016/09/10/klees-cognitive-legacy-and-human-rights-as-intercultural-transducers-modern-art-legal-translation-and-micro-spaces-of-coexistence/
Ricca M (2017) Ghostly spatialities in condominiums: nuisance law, legal geography, and intercultural chorology, pp 1–22. https://ssrn.com/abstract=3050729 or https://doi.org/10.2139/ssrn.3050729. Accessed 10 Oct 2017
Ricca M (2018a) Cultures in orbit, or justi-fying differences in cosmic space: on the significance of human rights under conditions of absolute a-territoriality. Int J Semiot Law 31:829–875. https://doi.org/10.1007/s11196-018-9578-5
Ricca M (2018b) *Ignorantia facti excusat*: legal liability and the intercultural significance of Greimas' "contrat de véridition". Int J Semiot Law 31:101–126. https://doi.org/10.1007/s11196-017-9529-6
Ricca M (2020a) Otherness, elsewhere, and the 'ecology' of law's implications: the semiotic oceans surrounding legal signification and its discriminatory exteriority/objectivity. Int J Leg Discourse 5(2):185–237
Ricca M (2020b) Don't uncover that face! Covid-19 masks and the niqab: ironic transfigurations of the ECtHR's intercultural blindness. Int J Semiot Law 19:1119–1143. https://doi.org/10.1007/s11196-020-09703-y
Ricca M (2022) Perpetually astride Eden's boundaries: the limits to the 'limits of law' and the semiotic inconsistency of 'legal enclosures'. Int J Semiot Law 35:179–229. https://doi.org/10.1007/s11196-020-09771-0
Sajò A (ed) (2004) Human rights with modesty: the problem of universalism. Martinus Nijhoff Publishers, Leiden
Sallis J (2015) Senses of landscapes. Northwestern University Press, Evanston

Savinio A (1992) Alberto Savinio: paintings and drawings, 1925-1952. Electa, Milano
Schuback MSC (2014) In-between painting and music—or, thinking with Paul Klee and Anton Webern. In: Sallis J (ed) The philosophical vision of Paul Klee. Brill, Leiden, pp 419–442
Watson SH (2009) Crescent moon over the rational: philosophical interpretations of Paul Klee. Stanford University Press, Stanford
Zumthor P (1993) La Mesure du monde. Seuil, Paris

Chapter 6
Errant Law

6.1 Inter-Subjectivity and Inter-Constitutionality: Transnational Mobility and Inclusive Citizenship

The inclusion of subjects within social contexts and related institutional circuits is a premise for democratic coexistence carried out under the sign of rights protection and Constitutionalism. Inclusive practices circle around the relationship between subjectivity and community. This is because the right to inclusion is delineated according to a specific conceptual and normative grammar. Caught in its main coordinates, this grammar goes under the 'citizenship' label.

A citizenship lexicon is inclusive if it is capable of integrating ordinarily shared differences (comprising values, principles, cognitive and communicative practices, rules, customs, etc.) extant in the social ground within a paradigm of sense/meaning. In a sense, in the relationship between inclusiveness and legal lexicon we can recognize the 'state of the art' of constitutional standards as developed within the liberal-democratic tradition. In the shadow of such standards, however, some problems take shape. They orbit around cultural contents and declinations of the platform of commonplaces often identified as indispensable assumptions for both social inclusion and cohesion. These main issues spring from the insufficiency of procedural versions of a grammar of subjectivity—elaborated by political philosophy and, then, adopted by legal thought—to assure equidistance, symmetrical coordination and responsiveness to law with respect to the lifestyles and the imaginaries articulated within the social ground of contemporary multi-religious and multicultural societies. I would therefore pose some questions that emerge from the exigency and difficulty of shaping inclusive features of cultural and legal subjectivity.

Who are the subjects who can aspire to inclusion? How and to what extent can the pluralistic dynamic bear the centrifugal force of differences without itself disintegrating? What are the features of subjectivity that can constitute the objects of inclusion processes? What is the relationship between inclusion and cultural difference with regard to the elaboration of a citizenship lexicon? And what aspects

M. Ricca, *Intercultural Spaces of Law*, Law and Visual Jurisprudence 10,
https://doi.org/10.1007/978-3-031-27436-7_6

of culture should be considered? Only the psycho-social features or also those that are normative-institutional? What is, therefore, the relevance of the multiple belongings of single subjects, and which should be included? How may normative and legal codes that are inherent to these different belongings reciprocally integrate within an inclusive legal lexicon of citizenship? And how should the autonomy and/or individual self-determination of subjects be recognized compared to the reception of normative items of legal and institutional systems to which migrants belong?

The set of questions proposed above constitutes the source but also the critical front of contemporary constitutionalism. Its matrix, as regards political-institutional legitimation, has much to do with the treatment of religious differences in the dawn of modernity. Actually, within the Western tradition, this issue seems to have reached a point of relative stability (save for its projections in post-colonial contexts). Currently, instead, it seems the dynamics of citizenships and democratic subjectivity are once again raising concerns.[1] But, what is the reason for this renewed coming to the fore of religious belonging in combination with the cultural features of people? Why do people appeal to religion to claim their own difference, their own right to difference? Such further questions can find answers and root precedents—or, at least, some of both—in the relationship between culture and equality.

The history of constitutionalism is doubtless intertwined with the geographical-colonial discoveries era.[2] European-Western thought is incline, on average, to asserts that 'such' history is completely 'modern.' Nonetheless, precisely because of such exclusive idea of modernity, this assertion constitutes a tenet that runs the risk of betraying an overall lack of historical perspective. What happened in Europe from 1500 onward is certainly woven into the coeval disclosing of new geographical and economic perspectives and possibilities. As Europe proceeded in its colonial 'enterprises,' the rise of jus-rationalism and, later, constitutionalism bestowed on its planetary expansion a surreptitiously universalistic aura, which, however, was a kind of 'emanation' from the political strategies devised to defuse the religious wars that had marked the dawn of the modern age in many European countries.

The ideas of equality and freedom supported and proclaimed by constitutional declarations and legal codifications sprang up from the exigency to neutralize the conflictive potentialities of religious difference, at least if used as a tool to legitimate polarized claims for political power. However, the religious differences inhabiting Europe at that time were flowing substantially within the riverbed of Christianity. Actually, the work of modelling social and legal subjectivity configured by

[1] Within the enormous literature on this topic, see Sullivan et al. (2011). For a perspective inclusive of the Asiatic world, backed up by an anthropological approach stressing that Western secularization is only 'one' of many possible forms of secularization, see the essays collected in Bubandt and Beek (2012). On this topic, I refer also to Ricca (2008, 2013b).

[2] See the interesting remarks proposed on this topic by Bhambra (2007).

rationalism and the Enlightenment gave very little space, if any, to Hebraism[3]; not to mention Islam, Confucianism, Buddhism, and Hinduism, at that time socially absent from the demographical ground of European territories—or, in any case, politically ignored. The grammar of equality and the patterns of subjectivities designed and forged by the legal and political language of modern Europe took root in Christian culture. Both drew their own constitutive substance from the conflation of Roman law and Christian theology realized between the Low Middle Age and the Proto-Modernity period.

Despite the forest of dualisms traced between politics and religion, internal and external *forum*, ethics and law, etc., drawn by modern thought, a deep semantic of legal subjectivity remained substantially unbroken, at least with regard to the coordination of quotidian coexistence. If the logic of natural and/or fundamental rights engendered a divide between public and private, authority and freedom, hitherto alien to the legal and political European lexicon, on the other hand, the forms of legal subjectivity of common laws (civil law, penal law, and so on) remained basically unchanged. In their essential structure, civil (contract, inheritance, etc.) and penal (typology of crimes, forms of responsibility) models were not altered, so passing through the Pillars of Hercules of modernity, they were substantially immune from any radical upheavals.[4] They iterated ancient forms, although nestled in an institutional structure emancipated from the control of ecclesiastical authorities and pivoted on freedom of conscience and individual autonomy. Nonetheless, those models were self-defining as universal. And they actually were universal, but only with respect to the grammatical-abstract form of their enunciations, certainly not in their cultural substance. Such legal forms conveyed, in this way, the universal potentialities enshrined within declaration of rights into the frames of meaning and legal experience imbued with Christian ethics and anthropology.

In this regard, actually, Europeans proved to be rather (culturally) myopic. They failed to figure out that the universality they professed was nothing but the mirrored image of their own cultural identity, at least in its basic articulations. This lack of critical consideration and self-distancing were probably dependent upon a specific contingency: modern legal language was presented, despite its semantic Roman-Christian matrices, as the result of a process of abstraction from difference. Beyond respective religious belongings (Catholicism, Lutheranism, Orthodox Christianity, Calvinism, Gallicanism, Anglicism, etc.), legal-social cartographies of civil and

[3]It is true that in *De jure belli ac pacis*, Grotius makes some references to the Hebrew ethical-religious universe, but they are only genealogical referrals to ethical-legal categories forged and remolded through the transition from the Roman legal tradition to the Christian-medieval one.

[4]These changes were especially significant toward the rhetoric of legitimacy underpinning legal rules, primarily contractual discipline. However, transformations that could appear extremely relevant from within the Western tradition's gaze, would appear instead almost insignificant if observed from another cultural point of view. Regarding the philosophical-normative continuities within the category of contracts through the different historical periods, see, among others, Gordley (1991); Decock (2013).

penal subjectivity aspired to appear as a kind of commonplace, the projection of a Reason shared by all human beings and, at the same time, a gift from a single God—even if made multifaceted through the spectrum of confessional differences—the Christian god. Probably, also as a consequence of this perspectival configuration, modern law processed by jus-rationalism was subsequently portrayed as free from religious influences and as a pure product of Human Reason.[5]

This false and illusive assertion of universality and *a*-religiosity is at its roots a twofold 'error' in the political perspective assumed by Europe. Modern Western law soon began to 'err' all over the planet, riding the grim steed of colonialism. In the face of this potent combination, all cultural differences, in turn ingrained in their own basins of sense anthropologically intertwined with religious experience, appeared to be irredeemably stained by an unacceptable superstitious connotation.[6] In this way, while its Christian matrices were dissimulated or concealed, Western law was simultaneously taken as a yardstick to accuse the normative models of people, the victims of colonization, of irrationality and religious/superstitious influences. In other words, while Western law was geographically *errant*, it was 'errant' about itself, on its own cultural coordinates, even if it was finding precisely in this error the fuel and legitimacy for its spatial and... missionary erring.[7]

Today that huge historical *error* is followed by another one, specular to the former, and traceable around the management of migration phenomena by contemporary Western states. Cultural Alterity—descended from the Otherness that was once the victim of colonial deeds—is breaking out today in Western social scenarios in the wake of migrations, triggering once again the phenomenon of fideistic-religious antagonism between differences. Such a process unfolds along a complex and meandering sequence that results also from the resilience of interpretive schemes of the colonial past inside the memory of its actors. The 'Other' that comes into view, is perceived and understood as a subject bringing a 'burden' of diversity. And this diversity depends on their culture, which is portrayed and understood as an

[5]In the passage from jus-rationalism to legal Enlightenment, the idea of a reason—and legal rationality—self-produced by human nature took shape. Such a rhetorical-epistemological move was also a political one. It led to its completion the process of emancipation of reason opened by the rationalism derived from Second Scholasticism. It is to be underlined, however, that the reason of Grotius was a human prerogative, hence universal, because it was however a God's gift. And it was precisely because of this gift, already enshrined in human nature, that reason—and ethical-legal reason, too—could boast and claim its own autonomy, its universal relevance regardless of the particular 'God' in which each individual was believing. In other words, the principles of natural law as thought by Grotius are to be considered as universal and valid for all 'even if God would not be' just because God has already given reason to human beings. Therefore, He could not avoid recognise Himself in something that is intrinsically good since it was previously made object of His giving on behalf of human beings. Behind these evident vicious circles, at that time, there were, in a permanent turmoil, the issues tied to the so-called controversy on universals—and, therefore, the ethical-legal universals, too.

[6]Although his theoretical approach to anthropology appears no longer acceptable, an extraordinary denounce of this attitude is in Frazer (2000).

[7]On these issues, see Glenn (2005).

alienating factor. But, in the eyes of those who host, culture and difference are, obviously, only features that are typical, idiomatic of the Other. Besides, that one's own culture tends to camouflage itself as nature, dressing in the guises of the commonplace, is well known. In this respect, the envisaging of the 'cultural' is a bit like the perception of smells. What is perceived are only the Other's smells (. . .or stinks). Conversely, inurement to our own *odors* makes them evaporate from the perceptive horizon.

The yardstick of the Other's cultural difference is—or, even better, has been for some time —the alleged absolute laicism and/or secularization of Western lifestyles and legal systems. And, since within the antagonism between identities polarization is always sharp and integral, if Western languages were self-proclaiming as secularized and rational, then those other-than-Western, because of their Otherness, could not fail to be qualified as folkloric and religiously featured. Difference has become so increasingly radicalized that it has transfigured into diversity, and then, in turn, into ethnic-religious polarization. Nonetheless this has proven to be a very dangerous play, if only because the Others have quickly been able to recognize the anthropological-cultural nature of Christianity. So, at one point, the mirroring effect, typical of all conflicts between identities, prompted the Others to recognize themselves, the cornerstone of their identity, precisely in the religiosity with which Westerners reproached them. Simultaneously, however, the same Westerners have been progressively re-wrapping themselves with the same Christian symbols that they presumed they had definitively dismissed and abandoned. In brief, universalism as derived from the process of rationalization-secularization that occurred inside modern Western culture was and still looks to be the offspring of an incomplete project. The problems with public and legal subjectivity, currently torn apart by conflicts between identities, are the ineluctable retaliation of that dissimulated incompleteness, in turn the consequence of the blind refusal to consider cultures swept away by the colonial wave as deserving the same respect and dignity afforded to the minds of victorious Westerners.[8] So, the 'elsewhere' that becomes near, by means of migrations, seems to make present and synchronic something that just yesterday would have appeared a-synchronic if compared with the Euro-American present.[9]

The same modernity embodied, acted, and 'grasped' by Others, by virtue of their readiness for geographical displacement, abruptly revives faith-based political conflicts. The pervasive power of the imaginaries that support the appeal to religion determines, thus, a radicalization of conflicts between differing visions of subjectivity and the framing of them in terms of a multiculturalism mostly gauged on a pre-ordered repertoire of religious belonging.[10] This interpretive pattern is widespread even today in public opinion. Notwithstanding the fact that its fortunes date

[8] See Muthu (2003).

[9] See Marramao (2008).

[10] Essentially, this was the tenet, anthropologically unacceptable but politically capable of an inauspicious success, proposed 20 years ago by Huntington (1996).

back many years, its rough schematism is nonetheless still shared. The pattern assimilates religions and cultures without any distinction between the denominational and the anthropological dimensions of religious experience. Furthermore, it ends up by pigeonholing cultural features into frames and systems of belonging classified in an aprioristic and stereotypical way. Some questions proposed above derive, at least partially, precisely from both the wide adoption of such models by social agencies and the resulting institutional consequences.

Freezing and packing individuals into systemic-normative patterns of subjectivity, as if persons were mass-coined copies, is at the source of some typical problems engendered by a multiculturalist governance of cultural and religious differences. This approach—despite the most recent attempts to actualize it by giving it a dialogical-pluralist semblance—[11]does not consider culture as a dynamic factor, and as such at the disposal of individuals' choices and substantially coincident with a creative competence that can be activated by each in tune with the relevant environmental contingencies. Quite the opposite, such a view produces, especially with regard to its legal implementation, an essentialization of cultures, reducing them to a repertoire of rules and practices. Cultural difference ends up, thus, being traced almost exclusively through its symbols, the most spectacular and self-evident morphological features—basically folkloric—related to its material expressions. But what goes missing, in this way, is the ability to articulate, just through one's own cultural competence, paths of sense and practice oriented to creatively construe the existential experience of persons.[12] So, the research and the understanding of cultural difference becomes coextensive with the possibility of finding objective/material evidence that proves certain ties between a given behavior and its indexes of systemic codification within various traditions, religious orthopraxis, and normative systems of both ethical and legal kinds ascribed to sharply distinct social and/or ethnic groups.[13] If observed from the point of view proper to state law, problems related to the inclusion of difference turn, consequently, into problems of the traceability and admissibility of norms/rules able to certify cultural habits. Here is, precisely, the deep reference of the alternative question raised above: will the result feature the inclusion of the psycho-social aspects of a persons' behavior or rather the normative criteria and patterns that rule an individuals' actions within cultural and/or legal systems of belonging and/or origin[14]?

---

[11] Among the many voices of authors related to this approach, see, for all, Modood (2019a, b).

[12] Regarding this reification or *cosification* of the webs of sense that give substance to culture, and the compromising and commodifying feature of so-called (and even too often praised) *accommodations*, see Ricca (2018, 2020). My criticism focuses on the tendency (maybe inevitable) to gauge accommodating negotiations on the morphological features of the symbolic indexes related to cultural identity and the consequential contrast of such practices with an understanding of culture as creative and self-transformative (therefore, coincident with the ability to continually renew people's experiential coordinates).

[13] See Renteln (2004), Renteln and Foblets (2009), Eisenberg (2005, 2009).

[14] An analysis of legal pluralism and its relationships (not coextensive) with interculture, can be found in Ricca (2013c, pp. 297–322). For an analytical-critical review of legal pluralism, see

Relationships between cultures are relationships between persons, thinking and perceiving individuals. Cultures are not things roaming the streets. Culture—as has been assumed above—is a 'knowing to do' embodied in dynamic praxis engendered by the use of habits and interpretive flexible schemes. This does not mean that origins, education, and stocks of knowledge have no importance in the interpretation of a personal action and its sense. Rather, it should be emphasized that each individual does not coincide with '*his own origin,*' his belonging. In other words, migration, and geographical displacements are 'removals,' trans-*lations* (to be intended according to its etymological roots), and transitions across contexts of meaning. Every contact between differences re-articulates cultural knowledge, if only because the mind has to react to and interpret answers from the environment and, in turn, interrogate it. All this triggers processes of metamorphosis that, in many cases, correspond to the need for change engendered precisely by the exigency to remain themselves even across different worlds, within contexts of signification different from those previously experienced.

The problems concerning cultural inclusion rise from inter-subjective relationships, their paths, their unfolding, and they have to find in them their semantic *metronome*. On the contrary, curtailing the inter-subjective plots of interculture by inclosing them into sequences of translation between normative schemes runs the

Melissaris (2009); Griffiths (2001). An anti-essentialist proposal concerning legal pluralisms is developed by Tamanaha (2000). A critical approach to not-definitional proposals regarding the issue 'what is law?', assumed as a kernel of the 'legal pluralism challenge,' is included in my analysis of intercultural law in Ricca (2013c, p. 27). See, moreover, the interesting essay of Dupré (2007), who calls for taking a praxeological approach to legal pluralism. Both in Tamanaha and Dupré, however, there is a sort of imprint deriving from the more general and traditional vision of legal pluralism, focused primarily on the definition of 'what law is' in and of itself: an issue that in the more or less recent past emerged from a criticism against legal statism and was dialectically colored by an ideological anti-statism waved in defense of so-called *unofficial laws*. The authors' view, actually, is not free from a vision from without. Their ideal goal, rather, seems to be oriented to demonstrate that if it is law, even not pertaining to the state, then 'state law' must listen to, or relate to, through symmetrical coordination, other forms and experiences of the 'juridical.' Also the praxeological and concretely anti-definitional proposal put forward by Dupré (in a sense more 'situated' and less abstract than the 'representational' approach of Tamanaha for whom law is anything and everything that people consider as such: a perspective that is rhetorically efficacious, but pragmatically indecisive) leads to an activity that merely recognizes, as if law were something that each scholar must only observe and not inevitably concur to produce, if only through its categorizations and qualifications. This vision—however paradoxical it might seem—is influenced and imprinted by the positivist and formalistic epistemology traceable also in the neo-Kantian framework elaborated by Hans Kelsen. Intercultural use of law—at least, as I imagine it—aims to produce and promote the same effects that Dupré believes visible in some forms of inter-legal connection conveyed by people's actions. Moreover, it is oriented—as its crucial feature—to determine intercultural inclusion through the use of the very same state law. This goal can be achieved producing conditions such that the state law collapses on its premises of legitimacy, which are in turn tied to and ingrained in the same cultural constants set in motion and remolded by the change of the chorological coordination of contemporary legal and social experience. On legal chorology, see below. In this regard, the initiative of Fontanelli (2010) to convey the legal pluralism theory proposed by Santi Romano in current international debate seems very praiseworthy, risk of caging the adaptation processes within a-prioristic frames detached from reality and the real needs of people. Facing coexistence problems from behind a desk, verifying the legitimacy of cultural claims according to their correspondence to normative codes certified authoritatively, delivering translation based only on a bookish knowledge of Otherness, trying to put texts in dialogue rather than persons, all of this stands to make a caricature of intercultural processes. The results of such strategies can only fail, leading to—what is worse—an increase of identitarian stiffening. The inefficiency of politics for inclusion and cultural integration will be inevitable as long as, rather than giving voice to people through a serious commitment to field research, both lawyers and public agencies think themselves capable of filtering the Others' claims through rigid and predetermined ethical-normative schemes. On their own, rules have nothing to say beyond majestically iterating themselves. Every rule is a product, an outcome of cultural processes, not their original and self-determining 'prime mover.' On the contrary, any condition that supports the engendering of intercultural inter-subjectivity is already an experience in and of itself, outright and new, which precisely for its novelty should be allowed to self-produce in a transactional fashion its own rules and codes of peaceful reproduction.

The problematic nature of integration managed by means of *comparison and accommodation of different sets of rules* nestles at the core of the very idea of inclusive citizenship. The issue of 'what is to be included' is faced, typically, in a legal-formal and/or institutional way. Taking as a model the hierarchical-normative taxonomy, subjectivity is considered as a mere projection of the legal system: as if the subject, observed under the lens of the law, could be wholly molded by legal words and categories.[15] Such a theoretical and operational paradigm is applied also to those who express and claim their own cultural difference. To assess such requests of recognition, their 'worthiness of protection,' scholars and institutional agencies undertake, first and foremost, the research of normative indexes that (allegedly) shape peoples' subjectivities. Anthropological, psychosocial, and cultural Otherness is turned, thus, into normative Alterity. Hence, the plurality of cultures undergoes a sort of mechanical conceptual substitution so as to transfigure itself and result in a plurality of legal systems. This operation seems to say that in the mirror of law (and in the eyes of lawyers) plurality can be nothing but the plurality and pluralism of legal rules.[16]

The formalistic-hierarchical-pyramidal configuration of legal experience and the related epistemological approach involve also human and/or fundamental rights and their uses. They are utilized as axes to introduce within the borders of state legal systems the normative sets that juridically qualify experiences and claims of the

[15]This is the traditional formalistic-positivistic approach to legal subjectivity and capacity. I have addressed this theoretical framework and its pragmatic implications with regard to the cultural and religious pluralism of contemporary societies more widely in Ricca (2013a). I refer to this essay for further bibliographical references on this topic.

[16]As regards the difficult relationships between legal pluralism and cultural plurality, and also for broad bibliographical references, Donlan (2011).

Other. The game of inclusion is played, therefore, according to the ascertainment of compatibility between normative codes used to 'recognize'—I would even say *to see*—Otherness, on one side, and human and/or fundamental rights, on the other. It is almost pointless to observe how in this way possibilities of intercultural negotiations substantially vanish as they are reduced to a 'calculation' of inter-normative compatibility carried out according to the exiguous rate of semantic transaction allowed by the rigidity typical of legal and prescriptive utterances.

Actually, the semantic flexibility and vagueness of more general normative provisions work with a particular intensity and can prove to be useful for the purpose of cultural inclusion when inscribed within the semantic spectrum of normative utterances and treated as concrete life situations rather than rules. If related to practical behaviors and common language expressions, the more abstract the words and categories employed by legal rules, the more ambiguous they will turn out to be, because it will be very difficult to determine what is inside and what must remain outside the borders of each category related to one rather than another social fact, behavior or object. But it is simply impossible to establish once and for all clear categorical borders. On the contrary, as soon as such borders are drawn, immediately and almost compellingly features and profiles of continuity between the semantic features inside and outside each specific category[17] come to the fore.

The *defining*, even if taken in and of itself, seems to engender the foundation to dispute critically the semantic *con-fines* or borders previously traced. This is because the descriptive parts of legal statements try (in vain) to capture a social reality that is continuously changing and mobile. Actually, things and events of the world do not have labels. Our attempts to superimpose an order onto the stream of phenomena, social as well as natural, have some inherent limitations. Categories make sense only if they prove capable of including within their semantic spectrum that which remains permanent over time. Permanency is, however, an abstraction drawn on the differences punctuated by the flowing of time, namely the succession of differences. This is the logical status of categorical generality. Therefore, the shape and borders of categories depend on our choices, ends, biological dispositions, and mental activity. Our conceptualizations of the world are outcomes of the interactions between environment and organism, between what is over there and what is in here. This interplaying is our *real* reality. Its interactions are continuously changing or, in any case, exposed and vulnerable to change. Categorical borders and *confines* previously established are seen to be, therefore, no longer consistent, because experience and the related interactions with the environment can reveal new or overlooked continuities between different semantic spectrums, as well as connotative (as well as denotative) discontinuities and differences within the same category.[18] Continuities

[17] Cfr. Bauman (1991), Blumenberg (2007), although these two authors come from very different points of view.

[18] This kind of continuity, in a sense, dismantles the implicit hierarchy that we assume to be extant between the different salience of what is considered to be inside a category and what is outside. Instead of this hierarchy the surfacing of connotative continuities determines a sort of horizontality between what was supposed out and what remained in. This kind of dismantled hierarchy applies

and discontinuities so emerging comprise the compositional elements of each category. Such connotative (and denotative) conflation and agitation compel us to redefine and remold categorical spectrums, both by unifying and by separating the pre-existent semantic borders. This effect is prompted by history, social change, experiential succession, and the overlapping and interplaying of different points of view and ways of life. In short, the same function of categories in their relationship with the environment determines just such an attitude to change and, therefore, an openness to the inclusion of the 'new' and the 'other.'

Conversely, when the poles of comparison consist in two or more legal utterances, what assumes semantic salience is mainly their morphological-linguistic difference. Such a difference becomes, therefore, the focus of comparison, so that the occurrence of formal linguistic differences between the poles of comparison ends up hampering the ethical and cognitive processes of cultural transactions and negotiations. In other words, form and morphological appearance, along with the partisan strains towards their maintenance, become a bone of contention. Despite their apparent clearness, both perceived exterior features and words when taken in themselves cloud the visibility and the same investigation of the context of sense (their indexical dimension), which instead would allow one to narratively situate their semantic potentialities, thus opening the door to teleological overlapping and, therefore, to an increasingly flexible inter-categorical and intercultural translation/transaction.

Following the formalistic-normative approach, on the other hand, the challenge of an inclusive citizenship seems doomed to remain entangled in the technical 'skirmishes' and polarizations of inter-legal pluralism (or inter-legality). Such an end point, however, is reached by overlooking the fact that the normative cartographies of citizenships constitute the effect, the consequence, of experiences of inter-subjective communication occurring along pathways of social action that spread and unfold throughout the quotidian life of people.[19] Nevertheless—it is worth repeating—every vocabulary of citizenship is construed, and could not be imagined merely by debating from behind a desk. Extending the metaphor, this vocabulary includes lemmas and definitions as wells as phraseologies. This means that it is resting on the implicit and the 'invisible/mute' dimension that are coextensive with the constant and mobile combining of social habits. It is precisely upon this

also to space, and particularly to legally ordered territorial spaces, such as sovereign space. So, under a chorological gaze (as I will show below) spatial and categorical relationships will tend to lose their hierarchical aspect to assume a horizontal and mobile one, as such open to translation-transaction. All this can have enormous consequences for the hierarchical use of human rights as interfaces to manage confrontations between different cultural claims: see Ricca (2023). As regards, instead, the conflation between 'connotations' and 'denotations' within a connotative *continuum* as an effect resulting from the (metaphorical) interpenetration between different 'categorical spaces' (namely, both semantic and experiential/physical) see, again, Ricca (2022a: especially 187 nt. 15).

[19] Within a literature on the topic of citizenship now reaching colossal heights, I think it worth mentioning, in the same direction traced above, the scholarship of Trnka et al. (2013), where the authors address the topic of psycho-political relationships extant between the vocabulary of sensorial perceptions and the lexicon of national belonging and citizenship.

background that inter-subjectivity takes its shape and can begin to assume its features, at the very moment that the Other appears on the public scene: that is, an intercultural subjectivity. In confining the dynamics of intercultural translation and transaction of sense within a cage of inter-normativity and inter-legal pluralism, both scholars and institutional agencies enable a top-down, substantially *dirigiste* governance of practices deleterious to the possible emersion of an inclusive citizenship. The result is, and will be, by and large defective, and doomed to get bogged down in the quagmire of identitarian hardening that is in many ways homologous and mimetic to the rigidity of normative apparatuses, in comparison.

Across the board, human and/or fundamental rights work as axes of claims for cultural recognition. This occurs also because within legal systems of belonging, the semantic potentialities of statements of rights are designed to meld with statutory laws and the related institutes that condense into themselves cultural codes of individual conduct. Migration transplants attempt to assert the equal legitimacy of their normative apparatuses of belonging with respect to the parameter of human and/or fundamental rights within the arrival context. The inter-normative comparison/confrontation is, therefore, re-envisaged as a comparison between contending interpretations of rights. Behind the scenes, however, there is an almost absolute silence about the anthropological ground of sense of different claims for respective cultural subjectivity; inter-normative comparisons inevitably lead to the adoption of the most self-interested and ethnocentric interpretations of human rights, thereinafter defended as prototypical. However, the consequence of such an output redirection appears to be dramatically disastrous precisely for the purposes of inclusion. This is because incompatibilities between the statutory laws from different legal systems or between state laws and other kinds of legal/normative sources will inevitably turn into a polarization between foreign rules and human and/or fundamental rights. Put more coarsely, the final outcome will be such that everything is found to be contrasting with 'our' way of implementing human rights, and because all elements will be evaluated in a prototypical fashion, they will be deemed for the same reason as incompatible, if not in-human.[20] So, in the blink of an eye, the human rights discourse will have transfigured, despite its initial potential as an extraordinary means of inclusion, into a powerful weapon for the exclusion and stigmatization of Otherness.

Along the argumentative path just outlined, the basic problem arises from the custom, so particular to jurists, to set up a sort of logical and chronological priority of inter-normativity with respect to inter-subjectivity. It is, upon closer assessment, a widespread and pervasive practice that connotes a phenomenon, in some ways even desirable, labelled at its highest levels as inter-constitutionality and, related to human and/or fundamental rights, as 'inter-jus-fundamentality.'[21]

The spreading of supranational rights declarations and the corresponding judicial authorities of guarantee—from the ECHR to the International Court of Justice, the

---

[20] See Chryssochoou (2004), Ricca (2008).

[21] See Silveira (2014), Canotilho (2011).

European Court of Justice to the International Criminal Court, and so on—fuel a phenomenon otherwise referred to as the 'migration of constitutional ideas.'[22] Solutions previously assumed by some national courts and/or by judicial bodies of supranational legal systems exert their influence on other national and supranational judges, and vice versa. This process of 'contamination' engenders a kind of common legal language that can work as a thread of transmission on a global scale—and supranational, at least—of normative patterns for inter-subjective relationships.[23] What is more, every judicial decision on rights deals with possible relations between individuals and state legal orders, and directly or indirectly, between individuals. Furthermore, since constitutional interpretation is triggered by the examination of practical cases, and these are, in turn, qualified by means of the spectrum of legal rules (and cultures) of various countries, somehow inter-legality tends to foster *legal transplants*, as well, that are concerned with more than just the parameters of human rights interpretation: along with those parameters, normative paradigms of common statutory laws are also on the move. Such a game of reciprocal contaminations could support the shaping of a transnational lexicon of legal subjectivity. Along and within its coordinates, even individuals could gain the possibility of obtaining protection for their requests for the 'juridification' of their needs, characterized by cultural features/ connotations. In this regard, many scholars argue about dialogue among courts and inter-legality, meanwhile some others, more recently, debate the emergence of a cosmopolitan constitutional law[24] and 'inter-jus-fundamentality.'[25]

Nonetheless, a possible, reciprocal attuning among legal systems and rules would represent, in any case, the outcome of processes and logic that have very little to do with the germination at the grassroots level of a transcultural and social inter-subjectivity.

In many cases, the tracks of contamination run along the routes of power and the economic-political influences engendered among the international relationships between states and financial potentates, not to mention the misleading plots of 'reasons' argued by a well-oiled propagandist rhetoric machine of human rights

[22] See Choudhry (2006).

[23] It is an idea strongly defended also within the functionalist paradigm of legal networks. See Teubner (2005, 2012); Joerges et al. (2004), Ost and Van de Kerckhove (2002). In some versions, it may be sourced in its philosophical inspiration to the rhizomatic paradigm proposed at the time by Deleuze and then taken over by Philippopoulos-Mihalopoulos (2010, 2012). From a different perspective see also Santos (2002) and Santos and Rodríguez-Garavito (2005). For a criticism of the post-modern tendencies that consider the activation of normative networks as an opportunity for the emancipation of individuals from state constraints and related serializing generalizations, I refer to Ricca (2013c). There, I express my serious concerns regarding the risk that macro-systemic dynamics, along with the schemes serializing social subjectivities and overwhelming differences, annihilate individual agency, so as to transform the subject into nothing but an epiphenomenon of reticular/rhizomatic interactions. The legal intercultural approach I propose is targeted instead to enhance and promote individual creativity.

[24] See Teubner (2012).

[25] See Silveira (2014), Canotilho (2011).

organizations.[26] Legal transplants and migrations lead to solutions that draw paths of sense that are completely different from those traced or traceable by people who migrate and engage in an attempt to adapt their own cultural knowledge to new social environments. The semantic synthesis realized, actually or potentially, by people takes place at an anthropological-cultural level, and goes hand in hand with processes of intercultural transformation, translation, and transaction that are often of a creative kind; therefore, such processes are (predictably) rather asymmetrical with respect to the results of mere inter-normative contaminations or transplants. In turn, however, the outcomes of such processes of intercultural 'invention' could well aspire to inscribe themselves within the semantic spectrum of human and/or fundamental rights, fueling an axiological-constitutional pluralism that might be competitive with inter-normative pluralism and related models of inter-constitutionality.

A precise synchrony and tight parallelism between the pluralism stemming from the social field—namely, from the bottom up—and the pluralism of institutional sources—thereby, from the top down—could turn into a defective protection of cultural difference. Precisely because it is classified according to normative-cultural paradigms recognizable and already recognized by legal systems and courts, the differences conveyed by an intercultural inter-constitutionality of a formal-legalistic kind could overpower and overshadow the interculturality processed at a social-anthropological level, up to the point of inhibiting and ultimately ousting its expressions. In other words, pluralism among legal systems and rules could make the interpretations of rights indifferent, deaf to the claims of legal-semantic qualifications ingrained in the transactions of sense produced at a grassroots level by social and communicative experience.[27] Facing this *blindness/deafness*—already consistently experienced in multicultural contexts where courts frequently resort to *cultural expertise*—the people in the role of 'Other,' if only to obtain the merely symbolic recognition of their own nominal difference, might resign themselves to representing their own needs and claims by appealing exclusively and rigorously to normative/legal schemes that are pre-ordered by their cultural, religious, political, or ethnical contexts of origin.[28]

Such behaviors would be induced not only because of an orthodox self-identification of people with their own cultural normative paradigms but also from a sort of fear of the alternative, that is, the possibility of an utter disregard for their difference and their consequential downfall into the (psycho-socially) stifling

[26] For a similar, but more widely elaborated critical assessment, I refer to Ricca (2013c).

[27] On such practices of normative/regulatory borrowings and their consequences see, however, below.

[28] See Holden (2011, 2023, forthcoming) and the essays collected in Holden (2019). Regrettably, the practice of cultural expertise, despite the good intentions and the declared commitment to bring to the fore the anthropological-ethnological 'stuff' of the cases at stake is sadly equivalent-as I have already warned above-to a normativization of flesh-and-blood people, i.e., real cultural agents; not to mention the cases in which anthropologists, also for reasons of effectiveness in dialoguing with judges rigidly anchored in their positivist approach, end up boiling down their anthropological assistance to the provision of comparative law and, partially, on private international law advices.

circuits of cultural assimilation. Finding themselves trapped in the vice-like grip of non-acknowledgement, on one side, and the compulsory nature of identity patterns stemming from legal-normative matrices on the other side, people end up demeaning their (inter-)cultural creativity and accepting, for merely symbolic reasons, identitarian schemes that are (inevitably) far from their effective existential exigencies. This discrepancy between cultural competence, intended as pro-active ability to 'engender culture,' and reified culture, understood as a repertoire of practices preconfigured normatively, produces grammars and lexicons of citizenship that are anything but inclusive.

The space reserved within legal systems for normative-cultural sets coming from other systems looks more like a piece of a jigsaw puzzle, a bit of patchwork, rather than an injection of difference well-harmonized into the fabric of a shared public and legal subjectivity. The social alienation of Others seems destined to couple with the sense of strangeness and estrangement produced by the cultural patterns and stereotypes imposed on them in the very name of protection of their difference. From this premise, the fall into an instrumental, symbolic, antagonistic, and strategic use of one's own cultural identity is but a very small step. And, actually, it is taken with an almost absolute regularity, even in if manifold ways. Paradoxically, pluralist imperatives for inclusion culminate in widespread practices of exclusion and subalternity, often surreptitiously encapsulated in the claims, and sometimes even in state law's recognition of personal laws and courts: a true mausoleum for any possibility of an inclusive and intercultural citizenship. The sheer struggle for power, for secluded and antagonistic social spaces, becomes at that stage, what is truly at stake in identity claims. But such polarizations, indeed, show themselves to be utterly *identical* in their greed for power, for the occupation of spaces taken away from the Other-than-Self, all this under the aegis of a cultural specificity turned into a mere rhetorical weapon and, therefore, deprived of any effective ties with a genuine experience of sense other than mere political and/or ethnic antagonism.

6.2 Cultural Differences and Legal Claims: What Do People 'on the move' Ask for from the Law?

Cultural difference shows its cognitive scope most genuinely within inter-subjective relationships. Normative apparatuses, both those from state and non-state systems (religious, ethnic, ethic, local, etc.), come into play only at a later time, sometimes obscuring the psycho-cognitive and social origins of their involvement through an effect of over-determination. Their relevance and visibility reach the highest degree when people face cultural conflicts of loyalty. The norms/rules from states or communities of origin and those of the host country overlap, in these cases, in their pragmatic implications and projections so as to set out incompatible experiential patterns and obligations. This is doubtless among the most evident pathological expression of subjectivities in transition or 'on the move'. However, it is not strictly necessary that the possible way out be reached exclusively on the ground of inter-normative relationships.

In order for a conflict between norms or rules to arise, the presence of a person who plays a conveyance role is always necessary. In any case, norms and rules hinge upon life situations, are devised to discipline them, and have as their targets individuals and groups (potentially) destined to embody them. Besides, without subjects in action, the raison d'être—but also the end—of any normative/legal provision would be lacking. Nonetheless, as I already emphasized several times, people are not the norms regulating or purporting to regulate their actions. Furthermore, individuals enjoy a wide margin of autonomy and space for maneuvering in determining their social conduct and, therefore, also in selecting and triggering the subsequent normative effects.

The margin just pointed out, this sort of grey zone between rules and their implementations, is available even when an individual lives and acts within the cultural and territorial context of birth. However, its width increases, at least potentially, if that individual is on the move, if they migrate across different existential contexts and legal circuits. In these cases, the public control of subjects by each system tends to fade in multiple directions and due to manifold factors. Such weakening may depend on an institutional power deficit. Those who migrate from one state territory to another become relatively exempt from the consequences of an eventual failure to obey the rules of their country of origin; simultaneously, they will be submitted to the constraints imposed by the law of the host state, the same constraints from which they were previously immunized by the curtain of protection supplied by the sovereignty of the state of origin. In these situations, the rate of submission of an individual with respect to the legal systems of origin and the hosting one can depend on the relationship between them, as ruled by public and private international law. In any case, the possibility to remold, recombine among them manifold heterochtonous legal effects, is—at least, to some extent—in the hands of individuals. Furthermore, migrating can impinge on the duality of bodily features, namely, persons taken as organisms, and the immaterial interests of people. And it is precisely with regard to the latter profile, typical of a psycho-social experience now widespread on a global scale, that scholars argue and debate about the (alleged) new phenomenon of the de-territorialization of legal subjectivity and the inter-legality produced by means of *law shopping* or *law fishing* practices.[29]

Subjectivities that are anthropologically and legally spread across space and positioned astride various territorial circuits of local power are an increasingly 'normal' phenomenon, idiomatic of our contemporaneity, although not available to everyone or, at least, not experienced by all in the same way. Flexible and/or transnational citizenship is an opportunity that is not lived univocally.[30] Some are

---

[29] See Santos (2002); Wai (2008); Jurčys et al. (2013).

[30] The emphasis on the substantially elitist fashion of the so-called *flexible citizenship*, initially devised by Ong (1999) as a new conceptual tool, constitutes by now an almost unquestionable fact in the anthropological-political literature. A different argument—and it is precisely that which is

able to experience it as actors, organizing their life in the best way by distributing their own activities and multifaceted subjectivity across various spatial and cultural grounds. At the same time, there are other individuals who find themselves overwhelmed by the spatial multi-relatedness of their place in life, and are therefore forced to accept the effects of choices and decision delivered elsewhere and by others as passive subjects.[31] In any case, it remains that the trinomial *system/norm/person* is not monolithic, and its embankment may crack as deeply as the multi-spatial and multi-dimensional spread of people widens. Nonetheless, such a flaw is not to be taken as a symptom of transactions of meaning actually and already achieved according to an intercultural subjectivity realized and experienced in a broad spectrum. These sorts of cultural and communicative transactions are quite opposite from the outcomes offered, in an only apparently similar way, by the practice of *law shopping* or *fishing*. In this case, the rules of the involved legal systems remain formally unchanged, although they are utilized by migrants—often without any awareness by the state institutional agencies—for contingent or extremely concrete purposes, sometimes even aligning the use of such rules with a hyper-orthodox respect of the cultural practices of their countries of origin or group of belonging. In all this there is really very little interculturality if it is to be intended as an axiologically pondered process of self- and mutual translation-transaction.

Much too often, migrants use the legal rules of host countries to incubate and hatch silent conflicts with the new environment and, simultaneously, even against their own infra-cultural circuit. Such conflicts can also remain hidden from the eyes of those who apply norms, that is, the legal operators (judges, lawyers, officials, etc.). Nonetheless, this use of hosting state law or, as an alternative, strange international-private legal mixing, can give rise to situations that are only seemingly intercultural, and are often characterized instead by a deep negative value if compared with the axiological and teleological premises of the same rules applied to each individual case. On occasion, scholars and legal operators show approval and contribute to the employment of such practices. In so doing, however, they are far from promoting social cohesion and inclusive dynamics capable of integrating different cultural subjectivities. In the most complete unawareness, they tacitly allow the illegitimate use of legal rules. The legally distorted outcomes of such ways of welding legal rules and cultural meanings could remain—as noted above—an outright dissimulation shadowed by the umbra of an apparent and formalistic inter-normative coordination. But, what is more, the cumulative result of such practices does nothing but exacerbate differences and polarizations between cultures and legal systems, whereas these should instead be managed as poles of a process of intercultural translation/transaction.

---

argued above—concerns the cultural and ethical-legal effects of an instrumental use of *accommodations* reached through the combination of normative/regulatory fragments of different origin that migrants often try to assemble in an inconsistent patchwork to achieve particular goals.

[31] See, in this regard, Tinnevelt and De Schutter (2010).

To wit, from a formal point of view, there is no question that each individual can in this way be guaranteed the possibility of selecting rules more suited to their case, or the legal system and related jurisdiction to which to entrust the protection of their interests. The legitimacy of such a choice, however, is to be contextualized. Otherwise, the application of a given normative and/or regulatory mixture could result in an illegitimate (and out of any control) heterogenesis of ends involving the same legal norms employed to rule single cases. On the other hand, then, there is the danger—emphasized and feared by many—that *law shopping* works, in fact, merely as an instrument to elude legal constraint. What is more, it is a risk that finds its counterbalancing in the tendency of national courts to methodically and concurrently remold the effect of *imported rules*. Precisely this circumstance has determined, at least at present, the rise and fall of the contemporary version of the so-called *lex mercatoria* of remote medieval ancestry. The double-faceted result of this revival is due to the attempt to view the development of extra- and supra-national legal devices created to regulate trade relationships as a new general frontier of legal experience, rather than as a specific, exceptional and, in a sense, even derogatory regime at the disposal of particular subjects: for the most part, multinational corporations, determined to design international arbitrations for the resolution of their reciprocal disputes. We need not even mention, then, the further and sometimes insurmountable difficulties tied to the attempts to assure consequential effectiveness to statements drafted as a result of international arbitrations within the different state borders through the indispensable intervention of national courts.[32]

Another cause of the failure of regulatory capacity and the binding grip of legal systems on individuals can be traced along the paths of *ignorantia legis*, that is, the lack of knowledge by the subjects of law about the norms and rules of their national, religious, cultural, and ethnic circuits of belonging or origin. The principle *ignorantia legis non excusat* represents a constructive feature that is endemic to the legal systems of the world and is, at least in the abstract, ethically absurd. The limitations of the applicability of this principle, stated by the constitutional and supreme courts of many countries in the case of highly technical rules, do not completely thwart its implications and constraints. On the one hand, how is it conceivable to establish the liability of a person for the infringement of a legal rule if they actually do not know that rule? On the other hand, calling into play the public obligation of knowing all the laws in force would be equivalent to reducing the legitimacy of the principle in question to a sort of institutional power to mockingly deceive people. What now? Why, despite everything, is the irrelevance of *ignorantia legis*, that is, the ignorance about the contents of law so widespread? Why is it never seriously questioned? Some reasons exist, and they are even good reasons, but they have nothing to do with the abstract force of law. Conversely, if the ignorance of formal law does not exclude liability, this is because people, on average, know how to avoid violating legal statements, even when they do not know their contents. It

[32]For a chorological-intercultural analysis of this normative hetero-integration phenomena, I refer to Ricca (2020).

seems to be a sort of miracle, or a collective exercise of occult sorcery, which is, nonetheless, iterated billions of times throughout the world; and yet it is not so.

The ability to avoid breaking the law, despite ignorance of its textual contents, depends on the folk legal knowledge people hold. This knowledge, or 'know-how,' is acquired and transmitted almost by means of a psycho-social osmosis through the iterated sharing of practices observed and acted from infancy. Anyone, within a sufficiently organized social context, is a jurist, even if they have no real awareness of having such a competence. Somehow, subjects obey the law for customary reasons, sometimes without any distinction between their knowing how to do things and the provisions and regulations of law as stated in regulatory texts. Put otherwise, the legal 'ought-to-be' is embodied, interiorized, and transmuted in 'social being' and spontaneous action. On the other hand, law in itself is, in turn, a result produced by values, ends and practices shared and disseminated in social contexts. All in all, *even* law stems from society considered as a fact, that is, from the 'social being.' If, therefore, people obey the laws of legal systems of belonging (a discourse that also involves both religious and ethnic normative apparatuses) this occurrence largely depends on factors and know-how that do not exclusively inhabit the words enshrined in legal texts or formalized rules. The obedience of the law owes quite a bit to the cultural habits acted out by people unawares.

When people migrate, what are the elements of legal knowledge they bring with them? And on behalf of what kind of law do they claim recognition? Is it the formal law of their contexts of origin or, on the contrary, the folk law encapsulated in their cultural and behavioral habits? Scholars generally restrain cultural pluralism into the straightjacket of normative/legal pluralism, and related claims are funneled into attempts at inter-legal integration. Nonetheless, the majority of people who migrate are primarily concerned with being able to maintain their cultural habits rather than obeying the imperatives of the formal legal rules—which in most cases they do not even know—of their country of origins or groups of belonging.

It is very unlikely that Indian, Chinese, or Arab individuals, upon arrival in a European country, and *vice versa*, calculate their cultural distance or potential confrontations with hosting state law in terms of an impossibility to respect a statutory or religious rule enacted by their country of origin. This is for the simple reason that common people, in their cultural contexts, know very well how not to break the law, although they almost completely ignore normative texts. It is perfectly consistent with their basic cultural 'baggage' that in their eyes the most important goal is to be informed about the laws of host country, on the one hand, and on the other, to interweave their own cultural meanings and habits within the semantic fabric of this legal language. This dual approach (and the related uses of law) constitutes a further opportunity for intercultural translation on legal grounds and, consequently, for an inclusive integration of Otherness. This is because cultural habits are more conspicuously flexible than normative statements. From a semiotic point of view, habits show a synthetic and radial structure. Adaptability to different contexts and situations is part and parcel of their significance and of their semantic potentialities. Habits are characterized by a teleological-axiological structure that makes them extraordinarily plastic with regard to the modulation of their semantic ingredients. Conversely, normative/legal utterances and statements are characterized by an inherent morphological rigidity and are usually interpreted according to lists of control that define the semantic elements and features/connotations pertinent to them in a strictly analytical way.

The differentiation just outlined is very relevant to the people's exercising of their cultural competence. If, in order to inscribe Otherness within the semantic meshes of legal discourse, the object of translation/transaction is a behavioral habit, then its semiotic adaptability and flexibility will be an integral part of its authenticity. Hence, if people take into consideration the semiotic possibilities and pragmatic tracks offered by the normative landscape of host countries, then they can properly reorient and adequately modulate the semantic projections of their own cultural habits. These new meaning devices can trigger, in this way, new possibilities of categorization and legal qualification, which can also be completely different from those tied to the apparently objective morphology of migrants' behaviors and words. Such transformations are possible and often even necessary because the morphological traits and features of the conduct of Others initially 'recorded' by natives (including legal practitioners and agencies) are far from being absolutely objective. They are 'considered objectively' only according to standards of judgement based on determined cultural and hermeneutical assumptions—those of the host country, in this case. Even so, even just by peeking into the 'implicit,' underlying every cultural habit, we can see entire connotative landscapes suddenly taking shape and making the initial morphologies and related categorical pigeonholes newly fluid. To produce such an effect, it is necessary to make use of a specific methodology, precisely, intercultural translation.

However, the consequences of intercultural translation do not involve only the observer, the subject placed outside a distinct culture, but also those who act from within the culture. Translating in an intercultural way works a little like a mirror. In order for people to be able to represent themselves to Others' accurately, they must look reflexively into their own minds and cultural patterns. Anyhow this self-reflexive gaze must allow itself to be oriented by the particular point of view that the Other's culture and the contingent exigencies of translation/transaction will induce them to assume when they explain themselves. If legal aspects are also involved in this process, then the self-transformative effect and creativity deriving from a lateral view on themselves may increase further—however paradoxical this could seem.

Actually, the discursive groundwork of law, if properly elicited, can produce immediate and significant pragmatic implications. Through the legal spectrum, the self-transformation ensuing from intercultural self-reflection appears to embody existential, effective, and concrete self-transformations. This is because the various and possible reactions of the legal system of the host country are tightly connected to the signification key that each foreigner or migrant will use to explain the meaning of behavioral or verbal expressions. If and when he or she will have acquired an awareness of the possibility of influencing and selecting legal reactions, then they will consent to a negotiation of habits underlying their claims for cultural recognition. Consequently, the foreign individual can coordinate their previous knowledge and perspective on their 'past Self' with future possibilities, so as to engender a sort of tuning between the potentialities of sense stemming from the cultural background of origin and the further chances of experience and meaning offered by the new environment. Linguistic/conceptual translation and spatial trans-duction, therefore the repositioning within new social and territorial contexts, will appear to be coextensive with some features of migration experiences or, more generally, of personal mobility.

What must be emphasized, in regard to the exercise of cultural creativity, has to do with the relationship between transformation and culture. Molding the interpretation of one's own cultural knowledge and anticipating its effects by gauging the potential reactions of the legal platform assures pragmatic effectiveness to intercultural dialogue and the possibility of realizing an inclusive integration. The option of mutual adaptation between law and cultural differences could rouse suspicions that only contingent, instrumental uses of both are going to take place. It is crucial to observe, however, that there is no law apart from contacts between its words, its schemes of qualification, the possibilities of their mutual combination, on one side, and the manifold categorizations and prospection of facts, events, behaviors or linguistic expressions, on the other side. At the same time, it makes little sense to speak of 'culture' independent from the transactions of meaning triggered and urged by the encounter between cultural knowledge and the environment that hosts it—an environment in which legal institutions are a far from insignificant component. In the game of specular self-transformations played by law and culture, the former elicits the emersion of cultural meanings and their ensuing practical-dynamical implementation; simultaneously, cultural differences educe the unfolding of potentialities of sense encapsulated in the discursive apparatuses of legal systems.

The authenticity of the use of both the host state's law and the related culture, on one side, and the binomial law/culture of the subjects 'on the move' takes its shape and is assured precisely by means of the convergence of the distinct paths of self-transformation just outlined. Moreover, there is no authentic space that does not intersect the semiotic crossroads engendered by and inherent to intercultural translation/transaction. In the midst of encounters between reciprocal cultural differences, that is, the social circuit of multiculturality, intercultural transformation is inevitable, even when it remains silent and invisible. It occurs always and in any case. The only way to establish authenticity is to make the transformation, the intercultural change, conscious and consequently, potentially under control. On the other hand, within new contexts or environments, only transformations and their acceptance allow for a continuity of sense between past and present, what people know (how to do) and what they learn (to do).

Fieldwork provides a kind of confirmation of the above observations; migrants made aware of the range of possibilities supplied to them by an intercultural and transactional use of law speak favourably of them. Their main concern appears to focus on the effectiveness of the legal protection afforded by such solutions. The discursive modality performed by people is particularly icastic and powerful enough to clearly show the sense and genuineness of their ongoing cultural transformations. They make statements such as, "But really, if I do so, then the [host] state law will allow me that result?" "And then, if indeed I do this, does the law protect me from other native citizens and even from my fellow countrymen?" In their concise vividness, these two standard questions fully transmit the anxiety and charge of expectations that comes with the creation of new shapes of cultural subjectivity; and, moreover, the emergence of difference, identity and their transaction within frameworks capable of sustaining inclusive integration. From another angle, these questions illustrate how behind intercultural confrontations the danger of infra-cultural conflicts materializes, perceived as anything but remote. These conflicts are frequently propelled by individuals 'on the move' and, just as often, by the related second generations that want to take advantage of the possibilities (cultural as well as economic) supplied by the migration experience and context.

More generally, what emerges from fieldwork is a passage from the perception of *multiculturality* understood as a fact, to the production of creative experiences marked by *interculturality* and envisaged as a horizon of opportunities. In other words, Others, if adequately informed of the possibilities at hand, show a strong inclination towards a pro-active citizenship, which indeed is the only kind that can support the social and cultural processes necessary to an equitable inclusion of differences. The discursive resources of law, if adequately accessed and elicited, can fuel and make viable the pursuit of similar paths. The intercultural use of law—at least, from the perspective I try to develop—is specifically designed to outline the conceivable and concrete possibilities in this direction.

6.3 Beyond Inter-Legality: Towards a Space of Pre-Litigation Intercultural Law

Translating behavioral habits rather than legal rules/norms is not, however, a very comfortable task. For a professional lawyer it can indeed be very difficult and even engender the sensation of lacking the methodological capacity to venture into such an enterprise. Why is this so? What is behind these difficulties? The origins of jurists' limitations are to be traced, in my view, to the training methods employed by academic institutions for the acquisition and use of legal knowledge of law practitioners throughout years of education.[33] The young law student is trained to deal mainly with legal texts and to qualify social dynamics according to the behavioral standards strictly predetermined in regulatory statements. The potential and manifold articulations of sense inherent in social actions do not fall within—or, better, are authoritatively left out of—the law student's targets. All of this, on the other hand, is exactly mirrored in the self-representations that institutional and academic circuits officially stamp on legal activity. Needless to say, in actual legal practice, in the so-called *law in action*, things work very differently.

[33] In this regard, see the insightful remarks proffered by Tully (2020) and Bryant and Peters (2014), and there for the referrals to other contributions on this topic.

The legal practitioner at work constantly translates from the common language used in social action into a legal technical language. Every undertaking of legal qualification consists in an act of translation and, as such, entails processes of semantic creation and abduction. Nonetheless, the translation effected by lawyers lies almost entirely in the shadows. This is likely due to the fact that in most cases legal practitioners share the same general culture of their clients and, therefore, of the recipients of their legal advice. So, precisely through those shared cultural coordinates, schemes of categorization and social phenomena to be qualified by the law eventually merge and blend. The 'cultural' disguises itself as 'factual,' and vice versa. In other words, the cultural component of judgements appears in the guise of natural, phenomenal objectivity, already encapsulated in the morphological appearance of 'things.' This occurs simply because facts already embody in themselves the results of a judgment and, consequently, the cultural coordinates employed to perform it, much like putting on a pair of glasses. Actually, as we act, it is very difficult to notice that we are availing ourselves of a cultural lens to 'see' the world. It should be observed that this already happens in the making of experience, therefore before we perceive, and then consciously represent 'reality.'

The mimesis of cultural variables within the infra-cultural communicative praxis conveys the image of a legal practitioner as a subject who merely applies semantic-deontic standards of a textual nature (namely norms) onto facts; accordingly, these are understood as things and events standing over there, beyond the jurist's mind, and appearing in total objectivity under the sovereign eye of the law. Nonetheless, the actual work of legal practitioners is instead crammed with cultural determinants and, thereby, with strains oriented to translate and, somehow, create (or, more technically, *abduct*) discursive devices suited to define the legally relevant essential terms of specific cases/situations. Those cultural determinants are the same ones that allow the jurist to decode the habits of social actors, grasping their invisible/silent, hidden/'mute' semiotic implications, usually doomed to lie confined in the invisible domains of 'implicitness.'

In fact, when an individual consults a lawyer or notary, very rarely do they ask the professional to apply a determined rule to resolve the situation that gives rise to their troubles. Much more often, clients portray a narrative story riddled with inter-subjective relationships and conflicts, accompanied by the indicative description of an *output* corresponding to their personal objectives. Legal professionals are usually able to gather the sense of the story, relying on habits of judgement and cultural behavior they share with the client. Those habits work to provide lawyers with an interpretive-semiotic access to the relations of sense underlying the words and gestures disclosed by the client. These shared habits, in turn, induce the legal practitioner to ask a series of question aimed at clarifying the case/situation by means of schemes of legal qualification that are postulated progressively as explicative hypotheses.

The dialogue between legal professionals and their clients will lead to a sequence of falsifications and verifications, questions and answers, up to the achievement of a sort of transaction between the representation of facts and the selection of the legal paradigms to apply in defining the normative situation, namely the portion of 'law in action and acted' embodied by single clients and their future and past deeds. This legally qualified 'shred' of factual landscape will be the outcome of a translating/translational synthesis between common language and legal language—incidentally, something similar occurs between the symptomatic folk language of patients and the scientific-medical language of doctors used in diagnosis and treatment/care. As already observed above, all this semantic crafting is part of an ongoing underground translation accomplished by playing on the 'invisible/mute' implicit sharing of cultural habits between professionals and common people.

These well lubricated processes of silent and unaware translations are destined to abruptly jam when the legal practitioner assists a subject of a different culture. In such cases, the implicit translation must necessarily become explicit, and this is precisely so as to avert massive (and sometimes tragic) misunderstandings. For this purpose, however, the professional jurist must acquire an awareness of their constant, though silent, role as a translator and, in some respects, as an ethnographer, roles they regularly perform under ordinary (infra-cultural) circumstances in the exercise of work. Moreover, this acquired awareness is to be followed by the arrangement and use of a methodology suited to managing legal translation that is to be carried out whilst straddling different cultural circuits. Unfortunately, the traditional know-how of the jurist stumbles over just this intercultural threshold and shows its deficiency in facing cultural differences efficaciously.

The list of difficult intercultural tasks jurists must achieve is long. The intercultural jurist must: 'recognize' the action of an heterochtonous cultural habit, make sure that it unfolds its underlying semiotic landscape, prompt explicative contextualizations, use their own cognitive competence as a deciphering eye rather than a hermeneutical cage to domesticate the key of sense articulated by the Other so as to pursue efforts for intersecting semantic transactions, perform simultaneously to this inter-contextualization a work of translation and sense transaction, forbear an authoritative and culturally ethnocentric use of legal/normative categories, exercise a demonstrated–and sometimes even shrewd–ability to creatively combine legal effects with the meaning articulations and needs expressed by the recipient of one's own professional activity. The list of skills required to accomplish an intercultural use of law is indeed extensive and tightly packed. Nevertheless, it does not call for superhuman abilities. The jurist—judge, legal practitioner, lawyer, or notary—is called upon to do with subjects of other cultures that which they do, as a rule, with their autochthonous clients, average citizens.

In these cases, what is needed is an anthropological support capable of supplying lawyers, but also clients, with adequate semiotic tools to explain the underlying relationships that can unveil the key of meaning inherent in what is said and enacted. As pointed out above, narrations, cross-contextualization, and intercultural translations/transactions are the three fundamental tasks that are to be cooperatively carried out by jurists, anthropologists and the subject-clients belonging to 'another' culture. Relying on these activities, jurists could find within the semiotic landscapes drawn by the Other particular 'connotative ingredients' capable of shifting the axes of categorical salience concerning the judgement of their legal qualification considerably. Consequently, they could find themselves compelled to make a different choice regarding the rule or the normative set to be utilized to accomplish his legal qualification objective.

Along the intercultural path just outlined, both the jurist and the foreign social actor would be induced to increase their awareness of their own cultural assumptions and, therefore, to adopt a questioning attitude, to develop a predisposition toward critical analysis, inseparably linked to the self-distancing inherent in the implementation of such practices. Variations in cultural self-awareness, thereby also in the cultural options chosen, and variations in determining the rules/norms to be adopted in the qualification of the legal meaning of facts, facts understood according to legal intercultural interpretations, can therefore be seen to be two sides of the same coin.

If all of this constitutes a sort of snapshot of an intercultural use of law in action, at the same time it also allows for the emergence of a horizon of possibilities for contemporary legal experience that takes place beyond the frontier of inter-legality. In the situations described above, the intention is not to make accommodations between different and reciprocally estranged normative statements, an approach which is in any case largely inadequate, and ultimately destructive. Conversely, what is at stake is the possibility to make state law capable of receiving and including the cultural cognitive/behavioral habits of Others within the fabric of its semantic potentialities. This approach appears to require a level of flexibility inconceivable in the case of merely inter-legal or inter-normative translation/transaction. Furthermore, it calls into play the same individuals that are, ultimately, the prime movers in the production of culture, as creative and thus political actors.

In many cases, however, the inter-normative and inter-legal approach is strictly necessary and inescapable. These situations occur when people put facts or legal qualifications that have already taken place and been legally defined elsewhere under the lens of the host country's law. Examples include the recognition and reception of personal legal status tied to the culture or legal system of origin, the legal effects of contracts concluded overseas, marriages celebrated in other countries, and so on. But the legal experiences of people are not confined to the past. In many cases, the legal effects of previous actions could still be re-negotiated and re-molded in connection with a systemic intercultural use of the host country's law.

The implications of private-international law are not absolutely cogent and can even become residual. Such a result depends on a combination of effects produced by the legal system of origin and that of the host country. It requires, of course, substantial legal skill and intercultural awareness. In this regard, the legal assistance of foreign people is essential, but only provided that both legal practitioners and their clients cooperate with anthropologists committed to promoting an intercultural use of law. If adequately acquainted with the possibilities of transformation of normative situations across multiple spaces of legality, social actors will be able to yield to intercultural modulations of inter-systemic legal connections through their personal choices. But there is more. People's lives continue even beyond the event of migration and the encountering of new state borders. In the new social environment, as noted above, ties and bonds with the legal system of origin tend to fade. This is not, however, exactly the same in the case of cultural, religious, and other anthropologically situated links and belongings. Nonetheless, the meaning of these ties is likely to interpenetrate the semantic potentialities of the host country's law, so as to engender creative solutions that come from the cultural competence of migrants as well as natives. This implies that the actors of an intercultural encounter are not the legal rules, but rather individuals who are able to act not only as vehicles but also as creative interpreters of the semantic matter of cultures and laws.

As stressed above, if interrogated, the norm, the textual rule, maintains a majestic silence. On the contrary, each person is the first and authentic interpreter of their own cultural conscience and has, in this regard, a kind of right to cultural self-representation.[34] Clearly this does not mean that a referral to culture can legitimate an offhandedly and impudently strategic, if not even selfish, use of one's own claimed difference. Putting up a breakwater against the possible misuses of the 'cultural argument' could, however, lead to the adoption of a rigidly *normativistic* approach— typical of legal multiculturalism and the related practice of so-called 'cultural defenses'— to the concept of culture and cultural difference. This solution would represent a remedy worse than evil because it would lead to making cultural belonging and otherness nothing but the other side of an *exceptionalistic* and ultimately secluding social logic, 'politically correct' but placed exactly at the antipode of any politics of true intercultural inclusion.

The intercultural use of law has nothing to do with attempts to carve out isles of privilege, exemption, or exceptionality. Inscribing cultural habits along the semantic routes of law by availing of potentialities of sense inherent in the legal language is an entirely 'normal' activity. It aims for a recognition of Otherness and plural difference; it can consequently re-negotiate the 'core,' so to speak, of categorical features of subjectivity. This could not be further from the logic of multiculturalism or the tendencies of legal pluralists committed to engendering circuits of 'juridical alternatives' to the state law, such as personal laws and jurisdictions.

On the other hand, it is possible to describe in detail how to enable this connotative re-negotiation of subjectivity and why it can subsequently spring from an activity of translation capable of triggering—the above emphasized—*crossed axiological and inter-contextual resonances* between different cultural encyclopedias. First, however, I would like to focus on the temporal aspects of an intercultural use of law, specifying which pathways can make space for a timely intercultural law.

Until now, the problematic dimension of cultural difference has found its place within judicial activities and before the courts. But perhaps it should be said that this is only where institutional analysts, political scientists, legal scholars, and jurists have acknowledged its presence. Consolidated academic currents that are labelled as 'multicultural citizenships studies' or 'multicultural rights' tend to focus on the judicial moment. The practice and doctrine of the so-called *cultural defense* is an idiomatic expression of this tendency and brings with it all the problems that inevitably derive from a pluralism that has been configured and guaranteed in an *exceptionalistic* and, precisely for this reason, segregating fashion. If this occurs, however, it does not depend on the assumption of a specific ideological perspective

[34] See Chryssochoou (2004).

alone. In my view, an unavoidable rigidity in prospecting cultural claims and their related identitarian inclinations descends from a specific circumstance: the legal process in and of itself, where the final verdict is determined by a class of judges whose intervention is always *post factum*.

The judge is always called upon to legally qualify events that have already happened, actions already accomplished, plans already realized. Examining different possibilities of signification in the interpretation of foreign people's conduct can undoubtedly promote an inclusive use of law. Nonetheless, this hermeneutical activity can be performed exclusively on that which has not yet occurred. What is lacking, in such judicial situations, is the possibility of negotiating and symmetrically transacting the respective cultural knowledge of people so as to meet the law in an 'adaptive' way. This is only possible when legal assistance (from lawyers, notaries, and, more generally, legal practitioners) is requested before the action takes place, that is, for consultative and pre- or anti-litigation purposes.

Legal advice represents the *culture medium* for the development of *law in action* and could work in the same way for *intercultural* law in action. On this ground, the most skilled professionals can give free rein to their creativity. As shown above, they can work in a dynamic intercultural way in at least two directions, by: *a)* meeting the exigencies and expectations of clients with regard to 'real life situations'; *b)* exerting the *ars combinatoria et interpretandi* to modulate and mold the responses of legal systems towards clients' claims and needs. In many cases, what takes place is precisely a transactional translation between the two sides of the relationship. This transactional/translating process sees the client as a pro-active and participating actor also, above all with regard to the redefinition of their own social and legal subjectivity. Being informed about both the discursive platform that law may afford and the modalities to adequately examine it constitutes a significant increase in individuals' knowledge of their social environment. Moreover, this knowledge can be coordinated with the paths of self-representation available to subjects— who are also clients—from different cultures.

The cognitive interpenetration between legal schemes and cultural ciphers of subjectivity often leads to pragmatic inventions that are intrinsically intertwined and embodied within the semantic meshes of legal utterances. This peculiar characteristic bestows a perspective of effectiveness to the teleological and practical prospections elaborated by clients because it inherently assures legal protection and cogency to their future achievements. Such practical and temporal projections in terms of effectiveness reach their highest intensity, obviously, when professional creations are endorsed by court decisions.

Court proceeding represents, however, merely one eventuality. It would be seriously misguided to assume that *law in action* can be reduced to only jurisprudential decisions. The life of law inhabits *normality*, disseminated among the folds of the daily existence of people who may or may not experience it in terms of social conflict. What arrives before the courts is only a little portion of the social universe put in motion by law and comprising all the inter-subjective dynamics equally punctuated by legal knowledge, either in its *folk* version or in that which is filtered and packaged by the skilled assistance of professionals. I would say even further that once people arrive before the courts, somehow the law has already failed in its mission to build and shape social action; in the face of this failure, people and the law will search together for a remedy, a 'thaumaturgical' statement of position allowing institutional authorities to 'save the day.'

In order to manage relationships with people from different cultures in the best way, a pre-litigation intervention of legal practitioners would be extraordinarily useful. This intervention would occur when people are still engaged with the planning of their actions, still focused on achieving their own social and personal ends. This would create a space for the creation of timely intercultural legal solutions that can allow Others to learn, choose, and mold their own cultural self-representations. For many Others, being acquainted with the inclusive potentialities of normative platforms would serve as an indispensable tool for experiencing a subjectivity that is newly aware, emancipated, self-determining and, above all, not trapped in an ignorance of the possible consequences of actions. I would emphasize once again, however, what was already highlighted above. To ensure that legal professionals can learn how to perform the necessary activities of cross-cultural translation/transaction, it is essential that legal firms cooperate with experts able to supply anthropological knowledge and methodologies.

Anthropological expertise—unlike what happens in the context of more dated multicultural experiences—should be extended beyond judicial situations.[35] This kind of advice, often required by courts of *common law* countries in the course of legal proceedings, should be anticipated. This is because by anticipating the preventive intervention of professionals, anthropological support would hugely increase its capacity of drawing possible, enhanced maps of inclusion and social integration of cultural differences within the state law and its guarantees.

Of course, persuading foreign people or people of different cultures to consult legal practitioners even before problems of integration become plainly evident is quite a feat. Legal professionals are not, as a rule, sources of charity. Their services come at a cost, and people who do not belong to dominant social groups typically lack both the predisposition as well as the economic resources to contact a legal practitioner before undertaking social actions. From this perspective, a particular—and not only privileged—position is that of the notary. The so-called Latin notary is called upon in his twofold function of professional and public official before the onset of conflicts or, at least, in the phase in which people have not yet given an official legal form to their plans of action. During this phase, the notary is in charge of determining the best match between the client's desires and the type of legal act that is to be performed: at least, in situations where the notary recognizes possible discrepancies between the formal solutions on the table, on one side, and the plans and expectations of clients, on the other. Promoting an increasing awareness of potentialities intrinsic to an intercultural use of law among notaries (in countries

[35] In many *civil law* countries (Italy included), the anthropological expertise in the course of legal matters is recognized only for a few legal areas. For more information about the case of Italy, see Ricca (2015, 2014b), Ricca and Sbriccoli (2015).

where this figure is institutionalized) could constitute a first step towards its dissemination.

If starting with the Latin notary, the experience of a timely intercultural law disseminated across social contexts and communities of foreigners/minorities could be the beginning of a 'virtuous circle,' especially in terms of the diffusion of a newly enriched legal education. Requesting assistance from lawyers and other legal practitioners in pre-litigation and anti-litigation phases could be increasingly useful and important, an approach capable of counterbalancing the deterrent effect of the high costs of services. Also, potentially, a growing demand for legal advice could be echoed by the emersion of legal-intercultural case studies eventually merged into the folk legal know-how of common people. The pre- and anti-litigation function performed by notaries could thus be adopted on a large scale by other legal and social agencies as a device for the management of socio-cultural conflicts. So, in addition to professional activity—delivered for a fee—one could envision institutional 'kiosks' offering free advice, committed to supplying legal-intercultural instructions provided by Municipalities or other specialized public agencies. Costs incurred by public agencies from the establishment of such offices would be largely compensated by the savings to be obtained in the avoidance, or at least diminishing of social conflicts arising daily in a world now irreversibly marked by flows of people and information embodying cultural difference.

If we could imagine a kind of political equivalence between migration flows and probabilities for an inclusive integration to be realized on a large scale, the intercultural and timely use of law would work as an independent variable in the determination of value to be recognized in the rigidity of national territorial frontiers. As boundary walls, those frontiers become thicker and higher as the inter-subjective distances expand or remain wide.

The rise of legal intercultural practices would be useful, surely, in relativizing the inter-subjective barriers between individuals of different cultures and, consequently, in promoting a revaluation of the political-spatial significance of frontiers. The more cultural Otherness and its inclusion results in a factor of social growth and development, the more the disclosure and flexibility of frontiers would evolve. Legal intercultural subjectivity and the interpretation of space would give rise to renewed teleological and axiological geographies. The co-implication between dynamics of cultural signification, law, and territorial-spatial distinctions calls into question, thereby, an ancient idea that goes back to the Plato's *Timaeus*, precisely the idea of *Kóra*, intended as a semantic-spatial *continuum*. Legal chorology is a partial transposition of such an idea and its implications on the semantic-spatial fluidities imparted by intercultural translation/transaction in the configuration and effectiveness of legal categorizations.[36]

---

[36]I suppose it is useful to specify here how my approach to chorology has little to do with Derridian idea *of Kóra* as my view does not coincide with the post-modern tendencies of this author and the related interpretations of Plato's *Timaeus*: see Derrida (1993). Some affinities with my chorologic reading of contemporary legal experience could be traced in John Sallis (1999) and Isar (2009a, b: spec. 46-48). In this last text it is possible to find an interesting comparison between Derrida's and

6.4 Legal Chorology and Intercultural Translation

What do space and criticisms of space have to do with intercultural translation for legal purposes? A possible answer to this question could rely upon—as I have already shown above—the declinations of critical geography emerging from certain Foucaultian approaches.[37] According to these approaches, spatial traces and distinctions, although appearing substantially as 'objectification in the empirical language of geography, are instead products and projections of exercises of power. The 'thinghood' of space would be, therefore, nothing but a device to dissimulate the grip of social control on the actions of people. Law, with its conceptual cartographies applied and overlapping onto space and its experiences, would be, consequently, a *medium* conveying the objectification of power and its purposes. Topographical-geographical punctuations and distinctions so realized would be nothing but a mystification of the arbitrariness inherent to the legitimacy of power and its political and legal foundations. Boundaries, houses, prisons, estates, buildings and so on, would be nothing but linguistic devices used to impose social constraints camouflaged as empirical evidence. By unveiling and deconstructing the axiological-political coordinates underlying the implications of such a disguising thingness, social subjectivity would be given the possibility to emancipate itself from these conceptual cages and promote their subversion.

As mentioned above,[38] this is the perspective embraced, in the wave of *Critical Legal Studies*, by the current of *Legal Geography* outlined and put forth above all in United States. On such premises, cultural differences could, thus, come into play as driving factors, precisely for their charge of Otherness and estranging power, so as to unmask the ideological roots and connections of legal-spatial categorizations. Nonetheless, the main problem with such an approach, although provocative, lies in its tendency to merely define a critique and not go beyond it. The deconstruction of the ideological-political features of empirical-reifying language, adopted by the law to disguise its partiality, opens the possibility of a struggle for space but does not envisage a peaceful way out. Analyzing the issue from an intercultural point of view, the principal outcome of legal geography would be the legitimation of new claims for the colonization of space to compete against others derived from cultural matrices already embodied in institutional/legal structures. Drawing the outlines of such a legitimate antagonism does not provide any explanation for how to move

---

Sallis' different interpretations of the platonic *Kóra*. Another important reference can be found, despite his post-modern vein, in the seminal semiotic-historical explorations of Zumthor (1993); see also Heritier, *Understanding Legal Semiotics: Chorologies (forthcoming)*.

[37] As for critical geography see G. Olsson (2007, 2011). As regards reinterpretations of the critical law-oriented approach to geography with a Foucaultian bent, see: N. Blomley (1994, 2003a, b, Delaney (2003, 2010, 2014); Blomley et al. (2001); Braverman et al. (2014); von Benda-Beckmann et al. (2009).

[38] See Chap. 4.

beyond the warlike logic of a polarized colonization of space, that is, the triad of subjectivity/space/exclusivity.

Notwithstanding the emphasis of the *Legal Geography* critical approach on political options related to the thinghood of spatial categories, it still seems entangled in a series of dualisms such as mind/reality, word/thing, language/empirical space, law/territory. It seems that the legal-geographical gaze and its related criticisms always target situations and legal categories that have somehow to do with physical space as characterized in common language. Scholars' analysis never appears to grasp that the engendering of (practical) action spaces is inherent to language and, especially, legal language.[39] *Legal Geography* fails to capture, for example, the spatial dimensions of contract law or inheritance law. It seems unable to make out (still) how every word, and even more every legal word, engenders spaces of action and cartographies of experience just because of its involvement in planning personal and social activities.[40] And yet if scholars' gaze were instead focused on the linguistic substance of every spatial category, probably they would perceive that within terms such as 'house,' 'prison,' 'street,' 'border,' etc., the primary presence of semiotic relations, the intrinsic architecture of semantic matter, is encapsulated in the words. It would show, then, how knowing how to maneuver within linguistic categories, promoting their self-transformation, is tantamount to producing the critical awareness and consequential actions conducive to possible renegotiations of lived spatiality. In this way, the relationships between experiential continuity and horizontality of space and word, physical and lived spaces, on one side, and categorical borders/spectrums, on the other, would emerge as crucial points. Starting from this basic acquisition, it would become feasible to foil—in a creative and, above all, constructive way—the reifying mystifications of spatial language encapsulated within legal devices. So, criticism would no longer result only in deconstruction and de-legitimization, but also and foremost in setting the appropriate premises to transform the semantic potentialities of legal categories—including those with spatial projections/connotations. Such a task could be accomplished precisely by taking into account the competing pluralistic articulations of sense and claims for categorical remolding that come from cultural differences.

[39] In the same direction, see, however within the same geographical studies area, S. Whatmore (2002); Anderson and Harrison (2010). These authors follow an approach that originates from the epistemological perspective proposed by Deleuze and, in a different key, by Latour. The legal implications of these epistemological views remain, in any case, far from that which I propose above: this is for the same reasons already emphasized with reference to the reading of personal agency offered by Philippopoulos-Mihalopoulos (2010, 2012, 2014). See, instead, from a political-anthropological perspective Trnka et al. (2013); in a cultural-anthropological and cognitive sense, Henare et al. (2007). Following different epistemological paths, I reach conclusions aligning with those proposed by these two groups of authors, connected both to pragmatist thought (Peirce, James and Dewey) and other theories concerning the embodiment of experience. As for the 'embodiment' topic, I refer, within a colossal literature, to Gibbs (2005). For further bibliographical references, see Ricca (2018).

[40] In this regard, for some remarks about corporality and sociality of the tight relationships between space and word, availing of an extraordinary historical insight, see again Zumthor (1993).

Another kind of answer to the question raised at the beginning of this section could come from the 'critique of space' conceived by Henri Lefebvre and, subsequently, by Michel De Certeau and again—although along different coordinates—Edward Soja.[41] What joins these critical analyses of space is their projection towards the future, therefore something beyond the mere deconstructive demystification of extant spatial categories and their conceptual-ideological genealogies. All three of these authors highlight, from different sides, the political connotation of space and its continuous renewing through the actions of subjects inherent to social experience. Firing fierce criticisms against modernity and its foolish ambitions to serialize and rationally control events and experiences, these three authors show the irreducibility and resistance to neutralization of individual action, when considered in its propensity to continuously trace pragmatic cartographies even within maps and paths set by a dominant institutional culture of knowledge and power. These scholars work just like entomologists engaged in the close observation of the inexhaustible work of ants, carried forward by each actor of quotidian life. They effectively identify the conceptual reshaping and re-signifying consistently realized by people along the edges of categorical/topographical frames of public/institutional language and its architectural/urban projections.

For the same reasons, when and where generality turns into ambiguity, the law becomes unclear, and borders evaporate because of the mobility of people. Just then, creativity discloses its regenerative potential through the germination of a myriad of micro-actions that cumulatively end up averting or neutralizing institutional (and dominant) aspirations to control and curtail social spaces. The logic of imponderability and unpredictability coextensive to post-modern visions championed by these authors is endorsed, however, also by some legal philosophers. These are the same who see in the porosity of the territorial divides of states and legal systems a matrix of effects such as: (a) inter-legality and interpenetrations of legal national frameworks; (b) the multi-situated condition of legal subjectivity; (c) the promiscuous cultural belonging of subjects; (d) the over-determining dynamics of normative webs with respect to local political frameworks; and, (e) de-territorialized legal experience connoted by inter-systemic pluralism.[42]

From this perspective, the emancipation of the subject from the hierarchical, aprioristic and 'curtailing' categorical frame of modernity pays the price, however, of a vanishing individual agency. Within a fresco of social inter-subjectivity so outlined, the standardized subject of modern law, forged by general and abstract categories that are deaf to the voices of difference, undoubtedly experiences a sort of crumbling. On the other hand, however, the *real* subject ends up being treated as nothing but an epiphenomenon of systemic dynamics. Emancipation from the conforming and serializing chains of modern law seems to commute, in the end,

[41] See Lefebvre (1974); Martin (2006) Butler (2012); de Certeau (1990); Soja (1996).

[42] See Philippopoulos-Mihalopoulos (2010, 2012, 2014); Santos (2002); Teubner (2005).

into a sort of political annihilation of the individual. I must confess I sense something rather ominous in such representations, somehow entwined in a sociology of complexity,[43] in which individual autonomy and even the subject's rationality appear to be mere silly aspirations before the crippling cognitive indecipherability of the (global) environment. I do not contend, obviously, that the power of complexity inherent to contemporary globalized society can neutralize the ability to forecast and control, which is traditionally related to individual self-determination. I fear, however, that to believe idolatrously in the overarching and ineluctable complexity of the world might make its unintelligibility even more overwhelming, so that it appears impossible to overcome. Moreover, I have serious doubts about whether worlds or natures seemed any less out of control or complex to humans in other eras. In the remote past—and, in many respects, even today—myths were used to help exorcise the unpredictability of events and creatively manage relationships with an environment that overwhelmed any human ability to control its phenomena.

This brief detour across the spatial reading of legal experience allows us to approach, now, the answer to the previous question concerning the implications between space and legal interculture with more sophisticated argumentative instruments.

The first step in such a direction is to highlight the pro-active nature of cultural knowledge. Cultures do not take place in a vacuum. They develop environmental and mental traces to engender the experience *of* space *across* space. Knowledge achieved through the making of culture supplies human beings with cognitive instruments to 'see' spatial distinctions, to 'perceive' them. What we perceive as placed over there, in the external world, is always the outcome of pro-active processes put in action by us in order to mold and categorize experiences. In turn, experience itself materializes from acts of categorization and creative symbolization of behavioral sequences and plans projected across space, in this case intended as the ecological dimension of life. This is because the same space we humans consider 'empty' is, instead, already semantically drawn. It consists of a horizon of possibilities corresponding to the potentialities of culturally configured human action.

The use of symbols and words presupposes a space previously imbued with innumerable and manifold connotative elements. But it is precisely there, in this 'semantically crammed space,' that the implications of the symbolic activity of mind will weave the plots of its pragmatic consequences. Representations of space, whether conscious or unconscious, specifically singled out or merely constitutive of experiential contexts, are embodied and epitomized in each single word and its meaning.

The above considerations lead us to postulate that there is no external space independent from what we do (and do not do) in and with it. We cannot merely perceive space as simple spectators without previously knowing something about it,

[43] See Philippopoulos-Mihalopoulos (2010). This author blends in his approach to *Spatial Justice* both Luhmann's functionalism and the Deleuze's rhizomatic topology, from which he expressively draws inspiration.

and this, in turn, is a consequence of what we have already made of it: and if not us directly, then certainly our ancestors who have left us a legacy of schemes that are biologically and culturally oriented towards successful interactions with the environment. Even when we imagine or fantasize about space, we do not create it but rather represent it according to conceptual categories that work abductively, that is, through the elaboration of hypothesis based on our previous experiences. But, as implied above, what human beings create within their environment is not independent from their cultural schemes, their activities of symbolization, conceptualization, and embodiment of space developed through experience and then transformed in neural patterns by virtue of our neural plasticity.[44]

Every symbol epitomizes the transactional projections processed in a bi-directional way between the organism and its environment. Said diversely, every word is the outcome of a twofold process of embodiment of experience put into the world and, in the reverse direction, of the *worldliness* of mind. Through the act of signifying, imagination simultaneously epitomizes and plans experience and its possibility of exertion across a space co-generated by the same human activity. To express the same concept in extremely synthetic terms, space does not show itself separate from what we make in it, whilst what we make in it is not disjoined from the categorical schemes we utilize to think and move in it. This means that every category projects and engenders a space of experience and every spatial contest is the consequence of conceptual cartographies. Hence, every culture and even every mind, in this sense, lives within the unique space that each of them concurs to engender.[45] As if to say that there is no 'prior to' within the relationship between

[44] See, in this regard, Ansermet and Magistretti (2008), where the topic of neural plasticity devised by Kandel and Spencer (1968) is developed in an interdisciplinary manner. In a very suggestive way, the authors assert that human beings are biologically determined to be undetermined. And this is due precisely to the neural traces processed and inscribed inside the brain structure by means of experience, intended both as practice and as noetic work (for example, the act of fantasizing).

[45] See Zumthor (1993, p. 30), who observed: "Sans doute ces fluctuations tiennent-elles à la nature problématique de ce que désigne le mot d'*espace* (ou ses équivalents dans les autres langues occidentales) et de ce à quoi réfère l'idée correspondante: réalité ambiguë, idée complexe, terme qui ne cesse de dériver en métaphores. Peut-être faudrait-il compter autant d'espaces que de découpages possibles de la «réalité». L'espace relève aujourd'hui des sciences biologiques et humaines autant que de la physique, et chacune de ces disciplines l'intègre à son ordre propre d'intelligibilité. L'historien des cultures ne peut donc le saisir que comme une catégorie irrationnelle, relative à la condition de l'homme sur son fragment d'univers: grâce à elle, l'homme déchiffre celui-ci tandis que, dans cet acte même, il se crée un environnement symbolique, en rapport instable de complémentarité ou de contradiction avec la nature ainsi pensée. C'est pourquoi sans doute le seul discours efficace sur l'espace est un récit, comme il pourrait l'être sur les lèvres d'un enfant: un *mythe*, au sens originel du mot. Tous les autres discours ne sont qu'une approximation de celui-là, s'attachant davantage, selon les présupposés ou les nécessités du moment, à l'idée de séparation ou à celle d'identité, à celle de permanence dans le mouvement ou à celle de mutation. D'où la fréquence des expressions figurées, de nos jours envahissantes: l'«espace littéraire» ou l'«espace des possibles», la métaphore provigne dans toutes les directions. Je voudrais, dans ce livre, éviter les embûches de ces demi-mensonges. Mais on peut s'interroger: ne trahissent-ils pas simplement l'impossibilité ontologique où nous sommes de ne pas prêter une

organism and environment. Both take place simultaneously and through a process of co-determination. All the rest, namely the universe of representations, consists in retrospective reconstructions, that are hypothetical and teleologically oriented, elaborated starting from the interactive and relational ground where each of the two poles, 'I' and 'World,' mind and environment, look like elements already included within the experiential relationship and forged by it for their semantic features.

The above neurological and psycho-cognitive excursions suggest that when Otherness breaks into the borders of a life context organized by the law, when the Other crosses the territorial frontiers of a state, they are not merely penetrating inside an empty space previously occupied and colonized by another culture. This is because that same culture is coextensive to the space on the internal side of the border, it coincides with the space, it *is* such a space. Consequently, the moving Otherness makes *itself* space and projects this space, conceptually connoted, inside another space. The subsequent cultural struggles and conflicts are, therefore, the *natural* or *instinctive* outcome of a radical pluralism, precisely, the pluralism of existential spaces. The problematic matter of intercultural encounters, in other words, does not come from the impossibility for two bodies occupying the same space—as Leibniz would have said. Rather, it is engendered by the impossibility of two bodies—at least, until they can be considered as two distinct bodies—and their pragmatic-experiential projections, to occupy space simultaneously, to be only one body, only one dimension of embodied experience. It is less a physical problem than a semiotic problem.

In the comparison/confrontation between reciprocal cultural Otherness there are not, thus, two different perspectives on the same empty space placed over there, but rather multiple semantic and teleological intersections and interceptions among categorical frames and categorizations of (pre-conceptualized) spaces that are incommensurable and incommensurably experienced. The only way out from such conflicted incommensurability is creative translation—a translation/transaction that is simultaneously inter-cultural and inter-spatial. At this point, it is immediately discernible—once again—that the Latin root of the term 'translate' (*trans-fero*: to trans-port, to carry across, taken in its twofold spatial and linguistic signification) already conveys something deeply ingrained in human experience. Actually, migration is at the same time a trans-*lation* or trans-duction across space(s) and an inter-categorical translation. The sources of conflict are not spaces, but rather the *continuum* extant among the ingredients constitutive of categories that allow and frame the conceptualization of those same spaces. This is an assumption of crucial importance that will be progressively addressed and explained hereafter.[46]

Intercultural dialogue and the efforts to translate/transact are strongly facilitated by the interweaving of narrative exchanges because narrations draw semantic landscapes full of connotations. Telling a story, with the aim to contextualize the

---

dimension aux choses, de ne pas considérer chacune de celles-ci, dans sa configuration, comme une reproduction du monde ? La civilisation médiévale, citée en témoignage, pousserait à répondre oui."

[46] See Ricca (2020).

meaning of one's own words or behaviors, can focus the attention of the Other on semantic features that would otherwise be completely overshadowed by the *apparent* morphologic clarity of the words or behaviors observed, at first glance, through their cultural schemes. Those features can demonstrate inter-categorical continuities capable of challenging the rigidity of borders drawn by the semantic checklists inherent to the categories of judgement used within each cultural circuit. In this regard, however, it should be emphasized how the generality of categories and thus the same epistemology of modernity and modern law in itself greatly increase the ambiguity of semantic borders.[47] This is because the more general a category is, the more the connotative ground that accords with its definition widens. Consequently, this wideness increases the probability that what is inside and what is outside the category are joined by a connotative *continuum*, namely the sharing of some features. This occurrence, in turn, blurs the categorical borders, making them vulnerable. In this way, the possibilities of an inclusion of Otherness capable of regenerating and renewing the semantic spectrum of categories takes shape.[48] This is the crucial wellspring behind intercultural translation/transaction.

The emersion of inter-categorical continuity is not, however, an outcome deriving from an activity of mere empirical ascertainment. The connotative *continuum* certainly has a descriptive source because it emerges from strains of intersected narration/contextualization. But assessing whether it allows for the remolding of categorical borders implies a creative, cognitive and, therefore, *political* action. Axiological-teleological evaluations will determine its possible directions, inevitably gauged, in turn, on the new inter-contextual dimension to which the interplaying narrations have given rise. As a whole, this is an effect of the dynamism that is coextensive to the same phenomenon of multicultural coexistence and the transformation of environment that is co-construed, unawares, by its actors.

These observations on the relationships between space and interculture allow us to show, now, how the connotative inter-categorical *continuum* is, simultaneously, a spatial *continuum*. The configuration of this coextensiveness depends on whether the categorical boundaries can begin to lose their rigidity, liquefying almost like the contours of Dalì's clocks. But it is precisely such liquefaction that corresponds to the conflating and the subsequent re-defining, in a new fashion, of inter-spatial borders. All in all, it is a process comparable, in many respects, to the generation of metaphors, which consist in the reciprocal and bi-directional *tran-sporting* (trans-*lating*, intended in its etymological sense), with losses and gains in both directions between the semantic elements of two original categories or domains in view of the creation of a third category/domain.

The fluidity of categorical borders revives from the bottom of experience, making the existence of a connotative landscape underlying and somehow pre-existing operations of mapping and framing space (previously taken for granted) newly intelligible. Conversely—and typically—insofar as that invisible/silent dimension

---

[47] See Bauman (1991).

[48] See Blumenberg (2007).

works in the background, each category can appear to be somehow coextensive to the web of relations making its semantic checklist and evident structure; to put it succinctly, categories coincide with these checklists. However, in some circumstances, the web of observable relations appears mobile, as if animated by a motility set off precisely by the ineradicable and ever extant connotative *continuum* between the inside and the outside of each category. Such a *continuum* makes the categorical borders fluid and blurred because it is capable of both widening and narrowing, as appropriate, the implicative connections and, therefore, the related contexts of signification. Furthermore, however tight the connection between meanings and context might be, it is not as powerful as the flexibility of the same contexts. And this is because contexts include implicative relations among ubiquitous connotations. This means that the same features appear in more than one categorical spectrum. But, in turn, the implicative connections are what engender and weave contexts of experience, thus determining what is close and what is distant, inside and outside, with respect to the semantic and pragmatic spectrum inherent to each category and drawn by them.

In Plato's *Timaeus*, he speaks of *Kóra* when he addresses the problem of the beginning.[49] A beginning, in this case, that precedes even the creation of the cosmos by Demiurge. In that ancient era, the same birth of time, even the elements—air, water, fire, and earth—are undefined, hovering and fluttering indistinctly. Their strange condition is nonetheless still recognizable in their inclination to transform from one into another as soon as they lose their stability (think of water and air, for example); or, perhaps, perceptible in dreams that haunt the 'semi sleep,' when the borders of 'things' and the links of pertinence supporting conceptual consistency seem to cloud; and yet, flash in the sparks of a burning fire that seems to blend with the air into which they scatter. Because they arise from a quite unusual mingling between connotations, and do not correspond to ontologically shaped ideas, the epiphanies of the *Kóra* about the threshold of consciousness have an opalescent, vaporous, spectral fashion, still perching astride Being and Non-Being.

To be clear, I do not think that the Platonic *Kóra* is interchangeable with the undetermined 'matter' in which Demiurge instills ideal forms in the course of the creation of the cosmos.[50] Rather, it is the connotative-material *continuum within* which object and thought, meaning and matter are still not distinguishable. Furthermore, it works as a living and dynamic background against which the merging of matter and ideas can take place alongside the emersion of categorical differences and the consequent birth of time (because without differences there cannot be time). Somehow *Kóra* is the conveyor, pre-existing even the cosmos, that allows ideas to

[49] See Sallis (1999).

[50] This particular understanding of *Kóra* corresponds to an interpretation of *Timaeus* deriving from Aristotle, which fails to grasp, however, the ambivalence of Platonic discourse, that is instead developed along a trajectory straddling eidetical/categorical spaces and physical/experiential spaces. Although still present and sometimes looming among the veils of oneiric images, *Kóra* and speculation on it have to do with a dimension that pre-exists the birth of the cosmos, distinctions, differences, and therefore time itself. See, once more, Sallis (1999).

be imbued with space and time. It is a conveyor, a *medium* that affects and permeates even geometrical forms through its creative, regenerative and thus over-categorical energy, engendering hybrid figures, not derivable through mathematical or geometrical progression from simple figures.

Now, beyond the epistemological perspective and ‘para-mythological’ configurations of *Timaeus*, the chorological dimension with its reference to origin, it seems plausible to describe the conditions that pre-exist the relationship between organism and environment in metaphorical terms—although it seems almost oxymoronic to consider. Nonetheless, the chorological dimension seems to come afloat right where previously established connections and borders of organism/environment relationships renew, creating a connotative *continuum* capable of engendering ever-new relationships of sense and categorical borders. Prior to—in an imaginary before, just as the ‘prior’ preceding the beginning of the cosmos is what *Timaeus* is about—the configuring of every category and experiential space, there is a situation of semiotic/semantic promiscuity and ubiquity; this is the same ‘before,’ the condition that looms—as in dreams, in an almost ghostly and protean fashion—over the process of intercultural translation and/or inter-categorical metaphor creation.

During the defining of each category, difference becomes visible, takes shape, restricts. This very difference enables the perception of time’s flow. But time itself is a semantic category, and depends on what inhabits it. Actually, coextensiveness between space and category, spatial and categorical spectrums, allows us to understand why the conceptualization of any space, calling into play semiotic and semantic elements (both connotative and denotative), constitutes a time synthesis, which eternizes and files differences within a hierarchically organized taxonomy.[51] But this is only a summary of the ongoing occurrence of a relational process. It is precisely for this reason that the temporal perspective should be included inside an understanding of spaces.

Situations, events, facts, and connections, spread over time can be epitomized in the semantic checklist of categories and that is made within their borders.[52] To understand such a process, one might imagine a footprint. Past, present and future—that is, the overall meaning and signification towards the subsequent experiences the footprint supplies—are summoned and actualized in the conceptual structure of every observed footprint. Its semantic elements, from a semantic point of view, comprise something that is not present in current time, that is strictly pertinent and close to the observational action itself; likewise, those elements do not lie in the space filled (or rather emptied) by the same footprint. Nonetheless, the *absent* elements partake and outline spatial coordinates essential to the experiential and, therefore, conceptual implications related to the footprint (they give clues about the

[51] See Deutscher (2010), Libet (2004), Fabian (1983). All three authors, from linguistic, neuronal and anthropological points of view respectively, highlight the conversion of temporal categories and phenomena into hierarchical-taxonomic schemes.

[52] See von Benda-Beckmann and von Benda-Beckmann (2014); Harvey (1996); Ronsenberg and Grafton (2010). From a linguistic-cognitive point of view and regarding the metaphorical equivalences between time and space, see T. Tenbrink (2007), and with a historical bent Zumthor (1993).

direction, distance, form, weight, physical conditions, etc., of the footprint maker). The temporal implications, on a general semantic ground, make synchronous what is a-synchronous, and would be considered as such with respect to the measure of time calculated referring to the procession of heavenly bodies (a kind of time, however, deriving from the spatial-conceptual *presentification* of something that is remote from a physical point of view). Sprawling over time, those implications draw a connotative frame that simultaneously molds a space of experience composed by their pragmatic and phenomenal potentialities, previously only imagined and then concretely feasible, but in any case altogether coextensive to the conceptual framework thus developed.[53]

Generalizations used in modern legal language, especially within the general and abstract statements typical of *civil law*, provide the spatial-temporal coordinates for the construction of sovereignty's circuit, which is nothing but a semantic-territorial synthesis. Claims for (inter-)cultural recognition aim to remold the categorical borders of legal language by leveraging the semantic-axiological continuities extant among morphologically different behaviors and/or symbolic expressions, sometimes even branded as incommensurable. This, inter alia, allows us to focus on a crucial matter regarding cultural differences and their reciprocal confrontations. Too often,

[53]The conversion of implications/consequences (even those emerging from experience) of something in categorical elements and the subsequent assimilation to the connotations of that same thing, fact or event pertains to a radial conception of categories. On the radial and implicative character of categorization processes, see Lakoff (1987) and, even before, Peirce (1868), as well a crucial observation proposed by Dewey (1926) and related to the famous definition of 'meaning' proposed by Peirce in the same essay just cited. It is worth briefly recalling the specific observations made by Dewey in his essay—perhaps not coincidentally, on a legal topic—regarding the subject-matter of corporations' legal personality. What is relevant, from a theoretical and semiotic point of view, lies in the fact that Dewey, in order to solve some legal problems addressed in that essay, makes an explicit referral to the pragmatist principle formulated by Peirce: "Consider what effects, that might conceivably have practical bearings, we conceive the object of our conception to have. Then, our conception of these effects is the whole of our conception of the object." Dewey broadens the gnoseological scope of the Peircean principle by calling into play an 'extensive abstraction' that applies also beyond the pragmatic or physical implications (*bearings*, in Peirce's words) and has as its object the entire scope of 'reciprocal relationships' (between signs). Dewey writes: "The mode of definition, however, has no inherent dependence upon pragmatism as a philosophy. It has been stated and adopted on the basis of analysis of mathematics and physics by writers who would be horrified to be called pragmatists. Thus stated, it is the principle known as 'extensive abstraction,' and assumes this form: "'. . .what really matters to science is not the inner nature of objects but their mutual relations, and that any set of terms with the right mutual relations will answer all scientific purposes as well as any other set with the same sort of relations'". Broad, *Scientific Thought* (1923: 39). The idea and the name are taken, however, by him from A. N. Whitehead. This is a more general statement than Peirce's, because it applies to mathematical concepts, such as "point," whose "consequences" are not physical effects. In concrete matters, the "mutual relations" which count are, however, of the nature of effects." The broadening hermeneutical option proposed by Dewey with regard to the pragmatist maxim had a pioneering socio-semiotic scope and is perfectly in tune with the conception of space, or rather with the spatial-connotative *continuum*, encapsulated in legal chorology, in turn inspired by Plato's *Timaeus*. In more general terms, and for a theoretical genealogy of the approach to categories and categorization proposed above, I refer to Ricca (2013c, p. 84 ff.; 2008, p. 217 ff.).

scholars and members of the general public alike portray and configure cultural polarizations as conflicts between values or axiological tenets, even when related to law. What is almost entirely absent, as a rule, is any of the primary cognitive substance or cause of such conflicts. Declarations of contrasts in values rely upon the 'objective' morphological features of behaviors or symbolic expressions. This kind of 'objectivity' is forged, however, according to the cognitive schemes of only one of the conflicting parties. Therefore, the alleged morphological objectivity could also correspond to tremendous mistakes of interpretation, depending on biases, stereotypes, stigmas and, above all, the absence of any effort or ability to perform an intercultural translation. Making room for an analysis of the cognitive side of the issue, instead, could produce, in many cases, an evaporation of the so-called values struggle. The self-transformation of the semantic borders of categories intrinsic to the process of intercultural translation/transaction, could lead to the drawing of a third categorical ground, within which an involvement of values and their pragmatic projections could also simultaneously undergo a transformative process.

Every (hypothetical) user guide to interculture should always include an invitation to ask the following questions: is what we believe we see really what we are seeing? Is its morphological appearance, the way in which the 'thing' empirically appears to us, truly universal and immune to the possible influence of different cultural schemes? Is it possible that a closer look at the Other's point of view and cultural patterns could change our categorization of the behaviors or words taken as sources of conflict between values? Have we made any attempts to translate interculturally before reaching the conclusion that we must engage in conflict, or face an incommensurability between different values and cultures? Can we make such an attempt to translate? How? What do we have to take into account? Lacking a prior commitment to formulate such kinds of questions and the attempts at intercultural translation that might follow, any possible efforts to 'accommodate' different positions, claims, and expectations, even if genuine, could run the risk of turning into an endless piling up of misunderstandings.

The Other's gestures and deeds, which cross and break into sovereign space, are always chorological transformations and synthesis. This is because they epitomize and engender spatial-conceptual implications that semiotically actualize, here and now, what happens at great distances, and is semantically codified according to coordinates of sense often rooted in *faraway* and *remote* events but nevertheless encapsulated in the 'know-how' of present individuals through their memory. By applying law, puzzling out words and behaviors, or interculturally translating the Other's deeds, what is distant in geographical space can become conceptually close, what is remote in a semantic-categorical sense can become spatially contiguous, and vice versa. The final effect will be that the inter-categorical translation will transmute into inter-spatiality and spatial translation—namely migration—will transfigure into inter-categoriality or a metaphorical conflation of categorical spectrums.

The overall phenomenon can be observed more closely to demonstrate how the specific characteristics of legal language make it more vulnerable, but at the same time more functional, than empirical or descriptive language to support such chorological intercultural syntheses.

6.4.1 *How the Re-Interpretation of Spaces Transforms Linguistic-Normative Categories*

To make readily understood the vision and important benefits to be had from the chorological-intercultural approach, it could be useful dramatize in an almost narrative fashion the relationship between an *average* legal professional and a foreign client or, alternatively, to outline some concrete inter-subjective relationships.

An interesting case could be that of a family business. In India or in Pakistan, family businesses are a widespread phenomenon. Many migrants to the Northwest hemisphere from those contexts are inclined to create family businesses also in their host countries. Not infrequently, the activity of a single business is developed astride the territorial-cultural contexts of both origin and destination. However, in many Western countries, the legal features of family business are not the same as those legally provided in the countries of provenance; in addition, in many cases the cultural patterns underlying the normative forms and conceptual structures defining family, its life, linkages, and inherent bonds, are also different.

In EU law there is no normative frame purported to regulate the family business. Consequently, I will use the Italian legislation regarding this institute and provided by art. 230*bis* of the Civil Code.[54] Among the most relevant aims of this rule is the prevention of the exploitation of family members, particularly women and children,

[54]Article 230*bis* of Italian Civil Code disciplines the family business as follows: "**Impresa familiare (Family Business)**. Unless consisting of a different relationship, the family member who works on a continuing basis in the family business has a right to maintenance, based on the income of the family and she/he has the right to share in the profits of the family business and the assets purchased with the profits, as well as any increase in the company's worth, also with regard to goodwill, in proportion to the quantity and quality of the work performed. The decisions relating to the use of profits and gains and those related to extraordinary management, productive guidelines and termination of the company are taken by the majority of the family members who participate in the company itself. Participating family members who do not have the full capacity to act are represented in the vote by those who exercise authority over them.

A woman's work is considered equivalent to a man's.

For the purposes of the provision in the first subparagraph, it is understood that the term *relative* refers to the spouse, relatives to the third generation and relatives-in-law to the second generation; as for family businesses, the term refers to the spouse, the relatives to the third generation, and relatives-in-law to the second.

The right to participate set in the first subparagraph may not be transferred, unless the transfer is made to a family member referred to in the previous paragraph and with the consent of all participants. Such right may be terminated by cash at the cessation of the work activity, for any reason, and also when the company itself is terminated. Payment can be made in more than one annual payment, to be determined by a judge if no previous agreement is reached.

In the event of a distribution of an estate or a company transfer, the subjects referred to in the first paragraph may pre-empt the company. If applicable, such right is applied according to the provisions of Article 732."

Family tacit co-ownerships in the agricultural field are regulated by usage if not in conflict with the previous regulations."

As regards family business see, within an expansive literature, Del Giudice (2010), Smyrnios et al. (2013).

when working for the business. To this end, family business becomes legally relevant in force of its mere practical occurrence rather than by means a formal foundational legal act.

In some European areas, for example the United Kingdom, Indians and Pakistanis often experience difficulties importing their family business practices. Conversely, in Italy, also by virtue of the provisions stated by the above art. 230*bis*, these people and their family business could probably find fertile ground. It is to be stressed, however, that in India the family business activity is allowed to be coordinated with individual enterprises, so as to parcel out the fiscal obligation. Indians and Pakistanis try to use a combined device of this kind also in the UK, but as a result find themselves subject to sanctions for violations of tax law.[55] In Italy, recent innovations in the field of individual enterprise targeting simplification (even if with results still to be assessed), could instead promote such combinations, especially given the informal nature of family business.

Thus far, one might observe, the subject-matter would seem in any case to pertain to inter-normative relationships. This is true, except that unfortunately the idea of a nuclear family as characterized by Italian culture and law does not coincide with the idea of extended family widespread in India and Pakistan. On the other hand, a merely comparative/inter-normative inquiry can bring this cultural discrepancy and how it precisely takes shape to light.

So, if an Indian was consulting a lawyer, with the intention to create an Italian branch of his family business, these two subjects might fall prey to a deep misunderstanding about the actions to undertake and their legal consequences. For example, it might be the case that the Indian entrepreneur had a nephew, son of his own brother, in Italy. In all likelihood, the Indian could feel the exigency, if not the moral obligation, to offer the nephew work in his family business branch. This is because the Indian would consider the nephew as an integral part of his extended family (or, at least, to be defined in this way in comparison to the Italian nuclear family). In contrast to the UK response, the Italian legal system could readily give him a positive response to such an exigency. Art. 230*bis* provides that the family business can include up to the third degree relative, and relatives-in-law of second degree. The client and the lawyer could thus converge on a common ground, where the latter could provide a positive solution for the Indian.

What the lawyer does not know is that extended family links and Indian family ethics in most cases do not permit the nephew to become co-partner of the family business and partake in enterprise decisions and profits. To understand the actual meaning of that which the Indian is asking for, the lawyer should have some information, inter alia, about the relationships between him and his brother, namely the father of the newly immigrated nephew, the discipline and situation regarding the

[55] On this topic and form, for a sociological legal-intercultural point of view, see the following text of Jyoti Dialani - Solicitor (England & Wales) & Advocate (Bombay): *Hindu Undivided Family: Tool for Tax Planning For Non-Resident Indians*, free download from www.Singhania.com/Publication/HUF.pdf.

portion of family business operating in India, and a whole series of cultural determinants, which without the assistance of someone expert or somehow acquainted with Indian culture—and, specifically, that segment of Indian culture to which the client belongs—would remain out of the lawyer's awareness. This is because those who are acting from their own culture are usually unaware of it, and above all, do not know how to provide analytical reports or conceptual-definitional explanations about its inner structures. Culture consists in a sort of background 'knowing to do,' which people are able to perform but not to symbolically outline. So, in the absence of objectified information about the implicit knowledge of his own client, the lawyer likely ends up giving *errant* or misleading advice.

In order to understand the meaning of his client's words and actions, the lawyer is required to make an imaginary journey across space. Only after having figured out 'how things are in India' can the lawyer hope to correctly puzzle out the cognitive schemes and, thereby, the actual meaning of behaviors and requests that the client makes of them. Once apprised of the intercultural and multi-sited 'semantic ingredients' of the situation at stake, the lawyer could then acquaint the Indian with a specific feature of Italian regulation of family business, that is, its residual function or 'residuality.' This means that if, between the entrepreneur and a relative within the third degree, or a relative-in-law within the second degree, another kind of legal relationship is established, then the occurrence and the related family business regulations become recessive. Concretely, and to refer to the outlined situation, the Indian could make sure that his nephew is able to work in the business, but in a role qualified as a 'dependent employee,' so as to avoid any entitlement of the nephew to partake in the larger family business activity or in the distribution of profits. Of course, it is up to the Indian, his modalities of self-representation and autonomous management of his own cultural coordinates to assess the best way to reach an appropriate solution, considering, naturally, any possible interference in relationships with his other relatives.

What matters from an intercultural point of view is that the solution of the case might remain hidden, out of reach for both client and lawyer, if the connotative landscapes used by each of them, in their actions and communicative performances, is not brought to the surface. The physical proximity of the Indian client-entrepeneur to the Italian territorial context transports (trans-*lates*), at least partially, within this different circuit the space of experience engendered in India by the combination of family and business (precisely, the family business). The two cultural-geographical spaces, Italian and Indian, come into contact just because they can intersect both in practice and through the symbolic planning of actions undertaken by migrant subjects. In turn, the work of the lawyer, as that of anyone dealing with an Italian-Indian family business, will produce consequences specifically related to this heterocthonous presence within national borders. If the lawyer is able to adequately interpret this spatial-categorical contiguity, namely the chorological dimension of the case, then they will have succeeded in envisaging the implications of their advice to the Indian regarding issues such as their future professional activity, the possibility of attaining additional Indian clients or not, the creation of a path to social inclusion, or rather exclusion of difference, the promotion of trade relations between

Italy and India, maybe even the avoidance of illicit behaviors, and so on. On the other hand, through the configuration of such an inter-space of experience, the lawyer will be simultaneously translating the categories of family behavior belonging to Indian culture into the Italian culture. This means that he will be remolding, in this way, the pragmatic consequences of public language, which will become—at least, for that portion—a *tertium*, namely a sort of *Italindian* or *Indalian*.

An intercultural use of law can, therefore, transform spatial proximity into categorical contiguity, giving birth to a new context of experience and sense through legal utterances alone. Apart from the obvious legitimacy of such an operation—which we can easily imagine benefitting innumerable analogous areas of social and legal experience—it could avail itself of the constitutional *medium* and its authoritativeness. The ties of family solidarity could easily find a place in the dome of Italian constitutional values—but this could apply to all national constitutions—so as to endorse and legitimate in both directions the choices of the Indian entrepreneur, that is: the intention to ensure his nephew a possibility to work in the family business and, on another side, the concern of protecting the interests of the more nuclear Indian family (father, mother, biological descendants and grandparents).

Beyond the relative morphological coincidence—that in this case might even be lacking— between Indian and Italian configurations of family business, there is something else that should be emphasized: the inscription of the behavioral habits of the Other within the axiological category of solidarity that could work as a metaphorical ground for the determination of semantic equivalence and, therefore, successful translation between respective legal-cultural schemes regarding both family and business. At the same time, there is nothing to prevent the lawyer from supplying a different answer that could produce deterrent effects with regard to the intercultural inclusion of (Indian) Otherness; the same effects that could spread, subsequently, on a transnational scale. The idea of an unavoidable nephew's partaking in the Italian branch of the family business—with all the related entitlements—could lead to a deterioration of the relationships between the Indian migrant entrepreneur and the other participants of the family business in India. Indeed, such a limitation might even induce the Indian entrepreneur to abandon plans to create a branch of the family business in Italy or, maybe, to select another national context in which to carry out an analogous project.

What is crucial, however, is the use of solidarity as a translational/metaphorical ground. This is because the use of such a ground, and in particular in the way shown above, allows for the renegotiation, through an intercultural interface, of the features of the respective lived subjectivities. Moreover, the 'invention' of that ground would produce a processive paradigm, a symbolic synthesis of inter-subjective dynamics, a new habit and a transactional scheme replicable indefinitely and adaptable to many different future situations. All this shows the *radical* difference between the practice of inter-normative or inter-morphological accommodations and the interdisciplinary approach to legal interculture. In the first case, people and institutions reach empirical compromise solutions, in most cases driven by a distorted selfish utilitarianism and wholly focused on the possible combination among the most striking and visible morphological 'protrusions' of cultural webs of sense. In the other case, that of a genuine interculturality, the final target coincides with the elaboration of ciphers of subjectivity that are inclusive and general, and in so far as they come from a process of re-modulation, are realized by means of the exercise of the cultural competence and creativity of each of the actors involved in the intercultural encounter. Under the first hypothesis, features and implication of cultural difference are merely combined, often by means of a reciprocal morphological amputation[56]; under the second, what takes place and has to be processed is the convergence among propulsive causes and generating factors of cultural difference, that is to say, among the cultural *engines* enshrined inside the minds and bodies of people. The distance and differences between these two approaches are enormous, and are the same as those identified between often axiologically inconsistent (if even acceptable) pseudo-utilitarian expedients, on one side, and a creative convergence of values and meanings, on the other.[57]

[56] A prime example of this accommodation by amputation can be found in Quebec's approach to interculturalism—utterly different from that proposed here. See, on Quebec's (inter-)cultural politics, Waddington et al. (2012). To understand the difference between Quebec's approach to interculturalism and my view of intercultural process through law, it could be useful to do a comparison centered on the cases reported within the above cited essay and those analyzed in this text; not to mention the cornerstones of intercultural coexistence (in reality, a sort of communitarian catechism of cultural subalternity and asymmetry) proposed by the Bouchard-Taylor Report on Reasonable Accommodation.

[57] On the nature of *accommodations*, dangerously tending towards possible *commodification*, I focused at length in Ricca (2013b), picking up some suggestions from Appadurai and re-gauging the scope according to the legal-intercultural dimension. I report here, for explanatory purposes, a fragment of that essay: "The term 'accommodation' is idiomatic to the jurisprudential Anglo-Saxon language and, partially, it was imported by European jurists, including Italian ones. Deriving from a topical conception of court jurisprudence and drawing on the dynamics of case law, *stare decisis* and the logic of the case, it is inclined to intertwine the results of the use of legal rhetoric, the rationale of the case, with institutional praxis and its tendencies. Good rhetoric can contribute to the invention of 'good meanings' and 'good contexts of argumentation', although it presupposes the distinction between arguing and signifying, the art of being right, and knowledge. The epistemological approach inherent to *accommodation* tends to leak back in an inevitably relativistic or post-modern conception of knowing. For my part, I do not believe that relativism is the only antidote against an absolute and absolutizing conception of truth or cultural cognitive patterns. From a semiotic perspective, the venture of knowing is and remains an open enterprise, merely oriented to objectivity and universality but keeping its inner pluralism; indeed, because it is pluralist, it is always revisable because hypothetical, transactional because adaptive and pragmatic, that is, targeted at experience and a responsive, renewing invention (although not a freehand construction) of reality. The relativism inherent in the practice of *accommodation* seems instead to articulate its dynamics, the dance of relative items, circling around something that, conversely, stays still, fixed and (relatively) steady. This 'something' coincides with a form of ossification, essentialization of the stakes—sometimes including objects, sometimes behavior or words—of cultural compromises (and certainly not cognitive transactions). A compromise, precisely, that is reached inevitably although perhaps unawares by means of a unit of measurement of cultural differences that are dramatically amenable to being used as a currency of exchange and selfish calculation by parties involved in only apparent confrontations of their cultural interests (see, on this topic, the collection of essays edited by Shweder et al. (2002), especially. part II, and, for some contributions, part I). All of this leads, in my view, to a fall off towards an ineluctable commodification of cultural encounters, intercultural translations and transactions. Down this path, there will be no room for reciprocal and

6.4.2 How Semantic and Normative Re-Categorization Can Re-Mold Spaces of Experience

To show the mirroring effects of legal-intercultural translation practices, I would report a case concerning an African Muslim woman (I omit her country of origin to better protect her privacy).

The lady, resident in Italy and planning to obtain citizenship, consults an Italian lawyer asking his assistance to, as she says, "make a division from my husband." The lawyer asks what she means by 'division from her husband.' Gradually, through dialogue it emerges that the foreign client does not have a marital separation from her husband (who belongs to her same faith and ethnic group) in mind, but rather a sort of division of the family home currently in joint ownership with him. The lady had previously gone to the Town Hall offices to demand that such a 'division' be legally defined so as to make the house's portion destined, in her view, to fall in her exclusive ownership, independent from the other part, virtually reserved to the husband. Faced with the refusal of the officer, justified by the impossibility of providing a division through administrative channels and upon the request of only one party, the lady resolves to ask, as mentioned above, the assistance of a lawyer.

The lawyer, at first, does not understand why the lady requests such a 'division.' So, he tries to guess whether it is a case of conflict between the spouses. If this were the case, the only way out would be a marital separation followed by her possible demand for ownership of the whole family house, the lawyer says. This solution, moreover, would be corroborated and made even more feasible by virtue of the fact that—as the lady asserts—she is the mother of five children. Soon, however, the lawyer realizes that a divorce is the furthest thing from the desires of his client. She does not want to separate from her husband, rather quite the opposite. She does not

bi-directional semiotic and cognitive transformations, only for mutual restriction of visions of the world, potentialities of action and signification. All subjectivities and their grammar will be thus doomed to remain identical to themselves, stiffened and sclerotized by the conviction of the 'cultural stakeholders' that they had to endure a sacrifice, although derived from a calculation of material benefits: something that is, in fact, a balancing evaluation performed according to criteria that pre-date the encounter between differences and make no use of any process or effort of reciprocal, intercultural translation/transaction. I conclude by stressing that *accommodation*, taken from this angle, ends up evoking and including a form of *commodification*, that is the transformation of the significant substance of things into mere equivalents of exchange value, namely consumption goods quotable on the market and configurable in the language of quantity. This term—even in the version '*commoditization*,' focused on the transformation of things into goods with an exchange value, see Appadurai (1986)—especially the section titled '*Commodities and the politics of value*,': 3 ff.—entered the legal language with referral to the danger of commercial exploitation of the human body or its parts. Within the economic field, *commodification* is instead referred to as the loss of idiomatic recognizability of products, therefore also of their idiomatic significance, deriving from the diffusion on a large scale of industrial technology, so that differences between the offered products will reduce exclusively to prices, since all the other qualities have become completely fungible or homologated. Things, in other words, if sucked into the commodification process, will no longer keep any significance except for a merely marketable-monetary one."

intend to behave like an Italian wife who feels herself insufficiently respected and loved by her husband. And actually, in addition to her request regarding home ownership, the lady begins to speak of a problematic situation tied to the unyielding intention of her husband to return to Africa, despite the fact that his passport has been confiscated. What is more, he is already an Italian citizen. Upon further narrations of her husband's vicissitudes, the lawyer learns that he has been convicted of insulting a public official, in fact, a traffic policeman, having escaped by force the imposition of a fine. As an additional penalty, his passport was confiscated. Nonetheless, the man is now firmly determined to leave for Africa.

According to the recounting by his wife, the reasons for the man's travel are tied to a desire to see his elderly mother who resides in Africa and, moreover, is currently receiving some medical treatments. The doubts immediately expressed by the lawyer about the plausibility of the husband's motivations in order to justify his travel—above all those regarding the absolute necessity to consult African doctors—bump up against, at least initially, a resolute silence from the client.

However, when she is confident enough that she has successfully managed to elude the lawyers' doubts, the lady returns to her need to obtain the 'division' of the family home, which at that point is going to take the shape of an inevitable judicial division. But, abruptly faced with the necessity to bear the costs of a legal process, the client, maybe already exasperated, lets out a revealing sentence: "...because I don't want *that* in my home! Just so, because he wants to bring *that* here! To me! I know it!"

At that point the lawyer, with fortunate intuition, realizes that the referral to 'that' must necessarily regard another person, likely a woman, currently not residing in Italy. Further encouraged, the client ends up revealing how 'that' is none other than her husband's second wife, who he had married during a journey home to Africa, made alone some years ago. Little by little, then, it turns out that the second wife, namely 'that,' lives in the marital house, located in Africa and originally acquired by the client along with her husband. But this is a situation that the lady, the client, feels as an invasion, and perhaps only a first invasion, now potentially repeatable even on Italian soil in the event the second wife were able to get there.

Abruptly... but only at the end of the conversation, the lawyer understands the genuine meaning of the request their client is making with regard to the 'division' of the marital house. A series of further questions, based on the lawyer's rough knowledge of Islamic law, elucidate the meaning of that claim even more clearly. The lady is a faithful Muslim, nonetheless she does not willingly accept the polygamy of her husband. Perhaps, if she had stayed in Africa, she would make the best of a bad situation. Instead, the migratory experience and her repositioning in a different socio-cultural environment, certainly more responsive to the exigencies of the women's emancipation, now make intolerable to the eyes of the lady-client what in her original country she could only endure. The claim for an exclusive ownership of a portion of the family house, reconsidered according to the intercultural transformations matured by the African client on the wave of her migratory experience, appears to be a gender issue, even better, a means of conveying an aspiration to personal emancipation. From that point forward, therefore, the lawyer figures out that the best way to meet the true needs of their client is not so much to address the ownership regime of the real estate, but rather the interpersonal relationship between the two wives. And this—the lawyer explains to her—because Italian law qualifies polygamy as incompatible with public laws.

Needless to say, perhaps, what a delightful surprise this unexpected information is in the eyes of the client. Gifted with this new possibility, she hastens to ask the lawyer: "Does Italian law really provide this? . . .that 'that' cannot come here? Ah! What a good riddance!" Meanwhile, a smile of satisfaction widens across her face. It is the sign of an unexpected joy that, however, induces the client to let out another revelation. So, she adds, full of happiness: "Well, so she cannot bring 'that other one' here along with her!" But this further referral to another "that" leaves the lawyer dumbfounded. Thus, he immediately adds: "Who is 'that other one', please?" This additional 'that' is none other than the second wife's son, deemed by his mother to be discriminated against—as usually occurs in these cases—with respect to the husband's other children, because this child cannot enjoy the benefits deriving from living in Italy. This new discovery regarding the existence of a second wife's son compels the lawyer, however, to dismantle the rosy hopes of his client of being able to exclude the second wife from a shared house in Italy: the same prospects that the client had seen shining ahead of her just a few moments before. Nevertheless, the lawyer cannot avoid apprising the client of the different situation arising from the existence of this (additional) son of the second wife. Actually, the father could ask for a family reunion with the child; hence, not as his wife but as the mother of his child, she could obtain a family reunion with her son and so come to Italy, as provided by the so-called soft public policy *Italian style*—somewhat different from a similar solution adopted in France—and the international protection of the fundamental rights of children.[58]

The subsequent, urgent question from the client in the face of this new information is the following: "But is it Italian law that says this?" Although decidedly not convinced by the consistency of Italian law (and who could blame her), at last the woman can only accept this new inauspicious possibility. Though heartbroken, even so she does not give up hope. So, contracting her face in a sly smile, she moves closer to the lawyer and, squeezing his arm, tells him with an accomplice's wink: "But this we will not tell my husband, Lawyer!".

The most striking aspect of this report concerns the intercultural transformations undertaken by the African Muslim lady-client. The climax of her cultural creativity is reached precisely at the end, when in her position against polygamy, despite the fact that this is a characteristic feature of her Islamic matrimonial tradition, she seeks an ally. So, we see a Muslim lady who tries to seek assistance from the Italian legal system, and thus even from a white Italian male (the lawyer). Astonishingly, she

[58] In this sense, Italian courts pronounced since the ord. Trib. Bologna 12 March 2003. On the same matter, see further, (Italian) *Corte Costituzionale*, decision n. 224/2005; and Cass. (Supreme Court), 2 March 1999, n. 1739. For other decisions on similar cases I refer to the journal «*Diritto, immigrazione e cittadinanza*». However, I addressed this issue more widely in Ricca (2008, pp. 331–336).

requests complicity from *him* in hiding from her husband the effective possibility allowed by Italian law to obtain a family reunion with the second wife's son and then with the mother.

All these events and changes seem to exemplify how profoundly an intercultural use of law can relativize the stiffening of identities and the rigidity of legal rules from both state and religious apparatuses. Furthermore, and simultaneously, the story just narrated shows the interspatial connotation of the interpretive shifts performed by the lawyer in the attempt to legally qualify the multi-sited situations lived by *his* client straddling two different territorial and cultural circuits, African and Italian.

In general terms, in order to arrive at efficacious solutions suited to the case, and therefore to select legal rules that are actually useful to meeting the client's needs, the lawyer must take into account what happens elsewhere. Although this may be a distant location, it inherits the semiotic circuit and thus the factual and legal categorization of the client's actions and plans. But it is precisely through this sequence of connections/implications that intercultural categorization becomes the hub of a process of change, and of re-configurations of the (effective) spatial dimensions in and through which experience takes its shape.

What course the family vicissitudes of the African lady-client took in the end I am not able to say, nor do I know the final advice of the lawyer assisting her. Regardless, however, the former and the latter, namely vicissitudes and legal advice, will have developed hand in hand, involving through intersecting representations, moves and countermoves, a whole set of actors joined by their actions in a transnational 'theatrical' scene. Nonetheless the theatre of such a story is precisely the trans-territorial and trans-categorical *Kóra* that punctuates, in the background and through a multi-sited polyphony, the inter-spatial and intercultural signification of its plot. What emerges and takes shape, in the end, is the semiotic frame for new spaces of action forged by new cultural meanings.[59]

Cultural anthropology and the anthropology of law notice and conceptualize, as regards similar cases, an increasing de-territorialization of both cultural experience and subjectivity.[60] These qualifications, derived also from the influence exerted by the idea of globalization, make sense, however, only in so far as we consider (even if only in the background and unawares) territory as a synonym of a 'spatial mono-cultural circuit.' By assuming a chorological perspective, instead, things appear quite different. Every place, since time immemorial and even from biological or botanic standpoints, is the result of inter-spatial processes epitomized within that which inhabits it. Entities presented in a particular place may have the most remote provenances. And these origins may be, in turn, very relevant to understanding features, implications, and meanings of that which researchers or common people

[59] See Ricca (2022a).

[60] As regards de-territorialisation and multi-sited anthropological analysis I want to limit here the references to Marcus (1995: 2006), Santos and Rodríguez-Garavito (2005: 1 ss.), Goodale (2007, p. 26) and, the now almost classic, Gupta and Ferguson (1997a, b), although I do not share these authors' post-modern approach.

find and must face when they examine or live in that place. Sometimes, just to figure out the meaning of what is present, we need to make physical or imaginary trips to these places of origin. So, these places will reposition within an 'inter-spatial' dimension or, perhaps, I should say simply within a new 'spatial' dimension. This seems almost obvious when we realize that there is no real distinction between territory and place, on one the hand, and space, on the other.

Once again, the space we experience appears not to be a thing, an empirical and empty entity over there, but rather a semiotic dimension, and as such capable of making close what is physically faraway and, vice versa, conceptually distant what appears empirically at hand. The key point lies not so much in the measurement of physical distance among objects as rather in their propensity to appear and function as (potential) reciprocal implications of one another. This view transforms objects, people and phenomena, which are close in such semiotic (inter-)space—provided that they are appropriately trans-*lated*—into potential elements/features of the same categories used to separate and distinguish other objects near to the former. In other words, physical proximity, although for a time marked by semantic distinction, could transform into categorical contiguity, also including during this process entities that are physically distant but semantically continuous. This is the case, for example, of the African lady-client, simultaneously 'close and distant' and 'distant and close' to her lawyer. In some sense, this could be considered as the most compelling recipe against xenophobia, racism and other forms of 'othering,' with a crucial caveat. How we define the ways and coordinates of these implications, how we make a cartography of the world and mold its inner distances of sense, remains a task *entrusted to* and not *immune from* the cartographers' values and ends.[61]

6.5 Errant Law: Cartographic Metamorphoses and Cognitive Deficit in Legal Qualifications

People migrate along with their spaces of experience. This means that in order to qualify what happens here and now, jurists have to embark on geographical-cultural routes they have never navigated before. To read 'present' situations, the law must become *errant*. The application of a rule belonging to a territorial legal system will have to transit (and simultaneously undergo a transition) along a process of normative and semio-cultural hetero-integration. To figure out what an individual from another legal system or culture is doing, thinking, and wanting, legal professionals of the host country will have to venture to journey towards a 'semantic elsewhere.' There, they will have to identify semiotic and contextual traces capable of bringing out the root sense of what is said and done by people here and now, or at least what is 'currently' made the object of interpretation within a particular, geographical space of experience.

[61] See Pickles (2004), Olsson (2007) et al.

In this regard, it is crucial to underline how inter-contextual 'travel' is not equivalent to neutral data gathering. The semiotic traveler's gaze creates semantic plots and events through a research endeavor. What is more, they have to take into account that their research is bi-directional, and its vectors are the experience, desire, and ability in cultural processing shown by all the actors of the chorological framework—including themselves. If they do not arrive 'beyond-borders' in their travels, if they overlook the cultural self-transformation experienced by people, then their understanding of situations under the lens of legal qualification will inevitably be incomplete, defective. But such an *errant* understanding would result in a legal assessment that does not correspond to the actual situation to be ruled, that is, the situation that works as a pivotal means/medium for the achievement of ends encapsulated in the rules selected for the case. In other words, a deficiency in the intercultural configuration of the facts would pave the way to a sort of heterogenesis of ends in the application of state legal rules and even religious, ethnical, non-state/non-official laws involved in the overall situation. Failing to trace the chorological landscape underlying the experience of people who are periodically involved in the circuit of the application of legal rules leads to a false representation of facts, and therefore a radical misuse of power by legal professionals and authorities. In this regard, it is important to stress how not only the state legal systems but also non-state/non-official laws are implicated in intercultural-chorological transformations. This is because the social environment of the state offers new potentialities for the development of the cultural competences of people belonging to religious, ethnic and other experiential or normative dimensions. Those potentialities can work, therefore, as semiotic and cultural connotations capable of engendering new hermeneutical tools in the understanding and use of normative systems of belonging. To put it another way, we could say that all the normative systems orbiting around paths of subjectivities could undergo a process of reciprocal and polyphonic learning and transformation.[62] Subjects, in short, act as semiotic vehicles in a process of communication and mutual adaptation/learning between the cultural, normative, and pragmatic dimensions of the chorological scene.

The configurability of some connections between the misuse of power and the lack of intercultural translation (within the legal qualification of migration or geographically-culturally multi-sited cases) delineates a central aspect of intercultural law. Its aim is not the achievement of aprioristically or dogmatically inclusive and postulated ends derived from an ideological striving towards a sort of *allophilia*. Rather, the driving force, the motor of intercultural law is of a cognitive kind. In order for state law to implement its own intrinsic ends and for its application to be consistent with the values upon which its legitimacy relies, it is indispensable to make intercultural translation part and parcel of legal competencies and tasks. Even more concisely and icastically, it could be said that an intercultural bent in the

[62] The capacity of legal systems and traditions throughout history to learn from one another is one of the topics most passionately studied and highlighted by Glenn (2005, 2013, 2014).

application of state laws proves necessary if they are to remain themselves, consistent with their own assumptions of legitimacy, even in the face of Otherness.

The error, the cognitive deficiency in puzzling out facts—in which the mind of the Other agent and the contexts of sense they use to plan their actions must also be included—may easily lead to being complicit in or responsible for an injustice, perhaps unwittingly. Such an injustice could even, in some cases, be found to be a violation of human rights, constitutional principles, or any other axiological-normative standard sufficiently vague and ambiguous to host within its semantic spectrum the cultural indices connoted by a semiotic distance from the native culture.

To produce systemically consistent effects, the law must become *errant* and so too must the related legal qualifications entrusted to its agents (lawyers, practitioners, judges, scholars and so on). It must *err* precisely not to 'err', that is, for jurists to avoid dramatic misinterpretations of the facts that the law is committed to rule. In this sense, the axiological charge of principles and their statements, particularly those included within the discourse on human and/or fundamental rights, make them similar to the so-called norms of *renvoi* and specifically, to those that work as presuppositions to the legal definitions provided by other legal systems about certain factual elements or situations.[63] A worthy example of this kind of *renvoi* is the concept of the "Chief of State" of one country as viewed by another. To define the *legal status* of a foreign Chief of State currently visiting within its borders, each state and its legal system must make a *renvoi* by presuming the legal rules of the foreign state to which the Chief of State belongs.

Now, just as this kind of legal *renvoi*, used especially in international law, presupposes regulatory definitions and factual descriptions contained in legal statements provided by foreign legal circuits, so too do legal principles and related axiological-legal categories project their semantic and deontic scope beyond the cultural and geographical borders of the state. They do this by accepting what occurs overseas and taking it as a hetero-integrative element of their own meaning and (legal) effects. What allows these cases and situations to straddle two or more territorial and/or legal circuits are people, their interests, and the paths of their life experience. The inclusive and hetero-integrative reaction of legal systems is possible and, in a way, even obligatory because the inclusive range of their semantic spectrum is extraordinarily wide and, above all, capable of embracing a high morphological plasticity with regard to the cases or situations to be placed under its umbrella. One example, I hope, should be sufficient to clarify the meaning of this assertion.

Consider categories such as 'joy' or 'solidarity.' Behaviors, events, objects, and phenomena that can be categorized under these two semantic domes can differ enormously in their morphological features, so much so that they may not show any common traits, at least from an analytical and empirical point of view. Considering situations of joy, for example, we might imagine navigation on a sailboat as

[63] See Ricca (1999).

well as a caress given to a child.[64] In the same way, among the acts of solidarity we might imagine a pragmatic demonstration of empathy towards the suffering of someone else as well as the funding of a scholarship on behalf of the most deserving.

In terms of correspondence among morphological features, members of the listed pairs share almost nothing. Even so, each may be associated with the others under the same categorical dome because of their axiological, emotive or teleological connotations. To be sure, categorical borders are nearly always axiologically or teleologically determined.[65] Each element of the semantic checklists can be considered as a means, a portion of the process of dynamic relationship/implication that results in what we, then, represent through the category and the word embodying the categorical spectrum. The determination of contexts and categorical borders depends

[64] In this regard, I would briefly highlight some points. In psychological theory, scholars often make distinctions between eliciting conditions of emotional reaction and emotions considered in and of themselves. Such a distinction, seemingly intuitive, relies upon a dualistic conception of experience. It works as if, precisely, the eliciting conditions were facts, taking place outside the mind and body, while emotion remained an inner reaction, emerging inside the body and psyche. However, the objectivity of facts and their apparently exclusive exteriority are consequences of ongoing relationships between an embodied mind and its environment (in which the same embodied mind is included as an integral and dynamic portion). Similarly, the mind/body entity is not a given outside its relationships with and within the environment. This means that emotions contribute to the determination of objects and phenomena taken to be external, while at the same time these are active parts in the generation of the bodily/mental transformations that substantiate and select the salient connotative aspects of facts and our perceptions of them. Emotional reactions penetrate and are inner parts of our perceptive activity even before we become conscious of them, exactly as occurs with empirical sensations and their categorization. This does not mean that reflective activity, as well as sentiments, cannot then have a retroactive effect on bodily/mental reactions, influencing, steering or even modifying their manifestations. Rather, conscious redirections of perceptive and emotive activities can become, over time, unreflective, transforming into habits unconsciously and automatically enacted by the mind/body. The emotional component, in many cases, can no longer be perceived by the conscience, making the qualitative, aesthetic, and axiological aspects inherent to all that is perceived, as well as the related categorizations and the process that conveys the emergence of experience, ultimately, invisible. In this way, the subjective, the inner, vanishes from the horizon of conscience. The counterpoint of this vanishing is the rise of outside objectivity, which becomes, instead, the place of condensation between subject and object. The achievement of such a condition of stability of the external world is, however, only momentary, never definitive, at least if we take these words in absolute terms. The angulations and perspective included in the subject/object relationship can always change, thereby reactivating emotional actions and conscious perceptions of the qualitative aspects of experience: this, in view of renewed configurations of objectivity, new synthesis between subject and object. These remarks taken as a whole allow us to assume, as in the examples given above, (sailing, the caress of a child, the empathetic pragmatic participation in the suffering of others, and finally, the funding of a scholarship), these actions as implications, constitutive connotations of the emotive categories of joy and solidarity, and not as mere eliciting conditions/premises or only pragmatic implications of the occurrence of purely mental/psychical events, as emotions would be from a dualistic perspective. With regard the enactivist approach underlying the above observations see, in a huge literature, at least Di Paolo et al. (2018) and, for its application to legal experience, Ricca (2022a, 2023). I refer to these two last text for further bibliography on enactivism.

[65] On these aspects, see Ricca (2013a, d).

on the ends and qualitative criteria (including the qualitative properties/connotations)[66] assumed to define them; but the meaning and content of the ends is in turn the outcome of the relationships among means; and, in the *end*, the overall set of ends defines the context. It is a circle from which we can escape only by virtue of a plasticity and an inclusiveness of axiological-teleological categories, qualities capable of relativizing the borders of morphological features, making it possible to cross them.[67]

The possibility of inscribing behaviors, words, objects, and events within the top axiological and, therefore, most open categories of legal systems (statements on fundamental rights are emblematic in this sense) can be activated through the explication of narrative landscapes rich with connotative ingredients. Relying upon such connotative landscapes it is possible to find semantic continuities between the forms of Other's behaviors and the semantic spectrum of axiological categories encapsulated within statements on legal principles. Once such lines of connotative continuity have been traced, it will be necessary to navigate a challenging and tricky path to ponder the salience of each of these connotations with respect to their cross-contextual resonance. In other words, when we decide in a specific case not to include under the 'value-principle umbrella of protection' Other's behaviors that appear to be morphologically different but within their own semantic spectrum comprise the same axiological connotations as other native behaviors that are instead authorized and guaranteed, a reasoned justification must be given as to why.[68] To take an example, let us suppose that in spite of all possible morphological differences, the process of a narrative cross-contextualization and intercultural translation/transaction leads to the singling out of an object, word or behavior as a religious symbol rather than as a blunt weapon (this is precisely the case of the *kirpan*: but the same scheme is suitable to numerous other cases of everyday life, such as contracts, successions, housing, enterprise, urban spaces, and so on). At that point, we should be able to find reasonable motivations to forbid an individual to carry a *kirpan* in public places and, at the same time, allow a Catholic to walk around with a metal cross weighing a pound.[69] Are there truly salient differences with regard to the high-risk public nature of these two objects and their possible uses or misuses? Or are their morphological and even obvious categorical differences (a *kirpan* is a little knife, and so a weapon, whereas an iron cross is a religious symbol) culturally determined? Could the *kirpan* be *rationally* categorized in the eyes of non-Western and non-Christian Others as a religious symbol, and the metal cross, instead, as a dangerous blunt object?

However, to reach the stage of intercultural cross-contextualization, the interpreter will have to make use of the statement of principle and the inherent value-

[66] See, on this, Dewey's seminal essay on the structural qualitative aspects of categorization (1931); and, for the implications of Dewey's approach in legal field, Ricca (2023).

[67] In this regard, see Ricca (2014c).

[68] On cross-contextual resonance, for wider arguments and references, see Ricca (2013a, d, 2014c).

[69] Cfr. Ricca (2013b, 2018, 2022b).

category as a kind of launching pad for excursions in semiotic-cultural territories far from those familiar to them. A genuine and non-ethnocentric implementation of 'that certain value' involved in the concrete intercultural situation requires, substantially, a semantic hetero-integration of the vocabulary and categorical borders usually utilized in the application of national normative apparatuses. This hetero-integration can include spaces of experience far away from those falling within the geographical range of efficacy of a particular national legal system. Nonetheless, the exigency to supply an interpretation that is axiologically consistent with the situation to be ruled will compel the interpreter to take into account and trans-*late* also what appears to be culturally and geographically remote.

In any case, the ascertainment and specification of the semantic-spatial web underlying the connotative relationships epitomized by behaviors, objects, words, and events, is nothing but an effort of chorological configuration of the situations to be ruled, and the related norms. Through the lens of intercultural legal chorology, it is perfectly coherent that the 'geographically distant' becomes close, and the morphologically discontinuous is revealed to be semantically continuous. This is so because the wellspring of perception and the configuration into the semantic/spatial is always semiotic. Within semiotic relationships, what determines the 'distant' and the 'close' are the chains of implication synthetized by creations of meaning, and the blocking out of their underlying connotative fabric, rather than distances measured in miles. This consideration can thus lead us to conclude that beneath a chorological gaze, an object that is physically close can become conceptually remote or *un-topical* because of its lack of implicative links to the semantic features of a particular category, and vice versa. In short, chorological implications could be schematized as follows: (a) physical or geographical proximity is not incompatible with connotative distance/discontinuity; conversely, (b) connotative distance/discontinuity is not incompatible with physical proximity; (c) connotative proximity/continuity is not incompatible with physical or geographical distance; (d) geographical distance is not incompatible with connotative proximity/continuity.[70]

Failing to correctly configure the chorological framework of acts, words, and objects can give way to instances of ineffectiveness, to the detriment of the apical values of legal systems. This ineffectiveness, furthermore, could also then make illegitimate the statutory or judicial choices it implicates. On the other hand, for the state sovereignty and its normative projections to turn outward and hetero-integrate with what is outside and beyond them from a semantic-spatial point of view would entail involving the acts of citizens belonging to other nations and/or cultural circuits. The activities of people continuously cross and supersede national borders; besides, even the protections of fundamental rights and the basic needs of populations rely upon factors that move along coordinates that are asymmetrical with

[70]Consider, once again, that over the course of the transpositional/metaphorical processes the distinction between 'denotations' and 'connotations' vanishes and all the ingredients (both morphological, implicit, visible and invisible, expressed and mute) of categories are *'flattened into '*— so to speak—a connotative *continuum*.

respect to intra-state laws and politics. So, if the denial to hetero-integrate national legal systems implies a violation of fundamental values or value-principles to the detriment of citizens, then the *renvoi* of presupposition (see above) performed by these axiological-normative standards will unleash its effects with the same force as in the case of cultural claims raised by migrants or people of other cultures.

From a complementary perspective, it must be underlined that cultural and/or religious circuits do not correspond at all to the apportionments and maps of the political geography and its national frames. Figuring out the genuine meaning of a religious claim raised here and now requires, not infrequently, a cognitive and axiological-legal hetero-integration of factors engendered and rooted in a 'territorial elsewhere,' sometimes even in non-physical places insofar as they coincide with spaces of transcendence and experiences of faith.

In general terms, it is to be observed, moreover, that legal statements are more vulnerable to the connotative continuity unveiled by the semiotic pressure of cultural difference than analytical-empirical sentences or concepts. Although all categories, even those abstractly analytical, include axiological elements, legal categories are intensely marked by values and their particular semantic characterizations. So, it is easier to inflect the semantic borders of linguistic categories playing on the semiotic (and, I would say, chorologic) plasticity of legal statements. This is because the law does not describe (or, at least, not only) but rather it prescribes. And for legal precepts to become imperative, they must show—especially in democratic-constitutional system—axiological-teleological value. If something is to be done, it is so because doing it is worthwhile. No type of legal imperative or formalistic theory of law can escape the grip of this constraint, which is also an anthropological premise of legal experience, at least at the level of the foundational principles or tacit assumptions of normative systems. So, as soon as we—in the guise of cross-contextual legal translators—are able to single out the axiological connotations of legal statements, often tied to their hierarchical-systemic presuppositions, then the chorological-intercultural approach will become openly viable. Along this way, though it may seem paradoxical, the very state law, the same deadly weapon wielded by colonialist oppressors and the Western dirigisme of the post-colonial era, can transmute, and become an efficient contributor to the self-collapse of ethnocentric, identitarian, nationalist, and similar discourses.

The indispensable *erring* of law along the routes of an intercultural chorology can be seen, here, as a specular portrayal of the *errant* swarming that punctuated the colonial 'enterprises'—in both the accepted meanings of the term 'err.' If once Western law lorded over peoples through its *erring* across the planet, driven by the wind of colonial imperialism in its sails, today it *errs* also in the face of the anthropic ebb tide engendered by migrations towards the West, and more generally, the 'Elsewhere.' In the past, the legal transplants imposed by colonial powers over other territorial contexts were marked by the crucial *error* of overriding the necessity of their translation into local cultural languages, so as to trigger process of intercultural transaction;[71] conversely, today, the same Western state law finds itself in need of translating Otherness, now dwelling within its own borders, in order to keep consistent with itself and avoid a collapse of its own legitimacy as a result of the interpretive *errors* and anthropological-cognitive deficiencies of its own legal agencies (judges, lawyers, notaries, and all the host of legal practitioners and officials). In other words, to prevent *erring*, by applying its own legal statements in an inconsistent and culturally asymmetrical way, Western law has to *err* in a chorological-intercultural sense. It is as if our modern history had overturned, and were now transforming in the upside down mirror of a colonial past. With the *geographical* parts reversed, this overturning is—in some respects—an effect of an *error* that is specular to past ones, while efforts towards an intercultural law—the very efforts that were not made in the past and that are still to be realized in the present—could represent a possible remedy.

The axiological-political coordinates of modern law had universality or, at least, an aspiration to universality as their originating ideal. Even so, for reasons tied to the so-called economy of possibilities, the alleged universality inherent in cosmopolitan declarations of natural/human/fundamental rights have found local implementations, that are territorially confined within national contexts and their borders.[72] The overall effect has coincided with the production of ethno-local experiences and concretizations of universality, that is, territorially and culturally situated versions of it—one could say even 'provincialized.' Declarations of rights welded themselves to the European legal categories of statutory laws, which were instead furrowed with historical-cultural wrinkles and crammed—as noted above—with Christian moral-theological predispositions. However, once the improper metonymical conflation between European culture and universality (*idest*: universalistic potentialities of statements on human/natural rights) had been accomplished, it was used as a means to legitimate the forced enculturation of colonial dominions. European identity was passed off as the 'universal' in itself, and this enabled the alibi to override and disparage the cultural 'dignity' of Others' ways of life.[73] Colonial imperialism flooded the planet, tormenting it with sails and cannons, but its arsenal also contained 'ideal' and symbolic devices, including legal forms.

The 'universality' betrayed by colonialism and nationalism, for all that, gets its comeuppance today, precisely in the trails of migrations. The achievement of de-colonization has unfortunately left many former colonies with a legacy that is

[71] All historical attempts at legal acculturation (irrespective of whether we refer to civil or common law), as for example the *adat law*, were substantiated rather by rough translations of the legal-ethical experience of colonized peoples into the categories and schemes of the systematic rationality of Western legal thought. And, when such operations resulted in complete failure, the lesson (presumptively) learned was univocal and certain: colonized people were evidently lacking any *sense of law*. The case of India at the time of English colonization is emblematic. See, in this regard, Lingat (1973) and Derret (1999).

[72] See. Habermas (1992); Benhabib (2004).

[73] See Muthu (2003).

hard to manage, to say the least. The dream of autonomy has uncovered, as building blocks of new regimes, the institutional instruments and political categories typical of Western culture. At the same time, however, it has been faced with all the difficulty of coordinating these government methods with traditional cultural imageries, that have finally wriggled free from the yoke of foreign oppression and been 'enabled' to work as legitimate sources for the self-representation of the political will of (autochthonous) peoples. The democratic 'dream' had to deal with the substantial asynchrony and incommensurability of many anthropological-symbolic categories of ethnic mentalities, often deep-rooted in religious traditions different from Christianity, and in contrast with the cultural coordinates of Western imagery. This discordance—not to mention the overhanging post-colonialism and the often artfully and rhetorically selfish uses of human rights made by the international agencies rigged by the Euro-American bloc—has been the explosion fuse of a diverse range of fundamentalisms. A trait common to these phenomena is their difficulty in devising forms of legal-social subjectivity that are capable of mutually condensing, including, and translating local cultures and traditions into categories deriving from modern Western law. Somehow, this is the poisoned apple concealed within the apparent gift-pack of deliverance from the colonial yoke *more or less* munificently 'proffered' by European states in the twentieth century.

The lack of intercultural translation, an offspring of the ethnocentric universalism championed by colonialism, crops up again, today, as a locus of challenges within the same contemporary Western states. The 'arriving Others' are loaded, *more or less* consciously, with the political-anthropological inconsistencies tied to the discrepancies experienced in their countries of origin between the imported modern Western categories (there) and the habits supplied by autochthonous religious-traditional imageries. So, their landing in Western territories, along the tracks of migrations, is realized on the wings of a prejudice borne from the hard efforts of coordination made in their countries between (Western) modernity and other traditions that are not infrequently managed in dialectical and oppositional ways. On the other hand, however, it is to be stressed how the past *error* of having passed off European identity as universality is not at all an attitude that can be automatically erased, corrected or eclipsed by the contemporary legal and democratic experience of Western countries. Consequently, the cultural difference acted by migrants finds itself engaged—I reiterate, with geographically reversed roles—in a struggle that is analogous to that already lost in their own home and renewed after de-colonization. On one side, we see the attempts made by the Others to make the most of universalizing and inclusive semantic potentialities of discourse on rights to inscribe it into their own cultural codes; whilst, on the other side, there is still the tendency to substantiate the lexicon of rights with the categories of Western legal cultures and the related anthropological ciphers assumed as its prototypical implementations.

Statements such as "whoever comes to our country has to respect our values and demonstrate that they share them," or "we have to establish some barriers to the integration of foreigners," "we will not be balkanized or Islamized," "foreigners must respect the rules of civil coexistence already established in our country," and so on, work as rhetorical alibis to justify a lack of intercultural translation and, above all, an ethnocentric and exclusionary use of human and/or fundamental rights. We should understand, instead, that it will be impossible to persist for too long in the betrayal of original (and genuine[74]) cosmopolitan aspirations inherent to the rights discourse. It is simply inconsistent to proclaim universality, assuming it as cornerstone in the construction of paradigms for a peaceful and civil coexistence, and simultaneously decline to understand it in a way that is integrally forged according to local cultures and their schemes. The busting of Otherness into the national borders of Western states gives rise to an implicit request—and necessity—to demonstrate how the universalistic cipher of modern Western law is authentic and concretely—that is to say, historically—viable. On the other hand, Western democracies cannot lightheartedly disclose, at this stage, that they are unable to include Otherness along an intercultural process capable of engendering a public and legal subjectivity that is equidistant from cultural differences and not asymmetrical in its recognition of manifold claims for validation. Otherwise, faced with such a historical evidence test, the overall modern project will have simply demonstrated its total moral and historical bankruptcy.

Now, although there are those who are looking forward to this occurrence or else proclaim that it has already occurred long ago, I cannot help—even if it is out of fashion—resisting this idea. I think that modernity is not (only) to be identified with its historical misuses, and universality is not only something *a priori* perched at our backs but rather what lies beyond our horizon, to be reached cooperatively by all of us humans, putting our cultural competence (and not our reified cultures) to work. Hence, I am unable to think of what could happen from a planetary perspective if tomorrow the thesis of the post-modernist ranks were to prove true, as if to say that the potentialities of modernity, of its universalistic grammar, showed themselves to be nothing but the corrupt use made of them by colonialism and post-colonialism. If modernity, at last, appears to be only the set of its deficiencies, I do not know where and how we could find, in the shortest possible time, a communicative platform to avert a blind war of all against all. My thoughts about modernity are not, however, mere examples of wishful thinking. The issue at stake is whether or not modernity is coincident with its misuses alone.

Many people, as crusaders of legal post-modernism and anti-state legal pluralism, believe that to avert and thwart conflicts between legal systems and cultures it would be sufficient eliminate the state and its experience, understood as the root of all evil and the very icon of modernity. I think, however, that the mere elimination of the state from the horizon of human experience would not be sufficient to automatically engender harmonious coexistence and mutual adjustment between differences and different ideas of law, ethics, culture, religions, and so on. This is only a pipe dream, and—what is worse—its existence can only be surmised behind the loud proclamations of pluralistic, relativistic, anti-modern and allegedly salvific creeds. Quite the opposite, I see the most important challenge in the possibility of making it so that the state collapses in on itself and its own premises of legitimation so as to self-transform

[74] Cfr., again, Muthu (2003).

towards the direction of an inclusive, pluralistic and intercultural declination of its modern roots.

Intercultural law and its anthropological-semiotic methodology of translation-transaction between differences, constitutes an attempt to realize the modern project, but by supplying it with culturally inclusive paths of realization characterized by a bottom-up responsiveness. The adoption of such a perspective induces us, inter alia, to imagine well-rehearsed answers to claims for making legal lexicons pluralistic: answers drawn from an inclusive use of the potentialities inherent in the semantics of rights. Such a purpose can be achieved—I think—by means of a vision of legal-cultural pluralism different from that currently prevalent and, consequently, through an understanding of inter-constitutionality and inter-jus-fundamentality that resists the top-down dynamics of today's supranational institutions and state agencies (including the courts).

6.5.1 Value-Based Pluralism vs. Rules-Based Pluralism

Legal pluralism is basically declined now as an inter-systemic pluralism. This approach induces, however, the classification of claims for cultural recognition raised by people within an operational frame ordered by international private law or, alternatively, conveyed by comparative law. In the first case, namely when legal agencies make use of international private law, the claims advanced by an individual or group are assessed according to their congruity with respect to normative/cultural apparatuses somehow already consolidated as legal or community rules. Perhaps, it is also by virtue of this method of classification that cultural difference claims tend to be clothed as petitions for the protection of religious freedom. Almost all religions of the world have produced over time codes and orthopraxis formalized in normative terms and handed down in this guise. Furthermore, claims for religious freedom enjoy a particular form of identification before and within secularized and laic legal systems. Secular jurisdictions have no competence to examine the axiological foundation of requests raised in the name of religion on their merits; otherwise, jurisdictional secular authorities would contradict their own laicism or, put diversely, betray their secularized presuppositions of legitimacy, therefore violating the sanctity of their *non-interference* in the realm of conscience and religious faith.[75]

[75] As for the claims for recognition of cultural difference clothed as petitions for religious freedom, see Ricca (2012), where I try to stress (especially in Chap. 1) the not-merely-strategic nature of such an option. In many cases, actually, it is motivated by the continuity extant at an anthropological level between current cultural features of legal subjectivity and imprints left on them (including Western secularized ones) by the centuries-old mingling of religion and culture. This consideration applies to all legal cultures and experiences. Unearthing the historically ubiquitous mix between religion and culture, and its resilience within contemporary legal languages, will become progressively more important as multilaterality and multi-directionality of processes of global cultural

Jurists, for their part, are more comfortable addressing (through their usual methodological toolkits) the indexes of cultural difference that can be assumed to be equivalent to or coincident with normative standards. From the legal practitioners' point of view, the tools for inter-systemic legal hetero-integration—principally the *renvoi*—have already been tested and complemented by devices (such as public policy) designed to limit and counter-limit their applicability (e.g. protection of refugees, asylum rights, violation of international *jus cogens*).

The crucial issue is, however, that cultural/ideal pluralism and its protection are not exclusively positioned on the ground of possible relationships among legal rules and their inter-legal implications. Cultural and ideal differences are conceivable—and actually in this way they are revealed within the various infra-national constitutional experiences—as components of an axiological pluralism embodied and acted by people along the paths of law-in-action and through the diverse interpretive reading of human and/or fundamental rights. On the other hand, statements on the protection of rights—apart from surreptitious dissimulations—show the intrinsic universalizing, trans-epochal and trans-local tension of the values and ends they include. Consequently, I see no reason why among the legitimate sources of this plurality of readings, cultural difference cannot also be counted. If it is taken for granted that all are equal before the law and entitled without any distinction of race, color, language, religion, political or other beliefs, then culturally oriented readings of constitutional and statutory laws must also be considered to be entirely legitimate.

The issue of legal and cultural pluralism is not necessarily best addressed on the ground of inter-legal connections/references, with all the inter-normative coordination and compatibility constraints this implies; or, at least, not only there. On the contrary, I think that the most important challenge takes place—provided that the curtain rises—on the stage of an interpretation of human and/or fundamental rights performed in a universalistic, inclusive, and bottom-up style. A possibility that occurs only if it is supported by continuous efforts of intercultural translation-transaction focused on practices and on the implicit aspects (the *invisible/mute parts*) of cultural/legal experience.[76]

This different approach, moreover, shows a twofold advantage. On one side, it allows us to place the claims for rights within an already structured semiotic web, precisely woven through a widespread and continuous activity of intercultural translation. This avoids, inter alia, the instrumental use of statements on rights and their related semantic vagueness: a use not infrequently aimed to aprioristically legitimize any request for protection, so as to reduce the law's attitude to provide directives for action, namely its prescriptiveness, to a sort of anomic void.[77] On the

co-implications increase, also in the wake of the planetary mobility of peoples and their interests (Ricca 2014c).

[76] About the *mute parts* of legal experience—completely different from what comparativist scholars define as 'mute law' see Sacco 1995. For a broad discussion, see Ricca (2013c).

[77] See Douzinas (2000); von Hildebrandt (2010). See, moreover, Ricca (2014a) and there the specific comments regarding the antagonistic and anomic consequences of a hierarchical rather

other side, a values-based (rather than inter-normative) and hermeneutical reading of legal pluralism would promote cultural self-transformations, as seen above, as a crucial feature of both the cultural competence exercise and the (potential) creativity inherent in a migration experience carried out in compliance with the possibility of personal emancipation.[78] All this would allow for the law of one state to be interculturally responsive to that which people *really demand and need*, an attitude that is often entirely absent when legal rules from countries of origin are instead transplanted and 're-enacted' by the legal systems of host countries. On the contrary, as field surveys show, migrants belonging to other cultures or faiths tend to generate cultural, as well as normative condensations (in this sense opposed to accommodating juxtapositions among norms or empirical features). People do not want 'either this or that,' according to an antagonistic and polarized logic of belonging that gives rise to a normative/cultural patchwork targeted at a rigid selfish logic bereft of any genuine and aware intercultural transformation; rather, they would prefer (quite legitimately, in my view) to opt for cultural and legal condensations that comprise little bits of both. People 'on the move' can envisage this option (which is the outcome of a creative and axiologically consistent reinterpretation of the manifold cultural patterns at their disposal) only if: (*a*) they are supplied with the indispensable informative supports regarding the possibilities and consequences of their actions; (*b*) they are enabled to ponder these possibilities and consequences on the basis of an intercultural coordination between their expectations and the reactions, including the legal ones, of the host society. In other words, they should be given the possibility to know in a timely way that there are viable intercultural paths to integration and potential interculturally featured requests for protection. Without such an awareness, the slippage of cultural self-representations towards identitarian caricatures of a folkloristic and antagonistic kind will be—and unfortunately nearly always is—almost ineluctable.

6.5.2 *Polycentric Plots of Intercultural Inter-Constitutionality and the Quest for a Bottom-Up Universality of Human Rights*

The passage from a purely inter-systemic/inter-normative pluralism to a values-based/intercultural one could assure room *within* the perimeter (or rather, network) of state sovereignty for circuits of 'difference.' The creation of such inter-spaces of experience allows lived inter-subjectivity to function as the very propeller of communication between different cultural habits and their relationships with law. In this way, normative or legal-systemic connections, webs, and so on, would lose their

than a horizontal and intercultural use of human rights statements when cultural conflicts are at stake.

[78] See Ricca (2013c).

primacy.[79] So, by virtue of the use of an intercultural infra-state constitutional interpretation, an effect of increasing polycentric alignment in legal-institutional practices of many countries could take shape. I will try to briefly outline the possible sequences of such a process.[80]

The existence of an enunciative set of human and/or fundamental rights, which is at least morphologically shared by many constitutions in the world, undoubtedly determines the cultural situatedness and spatial differentiation of their semantic scope and implications. And yet, the meanings of rights are an outcome of their *consequences*, their implications. In turn, the *consequences* of discourses on rights are outcomes of the combined potentialities of the meaning of legal statements, on one side, and the indexical landscapes underlying the various national political and legal systems called to elicit and trigger those potentialities, on the other side. Rights' universality is a situated one, as indeed is proper of every authentic form of universality. If this were this not the case, and if the 'inclination' to differentiate and situate rights so as to make their semantic platform capable of mirroring manifold points of view were lacking, then it would be no longer universality but rather a rhetorical dispositive contrived to impose overwhelming identity and homogeneity on differences.

However, the same communities belonging to the non-Western world, the so-called Rest, after a long period marked by their contestations of the logic of human rights as being ethnocentric, have recently veered off course. In addition to the multiplying of regional-universal declarations of rights, which are perhaps somewhat oxymoronic but at least demonstrate a genuine interest in legal universalism, the self-same anthropologists of law have remolded their initial criticism. Traditionally hostile to cosmopolitan paradigms of legal subjectivity, they most recently are willing to admit that there seems to have been a kind of poly-ethnic group resolution by non-Western people not to miss the chance to self-represent their cultural habits and claims, in some way supplied by the normative and discursive

---

[79]This way of envisaging intercultural relationships within law could be considered, in some respects, to align with Vanderlinden's (1989) and, even more with Macdonald's (2002, 2006 with Sandormiersky) subject-centered approaches to legal pluralism. However, there is an important difference between intercultural law and the subject-centered pluralism proposed, with different declinations, by these two authors. It consists in their understanding of the role played by the subject as an interface between more than one legal circuit, official or unofficial. In my view, culture is not law, and even if we can recognize in cultural habits some marks of normativity, these remain of a different kind from those of the law. Furthermore, in spite of this normativity, the plasticity of cultural semiotic landscapes and their indexical surroundings have to do with the creative production of sense continuously carried out by people rather than with the typical semantic stillness of norms.

[80]I should note, in this regard, that my idea of intercultural and chorological polycentricity is substantially different from other approaches such as those proposed through manifold visions by Petersen and Zahle (1995), Petersen (2008), or, with a philosophical bent, by Hirovonen (1998). Some interesting remarks about the implications of polycentricity for the Mixed Legal Systems experience can be found in Donlan (2015). See, for a different approach to the relationship between law and culture with respect to everyday life, Sarat and Kearns (1995).

platform of human rights.[81] Today, the current anthropological-political tendency seems to be making efforts to interpret the possible and potential meanings of universality in a culturally plural fashion. It is no longer understood in exclusively essentialized and ontological terms, but rather envisaged as a (regulative) horizon. In other words, universality is no longer represented as situated on the back of actions and their related cultural-political subjectivities, intended to work as a litmus test of their conformity and/or worthiness. Conversely, it is being assumed, little by little, as a teleological axis, and thereby as a procedural means of promoting polyphonic actions oriented to constructively and cumulatively achieve new horizons. All of this occurs along a potentially endless ongoing path because at each stage attained, the finish line for intercultural inclusiveness moves forward again. Indeed, it is the same with geographical horizons, which, as we approach move ever farther away.

From this perspective, I think that a values-based/intercultural pluralism should seek its vectors among subjects 'on the move,' taken as individuals, rather than among the inter-institutional migrations of ideas and hermeneutical trends about rights often generated by public authorities influenced by financial blocs of power. An Indian migrant, for example, will tend to propose in the host country interpretive approaches to rights that will echo (not only reproduce) those articulated in their country of origin. An adequate coordination between intercultural translation/transaction and claims for constitutional protection from the host country's legal system, could avoid the risk of anomy so often tied to the identitarian antagonism rooted in the hierarchical, top-down readings and uses of human and/or fundamental rights statements. On the contrary, these could work as a horizontal interface, as grounds for translation, in view of the creation of a legal-anthropological grammar of everyday life and its intercultural and interspatial dimensions.[82]

From one point a view, if all this were happening, a process of inter-constitutional communication could be engendered in the very wake of the inter-subjective/intercultural experiences traced by peoples 'on the move.' The outcomes of such a process would not, therefore, consist in patterns of inter-subjectivity drawn by means of normative and inter-institutional syntheses arranged top-down, as for example through the so-called dialogue among courts.[83] They would be drawn, conversely, from intercultural experiences, inherent to social multiculturality, and capable of acting both as an osmotic membrane for the interplaying of different hermeneutical perspectives on rights and, subsequently, on the constitutional dynamics spread throughout the globe.

Every 'place of multiculturality' could transform into a sort of local laboratory for global inter-constitutionality. Furthermore, the increase in multi-directional

[81] See Inoue (2004), Clarke and Goodale (2010), and for further bibliographical references on this topic, Ricca (2013c).

[82] I addressed the difference between hierarchical/top-down approaches and horizontal/intercultural uses of human rights specifically in Chap. 4.

[83] Legal polycentricity is understood precisely in this way by many legal scholars. See, for example, Christoffersen (2009, p. 562 ff.).

migration waves, which are not only from East to West, or from South to North, suggests that the possible unfolding of processes/laboratories for an intercultural multi-sited constitutionalism could be symmetrical and simultaneous in many countries. The overall result could be a new polycentric constitutionality of a non-*dirigiste* kind, that instead germinates from the bottom, from everyday life and is, at same time, capable of finding a point of global confluence in a legal-anthropological lexicon of subjectivity that is polyphonically 'inter-legible' by diverse local realities.

It would no longer, therefore, be a matter of 'glocality,' understood as a device for the adaptation of local to global and, at the same time, as a reaction of the global to the dialectic peculiarities of the local. Rather, what might emerge is the polyphony of intercultural-legal experiences processed into different spatial circuits and coordinated to progressively outline the synthetic features of a planetary subjectivity.

These postulations could also draw upon the existential multi-territoriality that marks the contemporary migration experience. He who moves toward new contexts of life, new social environments, does not always make a radical break from his contexts of origin, particularly if their migration paths are made to keep the channels of bi-directional communication with those who live in the countries of departure continuously open. If the states of the world were able to transact and synthetize their legal traditions and related schemes of subjectivity with the cultural differences of Others, and to do so by leveraging an intercultural constitutionalism, they could, in many cases, supply migrants with the keys to solutions that could be taken back home and adopted in the home context. All this communicative and trans-*lative* process would forge the 'pharmaceutical aids'—certainly late, but better so than never—to help remedy cultural discrepancies extant between the legal-institutional forms implicitly inherited from the West, and those in the margins of the imperialistic deeds of Europeans of yesterday, characteristic of post-colonial countries.

The global spread of social approaches and cognitive attitudes inspired to interculturality, and therefore to an intercultural use of legal knowledge, could engender a web of intersecting feedback among the different ways in which people, communities, institutions and states situate the rights discourse. It could take shape as the consequence of a kind of mutual anthropological-social pollination, the bees for which would be precisely migrants, the subjects 'on the move', and the transfer/trans-*lation* paths. Such occurrences, if underpinned and enhanced by law, rather than forced and caged by a legal practice deaf to cultural Otherness and its reasoning, could swarm, similarly to what happens in the fields during the flowering season. It is by looking at a landscape that we can see it is the result of the ubiquitous, spontaneous and simultaneous blossoming of flowers and so guess that spring is coming on, and certainly not on account of the fateful arrival of March 21st, merely determined by humans in their illusory conviction that they can mark the rhythm of the seasons through institutional decrees.

I think that we can find in the intercultural use of law a possibility for overcoming the winter of contemporarily revived religious and cultural antagonisms, so disavowing the mantra that human relationships can be efficaciously understood only as transaction forged by the Realm of Quantity and by financial units of measurement. The economic gospel, professed by its priests with an obsessive-compulsive attitude, is very similar to that of some old folks, who since the dawn of time have been blathering on about the notion that, 'there aren't any mid-seasons anymore.' Whether this is the case or not, whether or not we can exorcise Adam's (Smith's) fallacy and its invisible hand,[84] it is up to humans and humans alone. Interculturality and intercultural use of law are not meta-narrations with a predetermined final scene epitomizing ineluctable outcomes of history. Altogether, they constitute mere possibilities, workable paths. Making our way along such tracks is neither simple nor instinctive,[85] and for this very reason, it remains a matter of choice. Besides, one way or another, *errare humanum est.*

References

Anderson B, Harrison P (2010) The promise of non-representational theories. In: Anderson B, Harrison P (eds) Taking-place: non-representational theories and geography. Ashgate, Farnham, pp 1–36

Ansermet F, Magistretti P (2008) A chacun son cerveau: Plasticité neuronale et inconscient. Odile Jacob, Paris

Appadurai A (1986) The social life of things: commodities in cultural perspective. CUP, Cambridge

Bauman Z (1991) Modernity and ambivalence. Polity Press/Blackwell, Cambridge

Benhabib S (2004) The rights of the others: aliens, residents, and citizens. CUP, Cambridge

Bhambra GK (2007) Rethinking modernity: postcolonialism and the sociological imagination. Palgrave Macmillan, New York

Blomley N (1994) Law, space and the geographies of power. The Guilford Press, New York

Blomley N (2003a) From 'What' to 'So What?' Law and geography in retrospect. In: Holder J, Harrison C (eds) Law and geography. OUP, Oxford, pp 17–33

Blomley N (2003b) Unsettling the city: urban land and the politics of property. Routledge, New York

Blomley N, Delaney D, Ford RT (eds) (2001) The legal geographies reader. Blackwell, Oxford

Blumenberg H (2007) Theorie der Unbegrifflichkeit. Suhrkamp, Frankfurt a. M

Braverman I, Blomley N, Delaney D, Kedar A (eds) (2014) Expanding spaces of law: a timely legal geography. Stanford University Press, Stanford

Bryant S, Peters JK (2014) Reflecting on the habits: teaching about identity, culture, language, and difference. In: Bryant S, Milstein ES, Shalleck AC (eds) Transforming the education of lawyers: the theory and practice of clinical pedagogy. Carolina Academic Press, Durham

Bubandt N, Beek van M (2012) Varieties of secularism in Asia: anthropological explorations of religion, politics and the spiritual. Routledge, London

Butler C (2012) Henri Lefebvre: spatial politics, everyday life, and the right to the city. Routledge, Abingdon

Canotilho JJG (2011) Principios y "Nuevos Constitucionalismus". El problema del los Nuevos Principios. http://www.ugr.es/~redce/REDCE14/articulos/07JJGomesCanotilho.htm

[84] The expression 'Adam's fallacy' echoes the insightful title of Foley's book (2006).

[85] As regards the non-naturalness, or spontaneity of an intercultural attitude, which is instead something to be learned and practiced through specific training in "an unconventional (creative) thinking," I completely agree with Rozbcki (2015).

Choudhry S (2006) Migration as a new metaphor in comparative law. In: Choudhry S (ed) The migration of constitutional ideas. CUP, Cambridge
Christoffersen J (2009) Fair balance: proportionality, subsidiarity and primarity in the European Convention on Human Rights. Martinus Nijhoff, Leiden
Chryssochoou X (2004) Cultural diversity: its social psychology. Blackwell, Malden
Clarke KM, Goodale M (2010) Introduction: understanding the multiplicity of justice. In: Clarke KM, Goodale M (eds) Mirrors of justice: law and power in a post-cold war era. Cambridge University Press, New York, pp 1–27
de Certeau M (1990) L'invention du quotidien, vol. I, Arts de faire. Gallimard, Paris
Decock W (2013) Theologians and contract law: the moral transformation of the ius commune (ca. 1500-1650). Martinus Nijhoff, Leiden
Del Giudice M (2010) The Italian entrepreneurial outlook. In: Del Giudice M, Della Peruta MR, Carayannis EG (eds) Knowledge and the family business: the governance and management of family firms, The new knowledge economy. Springer, New York, pp 125–186
Delaney D (2003) Beyond the word: law as a thing of this world. In: Holder J, Harrison C (eds) Law and geography. OUP, Oxford, pp 67–83
Delaney D (2010) The spatial, the legal and the pragmatics of world-making: nomospheric investigations. Routledge, Abingdon
Delaney D (2014) Legal geography I. Constitutivities, complexities and contingencies. Progr Hum Geogr 39(1):1–7
Derret JDM (1999) Religion, law, and state in India. OUP, Delhi
Derrida J (1993) Khôra. Galilée, Paris
Deutscher G (2010) Through the language glass: why the world looks different in other languages. Metropolitan Books, Henry Holt and Company, New York
Dewey J (1926) The historical background of corporate legal personality. Yale Law J 35(6): 655–673
Di Paolo E, Cuffaro EC, De Jaegher A (2018) Linguistic bodies: the continuity between life and language. The MIT Press, Cambridge
Donlan S (2011) The Mediterranean hybridity project: crossing the boundaries of law and culture. J Civil Law Stud 4 [Also traceable as Donlan, SP, The Mediterranean hybridity project: at the boundaries of law and culture (February 26, 2011). http://ssrn.com/abstract=1874095 or https://doi.org/10.2139/ssrn.1874095]
Donlan S (2015) To hybridity and beyond: reflections on legal and normative complexity. In: Palmer VV, Mattar MY, Koppel A (eds) Mixed legal systems, east and west: newest trends and developments. Ashgate, Farnham, pp 17–32
Douzinas C (2000) The end of human rights: critical legal thought at the turn of the century. Hart, Oxford
Dupré B (2007) Legal pluralism, plurality of laws, and legal practices. Eur J Leg Stud 1:1. Retrieved from Cadmus, European University Institute Research Repository. http://hdl.handle.net/1814/6852
Eisenberg A (2005) Identity and liberal politics: the problem of minorities within minorities. In: Eisenberg A, Spinner-Halev J (eds) Minorities within minorities: equality, rights and diversity. CUP, Cambridge, pp 249–270
Eisenberg A (2009) Reasons of identity: a normative guide to the political and legal assessment of identity claims. Oxford University Press, Oxford
Fabian J (1983) Time and the other: how anthropology makes its object. Columbia University Press, New York
Foley D (2006) Adam's fallacy. Harvard University Press, Cambridge
Fontanelli F (2010) Santi Romano and *L'ordinamento giuridico*: the relevance of a forgotten masterpiece for contemporary international, transnational and global relations. Transnatl Leg Theory 2(1):67–117
Frazer JG (2000 [1927]) The Devil's advocate: a plea for superstition. Routledge, London
Gibbs RW Jr (2005) Embodiment and cognitive science. Cambridge University Press, Cambridge

Glenn PH (2005) On common laws. Oxford University Press, Oxford
Glenn PH (2013) The cosmopolitan state. OUP, Oxford
Glenn PH (2014) Legal traditions of the world: sustainable diversity in law. OUP, Oxford
Goodale M (2007) Introduction: locating rights, envisioning law between the global and the local. In: Goodale M, Merry SE (eds) The practice of human rights: tracking law between the global and the local. CUP, Cambridge, pp 1–38
Gordley J (1991) The philosophical origins of modern contract law. CUP, Cambridge
Griffiths J (2001) Legal pluralism. In: Encyclopedia of the social and behavioral sciences. Elsevier, New York
Gupta A, Ferguson J (1997a) Beyond "culture": space, identity, and the politics of difference. In: Gupta A, Ferguson J (eds) Culture, power, place: explorations in critical anthropology. Duke University Press, Durham, pp 33–51
Gupta A, Ferguson J (1997b) Culture, power, place: ethnography and the end of an era. In: Gupta A, Ferguson J (eds) Culture, power, place: explorations in critical anthropology. Duke University Press, Durham, pp 1–29
Habermas J (1992) Cittadinanza politica e identità nazionale. Riflessioni sul futuro dell'Europa. In: Habermas J (ed) Morale, diritto, politica. Einaudi, Torino. (collection of various texts)
Harvey D (1996) Justice, nature and the geography of difference. Blackwell, Oxford
Henare A, Holbraad M, Wastell S (2007) Introduction: thinking through things. In: Henare A, Holbraad M, Wastell S (eds) Thinking through things: theorising artefacts ethnographically. Routledge, London, pp 1–32
Hirovonen A (1998) Polycentricity: the multiple scenes of law. Pluto Press, London
Holden L (ed) (2011) Cultural expertise and litigation: patterns, conflicts, narratives. Routledge, New York
Holden L (ed) (2019) Special issue: cultural expertise: an emergent concept and evolving practices. MDPI
Holden L (ed) (2023) Cultural expertise, law, and rights: a comprehensive guide. Routledge (forthcoming)
Huntington S (1996) The clash of civilization and the remaking of world order. Simon & Schuster, New York
Inoue T (2004) Reinstating the universal in the discourse of human rights and justice. In: Sajó A (ed) Human rights with modesty: the problem of universalism. Martinus Nijhoff, Leiden
Isar N (2009a) Chôra: tracing the presence. Rev Eur Stud 1(1):39–55
Isar N (2009b) Chorography – a space for chorographic inscription. Bulletin of The Transilvania University of Breşov 2(51). Series IV:263–268
Joerges C, Sand I-J, Teubner G (eds) (2004) Transnational governance and constitutionalism. Hart, Portland
Jurčys P, Kjaer PF, Yatsunami R (eds) (2013) Regulatory hybridization in the transnational sphere. Martinus Nijhoff/Brill Publishing, Leiden
Kandel ER, Spencer WA (1968) Cellular neurophysiological approaches in the study of learning. Physiol Rev 48(1):65–134
Lakoff G (1987) Women, fire and dangerous things: what categories reveal about the mind. University of Chicago Press, Chicago
Lefebvre H (1974) La production de l'espace. Anthropos, Paris
Libet B (2004) MindTime: the temporal factor in consciouness. Harvard University Press, Cambridge, MA
Lingat R (1973) The classical law of India. University of California Press, Berkeley
Macdonald RA (2002) Lessons of everyday life/Le droit du quotidien. McGill University Press, Montréal
Macdonald RA, Sandormierski D (2006) Against nomopolies. Northern Ireland Leg Q 57:610–633
Marcus GE (1995) Ethnography in/of the world system: the emergence of multi-sited ethnography. Annu Rev Anthropol XXIV:95–117

Marcus GE (2006) What is at stake – and is not – in the idea and practice of multi-sited ethnography. In: Moore H, Sanders T (eds) Anthropology in theory: issues in epistemology. Blackwell, Malden, pp 618–621
Marramao G (2008) Cosmopolitismo della differenza. Il diritto dopo Babele. Daimon. Annuario di diritto comparato delle religioni 8:51–64
Martin J-Y (2006) Une géographie critique de l'espace du quotidien. L'actualité mondialisée de la pensée spatiale d'Henri Lefebvre. J Urban Res [Online] 2. free download at articulo.revues.org › Issues › 2 › Varia
Melissaris E (2009) Ubiquitous law. Ashgate, Farnham
Modood T (2019a) Essays on secularism and multiculturalism. Rowman & Littlefield, London
Modood T (2019b) A multicultural nationalism? Brown J World Aff 25(2):233–246
Muthu S (2003) Enlightenment against empire. Princeton University Press, Princeton
Olsson G (2007) Abysmal: a critique of cartographic reason. The University of Chicago Press, Chicago
Olsson G (2011) Mapping the taboo. In: Daniels S, DeLyser D, Entrikin JN, Richardson D (eds) Envisioning landscapes, making worlds: geography and the humanities. Routledge, London, pp 35–43
Ong A (1999) Flexible citizenship: the cultural logics of transnationality. Duke University Press, Durham
Ost F, Van de Kerckhove M (2002) De la pyramide au reséau. Pour une théorie dialectique du droit, Facultés Universitaires St. Louis, Bruxelles
Peirce CS (1868) Questions concerning certain faculties claimed for man. J Specul Philos 2:103–114
Petersen H (2008) Introduction: exceptionalism and normalization: ambiguity and honour in European integration processes. In: Petersen H, Kjæfer AL, Krunke H, Rask Madsen M (eds) Paradoxes of European legal integration. Ashgate, Aldershot, pp 287–298
Petersen H, Zahle H (eds) (1995) Legal polycentricity: consequences of pluralism in law. Dartmouth, London
Philippopoulos-Mihalopoulos A (2010) Spatial justice: law and the geography of withdrawal. Int J Law Context 6(3):1–16
Philippopoulos-Mihalopoulos A (2012) Law, spaces, bodies: the emergence of spatial justice. In: de Sutter L, Mcgee K (eds) Deleuze and the law (Deleuze connections). Edinburgh University Press, Edinburgh, pp 90–110
Philippopoulos-Mihalopoulos A (2014) The movement of spatial justice (Il movimento della giustizia spaziale). Mondi Migranti 8:7–20
Pickles J (2004) A history of spaces: cartographic reason, mapping, and the geo-coded world. Routledge, London
Renteln AD (2004) The cultural defense. OUP, Oxford
Renteln AD, Foblets M-C (eds) (2009) Multicultural jurisprudence: comparative perspectives on the cultural defense. Bloomsbury, Oxford
Ricca M (1999) Metamorfosi della Sovranità e ordinamenti confessionali. Giappichelli, Torino
Ricca M (2008) Oltre Babele. Codici per una democrazia interculturale. Dedalo, Bari
Ricca M (2012) Natura inventata e natura implicita nel diritto. Incursioni interculturali. In: Marrone G (ed) Semiotica della natura (natura della semiotica). Mimesis, Milano, pp 309–358
Ricca M (2013a) Pantheon. Agenda della laicità interculturale. Torri del Vento, Palermo
Ricca M (2013b) Il tradimento delle immagini tra kirpan e transazioni interculturali. Cultura vs. competenza culturale nel mondo del diritto. E|C Rivista dell'Associazione italiana di Studi semiotici: 1–31. http://www.ec-aiss.it/index_d.php?recordID=678
Ricca M (2013c) Culture interdette. Modernità, migrazioni, diritto interculturale. Bollati Boringhieri, Torino
Ricca M (2014a) Sapore, sapere del mondo. Tradizioni religiose e traduzioni alimentari. Daimon. Diritto comparato delle religioni 2014:33–66

Ricca M (2014b) I notai, don Chisciotte e la sincronica inattualità dell'Altro. Sociologia del diritto 1:7–31

Ricca M (2014c) Soggetto, diritto, religioni. Sentieri antropologico-culturali della capacità giuridica. E|C. Rivista dell'Associazione italiana di Studi semiotici:1–46. http://www.ec-aiss.it/index_d.php?recordID=705

Ricca M (2015) Intercultural perspectives for lawyers and the law. New possibilities for legal education and assistance. CALUMET - Intercult Law Humanit Rev 1:1–16. https://calumet-review.com/wp-content/uploads/2021/07/Ricca-pdf-Intercultural-Lawyers-EN.pdf

Ricca M (2018) *Ignorantia facti excusat*: legal liability and the intercultural significance of Greimas' "contrat de véridition". Int J Semiot Law 31:101–126. https://doi.org/10.1007/s11196-017-9529-6

Ricca M (2020) Otherness, elsewhere, and the 'ecology' of law's implications: the semiotic oceans surrounding legal signification and its discriminatory exteriority/objectivity. Int J Leg Discourse 5(2):185–237

Ricca M (2022a) Perpetually astride Eden's boundaries: the limits to the 'limits of law' and the semiotic inconsistency of 'legal enclosures'. Int J Semiot Law 35:179–229. https://doi.org/10.1007/s11196-020-09771-0

Ricca M (2022b) The 'spaghettification' of performativity across cultural boundaries: the trans-culturality/trans-spatiality of digital communication as an event horizon for speech acts. Int J Semiot Law 35:2435–2479. https://doi.org/10.1007/s11196-021-09880-4

Ricca M (2023) How to undo (and redo) words with facts: a semio-enactivist approach to law, space and experience. Int J Semiot Law 36:313–367. https://doi.org/10.1007/s11196-022-09912-7

Ricca M, Sbriccoli T (2015) Notariato e diritto interculturale. Un viaggio giuridico-antropologico tra i notai d'Italia. CALUMET - Intercult Law Humanit Rev 1:1–49. https://calumet-review.com/index.php/2015/05/06/notariato-e-diritto-interculturale-un-viaggio-giuridico-antropologico-tra-i-notai-ditalia/

Ronsenberg D, Grafton A (2010) Cartographies of time: a history of timeline. Princeton Architectural, Princeton

Rozbcki M (2015) Introduction – intercultural studies: the methodological contours of an emerging discipline. In: Rozbcki M (ed) Perspective on interculturality: the construction of meaning in relationships of differences. Palgrave Macmillan, New York

Sacco R (1995) Mute law. Am J Comp Law 43(3):455–467

Sallis J (1999) Chorology: on beginning in Plato's *Timaeus*. Indiana University Press, Bloomington

Santos BS (2002) Toward a new legal common sense: law, globalization, and emancipation. Butterworths, London

Santos BS, Rodríguez-Garavito C (2005) Law, politics, and the subaltern in counter-hegemonic globalization. In: Santos BS, Rodríguez-Garavito C (eds) Law and globalization from below: towards a cosmopolitan legality. Cambridge University Press, Cambridge, pp 1–28

Sarat A, Kearns TR (1995) Beyond the great divide: forms of legal scholarship and everyday life. In: Sarat A, Kearns TR (eds) Law in everyday life. University of Michigan Press, Ann Arbor, pp 21–62

Silveira AA (2014) Diritto dell'Unione Europea: dimensione culturale e artistica in un contesto di intercostituzionalità. Arte e critica, numero speciale 'Nuove Alleanze. Diritto ed economia per la cultura e l'arte':72-77; free download in pdf format www.decamaster.it

Smyrnios KS, Poutziouris PZ, Goel S (eds) (2013) Handbook of research on family business, 2nd edn. Edward Elgar, Cheltenham

Soja E (1996) Thirdspace: journeys to Los Angeles and other real-and-imagined places. Blackwell, Malden

Shweder R, Minow M, Markus HR (eds) (2002) Engaging cultural differences: the multicultural challenge in liberal democracies. Russel Sage Foundations, New York

Sullivan WF, Yelle RA, Taussig-Rubbo M (2011) Introduction. In: Sullivan WF, Yelle RA, Taussig-Rubbo M (eds) After secular law. Stanford University Press, Stanford, pp 1–22

Tamanaha Z (2000) A non-essentialist version of legal pluralism. J Law Soc XXVII:296–321

Tenbrink T (2007) Space, time, and the use of languages. An investigation of relationships. Walter de Gruyter, Berlin
Teubner G (2005) La cultura del diritto nell'epoca della globalizzazione. L'emergere delle costituzioni civili. Armando, Roma
Teubner G (2012) Verfassungsfragmente. Gesellschaftslicher Konstitutionalismus in der Globalisierung. Suhrkamp, Frankfurt a.M.
Tinnevelt R, De Schutter H (eds) (2010) Global democracy and exclusion. Blackwell, Oxford
Trnka S, Dureau C, Park J (eds) (2013) Senses and citizenships: embodying political life. Routledge, London
Tully LD (2020) The cultural (re)turn: the case for teaching culturally responsible lawyering. Stanf J Civil Rights Civil Liberties 16:201–258
Vanderlinden J (1989) Return to legal pluralism. J Leg Pluralism Unofficial Law 21(28):149–157
von Benda-Beckmann F, von Benda-Beckmann K (2014) Temporalities in property relations under a plural legal order: Minangkabau revisited. J Leg Pluralism Unofficial Law 46(1):18–36
von Benda-Beckmann F, von Benda-Beckmann K, Griffiths A (2009) Space and legal pluralism: an introduction. In: von Benda-Beckmann F, von Benda-Beckmann K, Griffiths A (eds) Spatializing law. An anthropological geography of law and society. Ashgate, Farnham, pp 1–30
von Hildebrandt M (2010) Human right as preconditions for intercultural society. Selected works of Mireille von Hildebrandt. http://works.bepress.com/mireille_hildebrandt/28
Waddington I, Maxwell B, McDonough K, Cormier A-A, Schwimmer A (2012) Interculturalism in practice: Québec's ethics and religious culture curriculum and the Bouchard-Taylor Report on reasonable accommodation. In: Besley T, Peters MA (eds) Handbook of interculturalism, education and dialogue. Peter Lang, New York, pp 312–329
Wai R (2008) The interlegality of transnational private law. Law Contemp Probl 71(3):107–128
Whatmore S (2002) Hybrid geographies. Nature, culture, spaces. Sage, London
Zumthor P (1993) La Mesure du monde. Seuil, Paris

Chapter 7
The Indigeneization of the World: Translating Spaces, Indigenizing Human Rights

7.1 Who Is Not Indigenous?

The gist of the approach to indigeneity adopted in this chapter is the conviction that it is much more than indigenous rights and the conflictive fashion that inevitably connotes the related judicial claims.

I would like to begin my discourse on the implications of an intercultural legal approach on indigeneity by analyzing the simple and somewhat whimsical question I offer as a title for this prologue. To this end, let me introduce myself: I was born in Sicily, thereby in Italy, to native Italian parents; I do not belong (at least, officially) to a decolonized territory, nor am I a member of any minority group or ethnicity (at least, by now…). I am a legal scholar, and a full professor at Parma University, Italy (…still). I cannot express any serious complaints about my ability to live (…survive?) in the *midst of* Italian culture and—*flaw of flaws*—my professional status ranks highly in Western society (…even if, in my mind, less and less so).

According to current assumptions about entitlement for claiming indigenous rights, there is no chance I would be recognized as indigenous. Certainly, the current concept of indigeneity is broader than it once was, as our ideas of indigeneity are no longer strictly connected to the misappropriations and plunders perpetrated by European colonizers since the dawn of (Western) modernity. Among those subjects legally entitled to consider themselves 'indigenous people' today are Asian, African, and even some European migrant communities or ethnic groups. On the other hand, the United Nations Declaration on the Rights of Indigenous People (UNDRIP) does not provide any definition of 'indigeneity,' and does not reference any particular territories or specific geographical areas. Traditional knowledge, cultural identity, communitarian self-awareness rooted in (allegedly) ancestral origins, and so on, constitute the *denotative* props necessary to claim the 'right' to be recognized as indigenous. In short, territoriality and indigeneity are no longer assumed as necessarily coextensive, although the struggle for territory and the related redress are the primary focus of most indigenous peoples' claims.

M. Ricca, *Intercultural Spaces of Law*, Law and Visual Jurisprudence 10,
https://doi.org/10.1007/978-3-031-27436-7_7

Nonetheless, my chances of being recognized as indigenous are pretty much zero to none. I would like to explore the reasons underlying this absence of possibility in order to better understand the anthropological consistency of the concept of 'indigeneity' used in political and institutional praxis, at least in recent years. In parallel, I will attempt to probe the degree of influence that political action on behalf of 'indigenous peoples' has had on the work of anthropologists and their elaborations of the idea of 'indigeneity' more generally.

Before going any further, however, I want to immediately tip my hand, so to speak. By raising the question of my actual potential as a would-be indigenous subject, my intent is to 'call the bluff' of the political and historical constraints that currently determine conceptions of the category of 'indigeneity.' As a point of departure but also as my endpoint, I assume that indigeneity is, actually, a planetary occurrence, completely coextensive with the advent of a symbolic-cultural species on the Earth that is prone to creatively adapt itself in order to face the massive variety of environmental challenges and stimuli. In short, indigeneity—as a matter of 'fact'—should be understood as a ubiquitous expression of the 'cultural nature' of human beings, and their creative tendency to 'produce culture' everywhere.

Although I am a lawyer, or perhaps because I am a lawyer, I think the *juridification* of indigeneity has for the most part had a negative influence on the anthropological understanding of this category, a negative influence that has resulted in a pernicious conflation between 'indigenism' and 'indigeneity.'

7.2 Indigeneity Is More Than 'Indigenous Rights': De-legalizing the Concept of Indigeneity, *de*-De-colonizing the Legal Approach to Indigeneity

The inherent flaw of 'indigeneity' as a category coincides, in my view, with its stemming from a context teeming with micro-struggles for survival by actors who have been geographically and historically identified. Actually, the backdrop against which this category took—political and cultural—center stage was the postmodern criticism of colonialism and postcolonialism. The UNDRIP, in the seventh paragraph of its Annex, anchors the motivation behind its provisions to a concern for the historical injustices suffered by indigenous people that were caused by colonialism. Hence indigeneity and indigenous rights have been intended, even by anthropologists, as two sides of the same coin, or at least closely related. This connection is understandable and even wise, given the necessity of assuring that the needs and claims of indigenous people are effectively met. If and when it listens and gives voice to its weakest subjects, the law is a means of redress that cannot be overlooked. Nonetheless, as a remedy for supporting people entangled in complicated plights—as many indigenous people have been and continue to be—the law sometimes proves to be defective. This is because legal language, especially that of positive law, operates within a kind of contradiction. It is a means to rule and solve conflicts by the recognition of rights, but also through the imposition of duties. In accordance with this dialectical and contrastive structure, subjects and situations are rigorously analyzed and determined. The ensuing game between parts and counterparts induces lawmakers and courts to establish precise requirements identifying which subjects are entitled to rights and which are burdened with specular duties. Most likely, this is why the legal recognition of indigenous rights tends to cast historical and geographical constraints on indigeneity that predispose it to political use. The result, however, is that 'indigeneity' becomes an instrumental category, whose phenomenal aspects and potentialities are overshadowed by a set of specific features that are conducive to judicial protection.

Guilt for the misdeeds of colonizers makes the voice of cultural difference much louder and more legitimate in the eyes of international and state jurisdictions. Unfortunately, however, such a psycho-historical vision results in an anthropological analysis of 'indigeneity' that is too often overly influenced by certain space-time constraints. Accordingly, the candidates for being 'indigenous', even from a purely anthropological point of view, must be non-Western peoples, individuals, or groups who are tied to a proven and dated tradition, even if the dynamics involved are cosmopolitan and/or mobile. Past conditions of exploitation by 'Westerners' appear to be the ground note that legitimizes classification as indigenous, in both anthropological and legal terms. Indigeneity, in other words, is latently connoted by difference: difference from the West, its individualism, its capitalist/industrial embodiments, and the polluting consequences of its exploitations.

I think this kind of approach results in an inadvertent conversion of indigeneity-as-a-fact into indigenism-as-political-strategy. If we address the category 'indigeneity' as if it were synonymous with 'indigenism,' then we can rightly assume that it is a historically situated category, which originates with contemporary criticism against colonialism and postcolonialism, and aims to redress the injustices, misappropriations, plunders, and displacements suffered by many peoples knocked over by the colonial wave and/or marginalized by capitalist world sprawl. I contend, however, that this is an excessively politicized definition of the experience of 'indigenizing.'

'Indigenous' cannot only refer to non-modern non-Westerners. Conversely, I think that those who produce 'indigeneity' constitute instead a much broader group that includes all those who undertake cultural processes by using symbolic resources to experience and interplay with the spaces they occupy.

I fear that the current approach to 'indigeneity' is much too political, and inclined toward identitarian interests rather than cognitive ones. The main basis for my view is that the human species gave course to its first act of 'indigenization' concomitantly with the initial stages of its dissemination on the Earth. From this perspective, it makes little sense to qualify as 'indigenous' only those populations pre-existing colonial invasions, or those affected by contemporary acts of displacement or destruction carried out by Westerners or Westernized governments and majority groups in the rest of the world. Furthermore, the anti-colonialist focus cordons off the experience of indigenization, which I view as a universal human attitude, within a sort of conservative frame that inconsistently separates it from all that occurred before the colonial era and all that might occur in the future.

How many people in the precolonial past were displaced or conquered by the same populations that later suffered upset and destructions carried out by colonizers? How many people in present times undertake, or will do so in the future, processes of mobility that lead them to indigenize other spaces, producing unprecedented cultural-spatial dimensions? Or, rather, did human history as well as human nature itself definitively stall with the onset of Western modernity, so that restoring the world as it was before colonialism and contemporary capitalist devastations would be nothing but an eternizing of that presumptive endpoint of history and evolution? My guess is that 'indigenism' is the normative interpretation of a phenomenon of 'indigeneity/indigenization' whose empirical substance and semantic potentialities are far broader than its current political and legal renderings. The normative version is, in my view, highly specious and deeply defective, if only because it is a sign of our inability as human beings to align our behavior to the due respect of cultural difference as such. As a result, unlike some scholars,[1] I do not think that the UNDRIP has usefully served to distinguish indigenous peoples' rights from those of all other minorities. Conversely, I argue that indigenism is a sort of remedy for a past and present unwillingness by the state and local/territorial authorities to give a serious cultural basis to the ideals of democratic pluralism.

I think that indigeneity can only gain its due legal recognition if anthropologists make a serious effort to develop the concept through a '*de*-decolonization' of its scope, and a de-legalization of its paths of analysis: that is, a cognitive enfranchisement from its legal implementations. A '*de*-decolonization of indigeneity' would be one in which anthropologists, as well as legal scholars, would work to liberate indigeneity from the current 'decolonizing approach.' I propose, in other words, that all of us—anthropologists and lawyers—undertake a dispassionate commitment to enlarge and generalize our views of indigenizing experience so as to include all cultural experiences inside its semantic borders. Otherwise, if the legal-political mainstream continues to hold its dominant position, I fear that the *differentialist* logic underlying it will end up dialectically and paradoxically subduing indigenous peoples' exigencies to the logic of Western cultural and legal patterns. Evidence of the kind of parabola that follows the dialectic differentializing approach can be seen in the regulatory protection of indigenous peoples' traditional knowledge, and its increasing inclination toward the reification/objectification of cultural experience. The logic of intellectual property protection is pervasive even if the real peril does not lie—as many authors warn—in the superimposition of individualistic property patterns over traditional ways to keep and use knowledge. Rather, the true danger should be identified in the inevitable ossification of all that is to be considered as simulacra of indigenous identity, which will have to demonstrate authenticity at an

[1] Kymlicka (2011, p. 99), Tobin (2014, pp. 41–45) and Brendan (2014). For a critical assessment of the current legalizing approach to indigeneity see Bhandar (2011, p. 227 ff), Birrel (2016, p. 9 ff.) and Hirtz (2003, p. 887).

immediate morphological and perceptive level now equated with a recognizable and self-evident difference from all that is from the West. On the other hand, differentialism embodies an out/out logic that transforms, sooner or later, into a drive toward an exclusionary use of space, things, symbols, ideas, etc. The search for authenticity, as an instrument to legitimize indigenous claims, gives practical substance to the Spinozian motto '*omnis determinatio est negatio.*'[2] This is precisely the oppositional logic that tends to locate differences along a *continuum*, thus concealing the silent imposition of a cultural Procrustes behind the apparent determination and defense of 'indigenous identitarian features.' Some attempts to configure holistic understandings of intellectual property have been made, so as to align legal protection with indigenous cosmological understandings of traditional knowledge.[3] But this cannot overcome the morphological stiffness required if indigeneity is to be considered as a 'good' endowed with an exclusionary and differentialist regime of legal protection. For better or worse, the legal protection of indigeneity requires a high level of determination, and this can only take a morphological and objectifying form.

The trap of a morphologizing and stiffened reading of indigenous culture is alluring, on the other hand, even to the representatives of indigenous peoples. Legal provisions provide the highest degree of semantic determination when it comes to deciding certain conflicts. And it is no coincidence if under the aegis of legal pluralism, the ancestral star of indigenous customary law has received, in recent times, significant political and academic attention.[4] More and more often the legal recognition of indigenous cultures, namely of indigeneity, morphs toward the assessment and reception by international or state law of the rules produced by customary law. In this way, culture is increasingly equated with customary law, so that political and legal agencies look for evidence of the cultural authenticity of indigenous claims in their traditional or pre-existing legalization. However much customary law proves to be plastic and fluid, or *untainted* by the rigidity that allegedly affects (the use of) statutory law, cultural habits are always different from legal rules, and people are not norms. If the aim of protecting indigeneity turns into a dwindling reduction of indigenous cultures into their legal expressions,[5]

[2] English translation: "All determination is negation."

[3] See Tobin (2014, pp. 158 ff., 164 ff., and *ibidem* 250 nt. 25) as for the referrals to the instrumental political-legal instruments adopted to protect indigenous peoples' traditional knowledge, biological diversity, access to genetic resources, and sharing of benefits arising from their utilization (Nagoya Protocol 2010) and the work of WIPO and its IGC. With specific regard to intellectual property regime implementation on behalf of indigenous people, see, most recently, Robinson et al. (2017). Also see, furthermore, Carpenter et al. (2009, p. 1027 ff.).

[4] See Tobin (2014, p. 57 ff.); UNDRIP art. 34; ILO convention 169 and the process of an increasing codification of customary law.

[5] Remarkably enough, this reduction, although politically understandable, completely overlooks the fact that custom, and even more culture, cannot be considered being exhausted by customary legal rules or directives. See, in this regard, Renteln Dundes and Dundes (1994, pp. 3–4).

this means that the price for obtaining recognition of indigenous rights will be the cultural ossification of indigeneity itself.

The relationships between the varieties of indigeneity and Western cultures or Westernized governments actually seem bound to take the shape of inter-legal accommodations.[6] This means that the possibility of achieving some degree of intercultural translation/transaction is hopeless from the start.[7] Indigeneity will have undergone, in this case, a double process of objectification and reification: its significance would be curtailed to the point of rigidly equating it to the morphological features of cultural habits, the evidence of which is moreover traced to customary legal provisions. Needless to say, this is nothing but a further demonstration that oppositional differentialist logic inevitably tends toward a homogenizing interpenetration of differences within which the possibility of a mutual creative cultural transaction and co-construction is doomed to be supplanted by a formal homologation, achieved through semantic amputations and instrumental/utilitarian short-sighted compromises.

Following from the above, an (at least) interlocutory de-legalized approach to indigeneity, coupled with a reading of indigenous rights less obsessively driven by the postmodern (Western) 'decolonizing mission,' constitutes an essential step towards a genuine intercultural and polyphonic harmonization of all the experiences to which the human attitude to indigenize gives rise, and canopies beneath itself.

7.3 Indigenization and the Semiotic Spatialization of Culture

Indigeneity is a direct implication of the spatializing work of culture. If we consider culture as a dynamic set of signs, then we must appreciate that this set has practical consequences. This means that culture unfolds *through* and *with* space. Through its spatial projections, it transforms space and its components into instruments of signification. As already observed, space itself is not something placed *out there*, something that can be grasped by the human body/mind unit as a simple self-evident datum. Conversely, it is always a result of the dynamic interaction between this unit (which is however a relational emergence) and its environment. In this sense, we can say that a 'void space' does not exist as an absolute experienced reality; rather 'void spatiality' is, in every case, an open horizon of semantic/practical possibilities, which are culturally, even if vaguely, determined. This is because in semiotic terms, spaces and categories horizontally interact along a connotative/signical or chorological *continuum*: there is no representation of space without categorization

[6] I have addressed the limits of the "legal accommodation" approach to intercultural relationships in Ricca (2017); but see also above Chap. 6.

[7] As for my approach to intercultural translation/transaction, see above Chaps. 3 and 5.

and no categorization without spatial projections (be they virtual or effective).[8] Such a semiotic approach allows us to overcome the mind/world, culture/nature, symbolic dimension/spatial dimension, material/immaterial divides. All of these assume, conversely, only a heuristic and instrumental signification, extremely important operationally, but devoid of ontological features.

From a semiotic perspective, cultural space is a proactive production through which living beings actively co-produce their environment. However, all living beings, and humans especially, elaborate signs through signical memory, which endows them with the ability to presentify past experiences and their semiotic traces so as to face present environmental challenges. This is the reason all words, images, practices, and habits are to be intended as both epitomes of past experiences and proactive projections of their future implications. The local, from this perspective and insofar as it is involved in human experience, is intrinsically ubiquitous and is interwoven with a multi-sited signical and relational space. Despite possible appearances, such an understanding of space is anything but an abstraction. It displays, instead, spatialities actually lived by living beings to a much greater extent, as they are symbolic and cultural creatures.

Territory and territorialities can thus be understood as a form of semanticization of spatial experience, powered by the universal attitude of human beings to produce and transmit culture. Both the categories 'territory' and/or 'territorial' are therefore products of this cultural work, which, in setting the coordinates of local experience, always includes signical elements deriving from somewhere else. In this sense, all indigenous experiences are in some sense heterochthonous. This is the mobile and trans-local rhythm of 'territorialization' that punctuates the human planetary enterprise. I would propose, then, to term the trans-epochal development of this multi-vocal and omnipresent activity 'indigenization,' and to use 'indigeneity' as the term for its (interlocutory and relatively) localizable results.

The nub of any experience of 'indigenization' is the production/invention of a territory (or place), which is thus a synthesis of the co-generative relationships between mind and space, immateriality and materiality. Territory embodies human presence in space, and human bodies proactively internalize space.[9] These paths of experience have a semiotic equivalent, in some sense isomorphic to their pragmatic projections, in what we can call 'noetic ciphers.'[10] They correspond to the processing sequences that the human attitude to produce culture has elaborated throughout the ubiquitous activities of indigenization. Noetic ciphers never have absolute pertinence to only one territory or place. They are, conversely, local and planetary at the same time, just like the story of humankind's presence on the Earth.

---

[8] With regard to the legal-chorological approach see Chaps. 4 and 6.

[9] As for a proactive and non-representational approach to the production of space see Anderson and Harrison (2010, p. 1 ff). The proactive approach to spatial experience allows for a criticism of traditional space/place dualism: in this regard, I proposed some possibilities in Mario Ricca (2017): see ibidem for further bibliographical references on this topic.

[10] In this sense, see Handler (2003, p. 355 ff).

In this sense, we can say that the division between indigeneity and cosmopolitanism is a false dichotomy, in part because today indigenous people are also on the move, and 'give place' to hybridizing contacts with other people in places different from those of their origin.[11] We can see the mark of cosmopolitanism within the cognitive core of all indigenous experience.[12] Moreover, I think it is precisely the semiotic ubiquity of the human cognitive attitude that should be at the center of a planetary ethics of 'indigeneities.' Such an ethics would be no different from that necessary to negotiate cultural differences—through mutual recognition/pollination—because there is no cultural experience without attendant processes of spatialization and, thereby, indigenization.

In this regard, I would like to emphasize that the territory[13] involved in, and produced by, all processes of indigenization should be distinguished from the physical concept of territory/land. If we embrace a semiotic approach to cultural experience, then territory will correspond to the real space engendered by flows of information and their relationships. It should not come as a surprise, therefore, if people craft spatial dimensions of indigeneity that do not correspond to geo-physical land boundaries. Territories or places, in cultural terms, should be understood as points of confluence for complex semiotic streams, of which the material/terrestrial components are only an aspect; the 'land' is thus to be considered central or not according to its relational significance, rather than its materiality. Recalling the question opening this essay, the territory of 'Sicilianity' is something that is now impossible to situate in a specific physical/geographical place or territory.

From this perspective, even the issue of origins—so often disputed when referencing the cosmopolitanization of indigeneity—undergoes a sort of dialectical inter-spatial transfiguration. Take, for example, one of the worst, even if sadly world-renowned, expressions of Sicilian indigeneity: the Mafia.[14] During the migrations

[11] Notwithstanding his usual deep insight in reading anthropological phenomena, this is nevertheless the core of the indigenous/cosmopolitan connection that James Clifford proposes (1997, p. 31 ff). For a bird-eye overview of the different approaches to cosmopolitanism/indigenism relationships and interpenetration see, however, Forte (2010, p. 1 ff). On the other hand, as Hannerz also observes, geographical mobility does not imply, in and of itself, an automatic conversion to cosmopolitanism: see Hannerz (2004, p. 71 ff).

[12] I think that this interplay among indigenism, trans-locality of cultural experience, and cosmopolitanism can emerge even in a trans-epochal fashion from a combined reading of, for example, Forbes (1998, pp. 15–27); Quinn, Jr. (1993, p. 34 ff) and Beck (2004, p. 131 ff.). Of course, the interplay between indigeneity and cosmopolitanism can overcome the dialectical opposition that the mainstream drove as a wedge between them if one accepts that 'cosmopolitanism' can be intended in cognitive/experiential terms rather than exclusive and tightly ideological terms as a doctrine embodying the imperialist universalism passed off by the colonizing West. For a de-ideologizing and de-Westerninzing reading of cosmopolitanism see, to begin with, Appiah (2006); Amit and Rapport (2012: Part II, chapters 5–9, exclusively authored by Rapport).

[13] See, regarding the web of projections of indigenous contemporary experience, Landzelius (2006, pp. 1–42); but also see, on the multi-site semiotic experience of space, Mallapragada (2014).

[14] With a plea to the reader to avoid assuming that in my consideration Sicilians are all members of the Mafia or, even worse, that I myself, because of my origin, am a '*mafioso*' too!

from Italy to the US in the late nineteenth century, it was born as a cultural reaction against the unification of Italy under the northern Savoy Dynasty, subsequently re-placing itself in America, and becoming the criminal organization 'Cosa Nostra.' Filled with traditional or even ancestral habits, in the new location the Mafia transformed so deeply that it eventually became a sort of beacon for its members still living in Sicily. In fact, when the Allied Forces invaded Sicily during World War II, they benefitted from the transnational support of Cosa Nostra and the Sicilian Mafia, something that vastly improved the sprawling expansion of these criminal organizations. In the aftermath of the War, the spatial coordinates of the Mafia/Cosa Nostra became inter-spatial; the territory of this now international organization changed its original location and, in a sense, became ubiquitous to such an extent that even Italians now use the terms 'Cosa Nostra' and 'Mafia' indifferently to refer to the same phenomena spreading all over the world.[15]

I use the example of the Mafia to provocatively draw attention to the possibility that indigeneity, in all its possible forms, is a worldwide occurrence, intrinsically dynamic and capable of trans-local territorializations (spatialized semanticizations of cultural experience). On the other hand, the culturally indigenous features of Cosa Nostra, as well as 'Drangheta, Camorra, etc., are well known by criminal police all over the world. Without a nuanced understanding of the behavioral habits embodied in their actions by the affiliated members of such organizations, it is almost impossible to prevent their criminal activities. At the same time, the code of their communication and practical actions now has multi-sited origins, and corresponds to a territorial dimension that has not coincidence with national borders or geo-political areas.

The observations offered so far show, once more, the necessity of moving the issue of indigeneity beyond the 'West versus Rest of World' polarization that results from contemporary assessments of the colonial and postcolonial dynamics of destruction and exploitation. Even if colonialism had never taken place, indigeneity would have had *its* place in the field of anthropological, political and legal analyses, with its intrinsic historical dimensions. On the other hand, there is no culture on the planet Earth that does not include a degree of knowledge that comes from some 'elsewhere,' and even a*s local cultural experience* it re-elaborates those *migrant* sets of information in an idiomatic way, and spatializes them in and through its specific territorial dimension. Consequentially, the process of the recognition of indigeneity should be multi-centered and should focus, if it hopes to be genuine, not so much on the morphological features or products of culture as on the processing of cultural/ adaptive solutions, so as to understand and recognize their noetic elaborative ciphers. When so conceived, all 'indigeneity' will become cognitively universal and cosmopolitan. In its noetic ciphers, in its idiomatic attitude to elaborate signical relationships along a path of creative semiosis—that is, the process through which the brain/ body units engender new meanings and vital methods—all cultures can mirror

[15]This is the same phenomenon also outlined in general terms by Pollock (2002, p. 39).

themselves and learn, in comparative/reflexive terms, something about the significance of their own habits.

A genuinely pluralistic understanding of indigeneity, that is, of the processes of spatialization in the human attitude to produce culture, should newly reveal the ubiquitous plasticity of the symbolic/pragmatic functions inherent in our humanity. This is the same capacity that binds and relates different cultural productions, and is behind the universal inclination to produce culture. In turn, the relational ubiquity of cultural experience, when considered with respect to its noetic ciphers, would result in a polyphonic and multi-centered indigeneity.[16]

Relationality, on the other hand, is also at the core of the self-consciousness of one's own indigeneity. The 'indigenous' can become aware of their indigeneity only when they can look at themselves in the mirror of an alterity that is both cultural and geographical (or better: spatial).[17] Ones' own indigeneity, in other words, is in any case the outcome of a reflexive action triggered by the encounter with alterity. Were such alterity absolutely absent, one would be unable to conceive ones' own indigeneity. In the same vein, searching for an authentic indigeneity would not make sense if there were no contact with the Other. People discover their own indigeneity and its authenticity in connection with, and because of, their relations with Others. Hence, indigeneity cannot be said to be 'authentic' only because of its direct coincidence or compliance with an original. This apparently paradoxical occurrence depends on whether the 'original indigenous' results from an encounter with Otherness. Indigeneity, by implication, can be continually reauthenticated through further encounters with other various alterities.[18] In this way, the most authentic indigeneity will always be the last, that is, the one remaining after a cumulative sequence of indigeneities have been determined, the outcome of a series of encounters with Otherness. In the end, we could even imagine that there will be many versions of one's own indigeneity, as various encounters with Otherness occur. In any case, these manifold indigeneities do not dwell inside everyone or each group in a parallel way. They reciprocally contaminate, cumulate, and conflate.

The above considerations lead us to relativize the exclusiveness of physical territory as a structural feature of indigeneity. Spatial projections of culture engender their own spaces, that is, the invention of many, various territories. But cultural spatializations and their territorial elaborations are semiotic dimensions that do not necessarily saturate the physical space. A single physical place can be traversed and interactively lived by many cultural spaces and experiences as well as their related territorializations. Spatial incompatibility among different cultures does not depend—as already observed—on the Leibnizian axiom in which two bodies cannot occupy the same space. Instead, if it occurs, such incompatibility is a semantic one; it

[16] See Inoue and Moreira (2016, pp. 14–17); Berkes (2012, p. 265 ff.); Wilson Cavender (2004, p. 71 ff).

[17] The pivotal signification of relational self-reflexivity is proved by the failing genomical attempts to interpret/normativize indigeneity: see TallBear (2013, pp. 9–12; 17–18).

[18] In this sense, see Goe (2006, p. 403 ff).

comes from the lack of translation/transaction between the semantic profiles of the different spatializations proactively drawn by the various cultural categorizations at play.

All the above argumentative steps seek to address the overlapping interplay of multiple indigeneities in both urban and rural contexts.[19] My idea is that the autonomy and the self-determination of indigenous peoples and their cultures is achievable by combining their conservation and their self-transformation through practices of symmetrical recognition and harmonization with all the 'other indigeneities' (namely cultural spatializations) of the world. In this direction, it is not physical isolation that will preserve indigeneity but rather the potential to share material space by ensuring different cultural subjectivities the possibility to creatively produce culture and reciprocally translate/transact their spatial projections. This does not preclude the fact that, in some cases, sole occupation of a territory could be the best way to assure cultural indigenous self-determination. This solution, however, should only be the final outcome of a semantic intercultural effort of translation/transaction between the noetic ciphers encapsulated in the cultural habits and morphological expressions of all the cultures aspiring to live in a specific place, urban or rural.

In saying this, I do not wish to underplay the injustices suffered by people displaced from their lands and dispersed throughout the world. As is known, all that was a consequence of colonial devastations/dispossessions and capitalistic exploitations of Others' living spaces, something mainly driven by a compulsive greed for self-enrichment. These tragedies took place and deserve meaningful redress. Nonetheless, I would like to warn against a formalistic use of the 'territory/self-determination' argumentative categorical couple. In many cases, the legalization of indigenous claims has spurred people to assert that their ancestral rights come directly from the land because this land and its cosmological significance dictate their customary law. These kinds of claims, above all if recognized in the name of a pluralistic normative conception of cultural difference, run the risk of giving course to an instrumental use of an indigenist argument dramatically doomed to turn into an exclusionary war for power over material space.

Although my following assertions may sound rather provocative anthropologically speaking, I have to say that territory in itself, if considered as material space, does not emanate any law.[20] I think that there is nothing holistic in the attempt to root

---

[19] On this topic, see in an expansive literature Deloria (2006) and the collection of essays included in Lobo and Peters (2001).

[20] See, *Permanent Forum on Indigenous Issues, Report on the Sixth Session (14–15 May 2007)*, Economic and Social Council Official Records Supplement, No. 23, UN Doc E/2007/43, E/C.19/ 2007; 12, para 4. See also Daes (2001); Gilbert and Doyle (2011, p. 291 ff); Tobin, *Indigenous Peoples* (2014, p. xix). A very interesting discussion on the derivation of Law from the Land in worldwide indigenous (self-)representations can be found in Coleman (2012, p. 15 ff); Battiste and Henderson (2000, pp. 45, 67). Drawing on non-dualistic assertions, Battiste and Henderson (45, 67), share and develop their idea that the indigenous category 'land' is synonymous with law. This follows because nature, from an indigenous view, is the final result of a series of

law in the land. On the contrary, and despite appearances, the rooting assertion enshrines a dualistic division between the nature/thing and cultural/symbolic dimensions. Human beings and territories, conversely, are inseparable because, from the perspective of their significance, culture and ways of spatialization are indistinguishable. Conceptualizations of spaces engender territories, which in turn can be recognized as sources of law. At the onset of this process there is a *continuum* between nature and culture, and this is to be recognized for indigenous people as well as for Westerners and other cultures. In my view, the real problem does not lie in the territory itself and its attribution or re-attribution to indigenous people. What should be preserved is the possibility to maintain and re-elaborate the noetic ciphers that join a specific culture to the territory that it engendered through its original, idiomatic experience of space. Actually, remaining in a territory or recovering a territory that no longer allows the implementation and self-transformation of those noetic/cultural ciphers does not make sense from the perspective of a genuine protection of indigeneity. This elementary observation shows how groundless it is to assert that law emanates from the land. As already observed above, territory or land is not a datum but rather is always the cultural result of experience and its inherent categorizations.

What has been elaborated so far, however, in no way undermines, but could instead even strengthen the right to claim redress for territory and its traditional use, at least in some cases. What I mean is that assuming the right to territory as an implication of the right to indigenous difference in itself, and therefore without any justification or attempt to translate its cultural ciphers interculturally, is merely an expression of an idolatrous war waged for physical space taken as an external entity—albeit instrumentally and ex-post crammed with wildly various symbols. This would be nothing but a morphological/materialistic approach to the human inclination to territorialize/categorize space and experience. But such a view is as immediate as it is deleterious, even if it might appear to be endowed with a sort of dazzling obviousness, such that it becomes a source of legitimation for indigenous claims; if nothing else, it looks like the opposite to the usurping territorialization/categorization superimposed by the colonizing West and its so-called advanced civilization. Nonetheless this is only an equal and opposite reaction, which westernizes Others, the indigenous, precisely by inducing them to objectify and 'reify' their culture by assuming the land as its axis. The materialized territory prompts the clinging of indigenous hopes to the illusion that it can preserve their culture and avert its end. But I fear that this would be a deeply mistaken approach. Conservation for its own sake would paradoxically relativize indigenous cultures and crystallize their

'contracts' between human activities and nature. This ancestral occurrence would make indigenous law very different from Western law, which would be rigidly rooted in an inflexible human/nature divide. The question arises: how much humanity is there in the law of indigenous land? And what about the Modern Doctrine of Natural Rights and its origins in medieval natural theology? Some historical insights from European legal history—I would suggest—could be useful to the cause of indigenous peoples' rights, and the possibility of engendering effective intercultural translations of their needs.

noetic dynamic sources: just a prelude to a future passively undertaken and out of any cognizant control.[21]

International and state rules providing for the participation and consent of indigenous people[22] in all the decisions potentially affecting their interests will serve little purpose if indigeneity is not expressed with reference to its noetic cultural motor, its capacity to self-transform and remain itself through and by virtue of its self-transformations. If indigeneity is not recognized and treated according to the inherent significance of culture, that is, as a source of renewing and renewable semiotic energy, today's material indigenous victories will soon turn into tomorrow's increasing ineluctable cultural ossification.

Against this danger, it could be observed that UNDRIP includes the 'right to develop' in many of its provisions: see Articles 11, 13, 23, 26.2, 31, and in several of the *considerata* included in the related Annex, for example. Nevertheless, the general aura of the Declaration and the bent of the legal implementation[23] of its guiding principles seem to be pervaded by a prevailing misoneism and conservative spirit. It is possible that future interpretations of this document will enhance the semantic implications of the term 'develop.' For this to happen, however, the change that needs to take place should directly involve a retooled idea of indigeneity, as well as a conflation between 'ought' and 'being' which includes a global, multifocal and polyphonic recognition.

7.4 Indigeneities as Cognitive Universes: A Path to the Dynamic Harmonization of Indigeneity's Protection and the Intercultural Use of Human Rights

My basic assumption is that indigeneity is a projection of the human attitude to produce culture, followed by the attendant cultural engendering of spaces. All experiences of indigenization, in this view, could be considered as targets or extensional projections of the 'indigenization of the Earth.' According to this view of human cultural action, 'Earthly Space' should be considered as an absolute or comprehensive metaphor for all past, present and future experiences of indigenization. So that it is, in a sense, the alpha and the omega, the original pattern and the semantic (future) synthesis of human presence on the Earth.

Against this backdrop, we could define in cognitive terms the reciprocal recognition of all 'indigeneities' and their actual and virtual spatial projections. My

[21] What, following Beck, could be defined as 'an unconscious and/or passive cosmopolitization': see Beck (2004, p. 134).

[22] On the participation and consent of indigenous people to the decisional processes regarding their territories and the maintenance of their cultural habits as tied to their 'living the land', see, in a vast literature, Doyle (2015).

[23] In any case, UNDRIP has no mandatory effect on the political action of national states.

argument is as follows: if each indigeneity stems from a universal human function, the 'production of culture and space,' then all indigeneities will feature noetic ciphers that reveal something about human cultural nature and the different ways of engendering an all-encompassing 'Earthly Space.' Recognition requires respect and dialogue; but dialogue, in turn, presupposes the possibility to exist and express oneself. If the manifold indigenizations are variations of the universal attitude to produce and semanticize space, then each of these experiences can teach something to the others and their human actors about their sense of Earthly enterprise. A refusal of this kind of learning can result in the physical and cultural genocide of indigenous targets, and of course also effects a self-defeating lack of self-knowledge. I would like to propose calling this condition a 'defective embodiment of earthly indigeneity.' From this perspective, recognition of Otherness is an activity that simultaneously pertains to both the realms of 'ought' and 'is.' It could be taken as a value or an end, but at the same time and insofar as it is embodied in current experience, it deploys itself as a means of knowledge. Our understanding of what earthly indigeneity 'is,' namely, our terrestrial Being, is a consequence of the act of recognizing Others. But, most importantly, this means that (human) Being depends, at least to a considerable extent, on what humans know about the interactions between themselves and the world. Through the spectrum of 'indigeneity,' then, 'ought' and 'is' show a tendency to converge. This tendency toward cognitive convergence should be assumed as a renewed ground for elaborating the overall discourse on indigenous rights.

From this perspective, I would like to return to the term 'noetic cipher' to better describe its significance and function. To begin, we can observe that all cultural products are semiotic-experiential syntheses of the interplay between mind, body, and the environment. What ultimately connotes this interactive process does not coincide with its final form or perceptive properties. These are only contingent expressions of a process, an experiential habit at work.[24] The inner significance of cultural products consists precisely in the compositional ciphers, namely in the noetic and behavioral patterns of adaptive adjustment underlying the birth of the 'thing' (objects, conducts, symbolic expressions, etc.). Given that space is not distinguishable from the experiences and objects that populate and punctuate it, and furthermore, that indigenization can be assumed as the meta-category for the human semanticization of space and environment, then all indigeneities should be understood and recognized through the noetic ciphers they include as a means of producing related and idiomatic spatial cultural experience.

Noetic ciphers are (cognitive) habits, processive schemes of adaptation, that only occasionally coincide with specific things, objects, physical territories, and so on. These and their external manifestations are projections, and consequences, but they do not exhaust in themselves all the significance of the noetic ciphers from

[24] The theoretical roots of this approach to the nature of things can be traced in Peirce's semiotics. See Peirce (1892/1893, pp. 19–22), where seminal cues regarding the chorological continuity between mind and matter, category and space can be found.

which they stem. On the contrary, such noetic ciphers hold an inner attitude to be metaphorically 'transduced' and implemented by the use of other material and spatial components. For example, a reindeer fur is a very useful garment if I am in Sweden or Finland during the winter; conversely, it would be a kind of torture device were I to wear it on a summer's day in the middle of the Saharan desert. The noetic cipher of 'wearing garments' can, however, remain the same in both locations and be recognized as such, notwithstanding the preferable choice of wearing a linen tunic in the Sahara Desert, for example. Paradoxically, if I were Swedish or Finnish, and determined to wear the reindeer fur also in the Sahara Desert so as to maintain my cultural indigenous roots, precisely by maintaining the morphological and objectified features of my habits, I would invalidate their significance.

When we think of the intercultural recognition of indigeneity, we have to assume the possibility of a multilateral understanding of the noetic ciphers at work in all the habits embodied by people who are party to the intercultural encounter.[25] What must be avoided are the morphological reification and objectification of one's own cultural noetic cipher as well as the tendency to reciprocally translate by means of the alleged discovery of functionalist equivalences.[26] It must be made clear: the intercultural translation/transaction between different noetic ciphers should always be carried out as an original act of cultural creation.[27] Which properties are to be selected in order to serve as a metaphorical ground for intercultural understanding and interplay between different indigeneities/cultures cannot be unilaterally or aprioristically identified. It is primarily for this reason that functionalism does not work. It usually proceeds through the identification of a particular set of features and uses them to support the idea that the common end shared by different cultural habits and their material expressions is a specific one. In most cases, we observe a tendency to convert Otherness into a regime that is compatible with one's own habits, obviously accompanied by the unfailing pervasive action of an ethnocentric gaze. Conversely, a genuine intercultural understanding requires a holistic and dynamic appreciation of the noetic and contextual components underlying the cultural habits

[25] An interesting example of co-grafting and co-pollination can be traced in the work of the South-African dancer and choreographer Dada Masilo. She merges classical and contemporary Western ballet traditions and techniques with South-African dances, and re-interprets the classical ballets—recent examples include *Swan Lake*, *Carmen* and *Giselle*—with the Dance Factory ballet company in Johannesburg. Interestingly, South Africa recently enacted the Protection, Promotion, Development and Management of Indigenous Knowledge Systems Bill (2016) to protect traditional indigenous knowledge of local indigenous communities from illicit use and misappropriation and, *inter alia*, to promote the commercial utilization of indigenous knowledge. To this end, the Bill creates the National Indigenous Knowledge Systems Office, with the official task of recording and certifying indigenous knowledge, as well as penalizing violators of its prescriptions. How should Masilo's choreography be classified? Are her ballets a development of, or rather a betrayal of South African indigenous knowledge? Meanwhile the Embassy of the Republic of South Africa advertises Masilo's ballets on its official websites in all the countries where they are performed.

[26] For a very thoughtful and, at the same time, icastic demonstration of the flaws inherent in the functionalist approach see Keane (2007, p. 223 ff).

[27] See above, but also Ricca (2008, 2013).

and subjectivities being compared. At the same time, the cultural subjects' freedom to choose what to leave behind and what to acquire through the process of intercultural transduction must be assured.

Against the foil of 'Earthly indigeneity,' a polyphonic dialogue between the different indigeneity and indigenization operations in action on our planet could be designated an 'inter-indigenization process.' This is—I argue—an existential task for humankind, one that recognizes that each culture contains noetic ciphers of adaptation to the earthly environment that could be helpful to understanding the sense of and future possibilities for human life on Earth.

The inherent translatability and transducibility of indigenous existential approaches are proven, on the other hand, by the legal regime—specifically as applied to intellectual property—provided and in some cases already jurisdictionally implemented to protect so-called indigenous and traditional knowledge. If this knowledge and its practical/objectifying implications are viewed, in the eyes of the same modern culture, to have universal utility, then why on earth would it need to be protected by intellectual property law? I raise this question even if it blatantly demonstrates a deep inconsistency. For what sense does it make, from a perspective of all-encompassing Earthly indigeneity, to assume that knowledge of universal significance can be ruled by a legal regime that allows for its exclusionary use and/or economic exploitation? This paradox and its constitutive elements, I contend, should be seen as the problematic kernel nestled within current conceptualizations and implementations of indigenism and indigenous peoples' rights. I think that until we humans understand that the main task within the need to recognize the value of indigeneity is the very cognitive function on which our existence on the Earth depends, then all political and legal attempts to assure indigenous rights will devolve into a self-destructive logic of appropriation and power, involving westernized cultures as much as indigenous ones. This is not a direct consequence of the individualistic quality of the Western concept of intellectual property, as it is so often argued. As matter of fact, Western iterations of private property also recognize many possibilities for collectivization, multi-personal use, functionalization to communitarian interests and values, and so on. To make use of these semantic variations of the Western idea of property within the spectrum of an intercultural translation of indigenous claims for territories, traditional knowledge, etc., global thought must wriggle free from identitarian and reifying conceptions of culture.[28] Examples of the inconsistent and culturally dissociative behaviors that an inadequate understanding of noetic ciphers underlying indigenous habits[29] provokes can be found, among the

[28] See Mezey (2007, pp. 2004–2046) and Comaroff and Comaroff (2009). As for the risk of objectification and reification resulting from the intellectual property regimes on indigenous traditional knowledge see, in a massive literature, Coombe (2009, p. 405 ff; 2017, pp. 373–400); and *ibidem* for further bibliographical references.

[29] See, regarding the idea of noetic ciphers the consonant considerations laid down by Ellen (1996, pp. 118–120).

myriad of similar cases, in two different stories respectively related to the Nuaulu people of South Asia[30] and the Kantu' of Kalimatan.[31]

I observed something similar during my fieldwork in Calabria, specifically in Riace, where a project for the repopulation of local villages was carried out by means of a plan of integration for migrants/refugees and the parallel recovery of traditional autochthonous knowledge and habits. Unfortunately, though the initial efforts were carried out with genuine inventiveness, the attempt to merge and co-pollinate Calabrian East Coast traditional knowledge and the cultural habits of new arrivals broke up on the reefs of economic, political and media exploitation of this social experiment. By and by, the focus on noetic ciphers and the possibility of their intercultural transduction/transaction lost its central positioning, and was eventually replaced by economic and identitarian accommodations between the interests of the natives and the foreign newcomers.[32]

The importance of centering the recognition and protection of indigeneity on its noetic ciphers is also proven by the current trend for harmonizing indigenous habits/behaviors and human rights. Ordinarily, the cultural differentiation of indigenous people is ruled by a double-faceted standard of self-determination/compatibility, which places—as dialectical poles—indigenous habits on one side, and state statutory law/international human rights regimes on the other. The tendency to interpret the relationships between indigenous cultures and the other cultures in identitarian terms leads to a reading of indigeneity that primarily orbits the morphological features of peoples' conduct.[33] These morphological features, then, are taken as indices to calculate their compatibility with human rights. At the same time, indigenous people try to include their claims to differentiate and self-determine their identities, taken in their material and practical consequences, under the semantic dome of human rights. No attempt at semantic translation takes place in these wars

[30] See Ellen (2008, p. 321 ff, and especially 326), where Ellen insightfully observes: "How people conceptualize nature depends on how they use it, how they transform it, and how, in so doing, they invest knowledge in different parts of it."

[31] See Dove (2011, p. 91 ff). I addressed diffusely the cases treated in the articles cited here and in the above note in Ricca (2012: spec. 320–328). The negative remarks proposed by Dove (2011) and Ellen (2008) are echoed, in terms of indigenous peoples' rights protection, by Love (2013, pp. 112–114; 116 ff) and Hirsch (2016, p. 103 ff).

[32] For more information about this case, see Ricca (2010). Notwithstanding the major attention given to the 'Riace case' by the newspapers and other media—even Wim Wenders made a film titled 'Il volo'—the mayor of Riace is now under investigation for misappropriation of funds and fraud against the Italian State and the EU, and has been sentenced in first instance.

[33] In this sense, the morphing of cultural heritage from ownership into stewardship can also be a form of instrumentalization and objectification of indigenous noetic ciphers. Against Carpenter et al.'s criticism of Mezey's arguments about the cultural defectiveness of indigenous property regimes we can observe that what law should protect, what should be recognized/shared, is the knowledge encapsulated in indigenous agricultural, animal breeding, and other habits, rather than their diversity or material usefulness in themselves. In this sense, see Wilson Cavender (2004, p. 71). See, moreover, Carpenter et al. (2009, pp. 1083–1084); Mezey (2007, p. 2004 ff). In this regard, see also the FAO Conference Resolution no. 5/1989 about so-called 'Farmers Rights.'

over the signification and guarantee implications of human rights enunciations. In these semantic struggles, there is no traceable explication/justification of differences; rather they are presented as self-bounded units to be considered as such, for their (alleged) empirical *givenness*. Needless to say, within this contrastive game, human rights can only play the role of imposing hierarchical standards, which are thereby dangerously exposed to political instrumentalization.

On the contrary, if the starting point of the protection of indigeneity focused on the noetic ciphers of the cultural parties at play, then the axiological 'ingredients' of human rights could be situated in the midst of the translational/transactive process so as to foster the collaborative creation of intercultural solutions. If all parties considered themselves as equal and full-fledged interpreters of different indigeneities, they could trace, in the connotative landscapes underlying their habits, the semantic components to use for calling into play human rights as translational interfaces. In this way, human rights could leave their hierarchical pyramidal positioning, and instead locate themselves on a horizontal plane, where they could function as a semantic bridge between different cultural and spatial universes.[34]

This intercultural use of human rights could give rise to the production of inter-spatial translations and therefore create new inter-spaces of experience, which in each specific place could give shape to a general formula of coexistence between indigeneities amenable to be implemented at an all-encompassing Earthly level. Rather than being trapped in a claiming/compensatory, reifying and anti-Western script, the discourse on indigeneity should endorse and include the view that, at least in absolute terms, there is no better or worse way to live on—and supported by—the Earth. It is true, colonialism and, more recently, the combination of contemporary technology and neocolonialism have caused and continue to cause great ecological changes and imbalances in bio-diversity. But human presence on Earth has also produced huge catastrophes in the past, especially if we consider human action from a deeply ecological point of view.[35] There is no indigenous people that is completely innocent if judged from this perspective. Human beings, as well as other creatures, are part and parcel of transformations that nature impresses on itself; this simply because the human being is itself nature, beyond and notwithstanding all possible dualisms. We should consider—with an appreciation for the paradox—that a conservative and *museifying* misoneism was born under modernity, and it cannot alter the trans-epochal process of cosmic signification that the appearance of humankind on Earth assumes. I argue that we, the humans, should modestly come to terms with this impossibility and, at the same time, with the innumerable and unforeseeable variations that the attitude to 'indigenize' space produces in all times. This is a task that can no longer exempt anyone from its accomplishment. Therefore, invoking the universal logic of human rights only to see the triumph of unilateral or conservative/ identitarian claims for redress is a contradiction that cannot long survive its

[34] See above Chaps. 3 and 6.

[35] On the anti-ecological consequences of traditional indigenous habits and agricultural practices, see Coombe (2017, p. 390 ff); see also Latour (2004, p. 232 ff).

consequences. In the human creative production of earthly spatialities, we must act all together, polyphonically, from the common understanding—even visually proffered by images from outer space—that the Earth is finite.

7.5 Some Concluding Remarks

Indigenous people deserve much more than to be reified in their role of 'Others' by Westerners, colonizers, and so on. They have been, are and will be interpreters of the human attitude toward the semanticizing experience of space alongside all other people on Earth. In my view, all humans can and should learn, with modesty, from the noetic/pragmatic devices that indigenous people have developed throughout their history. This disposition to learn, at least as a regulative ideal, should give rhythm to the respect for indigenous people, asking them in an equitable and interpenetrative way to imagine and construe a common human future on Earth. This is a duty for all of humanity insofar as indigenous people have not only the right to be entirely compensated and refunded for the plunders and despoliations they endured but also, and above all, to equal participation in the future process of indigenization of the Earth by humankind generally.

From this perspective, human rights are to be imagined as intercultural interfaces in the proactive translation-transaction of indigenous cultures in order to empower not only their rights to maintain their past identity but also their entitlement to unfold the cognitive 'energy' encapsulated in their cultural habits (including the injustice and marginalization they suffered) through the future indigenization of the Earth by all humans living on it. Precisely in this sense I think that any blindness to indigenous knowledge of any population on the Earth is not only an ethical and legal betrayal of the genuine bottom-up universalization inspiring the primeval human rights project (related to the modernity of Montaigne and Diderot, rather than that of Rousseau, Locke, or Hegel) but also a cognitive deficiency. Hence, any lack of equal involvement of indigenous people in the earthly indigenous enterprise that all humans must undertake is to be considered both a cognitive *error* and an axiological flaw, at once. The only way human beings will be able to understand their world in the future—its 'is'— will be a consequence of the implementation of the duty to involve all earthly peoples in planning the coexistence of human beings on our planet—its 'ought.' Vice versa, the Earth and planetary society we will be able to construe and sustain, will mold our 'being' and the axiological motor inside us. All this is beyond any naturalistic fallacy because 'is' and 'ought' are only the interactive and co-constituting sides of the ongoing process of 'being on the Earth', all equally indigenous, all equally earthly.

I can understand how all this might sound like a utopian/oneiric view of things, fraught as they are with the relentless presentification of the material consequences of injustice, exploitation, and disruption that indigenous people are having to endure. Nonetheless, if we assume a semiotic perspective, the idea of 'earthly shared and intertwined indigeneities' can be seen to be, on the contrary, inherently realistic and endowed, if adequately grasped, with huge practical consequences. The starting point is to consider 'indigeneity' as the result of a signical relationship between human agents and the spaces they live in. To use a Peircean lexicon, each 'indigeneity' is the interlocutory expression of a thirdness that is polyphonically engendered by living human beings on the Earth. In turn, each space or portion of space is the result of signical/pragmatic relationships, the epitome and, at the same time, the prophecy of their threads spread upon, through, and over the planet, its past and its future (insofar as these relationships will be consciously included in our semiotic and pro-active understanding of what earthly space is). Each environment is the result of the migration of information conveyed by living beings and the movements of the living entity that the 'Earth system' is. Seeds, spores, microorganism, and so on, all the way up and through human beings, travelled the Earth from the time of Pangea, during the continental drift, and the time span which hosted the evolutionary emergence of homo sapiens. There is no place that is not the consequence of this overall migration, the transformations it entailed, and the semiotic/phenomenal dialogue that it is carrying on with all the other places on earth. Spaces and places are not (mere) things, final reifications of past events, but rather semiotic agents involved in an ongoing process. Even the environments of indigenous peoples are the result of their ancestral migrations and the transformation that humans together with other living beings produced in 'that there' by their supervening occurrences and the semiotic heritage those beings brought with and in themselves. In turn, the consequences of those migratory events produced semiotic feedbacks on other parts of the planet. Only by becoming able to see the invisible semiotic/planetary threads concealed behind the dazzling and morphological appearance of places, environments, landscapes, plants, animals and peoples, can we grasp the real significance of what the indigenization process and its historical expressions are. Unfortunately, the logic and the rhetoric of rights claims must rely on a conceptual stiffening of places, subjects, needs, identities because of the dialectical, oppositional structure of judicial confrontations. The result is a kind of thinghood or thingness of what is at stake and the overshadowing of the semiotic, real processes which continue to unfold inside each place, living being, community and so on, and shape the signical/pragmatic consequences of their present existence, namely their actual meaning.

This view and its pragmatic relevance for indigenous peoples and for the whole of humanity has been insightfully expressed by an Amazonian activist, engaged in the fight against the last disastrous deeds promoted by the Brazilian former president Bolsonaro, whose interview I chanced to listen to just two years ago. That woman, dressed only in her tattoos—therefore, in the eyes of the average Westerner, the perfect imagine of an anthropological relic excluded from any global civilization process—explained, by means of an aware use of the telecommunications apparatus, the reasons behind indigenous peoples' claims more or less as follows: "People on the Earth, government and international powers have to understand the sacredness of our environment, the Amazonian landscape, and our way of life within it as a resource for the whole planet. Our relationship with the forest is a crucial factor in the ecological equilibrium of all of the Earth, it is a way of life on which the life of all civilizations, animal species, plant worlds depend. Humankind and political governments must recognize the importance of our needs, as Amazonian indigenous peoples, in order to understand themselves, their environments and the common future, because only through this ecological insight of the relationships that bind us, the Amazonian people to their environment, can they choose their future as inhabitants of the Earth. The Amazon's breath is the breath of all the Earth and all living beings on it." The Amazonian woman's speech gives the best explanation of the semiotic interrelatedness I try to draw in this chapter, the ensuing conflation of 'is' and 'ought,' the interpenetration between the reciprocal 'elsewheres' on the Earth including the related inhabitants and, finally, the need to consider indigenous people not only as victims or misoneist bearers of compensative rights but rather as primal agents in planning humankind's common future. The Amazonian activist's discourse is an extraordinary example of how transformation can encapsulate the best expression of authenticity by virtue of the semiotic, open-ended 'nature' of 'culture,' namely its inner signification as a form of a 'renewable source of semantic/experiential energy.' Her arguments, in my view, show a deep ability to see the invisible semiotic threads underlying the morphological appearance of things and an astounding savvy skill to discompose and recompose them in order to grasp the processive meaning of the actual experience she and all of us, as human beings, are undergoing on the Earth. Her view is all but utopian or oneiric. Conversely, she seems to embody the most radical and intelligent expression of cognitive and political realism against which the capitalist fashion of Bolsonaro's (hopefully faded) concerns appears as the unaware, capricious attitude of that immature child which humanity as a whole cruelly continues to be.

References

Amit V, Rapport N (2012) Community, cosmopolitanism, and the problem of human commonality. Pluto Press, London. Part II, Chapters 5–9, exclusively authored by Rapport

Anderson B, Harrison P (2010) The promise of non-representational theories. In: Anderson B, Harrison P (eds) Taking-place: non-representational theories and geography. Ashgate, Farnham, pp 1–36

Appiah KA (2006) Cosmopolitanism: ethics in a world of strangers. Norton, New York

Battiste M, Henderson J (Sákèj) Y (2000) Protecting indigenous knowledge and heritage: a global challenge. Purich, Saskatoon

Beck U (2004) Cosmopolitical realism: on the distinction between cosmopolitans in philosophy and the social sciences. Glob Netw 4(2):131–156

Berkes F (2012) Sacred ecology, 3rd edn. Routledge, New York

Bhandar B (2011) Plasticity and post-colonial recognition: 'Owing, Knowing and Being'. Law Critiq 22(3):227–249

Birrel K (2016) Indigeneity: before and beyond the law. Routledge, London

Brendan T (2014) Indigenous peoples, customary law and human rights—why living law matters. Routledge, London, pp 41–45

Carpenter K, Katyal SK, Riley AR (2009) In defense of property. Yale Law J 118(6):1022–1125

Coleman D (2012) Toward an indigenist ecology of knowledges for Canadian literary studies. Stud Can Lit 37(2):1–31

Comaroff J, Comaroff J (2009) Ethnicity, Inc. The University of Chicago Press, Chicago
Coombe RJ (2009) The expanding purview of cultural properties and their politics. Annu Rev Law Soc Sci 15:393–412
Coombe RJ (2017) Frontiers of cultural property in the global south. In: Anderson J, Greismar H (eds) The Routledge companion to cultural property. Routledge, London, pp 373–400
Daes EI (2001) Indigenous peoples and the their relationship to land: final working paper. http://www.refworld.org/docid/3d5a2cd00.html
Deloria PJ (2006) Indians in unexpected places. University Press of Kansas, Lawrence
Dove MR (2011) Rubber kills the land and saves the community: an undisciplined commodity. In: Dove MR, Sajise PE, Doolittle AA (eds) Beyond the sacred forest: complicating conservations in South East Asia. Duke University Press, Durham, pp 91–122
Doyle CM (2015) Indigenous people, title to territory, rights and resources: the transformative role of free prior and informed consent. Routledge, London
Economic and Social Council Official Records Supplement, No. 23, UN Doc E/2007/43, E/C.19/2007; 12, para 4, Permanent Forum on Indigenous Issues, Report on the Sixth Session (14–15 May 2007)
Ellen RF (1996) The cognitive geometry of nature: a contextual approach. In: Descola P, Pálsson G (eds) Nature and society: anthropological perspectives. Routledge, London, pp 103–123
Ellen RF (2008) Forest knowledge, forest transformation: political contingency, historical ecology, and the renegotiation of nature. In: Dove MR, Carpenter C (eds) Environmental anthropology: a historical reader. Blackwell, Malden, pp 321–328
Forbes J (1998) The urban tradition among native Americans. Am Indian Cult Res J 22(4):15–27
Forte MC (2010) Introduction: indigeneities and cosmopolitanism. In: Forte MC (ed) Indigenous cosmopolitans: transnational and transcultural indigeneity in the twenty-first century. Peter Lang, New York, pp 1–16
Gilbert J, Doyle C (2011) A new dawn over the land: shedding light on collective ownership and consent. In: Allen S, Xanthaki A (eds) Reflections on the UN Declaration on the rights of indigenous peoples. Bloomsbury, pp 279–328
Goe J (2006) Becoming indigenous peoples: difference, inequality, and the globalization of East African identity politics. Afr Aff 105(420):399–420
Handler R (2003) Cultural property and culture theory. J Soc Archaeol 3(3):353–365
Hannerz U (2004) Cosmopolitanism. In: Nugent D, Vincent J (eds) A companion to the anthropology of politics. Blackwell, Oxford, pp 69–85
Hirsch E (2016) Mediating indigeneity: public space and the making of political identity in Andean Peru. Polit Leg Anthropol Rev 39(1):95–109
Hirtz F (2003) It takes means to be traditional: on recognizing indigenous cultural communities in the Philippines. Dev Change 34(5):887–914
Inoue CYA, Moreira PF (2016) Many worlds, many nature(s), one planet: indigenous knowledge in the anthropocene. Revista Brasileira de Política Internacional 59(2):e009:1–19. http://www.scielo.br/rbpi
Keane W (2007) Christian moderns: freedom and fetish in the mission encounter. The University of California Press, Berkeley
Kymlicka W (2011) Beyond the indigenous/minority dichotomy. In: Allen S, Xanthaki A (eds) Reflections on the UN declaration on the rights of indigenous people. Hart, Oxford
Landzelius K (2006) Introduction. In: Landzelius K (ed) Native on the net. Indigenous and diasporic peoples in the virtual age. Routledge, London, pp 1–42
Latour B (2004) Politics of nature. Harvard University Press, Cambridge
Lobo S, Peters K (eds) (2001) American Indians and the urban experience. Altamira Press, New York
Love B (2013) Treasure hunts in rural Japan: place making at the limits of sustainability. Am Anthropol 115(1):112–124
Mallapragada M (2014) Virtual homelands: Indian immigrants and online cultures in the United States. University of Illinois Press, Urbana

Mezey N (2007) The paradoxes of cultural property. Columbia Law Rev 107:2004–2046
Peirce CS (1892/1893) Man's glassy essence. The Monist 1:19–22. https://isidore.co/misc/Res%20pro%20Deo/Peirce/The%20Monist%20papers/4.%20Man%27s%20Glassy%20Essence%20(1893).pdf
Pollock S (2002) Cosmopolitan and vernacular in history. In: Chakrabarty D, Bhabha HK, Pollock S, Brenkenridge CA (eds) Cosmopolitanism. Duke University Press, Durham, pp 15–53
Quinn WW Jr (1993) Intertribal integration: the ethnological argument in Duro and Reina. Ethnohistory 40(1):34–69
Renteln Dundes A, Dundes A (1994) What is folk law? In: Renteln Dundes A, Dundes A (eds) Folk Law: essays in the theory and practice of *Lex Non Scripta*, vol 1. The University of Wisconsin Press, Madison, pp 1–4
Ricca M (2008) Oltre Babele. Codici per una democrazia interculturale. Dedalo, Bari
Ricca M (2010) Riace, il futuro è presente. Naturalizzare il 'globale' tra immigrazione e sviluppo interculturale. Dedalo, Bari
Ricca M (2012) Natura inventata e natura implicita nel diritto. Incursioni interculturali. In: Marrone G (ed) Semiotica della natura (natura della semiotica). Mimesis, Milano, pp 309–358
Ricca M (2013) Culture interdette. Modernità, migrazioni, diritto interculturale. Bollati Boringhieri, Torino
Ricca M (2017) Ghostly spatialities in condominiums: nuisance law, legal geography, and intercultural chorology, pp 1–22. https://ssrn.com/abstract=3050729 or https://doi.org/10.2139/ssrn.3050729. Accessed 10 Oct 2017
Robinson DF, Abdel-Latif A, Roffe P (eds) (2017) Protecting traditional knowledge: the WIPO intergovernmental committee on intellectual property and genetic resources, traditional knowledge and folklore. Routledge, London
TallBear K (2013) Genomic articulations of indigeneity. Soc Stud Sci 43(4):509–533. Special Issue: Indigenous body parts and postcolonial technoscience (August 2013)
Tobin B (2014) Indigenous peoples, customary law and human rights – Why living law matters. Routledge, London
Wilson Cavender A (2004) Reclaiming our humanity: decolonization and the recovery of indigenous knowledge. In: Mihesuah Abbot D, Wilson Cavender A (eds) Indigenizing the academy: transforming scholarship and empowering communities. University of Nebraska Press, Lincoln

Chapter 8
The Invisible Ubiquity of Sacred Places

8.1 Prologue

In this chapter, I would like to try to draw some conclusions from the theoretical path undertaken so far by going back to the interpenetration among culture, religion and secularization. The aim is to focus on the very thorny issues tied to the legal protection of 'sacred places.' The goal behind this thematic choice is to show that the intercultural treatment of experiential spaces, especially what I call the *surroundings* of 'sacred places,' is the only viable starting point to defuse the conflicts apparently triggered by the visible and material presence of 'sacred things.'

As things, actually, the items of the so called 'religious heritage' are placed astride the internal and the external domain. And besides, without this embodied hybrid spatial/semantic pertinence, and therefore lacking the implicit recognition of an active intermingling between materiality/exteriority and immateriality/interiority, those places cannot be defined as 'sacred.' Nonetheless, the 'thinghood' of sacred places is at odds with the imaginary of secularization and the alleged privatization of religion. According to its rhetoric, the 'religious' should be safeguarded but simultaneously maintained *on the internal/private side* of the subjectivity and the spatial projections of its activity. And yet, the 'sacred place' embodies and makes visible the invisible, exteriorizes the internal, publicizes the private. A source of further problems is that the 'sacred place'—as I will try to argue—is an epitome and, at the same time, a pre-figuration of the projections of religion, if intended in its overall anthropological significance, through the daily spaces of people's life. Many conflictive situations originate from the silent resilience of religion inside cultural habits and its dilution—as it were—in the worldly practices of each geographical and political context. When the pragmatic threads emanating from sacred places meet the cultural texture of spatialized daily experience, for example in urban landscapes, a struggle for space and the prevalence of the related patterns of semanticization tacitly takes place. But insofar as people are not completely aware of the spatialization of their cultural differences, and lack intercultural translational/transactional skills, sacred

M. Ricca, *Intercultural Spaces of Law*, Law and Visual Jurisprudence 10,
https://doi.org/10.1007/978-3-031-27436-7_8

places become—but already they are so—the fetishized catalyst of the inability to reciprocally translate the multiple experiential spaces and the related categorical schemes. The rhetoric of secularization and the alleged absence of religion from a neutral, pluralistic or, in the worst case, merely tolerant public sphere, ends up increasing the conflicts. And this precisely because that rhetoric conceals the resilience of religion within the presumed secularized cultural lexicon and, consequently, prevents people from becoming cognizant of the need for an intercultural translation of their experiential space oriented to reconfigure their difference in view of a polyphonic understanding/construction of their space of coexistence. As I will try to illustrate, the conflicts orbiting sacred places stem from 'what is not said' about the patterns of semanticization of the spaces surrounding them.

The problem with the privatization of religion is not only that it never took place but also that its indirect implication coincides with an (allegedly) objectivizing epistemology, precisely the epistemology of secularization. This epistemology conceals, however, how much religion is resilient in the Western conceptualizations and the related categories. Such resilience has to do not only with political or institutional discourse, but also with daily life, its scripts, habits and cognitive schemes. An area strongly influenced by this 'non-perceived' cultural/anthropological action is the legal one. What I call *legal theology* is goes far beyond the scope of Schmitt's political theology as well as the three strains that have been acutely identified as the multifarious projections and/or declinations of secularization: that is, the political, the ideological and the institutional ones.[1] When I refer to the 'epistemology of secularization,' I intend a mind/world divide that is reified in the semantic structure of 'things', the same things we assume to be 'real', 'out there', distinguished from 'the subjective dimension' and, consequently, the domain of values and the internal forum. The 'external forum' is a kind of constellation of these items. Their epistemic neutrality/self-evidence, gauged on the immediate and universal signification of the so-called primary qualities, is assumed by modern Western secularization as both the shield and buttress for freedom—which can remain, in this way, protected/secluded within the domain of conscience. Unfortunately, but also predictably, this protective seclusion, over time, turned into a sort of cage. Such effect is also due to the fictitiously self-evident and not-construed morphological features of the external objects and the presumed representational (almost isomorphically mirroring) schemes through which we categorize them. The real state of affairs regarding all kinds of categorizations, however, is that the checklist constituting them stems from a selection from the stream of perception. Perceptions, however, are not to be intended as a collection of stimuli issued from the objective structure of the world out there, and not even a representational rendering of them by virtue of our schemes of judgment, which are then projected again onto the external phenomena. The so-called *data* are not *given* but somehow *made* by means of an unremitting and co-generative process of mutual adjustment between the organisms and the world of experience—something different from the Kantian aprioristic and representational

[1] Casanova (2009).

understanding of human knowledge. On the other hand, the etymological origin of the word 'facts' is too often overlooked. Actually, it comes from the *Latin* 'facere'—which precisely means 'to do', or better 'to make'. 'Data,' precisely in this sense, result from the dynamic process of mutual responsiveness ongoing between the world and mind/body units. This process, however, is stirred by values, both biological and cultural—which are to be assumed as deeply intermingled with one another along a relational *continuum* and not ontologically insulated from one another.

Becoming aware that the categories related to the so-called 'things of the world out there' are laden with values/ends is a crucial step towards grasping the epistemological depth to which secularization and its cognitive and socio-communicative implications unfold, which is in many respects a silent occurrence. This is because each culture construes its own world of facts. It obtains this result by subtracting the axiological/subjective component of the cognitive process, previously involved as an enactive and proactive factor to carry on experience. By means of this subtraction, what results from that process is communicatively transformed in a field of inter-subjective self-evidence. This is the dimension of objectivity, the universe of communicative self-evidence, in short, the external world of (the 'real') facts. The consequence of this concealment of subjectivity is that Otherness, that is, the axiological/teleological factors of Others' 'factualizations' of the external world, is dubbed as 'subjective.' What is very interesting—and tremendously deceptive—in this epistemic disposition, is that the Other's external world is disqualified as 'replete with subjectivity:' namely superstitious pseudo-cognitive inclinations, wishful thinking, naïve and anthropomorphic beliefs.

The modern liberal political and cognitive setup—as it were—employs a variety of strategies to assure protection from these 'ineffable and fanciful' exudations of human psychological dispositions. Among them can be counted their insulation, if not relegation, within the 'reserve of freedom,' the golden cage of the private realm. Unfortunately, the parallel portion of subjectivity nestled in the external and objective world that was previously engendered by the communicative practices of dominant groups and cultures—nobody knows exactly how and when—disappears. The remnant/resulting objectivity transmutes, then, in a pantograph used to draw the geography of the social world, a cognitive-pragmatic instrument which marks out the border beyond which freedom has no public and rational citizenship.

In my view, the problem of secularization is eminently epistemological rather than political. It is so because the power inherent in saying how the world 'is' includes a huge coefficient of 'dissimulated ought,' and in the end results in a much more pervasive liberticide than any other explicit authoritative attitude. The power of making the world, however—and here lies the distance of my argument from the Foucaultian one—is not a distortion of the cognitive activity. The very challenge is, rather, to recognize that 'objectivity' is coextensive with inter-subjectivity. An intersubjectivity that is inherent even in the relationship between the same subject, respectively considered in its past and present instantiations, who reflexively thinks of itself and its past experience as *facts* but, precisely for this reason, also as signs to be interpreted. The interpretive tools silently and invisibly involved in the perception of the 'real world,' the world of *facts*, dwell, however, in people's minds and coincide, more precisely, with the network of semiotic relationships stored in their memory—provided that such networks, in turn, are the result and simultaneously the epitome of previous enactive exchanges between the individual organisms and their environment. Only by becoming aware of, and available to dis-compose, the semiotic landscapes underlying the allegedly *objective morphological appearances* of one's own world is it possible to renew the selective activity that axiologically and teleologically can lead human beings to 'enactively make their world meaningful' even when they are called upon by experiential circumstances to face Otherness. The inability to carry out a continuous renewing of the experiential world gives rise to an *immodest use* of categories that in each cultural context are assumed to correspond to the scaffolding of the 'real world.' Symmetrically, this defective epistemic attitude fosters the tendency of the 'subjective side of the moon,' namely the field of freedom, to sprout absolute, radical and absolutely non-transactable self-assertive dispositions.

I think, however, that what I have outlined above is somehow an anthropological epistemic tendency, which in Western secularization has found only a paroxysmal expression. On the other hand, that secularization is distant from the enactive and relational approaches in its conception of world-making can be seen in the overall trend to recognize the misleading, and even deceptive, features of the corresponding meta-narrative in the political domain and in constitutional or public law rather than in private law and criminal law areas. Nonetheless, as already observed,[2] it would not be difficult to find the footprints of Christian moral theology in the anthropological/ethical imaginaries underlying the category of contract, the conception of guilt, the idea of person (and also corporation), the patterns of obligation, equity, good faith, responsibility, and the overall encyclopedia of 'factual features' that these categorical legal apparatuses bring along.[3] But all this 'material' seems to have escaped the criticism of secularization. Nevertheless, the above instruments—as it were—give rhythm to daily life for most of the world, much more than weapons or even financial strategies. This 'fact,' however, seems to be accepted almost as if it was intrinsically, clearly, and necessarily universal. Conversely, I think that this kind of cognitive strabismus is another tacit effect of secularization, and precisely one of its aspects that can be traced back to Grotius and the interplay he orchestrated between the medieval problem of universals and the early modern transformation of ethical and legal concepts.

Criticism of secularization has never focused on the need to rethink the grammar of subjectivity in pluralist and multicultural societies in the West, as well as in the post-colonial Rest, by redefining the categories of contract, obligation, responsibility as they have been molded in the European/Christian cultural context. On average,

---

[2] See above, Chap. 2.

[3] See, about the 'factual features' embodied in legal language regarding categories as 'contracts,' 'ownership', 'guilt,' etc., and therefore the lack of self-referentiality of law and its deontic discourse Ricca (2022).

claims against ethnocentrism pivot upon human rights rather than private law (with the exception of marriage and family law) and even some fundamental aspects of criminal law. This is a consequence of a strong inclination to respectively underrate: (a) that the social communicative fabric is first and foremost imbued with the language and practice of property, contracts, inheritance and various categories of crimes; and (b) that it rests on a communicative/experiential terrain already inseminated by such schemes, the very ones that human rights discourse depends upon. The question is: why is there a cultural blindness that prevents seeing the relationship between secularization and the worldwide dissemination of Western contract law, criminal law, etc. as patterns of behavior or, in more general terms, the legal grammar of daily life resulting from their continuous and pervasive implementation? My idea is that these theological-legal 'source channels' of Western secularized discourse are under-considered because they are so close to the daily life language of things and pragmatic exchange as to appear implicitly embodied in things themselves. What is to be underlined is that such a language of things is the same one that is molded by the modern secular theorization of a divide between internal forum and external forum, the objective world and the subjective world, the realm of public life and the private domain of freedom. The final outcome is that factual language and legal schemes have progressively intermingled with one another so as to reciprocally underpin and create a kind of semio-ideological 'whole.' Within this 'entirety,' thinghood and legal schemes mutually buttress their own semantic rigidity through the invisible and tacit unfolding of habits and their practical implementations. In this way, however, experience communicatively locks itself down, engendering a kind of unsustainability of Otherness. This is a consequence of the complete blindness to difference stemming from its semantic irrelevance with respect to the dazzling self-evidence of morphological and empirical categorization that overshadow, under their only apparent obviousness, the universe of mobile and fringed relationships they epitomize.

At this point, I can connect the arguments I have deployed so far with sacred places, the intercultural sustainability of their protection and religions. Insofar as sacred places are understood as 'things', the invisible threads of their semantic and pragmatic implications will be doomed to remain concealed and silenced. As I will strive to show, the real struggle in their regard, however, has to do precisely with the implementations and projections of the habits they represent and symbolically summarize throughout the spaces of life, for example the urban areas surrounding them. Social behavior, in these areas, is given rhythm—so to speak—by the patterns of conduct stemming from legal categories molded by law and, usually, by dominant groups. By combining with the material element of experience, those patterns produce phenomenal effects that give rise to 'landscapes of thinghood.' Against these only apparently exclusively empirical landscapes, in turn, the semiotic and pragmatic consequences of sacred places, even more if related to faiths of minority or foreign communities, end up colliding. To put it diversely, the problem of the protection of sacred places is an environmental/*ecological* one. As long as people called upon to apply law, as well as people inhabiting living spaces, do not look at the semiotic and pragmatic relationships underlying the 'thinghood' of sacred places and their surroundings, it will be impossible to get to the bottom of the conflicts stemming from them. This is a problem of semio-ecological sustainability of difference that is not much distant from the traditional issues related to environmental sustainability. As I will show below, this applies to both the local and international/planetary dimension of such conflicts and the relevance of sacred places. Proposing an analogy between these two kinds of *eco-logical* questions and the related solution strategies could be useful to better introduce what follows.

My idea is that until the language of things and the legal language of quotidian life drop the illusion of an objectivity of the external world and an externum/internum divide, it will be impossible to spawn a genuine ecological and, therefore, inclusively planetary experience leading toward a sustainable relationship with the global environment. The assertion according to which each factual category is genetically and constitutively hinged upon values/ends is to be matched, today, with the responsibility human beings have with regard to the future development of their environment—in some sense, echoing Jonas' '*Principle Responsibility*.'[4] This means that the outcomes of nature cannot be considered a constant ground, immune from human action. The environment is no longer a set of unchanging boundary conditions of human life even because it is not (relatively) immune from its developmental paths—as it was in the ancient past. This means that things, or better the 'thinghood' of the world, are to be prospectively thought of processively, interplaying with human choices, values and ends. Secularization's cognitive imagery finds itself, therefore, caught between two impinging and somewhat confuting factors: on one side, its allegedly descriptive/representative 'factual categories' that are impelled to show their genetic axio-telic and relational origins;[5] and, on the other, the perspectival status of the world's facts that are to be determined by a responsible human action.

The inter-temporal connection just outlined between facts, values and ends is strictly tied to the role of law and shows its twofold potential significance as both a source of legitimation and a means to plan future facts. From this perspective, 'facts' are to be thought of as steppingstones towards a factual future, that is to say that they are to be understood as transformative means. But, if this approach is plausible, what about, then, the exterior, subject-independent status of the objective facts in this different figuration of experience? And, more specifically, how to treat the 'fact' in the process ordered to construe the medium term of the legal syllogism? Usually, the rigidity of facts, in social experience, is the other side of the alleged secularization of private and criminal law's categories because of their close interplay in daily life imagery and dynamics; at the same time, the normative force of these legal institutions shores up the presumed objectivity of facts. This situation, as observed above,

---

[4] Jonas (2012).

[5] What is in tune with the enactive approach, which is something different from the Kantian universal human relativism of knowledge. As for the legal implication of the adoption of a semio-enactivist approach see Ricca (2022); more in general, about enactivism, see Di Paolo et al. (2018).

is doomed to vanish from the picture of an intelligent (sigh!) human action. Things, and therefore the legal rules identified to qualify them, should be re-categorized in view of an aware teleological and axiological selection of the reflexive and ongoing relationship with the environment. Operatively, this means that things are to be dis-composed in their semiotic components and re-combined keeping in view the values/ends involved so as to select what is to be included in the categorical checklists and what is to be excluded. But thinking of things through a consideration of values/ends as processive ends—exactly like a horizon, which metaphorically is the most iconic means of all means in prompting the movements of bodies and minds—has a precise implication. It is that *all* cultural imageries could be potentially legitimized in the effort to define the future, interpreting legal values/ends as means to orient the making of facts. If this is the all-encompassing situation, even the role of religious imageries, their intercultural worldwide mobilization and the critical excavation of the secular language in order to bring to the surface the religion resilient within it, all these factors become part and parcel of planetary efforts to plan a world of 'future facts,' as well as their significance for the present. This is mainly because religious imageries cannot be detached from cultural ones at least in their relevance in people's daily life. But, as already observed, it is exactly the 'facticity of daily life,' its semantics, that are to be renewed to reach an efficacious multi-perspectival sustainability.

Let me provide a practical example to make more explicit what I mean. Consider the case of water—an element that has come to the fore today around the world because of increasing global drought. Water is certainly a 'thing.' And yet, its meaning epitomizes innumerable relationships, including human activities. These activities are inherent in the meaning of water, which is much more than the set of its morphological material features. Even if the representation of its static features seems to correspond to what is objective and external among its components, on closer examination this will turn out to be a false assumption. All the practical implications of what we call 'water' have external consequences insofar as they involve dynamic relationships between human beings and their environment. From this perspective, the meaning of 'water' is reticular and interweaves with the cognitive habits and pragmatic scripts that steer human action, including all the other 'material elements' that are involved. In a sense, these implications are inherent in the semantic structures of water in the same way in which its atomic composition is, despite the invisibility of both. The semantic spectrum of 'water' includes, therefore, these activities, their means and the related teleological/axiological horizons. The determination of these ends/means stems from cultural activity and is subsequently summarized in what we call the semantic spectrum of the denotative and connotative elements constituting the category 'water.' Religions have a powerful role in defining the connections of water with human conduct, as well as the semiotic and epistemological ideology of secularization. The task of rethinking the relationship of water with regard to its ecologically sustainable human use can be accomplished only by means of a coordination among the imageries, including the religious ones, underlying the uses of this substance. From this point of view, its conceptualization as 'a thing out there,' independent and detached from human thought and action, is a cultural approach to water that is not necessarily conducive for promoting ecological and, therefore, intercultural sustainability. For example, storing huge quantities of water, intended as a rough external material, could prove to be a faulty solution precisely because it leaves unaltered the cultural and pragmatic schemes of behavior that condition its 'life' within an environment populated by human beings. On the contrary, what should be focused upon is the relationship between water and human habits, cultural imageries, social organization, and many other environmental projections engendered by the interplay between the 'life of water' and anthropologically interpreted experience. In this regard, consider, in sequence, the structures of urban landscapes and the way in which they involve the use of water; cultivation technologies; or, still, the activities involving water and related to health, hygiene and sanitation; the apparatuses capable of exploiting the air's humidity and, therefore, the different status of water (in this sense, imitating the survival strategies of flat plants in desert environments). From this angle, the translation and transaction between the various religious/anthropological habits regarding, in the various cultural imageries, the relationship between body cleaning and purity could lead to a renewed understanding of which path of ecological/intercultural sustainability should be undertaken. In many places and in many ways, water has sacred significance, which in turn corresponds to specificities and differences in its uses, its collection, the methods to save it, its interplay and interpenetration with other 'material elements' involved in human experience and therefore its experiential, *factual*, meanings (both the actual and conceivable ones).

From a legal point of view, and specifically with respect to the construction of the medium term of legal syllogism in legal cases, all these apparent 'surroundings' of water should be understood as profiles with legal relevance/pertinence. And this relevance involves all the legal values/ends nestled in constitutional and human rights declarations' provisions. On the other hand, 'water' is a bundle of relations, and these relations extend far beyond national legal systems and cultural areas. This means that overcoming the secular gaze on the presumed 'thinghood of water' also implies the redefinition of state sovereignty and its projections on a global and intercultural level. Consequentially, a translation/transaction between the cultural and religious imageries regarding water, including the way in which some remain resilient within the secular language (and its legal consequences), becomes of the utmost importance if we are to re-weave, and actually inter-subjectively re-invent on a planetary scale, the 'objective' meaning of what is chemically defined H_2O.[6] This path requires a radical overcoming of the epistemology of secularization as well as the Christian anthropological schemes silently and thereby uncritically resting on its semantic seabed (i.e., background). The same discourse is to be applied, in my view, to that 'thing' called sacred places. I proceed, now, to try to show why.

[6]For an elaboration of the 'fluidity' of conceptions of water and the resources available once the rigid mantel of secularist assumptions is lifted, including the resulting empirical implications, see Vazquez (2018).

8.2 Words Making Spaces

Any analysis of the legal protection of sacred places/sites requires a prior understanding of these symbolic and spatial entities in their phenomenal signification.[7] The experience orbiting around such spatial *entities*, and revolving on their ritual dynamic axis, shows us that sacred Place and sacred Word are two sides of the same signical coin.[8] Just as the sacred Word is to be interpreted, the sacred Place is to be acted/lived, and vice versa. This parallel comes from the inherent *embodying* of the Sacred Word in the world, at the moment of its expression.[9] Logos, as such, is immediately, even if often invisibly, spatialized. It fills space even when human eyes are unable to see this incarnation. Rite and/or liturgy are, precisely, the spatialization and dynamic process of embodiment through which the sacred Word acquires its transient and fleeting visibility. In a sense, liturgy is a metaphorical reiteration of Creation or—depending on the differing faith perspectives—the generation of the Cosmos. All things and humans participating in rites or liturgies change, even if they appear to remain the same. They are renewed in their own inner significance. Isomorphically, the place of the rite transmutes into another kind of space because it is re-signified, and then re-spatialized, as a consequence of the filling and regenerative action of the sacred Word *in-action*.

On the other hand, chthonic beliefs,[10] which do not appear to orbit the theology of the word in the same way as monotheisms, give shape to sacred places, and identify them through acts of signification. They select specific areas, and the entities they

---

[7] I will rigorously avoid any definition of sacred place. This choice is prompted not only by the inherent difficulty of such a task, but also because of the manifold connotations of the sites and places considered sacred by world religions: see Petkoff (2014, pp. 58–60). My decision to eschew any definition of sacred places is due to a refusal to engage in any reification of them and, consequentially, of the target of their legal protection. The materiality of sacred places is not devoid of signical implications. On the contrary, in my view, that materiality is an epitome of the signical fluxes that the semiotic relatedness of each sacred place and/or site to the world and believers' action inspires wherever it happens. I only assume a distinction between sacred places and memorial sites, at least until a specific memorial site is transformed into a ritual or ceremonial place. This is only because the spatial-semantic expansiveness of ritual/ceremonial practices is highly particular. My perspective includes the assumption of a wide and elastic categorization of ritual/ceremonial activities so as to include to the greatest extent the varieties of sacred experiences, including those of native peoples. As for the definition and protection of indigenous peoples' sacred sites, see the recent overview proffered by Newman et al. (2017, pp. 11–26). Della Dora (2011, pp. 163–184).

[8] Provided that the 'Sacred Word' might also be a 'mute word,' that is to say a signifying gesture, or event, which breaks the extant (normal) semantic structures of objects, events, living beings, places, and frames them into an unprecedented indexical context. Hierophany is always an act of re-signification with respect to the current (profane or mundane) cultural categories.

[9] The symbolic dimension revitalizes and re-semanticizes the material world in any hierophany. In this way the sacred unfolds itself through the space and the spatial entities which substantiate it. The symbolic signification of the sacred coalesces with the spatialized matter and renews its nature. About the renewing implications of hierophany on the world's matter and spaces, see Eliade (1958, p. 367 ff.; or. 1948); Eliade (1959, p. 21 ff.).

[10] Glenn (2014).

contain, from space or spatial fluxes thereby forging the geographical features of sacred places. Such a process of sacralization occurs when these areas and the items they include are able to host something other than their visible and touchable materiality.[11] Nonetheless, the sacred dimension does not erase that materiality but instead renews it from within; in a sense, the sacred *indwells* in space. In this way, space becomes a specific sacred place through an act of semanticization that coincides with the manifestation or expression of sacredness. This also applies to the case of chthonic beliefs, where space and word, word and space, are somehow marked by co-extensiveness. But this should be understood in an even more deeply pragmatic sense.

In all religious experiences, regardless of their transcendent or immanent inclination, words and spaces are transmuted in signs of Otherness: a kind of Otherness that, however, is embedded in the world and the entities it comprises. The signical substance of belief consists in an invitation to humans to recognize and understand these signs of divine Otherness and discover their significance by grasping them in the mirror of the worldly experience. Although divided from the world because of their Otherness, holy words and holy places can produce sense only through communication. They are like doors to be passed through; otherwise, in the absence of such passing, the taking shape of sacred words and spaces—their irruption into history and human experience—would remain bereft of any sense or function. In short, they would be doomed to remain silenced and eternally enclosed in their unbridgeable Otherness from the world.[12] Conversely, holy words and holy places are inherently open to mediation. And such mediation is precisely the 'passing through,' namely a work of trans-*lation* of their significance in the world and, vice versa, of the world's signs in them. Interpretation and rites constitute the Thirdness by, and in which, that mediation happens. Human beings, through their understanding and action, function as interfaces; when they cross the morphological threshold of sacred words and sacred places, they renew the space of experience, allowing the sacred origin to become contingently visible. Such a renewal involves a *creative action*, in the specific sense that it acts as a kind of continuation of the creation or generation of the cosmos.

---

[11] This does not mean that the materiality of things is completely annihilated. Rather it is transfigured by a semiotic motor—precisely the manifestation of sacred—that reshapes the connotative projections which the pre-existing material 'object' epitomized. See Keane (2007, pp. 110–127).

[12] As is well-known, this kind of *separatedness* was deemed inherent in the concept and experience of sacred places by Mircea Eliade, relying upon Durkheim's vision of sacred/mundane relationships. However, this assumption was somehow emphasized by subsequent readings of Eliade's work. See, for example, Smith (1978, p. 88 ff.) Chidester and Linenthal (1995, p. 16 ff.); Holloway (2003, p. 1962). To relativize such reading, on the other hand, it is enough to consider Elia's description of the erection of the Vedic altar for sacrifice and its twofold, simultaneously cosmogonic/spatial and chronological, symbolism: Eliade (1958, p. 372). More broadly, see his referral to the *orientation* and the underlying cosmology in the consecration of sacred space: *ibidem*, 369. Sacred space is separated and at the same time genetically continuous to the cosmos, namely not divorced from it. A more nuanced reading of Eliade's sacred/profane divide can be found in Hamilton and Spicer (2016, pp. 1–25).

In the same vein, human beings can grasp the signification of holy words and places only via the *interpenetration* between them and the world, namely the sacred signs and the *worldling* action. The eternal dimension of sacredness goes through a process of presentification and contextualization within the worldly time stream. Human beings can participate in this process by using their memory and symbolic imagination, harmonizing the worlds' signs and the flow of their actions, respectively, in the sacred words and places, and vice versa. Sacred words and sacred places become, from this perspective, living and regenerative mirrors of the cosmos. Through recitation, interpretation and ritual action, words and sacred places achieve a culmination of their interpenetration: although ephemerally, all creation finds synthesis.[13]

8.3 The Semiotic Ubiquity of Sacred Places

Sacred words and sacred places host the world and its Otherness. This means that the Otherness of the sacred meets its Other-than-itself, namely the world and natural experience. The trace occurrence of such Thirdness is reproduced through the human mind and human conduct, as well as through space and time. At least potentially, this semiotic emanation can involve the whole Earth, if not even the Cosmos, and all of history. It is so because sacred experience is open to being trans-*lated* in the daily life of believers, merging into their worldviews and actions. In this sense, the meaning of

[13] Something similar can be found in the paths of conversion across all the faiths. Conversion is always connoted by projections into the environment through proactive behaviors capable of renewing the believer's life and her/his action in the world. In conversion studies there are two theoretical strains. The first places the act of conversion in a psychical and self-narrative dimension, namely the *hearth*; the second casts a holistic, social gaze on it and its causes, tracing its origins and consequences within the social contexts and the actions of its determinants. These two approaches can be respectively dubbed *intimist* and *situationist*. For more on this, see Ricca (2016, p. 95 ff.): *ibidem* for further bibliographical references. However, even in the intimist interpretation, the conversion and the evidence of its authenticity are tied to and ensue the assumption of worldly behaviors. Mind and world, soul and body, transcendence and space, sacred and mundane are always co-involved in the phenomenology of the participation in the divine dimension and its revelation. From this point of view, the psychological *intimist* approach and the anthropological/sociological *situationist* one could be considered as two different gazes on complementary aspects of the same phenomenon. Neither the psycho-ontological dimension nor the social/political one can be considered as the exclusive source and/or determinant of conversion. Analogically, in my view, the same can be observed regarding the relationships between sacred places and profane/everyday social circuits. In this sense, the traditional 'ontological' approach to sacred places and the most recent *situationist* and *narrativist* one, based on an analysis of social dynamics, can be considered as two sides of the same psycho-embodied and socially proactively projected human experience of the sacred. In this sense, Halloway's proposal (2003: 1966) should be read against the foil of the theorization of conversion practices. The same could be said of the situationist/narrativist approach proposed by the geographer Chidester Linenthal (1995); Kong (1993, pp. 23–45; 2001, pp. 211–233; 2002, pp. 1573–1586). For a chronological, critical overview of geographers' manifold approaches to the 'sacred places' issue, see Della Dora (2015).

sacred words and places is inherently dynamic, and is readily embodied in rites and, in parallel, all aspects of life, as in the concentric circles of a semiotic propagation wave.[14] In turn, this spatial and semantic diffusion engenders a sort of semantic ebb that flows back towards sacred words and places. The real significance and experience of sacred words and places is, in short, ubiquitous. So, with specific regard to sacred places, we could say that they are always (*also*) *elsewhere* than their physical earthly location; at the same time, their geo-semantic position is, at least potentially, *everywhere*. These arguments, however, shall be articulated further.

Consider for a moment the world, filled with minds dispersed across the planet. Now imagine that within multitudes of these minds, the idea of a famous Sacred Place may be simultaneously in motion. While one thinks of Jerusalem in one place on Earth, elsewhere another is dreaming of the same place. Of course, we could similarly imagine Lourdes, Mecca, or Noahavose (Bear Butte), sacred to the Cheyenne Native Americans. The synthesis of all these peoples' 'wheres,' and the embodiment of the iconic image of their sacred places, *are* the true *being-where* of each sacred place. This is the cosmic potential signification of all genuine Sacred Places. In this regard, it could be helpful to think of the *chôra* (dynamic space) projected by the Byzantine Icons during their Sacred rites; a space that makes visible the invisible presence of a generative God's action inherent in the world.[15] The similar but enlarged concept of *chôra* can be traced—once more—in Plato's *Timaeus,* and operatively translated in the blurring of categorical and spatial borders equally traceable in dreams, as well as in the experience of cultural and cognitive turmoil.[16] In these situations, the sharpness of the distinctions between categories withers away to the extent that what is remote or dissimilar conflates with what is close or similar; and vice versa. In the same vein, the 'placeness' of sacred places is ceaselessly on the verge of transmuting into 'Space' (that is, a place reopened to infinite interpretation) by means of the scattered semiosis processes at work in all Earthlings' minds (whether they are believers of a specific faith or not).[17]

In addition, liturgy—if taken in its etymological sense—means "the place to carry out public affairs." It comes from the Greek *leitūrgĺa,* as such derived from *leitūrgós*, which is composed by *lḗiton* (place of public affairs), in turn connected to *laós* (people), and *érgon* (action, work). Liturgy can thus be assumed as an iconic

[14]This metaphorical expansiveness and the pragmatic exceeding of rites, and therefore of the pairing sacred word/sacred place, is powerfully embodied by sacred art and the pedagogical, ethical and political maps it supplies to believers. See, in this regard, Walker and Luyster (2016, pp. 1–16).

[15]In this regard it is interesting to consider the concept of 'hierotopy.' See Lidov (2006, 2008, 2009. 2014, 2016) Isar (2006, 2009a, b).

[16]See Sallis (1999). It is to be pointed out that Sallis' approach is quite different from that proposed by Derrida (1993).

[17]In this sense I can agree with Tuan's idea that the physical places that are very remote for someone can instead be very close to them if considered from a humanistic/affective point of view. See Tuan (1977). However, I do not share the divide he proposes in the same text between place and space because I think that space is in any case a horizon of semanticized (and to be continually re-semanticized) possibilities. See above Chap. 6.

material metaphor of the way people should live and act in the world.[18] Therefore, sacred places cannot be grasped in their real and experiential significance as something existing *out there*, but must instead relate to the practical embodiments within human actions of the message, the directives for action, and the interpretation of the world that those places enshrine and emanate by virtue of their iconic power of signification.

The sacred words of rites and holy liturgies carried out in sacred places supply, in all religions, a metaphorical model to be translated and implemented in human conduct. This is true, for example, for both Vedic texts and rites, and Christian holy words and celebrations.[19] The meaning that people give to sacred places concretely, even if partly unaware, is steeped in these traditions of pragmatic mediation/translation. And believers from the most remote corners of the world presentify sacred places in their experience by means of this semiotic trans-*duction* of significance, given off by the rites that are performed inside them. These translational and actualizing schemes of widespread signification regarding sacred places can also be recognized in the traditional/historical practices of '*trans-lation*' of relics or even material components of sacred buildings or locations. The relics, or the pieces of a sacred building, serve as sources of meaning that convey the replication of rites, and the related forms of daily conduct. Of course, these spatial transferrals also produced semantic re-contextualizations, which could also exert their influence on the process of signification of the original places, along with the many social, psychological and political implications.

The sacred dimension (and its Otherness)—either in personal-transcendent faiths or in immanent ones—always requires a path of knowledge. Its mysterial domains can only be penetrated, however, in the mirror of natural experience, and its transfiguration only in the light of sacred Otherness. In this sense, we can recognize a double movement, whether in monotheisms or polytheistic forms of panpsychism. The more the penetration of sacred mysteries or dogmas proceeds,[20] the more its semantic projection in cultural life practices expands. On the other hand, we might note that religious conversions (and their authenticity) are also tied to, and verified through, the practical conduct of the converted. The spiritual/noetic moment of conversion is never detached from the life conduct of the converted, nor can its

[18] In this regard, consider the prototypical example of the *Veda* and the related texts of *Dharmaśāstra*, which translated *Vedic* ritual instructions. These were taken as immanent metaphors of the cosmos and were interpreted to determine the sacred activities to be carried out inside the temples, in directives to rule the inter-subjective relationships of the Hindu people. On the metaphorical and pragmatic significance of Vedic rites see, recently, the interesting essay of Einoo (2016). Bell (2009).

[19] On the liturgical and hence socio-political embodiment of Christian rites in Byzantine Medieval rites see, most recently, Bogdanović (2018, p. 1 ff.; 190 ff.).

[20] For example, as regards the Catholic conceptualization of 'dogma' as *a path to truth*, rather than the truth in and of itself, and therefore as a sign, see Denzinger (2009); but see also *Motu proprio, Ad tuendam fidem*, 18 maggio 1998, *Lettera Apostolica* by Giovanni Paolo II, which aimed to amend canons 750 and 1371, n. 1, of current *Codex Iuris Canonici*, and canons 598 and 1436 of the *Codex Canonum Ecclesiarum Orientalium* (in *Acta apostolicae Sedis*, 1998), pp. 457 ff; 544 ff.

authenticity be assumed or immune to being tested by evaluating the deeds of the 'new' believers. In any case, practice unfolds in and through the world.[21] Thus, all conversions and sacred experiences tend to induce cognitive and social upheavals. Previous ways of judging, categorizing and assessing are often washed over by the worldly projections of the knowledge about the (new) sacred dimension. If we assume that each form of categorization, even identitarian ones, involves the creation of borders between what is inside the category and what is outside it, and symmetrically between the Self and the Other, then we can conclude that religious experience and the hermeneutics of the sacred dimension include a renewed semantization of Otherness and thereby some sort of openness toward it.

The above remarks may seem to be somewhat odd and counterintuitive, especially if we consider the exclusiveness that is often claimed by the sacred Otherness of each faith or belief. This is particularly true for monotheisms, whose narratives depict the revealed truth as a 'jealous privilege.' Nonetheless the meaning of revelation cannot be known by blinding oneself to the world and adopting exclusionary attitudes. The communicative pith of sacred words and rites—and therefore the spatial semiotic propagative scope of sacred places—passes through a *pistic* or *pistemic* (as such distinct from epistemic) disposition endowed with a pragmatic projection towards the world. Only by means of this effort of mediation can a human being embody the sacred dimension and advance their understanding of sacred Otherness. It is at the intersection between sacred Otherness and World Otherness that human beings can dynamically incorporate, like the crucial middle of a chiasma, the presence of the 'sacred' in creation and improve their understanding of what the holy words and places are signing.

The potential semiotic expansiveness (and/or exceedance) of sacred words and places towards Otherness is boundless. Even the most insignificant entities of the world enshrine the cipher of this creational principle and human beings, as believers, are called upon to glean, out of all existence, this cipher.[22] This also means that even the most remote element of a category can become close to it in the light of sacred hermeneutics and *pistemically* inspired praxes. Such semantic mobility between remoteness and closeness concerning categorical borders impacts, however, the spatial coordinates of practice. An event, a thing, an experience (if considered with regard to the double understanding of the sacred dimension and the worldly one) could reveal its semantic closeness to a sacred space in which some faith has its original source, despite its physical remoteness. To put it more synthetically, the semantic closeness of a religious experience (and thereby its *actual* spatiality) relativizes physical geographical distances.[23] Consequentially the 'here' or 'there'

---

[21] See Ricca (2016).

[22] With regard to the widespread and omni-placed presence of divine creational ciphers, it is very interesting to note the continuity extant between the thought of the Christian church fathers and that of the Islamic *Mu'tazilit* school (for example, Al-Jahiz). See, respectively, Della Dora (2016, p. 57 ff.), Miller (2013); Ricca (2019).

[23] Such relativization is to be considered a cultural outcome, the cause of which was the same that spurred the believers' imagination to place the sacred place at a center of their mappings of the

of sacred places are to be understood less as specific topographical locations than as semiotic points of confluence, the meaning and scope of which is produced by peoples' worldwide, faith-based, actions and interactions.[24] Nevertheless—as I will show below—even secularized conduct and processes of interpretation, together with the related practical consequences, cannot be ignored in the determination of the meaning of sacred places.

8.4 The Planetary Projections of Liturgical Spaces

The actual signification of each sacred place—no matter of which faith or belief—is an extension of the all-inclusive semantic potentialities of the sacred word, taken as the sign of the cosmos' origin. The entire terrestrial circumference can serve as a liturgical field; the actions of the world's people unfold in the practical directives that are metaphorically ciphered in the rites performed in sacred places. Thus, any offence or damage to a sanctuary or a consecrated ground/land signifies (is felt as)—at least potentially—an attack on all the practices that in any else 'where' replicate the message encapsulated in the rites or liturgies hosted in that sacred place. This is because by means of rites and liturgies, sacred places aspire to host in that 'there' *simply* all the world. This kind of *hospitality* is also a cognitive one, if only because through its fruition, the 'divine' and the 'worldly' achieve a condition of immanent visible coexistence in the eyes of believers.[25] It is precisely this coincidence that turns any aggression against the practices replicating and unfolding through rites and liturgies into an attack on the related representative sacred places, and vice versa. It is historical and contemporary experience that illustrates this way of perceiving sacred places. Such spatial-semiotic ubiquity is attested by the reactions, just to name a few, of Catholic, Islamic Umma, and Hindu communities, as well as the indigenous believers. If one believer is under attack while they are practicing rites related to their religion, the source of which is spatially traceable to a particular sacred place, the attack is perceived as a strike against the sanctity of the sacred place as well. Any aggression against an individual for their own faith is—just to reference the examples above—an attack on the Catholic Church or the

world. See, for example, Smith (1978: spec. ch. 4, 6 and 7) and his observation about the sacred geography of diasporic communities; see also Della Dora (2007). In this sense, with specific regard to the Islamic faith, see the beautiful essay by Pallavicini (2014, p. 114). As for the co-implicative relationships between category and space, categorization and spatialized experience, see above Chap. 4, and therein for the related bibliography.

[24] On the relationship between sacred Word, sacred spaces, landscapes and the whole of nature see the very insightful work by Veronica Della Dora (2016, p. 68 ff.).

[25] A very interesting study that gives psycho-bodily evidence of this emotional and experiential ubiquity has been carried out by Klingorová (2018). More generally, on the overcoming of the sacred/profane divide by the hierophany and the experience of it in the everyday, see Holloway (2003, pp. 1968–1969, 1972).

Indigenous Community, on St. Peter's Basilica or Sacred Land, wherever the offended believer is. In this sense, we could say that the protection of sacred places applies to actions that may embody their signification anywhere in the world.

Evidence of the dynamic and action-embodied omnipresence of sacred places can be traced in the historical, as well as contemporary, experience of pilgrimage.[26] During the Middle Ages, pilgrims enjoyed a special regime of protection, traceable to the so-called *Lex Peregrinorum*.[27] These provisions assured the pilgrims the right to a safe journey towards their own sanctuaries. In a sense, pilgrims were viewed as if, through their sacred travel, they were moving along an alternative geographical path. Their sacred destination projected its semiotic threads over the pilgrims' itineraries so as to spatially re-categorize their presence while they traversed the different countries. It was as if the pilgrimage routes uncoiled through a spatial dimension *other* than the territory under the political sovereignty of the various kingdoms they passed through. This multiplication of spaces was not a fiction, but rather an effect of the pluralities of the semantic layers produced by human action. Pilgrims were actually moving through a parallel space-meaning dimension that carved out its own spatial coordinates amidst the political/geographical ambits of the various kingdoms. Their paths were a means to the sacred end that the sanctuary of destination incorporated. The recognized illegitimacy of harming them or obstructing their journey was a consequence of the spatial plurality stemming from the common source of legitimation that sacred places and earthly political power shared: God's Will. The immanent presence of God, which enlightened the pilgrims' routes, made sovereign space and pilgrimage paths somehow different.

On the other hand, the pilgrims' travel in itself was a kind of trans-*lation*. The sacred place of destination radiated its semiotic/pragmatic field of signification toward the various places of the pilgrims' departure so as to elicit their desire to travel to them. But a symmetrical effect also applied to the journey back home, and the subsequent social positioning of pilgrims there. The successful pilgrimage re-qualified the social role and distinctiveness of those who had undertaken the sacred journey and had come back with the signs (badges) of their holy visitation. In a very practical sense, the sanctuary's presence was ubiquitous: it exerted the power of the semantic and social renewal of space.[28] From this perspective, the places of

---

[26] An overview of pilgrimage from the past to present in world religion can be found in Coleman and Elsner (1995). See also Chareyron (2000). On contemporary sacred pilgrimage, in a vast literature, see Coleman and Eade (2004), who emphasize, *inter alia*, (a) the process of the semanticization of sacred places by virtue of the spatial mobility symbolized by pilgrims; (b) the inner transformative meanings of the journey; Stoddard and Morinis (1997). This text features a comparative examination of religious pilgrimages together with a proposal for their classification (*ibidem*, Stoddard); but also, Morinis (1992, pp. 2, 8–13). An interesting non-Western centered perspective is offered by Tagliacozzo (2013). On pilgrimages and the related conceptualization of sacred places and their geographical significance, see Jacobsen (2012), Singh Rana (2013).

[27] See Bird (2012), Birch (2000), Gilles (1980, pp. 161–189).

[28] From a semiotic point of view, the overlapping between remoteness and proximity determined by mobility, both physical and virtual, is to be considered a common trait of the ancient world as much as of the contemporary technologically networked world. On the communicative and thereby

departure and the sacred arrival destination were dialectically conjoined by means of the act of trans-*lation* substantiated by the pilgrims' lived paths.[29] Place of departure and place of destination somehow functioned as the spatial poles of a liturgical/ transfiguring action that unfolded along and through the pilgrimage's route. God's presence indwelled this triadic relation and re-generated at the same time the outward space of action and the inner spiritual 'spatiality' of the pilgrims. Conceptually, the pilgrimage was a journey to be carried out simultaneously outside and inside pilgrims' bodies and souls. God's presence pervaded the lived space of the pilgrims; nonetheless it filled that spatiality without erasing or apparently transforming its physical appearances.[30] Through their sacred pilgrimage, people engendered another space and moved inside it. The membrane, the interface of translation and coordination between the political-territorial worldly space and that of the pilgrims was the religion/faith itself.

The re-spatializing and, in a sense, immunizing effect of the sacred journey often enjoyed an interreligious recognition.[31] The spatialization of the human/divine relationship produced a trans-religious significance, as such capable of relativizing the worldly territorial projections of the political powers which could be legitimated by the different faiths. Local authorities, in other words, perceived the transient presence of pilgrims as if it did not (at least, not fully) occupy their territorial space although it moved exactly through it. This was because in pilgrims' action, belonging to any faith, the presence of the divine was felt as if it were topical (present).

Today, the legal spatial regime of pilgrimages cannot leverage the same source of legitimation/signification. In a widely secularized world, the space that pilgrims trace along their routes has nothing to do with the foundation from which secular political power arises. The spatial plurality engendering their legal protection results—or should result—from the universal recognition of religious freedom. However, the dualism inherent in the secularization logic, which is also a semantic-spatial dualism,[32] tends to objectify the signification of sacred places and the journeys to them. This objectification concurrently produces a kind of alienation of the sacred dimension that makes almost impossible the political-legal translation of the invisible web of sense underlying the sacred places and the human experiences that irradiate from

experiential continuity between the 'close' and the 'remote' in contemporary world, see Urry (2000, 2002).

[29] See Gregorič Bon (2016, pp. 74–77).

[30] In this sense, it could be useful recall the Sallnow's formula, which termed pilgrimage as 'a kinaesthetic mapping of space'. See Sallnow (1987, p. 184 ff.).

[31] Although this recognition was intermittent throughout history, and encountered many obstacles due to the political struggles. The pilgrimage to Jerusalem—see Chareyron (2000)—is a clear example of these changing fortunes of the pilgrims' *immunitas*.

[32] Some interesting cues about the relationship between modern Western secularization and the divide sacred space/profane space can be found in Coster and Spicer (2005, pp. 1–16). But see also Knott (2014).

them.[33] But I shall come back to this occurrence and its political/legal consequences more broadly below, with regard to the phenomenology of contemporary desecration and damaging attacks on sacred places.

However, before going further, I would like to dwell for a bit longer on the ubiquity of sacred places and its deep connection with the dynamic of liturgy. Consider, in this regard, the modern tradition of staging the *Via Crucis*, celebrated every year in Rome on the occasion of Catholic Easter, inside the walls of the Coliseum. This monument originally was and currently is everything but a sacred sanctuary.[34] What contingently transforms it into a holy place is precisely the mere fact that, once a year, the *Via Crucis*, portraying Jesus' path to crucifixion, is staged inside it. The choice to celebrate this rite there is packed with historical significance. As is well known, during the Roman Empire the Coliseum was one of the places in which the persecution of Christians reached its final stage: martyrdom. The contemporary celebration of *Via Crucis* inside the Coliseum presentifies that past but is intended to serve, at the same time, as a sort of dialectical reversal of it. Once a year, this place of ancient desecrations contingently becomes consecrated by virtue of the *Via Crucis* event that fills the Coliseums' spaces, renewing them through the ritual action. Jesus and other ancient martyrs are present there and in a sense are made visible even if they do not occupy the space. The Pope himself embodies the painful path of Jesus toward his crucifixion even if the Pope is not Christ. The celebration is broadcast around the world. It embodies the sacrifice of Christians that occurred throughout the ages, wherever and whenever they took place and will take place. Just like a geometrical cross, in the Coliseum the *Via Crucis* projects its significance both vertically and horizontally, that is, respectively through space and time. In this sense, the Coliseum actually assumes both temporal and spatial ubiquity. Remote and close sacrifices converge in the rite's space so as to draw a movement of reciprocal substitution, replacement, sequencing, appearance and disappearance, which makes visible and understandable God's presence throughout history and space: in short, his omnipresence. Simultaneously, however, the Coliseum also conjures up the conflictive relationships between the Catholic Church and other faiths throughout history. From this perspective, it also embodies the flip side of Christian martyrdoms, namely the violence that Christians inflicted on people of other faiths and beliefs along the Catholics' earthly pilgrimage through history. The dynamics of this presence-absence allows for the emergence of a chorological dimension within which remoteness and closeness, at once spatial, temporal, and categorical, conflate so as to make forms morph into one another and give human beings the fleeting perception of generative and re-generative cosmic Godly action. As soon as the

[33] From this point of view is very important to remark that the sacredness of places does not coincide with the place in itself but it is a result of the interplay of people's representations and actions related to that place: including journeys to it and the practices of hospitality. See Digance (2003: spec. 146).

[34] I think that it could be considered as a 'memorial site' for the martyrdom of so many Christians during the Roman Empire and its persecution against them. It is not a sacred place when it does not host the *Via Crucis* or other rites. In the same vein, I do not share the idea that Auschwitz can be considered a sacred place as opposed to a 'memorial site.'

celebration ends, the Coliseum reverts to its archeological 'materiality,' as an ancient Roman amphitheater, an arena. But as long as the *Via Crucis* lasts, the Coliseum is—at least potentially—everywhere and all 'wheres' are inside its inner space. Its 'placeness' transforms contingently in space, or better, in an indeterminate and thereby omni-directionally 'semanticizable' spatiality, which vanishes as soon as the *Via Crucis* reaches its endpoint.

The circularity of the Coliseum echoes cosmic dimensions and its inclination to contain all things, creatures and events. *Mutatis mutandis*, the same circularity undergirds the dialectics between whither and whence, arrival and homeward, that joins the pilgrimage to sacred places. Everything that happens within the phenomenal space of the pilgrim's journey, all actions and thoughts, are potentially categorized as existential inflections stemming from the semiotic radial influx exerted by the liturgical/cosmic signification of the sacred place of destination. In other words, it expands the liturgical immanent and, at same time, representative embodiment of the cosmos towards the cosmos itself, and therefore the space outside the holy borders or walls. An effect that is realized by means of the semiotic incorporation into human action of the divine/human signification that sacred places produce.

8.5 The Legal Consequences of the Secular Reification of Sacred

The above arguments lead to the assertion that the meaning of sacred places is coextensive with, or at least includes, their spatial pragmatic projections. Beyond their topographical coordinates, the *real* spatial experience that emanates from them can be traced to their praxeological ubiquity, or simply in the actions people undertake while thinking of their dynamic (thereby also liturgical and/or ritual) significance.[35] If this is correct, then an appropriate legal protection of sacred places should include the actions that embody their signification. This means that legal agencies should focus on the reasons and ends underlying the human behaviors enacted as a consequence/inference of the sacredness of places, which in turn immanently enfolds the sacred words or ways of categorizing the world. To put it more explicitly, legal protection cannot be confined to only sacred places/sites taken as things.[36] Their reification would prevent legal agencies from understanding and publicly communicating what the sacred places are trying to make visible and actual. If these attempts are ignored, sacred places run the risk of being alienated from the mundane world, encaged in their enchanted Otherness, without any possibility to be mediated and traduced according to what people draw from them in terms of

[35] Very insightful remarks are proposed, in this sense, by Yahya Pallavicini (2014, p. 114).

[36] Unfortunately, this is the almost typical inclination of all legal provisions and activities regarding the understanding and protection of sacred places/sites in terms of property rights protection. See, in this regard, Petkoff (2014); but also, as regards international legal provisions, Leanza (2014).

significance and pragmatic directives. Insulated in their religiously territorialized materiality, they would remain untranslatable and therefore unintelligible to secular as well as religious Otherness, namely the world Other-than-themselves, and the various universes of faith they incorporate. Any protection of them under the aegis of religious freedom would inevitably wind up being merely formal. Their significance would therefore become destined to remain sealed in a semantic and practical irreducibility to all-that-is-Other-than it. The immediate consequence of this is, however, itself a conflict.[37]

Unfortunately, international legal provisions seem inclined to entangle the protection of sacred places in the dualistic oppositional logic idiomatically inherent to modern Western secularization. If, for example, one looks at the UN website under the heading 'places of worship,' they will immediately find the following list of provisions:

> 1981 Declaration of the General Assembly
> Art. 6 (a): The right to freedom of thought, conscience, religion or belief includes the freedom, "To worship or assemble in connection with a religion or belief, and to establish and maintain places for these purposes;"
>
> Human Rights Council resolution 6/37
> 9 (e): The Human Rights Council urges States, "To exert the utmost efforts, in accordance with their national legislation and in conformity with international human rights and humanitarian law, to ensure that religious places, sites, shrines and symbols are fully respected and protected and to take additional measures in cases where they are vulnerable to desecration or destruction;"
>
> 9 (g): The Human Rights Council urges States, "To ensure, in particular, the right of all persons to worship or assemble in connection with a religion or belief and to establish and maintain places for these purposes [...];"

[37] On the difficulties inherent in underpinning a pluralistic and multi-religious regime of coexistence by means of a social reciprocal recognition based on a syncretistic interpretation of religious symbols and sites, see Hayden (2002); Hayden et al. (2016: spec. 60–65). Similar attempts tend to obscure the social implications of religions and thereby end up excluding them from the (hoped for) dialogue. The result is, rather, an instrumentalization of religion and its antagonistic use; but precisely such an effect, in turn, fuels the religious intolerance making people blind to the consideration of their social habits rooted in religious orthopraxis and the possibility of their translation: in short, a vicious cycle that escalates the conflict among religious and cultural differences. Some indications on the importance of the social 'surroundings' and the intersecting narratives of peoples' practices as an efficacious motor to engender the sharing of sacred places can be found in the collection of essays edited by Bowman (2012); but see also the wonderful essays by Barkan and Barkey (2015), and all the essays collected in this book.

Human Rights Committee General Comment 22
Para. 4 : "The concept of worship extends to [...] the building of places of worship."

Reading such a list one can easily grasp the derivative connection that the UN establishes between religious freedom and the protection of sacred places.[38] The ideal divide between reason and faith, so axial for modern political thought and epistemology, is replicated in the legal cartography of material spaces. Sacred places are considered primarily—if not exclusively—as things, buildings, monuments, topographically bounded areas, etc. They are to be protected as part of the 'enclosed' realm of religion and, hence, religious freedom. It is no coincidence that national states seek to align their legislation to the legal standards arising from international human rights and 'humanitarian law' in order to assure a spatial zone of protection for everything that orbits worship within their territory. Although such provisions could seem to be almost obvious and utterly reasonable, nonetheless they fail to capture the ubiquitous and dynamic projections of sacred places. On the contrary, they end up strengthening the Otherness and, in a sense, the *alienness* of their spatiality and significance from the cultural and legal secular field of the different nations. Underlying these kinds of provisions there is always a differentiating and exceptionalist logic that eclipses the possibility and the necessity to translate the meaning of sacred places and their pragmatic ubiquitous projections in the social warp and woof of the spaces where people live. Sacred places are protected as *special things* related to *separate areas*. As in nesting Chinese boxes, a hierarchical categorical/spatial scale is at play. The biggest container is the global extension/international law, inside it are the regional dimension/regional laws, and then inside these we find national territories/state legal systems; it is within this last 'hold' that sacred places should get their differentiated topographic/normative protection. Where—I ask—does this scalar structure make room for the mediation and translation in the common spaces of life of the semio-pragmatic threads moving from the chorological and potentially cosmic significance of what occurs inside the sacred places?

The above question reveals itself to be inescapable as soon as we consider that protecting sacred places is most relevant when and where their presence (and spatial worldwide projections) faces cultural and religious environments that are largely 'foreign' to or unfamiliar with their significance. In such cases, however, the hierarchical/pyramidal view of legally protected human rights inevitably endorses an oppositional differentiation between sacred places and the surrounding social/

[38] Of course, the same can be said regarding the UNESCO provisions: the Convention Concerning the Protection of the World Cultural and Natural Heritage, and the related Guidelines (respectively 1972, 2005). Both these texts have often been used to arrange some protection for cultural places/sites of religious interest. In this regard, see Benzo (2014, pp. 17–23), and the inevitably reifying/cosifying and property-centered pervasive connotation of his attempt to give a list of definitions on sacred places/sites. Things do not change with the Universal Code of Holy Places (2011), available at http://www.kas.de/wf/doc/kas_12037-1442-1-30.pdf?140204080404.

cultural environments. The other side of this oppositional bent is the othering reification/cosification of sacredness, in particular when it coincides with the sacred dimension of a minority group. But othering/reifying the spatial areas of people's sacred symbols and material expressions also entails compartmentalizing the pragmatic cultural implications of their belonging. In this way, I fear, the motivational seeds of eventual desecrations will be widely scattered on the field of social coexistence. One does not need to be a prophet or a visionary to understand the potentiality of ubiquitous expansion gushing up from these polarized spatial/cultural relationships. In this sense, the categorical/pragmatic chorology of sacred places becomes almost obvious. Jerusalem and its conflictive inter-religious/intercultural conflicts prove to be really everywhere. The inter-sacred polarizations that *take place* there reiterate, almost pushing their way into the biggest box of the above spatial/legal nested Chinese boxes, at a global scale and in every context in which sacred places of some faith have come to terms with the different religious/cultural environment in which they find themselves. This applies to mosques or Hindu temples in Christian areas, as well as to Christian churches in Islamic or Hindu areas, and so on.

Things do not improve if we shift our focus to multicultural conjugations of religious freedom and the related protection of sacred places. In this respect, I would like to share another excerpt from the UN Human Rights website on religious worship, in this case regarding the Timbuktu mausoleums:

> In July 2012, the sacred sites and mausoleums of the World Heritage site of Timbuktu in Mali were attacked with axes and shovels by fighters from the Ansar Dine group, an armed Islamist group which controls the northern part of the country.
>
> The sites in Timbuktu were included in the UNESCO's List of World Heritage in 1988. They are reminders of Timbuktu's past as an intellectual and spiritual capital, and a focal point for spreading Islam in Africa.
>
> The UN expert on cultural rights, Farida Shaheed, condemned the violent destruction of "a common heritage of humanity" in a joint press release with the UN expert on freedom of religion or belief, Heiner Bielefeldt.
>
> Shaheed further stated that "it is a loss for us all, but for the local population it also means denial of their identity, their beliefs, their history and their dignity."
>
> Under the International Covenant on Civil and Political Rights, States parties must protect people's freedom, either individually or in community with others and in public or private, to manifest their religion or belief in worship, observance, practice, and teaching. In addition, in those States parties in which ethnic, religious or linguistic minorities exist, persons belonging to such minorities shall not be denied the right, in community with the other members of their group, to enjoy their own culture, to profess and practise their own religion, or to use their own language. Under the International Covenant on Economic, Social and Cultural Rights, everyone has the right to take part in cultural life, which implies, according to the Expert in the field of cultural rights, the right of everyone to access and enjoy cultural heritage.

The verbal formulas used in this document to emphasize the legal foundations for the protection of Timbuktu and the condemnation of the destruction/desecration acts carried out by the Ansar Dine group are as follows: "intellectual and spiritual capital," "common heritage of humanity," "freedom of religion or belief," "identity," "beliefs," "history," "dignity," "people's freedom [...] to manifest their religion or belief in worship, observance, practice, and teaching." Moreover, the excerpt relies upon the obligation of national states to recognize the right of ethnic, religious or linguist minorities to enjoy their own culture, profess and practice their own religion, and use their own language. Finally, there is a strong referral to the right of everyone to take part in cultural life by means of their access and enjoyment of cultural heritage. However, despite the incidental reference to the right to take part in cultural life, the above excerpt concludes with an apotheosis of reification embodied by the concept of 'cultural heritage.'

Reflected in this document we can find the granitic idea that cultures are to be protected as such, as they are, according to an almost compulsive identitarian museum-making global mission. This is nothing but the model of a legal protection rooted in the multiculturalist view (in its most radical versions, no less). I think that this way of considering the relationships between cultures is, in turn, a consequence of secularizing Reason that causes an othering and reifying understanding of the significance of sacred places and the religious universes they incorporate. In this perspective, the culture and religion of Others are always conceived as something irreducibly 'else.' To avert the secluding effects of such an approach to Otherness, however, it is futile to emphasize that in an ideal multicultural social landscape everyone should be considered equally Other to everyone else. A pluralistic insulation cannot mature harmonic interpenetrations; on the other hand, defective accommodations based on the logic of compromise will produce the fatal result of a growing commoditization between untranslated—and gradually less and less translatable—differences.[39]

Meanwhile, in all contemporary Western multicultural contexts, the logic of secularization, the normalization of the invisibility of cultural and above all legal backdrops inherited from the past, silently continues, unquestioned.[40] It is as if

[39]For these reasons I do not think that in the long-term perspective the 'defective' and procedural approach to the governance of sacred places/sites proposed by Hayden (2002), Hayden et al. (2016) proves to be conducive to a peaceful coexistence between peoples with different cultural/religious claims regarding their use and enjoyment. A symptomatic example of the liberal and, at the same time, authoritative legal implications of such an approach can be found in Sapir, Statman (2016), where religious freedom or the right to cultural difference, taken as the basis for the public protection of sacred places, are understood without any attempt to cognitively translate/transact the behavioral habits stemming from religion intended as anthropological agency.

[40]Among scholars of Hindu culture, it is possible to find a more nuanced sensibility which, however, is far from able to influence Indian legal-policy makers and the legislative measures they adopt. See, for example, Bhargava (2008, 2011); De Roover et al. (2011). As for Islamic religion see Modood (2009, p. 164 ff.). All these writings are the result, however, of a gaze cast from without onto everyday practices and the legal categorizations that give shape and rhythm to them. In their arguments, almost exclusively developed on a political plane, there is no reference made to the central categories of socio-legal life, such as contracts, the classification of crimes, corporate and commercial laws, inheritance, and all the legacy of moral theology that is encapsulated in the related institute. I developed such an analysis of secularization and its intercultural perspectives in other writings and refer to these for an explanation of my approach, including the bibliographical references. See Ricca (2016 [A Modest], 2013a, c, 2008). See also above, Chap. 2.

people and scholars were blind to the cultural influxes of tradition in common life and their pervading presence exactly where their camouflage makes them almost invisible. Let me iterate briefly and for the last time one of the leitmotifs of the entire book. On average, cultural 'stigmata' are caught only when their difference is glaring and already conflictive. Almost nothing is pragmatically investigated from a multicultural point of view with regard to ownership, contract law, obligation, general conceptualization and classifying of crimes, guilt, responsibility, associative forms and corporations, general ideologies of inheritance, and so on. In all these areas of both experience and legal regulation, the dominant paradigms remain and exert their influence nearly unhindered. The worst cases are the legacy of colonization and post-colonization, with the result that Western legal templates concerning these areas of social experience have been imposed all over the world. The resilience of those past events makes it so that in either Christian or ex-colonial countries, multiculturalism floats across a discursive ocean imbued with the cultural coordinates that Western secularization inherited from pre-modern Christian moral theology and still encapsulates in its legal institutions. What is different becomes visible only insofar as it surfaces contrastively in that cultural/legal ocean, but only to acquire its contours as if it were a newly emerged island.

Against the foil of colonial and post-colonial experience and contexts, Western secularization—and specifically, its legal manifestation—displays all its cultural provincialism. The same public/private divide developed alongside the idea of religious freedom is deeply embedded with such provinciality.[41] The possibility to design, in a liberal fashion, a private space inside which 'to consume' one's own religious belonging and freedom is strictly tied to the pervasive presence of Christian theological moral vestiges in the discursive apparatuses of public life, especially in the legal lexicon. The secularization process begun by Grotius removed the theological moral features that Second Scholasticism had superimposed on ancient Roman law from the legal institutes. Theological principles were substituted by rational/natural essences that were equally recognizable, and thus applicable to, people of different faiths. Still the current common law apparatuses and civil law codifications can be considered the long-term offspring of Grotius' and his followers' efforts. Unfortunately, his massive rhetorical and communicative operation was carried out within the culture of a Christian moral-theological and legal tradition. The result was that legal modern secularism passed off its rationalistically winnowed out and dressed up tradition and identity as if it were the expression of an all-encompassing universality.

Nonetheless, the resilience of moral theological frameworks within the rational secularized legal grammar constituted the pivotal condition for the public/private divide—so closely aligned to the modern idea of religious freedom—to succeed. In this regard, it is of the utmost importance to underscore that religion is something different from denomination. If considered in all its anthropological scope, religion

[41] An analytical examination of all the consequence of the modern public/private divide with regard to the legal and political regime of sacred places/sites can be found in Tan (2007).

goes far beyond the strictly sacramental dimension. Religions, unlike their denominational institutions, forge cognitive and social habits aimed at pervading the social life of people. The alleged absoluteness of the public/private, 'public reason/inner individual faith' divides is plausible and pragmatically viable only if the co-ordinates of the social landscape are aligned with the theological moral projections of the peoples' different religious universes of sense. Though Western modernity has drawn a deep rift between politics and denominational institutions, the resilience of religion within the secular legal and social grammar has remained, and is still too often passed over in silence. Of course, if this was comprehensible within the historical cultural European borders that saw and accompanied the dawn of the modern era, it is unacceptable and almost inconceivable now that the cultural and theological moral homogeneity of national social landscapes is continuously challenged.

The cultural provinciality of Western cultural (and particularly: legal) secularization is also the main cause of its incompleteness and relativeness. Such cultural relativeness is not to be intended, however, only as a cultural connotation related to a geographical-political macro-area, to wit: the West. Its influence is recognizable and produces its effects also within the microcosm of quotidian life spaces. The public/private and reason/faith dualisms, as well as that of morality/politics, replicate simultaneously in the practical and micro-spatial divides. The reification of sacred spaces and the insulation of their presence are also a direct result of secularizing liberal logic.[42] This derivation can be easily ascertained as soon as one realizes that the temple and the city, liturgy and street life, could be divorced conceptually only because—tacitly—they remained semantically and pragmatically continuous. If we were to view this continuity as culturally and spatially broken, we would immediately see the chorological and ecological extended significance of the sacred place come to the fore.

[42]The best evidence of this implication can be found in the reifying effects ensuing the adoption of religious freedom as a jurisdictional tool to assess the Indian American Indigenous peoples' claims to enjoy their sacred sites and space. The lack of intercultural translation in the balancing judgments of US Courts is plainly displayed in the essay by Wiseman (2017). The failure to understand the cultural and religious at stake, when the balancing test between competing claims is exerted relying on the morphological appearance of cultural habits, is icastically shown by the flaws inherent in the 'intermediate proposal' put forward by Skibine (2012). But see also the self-critical descent toward a reduction to 'property rights' of Indian claims regarding their sacred places traceable in Carpenter (2005). At the end of this essay, the author appears to be somehow aware of the multiplicity of spatialities that different peoples project onto an allegedly 'unique' out-there space, and therefore the need to grasp such an intertwining so as to provide transactive/translational patterns of justice. In this sense, see Carpenter (2006).

8.6 The Intercultural Translation of Sacred Spaces Through Human Rights

What a semiotic analysis of sacred places illuminates is that their spatiality is made by people's actions, and these draw inspiration from the metaphorical behavioral directives of rites, ceremonies and liturgies. Sacred places are dynamic entities; their meaning is continually made the object of mediation and translation in the semantic fields of common life and social spaces. If law is to appropriately protect Sacred Places, it has to gauge such protection on their *real* ubiquitous and pragmatic significations/projections. Thus, an appropriate implementation of human rights cannot engage with Sacred Places as something existing *out there* or as a cosified inheritance, a 'capital' that can be preserved by means of insulation, or some kind of setting apart.

In this direction, the hierarchical/pyramidal approach to human rights interpretations and implementations for the protection of sacred places must be promptly left behind.[43] What is needed, conversely, is to use human rights, caught in all their semantic and pragmatic extension, as an interface of translation across the different behavioral implications of sacred places. In other words, to avoid destruction, desecration and the denial of the enjoyment of sacred places and sites, law should exert its influence on mutual translation between life spaces and the sacred words and spatial proactive framework they forge, and that are forged by them. This is the only way to dismantle the inherent alienness to which liberal secularism has condemned sacred places, which appear twice divorced from public life: first, as religious entities divided from secular spaces and semantics; second, as identitarian symbols of religious and/or cultural minorities that are frozen in a misoneistic portrayal, as a condition of their legal protection. To paraphrase an ancient Chinese saying, I suspect that such a strategy—which *inter alia* corresponds to the current political mainstream in the implementation of human and cultural rights—is like

[43]The lack of translation and the reification of sacred places/sites under the dome of religious freedom or cultural autonomy inevitably produces defective results. The best evidence of such a consequence and the blindness to the inner sense of sacred places and sites is embodied by the so called 'burden test' that US Courts apply when they review American Indigenous peoples' claims for the use of their sacred sites. The 'burden test' is ordered to assess the occurrence of a 'substantial burden,' provided that it exist "only when individuals are forced to choose between following the tenets of their religion and receiving a governmental benefit or coerced to act contrary to their religious beliefs by the threat of civil or criminal sanctions." In this regard and for the case law referrals to the 2008 Ninth Circuit decision see Wiseman (2017, p. 153). A broader interpretation of the Religious Freedom Restoration Act (RFRA) bumps against the fear that "because Indian religions are perceived as mysterious and because the location of sacred sites can be at times ill-defined, once claims to sacred sites are recognized, the floodgates may open, leaving nothing to stop Indians from claiming vast areas as sacred, thus freezing economic activities over numerous tracts of federal land": in this sense see Skibine (2012, p. 289). See also, for a comparative analysis of US politics regarding the indigenous peoples' sacred sites that shows, in the end, the importance of negotiations to overcome the implicit stiffening ensuing from the liberal secular approach to the sacred, McDonald (2004).

climbing a tree to catch fish. Its continuing implementation will achieve nothing but an antagonistic and conflictive perception of sacred places in an environment that is not culturally in tune with them as symbols of an untranslatable and untransactable Otherness.

As the history of past religious interplay shows, interreligious translation is possible either as a result of a semantic commitment, or as the outcome of spatial inter-penetration among different sets of practices.[44] With particular regard to sacred places, this possibility is proven by the multi-religious uses that many communities make of the same temples, buildings or sacred areas in the shadow of secularization.[45] This practice does not imply any blurring of the theological meaning of these places, nor any kind of conversion. Rather, people meet and share sacred spaces because they are able to translate the different behavioral spaces and quotidian cartographies that each faith draws from these environments.

Sacred places become, then, spaces of translation that are capable of projecting their semiotic action beyond their borders and walls, towards and into the social environment. Their destruction and desecration, in such cases, are in some sense automatically neutralized by the social sharing and translation of their extended signification. Just as mind transforms environment and the entities that populated it in prostheses enhancing body action, so as to include them in an extended and ecologically embodied operational mind, in the same vein the widened pragmatic signification of sacred places could function as a vehicle to trans-*late* these experiences of sharing into the common grammar of social coexistence. Legal action, however, should also move along a reverse-path. It should start from the translation of the worldwide behavioral consequences of faith directives, going as far as to include a dynamic reconceptualization of sacred places that are understood in their extensible significance.

To achieve this result, it is crucial to acknowledge that space is never something out there, but rather a pragmatic and operational projection/transaction between the human activity of categorization and the environment. If considered from an experiential perspective, categories and spaces are continuous, if only because any categorization involves actual or imaginative spatializations while any conception or perception of space includes its categorization. In both cases the human mind is working with signs.[46] From this perspective, the struggle for space is not to be conceptualized as a fight for a single outside objective space, one which each competitor represents differently and tries to occupy exclusively. The real conflict is always between different spaces, some features and connotations of which can be

---

[44] In this sense, it is very interesting to note the existence in Ancient Egypt or the Assyrian Empire of officials tasked with the inter-theological translation of treaties, when such were concluded among countries and authorities of different faiths. On this topic see, Assmann (1996, p. 25 ff.).

[45] See Della Dora (2016/2018).
https://doi.org/10.1177/0309132516666190).

[46] Some interesting insights on the co-extensiveness between categories and space can also be found, beyond the semiotic field, in phenomenology. See Blumenberg (2007). But see also Bachelard (1957) and Zumthor (1993).

on a collision course. Fetishization, reification of Otherness and its spatial projections are the semiotic fuel that moves the conflict forward. With dazzling blatancy, they obstruct any channel to possible translation that might otherwise be able to creatively draw out connotative and pragmatic continuities from different ways of spatializing experience, rather than their discontinuities. I refer to this as a creative activity because there is no achievable objective inter-spatiality; the only solution comes from the competitors' awareness that through the reciprocal translation of their own spaces, they are giving shape to a Third dimension of which they are the exclusive authors and guarantors. Translating activity should be anchored to an intercultural use of human rights. Their axiological 'ingredients' should be taken as metaphorical interfaces, or as the ground beneath the religious/cultural differences and their related spatializations.[47] As I stressed above, sacred places are the material media of communication and convergence between an openness to God and an openness toward the world, including human Otherness. Cognition rather violence and exclusion thus emerges as the multi-centered authentic meaning of religious experience. Translation and cognition, on the other hand, are inseparable and mutually inclusive. The awareness of this could give course to the possibility to draw from the different sacred places the semio-pragmatic means to conceive and co-orchestrate, through the intercultural use of human rights, the patterns affording different universes of sense and the related spatial geographies to fruitfully coexist on the Earth. The protection of sacred places would become, then, an epiphenomenon of reciprocal translation among the semio-pragmatic projections of sacred places all over the world.

The chorological shrinking and relativization of distances ensuing from an understanding of the dynamic and trans-spatial significance of sacred places prompts me to imagine the planet as a big city, in which Jerusalem and the Ganges, St. Peter's Basilica and Aboriginal sacred paths, are close and interrelated, just as people of different faiths live, move, and breathe side by side in the multicultural megalopolis of the world. But the space of such an only apparently imaginary city would be nothing but the result of the semantic interrelationships between all these sacred places and their praxeological consequences.

The interreligious respect for the pilgrimages that drew and connoted their particular political ecology in the past proves that a worldwide communicative network among sacred places is possible. In a way, the de-territorializing effect that we attach to the world wide web was already a semiotic reality in the Middle Ages (and even before).

[47] A for the intercultural use of human rights I refer to my previous works: see Ricca (2008, 2013b), and above.

8.7 Sacred Places *vs.* the Space of Atheism: *Ciclopean* Issue

In the planetary semio-eco-logical scope of the meaning and legal protection of sacred places, however, there remains a sort of blind spot. It is constituted by the secularized and atheist visions of sacred places and religious universes. No one can ignore the fact that the desecration and destruction of sacred places, at least historically, were also carried out by atheist activists or political authorities. Needless to say, their attitude towards sacred places and religions is further stimulated by the cognitive and spatial alienness produced by the semantic/spatial secularization divides. Nonetheless, I think that the translational functions of a horizontal use of human rights as metaphorical interfaces could also be extended to the relationships between atheists and religious spatialized expressions, including sacred places. All the same, it would remain a hopeless effort to ask atheists to recognize the mediating function between a sacred dimension and the worldly one that sacred words (or frameworks of sacred acts of semantization) and sacred places inherently represent for believers. However, no atheist could wisely ignore the materiality of the consequences of faith. This would be equivalent to a failure to know his own 'enemies.' The risks ensuing from this kind of willful and othering blindness towards those who invoke the religious sources of their action cannot find any better evidence than Homer's Odyssey, and the sad story of Polyphemus. Consider the following short passages from the Odyssey.

When Ulysses meets the Cyclops in his cave for the first time, the Achaian warrior addresses these words to him:

> As for us, chancing to come here we lay ourselves at your feet in entreaty, in the hope you may offer us a stranger's present, or give us a gift in some other way, as is the proper custom with strangers. Come now, my dear fellow, show respect before the gods: we are the suppliants, you know, and Zeus it is who watches over the rights and wrongs of suppliants and strangers, the stranger's god, who accompanies strangers deserving of respect.

Despite Ulysses' invocation of divine protection, Polyphemus gives him the following rebuttal:

> So I spoke, and he at once replied with a pitiless heart: 'You are being silly, stranger, or you have come from far away, telling me either to fear the gods or keep out of their way. The Cyclopes take no notice of Zeus the aegis-carrier, or the other blessed gods, since we are much superior to them. I would not spare you or your comrades to avoid the hostility of Zeus unless my heart told me to.[48]

Everyone knows how the story continues... and ends. The intentional cognitive blindness of Polyphemus will transmute into an actual physical one.[49] This occurs because he gives too much relevance to his physical superiority and the force imbalance existing between him and human beings. So, he refuses to give course to the ritual of hospitality, which is—as Homer is still teaching us—nothing but a

[48] For the translation from the Greek of Homer's Odyssey, see Dawe (1993, pp. 371–372).

[49] On Polyphemus' inhospitality as cognitive blindness see Ricca (2011).

strategy for knowing Otherness. Unfortunately (but only for the Cyclops), Ulysses transforms him into a sign, and by means of his power of symbolic representation changes the trunk of an olive tree in a terrible sharp weapon with which he pierces out the eye of the Cyclops. Only at that point the Polyphemus' lack of hospitality proves to be essentially his real blindness, the cause of his dramatic refusal to know Otherness and, more generally, the world. But what has the tragic sort of the Cyclops in common with atheists and sacred places?

As we see above, rites and liturgies transform sacred places into hosting areas where the world and the divine can conflate. This hospitality is immanent to rites, but it also engenders and symbolizes a cognitive-practical improvement. As I have already emphasized, when religious rituals/ceremonies allow believers to know the world as a result of its inter-penetration with the divine dimension, they simultaneously urge them to translate this knowledge in their behavioral habits through the same world. Like Polyphemus, no atheist should be so confident in his own superiority as to ignore Otherness and its sources of interpretation of the world; and, vice versa, no religious believer can disregard or refuse to know the atheists' universe of sense.

8.8 Epilogue

Taken from an anthropological perspective, religion demonstrates its materiality, which deserves, as such, to be considered as an element and a force at work in the social environment. Insofar as the semio-practical consequences of religions are spatialized in and beyond sacred places, they can also be translated by using the human rights semantic and axiological apparatus as a metaphorical interface to shape a grammar of coexistence. No conversion or religious contamination is inherently or inevitably involved in this kind of translation between religious pragmatics and atheist ones. On the contrary, it seems able to outline the possibility to configure public inter-space of coexistence between different cultural and religious orthopraxes based on an intercultural and multivocal process of secularization. The only *immense caveat* is that universal human rights must be put into use as immanent tools or operational ends, much like the horizon which provides both an asymptotical arrival point and a stimulus for our endless motion toward it. Human rights' processive teleology is to make their axiological-semantic platform and its inherent vagueness available, so as to spur the human attitude toward universalization, which is nothing more than an ability to engender and ceaselessly renew categorical schemes and their projections in the making of spaces.

A polyphonic harmonization and inter-translation of sacred spaces is the pre-requisite to align their legal protection with their chorological (namely semantic/spatial) significance. But this achievement requires that human rights be interpreted and implemented not only at inter- or supranational levels, but also from a planetary perspective. In order to ensure that the human actions that stem from, and interplay with, the semio-practical trans-local consequences of each genuine sacred place are co-present everywhere, and reciprocally attuned, human rights must be used as horizontal interfaces between different behavioral and semiotic ideologies. Jerusalem, St. Peter's Basilica, Aboriginal Sacred Stones, Meteores, and so on, can be everywhere on the Earth, and maybe even beyond its atmosphere, as perennial icons of the divine/human creational potential.

References

Assmann J (1996) Translating gods: religion as a factor of cultural (un)translatability. In: Budick S, Iser W (eds) The translatability of cultures: figurations of the space between. Stanford University Press, Stanford, pp 25–36

Bachelard G (1957) La poétique de l'espace. Presses Universitaires de France, Paris

Barkan E, Barkey K (2015) Introduction. In: Barkan E, Barkey K (eds) Choreographies of shared sacred sites: religion, politics, and conflict resolution. Columbia University Press, New York, pp 1–31

Bell CM (2009) Ritual theory, ritual practice, 2nd edn. OUP, Oxford

Benzo A (2014) Toward a definition of sacred places: introductory remarks. In: Ferrari S, Benzo A (eds) Between cultural diversity and common heritage: legal and religious perspectives on the sacred places of the Mediterranean. Routledge, Abingdon, pp 17–23

Bhargava R (2008) Political secularism: why it is needed and what can be learnt from its Indian version. In: Levey GB, Modood T (eds) Secularism, religion and multicultural citizenship. CUP, Cambridge, pp 82–109

Bhargava R (2011) Beyond moderate secularism. In: The immanent frame: secularism, religion, and the public sphere. http://blogs.ssrc.org/tif/2011/09/16/beyond-moderate-secularism

Birch DJ (2000) Pilgrimage to Rome in the Middle Ages: continuity and change. The Boydell Press, Woodbridge

Bird J (2012) Canon law regarding pilgrims. In: Taylor LJ et al (eds) Encyclopedia of medieval pilgrimage. Brill, Leiden, pp 2213–2139

Blumenberg H (2007) Theorie der Unbegrifflichkeit. Suhrkamp, Frankfurt a. M

Bogdanović J (ed) (2018) Perceptions of the body and sacred space in late antiquity and Byzantium. Routledge, Abingdon, VA

Bowman G (ed) (2012) Sharing the sacra: the politics and pragmatics of inter-communal relations around holy places. Berghahn Books, New York

Carpenter K (2005) Old ground and new directions at sacred sites on the Western landscape. Denver Univ Law Rev 83(4):981–1002

Carpenter K (2006) The interest of "peoples" in the cooperative management of sacred sites. Tulsa Law Rev 42:37–56

Casanova J (2009) The secular and the secularism. Soc Res 76(4):1049–1066

Chareyron N (2000) Pilgrims to Jerusalem in the Middle Ages. Columbia University Press, New York- Chichester

Chidester D, Linenthal ED (1995) Introduction. In: Chidester D, Linenthal ED (eds) American sacred space. Indiana University Press, Bloomington, pp 1–42

Coleman S, Eade J (2004) Introduction: reframing pilgrimage. In: Coleman S, Eade J (eds) Reframing pilgrimage: cultures in motion. Routledge, London, pp 1–20

Coleman S, Elsner J (1995) Pilgrimage: past and present in the world religions. Harvard University Press, Cambridge

Coster W, Spicer A (2005) Introduction: the dimensions of sacred space in reformation Europe. In: Coster W, Spicer A (eds) Sacred space in early modern Europe. CUP, Cambridge, pp 1–16

Dawe RD (1993) The Odyssey: translation and analysis. The Book Guild, Sussex

De Roover J, Claerhout S, Balagangadhara SN (2011) Liberal political theory and the cultural migration of ideas: the case of secularism in India. Polit Theory 39(5):571–599
Della Dora V (2007) Geostrategy and the persistence of antiquity: surveying mythical hydrographies in the Eastern Mediterranean, 1784-1869. J Hist Geogr 33(3):514–541
Della Dora V (2011) Engaging sacred space: experiments in the field. J Geogr High Educ 35(2): 163–184
Della Dora V (2015) Sacred space unbound. Environ Plann D Soc Space (13). https://pure.royalholloway.ac.uk/en/publications/virtual-issue-13-sacred-space-unbound. Virtual Issue 13
Della Dora V (2016) Landscape, nature, and the sacred in Byzantium. CUP, Cambridge
Della Dora V (2018) Infrasecular geographies: making, unmaking and remaking sacred space. Progr Hum Geogr 42(1):44–71
Denzinger H (2009) Enchiridion symbolorum, definitionum et declarationum de rebus fidei et morum, Bilingual Edition on 40th edition, edited by Peter Hünermann. EDB, Bologna
Derrida J (1993) Khôra. Galilée, Paris
Di Paolo E, Cuffaro EC, De Jaegher A (2018) Linguistic bodies: the continuity between life and language. The MIT Press, Cambridge
Digance J (2003) Pilgrimage at contested sites. Ann Tour Res 30(1):143–159. https://doi.org/10.1016/S0160-7383(02)00028-2
Einoo S (2016) Rites for rain in the Vedic and post-Vedic literature. In: Brereton JP (ed) The Vedas in Indian culture and history: proceedings of the fourth international Vedic workshop. SEF, Firenze, pp 243–258
Eliade M (1958 [1948]) Patterns in comparative religions. Sheed & Ward, London
Eliade M (1959) The sacred and the profane: the nature of religion. Harcourt, Brace and World, New York
Gilles H (1980) Lex peregrinorum. Le Pèlerinage, Toulouse, Privat, Cahiers de Fanjeaux 15:161–189
Giovanni Paolo II (1998) Motu proprio, Ad tuendam fidem, 18 maggio 1998. Lettera Apostolica
Glenn PH (2014) Legal traditions of the world: sustainable diversity in law. OUP, Oxford
Gregorič Bon N (2016) Rooting routes: (non-)movements in Southern Albania. In: Gregorič Bon N, Repič I (eds) Moving places: relations, returns and belonging. Berghahn Books, New York, pp 63–84
Hamilton S, Spicer A (2016) Defining the holy: the delineation of sacred space. In: Hamilton S, Spicer A (eds) Defining the holy: sacred space in medieval and early modern Europe. Routledge, Abindgon, VA, pp 1–25
Hayden R (2002) Antagonistic tolerance: competitive sharing of religious sites in South Asia and the Balkans'. Curr Anthropol 43(2):205–231
Hayden R et al (eds) (2016) Antagonistic tolerance. Competitive sharing of religious sites and spaces. Routledge, London
Holloway J (2003) Make-believe: spiritual practice, embodiment and sacred space. Environ Plann A 35:1961–1974
Isar N (2006) Chorography (chôra, chorós) – a performative paradigm of creation of sacred space in Byzantium. In: Lidov A (ed) Hierotopy. The creation of sacred spaces in Byzantium and Medieval Russia. Progress-tradition, Moscow, pp 59–90
Isar N (2009a) Chôra: tracing the presence. Rev Eur Stud 1(1):39–55
Isar N (2009b) Chorography – a space for chorographic inscription. Bulletin of The Transilvania University of Breşov 2(51). Series IV:263–268
Jacobsen KJ (2012) Pilgrimage in the Hindu tradition: salvific space. Routledge, London
Jonas H (2012) Das Prinzip Verantwortung: Versuch einer Ethik für die technologische Zivilisation. Suhrkamp, Frankfurt am Main
Keane W (2007) Christian moderns: freedom and fetish in the mission encounter. The University of California Press, Berkeley
Klingorová K (2018) 'God was with me everywhere': women's embodied practices and everyday experience of sacred space in Czechia. Gender, place & culture. J Femin Geogr 25(1):37–60

Knott K (2014) The location of religion: a spatial analysis. Routledge, Abingdon, VA
Kong L (1993) Ideological hegemony and the political symbolism of religious buildings in Singapore. Environ Plann D Soc Space 11(1):23–45
Kong L (2001) Mapping 'new' geographies of religion: politics and poetics in modernity. Progr Hum Geogr 25:211–233
Kong L (2002) In search of permanent homes: Singapore's house churches and the politics of space. Urban Stud 39:1573–1586
Leanza U (2014) General problems of international law concerning sacred places. In: Ferrari S, Benzo A (eds) Between cultural diversity and common heritage: legal and religious perspectives on the sacred places of the Mediterranean. Routledge, Abingdon, pp 37–55
Lidov A (2006) Hierotopy. Creation of sacred spaces as a form of creativity and subject of cultural history. In: Lidov A (ed) Hierotopy. The creation of sacred spaces in Byzantium and medieval Russia. Progress-tradition, Moscow, pp 32–58
Lidov A (2008) The comparative hierotopy. In: Liadov A (ed) Hierotopy. Comparative studies of sacred spaces. Indrik, Moscow, pp 9–12
Lidov A (2009) Hierotopy. Spatial icons and image-paradigms in Byzantine culture. Theoria, Moscow
Lidov A (2014) Creating the sacred space: hierotopy as a new field of cultural history. In: Cremonesi C, Carnevale L (eds) Spazi e percorsi sacri. I santuari, le vie, i corpi. Libreriauniversiataria.it edizioni, Padova, pp 63–92
Lidov A (2016) Iconicity as spatial notion: a new vision of icons in contemporary art theory, pp 1–12. http://hierotopy.ru/contents/IconicityRijeka2016lidov.pdf
McDonald AL (2004) Secularizing the sacrosanct: defining "sacred" for Native American sacred sites protection legislation. Hofstra Law Rev 33(2):751–783
Miller J (2013) More than the sum its parts: animal categories and accretive logic in volume one of Al-Jāḥiẓ's Kitāb al-Ḥayawān. PhD dissertation, Department of Middle Eastern and Islamic Studies, New York University
Modood T (2009) Muslims, religious equality and secularism. In: Levey GB, Modood T (eds) Secularism, religion and multicultural citizenship. CUP, Cambridge, pp 164–184
Morinis A (1992) Introduction: the territory of the anthropology of pilgrimage. In: Morinis A (ed) Sacred journeys: the anthropology of pilgrimage. Greenwood, Westport, pp 1–28
Newman D, Ruozzi E, Kirchner S (2017) Legal protection of sacred natural sites within human rights jurisprudence: Sápmi and beyond. In: Heinämäki L, Herrmann TM (eds) Experiencing and protecting sacred natural sites of Sámi and other indigenous peoples: the sacred Arctic. Springer, Cham, pp 11–26
Pallavicini Y (2014) 'God has made the earth like a carpet': the Sacred places in the Islamic tradition. In: Ferrari S, Benzo A (eds) Between cultural diversity and common heritage: legal and religious perspectives on the sacred places of the Mediterranean. Routledge, Abingdon, pp 112–137
Petkoff P (2014) Finding a grammar of consent for 'soft law' guidelines on sacred places: the legal protection of sacred places within the existing public international law instruments and grass-root approaches. In: Ferrari S, Benzo A (eds) Between cultural diversity and common heritage: legal and religious perspectives on the sacred places of the Mediterranean. Routledge, Abingdon, pp 65–84
Ricca M (2008) Oltre Babele. Codici per una democrazia interculturale. Dedalo, Bari
Ricca M (2011) Polifemo. La cecità dello straniero. Torri del Vento, Palermo
Ricca M (2013a) Il tradimento delle immagini tra kirpan e transazioni interculturali. Cultura vs. competenza culturale nel mondo del diritto. E|C Rivista dell'Associazione italiana di Studi semiotici: 1–31. http://www.ec-aiss.it/index_d.php?recordID=678
Ricca M (2013b) La fabrique coupable des malentendus innocente. Étrangers, diffractions culturelles et strategies politiques du non savoir. Revue des Sciences Sociales, Malentendus 50:60–68

Ricca M (2016) Klee's cognitive legacy and human rights as intercultural transducers: modern art, legal translation, and micro-spaces of coexistence. CALUMET - Intercult Law Humanit Rev 3: 1–40. https://calumet-review.com/index.php/2016/09/10/klees-cognitive-legacy-and-human-rights-as-intercultural-transducers-modern-art-legal-translation-and-micro-spaces-of-coexistence/

Ricca M (2019) Signs across races: Al-Jahiz's cosmo-semiosis and his trans-racial mapping of the "human." CALUMET - Intercult Law Humanit Rev 8:21–40. https://calumet-review.com/index.php/2019/06/11/signs-across-races-al-jahizs-cosmo-semiosis-and-his-trans-racial-mapping-of-the-human/

Ricca M (2022) Perpetually astride Eden's boundaries: the limits to the 'limits of law' and the semiotic inconsistency of 'legal enclosures'. Int J Semiot Law 35:179–229. https://doi.org/10.1007/s11196-020-09771-0

Sallis J (1999) Chorology: on beginning in Plato's Timaeus. Indiana University Press, Bloomington

Sallnow MJ (1987) Pilgrims of the Andes: regional cults in Cusco. Smithsonian Institution, Washington

Sapir G, Statman D (2016) The protection of holy places. Law Ethics Hum Rights 10(1):135–155. https://doi.org/10.1515/lehr-2016-0005

Singh Rana PB (2013) Hindu tradition of pilgrimage: sacred space and system. Dev Publishers, New Delhi

Skibine AT (2012) Towards a balanced approach for the protection of Native American sacred sites. Mich J Race Law 17(2):269–302

Smith JZ (1978) Map is not territory. Brill, Leiden

Stoddard RB, Morinis A (eds) (1997) Sacred places, sacred spaces. The geography of pilgrimage. Geoscience Publications, Baton Rouge

Tagliacozzo E (2013) The longest journey: Southeast Asians and the pilgrimage to Mecca. OUP, Oxford

Tan CL (2007) The effect of the "public–private" dichotomy on the concept of Indigenous "sacred place" in the religious freedom and heritage protection laws of Australia, USA, Canada and New Zealand. PhD thesis, University of Western Australia, Perth. https://api.research-repository.uwa.edu.au/files/3228592/Tan_Carolyn_Lian_2010.pdf

Tuan Y-F (1977) Space and place: the perspective of experience. University of Minnesota Press, Minneapolis

Urry J (2000) Sociology beyond societies: mobilities for the twenty-first century. Routledge, London

Urry J (2002) Mobility and proximity. Sociology 36(2):255–274

Vazquez ML (2018) People moving water: religious and secular perspectives at play in legal water management. Quaderni di diritto e politica ecclesiastica 2:437–466

Walker A, Luyster A (2016) Mapping the Heavens and treading the Earth: negotiating secular and sacred in medieval art. In: Walker A, Luyster A (eds) Negotiating secular and sacred in medieval art: Christian, Islamic, and Buddhist. Routledge, Abingdon, pp 1–16

Wiseman TA (2017) Because the law on the restoration of religious freedom cannot protect sacred sites. Am Indian J 5(1):140–166

Zumthor P (1993) La Mesure du monde. Seuil, Paris

Chapter 9
Conclusion

Interculturality and the Reinvention of the Space for Democracy's Survival

I would like to begin this conclusion by calling into play a simple object: a glass. As a second step, I would metaphorically attach to it two questions. What is the implicit geography of that glass? And what is the relationship between such geography and the meaning of that glass? I ask whoever is reading these lines, to imagine a glass or—perhaps—to look at the glass sitting before them. 'It is in front of me'—could be the answer to the questions. Nonetheless, the pronoun 'me' makes such an answer rather elliptical. That 'me' is implicitly assumed to correspond to a being with a 'mouth.' And, in addition, a 'mouth' that is made in a specific way. Storks also have a mouth—just to evoke one of Aesop's well-known fables—but they would not know what to do with a glass too low and small to fit their beaks/mouths. Let alone beings without 'mouths'... but also without hands, arms, tongues... More in general, in a world populated by beings without mouths, arms, hands, tongues, etc., would the glass still be a 'glass'? (And this even apart from the not negligible circumstance that, in such a situation, most likely also the glass makers would be absent).

The morphological appearance of the above glass, the quintessence of its 'form,' its inherent structure, enshrines inside itself a relationship, or better a network of relationships, which are the subject of semiotic generalizations engendered by means of cultural communication processes. What is, therefore, 'more real'? The network of semiotic relationships or the morphological 'figuration' of the glass? This simultaneously simple and very complicated question could seem to reopen the eternal issue of 'universals.' But actually, it is something else. This is because the relationships underlying the glass are both imagined and acted: that is, insofar as they are imagined, they are means that can transform what a living being endowed with a mouth can do with what they have before them... precisely, a glass.

But there is more to say. The glass can be made of countless materials. As it is an artifact, the manifold materials—far beyond being mere secondary attributes—are *pieces of the world* that are transformed in elements operatively co-constitutive of the glass at stake. The idea of drinking can conjure a glass, or a cup made of plastic, of paper or something else. From both a genealogical and a sensorial perspective,

M. Ricca, *Intercultural Spaces of Law*, Law and Visual Jurisprudence 10,
https://doi.org/10.1007/978-3-031-27436-7_9

this activity means calling implicitly into play various geographies, relational modalities and dynamics through which the space is lived and managed, including the elements comprising it. A glass, for example, is the epitome of a particular chain of gestures, relationships with the environment and activities designed to transform raw materials. A plastic cup sums up in itself largely different relational/dynamic and—I would say—kinetic concatenations (that is, including activities mediated by human bodies): just think of the oil extraction activities needed to produce the plastic used in the construction of the cup. Many different 'wheres' and 'hows' are assumed *inside* a glass or a plastic cup, as well as in their respective process of production. Those 'wheres' become *materials* and, thereby, as such they will affect the use and the local and topical environment embodied in the dynamics of fruition related to the glass/cup and its relationships with the 'mouths' for which it is intended.

The 'life prospects' of a glass, a plastic cup or a paper one, largely diverge. They depend on the 'wheres' and the manner in which they are stored and preserved, and the possibility of re-use, destruction and eventual recycling, as well. At least in some cases, if someone could follow the spatial and therefore relational destiny of a glass (be it made of glass, paper, or plastic), once it had gone beyond their immediate experiential horizon, they would no longer envy those who take cruises around the world. In short, the glass, either concretely used or only imagined, seems to equal a relational crossroads excerpted from a chain of semiotic and experiential connections. In this regard, an epistemological question arises: how legitimate is it to limit the cognitive consideration of the above relational chain by extrapolating from it only certain elements, subsequently combined and reduced to a categorical checklist of morphological features/properties? This elliptical rendering can even find justification in cognitive and practical economy—irrefutably. Nevertheless, this reasoning simultaneously draws a spatial framework that interplays with a web of further, innumerable relationships. But the meaning of the glass is not *immune* to these *other* relationships from both the cognitive and practical perspectives. What if, therefore, these presupposed, apparently invisible relationships became defective or were missed? Could the categorical abstraction of the glass—from an ontological perspective—legitimately remain unchanged? Or, rather, should the way to categorize that 'piece of world' that we define 'glass' also be revised?

Someone could in all likelihood wonder what this discourse has to do with intercultural law, spatial justice, law and the efficiency of democratic processes. These conclusive pages are designed to provide a simple and concise answer to this question as a kind of resumé of the theoretical gist of the overall book and a path towards further projections. I will raise, in this respect, some further questions. Can the portion of relationships (morphological, structural)—which I would define as relationships between factual elements and, simultaneously, their dynamic and pro-active interpretation—that we typically use to define the glass assure the permanence/stability of all the other ones? Or is that relational portion capable of remaining immune to the other relationships' potential for change on both an experiential and abstractly categorical plain?

In many cases, it is possible by virtue of both a time and space diffraction. Consider, in this regard, traditional glass. Glass can be obtained, in principle, from any liquid by preventing it from reaching crystallization during the process of solidification. However, to produce glass it is almost indispensable to have materials that solidify slowly enough: e.g., arsenic anhydride (As2o5), silicon oxide (Sio2), germanium dioxide (Geo2), phosphoric anhydride (P2O5), or boric anhydride (B2O3). To procure these materials implies, in most cases, activities that are 'remote' in both space and time from the *common* moments and places where the glass is utilized. This is the reason why the chain underlying their production and processing is usually keep 'distant,' if not even 'outside,' the definitional perimeter of the category 'glass': that is, what we ordinarily recognize, think of, experience as a 'glass;' or better, what we believe that we can consider, recognize, experience as a 'glass.' The same could be predicated—with a further dispersal in both space and time—for a plastic cup.

The crucial point—at least, in my view—is that neither the 'cognitive' nor the 'geographical' distance can assure the stability of all the relationships it presupposes. When this stability fails, even the above (categorical) distancing shows its artificiality and contingency, its being situated within a semantic and experiential greed that is neither eternal nor unalterable. It so happens that when the 'implicit,' the 'presupposed,' undergo some change, then the 'remote,' the 'apparently unrelated,' prove to be close, co-implied in the 'present,' in what is 'here' and 'now', as well as in the related experience. To get back to the glass, its being an epitome of productive chains spread out over space and time makes so that the alterations taking place in the 'elsewhere' can immediately impinge on its present and situated availability, its production, the material utilized to produce it, its shape, its dissemination, and so on. Think of the Covid pandemic and the recommended use of straws in public places... just to offer a bit of immediate evidence.[1]

Leaving aside, now, the metaphor of the glass and broadening the scope of the analysis to include any object-means of local experience, it is not hard to see how the relational and phenomenal substratum underlain by each 'entity' and the corresponding category is asymmetrical to the geographical/spatial distances. From a semantic perspective, the 'elsewhere' can prove to be dramatically close, to the point of compelling a re-drawing of the relationship between the denotative and the connotative elements of each category, between the center and the periphery of its semantic spectrum. Far from being an exclusively speculative discourse, these observations have immediate practical and political relevance.

Democratic political institutions find their legitimation in the idea of individual self-determination. Individuals' ability to self-determine, however, is necessarily rooted in the availability of information. More specifically, it depends on the close connection between information and the cognitive schemes that individuals develop and process in order to map their world and plan their activities. Technology and interdependence have made the interplay between places and spatial circuits with respect to the production of human experience more and more dense. The same can be said, moreover, regarding the meaning of that experience: to be intended as the

[1] See Ricca (2020).

result stemming from the dynamics inherent in the web of semiotic relationships involved in human existence and action. As such, meaning is inherent in any entity, object of knowledge and, therefore, the unfolding and the expressions of subjectivity. However, the knowledge of individuals is still closely anchored and corralled into the local dimension. *Common people* know very little about the real dynamics of the semio-spatial relationships that underlies the objects, places, individuals and phenomena they perceive. A consideration that applies both to what is presupposed—that is, what belongs to the production chain of what is present—and to what follows the current fruition of the 'perceived items' or their imminent inclusion in individual and collective action plans.

Differently from the so-called global actors, common people are devoid of a semantic-spatial awareness that allows them to connect the presuppositions and consequences of what they *desire*, pursue, assume as integral parts of their lives, targets of their own freedom, pre-conditions of their dignity, basic ingredients of their being and feeling on an equal footing with others. The paradoxical outcome is that people often do not really know what they believe they want and, conversely, do not long for that which they are actually in need of in order to achieve their goals and to update them and make them in tune with the state of the world.

The 'elsewhere' is pervasively close to the democratic actor but remains simultaneously silent, blurred and sometimes even hidden. All this engenders anthropological separation and, at the same time, political polarization in the field of daily experience on a global scale. By opposing their unknown and allegedly distant Other, individuals abide by the as-traditional-as-fictitious logic of the contrastive relationship between different territorial/national areas. In this way, however, they behave as unaware enemies of themselves. In the asymmetric game between global actors and local democratic subjects the overall scene is dominated and haunted by the practical consequences of an ancient motto, which seems to hover over the planetary stage: namely, the well-known *divide et impera*. It is Julius Caesar's motto, nothing but the generative and strategic cipher of ancient and modern imperialism. Under renewed guises, it also applies to the contemporary cultural contrasts and divisions. The adjective 'multicultural' and the substantivized attribute 'multinational' resonate with a phonetic coincidence that is politically more devious and mystifying than can be imagined at first glance. The identitarian discourse, nub of the so-called multiculturalism, is ironically but also tragically in tune with the cynical interest of multinationals to prevent a global public opinion from arising and taking shape. Should individuals, closed in their national and/or local sociopolitical *corrals*, realize how much the elsewhere and its cultural otherness is already inherently embedded in their daily experience, they would understand that blindly and aprioristically opposing Others is tantamount to fighting against themselves. For the Other than Self is also the Other of Self, an inner part of both one's own past and future, the very meaning of each individual.

The global pandemic predicament has made visible the pathological proximity of bodies geographically spread out across huge distances by virtue of the biological communicative corridors coextensive with the genetic information nestled in the SARS-CoV-2 virus. But it has done nothing but plainly evidence the asymmetry extant between the symbolic-political-territorial imageries and the semiotic *continuum* underlying the transmission of bio-information. A *continuity* that has been blatantly ignored and strategically exiled outside the world population's conscience, and yet strikingly present and selfishly managed by the savvy players of the global economy. Players who, riding the pandemic wave, attempted to conceal—especially in the early stages of breakdown—*non-geographic* proximity by keeping the same people doomed to contract Covid 19 in a condition of cognitive blindness regarding its consequences. But it is a strategy that, despite its catastrophic implications, continues today and fuels propaganda for a stolid, unresponsive and indifferent exercise of freedom. For it is almost compulsively gauged on the claims for the stubborn reiteration of past behavioral schemes under the common people's illusion that they can float in a condition of careless ignorance about the semiotic relationships populating and determining the real dynamics of their experiential space, and therefore the connection between expectations and consequences, prognosis and outcomes.

Someone could ask: what about the Internet? Don't most people have access, today, to this *translocal* information portal? Isn't it capable of shunning and defusing the compartmentalization and manipulation of information, which in the past was at the sole disposal of the state and international agencies? The Web—indisputably—is spatially and thereby also semantically more isomorphic to the weft of semiotic relationships weaving experience than the traditional physical communication anchored to the local circuits and/or the conveyance of paper material. But what still seems difficult to transmit to people is the use of virtual space as a public square for freedom, for the creation of a global public opinion. More specifically, what is still missing in collective awareness is the ability to psycho-cognitively transfer the 'elsewhere' within the understanding of each individual's lived space, which is more or less corresponding with the place of ordinary physical dwelling.

Beyond any rhetoric of hidden reasons, I am persuaded that the global latching on to online learning is the consequence of a specific and 'weighed' fear on the part of the most powerful global actors and their representatives (or better, inside men) within national and transnational institutions. It is the fear that a virtual public square could materialize which, by and by, could remove the asymmetry from the cognitive and experiential space of political conscience, including the productive forces and their related economical-geographical implications. The possibility for multinationals and the subjects leading the global exploitation of the so-called comparative costs and delocalizing is by now a crucial hindrance to the political-economic self-determination of peoples. It would be reasonable to expect that a global public opinion, if adequately trained to perceive the *continuum* between Others' spaces and one's own in terms of co-implication, meaning, and semantics of local individual daily experience, could bring about a rebalancing between peoples' informative horizons and the decision-making spaces. If the local actors all over the planet (more or less) learned to simultaneously refuse to play along, then comparative costs and financial strategies would have few advantages to secure the turbo-capitalist plutocracy. Such realigning and mutual *translation* between spaces and information is today only achievable through a skilled and well-trained aptitude to learn and read the 'elsewhere' as relationally close. Failing that, democracies seem to be destined to an inevitable inanity and a condition of risible impotence, capable of unleashing mass frustration and gut reactions, as such very often vulnerable to political manipulation.

To avoid this already diffuse folly, education is a crucial tool for learning to navigate digital spaces and handling them intelligently in view of their interpenetration with physical spaces so as to make ubiquitous every *here* and each *elsewhere*. This kind of education, to be necessarily set out according to an intercultural translational and transactional perspective, is both inseparable from and a condition for the future of democracy. Without such education, democracy will become (as it already is) a farcical travesty of itself, a void ghost doomed to become ever more evanescent.

To return to the metaphor of glass, everyone should learn to wonder, precisely at the moment they quench their thirst, how much China there likely is in their glass; in the same vein, how much of the Middle East could be traced in their plastic cup; and still, how much Amazonia could be glimpsed, should the drinker be an ecologist, in their paper cup. This—if anything and just to cite Leibniz—because whosoever wants something, must also want its consequences (namely, both its past and future implications); otherwise, they do not want that thing. In the alternative scenario, people will go on mechanically wishing for 'objects' of desire only formally identified as such but pre-determined by others or, even worse, by headless but not less heteronomous and oppressive chains of algorithms produced by a technology-driven economy. If we fail to make haste in the effort to educate ourselves on how to manage digital communication so that we might finally *become aware* of the semiotic threads connecting physical and virtual spaces on a global scale, the very possibility of democracy will die. Failing to understand the semiotic interpenetration among the multiple spaces entailed in the production of meaning and the material items involved in the unfolding of human experience is equivalent to losing our conscious grip on the ecology of individual life. Only an open and far-ranging communication, capable of reciprocally showing the lived spaces of Others, the experiential fabric of their beliefs and cognitive patterns, the embedding of people's bodies in the interaction with different and yet semiotically interplaying environments, could allow individuals to grasp the story epitomized in every desired object, its real status as a 'good.' Only an awareness of the semiotic plot recapitulated in each commodified item could avert the formalism of money, its absolutization as a unique translational interface for the meaning and qualitative value of 'the matter of the world.' It is true that the functionalization of production and ideation gauged on the abstract measure of evaluation and exchange of money can defuse the human tendency to fall into the quagmires of reification and the sacralizing ossification of practices and cognitive patterns. Nonetheless, the semantic and pragmatic mobility triggered by the market communication/translation among different goods can make people blind to the presuppositions and the consequences of what is desired and exchanged, namely its semiotic, experiential, ethical and aesthetic paths of production. The psycho-social outcome of such a situation is a kind of misoneist attachment to renewing targets of desire and behavioral schemes, which change only externally while keeping their inner structure unaltered. It is as if the planetary population were affected by a compulsive collector syndrome, for whom the last not-yet-obtained item for their collection is a reason for living, but only until they find they cannot include it in their collection. Whereupon that precise desperately desired object will ineluctably slide in the shadowy pit of the 'already acquired items'... to be replaced by another target of desire. In this way, rather than being the source of creativity and a psycho-anthropological resource to upset the stagnant landscape of frozen semantic cages, desire becomes a cause for alienation and an unconscious iteration of existential schemes. In this scenario, the more different spaces of experience are translated and thereby made categorically close through money and the logic of exchange coextensive to the market, the more those spaces become distant and non-communicating worlds within people's imaginaries. This is due to a diffraction between economic trans-*lations*/transactions and cultural ones. Through it, a seclusive circuit takes place outside of which the qualitative aspects of cultural and spatial differences connoting the lived experience of people remain. When national societies continue to think of themselves through the spectrum of a freedom-from-others that is ultimately an attitude of indifference to Otherness[2] and Elsewhere, they find themselves progressively affected by both an ungrateful ignorance of their past and a helpless unawareness of their future. And besides, the tendency to duplicate also on the web the creation of a communicative space immune to differences and unmoved by anything that cannot be immediately translated in financial/quantitative terms is already a matter of fact.[3] The strategies to control access to online platforms have been established for some quite time now by the most powerful economic actors in the world. At the same time, these plutocratic agents are today committing to exclusive, reserved virtual dimensions, where their avatars can enjoy an eco-communicative space accessible only to the wealthy. Such an excluding hierarchization of virtual spaces, however, could be an attempt to radicalize the cognitive/spatial asymmetry already extant at a global scale, as illustrated above. Consequentially, whoever takes care of democracy's destiny, should engage in socially responsible action designed to make people cognizant of the horizontal continuity between virtual and physical spaces. In this sense, a public movement should be organized to allow people to learn how to take advantage of the potentialities of the web in making 'elsewheres' present; one that highlights the continuity between the virtual informational environment and the importance of interpenetration between the global and the local for the meaning of the physical spaces of experience. Conversely and ironically, ordinary access to the Internet and its communicative corridors is on average channeled communicatively through almost asphyxiated relationships, discursively rather frugal and laconic exchanges, and economic transactions, and this when the banality of the content does not devolve into hate speech and mere

[2]For a historical-critical approach to the conflation between the indifference to Otherness deceptively included in the idea of freedom, including its apotheosis in the neoliberal worldview, and the contemporary defective understanding of human rights, see Moyn (2018); but see also Filip (2020).

[3]For some interesting insights on this topic, see Zuboff (2019).

vulgarity. All this, unfortunately, winds up frustrating the educational and informative improvement that the web could, in theory, propel. It also increases the cognitive divorce of people from the effective scope of their life spaces. Using the web in an emancipatory direction requires education and, at the same time, a specific training in developing an essential ability to protect oneself from the effects stemming from a naïf misuse of the semio-electronic pluriverse, and exposure to the deceptive messages it can convey.

Communicative corridors, of course, are a necessary but insufficient condition for translating different and distant spatial frameworks involved in the production of local experience and meaning. Intercultural skillfulness and the ability to communicatively engender a thirdspace of signification and experience is not a negligible ingredient in the process of developing a widespread consciousness about the semiotic interpenetration among reciprocal 'elsewheres' that proceeds hand in hand with daily planetary biological and social phenomena. This skillfulness requires the acquisition of a specific methodology and a good degree of acquaintance with a chorological approach to categorization capable of making people prepared to 'see' and transform the physically distant as semantically close, and the categorically distinct as experientially co-implicated. This is the only way to give course to the progressive development of a planetary public opinion that can function as the collecting basin of a polyphony of voices stemming from, and reciprocally translating, the spatial socio-anthropological circuits hosting human experience and the different subjectivities spread all over the world.

The role of law in this process of spatial and intercultural alignment among the different players of globalization is crucial. This is because law can support the unfolding of the process by means of its normativity and its inherent axiological/teleological elements, which as such could actively convey a process of cognitive/intercultural remolding of the categorical checklists to be used in the translation/transaction of the meaning/fact of relationships. In this sense, law can function not only as a prescriptive *dispositive* destined to order and sanction *ex post factum* the infringement of imperatives but also as a tool to plan the production of facts by means of a planetarily pluralistic renewal of both their schemes of categorization and the behavioral/pragmatic habits entailed in human relationships with the living environment.

A useful example of how interculturality, spatial chorology and law can fruitfully combine is suggested, once again, by the recent pandemic and its dynamics. The rapid spread of the COVID-19 virus has undoubtedly been due to the global mobility of people. This *geo-semeiotic* factor is destined to increase exponentially in the future. Therefore, any preventive politics designed to intercept future pandemics must take into account the renewal of cultural habits involved in the treatment of animals, the processing of their feed, and their consumption: all this in view of an improvement of the human control over health consequences. Without an intercultural and synesthetic transdusction between different food traditions, a multiplicity of local productions, and the related environmental interplay among human beings and their nutritional exigencies, the exploitation of natural resources, economic global constraints, etc., any renewal of the 'health & food' binomial will be futile. Culture, taste and the materiality of food and bodies are relationally and dynamically connected. It is precisely for this reason that without an intercultural approach there can be no viable politics for global health. On the other hand, not even law could disregard the cognitive dimension underlying the perception and categorization of food. Any legal top-down imposition of rules intended to change the embodied habits of food consumption would run the risk of turning into an unavoidable—and announced—shipwreck. Only a translational/transformative process could succeed in combining healthy exigencies with the anthropological and spatial projections stemming from and surrounding food, its production, consumption, and its psycho-social significance on a global scale. A genuine process of translation could discover, along the multiple paths of signification that arise from any recipe, a semiotic landscape that could be interculturally and *transpatially* transduced by using the values/ends enshrined in human rights semantic platforms; the result would be a legal provision in tune with cultural circuits of meaning. Such an outcome could also lead to a recombination of different cultural traditions in view of the elaboration of safer food and health standards which could be, *inter alia*, useful in the attempt to decrease the threat of new pandemic waves related to eating and hygienic habits.

My hope is that this book can help proffer the methodological instruments to support the intercultural knowledge needed to assure a future to democratic life on both a local and global scale. And this simply because if democracy does not become polyphonically and chorologically global from the bottom-up, it will no longer be democracy.

References

Filip B (2020) The rise of neo-liberalism and the decline of freedom. Palgrave Macmillan, Cham

Moyn S (2018) Not enough: human rights in an unequal world. Belknap Press of Harvard University Press, Cambridge

Ricca M (2020) Don't uncover that face! Covid-19 masks and the niqab: ironic transfigurations of the ECtHR's intercultural blindness. Int J Semiot Law 19:1119–1143. https://doi.org/10.1007/s11196-020-09703-y

Zuboff S (2019) The age of surveillance capitalism: the fight for a human future at the new frontier of power. Profile Books, London